SPIRITUS 'MAGIS'

Spiritus 'Magis'

150 Years
OF
Saint Ignatius College Preparatory

Paul Totah

Saint Ignatius College Preparatory · San Francisco

Published by Saint Ignatius College Preparatory
2001 37th Avenue
San Francisco, California 94116

Portions of this book first appeared, in different form, in *Genesis IV*,
the alumni magazine of Saint Ignatius College Preparatory.

Library of Congress Cataloging-in-Publication Data

Totah, Paul.
    Spiritus magis : 150 years of St. Ignatius College Preparatory / by Paul Totah.
       p. cm.
    Includes bibliographical references and index.
    1. Saint Ignatius College Preparatory (San Francisco, Calif.)--History. I. Title.
    LD7501.S35355T68 2005
    373.794'61--dc22

                                                  2005000920

ISBN 0-615-12786-X

Designed by Douglas A. Salin

www.siprep.org

TO FR. ANTHONY P. SAUER, SJ

A MAN FOR OTHERS
&
A MODEL FOR US ALL

The first Saint Ignatius Crest, designed by George Lyle '09.

CONTENTS

PREFACE: AMDG

It is hard to imagine a less auspicious start for our school. When Fr. Anthony Maraschi, SJ, opened the doors of the first St. Ignatius Academy on San Francisco's Market Street, expecting to see a crowd of Catholic boys eager for Jesuit education, only three small faces peered at him on that October day in 1855. As the day progressed, no one else came. When the term ended early in February, the school had managed to attract only 23 students in all.

Despite a slow start, St. Ignatius College (which later split into the University of San Francisco and St. Ignatius High School) took root in the shifting sands of Market Street, and then transplanted itself five times before landing at the sixth and present site in the Sunset District.

Many themes capture the spirit of the Jesuits who established SI and who persevered despite earthquake and fire, poverty and debt, and the social upheavals that have marked San Francisco since its founding. Of these themes, one word stands out: *magis* — the greater good.

When Jesuits use this Latin word, they use it in the specific context of the Spiritual Exercises of St. Ignatius of Loyola, the group's founder. In his guide to mystical prayer, Ignatius asks us to bring before God any decisions we have to make, and to ask for divine help to discern and choose the option that "leads more to the original purpose for which we were created"; i.e., to "praise, reverence and serve God."[1]

This idea of *magis* helps to explain why the Jesuit

fathers John Nobili and Michael Accolti set out from Oregon for San Francisco in 1849. Initially drawn to the Pacific Northwest (headquartered in Oregon's Willamette Valley) to stake out the territory for the Catholic Church and evangelize among the Native American tribes, they saw the epicenter of the West suddenly shift when James Marshall discovered gold in the American River. They left Oregon because they believed they could do greater good in California, ministering to a greater number of immigrants, many of whom had come from Catholic Europe, in that mad rush for gold that changed California and the West forever.

There's another way to look at *magis*. Over the years, the word has taken on a different connotation from the one envisioned by Ignatius. Some see the word (for better or worse) as an invitation never to be complacent, never to be satisfied and always to strive for excellence. That spirit of competition, with oneself and with others, has been as much a guiding force for SI since its inception as the Phoenix has been a symbol for San Francisco.

Why did the first Jesuits come to San Francisco and Santa Clara? Simply put, to beat the Protestants to the punch and to claim for the Roman Catholic Church the cities named for St. Francis and St. Clare through the education of their children.

By the time Fr. Maraschi opened St. Ignatius Church in 1855, a few months before the school, San Francisco had only four other Catholic churches among a sea of 23 Protestant churches. By building St. Ignatius Church and Academy on Fourth and Market Streets, west of the established city, the Jesuits were doing what gold miners were doing in the hills: staking their claim to a place that one day might reap rich rewards.

Their efforts paid off. Over the years, the Jesuits struck the mother lode time and time again, though certainly not financially; in fact, the school was in debt throughout most of its history. The Jesuits measured success by the number of students they attracted, by the depth and breadth of education they could offer, and by the sheer goodness of the students who graduated from SI.

Their choice of locations also proved fortuitous. Just look at the sites of the first three campuses. The Market Street site of the first two campuses would later become the home of The Emporium department store (soon to be a new Bloomingdale's), its third site (the one destroyed by the 1906 earthquake and fire) is now the Louise Davies Symphony Hall in the center of the city, and the fourth site is now adjacent to St. Mary's Hospital.

The spirit of *magis,* of seeking the greater good, has kept SI competitive with itself and with other insti-

tutions. Each year teachers try to do their jobs better than the previous year. Each semester students try to move from a B+ to an A- in one more class. Each day athletes train to shave a tenth of a second off their time or jump a little higher. When alumni look back at their glory days at SI, they sometimes think of the Bruce-Mahoney Game or the Doc Erskine Trophy, symbols of that same competitive spirit that pushes SI and its students to attempt to excel in all things.

The U.S. Department of Education recognized that desire for excellence when it named SI as one of the top 60 prep schools in the nation in 1984. Also, from the late 1990s to the present, the school has consis-

The first St. Ignatius Church and School, built in 1855 on Market Street

tently ranked in the top 30 nationally in the Advanced Placement program and was recently named as one of the top 12 Catholic schools in the country for professional development.

Some would say that this push for excellence has its downside. Over the years, SI has been called elitist, and its students have been accused of arrogance. Certainly some of this is true. But if we look at the big picture, we see that the spirit of *magis* has created generations of Ignatians who know how important it is both to lead and to serve. Look at the number of great public servants who have graduated from SI, and expand your definition beyond "politician." Think of all the priests, bankers, teachers, doctors, police officers, firefighters, lawyers, carpenters, plumbers, CEOs, judges, writers — you name it — who do what they do AMDG (for the greater glory of God), echoing in their adult lives what they once wrote out every day in class atop each piece of paper they used.

Also, this talk of competition may be a little misleading. The Jesuit priests who founded SI and who have worked here these past 150 years did so not just to beat the Protestants to the punch, win athletic trophies or rack up top SAT scores. They came here and stayed a century and a half for reasons far more profound. Ask today's faculty at SI — lay or Jesuit — why they teach, and they will tell you that they are devoted to helping their students. What this bespeaks is a genuine love for these young men and women; a desire to give them knowledge and skills; a hope to shape them into men and women of competence, conscience and compassion; and a deep conviction surrounding their own vocations. This is why the first priests came from

half a world away, why they stayed and why they prospered.

Finally, *magis* connotes a spirit of balance. As the late Jesuit theologian Karl Rahner, SJ, noted "unless we operate on a principle of spiritual balance and the *Magis*, there is a danger in life of self-centeredness, a danger of going from one excess to another."[2] This sense of balance defines the modern SI. We tell our students that the three parts that make up the school day — academics, extracurriculars and campus ministry — are equally important. SI hopes to educate the whole student and to touch the creative, athletic, intellectual, emotional and spiritual heart of each young Ignatian.

With this book we celebrate 150 years of Jesuit history in San Francisco. We also celebrate a great school that, from the days of the Wild West, has turned boys (and, since 1989, girls) into people for and with others, into servants who know how to lead and leaders who know how to serve, and into educated and civilized people actively building the Kingdom of God.

We are grateful for this long and rich history and for the giants on whose shoulders we stand — all the great teachers and priests, scholastics and brothers, alumni and administrators, benefactors, parents, and students — who have come before us. May all of us continue to serve the youth of the Bay Area for the next 150 years with the same spirit of *magis* that has marked the first 150. If we can do this, we will truly be blessed.

— *Paul Totah '75*

Spiritus 'Magis'

I. THE FOUNDING
OF ST. IGNATIUS COLLEGE
(1849 ~ 1861)

Six years after the Jesuits arrived in California, St. Ignatius College appeared on Market Street as a one-room schoolhouse with the mixed blessing of Archbishop Alemany. What makes the history of SI so remarkable is that six years after the construction of this small school, SI built an impressive college right next door and attracted an impressive faculty, as some of the best Jesuit minds of Europe, fleeing anti-Catholic sentiment, found their way to teach at this outpost college on the edge of the continent. The school quickly earned the respect of the citizens of San Francisco who sent their sons to learn from the good Italian fathers. These first few years also saw SI acquire a staggering debt that would cast a cloud over the school until the middle of the 20th Century.

Gold Rush Beginnings

Imagine San Francisco before the Gold Rush: only a few low scrub oaks, only a few settlers' homes, only a ship or two in the harbor. All that changed within months after the discovery of gold on January 24, 1848. No one, least of all the Catholic Church, was prepared for the rush of people through the Golden Gate on their way to the gold fields. Fr. José Maria de Jesus Gonzales Rubio, a Franciscan missionary and administrator of the Diocese of California, in a letter written four months after the discovery of gold, wrote of his difficulty in ministering to these newcomers:

"Day by day we see that our circumstances grow in difficulty; that help and resources have shrunk to almost nothing; that the hope of supplying the needed clergy is now almost extinguished; and, worst of all, that through lack of means and priests, divine worship throughout the whole diocese stands upon the brink of total ruin… Oh! How we should fear, dearly Beloved, a chastisement so dread! A chastisement the greatest assuredly that could befall us from Heaven's anger, which, it would seem, we already begin to experience, since God in his inscrutable judgments has, for the past few years, allowed that in this our country everything should be thrown into confusion; that the missionaries should die or abandon the country, while I have no hope of replacing them; that religious education should day by day disappear…"[1]

In the autumn 1848, Fr. John B. Brouillet, vicar-general of the diocese of Nesqually, Oregon, landed in San Francisco hoping to minister to Catholic miners headed for the gold fields. Fr. Antoine Langlois, a diocesan priest on his way to Canada to join the Society

Opposite page: San Francisco in the 1850s.

of Jesus, joined him a few months later. Fr. Brouillet asked him to stay in San Francisco, and he wrote to the Jesuit superior in Oregon for that permission. The answer: "He should labor in San Francisco, and leave the future in God's hands."[2]

Later, both Brouillet and Langlois, desperate for help, encouraged Fr. Michael Accolti, SJ, working in Oregon's Willamette Valley (a part of the Jesuits' Rocky Mountain Mission) to visit San Francisco, and they continued their work to minister and convert. In his journal, Langlois noted that this work continued "in spite of the natural obstacles thrown its way by the thirst of gold; gold, of which all had come in search from every part of the globe; in spite, moreover, of the drawbacks of uncertain employment, of various inconveniences, of the intermingling of people, strangers to one another, and this in tents for a considerable number; in spite of the temptations of bar-rooms and saloons on every hand for the multitudes that frequented them, to amuse themselves, drink and spend their time…"[3]

Brouillet wrote to Accolti that "the people [of California] desire you warmly and are urging you to come. Everybody is asking for a Jesuit College and here is what they put at the joint disposition of yourselves and the Sisters of Notre Dame: an entire mission, one of the finest and best equipped in the whole of California, with a magnificent church … on condition that a college and convent be set up there with the least possible delay…."

Accolti and the Jesuits in the Oregon territory had met with challenges working with Native Americans, especially after the inundation of whites into that region. Accolti wanted to work in California, but all the Jesuits were faced with an order by the Jesuit Father General John Roothaan barring his priests from seeking new mission work there, in part because he did not want to see the efforts of the Society stretched too thin and because of past prohibitions by the Mexican government against Jesuits traveling in its territory. Those prohibitions ended with the cession of California from Mexico to the United States on February 2, 1848, by the Treaty of Guadalupe Hidalgo, and Accolti believed that enough had changed since Roothaan's order to warrant the journey, especially with the discovery of gold. "All the white Catholic population around Oregon City had left for California," noted SI Archivist Michael Kotlanger, SJ '64. "The success of the Indian mission work was slow and grudging. Greater good seemed to lie in California where the Rocky Mountain Mission was forbidden to expand." Despite this prohibition, Accolti repeatedly petitioned his superior, Fr. Joseph Joset, SJ, for permission to sail to San Francisco; Accolti finally wore Joset down and permission was granted.[4]

(Accolti, the founder of the California Province of the Society of Jesus, pursued his dream of establishing churches and schools in California with amazing vigor. SI owes its origin as much to Accolti as to the school's founder, Fr. Anthony Maraschi, SJ. Without Accolti's years of campaigning, letter writing and personal appeals, the Jesuit mission in California might never have been.)

Joset asked Fr. John Nobili, SJ, who had met with poor health working at an isolated Indian mission post in British Columbia, to accompany Accolti to California. On December 3, 1849, the two boarded the O.C. *Raymond*, a lumber ship heading down the Columbia River for California, and arrived in San Francisco the night of December 8, on the feast of the Immaculate Conception.[5] In Fr. Accolti's memorial on the subject, he wrote that "the next day we were able to set foot on the longed-for shores of what goes under the name of San Francisco, but which, whether it should be called a villa, a brothel, or Babylon, I am at a loss to determine; so great in those days was the disorder, the brawling, the open immorality, the reign of crime which brazen-faced triumphed on a soil not yet brought under the sway of human laws."

Fr. Accolti initially entertained the idea of heading to the hills to dig for gold, but gave up that plan. In a letter to Fr. Roothaan three months after his arrival, he wrote the following: "Here we are in California, come not to seek gold in this country of wealth and treasure, but come to do a little good. Though at first there was thought of sending me with two brothers to the mines to seek means for the support of our missions, on further consideration, it was thought best to abandon such a project, which has its dangers, however you look at it. The object of our expedition to this country, according to Father Joset's instructions, is threefold: 1. To exercise the ministry, especially in assisting the sick, who are always numerous in this city; 2. To see if things are favorable to the establishment of the Society as the Rev. Mr. Brouillet wrote us; 3. To make a collection in favor of the missions."[6]

Accolti also wrote to Fr. Gonzales in Santa Barbara, the diocesan administrator, telling him of their arrival. They received a reply dated March 5, 1850, in which Fr. Gonzales wrote of his hope that "two colleges of the Society of Jesus should be established here; one in the north where you are, and another here in the south.... I desire [the establishment of the Society of Jesus] here. I desire it and have yearningly desired it; I have begged it of God with earnest pleadings..."[7] He also promised financial assistance in the founding of these schools, though that money never materialized.

Accolti, clearly delighted by this invitation to the Society of Jesus to work in California, wrote back on April 9 that "the hopes of Catholicity in these parts lie mainly in the training of youth in religion, morals and letters" and that "what pleases us most is that your desires have spontaneously the same object as our own, in that your Reverence urges and exhorts us to build a college, although our letters written on January 28th and containing our humble request for such permission, had not as yet reached you."[8]

He added that his first effort to build a school would be in San Jose both because it was "the chief city of Northern California" as the state capital at the time and because "some property and some money for the putting up of a part of the buildings have been freely offered by the faithful."[9]

The Latin word *collegio*, it should be noted, had a different meaning in the 1800s than the modern meaning of the word "college." It referred to the European model of a school typically comprising students from ages 6 to 18. St. Ignatius College, similar to Jesuit colleges throughout the world, remained primarily a grammar school and high school for much of the 1800s. It awarded its first bachelor of arts degree in 1863 but very few others until the 1900s. In 1864, for instance, only one-third of the 450 SI students were studying subjects on the college level, and most of those college students were between 16 and 18 years old. Between 1863 and

Fr. Michael Accolti, SJ, the founder of the California Mission of the Society of Jesus.

1880, SI issued only 57 academic degrees (31 Bachelor of Arts degrees, 11 Bachelor of Science degrees, one Master of Science degree and 14 Master of Arts degrees). "When the total number of 57 is compared with the number of students [enrolled] during this almost two decades being considered here, it becomes evident that most of the students were either in the preparatory or elementary divisions of the 'College.'"[10] Not until the GI Bill gave returning World War II veterans inexpensive access to college did the number of college students grow at USF and at most American colleges.

Fr. Francis Veyret, SJ

On May 31, 1850, Joseph Alemany, O.P., was ordained the Bishop of Monterey (a diocese embracing most of upper-California at the time). In March 1851, he turned over the parish of Santa Clara to Nobili and asked that he establish a Jesuit college there. What happened next was perhaps the most important step in the history of the Jesuits in California.

Accolti, frustrated that his letters to his superiors met with no response — they took on average two years to travel to Rome and for a response to be sent back — left for Rome in 1853 to meet personally with Father General Peter Beckx, SJ, to convince the Jesuit General to send more priests to California.[11]

Tensions in Europe would work to Accolti's advantage. In the mid-1800s, Europe was rocked by revolutions. Liberal masses attacked the conservative restoration governments that returned to power

following the final exile of Napoleon Bonaparte. The Jesuits generally supported the conservative regimes; thus, they, along with most of the Church, drew the enmity of an angry populace. This was especially true during Italy's *Risorgimento*, the Italian unification movement that sought freedom from foreign control, including the Catholic Church.

As fate would have it, some of the best and brightest Italian Jesuits, including those in the Turin Province, were in exile or hiding and needed to find safe harbor. In 1854, Beckx asked Turin Provincial Alexander Joseph Ponza, SJ, to administer the California mission. Turin would benefit by having a central place for its priests to gather, to teach and to train novices, and Santa Clara College (and soon St. Ignatius College) would have sorely needed manpower and world-class scholars. The Turin Province administered the California mission until 1909, when the California Mission earned status as a separate province of the Society of Jesus.

Lot 127 Changes Hands

St. Ignatius College was not the first Jesuit school attempted in San Francisco. Fr. Flavian Fontaine (a member of the Congregation of the Sacred Hearts of Jesus and Mary who were staffing Mission Dolores) acquired land in 1853 and erected a brick building, which, he hoped, would educate both day students and boarders. After spending all the money he had and borrowing $2,000 more, he started construction on a site at what is now 14th and Walter Streets for the Catholic College of Mission Dolores. Unable to pay his debts, he fled San Francisco in September 1853 for Panama where he died.

With Accolti in Rome, Nobili saw a potential bargain in the new but empty college building. With the urging of Alemany, who became the first Archbishop of San Francisco in 1853 and who was eager to see a Catholic school thrive in San Francisco, Nobili purchased the property for $11,000. Fr. Flavian's creditors demanded payment, and Nobili had to surrender more than $10,000 to secure rights to the building. When Accolti returned from Rome, he questioned the wisdom of Nobili's purchase for good reasons.

The Jesuits did open a school in this building toward the start of 1854, but no records exist as to the specific date it opened or how many students it served. Fr. Francis Veyret, SJ, sent from Santa Clara College to be its president, was its only teacher. The school failed, despite its prominence as a two-story hillside structure, in part because students had a hard time walking to it and found the hillside a poor playground. The city's buildings stopped at Third and Kearney Streets, and to the west lay sand dunes stretching to the ocean. To get to school, students had to take a stage down Third to Mission and then navigate a rickety plank walkway to the school through sand and brush.[12] The school lingered until September 1854 when it closed forever, a costly experiment that continued to plague future Jesuit administrators for years. This educational experiment would be known from this point on as the "College of Sorrows," both because of its sad history and its proximity to Mission Dolores. Despite this failed first

attempt, even after losing the most valuable part of the property in litigation, the Society of Jesus refused to surrender the idea of establishing a school in San Francisco.

That idea became reality thanks to SI's founder, Fr. Anthony Maraschi, SJ, who was born in Oleggio in the Piedmont region of Italy on September 2, 1820, and joined the Jesuits at Chieri in 1841. He taught for three years in Turin where his associates were greatly impressed by "his virtues and sterling character. His piety was sincere and deep, but it was an unobtrusive piety revealing itself in strict fidelity to duty…. The pupils given Fr. Maraschi were famous for dullness and inattention, yet there was no complaint from their teacher for his wasted toil, no apathy or discouragement. On the contrary, day after day one would generally find him carefully examining and correcting the wretched themes of his unpromising charges."[13]

The College of Sorrows

As a Jesuit, Maraschi seemed to his friends to "be cold and distant, but for all of that, possessing a warm heart."[14] He served as a "substitute procurator" (treasurer) and prefect of the boarders at the Jesuit college in Genoa in 1847, and then taught at the Jesuit college in Nice in 1848, but had to flee anti-clerical persecution that had plagued the Jesuits in Europe for years. The Jesuit house in Nice was attacked and the community driven into the streets by a crowd suspicious of Jesuit ties to the old monarchy. He lived in hiding at a friend's house until Fr. Roothaan called him to Marseilles. There Monsignor De Mazenod, the founder of the Oblates of Mary Immaculate, ordained him on April 30.

Soon after, he set sail for America where he studied and taught at Georgetown College. He later taught philosophy at Holy Cross College in Worcester, Massachusetts, and at Loyola College in Baltimore. He pronounced his final vows as a Jesuit on August 15, 1854, and then received orders from Fr. Provincial Ponza in Turin to journey to San Francisco to assist in the new Jesuit mission there. When Fr. Maraschi told Archbishop Francis Kenrick of Baltimore of his orders, Kenrick showed him a letter he had just received from Bishop Alemany in which he shared his dream of establishing in San Francisco "a good college for the education of male youth."

Maraschi did not leave Baltimore alone. Two other Jesuits accompanied him — Fr. Charles Messea, SJ, and Fr. Aloysius Masnata, SJ (who would later become SI's rector-president from 1873–76). Along with crowds of men hoping to find California gold, the three priests

Fr. Anthony Maraschi, SJ, a Jesuit from the Turin Province, founded SI in 1855.

left New York on October 8, 1854, for Panama. There they made the difficult and dangerous overland journey across the isthmus to a Pacific port before embarking on the steamship *Sonora* bound for San Francisco. The three priests arrived on All Saints Day, November 1, into the wilds of the Barbary Coast district.

The city that Maraschi found was one hard to imagine for present-day San Franciscans. Between 1849 and 1851, a series of fires raged through the city, and thus it was constantly rebuilding itself (hence the symbol of the Phoenix rising from the ashes on the seal of the City of San Francisco). Newcomers could easily find the gambling halls and brothels that gained the Barbary Coast district its notoriety, but they could also find places of Christian worship among San Francisco's 27 churches. In the city named for St. Francis of Assisi, however, only four of these churches were Catholic — St. Francis on Vallejo Street, St. Patrick's on the site of what is now the Palace Hotel, Mission Dolores and St. Mary's Church on California and Grant, completed in 1854. Also, despite the wealth enjoyed by the first gold-seekers, the city was filled with thousands of miners who came down from the hills never having struck it rich or who wintered there waiting for the Sierra snowmelt. They had no money for the high-priced goods that lined store shelves, and by the end of 1854, more than a third of the city's 1,000 stores stood empty. In short, Maraschi landed in a city with few Catholic institutions and facing its first economic depression.

Maraschi reported to Archbishop Alemany who assigned him to work at St. Francis Church. Two months later, in January 1855, he was transferred to St. Patrick's Church on Market near Third Street, on what was then the "western outskirts of the city" where he worked for seven months.[15]

Maraschi had come to San Francisco not only to

serve as a parish priest but also to open a college. He saw the success of Santa Clara College to the south with its boarding students and felt that one boarding college was more than enough for the fledgling state at the time. He hoped to open a school for day students and sought permission from Archbishop Alemany. Encouraging him in this venture was Fr. Nicolas Congiato, SJ, who arrived in San Francisco on December 8, 1854, to serve as the superior of the Jesuit mission in California and who would later serve as the second president of St. Ignatius College.

Maraschi soon discovered that Alemany, while supportive of a Jesuit school, was not eager to see the construction of a Jesuit church, especially one that would not be under his control. Church laws at that time were ambiguous regarding ownership of church property; religious orders and bishops each claimed ownership of church deeds. Alemany also worried that the Jesuits, with their penchant for preaching, would lure away parishioners and their offerings from the archdiocesan churches.

In "A relation of the facts connected with the foundation of Saint Ignatius College of the Society of Jesus in San Francisco, California," written by Maraschi in 1863, he writes of this tension and of the permission Alemany finally gave for the building of the school. (Note that Maraschi refers to himself in the third person):

"Several pieces of ground were offered for our establishment, but his Grace, after whose pleasure Fr. Maraschi had been directed to inquire, objected to the best of them because they were too near the other churches. We may mention in particular the house and lot of Mr. Dillon, the French Consul who was quitting San Francisco with his family. When Fr. Maraschi proposed it to his Grace, he got for an answer that he might open the College there, but for the church, he should never think of opening it there, because it would take away the people from the Cathedral and the church of St. Francis. Indeed, the situation of that property was such as to be near the upper angle of an isosceles triangle, the two churches above mentioned being at the two extremities of the base.

"We had thus come to the beginning of April [1855] without doing anything, when Fr. Maraschi requested his Grace to open his mind plainly with regard to the part of the city where he desired we should start our establishment, it being the will of the Superiors of the Society not to depart from his views on the matter in question. Then His Grace pointed with the pen on the map of the city, just to the place where we are, saying that thereabout was the place where he would like we settle ourselves. It pleased Almighty God to dispose that precisely the very lot which His Grace had marked out with his pen, should be for sale a few days afterwards."

About this location, Maraschi is reported to have said, "Here, in time, will be the heart of a great city." History proved him an apt prophet.

Fr. Joseph W. Riordan, SJ, in his history, recounts this incident differently, noting that Alemany pointed to the parcel not with a pen but with "a sweep of his hand toward the unoccupied lands," and telling Maraschi to build "any place over there!" Whether Alemany pointed with pen or with a sweep of the hand, it is easy to speculate that his primary desire in locating SI so far from the people of San Francisco was to protect his own struggling churches from competition with the Jesuits.

Alemany insisted that the Jesuits not take up a collection to fund their new school and church, forcing the Jesuits to fund the venture through loans. Maraschi added that "whilst we were building, somebody spread through the city that we were doing it without permission and against the will of His Grace." The archbishop dispelled that rumor by preaching at the church's opening. However, he also arranged a meeting between the Jesuits and his diocesan priests to fix "the limits of the district attached to our Church, subject to any change which the Ordinary might make from time to time."

Maraschi purchased the land, known as Lot 127 on Market Street between Fourth and Fifth Streets. The parcel measured 127 feet by 275 feet and was owned by Thomas O. Larkin, the first American Consul in Monterey, who sold it for $11,500. "The title proving satisfactory, the deed was made out in favor of Father Congiato on May 1, 1855, and the price was put down in cash, the money being borrowed from the French firm of V. Marsion connected with the firm of the same name in Paris and Havre, France." The bank charged 1.5 percent interest per month on this $11,000 loan, increasing the Jesuits' debt to $26,000.[16]

One might easily make the mistake of conjuring visions of the present day Market Street with its traffic and landmark buildings. In 1855, Market Street made an abrupt stop at Third Street, and only sand dunes and low dune plants, with an occasional shanty, could

Fr. Joseph Bixio, SJ, helped Fr. Maraschi open the first school.

be found to the west. The first site of St. Ignatius College ran along a street that existed only on planners' maps, in an area known as St. Ann's Valley (though it was far from a verdant valley) in a narrow depression between two sand hills. Each time Maraschi went out to inspect the property, he found it looked a little different as the dunes constantly changed shape with the shifting sands.[17]

Also, if the $11,000 price Maraschi paid seems exorbitant for land in the middle of uninhabited sand dunes, the amount seems even more extraordinary when we learn that, in today's dollars, the price would be more than $200,000. San Francisco real estate, among the most costly in the nation today, sold at a premium ever since the Gold Rush.

Maraschi wasted no time in hiring workers to construct a simple wood and plaster church on the site. The simple structure with "a plain gable roof on four plain walls, neat and decent in every particular" cost $4,000 and was ready for its dedication on July 15, 1855.[18]

Educating the Youth
of the Bay Area Since 1855

At the dedication of St. Ignatius Church, Archbishop Alemany preached and declared that he was "most happy to have the members of the Society of Jesus as his cooperators in the work of promoting the salvation of souls and in giving a good education to the youth of the diocese and especially in the city of San Francisco." Nobili, now the president of Santa Clara College, traveled the 50 miles to take part in the ceremony of blessing and dedication. Maraschi and three other Jesuits (Decius Solari, SJ,

Urban Grassi, SJ, and Joseph Carreda, SJ) also took part in the dedication ceremony. As a newspaper account noted, "There was a large attendance on the occasion, a considerable portion of whom were ladies."[19]

Maraschi was now the pastor of St. Ignatius Church, which measured 75 feet long by 35 feet wide and had enough pews for 400 people. His first assistant pastor, Fr. Joseph Bixio, SJ, arrived in California in early July, and only stayed a year in the city before being transferred to Santa Clara.

(Fr. Bixio, described as a "strikingly handsome, nervous man with an athletic build and a commanding, genial presence" later gained notoriety by serving as a chaplain during the Civil War, ministering to both sides in Virginia and West Virginia.[20] He was eventually arraigned before General Philip Sheridan before being released and earned an unwarranted reputation as a spy.[21] He eventually returned to live at SI from 1866–1870, and after a stint in Australia, returned again in 1880 carrying with him botanical samples from that country for the SI science labs. He died March 3, 1889. For more on this adventurer-priest, read the account by Fr. Cornelius Buckley, SJ, in the spring 1999 issue of *California History.*)

Maraschi then set workers to build the simple wood-frame one-room school building 20 feet behind the church and a two-room residence for himself and Bixio. The first St. Ignatius College (advertised in its first year as "St. Ignatius Academy") was not an impressive edifice. The one-classroom school building measured 16 by 26 feet (according to McGloin) or 25 by 40 feet (according to Riordan) and cost $750 to construct. A portion of the classroom served as the residence of the school's first teacher, a layman by the name of John Haley.

On the first day of classes, October 15, 1855, the school opened its doors to its first students. We can only imagine what Maraschi, Bixio, and Haley expected to find that first morning. If they had hoped to see a long line of students or a crowd pushing to get in, they must have been gravely disappointed to see only three students looking up at them.

Of the three, we know the name only of Richard McCabe, though an 1878 report mentions that all three pioneer students of St. Ignatius Academy had become "well known professional men of San Francisco."[22] Of SI's first student, the *Langley San Francisco Directory Book* lists two men by the name Richard McCabe. One was listed as a lithographer and zincographer who worked first at Britton & Rey Company (one of the big printing firms in town) and later for A.L. Bancroft & Company on Market Street, which did quality fine printing and engraving and which appears to have handled much of the financial district printing including stock and bond certificates. The other Richard McCabe was listed as an organist at St. Francis Church. (Fr. Kotlanger, archivist for both USF and SI, suspects the SI McCabe to be the former of the two.)

Over the next several days and weeks, only 20 more students joined the original three. These stu-

SI's first student, Richard McCabe

dents came from 14 families, as they included several siblings, with each child paying about $2 a month in tuition. Maraschi made the decision to close early for the year, and, by February, Haley vacated his premises in the front of the classroom. Several of the Jesuits took up residence in the school building during this hiatus including Accolti, who had replaced Bixio after Alemany sent him to minister to Catholics living on the Peninsula. Another Jesuit in residence was the newly arrived Br. Albert Weyringer, SJ. This young brother, 50 years later, commented on the early days of the school for Riordan's book:

Br. Albert Weyringer, SJ

"We lived in a hole surrounded by sand hills. Toward the city, which was some distance to the east, and from which we were cut off by barriers of sand, there was but one house, [that of] the shanty of a milkman on the adjoining lot. Westward there was the Lincoln School standing out considerably into what is now Market Street, but during my residence in St. Ignatius the buildings were unoccupied.

"Behind us rose a sand hill which sloped again towards Mission Street, and served as neutral territory between our college and a public school which had been built there. This neutral ground, however, was often invaded from the school mentioned, for a Jesuit in cap and cassock was a rare object of curiosity to the children of those days in San Francisco; and, perched on the hilltop, they surveyed the scene below, making Father Maraschi the butt of many a remark, much to the mortification of their teacher who could not repress their rudeness.

"The residence was small and poor, and the accommodations so scant that, for a time, Fathers Accolti and Maraschi shared the same room. But as for sleeping, Father Maraschi used only a mattress, which he rolled up by day and spread on the floor by night, his part of the furniture was easily housed....

"[After the term ended] my chief occupation consisted in cutting a road through the sand behind the house, the intention being to establish communication with Mission Street. My labor was quite successful for a time, and even the strong winds which at that season prevailed, kindly gave me valuable assistance; for all that was required was to lift the sand with my shovel and toss it into the air, and presently it was scattered far and wide to my intense pleasure.

"I had gotten indeed to like the wind and even to look on it, in a manner, as a partner in my toil, when all of a sudden the rude awakening came. One night this very wind, which had dealt with me so kindly, came in great gusts from the ocean. How it howled and shrieked around our little buildings, which rocked under its rude touch, as it hurried by! And my road? The wind came, and went — and my road with it. Morning showed an unbroken hillside beneath which my planks were buried, and I was out of a job, since it was evident that so long as the hill remained, no matter what labor might be expended, the permanency of the road could never be assured."

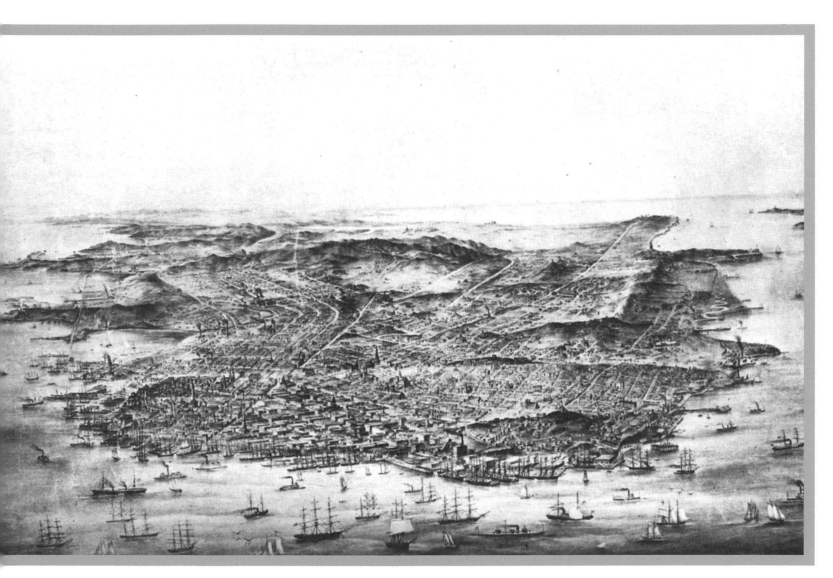

The San Francisco Peninsula shortly after the Gold Rush.

Weyringer went on to speak of how the sand covered the vegetables and flowers in the Jesuits' garden, how the remoteness of the site left the Jesuits free of the "excitement attending the days of the Vigilance Committee," and how they were rarely disturbed except for "spiritual ministrations" by the locals in need of a priest. He also wrote about finding a colorful plant and transplanting it in front of the church door with the hopes of training it around the doorway. He removed it only after Fr. Maraschi informed him that the plant was Poison Oak.

(Among those who needed spiritual ministrations were Charles Cora and James Casey, both victims of the San Francisco Committee of Vigilance. Both Maraschi and Accolti gave last rites to these two men before their death by hanging on May 22, 1856. Maraschi also witnessed the marriage of Cora to his mistress, Belle, on the morning of his execution.)[23]

Fr. Richard Gleeson, SJ

School is in Session

The school re-opened the following fall, this time drawing 89 students for the 1856–57 term. These students, primarily the sons of Irish and Italian immigrants, went to a school whose purpose was distinct from that of public schools in the U.S. The purpose of Catholic, Jesuit education was not only to train students for a career but also, in the words of Nobili, "to cultivate the heart, to form and cherish good habits, to prevent and eradicate evil ones."[24] Maraschi, in establishing SI Academy, was carrying forth the spirit of Jesuit education laid out in the *Ratio Studiorum*, a guidebook for the establishment of Jesuit schools first published in 1599 and revised in 1832.

This "Magna Carta of Jesuit education" the *Ratio Studiorum* gave both St. Ignatius and Santa Clara colleges nearly the same prescribed curriculum as every other Jesuit school around the world. It included a study of the classic languages (Latin and Greek), the humanities (drama, history, and literature), theology and philosophy (which included natural sciences and mathematics). This new system of education "assumed that literary or humanistic subjects could be integrated into the study of professional or scientific subjects; that is, it assumed that the humanistic program of the Renaissance was compatible with the Scholastic program of the Middle Ages."[25]

Fr. Richard Gleeson, SJ, described the *Ratio Studiorum* this way: "In that system, the teacher exacts either by himself or through the boys themselves the memory exercise. He then gives ... whether [for] one of the ancient classics or the modern, a Prelection so-called. A passage is read and thoroughly gone over with attention to the grammatical structure and idioms in the lower classes, to the various beauties of style in the intermediate classes, to the structure and imagery and rhythm in the class for Humanities or Poetry, and to the principles of oratory in the class of Rhetoric. A similar Prelection is given in the precepts of grammar, of poetry, of eloquence in the respective classes, with insistence not so much on the diction of the author followed, as on his thoughts. These Prelections are exacted from the individual students on the following days. Weekly repetitions, monthly repetitions; half-yearly and yearly repetitions go over the same matter. It is drill, drill, drill. The teacher is alive and he keeps his class alive. The Prefect of Studies visits the classes systematically, inspects the work, encourages pupils and teachers, and, when there is need, corrects the former and instructs the latter. The ideal teacher will draw out his individual pupils. He will train them to think, to think clearly and deeply and promptly. He will train them to express their thoughts quickly, elegantly, forcibly. The boy is being equipped for his work in life, professional, mercantile, mechanical. He will be able to concentrate his powers on any matter that comes for his consideration and give an account of his thoughts and his investigation.... In all this training one point cannot be sufficiently noted — the individual touch. Each teacher in this system reaches out to and affects each of his pupils in whom he is personally interested." [26]

While the SI curriculum included such traditional fare as Latin, Greek, English, French, Spanish, poetry, rhetoric, elocution, history, geography, arithmetic, and moral philosophy, Maraschi felt pressure from students and parents to teach practical, vocational courses. As one Jesuit noted in 1866, "Oh what a waste of time are Latin and Greek, for so many students that I now see [are] working ... as grocer, butcher, and who knows what else!" [27] Jesuits believe in adapting their programs to fit the needs of the place in which they minister; thus, from the first, SI offered bookkeeping and "natural philosophy," which translated into a study of practical sciences such as mineralogy, assaying and chemical analysis to prepare students to work in the mining industry. In fact, miners brought their ore samples to the priests for assaying because the Jesuits had a reputation for honesty and accurate analysis.

Later, SI's physics and chemistry cabinets (laboratories and collections) would grow to be among the best in the country. A national survey of science courses polled 500 American colleges and universities in 1880 and listed SI among 120 institutions judged to

An early advertisement for St. Ignatius Academy

Fr. Nicolas Congiato, SJ, served twice as SI president, from 1862 to 1865 and again from 1866 to 1869.

be "superior." SI's science courses were described as being "unusual" or "remarkable."[28]

Younger students in the preparatory department studied spelling, reading, writing, the elements of arithmetic, history and geography.[29] Students learned their subjects by writing compositions and engaging in discussions, disputations and contests. As in Italy, the academic year ended with a series of public examinations called *saggi*. One Jesuit noted that these events (where one had to show mastery of a subject such as Latin or rhetoric) "would have honored the Roman College to say nothing of any other college of our Italian provinces."[30]

The Jesuits reined in their young charges with strict discipline, and Accolti bragged that his students showed "exact compliance with the rules of discipline." Jesuit schools, he added were strict, but "of course not so stringent as that enforced at West Point."[31]

This standardized system, which saw education not as an end but as a means (to glorify God, to perfect the self, to assist in the service of others), allowed priests to come from Europe and easily start teaching at SI and to move between Santa Clara and St. Ignatius Colleges with little difficulty as the curriculum, textbooks, examinations and philoso-

phy of education were the same. "This allowed for plug-in teachers who could be moved as needed," according to Fr. Kotlanger. This practice continued well into the 20th century when centralized oversight ended.

The priests and brothers sent by the Turin Province established the reputations for years to come of both St. Ignatius and Santa Clara Colleges. Up until 1909, when California became its own province, nearly 100 priests, brothers and scholastics from Italy came to California and the Pacific Northwest to work as teachers and missionaries. In fact, of SI's first 14 rector-presidents, only four were non-Italians.[32] Later, with the establishment of the novitiate in Santa Clara, many native-born Americans joined those Italians.

One Irish-born teacher noted that the Jesuits from Turin were "like the Greeks after the fall of Constantinople. They brought with them libraries, scientific instruments and the education and habits, which fit men for the life of teaching. The Fathers, however, labored under one defect — both in the pulpit and in the classroom. They spoke and taught in a language not altogether English, and their manners and ideas were too Italian to meet the taste of the young Republicans of the West."[33] Because of this limitation, Jesuits from the East Coast came to help their California brothers.

These refugee priests included "gentlemen of great culture and personal charm" as well as "impressive academic credentials" such as Fr. Aloysius Varsi, SJ, who, to prepare himself for a career as an astronomer in the Jesuit-run Imperial Observatory in China, studied at the University of Paris, the same college that Ignatius and many other Jesuit scholars had attended. Other noteworthy scholars included

Fr. Joseph Bayma, SJ, a mathematician, philosopher and theoretical physicist whose *Elements of Molecular Mechanics* "earned him recognition as a pioneer in stereochemistry," and Fr. Anthony Cichi, SJ, and Fr. Joseph Neri, SJ, both skilled scientists. Neri was the first to introduce electric lights to San Francisco and lit Market Street in 1876 with "arc lights of his own invention" to help celebrate the nation's centennial.[34] (More on these men in upcoming chapters.)

These great priests also brought with them a devotional life that was alien to much of the western United States. They structured the school calendar around feast days and holy days of obligation. "Pilgrimages to the shrine of St. Joseph [the patron saint of the California Province] in March, Marian devotions in May, Corpus Christi processions in June, the construction of elaborate crèches at Christmastime — all were standard fare. These rituals of Mediterranean Catholicism nurtured a sense of solidarity and reminded practitioners that their church was universal." This structured practice became popular as the Catholic population of the state grew with the influx of Irish, German and Italian immigrants.[35]

Years of Growth:

1856–1860

SI started in debt and continued in debt until well into the 20th century. By the end of 1856, SI owed nearly $20,000, and was operating at a loss. The school's net revenues were barely half of what was paid on the annual interest ($1,489) toward its debt.[36] To pay off this interest, Maraschi simply borrowed more money.

He also needed funds to hire a new teacher for the school's second year. Peter J. Malloy, like SI's first teacher, was an immigrant from Ireland. (Malloy would later become California's first Jesuit candidate for the priesthood when he entered the Jesuit ranks at Santa Clara College on September 1, 1857. He died several months later, on December 20, 1857, and is buried in the Mission Dolores cemetery.)

The school grew in 1858 when Maraschi built two new classrooms behind the first school building. That year he also purchased a collection of shells for the school's museum and bought scientific instruments. "We do not deny that the museum and [scientific] cabinet of 1858 were very small affairs," writes Riordan. "We merely wonder that there were any at all … when we reflect that their inception coincides with a period of great financial depression in San Francisco, when the city was in great part depopulated by the mad rush to the gold fields of Frazer river."[37]

Fortunately, the 1858–1859 term saw an increase in the number of students (75) and faculty. In addition to the laymen William Barry, John Grace and John Egan, several priests were active in the faculty. Maraschi taught Greek and Spanish; Fr. Emmanuel Nattini, SJ, taught music; Fr. Urban Grassi, SJ, taught English and mathematics; and Fr. Alphonse Biglione, SJ, taught Latin, English, French and Algebra. Fr. Biglione also established the Students' Sodality of the Blessed Virgin Mary, marking the start of a tradition that lasted until the 1970s with the start of Christian Life Communities at the Sunset District campus. (Fr. Grassi had earlier taught at Santa Clara College. His transfer to SI marked the start of ebb and flow of teachers between these two schools for years to come.)[38]

The *Monitor,* the Catholic newspaper for San Francisco, published this ad in its April 3, 1858, edition:

DAY SCHOOL

The third annual session of the Day School at St. Ignatius Church, Market Street, between Fourth and Fifth, directed by the Fathers of the Society of Jesus, commenced on the 1ˢᵗ of September. The hours of attendance are from 9 o'clock a.m. to 3 o'clock p.m. Pupils of all denominations admitted.

TERMS

English, Spanish, French, Italian, Latin, Greek, Elocution, Arithmetic, Bookkeeping, Mathematics, History, Geography, per month, $8

Preparatory Department, $5. Three lessons weekly will be given in drawing for $2 per month. No extra charge for vocal music and stationery. Payments to be made monthly in advance.

For further information apply in the forenoon to A. Maraschi, S.J.

Before the end of the term, on April 30, 1859, the state legislature granted a charter to the school, and SI officially incorporated under California state law. St. Ignatius Academy changed its name to St. Ignatius College and had the right to confer degrees. That August, the *Alta California* published an article praising Maraschi as "eminently qualified for the position [of college president], being a finished scholar and a man of high moral character.

He has labored incessantly to advance the interests of those placed under his charge and the examination of the several classes exhibited the complete success which has attended his efforts."[39]

The faculty continued to change throughout the 1850s and 1860s as priests were transferred between Santa Clara and SI and as lay teachers came and went with each new discovery of gold or with the lure of a higher-paying job. The one constant was Maraschi who, in typical Jesuit fashion, wore many hats. In addition to serving as college president, he acted as treasurer; an instructor of Latin, Greek and Spanish; and parish priest for St. Ignatius Church where he (as with all Jesuits stationed at SI) celebrated Mass, heard confessions, visited the sick, kept the books and maintained and expanded the facilities. Maraschi served as president until 1862 when he turned the duties over to Fr. Nicolas Congiato, SJ, but he stayed on at SI where he served as treasurer and teacher until his death. SI thrives still because of Fr. Maraschi's careful stewardship, his desire to build SI into a world-class college and his loving devotion to the students, the faculty, and the people of San Francisco.

(As an interesting aside, Fr. Maraschi spent some time surreptitiously tutoring a young woman, Charlotte McFarland, who had been orphaned in infancy and given over to her aunt to raise. That aunt was both staunchly anti-clerical and opposed to the formal education of women. Charlotte somehow contacted Maraschi who agreed to teach her to read. Charlotte had to hide her books from her aunt, who would burn them upon discovery. "But both Fr. Maraschi and my mother were persistent," said Jack Gibbons '37, Charlotte's son. "She was an extremely bright woman who, later in life, would read the *Wall Street Journal* and the racing form every day. She thought the sun rose and set on Fr. Maraschi.")

Snapshots of School Life: 1860-61

By 1860, the school consisted of several ramshackle classrooms that lacked "a oneness of plan" that made for "an unsatisfactory patchwork."[40] Maraschi was reluctant to build anything that would increase the school's sizeable debt, and through prudent administration, he was able to cut that debt by $1,200 and purchase more scientific equipment including "a steam engine, an electric machine and appendices, an air pump and appendices, articles bought at San Francisco College, a theodolite, a compression fountain…. [and a] telescope, a very fine instrument, and for many years the best in California."[41] (San Francisco College, which operated briefly, was forced to close due to lack of patronage.)

By December 1860 the sand hill behind the school had been leveled to create a playing field, and Maraschi instituted the school's first athletic program by giving students a ball to play with. Students provided their own organization and coaching for whatever games they devised. (It would take 50 more years for a formal sports program to emerge when SI joined the city's Academic Athletic League in 1910.

Enrollment at SI increased as people gained easier access to it, thanks, in large measure, to the Market Street Railroad Company, which, on July 4, 1860, opened a line on Market Street from Third to Valencia Streets, running both horsecar and steam train lines. Students could also use a wooden plank walkway that connected the church and school to the city through what would become Union Square. In the spring and summer of 1861 work crews graded and "macadamized" Market Street, making it easier for students to walk to school.

One of those students was John J. Cunningham, who was listed in the school's first college catalogue of 1861. (The catalogue, also called the prospectus, was an early non-illustrated version of the yearbook, listing students, teachers, courses and prizewinners for each year.) He had enrolled the previous year at the age of 6 and later wrote about his first day at school:

"I remember the adventure as if were just this morning. [My mother and I walked up Jessie Street to Fourth Street to a gate] that led to the ascent of the hill of learning, along the rough pine planks that furnished footing for the children that went to the school on top of the hill. Ushered into the room, my awe-stricken eyes beheld my future pedagogue, Mr. John Egan, who presided over the educational development of some 30 urchins, ranging from 5 years of age to 13 or 14. My name was registered; I was assigned a seat; I was kissed goodbye by my mother,

Charlotte McFarland was secretly tutored by Fr. Maraschi.

who warned me not to eat in class and to be home early for dinner…. I recall that, in June 1861, St. Ignatius College held its closing exercises in the open, at the rear of the church. The year following, we had a wet winter and our classes were held in the basement of the church, the floors of which had to be raised by planking that we boys might go dryshod to our classrooms."[42]

(Cunningham would later become the first native-born Californian to enter the Society of Jesus, and he spent nearly 60 years in the order before his death in 1931. He distinguished himself by directing the Gentlemen's Sodality of St. Ignatius Church and would be the first of a long line of SI alumni who would return to their alma mater to teach.)

The catalogue that included Cunningham's name also included the school's rules of behavior: "All must treat their companions as becomes persons of polite education. Anything, therefore contrary to a decent behavior, all wrestling, laying hands on each other, all improper language, all disorderly conduct in going to or returning from school, are strictly forbidden. "The school room is to be considered at all times, sacred to silence and study … all cutting of benches, or otherwise injuring any of the furniture or walls, or writing upon them, is strictly forbidden."

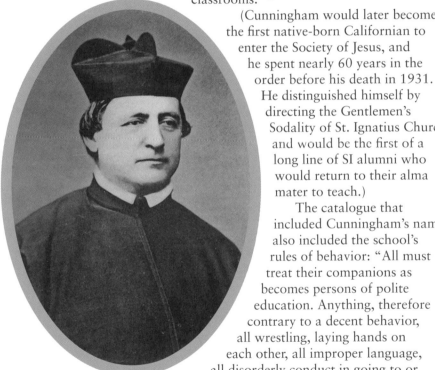

Fr. Burchard Villiger, SJ, SI's 3rd President (1865-1866)

The following year's catalogue emphasized that the school's purpose was to give "a thorough classical, mathematical and philosophical education…. Experience has proved that by this method are imparted the best literary education, the fullest knowledge of English, and the most perfect training of the mind; and, on the other hand, exemptions in this regard have been found to be a great source of idleness and indifference to study."[43]

Students were also kept from "idleness" by attending Mass each Monday, Wednesday and Saturday and by assisting "at the explanation of Catechism on Tuesday and Friday as well as receiving the sacrament of penance once a month." Note that the two days off for students were Thursday and Sunday, as the school followed the Italian system of education. This schedule did not change for many years.[44]

Riordan offers us another glimpse inside the life of the students and teachers in his description of the "good, simple Fr. Benedict Piccardo! Who does not remember him of the facile pen, from which Latin hexameters flowed with astonishing ease and elegance? Who that ever came in contact with him has not seen him glow with enthusiasm at the mere mention of the name of Virgil, the *Aeneid* of whom he almost knew by heart? Start a line at random, and Fr. Piccardo, even in his declining years … would immediately continue the text. His devotion to Virgil, for it would be hard to speak of it by any other name, may indeed at times have amused by the very intensity of its earnestness; but it never failed to produce its effect upon the minds of his pupils, and stir up a spirit of loving regard for the classics."[45]

The Jesuits at SI entertained a few noteworthy

visitors including the famed Jesuit missionary Peter DeSmet, who had recruited many of the first Italian Jesuits to come to North America and who was a well-respected "Black Robe" among Native American tribes in the Great Plains and Rocky Mountain regions. Another noteworthy visitor was Fr. Felix Sopranis, SJ, the visitor general of the Jesuit houses in America, who had arrived on March 25, 1861, to make an official inspection of SI. He spent two months in California, mostly in San Francisco, and recommended that the school, though deep in debt, borrow more money to expand. He also asked Maraschi to wait until the arrival of Fr. Burchard Villiger, SJ, the new superior of the California mission.

Villiger arrived in May and took over as president of Santa Clara College, where he turned the one-story adobe classrooms there into a grander college. He also felt that SI should build a school befitting the new city of San Francisco and instructed Maraschi to raise funds to build a three-story brick building adjacent to the church.

Villiger knew that Americans equated great education with grand buildings. As Fr. McKevitt writes in his history of Italian Jesuits in the United States, "Wherever they went, the émigrés [Jesuits] were torn between two conflicting desires: to adhere to European conventions and to adapt to the exigencies of American culture. When erecting schools and churches, the exiles quickly learned that handsome buildings were essential in their adopted homeland. 'Appearances count for a lot here,' a Neapolitan Jesuit wrote. 'The American, more than any other nationality is impressed by appearances, and believes in what he sees.' They believe 'a beautiful building must signify an excellent school,' and hence 'we

must adapt to this weakness of theirs.'"[46]

Despite a debt of $24,000, Maraschi appealed to the St. Ignatius Church parishioners and SI parents to help with the construction of the new school. Up until then, Maraschi had not troubled his parishioners by asking for donations, and they were grateful for this reticence. They responded well to his request for school funding also, in part, because the popular six-year-old school had proved a success. The first gift of $100 came from a Mr. D. J. Oliver and several other sizeable gifts followed. In August 1861, Maraschi purchased for $11,000 the adjoining lots to the west of the school as the site for the new college and church.

The men of San Francisco supported SI in other ways, too. As a student Sodality had already been formed, the Jesuit fathers thought a men's Sodality would be a fitting addition. They invited the men of the parish and fathers of students to meet November 6, 1861, to organize a Sodality of the Blessed Virgin Mary. It eventually included "the most prominent Catholic laymen of the city; and there was every reason to hope much both for the private spiritual welfare of those who composed it and the general good of Catholicity in San Francisco, from an organized body of men not ashamed to profess publicly the piety of their hearts." The Gentlemen's Sodality remained a prominent part of St. Ignatius Church activity until the late 1960s.[47]

This group found its counterpart in the Ladies Sodality of the Blessed Virgin Mary. It started when "the ladies of the congregation … began to look with envious eyes upon the [men's] organization, and to ask why they, too, might not have a like Sodality. Surely they were as devoted to the virgin Mother as the men; if any doubt existed, well just

give them a chance to disprove it." Thus, on May 14, 1862, that organization sprang into being. "So generous was the response to this invitation, and so rapid the growth of the [ladies] sodality, that by the end of the month it far outnumbered that of the men [and] could boast a regular membership of 290."[48]

The Eloquent Indian & The Archbishop

In August 1861, SI appointed its first prefect of discipline in the form of Fr. James Vanzina, SJ, "who received from Superiors the task of mastering the difficulties of the character of the American boy … while he, at the same time, sought to master those, even greater, of the English idiom."[49] That same month also saw the arrival of the most famous Jesuit preacher of his time, Fr. James Chrysostom Bouchard, SJ. Bouchard was the son of Marie Elizabeth Bucheur (or Beshard) who had immigrated to the U.S. from France with her parents. When members of the Comanche tribe killed her parents during a raid, she was adopted by the Lenni-Lenappi tribe, an offshoot of the Delawares, and later married the tribe's chief, Kistalwa. They had two children, the younger being Swift-Foot, the future priest. "It is said that even from infancy he showed a remarkably religious spirit and would gather his little companions around him and tell them what he had learned from his mother about the Great Spirit."[50] When he turned 12, his father died when the tribe attacked the Sioux. A Presbyterian minister took him to study at Marietta College in Ohio, and he eventually became a minister. While visiting St. Louis, he heard Fr. Damen preach to children. Riordan writes that "he listened, was impressed by what he heard, sought more light and was received into the

Church in January 1846."

After entering the Society of Jesus in 1848, he gathered large crowds wherever he preached. Upon his arrival in California, he used SI as his base of mission operations — maintaining a room there for 30 years — while preaching to throngs at St. Ignatius Church and throughout the western states in cities, towns and mining camps.

Bouchard's popularity, while a boon to St. Ignatius Church, caused a problem for Alemany who was besieged by the complaints of many of his parish priests, already heavily in debt, who were losing parishioners to the Jesuits. Alemany, himself, was also losing patience with the Jesuits, especially with their autonomy in relation to St. Ignatius Church and parishes. The problem came to a head in the 1860s with SI's plan to build a new school next to its first Market Street site.

In an 1862 letter to Archbishop John Baptist Purcell of Cincinnati, Alemany mentioned some of his frustrations with SI, noting that he had invited the Jesuits to open a school "with a view to have the Catholic boys of this city taught almost gratuitously." Now they "charged rather too much." Further, "until recently they had but a small school.... Now they have placed a large number of Fathers in their establishments here, some of whom preach with much satisfaction to the people; they carry on an immense building to be used principally for church and their residence; they seem to spare no means to attract all, and, by means of confraternities, they seem to obtain large numbers from other parishes to their church. This naturally has excited most of the secular priests.... This puts me in a fix; for while I should like the good will of the Fathers.... I should not let the flocks be diverted from their pastors...."[51]

In 1862, Alemany sent Fr. Nicolas Congiato, SJ,

then president of St. Ignatius College, a letter making a surprising request for evidence: "To comply with what I consider my duty, I must inquire of you whether you have permission from the Holy See for the erection of your college or institution of St. Ignatius in this city — and, if so, what is the date of this permission? I must also ask of you a list of the Fathers and Brothers attached to St. Ignatius with their respective ages, and whether they be professed or simple novices. I fear that there is not prudence enough used by all under your care. The love of God demands that we should be prudent."[52]

Congiato forwarded this letter to his superior in Rome along with this commentary: "Here is another of those sweet and consoling letters which have been emanating from His Grace the Archbishop for the last few months ... I am at a loss to understand what the Archbishop means by what he asks and says of us. As far as I know, no imprudence in any way has been committed by any under my care here in San Francisco of late. The poor Archbishop is led by the nose and believes whatever is told about us by those who surround him."[53]

Those who led Alemany "by the nose," according to Congiato and other SI Jesuits, were the dozen parish priests on his diocesan council. In 1863, Alemany asked these priests to comment on the "harmful" ac-

Joseph Sadoc Alemany, San Francisco's first archbishop.

Opposite page: Fr. James Bouchard.

tivities of the San Francisco Jesuits. Their replies were lengthy and vociferous, accusing the Jesuits of luring away parishioners by encouraging membership in the sodalities and by the "lavish distribution of the St. Ignatius Water ... a beverage, in fact superceding the Napa Soda Water and the various 'nostrums' guaranteed for the infallible cure of all the maladies of human nature."[54]

Alemany responded to his priests' concerns by writing to Fr. Congiato reiterating his demand for the deed to St. Ignatius Church or face the consequence "that if this was not done ... I should declare your Church here to be no longer a Parish Church." Losing status as a parish would mean losing revenue that came from weddings, funerals and baptisms — crucial funds that supported the school. (The archbishop tended to look the other way when Jesuits performed last rites, as he felt it did the parishes no harm and served the common good.) Without those monies, SI would sink further into debt. However, the Jesuits chose not to surrender title to their beloved Church. Thus, on October 2, 1863, Alemany sent a letter to Maraschi, who served then as pastor of St. Ignatius, announcing that the church would lose its parish status. The neighboring parishes of St. Patrick's, St. Joseph's and St. Mary's gobbled up the St. Ignatius Church parish territory, and the Jesuits announced this sad news to their former parishioners at Mass.[55]

Accolti tried to make peace between the Jesuits and Alemany with lengthy letters to both parties urging patience; those letters helped, but did not change anyone's mind. Alemany still believed the Jesuits were intentionally luring away parishioners, while many Jesuits believed that San Franciscans came to them simply because they were the better preachers.

Foremost among these better preachers was Fr. Bouchard, the "Eloquent Indian," who remained one of the focuses of the tensions between the Jesuits and the Archbishop. At times, Fr. Congiato found it prudent to "remove him from San Francisco from time to time so as not to make his presence obnoxious to Archbishop Alemany." Alemany did not approve of, and, in fact, sought to dismantle, the two sodalities of St. Ignatius Church that Bouchard helped to establish, as he worried that the fund-raising by these groups hurt the fund-raising efforts of his own parish priests.[56]

He had another problem with Fr. Bouchard, one that dealt with his rather lengthy beard that he started growing shortly after his arrival to California. Alemany wrote to Fr. John Ponte, SJ, the Jesuit superior, that he preferred for Bouchard to "cut the hair short with the scissors, as practiced by St. Alphonsus, and have the neck protected with something warm, which, I feel confident, would have the desired effect...." Despite an order from Archbishop Charles Seghers of Portland to Bouchard to "shave off your beard as soon as the present 'cold spell' ceases," Bouchard never did. He let it "grow and prosper until it became quite a distinctive and personal trademark ... in his journeyings throughout the Far West. With it he lived and with it he died!"[57]

Difficulties between the Jesuits and Alemany flared again when the Jesuits sought permission to move from Market Street to Van Ness and Hayes — a site far too close to the proposed cathedral to suit Alemany. (This controversy will be discussed in the next chapter.)

Fortunately, Alemany and the Jesuits made peace toward the end of his term as archbishop. As Fr. Parmisano writes in *Mission West*, "on the 19th of May, 1885, Father Sasia, in company with Fathers Kenna and Congiato, waited on the Archbishop to wish him Godspeed and, five days later, he departed.

Whatever differences had existed between him and the Fathers had long since been healed — differences, in fact, which were rather due to external influences which had been brought to bear upon the pious prelate than to anything spontaneous on his own part. An ornament to his noble Order and to the Archdiocese, he left behind him no sincerer admirers of his many virtues than the Fathers of St. Ignatius."

The question of St. Ignatius Church regaining its parish arose again in 1885 when Alemany's successor, Archbishop Riordan, asked the superior of the Society of Jesus for permission to reinstate that status. Ironically, the SI Jesuits declined that request, as they sought to keep their college church free from the burden of parish duties. St. Ignatius Church would not regain its status as a parish until 1994 with the reorganization of the San Francisco Archdiocese undertaken by Archbishop John Quinn.

HOW THE IRISH ROMAN CATHOLICS BLOCKADE THE SIDEWALK EVERY SUNDAY, IN FRONT OF THE JESUITS R.C. CHURCH ON MARKET STREET, AFTER LAST MASS

From Colonel Thistleton's Jolly Giant, an anti-Catholic weekly magazine published in San Francisco during the 1870s. This is from the March 28, 1874 issue. Reprinted from "Eloquent Indian," by Fr. John McGloin, SJ.

II. St. Ignatius College Comes of Age (1861 ~ 1880)

*I*n its second campus, just next door to its first *Market Street school, SI became one of the leading colleges in the Bay Area thanks to three great peda-gogues — Frs. Varsi, Bayma and Neri. Fr. Neri shined the first electric light in San Francisco from the window of St. Ignatius College, Fr. Bayma authored several major texts on religion and "molecular mechanics," and Fr. Varsi studied astronomy at the University of Paris. These men produced generations of Ignatians steeped in both classical and modern education.*

These early years saw the birth of several SI traditions, from the Sanctuary Society to drama, with SI students performing the first school play west of the Mississippi. It did not take long for SI to outgrow its new campus, however. This, and the sting of high property taxes levied on Market Street buildings, led to the decision to build the third campus on Hayes and Van Ness Avenues. That building campaign met opposition from the people of San Francisco, upset that SI had hired Chinese brick makers, and from Archbishop Alemany, fearful that the new church and school would be too close to the proposed cathedral. SI faced all these obstacles, and more, as it continued to grow and define itself.

The Opening

of the Second Campus: 1861-1862

Tension between SI and the archdiocese convinced Maraschi to put plans to build a new church on hold as early as 1861. Something had to be done, however, as the old church was far too small. When Fr. Bouchard preached, "the little edifice [of the church] was taxed to its utmost, so that crowds stood without, unable to gain admission. Still his voice, which was remarkably powerful, reached even to these; and they stood in rapt admiration, for never before had they heard a man speak like this man."[1] In order to hold the crowds, Maraschi decided to use the upper level of the new college as a large hall, which could be used as a place of worship, and classrooms would occupy the first floor. From the base of the brickwork to the top of the cross, the school would measure 75-feet high.

On January 21, 1862, Maraschi stepped down as SI's first president-rector at the end of the usual six-year term, and Fr. Congiato, an old friend of Alemany and the former head of the California mission, took over. The Jesuits hoped that Congiato's close ties with

The Jesuits built the second campus next door to the first in 1862.
They left it only when property taxes for the Market Street property grew too burdensome.

An 1860 drawing shows the original church and school adjacent to the new campus.

Alemany would delay any decision regarding the St. Ignatius parish, as Sunday contributions were essential in keeping the school running. Also, the overworked Maraschi needed more time to attend to finances, teaching and parish work.

The official announcement to the people of San Francisco that SI would build a new college came from Bouchard on February 23, 1862, who proclaimed that the Jesuits hoped "to erect a more commodious building and place of worship and also a college for the youth now growing up in our midst…. We are but poor Jesuits, but with God's help, we anticipate no apprehension of failure. Our work here is to promote the honor and glory of God by affording means of worshipping Him in a suitable temple."[2]

Building soon began, and after workers had laid the foundations of the Jesuit residence and college,

the school held a ceremony in May 1862 that marked the laying of the cornerstone before a crowd of 3,000. Among those attending were Fr. Villiger from Santa Clara College and a Jesuit novice, Hugh McKeadney, who was also a talented architect and builder. He had drawn the plans for the new school and would serve as the project manager.

By July, SI had spent $60,000 on the new structure, $55,000 of that lent by the Hibernia Bank with a monthly interest rate of 1 percent. Due to the dispute over the church's status as a parish, the Jesuits could not raise funds throughout the city but had to rely on voluntary gifts. "To tell the truth," writes Riordan, "the offerings were generally small; $250 was certainly not a large amount, yet it was the largest individual gift that the fathers received, and the number of donors could be counted on the fingers of one hand." Among those donors, Riordan notes, were several parish priests who were friends of the Jesuits.[3]

In August 1862, SI purchased a three-ton steel bell, measuring 6 feet at its mouth, cast in Sheffield, England. One of the city's voluntary fire companies had ordered the bell, but by the time it arrived, the company had no funds to pay for it. The bell, christened the "San Francisco" went up for sale, and Villiger and Maraschi discovered it in an iron foundry while walking one day. "Father," said Villiger to Maraschi, "that would be a fine college bell, but we have no money to buy it." The two went to see the foundry's owner, and Villiger asked for the bell, noting that "it would be a fine college bell, but we are too poor."

Three weeks later, workers at Conroy and O'Connor Foundry marched the big bell up Market Street to the college and left it in the middle of the garden along with a letter indicating that the priests could take as long as they wished to pay the $1,350 bill for the bell. The Jesuits built a 30-foot tower in the garden and hung the bell atop it, ringing it "regularly for the college exercises and the Angelus, and its peal resounded for miles around."[4] (That same bell was moved to the school's third site and crashed to the basement of the church during the 1906 earthquake and fire. The bell was rescued and installed in the bell towers of the following two St. Ignatius Churches. It was refurbished in the 1990s and still rings each day at noon, the oldest bell in daily use in the city.)

By Christmas Day 1862, the Jesuits had spent $102,500 on the new school and had amassed a debt nearing $140,000. With great faith that the school would succeed, they opened the great hall in the new building for worship. Visitors found the new brick building to be "severely plain in style but substantial and commodious.... The classrooms were large and airy and extended the whole length of the building.... Two rooms on the ground floor of the Fathers' residence, and fronting Market Street, were devoted to science. Between these last, there was a permanent partition; not so, however, between the others. With these, everything save the outer walls was moveable." Those who toured the new facility walked westward on wooden sidewalks and a newly graded Market Street past the old school and church (now used as a chapel for the sodalities). They passed the Market Street entrance for the new church and then turned south at Jessie Street where they found SI's front doors. In short, what these Christmas Day visitors saw was a church and college that "were the best in the city" and by the end of the year, the student body swelled to 457 who were drawn to this impressive new school. The number of faculty, too, had increased to care for these new students. In 1861, SI employed four

Jesuits and three laymen, and those numbers grew to eight Jesuits and four laymen by the end of 1862.

Two years later, in 1864, one San Francisco newspaper wrote of the new SI: "Today the Jesuits have built the most prosperous and populous education institution in California."[5]

Stability & Earthquakes: 1863-68

The debating society began February 4, 1863, with the unwieldy name of the "Philodianosian Society." Riordan writes that this name "must have been a matter of long and deep consideration. It had to be learned, uncommon, drawn from the parent Greek and with enough roll to it to give due distinction to such as fortune favored sufficiently to admit as members."[6] The society's first officers were Prof. W.J.G. Williams, president; A.J. Bowie, vice-president; H.P. Bowie, secretary; G.K. Pardow, treasurer; A.A. Pardow, librarian; and A.A. O'Neil, censor. The society lasted only one year, but would soon resurface the following October as the Philhistorian Debating Society "since history was to supply the main themes for discussion."[7]

The 1863 school year ended with an impressive exhibition. By removing the wall partitions, students transformed the entire first floor into an exhibition hall,

August J. Bowie, Jr., received SI's first Bachelor of Arts degree.

arranged chairs in tiers and built a stage. The morning session offered literary, musical and scientific demonstrations by students, with music supplied by the Santa Clara College Band. The evening session included a dramatic presentation entitled "Joseph and his Brethren" with James M. O'Sullivan (later to become a Jesuit priest) as Joseph. Playing the roles of Joseph's brothers, Issachar and Nepthali, were Jeremiah F. Sullivan (SI 1870) and Frank Sullivan, brothers who would later become judges. (Jeremiah would go on to become an associate justice of the California Supreme Court, and his younger brother, Matthew Sullivan (SI 1876) would advance to become Chief Justice and later the first dean of the SI School of Law.) This play, a popular one for Catholic schools in the 19th century, was most likely the first dramatic show staged at SI and the start of a long and continuous tradition of student theatre. (USF's College Players and SI's drama department both point to this play as evidence that they are the oldest theatre companies west of the Mississippi.) These end-of-term exhibitions, which continued for 50 years, also provided great entertainment for the citizens of San Francisco, many of whom came even though they had little or no connection with the school.

That commencement ceremony also marked the first time St. Ignatius College conferred a Bachelor of Arts degree. The recipient was Augustus J. Bowie, Jr., who went on to study in Europe and earned a Doctoral degree in engineering. (Only recipients of Bachelor's and Master's degrees took part in graduation ceremonies; other students simply matriculated to the next grade.) This first degree was proof of a claim the school advertised in the 1863 *City Directory of San Francisco* in which the Jesuits noted that they were empowered by its 1859 state charter to "confer degrees and academical honors in all the learned professions and to exercise all the rights and privileges common to any other literary institution in the United States.... [The] design of the institution is to give a thorough English, Classical, Mathematical and Philosophical Education ... provided with a full staff of professors, this institution presents considerable advantages for the mental and moral training of the students; a complete Philosophical apparatus has been ordered from Paris and the Laboratory contains over 250 pure chemicals and all that is necessary for the most complicated manipulations and analysis.... The College has, moreover, a complete photographic gallery; a telegraphic apparatus has also been provided which, through the kindness of the California State Telegraph Company, connects St. Ignatius College with Santa Clara College." The advertisement listed monthly tuition as $3 in the preparatory department, $5 for the grammar department and $8 for the higher department.[8] In today's dollars those figures translate to $40, $70 and $110 per month — a significant sum.

Perhaps the school had to advertise so extensively because it faced serious competition for the first time in its career. San Francisco boys could now choose from among five colleges: SI, Santa Clara, Sacred Heart College (later to become St. Mary's College), Union College and San Francisco College. Also, the loss of parish status in 1863 led to a drop in income. Helping to spend what little money the school had was Fr. Anthony Cichi, SJ, an eminent chemist, who purchased "magnificent photograph apparatus." Maraschi continued to keep the books and kept track of every penny spent, including the purchase of figures for the manger scene of "houses, shepherds and even St. Joseph ... camel and horses for the wise kings." By the end of 1863, the debt grew by $18,000.

Fortunately, 1864 began with good news. Though

SI opened in 1855, it did not receive official recognition from the Society of Jesus until 1859, when it was granted the status of "*Collegium inchoatum*" or "College commenced."[9] In 1864, Rome upgraded that conditional status to make it a "complete institution."[10]

The fine libraries of SI and USF had their start in 1864, when the school purchased a complete edition of the works of the Fathers of the Church and solicited donations from students, families, friends and benefactors. Soon the Jesuits accumulated a large collection of volumes in the college library. (All these books were destroyed in the Great Earthquake and Fire of 1906.)

SI welcomed its third president on July 2, 1865, after Congiato was assigned the general superiorship of the California mission. He appointed Villiger as his successor and he, in turn, handed over the presidency of Santa Clara College to Masnata. His term would only last one year, as his superiors recalled him to the Maryland Province to serve the Church there as an administrator. Before he left, he cancelled SI's elementary program and vocational courses. He hoped to institute a strictly classical curriculum, similar to those of Jesuit colleges in Europe and on the East Coast. As a result of this unwise decision, SI's enrollment fell to 188, though it grew to 236 the next year when a commercial course was

reintroduced. As Riordan notes, "the San Francisco of that day was certainly not prepared for classical standards."[11]

During much of the 1860s, the Civil War had little effect in California and while it stirred the interests of SI's students and faculty, few were directly touched by this bloody conflict. All, however, were profoundly shaken by the assassination of President Abraham Lincoln. When he died on April 15, 1865, a mob ransacked the newspaper office of the *Monitor* (the Catholic newspaper) and crowds talked of doing the same to Catholic churches and institutions. Riordan blamed the mayhem on "bigots [who] are [ready] to take advantage of whatever may be distorted to the prejudice of the Catholic Church [and to] invest the dastardly deed with a religious significance which it

This view of the second campus shows the clock tower built to house a bell puchased by the Jesuits. However, the priests could not afford to buy the clock itself, and so they painted on a clock face instead.

did not bear."[12] On the day of the funeral, SI draped its exterior walls in mourning and the school's 490 students and 17 faculty (12 Jesuits and five laymen) marched in the April 19 funeral procession.

Two years later, the SI Jesuits petitioned Archbishop Alemany to allow them to minister to the growing number of African-Americans coming to San Francisco. Alemany wrote to Congiato, who was in his second term as college president (1866-69), that he preferred "to wait before availing myself of your charitable offer."

(Later, in 1871 and 1874, the Jesuits turned down two requests by Alemany to minister to the Chinese community in San Francisco. As Fr. Riordan writes: "burdened as the Fathers were with many duties flowing from their educational commitments as well as those coming from the maintenance of a large church … it was felt, and this after proper consultation with superiors in Rome, that it was not expedient to undertake a work so excellent and so desirable which must necessarily interfere with other works already accepted and established.")[13]

In August 1865, several more Italian Jesuits joined their SI brothers, the foremost among them being Fr. Joseph Neri, the skilled chemist who would later illuminate Market Street for the nation's centennial celebration. Also that year, James M. O'Sullivan became the first SI graduate to enter the Society of Jesus.

A new tradition began in 1865, when students started serving Mass at St. Ignatius Church as altar boys. This group later became known as the Sanctuary Society and continued until the 1960s when SI moved to its Sunset District campus. As McGloin writes: "Many Jesuits who have served or are at present serving in the Jesuit apostolate in San Francisco can trace their religious vocations from their first contacts with

this organization."[14]

(Many alumni from the Shirt Factory and the Stanyan Street Campus have fond memories of being in the Sanctuary Society. Priests said Mass from 5:30–7 a.m. and then, in later years, treated the altar boys to a simple breakfast. Peter Devine '66, tells one story of a time when his father, George Devine '19, sat down for breakfast along with dozens of other boys. "Fr. Mootz, the prefect of discipline, had the bright idea to order donuts for the kids. After everyone had a donut, they asked for a second one. When he refused, they playfully grabbed the box out of his hand and began throwing the donuts at him. Even though he was the prefect of discipline, he was a pushover. Just then the rector walked in and accused the boys of assaulting a priest, a crime he called a sacrilege. It made a big impression on those kids!")

The school population increased in 1867 with the reintroduction of the elementary classes, and the Jesuit apostolate in San Francisco grew too, when Accolti returned that year to serve as chaplain at San Quentin Prison and to teach at SI. (Over the years, other Jesuits who lived at SI also worked at a number of apostolates including San Francisco General Hospital, the city jail, Alcatraz, and the Presidio.)

Alexander A. O'Neill received the school's first Master of Arts degree in 1867, though not due to any work completed at SI since the conferring of his Bachelor's degree two years prior. The college awarded a Master's degree to anyone who completed two years of study at any institution after leaving SI, and O'Neill had studied medicine elsewhere to earn this distinction.[15]

Stephen M. White, the first in a long line of SI alumni to make a name for themselves in politics, enrolled at SI for the 1867-68 term and stayed until

1870, when he transferred to Santa Clara College. He later served as the U.S. Senator representing California from 1893 to 1899 and was known as the "Father of Los Angeles Harbor."

This relatively stable period in the life of the school was disrupted by several earthquakes, the first occurring on October 8, 1865, and another one day later. Then, on October 21, 1868, a 42-second jolt caused major damage throughout the city. Two chimneys on the church and school building collapsed, and plaster ornaments inside the church fell and shattered on the floor; fortunately, no worshippers suffered injury. Students were dismissed from class between Wednesday, October 21, and Monday, October 26, for fear the frequent aftershocks might bring the school down on their heads.

Other churches in the city suffered severe damage, and SI allowed the Lutherans to use their old wooden church, which had been converted into a chapel for the various school sodalities. "It was with great pleasure that the Fathers were able to do them this act of kindness, for the most cordial relations had always existed between St. Ignatius and the German pastor and his flock."[16]

Fr. Joseph Bayma:

SI's Fifth President: 1869-1873

Born in Piedmont, Italy, Joseph Bayma entered the Society of Jesus in 1832 and began a distinguished career as a teacher of literature, mathematics, physics and chemistry. (Look for more on Bayma's scholarship in the next section.) While administering an Italian seminary in 1860, Bayma found himself in the middle of anti-Catholic riots, forcing him to flee to England where he taught at Stonyhurst for seven years. He left for California in 1868 and became SI's fifth president in 1869 before moving to Santa Clara College three years later. He taught there until his death in 1892.

For his first task, Bayma borrowed $30,000 for the construction of 16 classrooms in a three-story wooden addition to the school, and the new wing was completed by December 1869. This expenditure, of course, simply added to the vast debt. Despite swimming in red ink, the Jesuits still committed themselves to educating those who could not afford to pay tuition. A reporter noted this in the January 8, 1870, edition of *The Monitor*: "The rules of the college require pay, but there are many attending whose parents cannot afford the pension, small as it is, so the good Fathers teach their children gratis. But all that can afford are required to pay regularly. There are about five hundred boys attending the college; nearly one-half of them, we are informed, do not pay a cent." (Every Jesuit school still follows the policy that no child be denied an education because he or she cannot afford tuition.)

Two years later, when the Jesuits heard of rumors accusing them of a lack of generosity, Bayma sent this letter to the editor of the *Monitor*: "As we have heard on unquestionable authority that, in a certain public place in this city, in discussing the merits of Catholic schools, it has lately been asserted that, at St. Ignatius College, the Jesuits make their scholars pay very well, and that very few receive the privilege of a gratuitous education, we think it proper to bring before the public the following facts…. Our yearly receipts pay for an average of 184 pupils at most, leaving a balance of 201 pupils per year, from whom we receive no compensation. When this is taken in connection with the nature of our institution, which is not a common school, but an incorporated college having all the rights and prerogatives of the best universities, imparting to her pupils every branch of knowledge and fitting them for the highest positions in society, it will be evident to any unbiased mind that the assertions we criticize are illiberal and uncharitable. Those who made them could do something more useful to the community than dissuade Catholic parents from sending their children to a Catholic college. Their zeal would show to better advantage if they spoke of helping Catholic schools to teach the thousands of Catholic children in this city, whom Catholic schools are unable to accommodate. As it is, we do not require payment as a necessary condition of admission; but we do require quiet behavior, close application and gentlemanly manners. A deficiency in these requirements, especially the last, and not that of money, justifies a refusal either to admit or to keep a pupil. Time and again have we admitted deserving pupils who had been refused admission into other schools, for the reason, we were informed, that they could not pay. Were it our primary object to make our college a paying institution, we would certainly adopt a different policy. But we can inform our patrons and the public that our expenses are considerably greater than our receipts, and this is the best apology we can offer for inviting our friends to the College Hall sometime next month, that we may dispose of some gifts at the 'Ladies Enterprise' for the benefit of the school."

As a symbol of the school's commitment to the people of San Francisco — and of its poverty — the Jesuits erected a tower for the 6,000-pound bell on December 28, 1869, but the priests couldn't raise enough funds to build a working clock atop the tower. They did paint hours on the face of the clock, but had no money to buy hands or the clockworks. The big bell, writes Riordan, "[rang] out the old and [rang] in the new; though to our thinking, the new that it rang in for St. Ignatius was only an increase of the old that it rang out — debt — debt — debt…."[17]

Despite the money owed by SI (more than $170,000

by now), Bayma and his brother priests began discussing the need to build a larger college and church in a quieter part of San Francisco. The primary reason for the move was the large tax-burden the Jesuits faced ($12,000 in 1877) for their valuable Market Street real estate. As Riordan adds: "those that scanned the future knew that, on the present site, permanence could never be."[18]

Maraschi believed SI could best provide for its future by investing in real estate. Toward that end, he purchased a portion of the San Pablo Ranch in the East Bay. No one farmed this barren land, but Maraschi saw it as valuable as it bordered the deep water of the San Francisco Bay. The sale of this land in 1902 for $200,000 would help SI repay its debts.

Not all the Jesuits approved of Maraschi's money-making schemes. At one point, he encouraged his friends to buy stock in a company that owned a gold mine. When that company went bankrupt, the Jesuits were afraid that they would be liable and that Maraschi would be accused of being an accessory to fraud. Maraschi also rented out apartments and organized an informal insurance company. Fr. Henry Imoda, SJ, SI rector in 1888, wrote to his superiors of his concern, noting that if Maraschi died without a will, the Society of Jesus could face numerous lawsuits.

Life at the school continued despite earthquake and debt. In 1871 the school inaugurated a new Debating Hall and instituted the Ignatian Literary Society, dedicated to "the improvement of all connected with it, in debate, social advancement and general literature." The group barred any discussion "bordering on immorality, sectarianism and direct politics," and set the minimum age of membership at 16.[19] Also, the first school band and choral group formed on February 12, 1874, "to cultivate music for innocent social enjoyment and to add solemnity to civil and religious festivals."[20]

Three Greats: Bayma, Neri & Varsi

Throughout the 1870s, the school's fame increased as a result of the work of three key professors: President Joseph Bayma, SJ, Fr. Joseph Neri, SJ, and Fr. Aloysius Varsi, SJ.

Bayma authored several major works including *The Love of Religious Perfection* in 1863, *Treatise on Molecular Mechanics* in 1866, *Force and Matter* (published posthumously in 1901), and a series of high schools texts on algebra, geometry, analytical geometry, trigonometry and calculus. "The series was unique and revealed his specialized genius in that no proofs or methods were presented from other persons — all were derived from his own speculations and research."[21]

In his major work, *Treatise on Molecular Mechanics*, Bayma, along with the noted Jesuit scientist Roger Boscovich, "reduces all matter to unextended points, centers of force acting in the inverse square of the distance; thus acting upon one another, but of course not touching." This work was studied in Oxford and Cambridge and at science departments of other noteworthy universities. Bayma

Frs. Bayma, Neri & Varsi cemented SI's reputation as one of the leading colleges on the West Coast.

wrote poetry, too, and was considered an English scholar, remarkable for a man who started learning the language at 32.[22]

Fr. Neri at SCU in 1904. He was 68 and going blind. In 1871 he introduced electric light to San Franciscans, & later had an outstanding career as scientist, spiritual director & chaplain.

Neri, an early experimenter of electricity, built and perfected his own electrical lighting system in 1869 to use during his lectures, and he became the chairman of the natural sciences department in 1870. To illustrate his lectures on electricity, he built the city's first storage battery (a peroxide of lead combination with about 30 plates), and his exhibitions of electric lights in the 1870s drew huge crowds. The first such demonstration occurred in 1871 when he showed an amazed crowd an electric arc light from a window of the college facing Market Street in what was the first known use of electricity in San Francisco.

On July 4, 1876, for the Centennial Celebration of the Declaration of Independence, Neri lit Market Street with arc lights, Foucault's lamps and reflectors, the first exhibition of public arc lighting on the Pacific Coast. From the college roof to the other side of Market Street, Neri hung several wires from which he suspended three arc lights to illuminate the night parade. "They threw a stream of soft, mellow light all along the line of march of the military and civic procession down to the ferry at the bay...."[23]

A decade would pass before other cities tried this method of street illumination. Even Thomas Edison's first incandescent lamp would not shine until 1879, and it took until 1881 before New York installed the first central electric power plant. Neri's electric demonstrations impressed the city fathers to the point where they installed "an electrical system of illumination then regarded as the largest in the world."[24]

The machine that gave Neri the ability to conduct those electric experiments was a large electro-magnetic device (called the Alliance Machine) that had been used in the second Siege of Paris during the Franco-Prussian War for "lighting defensive work."[25] Tiburcio Parrott, a great friend and benefactor of SI, purchased this machine and donated it to the school.

This machine was featured in an 1874 notice advertising one of Neri's public electrical experiments: "The experiment will be an exhibition of the electric light, with the new mammoth magneto-electric machine lately received from Paris, from the Compagnie l'Alliance, with a new electric light regulator for first-class lighthouses, spherical mirror and large Fresnel lens *a échelons*, mounted on a rotating table to project the light to the most distant points around San Francisco and the bay within the range of the tower. The light is such as to be seen at a distance of two hundred miles.... The apparatus used on the occasion alone, and for the purpose indicated, represents over $5,000..." Neri improved upon the machine by strengthening its magnets by current from a storage battery.[26]

According to Riordan, Neri hoped to "popularize

The Alliance Machine, used in the Second Siege of Paris, gave Fr. Neri the ability to conduct electrical experiments.

and spread as much as possible the discoveries of science, freed from the errors with which infidel scientists ever sought to yoke them; and he thought,

The Jesuits added new stairs leading to the church and school. Note the horse-drawn carriage parked outside on Market Street.

and thought well, that this was an excellent form of missionary work, since it removed prejudices from the minds of non-Catholics, helping to strengthen the faith of ill-instructed Catholics, and make good Catholics prouder of the old Church of the Ages, by demonstrating practically that there was no true advance of science that she could not bless; that there was not, and could not, be any conflict between true science and true religion."[27]

In 1876 Neri came to the rescue of the Mechanics Institute of the University of California. That institute held an annual industrial fair, but faced stiff competition that year from Philadelphia's centennial celebration. Neri lent the institute nearly all of his scientific apparatus, which was moved to the Mechanics Pavilion where it was displayed and operated. For most of August and September that year, Neri offered lectures and demonstrations twice weekly with help from SI students. He also helped to power the first miniature electric train to run west of the Mississippi.[28]

The Institute directors praised SI for its aid, noting that "we may well congratulate ourselves for possessing within our midst, in this young city and state, such facilities for scientific education as St. Ignatius College affords to our rising generation, and such a cabinet of [scientific laboratory equipment], second to none in the United States."[29]

Neri's scientific exhibitions and demonstrations were also a part of the three-day commencement exercises that marked the end of the school term and the conferral of advanced degrees on college-level students. (High school-level students did not celebrate their own graduation exercise until 1916.)

By the time he turned 75, Neri suffered from near complete blindness. His eyesight was always defective, but years of working with spectroscopes ended his vision. By the time of his death, Neri had amassed scientific equipment worth nearly $100,000 and gave SI the most notable science department in the West. A commission from the Smithsonian Society rated SI's collection of scientific apparatus among the top five in the United States.

Another gift helped make SI the leading scientific institution of the West. In 1875, Joseph Donohoe gave to the school an extensive collection of stuffed birds, minerals and Native American artifacts. "As generous as was this gift," notes Riordan, "it was outdone by the richness of the cases that contained it…. The cabinet contains … remains, shells, coins, rarities, curiosities and historical records of various kinds, collected in the course of many years, and contributed by donors from different parts of the world. The collection made up three or four wagon loads in transportation." The gift also gave SI one of the best ornithological collections in the United States.[30]

The final teacher in this distinguished triumvirate was Aloysius Varsi, a nobleman, born at Cagliari on the island of Sardinia of Corsican parents on March 9, 1830. He joined the Society of Jesus at 15 and studied in Chieri, near Turin. In 1848, revolution forced the Jesuits to flee, and, according to an account given by Fr. Richard A. Gleeson, SJ, Varsi and his comrades barely escaped with their lives. "They took refuge with the Brother Hospitallers of St. John of God, living, as they did, on alms collected from door to door."

Varsi studied in Belgium and France and became "a deep philosopher; a profound theologian; a beloved pupil of Father, afterwards Cardinal, Franzelin…. Owing to his extraordinary ability as a mathematician and a scientist, he was sent to Paris where he attended the lectures of the most distinguished scientists of the day, who found in him a prodigy. This training was to prepare him for the Mission in China, there to take charge of the Imperial Observatory."

Ordained in 1856 at 26, Varsi eventually came to the U.S. in 1862 where he served as a chaplain in the Civil War. Later he taught at Boston College and at Georgetown, where an Italian artist selected him as a model of St. Charles Boromeo for a fresco above the main altar in the Church of St. Aloysius in Washington, D.C., depicting the first communion of St. Aloysius. (That fresco can still be seen in this Jesuit parish church.) While in Boston, "he gave a public lecture with experiments on electricity, the first of its kind to be given in the United States."

Varsi's superiors, knowing the needs of the California mission, sent him there instead of China. McGloin describes him as being a "cultured and mellow person with a gift for friendship," and Br. Tom Marshall, SJ, former archivist for the California Province, calls him a "giant of a man, bigger than any of the men around him." His greatest contribution to SI was his astute administration and fund-raising during a time of great expansion. Thanks to his leadership, the Jesuits built SI into one of the finest colleges in the world and St. Ignatius Church into a beautiful house of worship, all in the center of the city.

Another Battle with the Archbishop

In 1873, Bayma stepped down as president, and the next two presidents — Fr. Aloysius Masnata, SJ, and Fr. John Pinasco, SJ — began making plans to move the school and church westward to Hayes Street and Van Ness Avenue, the present site of the Louise Davies Symphony Hall.

For all the success of the school, the Jesuits were fearful of losing SI College. Property taxes on Market Street, already at $12,000 per year, kept climbing as the property rose in value, and the school's debt kept growing along with it. SI needed to move to stay alive, and it had to act fast when property became available. However, the Jesuits ran into a rather formidable roadblock in the person of Archbishop Alemany, who opposed the move on the grounds that any new church would lure parishioners away from the second site of the Cathedral, planned for Van Ness and Geary (and dedicated in 1891), and from neighboring churches, especially St. Joseph's, which would soon move to larger quarters at 10th and Howard Streets.

The Jesuits needed to do something to continue their ministry in San Francisco. In desperation, they sent Varsi to Rome to seek permission with the Congregation for the Propagation of the Faith, which had all U.S. churches under its jurisdiction. Varsi eventually met with its prefect, Cardinal Franchi, who had the final say in the matter. "Varsi submitted maps of San Francisco to the Cardinal, indicating two lots which were located closer to Market Street than the site ultimately selected. [The Cardinal's answer] which was to afflict Alemany and to cause him to renew his opposition to the move [was] *'Facciano pure'* (Let them by all means.)"[31]

Even with permission from the Cardinal, the Jesuits knew they had a fight ahead of them. To give Varsi more stature in facing Alemany, Beckx appointed him superior of the California Jesuit mission in October 1877. He returned to San Francisco, bringing with him 13 Jesuits from Europe and the East Coast. (More on this in the next section.)

Shortly after Varsi's return, land owned by D.J. Oliver became available in the Western Addition. The Jesuits paid $200,000 for a city block of land bordered by Van Ness Avenue, Hayes, Franklin and Grove Streets on October 29, 1877. The figure was high for its day, but the land was about to be sold in subdivisions, prompting the quick decision by the Jesuits to purchase the property.

Even with Vatican permission and with the sale a fait accompli, Varsi waited nearly a year before writing to Alemany to seek local permission. In a letter dated June 21, 1878, Varsi wrote the following:

"Most Reverend Archbishop:

"I have received information from Very Rev. Father General Beckx that it has been decided in Rome by the proper authority, that we are at liberty to remove St. Ignatius Church and the College to lot 74 of the Western Addition; and Father General says that we should commence building at once.

"This decision relieves me of a very great anxiety; but yet I should feel very much grieved if I were to proceed without first obtaining Your Grace's blessing on it. I therefore most humbly beg Your Grace, for the love of Jesus' Sacred Heart and of St. Aloysius, whose feast we celebrate to-day, to grant us this favor; for which we shall ever feel most grateful.

"Hoping to receive a favorable answer soon, I remain, with the most sincere respect,

"Your Grace's very humble servant in Christ,
— A. Varsi, SJ"

Alemany wrote to Cardinal Simeoni in Rome seeking confirmation of this news. When he received it, he sent a sad reply to Seimeoni on July 22, 1878, noting his displeasure with the judgment: "I bow my head and accept your decision with holy resignation." The August 5 letter Alemany penned to Varsi had a more contentious tone; in it, he insisted on being compensated for losses and expressed his concern for the financial well-being of the archdiocese. The tone of the letter hints at Alemany's anger over Varsi's Roman maneuvers:[32]

"Very Reverend and dear Sir:

"The Cardinal Prefect informed me that considering what had been done, the immense injury which would accrue to you if your new building was not built in your new lot, purchased with a most

heavy sum, etc., you may be allowed to proceed; consequently, I can have no objection. The Cardinal, however, intimates that should any injury result to the Cathedral (and I request the same in regard to St. Joseph's) from your proximity, it would become necessary to have such compensated. When answering His Eminence, I added that, in case to avoid trouble it was deemed prudent to build [a] new Cathedral elsewhere, and the heirs of N. Hawse would sue and recover the lot donated for a Cathedral at [the corner] of 10th & Howard St., I would expect to be indemnified. "Yours truly in Christ,
+J.S. Alemany, A.S.F."[33]

The Memoirs of Fr. Richard Gleeson, SJ

As mentioned in the previous section, Varsi returned to the states with far more than permission to relocate the college. He brought with him 13 Jesuit novices, much needed recruits for the school in a time of dwindling vocations. Among those young men was Richard A. Gleeson, SJ, an enthusiastic 15-year-old. The following accounts of Gleeson's meeting with Varsi and of his journey west are taken from *A Memoir: Richard A. Gleeson, SJ*, by Alexander J. Cody, SJ, and from *My Golden Jubilee Thoughts,* by Richard Gleeson, SJ. These accounts offer a glimpse of what life was like for Jesuits in the 1870s, especially as they traveled across a burgeoning America.

"Father Ferrari, one of Richard's teachers, was expecting a distinguished visitor in the person of a fellow Jesuit priest, Aloysius Varsi, just returned from Rome, then in New York and on his way back to California. He had been looking through Europe for recruits to serve on the Jesuit Mission in California and had some 12 young men awaiting him in New York. He was to come to Philadelphia in search of possible others."[34]

Gleeson was called out of a Latin class and taken to a parlor in the rectory of the Gesu in Philadelphia to meet Varsi. There, Gleeson's teacher said, "Father Varsi, this is Richard Gleeson. He may go with you to California." Gleeson felt that "the piercing eyes of the stranger-priest read me through. He arose, approached, his face lighted with his inexpressible smile, took my hands into his large warm hands, and sat me beside him on an old-fashioned sofa. Before he said a word I was captivated. I was ready to go with him to California, China, Africa, anywhere in the wide world. In a few minutes he was satisfied that I had a vocation to the Society of Jesus. Within two hours I had returned joyfully with the permission and the blessing of my truly Christian Father and Mother and the next day, the Feast of St. Matthew Apostle the Evangelist, I was on my way to California with 13 others, who formed the band gathered in Europe by Father Varsi, for the Jesuit Mission by the Golden Gate. From my first meeting with Father Varsi until this hour he has been an inspiration and an ideal."[35]

Gleeson's fellow novices on the trip came from England, Ireland, Belgium, Poland, Holland, Germany and Italy, and eight of the group barely spoke English. The group boarded a train in New York for the week-long journey to California, with Gleeson, the youngest member, spending much of the time teaching English to his fellow novices.

"Generally the days were dull and uneventful; and as far as the classes in pronunciation went, to the embryo teachers, most disappointing. The evenings were better, when the rosary was said in common; afterwards, everyone joined in a sacred concert of Latin hymns and of a Latin version of the Litany of Loretto. Fellow travelers who had sedulously avoided the coach through morning and afternoon hours then cautiously peeked in and invariably stayed to listen. They could not really be blamed for their suspicion and their caution. It was indeed, a motley group, each member tailored to his own national costume, which, in turn, was not too new, and, sometimes, not too well-fitted. Be-

The bricks used to build the third campus caused turmoil for the Jesuits. The one pictured above was found during the construction of the Davies Symphony Hall. Note the cross that identifies the brick as one made by Christian workers.

sides, each member spoke some foreign language, and for a long period in American history foreign languages were anathema to native American ears. The group, also, were an odd lot. They served themselves two meals a day out of their own capacious hamper baskets. They ate the third in the dining car. Invariably they walked in, following the same leader, who, the more boldly curious learned, answered to the name of Allen; and the more boldly curious learned, too, just the exact bill of fare. On a particular morning the leader ordered spring chicken; the group ordered thirteen more; the leader followed with a second order for lamb chops; the thirteen solemnly repeated "lamb chops." Foreigners, evidently, ate as heavily as Americans. On leaving the diner when Father Varsi answered the steward's casual query, 'Were the boys satisfied?' with the off-hand reply that he had heard no complaint, the dining-car manager burst out with 'Complaint! I never met such a crowd! It will take a couple of trips to Omaha to make up for it.'

"It was different, though, the natives reasoned, when it came to singing. The group, really, could be an opera company. When the train reached the North Platte River country in the midst of an electric storm it was delayed for a day at North Platte. The bridge behind collapsed just after the train's crossing and the rails to the westward were partly washed out and needing immediate repair. One of the passengers mustered up courage to speak to Richard Gleeson, for his language, it was noticed, was just as theirs. Richard Gleeson at that moment was in sore need of merriment. A twenty-four hour wait to a 16-year-old boy can be unbearably long, even with the adjuncts of lightning and cloudburst and flood and buckled railroad tracks. Confidentially, the passenger asked, was it a theatrical troupe? 'Yes! Yes!' There were eager possibilities. 'Would you boys put on a show for us tonight at the theatre in town?'

"'Quite willingly!' The words held every enthusiasm and consideration that a young, and an obliging, and a hoping actor could put into the phrase, but they were bolstered conditionally with an appealing glance towards the riverbank and the intimated submission to official management.

"Now Richard Gleeson knew Father Varsi as a nobleman of Cagliari. He knew, too, that while at Georgetown, Father Varsi had served as a model for the Cardinal, St. Charles Borromeo…. But his questioners knew none of this and saw neither the blue Mediterranean nor the robe of cardinal red; they beheld merely a silent, elderly Italian, presumably a temperamental impresario, studying the river's flood in the whipping wind and rain. One look was enough. They made no appeal.

"The train at length got started. At Cheyenne the night grew bitterly cold. Father Varsi wrapped his great overcoat as a blanket over the sleeping Richard and sat motionless in the freezing dark until the dawn. The lengthening miles clicked along to the far West. The snow-clad Sierras swept down into sunny valleys and to marsh lands and to the margin of San Francisco Bay."[36]

Arson and Racism, Bricks and Crosses

Hugh McKeadney, who as a Jesuit novice had designed SI's second Market Street school, began drawing plans for the Van Ness campus. He designed the school in the shape of an "E" — with rooms and corridors extending alongside the church. Varsi first wanted the church to face Van Ness but decided to abandon this plan due to the clouds of dust that blew down the avenue from time to time, and they moved the church façade to Hayes Street. Construction of the new church, campus and residence buildings lasted from 1878–1880 and cost $323,763.

The one controversy surrounding construction had to do with the company supplying the 7 million bricks used to build the church and school. San Francisco was suffering from an economic depression and thousands of men were out of work. Anti-Chinese sentiment ran high as the unemployed blamed Chinese immigrants for taking jobs away from whites by accepting low pay. In the midst of this resentment, a rumor began to circulate that the Jesuit fathers were purchasing bricks "of Chinese manufacture." The *Call* published an article July 2, 1878, claiming that Maraschi "had been waited upon by members of brick-making firms where white labor is employed, and these made offer to supply the bricks at the same cost as the chinamen [sic]; but they had received no encouragement from the Reverend Father. In fact he declined to meet with them. Some very bitter comments were made by the members at their meeting yesterday over the proceeding. White labor, it was said, was employed in response to a general demand; but unless the firms employing it receive more encouragement than heretofore, the men will have to be discharged."[37]

Another newspaper accused the Jesuits of purchasing 15 million bricks and claimed the priests bypassed firms that hired "white men only." The next day, July 3, 1,500 men, most of them members of the Brick Makers' Protective Union, staged a rally on Market Street in front of the school denouncing SI. The newspaper articles and rally enflamed emotions and led someone to set fire to the Market Street college during the Fourth of July parade. Fortunately, the fire was discovered and extinguished in short order and caused only $200 worth of damage. Varsi responded to this incident with a letter published July 7 in the *Call*, which corrected many of the accusations against SI. No Chinese brick company existed, he noted; the Patent Brick Company, from which SI had purchased the bricks, "employs Chinese men but not to the exclusion of white men." He went on to warn that "should we … be compelled by the undue dictations of your publication to adjourn the work to another indefinite season, the workingmen would be the losers."[38]

McKeadney, too, published a statement noting that he alone had signed the contract with the company in question. "We simply wanted first-class hard brick, for which we were to pay hard dollars. It did not occur to us to demand a stipulation that the

Fr. Michael Accolti, SJ, who helped to found the California Mission of the Society of Jesus, died November 7, 1878, shortly before the completion of the third campus.

brick should be made exclusively by white men, any more than it did to the sellers to demand that the gold of the coin should be mined by such."[39]

The letter worked, and the diatribe against the Jesuits ceased. The *Examiner* blamed the *Call* for setting workers against the priests and added: "We hope to see [the college and church building] completed and bounteously endowed, to be at once an ornament to the city and a blessing to all."[40]

The Jesuits, sensitive to the racist demands of the white-controlled unions, did make one concession that modern readers would find most objectionable. They agreed to pay an extra 50 cents per thousand to ensure that white men only would make the bricks used to build the new church and school. The *Evening Post* noted that "in order that no bricks might be delivered other than as agreed, a mold was stipulated to be used that should identify the manufactured articles." That mold was a cross to show that Christian men made the bricks.[41]

The Jesuits and white union leaders discovered a hitch in this compromise. According to the *Evening Post* "there is one portion of the work where white labor is unwilling or unable to compete. This is in taking the heated bricks from the ovens. About twenty men are so employed, and the ovens reach 240 degrees of heat. The Chinamen [sic] who have been engaged for some time at this work are said to be bleached white with the intense fires to which they are subjected.... Just here comes in the necessity of a little common sense in the matter.... It is impossible to correct all the evils of this Chinese plague in a moment or a month, and it is the part of wisdom to always do the best we can under the circumstances, never throwing away an advantage because it is not greater." Thus, in the end, the Christian bricks of SI were made

with the combined effort of white and Chinese labor, in spite of the fear, racism and shortsightedness of those involved.

(When the workers were building Davies Symphony Hall in September 1978, they uncovered a large cache of these bricks, marked with crosses. Kevin Starr, an alumnus and former faculty member of USF, wrote of this discovery in "Free to Speak a Secret," published by USF: "David H. Zisser, an attorney employed as contracts administrator for the Southern Pacific Communications Company, was taking a break from a bout of research in the law library at City Hall. He strolled over to the construction site to get some fresh air and to watch the spectacle of the great bulldozers moving tons of earth. Zisser noticed that among the earth and debris being cleared were countless bricks, many of them marked with the sign of the cross." A graduate of USF, Zisser knew the history behind these bricks and contacted USF, which had them mounted and presented to those who donated $1,250 in honor of the school's 125th anniversary.)

Workmen began laying the foundations for the new school July 11, 1878, and the school celebrated the dedication of the cornerstone on October 20 with 6,000 in attendance. The text of the Latin dedication read by Fr. Bouchard was placed in the cornerstone. (After the 1906 earthquake, the Jesuits recovered that cornerstone and its contents. You can find that same cornerstone outside the entrance to the bell tower of St. Ignatius Church on Fulton and Parker Streets; the contents, however, were removed and placed in the cornerstone of the present church.)

Accolti, who worked so tirelessly to found the California mission, never saw the new school completed. He died November 7, 1878, of what was most likely a massive stroke. His funeral was held in St. Ignatius Church two days later, and he was buried at the Jesuit plot in the Santa Clara Mission cemetery.

The new buildings were dedicated February 1, 1880, and the school opened July 2, 1880, with three distinct sections — the Preparatory Department, the Literary and Commercial Department and the Philosophical and Scientific Department — which occupied separate floors of the three-story college. Most would agree that the new church and school "were among the finest structures in all of San Francisco" up until their destruction in the 1906 earthquake and fire.[42] Among those who helped decorate the interior of the church, especially the elaborate side altars, were many women benefactors, foremost among them being Mrs. Bertha Welch who, in 1890, donated $50,000 to provide for the interior adornment of the church. Among those adornments were 24 stained-glass windows crafted in Munich, decorations by the famed Italian artisans A. Moretti and Trezzini and paintings by the European-trained Domenico Tojetti, one of the city's most famous painters.

Five years later Mrs. Welch gave the Jesuits another $50,000 towards the purchase of a church organ, with 85 stops and 5,301 pipes. Its various parts arrived packed in four extra large railroad cars in September 1896. After a performance, the famous soloist Clarence Eddy judged the organ to be "one of the greatest and finest" in the world.[43]

In 1880, the Jesuits faced a total debt of $862,510 and paid $42,500 in annual interest. Given these

St. Ignatius College included a grammar school for many years. This 1888 photo shows one such class.

numbers, we can understand why the Jesuits grew angry whenever the papers referred to the "million dollar home of the Society of Jesus in San Francisco."[44] Varsi chose to ignore these remarks in public but told his supporters, in private, the size of the debt that supported this "million dollar home."

He also ensured the success of this third campus by hiring more teachers for the 680 students and appointing Fr. Robert E. Kenna, SJ, as the school's eighth president. Kenna, born in Mississippi and raised in San Francisco, was the first non-Italian president the school had since Maraschi opened the doors of the little wood-frame school in 1855.

ST. IGNATIUS CHURCH & COLLEGE, OCT. 15, 1905,

TURRILL & MILLER, PHOTOGRAPHERS SAN FRANCISCO, CAL.

III. THE GREAT JEWEL OF EDUCATION (1880~1905)

*I*n its third campus on Hayes and Van Ness, SI became the premier college on the West Coast, with
the greatest enrollment of any Jesuit college and
*some of the finest scientific equipment and collections
found in any university in America. Many consider
this the Golden Age of SI, when, it seemed, nothing
could diminish the school's luster.*

*Adding to that sheen were several distinguished
alumni, among them John Montgomery '78, the first
person ever to make a successful glider flight. SI students also added to the school's history when they
played rugby against Sacred Heart College in 1893,
inaugurating the oldest athletic high school rivalry
west of the Rocky Mountains.*

*In 1905, when SI celebrated its 50-year anniver-
sary with grand parties and high Masses, everyone in
the community felt on top of the world. They did not
know tragedy would befall them one year later.*

John Montgomery Makes Aviation History

One of the rising stars of SI's science program at
the time of the transition from the second to
the third campus was John Montgomery (SI
1878), who later made aviation history by being the

first person to fly in a heavier-than-air craft when he
soared in a glider near San Diego in 1883.

Born in Yuba City on February 15, 1858, Montgomery moved to Oakland with his family in 1864
and began his study of bird flight and wing structure.
He formulated a theory, which he later proved, that
the curved surface of a bird's wing gave it the lift needed for flight. As a young child, he enjoyed stretching
out on a pillow and pretending to fly, and after attending a July 4 celebration in Emeryville, where he saw
a steam-propelled hydrogen balloon called the Avitor,
he raced back home and built his own version of that
aircraft.

He attended Santa Clara College in 1874 for one
year before transferring to SI, where he studied under
Fr. Neri. He received his Bachelor of Science degree in
1879 and his Master of Science degree in 1880. After
leaving SI, he worked as a foreman on his family's
farm in the Otay Valley near San Diego.

With his sister, Jane, he worked with a steam boiler and bellows to form ash strips into parabolic cambered wing ribs. Apparently these activities did not
earn him the respect of his neighbors, some of whom
"thought him a bit daft." In fact, when he went out
with his brother James on August 28, 1883, to test his

*Opposite page:
The third
campus was
dedicated in
1880.*

of Otay Mesa, assembled their gull-winged glider (later named *The Gull*), which was "as wide as a baseball coach's third base box," and waited for the wind to pick up. When it did, they were ready. James positioned himself 12 to 14 feet below the glider, holding on to a rope attached to its front, and John, at all of 130 pounds, sat inside the glider. When John cried, "Now," James ran, and John rose 15 feet high. He landed at least 300 feet from the point of takeoff. (Some historians claim the distance was as great as 600 feet.) He landed on his feet, holding the 38-pound craft in his arms. All of this happened 20 years before the Wright brothers flew their plane at Kitty Hawk.

Montgomery, in a 1908 speech to the Aeronautical Society of New York, had this to say about his historic flight: "There was a little run and a jump, and I found myself launched in the air. I proceeded against the wind, gliding downhill for a distance of six hundred feet. In this experience I was able to direct my course at will. A peculiar sensation came over me. The first feeling in placing myself at the mercy of the wind, was that of fear. Immediately after came a feeling of security when I realized the solid

John Montgomery (SI 1878), was the first person ever to fly a glider.

glider in the mesa at the edge of the farm, he brought along two rifles to explain to anyone they met that they were only out hunting. Neither wanted to answer questions (fearful of being ridiculed) about the disassembled 38-pound wood and fabric craft they had hidden in a hay wagon, covered with straw.[1]

The two brothers pushed their wagon to the edge

support given by the wing surface. And the support was of a very peculiar nature. There was a cushiony softness about it, yet it was firm. When I found the machine would follow my movements in the seat for balancing, I felt I was self-buoyant ..."[2]

In 1885, he continued testing glider designs and wrote in a letter to his sister: "My attention is still fixed on my flying machine, and I am getting along fast enough to suit myself. Since I last wrote you, I have performed hundreds of experiments and discovered some important facts and laws. I have had many failures and discouragements, but have become convinced more than ever of the correctness of my ideas and plans."

He ended his glider studies in 1886 and focused on studies related to the theory of flight, perhaps because not everyone in the scientific community embraced his notions. Montgomery eventually joined the faculty at Santa Clara College in 1896 and earned a doctoral degree in 1901. During this period he experimented with tandem wing designs.

In 1905, he built a new glider, *The Santa Clara,* a red and white aircraft with a staggered-biplane design. He hired a circus performer to fly it in a daring stunt before 1,000 onlookers and reporters. That performer, Daniel John Maloney (who went by the alias Professor Lanscelles and who wore red tights for the occasion), raised himself by a hot-air balloon in the glider to 4,000 feet above the ground, and then cut himself loose.

That event is described in *A Memoir: Richard A. Gleeson, SJ,* by Alexander J. Cody, SJ: "The greatest event in the closing years of Santa Clara College before it changed into the University of Santa Clara was

had on President's Day, 1905. During Father Kenna's term of office, the President's Day fell on the feast of St. Robert, April 29. This [memorable day] saw the first heavier than air plane, the invention of Professor

John J. Montgomery of the College Faculty, pursuing its undulating course under the force of gravity and the resistance of the atmosphere....

"A nearby hot-air balloon tugged at its moorings. Dan Maloney, an assistant, stood by ready to mount the plane's saddle. Father Kenna blessed the [plane], naming it *The Santa Clara.* Professor Montgomery, hat in hand, led the crowd in a further prayer; then Professor Montgomery signaled to his assistants. A rope was attached to the balloon and to the monoplane; the bag shot skyward and so did Dan Maloney aboard the glider. Four thousand feet up, the two skyships parted. Maloney then began his long glide, mak-

Montgomery flew his glider in south of San Jose. He named his glider "The Evergreen," for the fields over which he flew. (Photos courtesy of San Diego Aerospace Museum.)

ing figure eights, ascending on the rising air-currents like a soaring bird; and because Dan Maloney was a true aerial gymnast, he gave himself over to steering and diving movements that were not outclassed until after 1910 by such stunt fliers as [Lincoln] Beachy. For more than 20 minutes, Dan Maloney kept aloft, at times attaining a speed of 60 miles an hour. When he landed, he came down so gently that he remained upon his feet (supporting the glider with his hands) at a spot decided upon three quarters of a mile from where the balloon had been released. 'I landed like a bird,' was Dan Maloney's jubilant remark. He posed for his picture and then bicycled back to the college. He said later that his two greatest joys were that he had flown a plane blessed by a priest and that he had shown Professor Montgomery's doubting friends that the Professor's 'youthful pranks' had paid off.

"When Professor Montgomery was asked what things gave him the greatest satisfaction, he answered, 'Mainly these: the solemn blessing of the aeroplane and the presence of my aged mother.'

"That 'soaring machine' was strange and quaint, built of light hickory, braced with piano wire, covered with thin, oiled muslin; its wingspread was 24 feet. In the space between the slightly curved and rigid wings, a small bicycle seat was mounted, with handrails above for the flyer to grasp; a semi-circular tail arrangement was attached to the rear wing to be manipulated through pulleys in directing the course of flight. The whole apparatus weighed 42 pounds."

Among those who praised Maloney's flight and Montgomery's glider were Alexander Graham Bell, who claimed that "all subsequent attempts in aviation must begin with the Montgomery machine," and Victor Lougheed (half-brother to the founder of Lockheed Aircraft), who called the flight "the great-est single advance" in aviation. The press also praised Montgomery's achievement and used Montgomery's term "aeroplane" to refer to the entire craft — the first time the word was used to mean more than a part of the machine.[3]

For the next three months, Montgomery flew *The Santa Clara* himself, gliding low enough to buzz the large crowds who had come to watch him. Unfortunately, when Maloney repeated the stunt three months later, he failed to see a tangled cable that broke a strut and led to a fatal crash. As he fell, Maloney offered "a gallant wave just before the impact."

Montgomery continued experimenting with designs with 4-foot and 8-foot models that he tested in wind tunnels, trying to perfect wing design and controls. He also proved expert in other new technologies. At Santa Clara College he helped Fr. Richard H. Bell, SJ, improve the Marconi Wireless, and he designed an electric typewriter. He also received patent No. 831,173 "For Improvements in Aeroplanes," and that patent became the basis for a lawsuit brought by his widow, Regina Cleary Montgomery, in 1921 against the Wright Brothers claiming that her husband was the inventor of the airfoil, the crucial design that allowed for flight.

Despite his physician's advice to stay on the ground, Montgomery continued to fly. At a camp in Evergreen, south of San Jose, Montgomery made 55 successful flights in his most advanced glider from a place now known as Montgomery Hill on the Evergreen College campus. This craft was a monoplane design with a complex longitudinal, lateral and roll control system with a hand yoke and hand-held rudder. For *The Evergreen*, Montgomery used a rail launch system that took the glider downhill for it to gain enough lift to take off. In the past, he had even experimented with horses to give the glider enough speed for takeoff. For *The Evergreen*, however, he had great plans. He hoped, at the conclusion of his experiments, to install an engine to give it powered flight.

His 56th flight on October 31, 1911, proved his last, as the craft stalled and crashed. A stove-bolt, used to hold the main wing support to the fuselage, entered Montgomery's head behind the ear, and he died before help could arrive. (Montgomery's mechanic had wanted to trim that bolt, but Montgomery insisted the bolt remain in case he wanted to "make some change that needs more length."[4)]

Montgomery remains a controversial figure in aviation history, with some arguing that his pioneering work has been overlooked, and others claiming that it has been exaggerated and mythologized over the years. "His development of some of the principles of aerodynamics helped in a modest way to lay the foundation of modern aviation. Montgomery did not invent the curved wing, but he did demonstrate the lifting power of the curve and its use in maintaining flight equilibrium. Nor did he invent wing warping, but he made effective use of this wing shape in his earlier gliders."[5]

Montgomery's achievements were dramatized in a full-length 1946 Columbia Pictures feature, *Gallant Journey*, starring Glenn Ford and Janet Blair, and recounted in a 1967 biography, *John Joseph Montgomery: Father of Basic Flying* by Arthur D. Spearman, SJ. The original gliders don't exist, but parts of the originals are housed at the Smithsonian, and parts from *The Evergreen* were used in a facsimile, which is on display at the Hiller Aviation Museum in San Carlos along with replicas of *The Gull* and *The Santa Clara*.

The museum also displays a brass plaque with this inscription: "International Historic Mechanical Engineering Landmark, Montgomery Glider 1883: This replica represents the first heavier-than-air-craft to achieve controlled piloted flight. The glider's design was based on the pioneering aerodynamic theories and experimental procedures of John Joseph Montgomery who designed, built and flew it. This glider was way ahead of its time, incorporating a single parabolic cambered wing with stabilizing and control surfaces at the rear of the fuselage. With his glider's success, Montgomery demonstrated aerodynamic principles and designs fundamental to modern aircraft. The American Society of Mechanical Engineers, 1996."

To honor Montgomery, the City of San Diego formally renamed Gibbs Field, which opened in 1937, as Montgomery Field, with the formal dedication taking place May 20, 1950, to honor the man who made the first controlled flight in a fixed wing aircraft. Montgomery's legacy remains at SI, too, as many of his descendants attended St. Ignatius High School and College Preparatory. Montgomery married Regina (Gene) Cleary, the sister of Frank Cleary (Class of 1882) and Alfred J. Cleary (Class of 1900). Both men sent their children and grandchildren to SI, including Mark Cleary '64, who was named chairman of SI's Board of Regents in 2002.

Mark, who served as an altar boy at his aunt Regina's funeral, recalls that even as an adult she would love driving around the city with her brother, Al, who served as San Francisco's first chief administrative officer. "She loved riding with the siren blaring," recalls Mark. "After her brother's death, she had no sirens to play with. She tended to 'faint' in public just to ride in ambulances and hear the sirens. In the movie version of Montgomery's flight, *Gallant Journey*, the actress who played my aunt fainted, and my father commented how true to form it was."

Students went on vacation January 21, 1880, but most returned the next day to help move furniture from the old school on Market Street to the new school on Van Ness Avenue. Bouchard preached

3055.   Class of Rhetoric. St. Ignatius College.   J. M. Hoffman, Photo.

1 E Cullinan   2 D. J. Mahony   3...

A Class of Rhetoric from the third campus (date unknown).

his last sermon January 25 in the church that for years had existed on the second floor of the old school, and on January 31, the SI Jesuits heard confessions there for the last time.

Those same priests were on hand for the February 1 dedication of the new Hayes Street Church, presided over by Archbishop Alemany and Bishop James A.

Healy who delivered the homily before nearly 7,000 people, only half of whom could fit inside the church. Those who could not fit stayed outside during the Mass. By the end of the day, 15,000 people visited the church and school buildings.

At the February 10 dedication of the school's exhibition hall, Bishop Healy told the SI students that "yours is a great state and a great city. You have great mountains, great trees, and I might say a great college…. I would like to impress upon the minds of these young gentlemen that labor is necessary in every walk of life. What you acquire easily is of little value…. Above all it is essential to possess an experimental knowledge of Christianity, not that which is culled from the catechism, but that which is felt in the heart. This is the great jewel of education."[6]

Fewer students took advantage of that jewel of education in the 1880 term, as the new location made it more difficult for them to commute to school. Enrollment fell to 652. Ironically, student population increased on an unexpected front. In 1881 the Jesuits started a Sunday school program for girls and began with nine pupils and one teacher. One year later, the program numbered 700 girls and 45 teachers. This foreshadowing of coeducation came to an end in 1891, according to Riordan, "only when it could be done by others."[7]

The new college also elicited praise from the local press. A *Journal of Commerce* article from the 1880s held that the "new college is to be preferred to the old one…. There is certainly not a better equipped college in this city, as we said before, and the low rate of tuition excites surprise; but this is explained in the foregoing where we mentioned that the aim of the Jesuits was not to gain money but to give education."[8]

Those who had previously benefited from that ed-

The Philhistorian Debating Society Hall inside the Hayes & Van Ness Avenue campus.

ucation gathered in 1880 for the school's first official Alumni Association meeting, with the Hon. Jeremiah F. Sullivan as its inaugural president. "The devotion of the old boys to Alma Mater … had made Father Kenna's task a comparatively easy one." Even before this formation, the classes of 1875–1877 held a joint reunion on May 30, 1878, at the Maison Doree, presided over by Alfred Tobin (SI 1876). "The gathering was large and enthusiastic. The trials, and successes, and varied incidents of college life were rehearsed amid much applause, and when it was proposed to renew college friendships by a yearly banquet, there was no dissenting voice."[9] This reunion was the first for any Catholic college on the Pacific Coast. This organization, quite active at first, eventually grew dormant until the school resurrected it in 1902.[10]

St. Ignatius Church also enjoyed a remarkable popularity in the early 1880s. When two East Coast Jesuits, Fr. Bernard Maguire, SJ, and Fr. Jeremiah O'Connor, SJ, came to St. Ignatius Church to give a two-week mission in February 1881, they drew as many as 15,000 to their services. People were turned away each night for want of room and 17 priests heard confessions until midnight one night. On the Sunday of the mission, priests started distributing communion at 5:15 a.m. and didn't finish until late in the morning.[11]

That year, the church again drew massive crowds on September 19 upon the death of President James Garfield, who had been shot July 2 by an attorney angered that he had been denied a consular post. At the September 26 Solemn High Mass in memory of Garfield, Fr. Kenna eulogized the president and warned parents "concerning the evils that flow from a lack of respect for authority, especially in the young."[12] As with Lincoln's assassination, the Jesuits draped their

school in black for this sad occasion.

For the march commemorating Garfield that day, 500 of the SI student body walked from Grove Street to Market Street. After waiting for two hours, they learned that the Industrial School Band was to lead their part of the parade. The boys grew angry, having imagined that they would be at the head of the procession and fearful that people might confuse the two groups. They threatened not to march, but the Jesuits persuaded them not to cause trouble on this solemn occasion. "No sane mind would mistake them for boys from the [Industrial School] reformatory," they argued, and the students agreed to follow the band.

In 1883, Fr. Joseph Sasia, SJ, took over as college president and also took over the enormous debt of $1,008,511 — a staggering figure for those days. Interest on this grand sum for the past eight years had amounted to $285,264. Fortunately, Mrs. Abbie Parrott (whose husband, Tiburcio Parrott, had earlier acquired

Opposite page: The Sanctuary Society at the third campus.

The physics cabinet held state-of-the-art equipment.

and donated to SI the electro-magnetic machine used in the Siege of Paris), purchased the old Market Street school site for $900,000 in 1886, paying far beyond the value of land and buildings in order to help the Jesuit fathers pay down their debt. Her family later built The Emporium on the site, which closed in the 1990s. (A brass marker near the main entrance of the building, soon to open as a Bloomingdale's, commemorates the site of the first St. Ignatius Academy and College. The school also celebrated its 125th anniversary there in 1980 and added a new plaque to the site.)

The year 1883 also saw the school's enrollment rise to 704, making it by far the largest Jesuit school in the country. Of the Society's 23 colleges, only three schools, aside from SI, had more than 300 students.[13]

Fr. Imoda, took over as president in 1887, and his term would last until 1893. During his tenure, fire destroyed the old church and school on Market Street, which had become a cheap lodging house and a warehouse for a furniture company. While the Jesuits mourned the deaths of three who died in the fire, they were not sad to lose the old buildings, which "had long been an eye-sore to the public and a heart-sore to the Fathers, who, had circumstances permitted, would have torn the buildings down rather than have seen them turned to profane uses."[14]

Imoda turned the administration of the college over to Fr. Edward Allen, SJ, in 1893, and he would lead the school for three years. Imoda, the head of the California Mission, believed the college could support itself without tuition from college students enrolled in the "classical course" (meaning those in the grammar, literary and historical departments who had added Latin and Greek to their studies). The Jesuits, hearkening back to their traditional European roots, also decided only to award degrees to students taking this

Opposite page: Students sit in JUG in an 1890s classroom.

classical course; thus, despite the free tuition, enrollment went down when the 1893 term began.

The Jesuits hoped to raise those numbers through an advertisement that read: "We fear that many Catholics in this city and state are not aware that, following the rule of their founder, where it is possible to do so, the Jesuit Fathers have made of St. Ignatius College a FREE COLLEGE, in all that pertains to superior education, classical and ordinary. To all young men of good character, the Society of Jesus will give education absolutely gratuitous, not an ordinary education but a superior education comprising classics, mathematics, science, philosophy and all cognate matters. To those who do not desire a classical education, the ordinary commercial branches will be taught. Any young man who may desire to acquire knowledge in its fullest sense, to prepare for the professions, for a full university course, has here an opportunity which few in this country possess. San Francisco is, we believe, the only city in the United States which is so blessed, and our young men ought to take advantage of this splendid opportunity offered them. In this respect, the rich have no advantage over the poor, since no other condition is required than a good character and a determination to study."

In 1896, the experiment with free tuition ended, due in large part to the school's enormous debt. The Jesuits once again charged tuition, with college students paying $8 a month and another $10 to receive an academic degree. High school students paid $5 monthly while sixth through eighth graders paid $3.

Joseph Stack was one of the students whose parents paid for him to attend SI in those years, even though he was a reluctant pupil. When he was 16, Stack found himself assigned to a Latin class by the "formidable" prefect of studies, Fr. Henry Woods, SJ.

Students in 1890.

Many years later, Stack wrote the following account of that class:

"At Christmas time [in 1895], Fr. Woods suggested that I move up to a poetry class taught by Mr. John Hayes, SJ, a scholastic. Here I found myself with those who had already mastered Latin and Greek grammar and who were reading Homer in Greek and Virgil in Latin with great facility. I had to sweat to keep up with these branches. I recall writing a bit of verse, which Mr. Hayes remodeled for me. He wished me to read it at one of the class specimens given before the whole student body. Fr. Woods refused permission, using a familiar argument of his: the verse was too well done for me to be the author and too poorly done if the scholastic were to acknowledge himself as the writer!" Stack later grew fond of his classes at SI and, after graduating in 1896, entered the Society of Jesus and served as a teacher and retreat master.[15]

The Great Rivalry

This era of the school also marks the start of a great athletic rivalry between SI and Sacred Heart, the longest of any school west of the Rocky Mountains, which started with a rugby game played on St. Patrick's Day in 1893. (The centenary of that rivalry was celebrated in the fall of 1992 at Kezar Stadium with a crowd of 7,000 witnessing SI's 7–3 victory over the Irish. Mention of this grand tradition can be found in the 2002 *National High School Sports Record Book* on page 151 under the "Oldest Current Rivalries" section. There, the SI vs. SH match-ups are tied for ninth with two other schools. The oldest rivalry dates from 1875 between New London and Norwich Free Academy, both of Connecticut.)

San Francisco Chronicle writer Will Connolly '28, in the November 4, 1949, edition, wrote about that first game in an interview with Warren White '39, an English teacher at SI at the time who had researched the history of the rivalry. He told Connolly that the game began when Cornelius Kennedy, a Sacred Heart College student, "bought a pamphlet on 'How to Play Football,' written by a young man under the style of Amos Alonzo Stagg. Kennedy collected a team at Sacred Heart and elected himself coach and captain because he owned the textbook and the football. He had an investment of $12 and needed competition to protect it. So he visited St. Ignatius and cajoled the boys into fielding a team. Kennedy was magnanimous. St. Ignatius had no coach, no team. He generously agreed to teach them the fundamentals gleaned from the Stagg book. For two

59

When SI's first rugby team played SH in 1893, it marked the start of the oldest high school rivalry west of the Rocky Mountains. That rivalry took on new dimensions in 1946 with the Bruce-Mahoney trophy games.

weeks he tutored the Ignatians late in the day, after putting in licks with his own Sacred Heart eleven.

"The game was played on March 17, which is St. Patrick's Day and a holiday for the schools…. The game was held in Central Park at Eighth and Market streets where the Crystal Palace now stands. Fifty-seven years ago, the corner was on the outer fringe of the downtown district, virtually in the sticks. Both Sacred Heart and St. Ignatius had to practice surreptitiously, for the Brothers and the Jesuits considered football a brutalizing sport at that time and a distraction from scholarly pursuits. The way it was played, they were right. Injuries were common.

"Sacred Heart won, 14 to 4. The Irish of SH were accoutered in canvas jackets, red and yellow stockings. St. Ignatius wore black and gold, a radical change from the colors they now affect. You could suspect that Kennedy deliberately under-coached St. Ignatius. As a matter of fact, he gave his best effort. The game was close. Under association rules … at that time, a touchdown counted 4 points and a field goal 2."

Connolly also noted that "the Kennedy in question later embraced the sacerdotal cloth. He is now pastor of St. Paul's, a basic parish in the Mission. Surely the Rev. Cornelius Kennedy, in his salad days, wouldn't have stooped to trick the poor, benighted Ignatians. He was simply trying to help."

The Sodalists' procession to St. Joseph's statue in the Father's Garden was an annual event that began in 1883. Fr. Francis Prelato, SJ stands up against the banner on the right.

Passing the Torch: The Death of Fr. Maraschi

In 1896, Fr. John P. Frieden, SJ, succeeded Allen as president, and he served for the next dozen years, leading SI through the triumph of its 50th anniversary celebration and through the tragedy of the destruction of the school and church in the Great San Francisco Earthquake and Fire of 1906.

Born in Luxemburg, Frieden had worked as a teacher even before entering college. He entered the Society of Jesus after completing his college work and,

come into contact with thousands of San Franciscans who knew and loved him for his charity.

A newspaper account of the funeral Mass offered this commentary: "With impressive simplicity, without pomp or ceremony, a low Mass of requiem was offered yesterday morning (Saturday, March 20), by Fr. Frieden, president, at 9:15 in St. Ignatius Church for the repose of the soul of the late Fr. Anthony Maraschi…. There was no sermon, no word of commendation for the dead, no account of his deeds of sacrifice and acts of holy zeal. But deep in the hearts of the vast concourse that filled pews and aisles and pressed against the sanctuary rail, the eulogy of that life was engraved in indelible characters."[16]

As a testament to how many people loved Maraschi, "a continuous stream of people commenced moving along the line of Hayes Street toward St. Ignatius Church, growing more dense" as more people joined the throngs coming to mourn the late, great priest.[17] Even the Southern Pacific Railroad Company transported his body to Santa Clara for burial at no charge.

Of Maraschi, Riordan offers up this accolade: "Prominent businessmen of the city sought his advice in business matters, while the poor and ailing found in him equally a friend, for he was no discriminator of persons. Many believed that he could work miracles and begged his assistance in all manner of diseases;

while still a novice, traveled to Missouri where he taught at St. Louis University. After several other assignments, he became president of Detroit College in 1885 and, in 1889, head of the Missouri Province. He trained novices before his appointment to SI.

Even before Frieden came to SI, most of the Jesuits who were involved with the founding of the school were in failing health or had died. On March 18, 1897, Maraschi, SI's founder, died, and his body was borne to the Gentlemen's Sodality chapel. As the school's founder, first president and treasurer, he had

and, indeed, it seems certain that, whether in recompense of their faith or the merits of Father Maraschi, more than one special favor answered their requests. He was a man of action, not words; seemingly cold and distant, but, for all that, possessing a warm heart. He has every right to be considered the founder even of the present church and college, for it was the property on Market Street and the land near Richmond, both acquired through him, that supplied the funds to build St. Ignatius and to liquidate its debt."[18]

Fortunately for the Society of Jesus, just as it was losing members of the old guard to death, young men were entering its ranks. One such Jesuit, George P. Butler, was ordained a priest in June 1897, the first SI alumnus of the Van Ness campus to have that distinction.

During this period, the school stopped offering classes for elementary students as the Jesuits attempted to solidify the school's reputation as a world-class school of higher learning and as more and more parishes opened their own grammar schools. As a result, enrollment fell; "it was hoped, however, that the raising of the standard of the college would more than compensate for any numerical loss."[19] The school still struggled to repay its debts, and by 1899 it re-established the Ignatian Society, friends of the school who had earlier provided the school with financial assistance.

In 1901, President William McKinley visited San Francisco, and SI dressed itself up to honor the president, who passed by the school in a grand procession. "The pupils were ranged on the steps and balconies of the building and gave three rousing cheers as the President passed. To mark his appreciation, Mr. McKinley stopped his carriage and gracefully returned the salute of the young men. He made no effort to conceal his pleasure, and turned several times to look back and admire the beauty of the buildings in their festive attire."[20]

That same year, Mrs. Regina Pescia created what may be the college's first named scholarship in honor of her husband, Dr. Joseph Pescia. The scholarship provided a student with an annual gift of $130 for four years. Students competed for this academic honor, and its first recipient was Owen McCann.

Young Owen was not the only financial beneficiary that year. The East Bay land near Richmond that Maraschi had purchased in the 1870s, and adjacent parcels that he had acquired over the years, had grown in value as they were near the Santa Fe line and Standard Oil's property. The Jesuits sold the land for $200,000 in 1901, and for the first time in its history, the school was out of debt. The Jesuits thanked the donors of the Ignatian Society and disbanded this organization. They looked to the new century with confidence and, for the first time, with solvency.

Celebrating the First 50 Years

The first years of the new century proved to be propitious ones for the school's drama program. Students staged *Macbeth* in January 1900, and *Julius Caesar* a year later. In 1903, they performed *Richard III* and, in 1905, *Henry V*. The school also experimented with its classical program by introducing, in 1902, practical business courses such as bookkeeping and stenography at no extra cost to students.

Also, as part of their commitment to *mens sana in corpore sano* (a sound mind in a sound body), the Jesuits strengthened their athletic program in 1902 by building two handball courts and, in 1903, a

The SI community celebrated the 50th anniversary of the founding of the school on October 15, 1905.

$40,000 gymnasium for use by students and members of the Gentlemen's Sodality. Riordan writes that "on February 2, 1903, after assisting at Mass, the students repaired to the college lot on Franklin Street, there to assist at the beginning of the work."[21] This use of student labor by the Jesuits was typical for its day.

The 10,000-square-foot gym contained handball courts, a billiard room, a reading room, a bowling alley, a 50x15-foot plunge bath, a boxing ring, gymnastic equipment, a locker room and a running course on the upper level of the 35-foot-tall structure.

To prepare for the 50-year celebration, 130 members of the Alumni Association gathered at the Palace Hotel on October 8, 1903, just a few blocks down the street from the site of the first SI. Others gathered to celebrate, too, though in an unusual place. In the basement of SI college, the women members of the Francesca Society (named in honor of St. Frances of Rome), had set up a free school for 240 girls to teach them sewing and cooking. During Christmas 1903, the teachers and Jesuits distributed presents to the girls and gave them a tree to decorate.

The jubilee year of 1905 began with an announcement that the school term would, from this year forward, begin in September and end in June. The Archbishop made this request to encourage uniformity among the schools and colleges in the archdiocese. The Jesuits also announced that no diplomas would be conferred during the May commencement exercises that year; instead, graduates would receive them in October during the Jubilee celebration.

In September, SI president Fr. Frieden received this note of congratulations from the Society's Superior General, Louis Martin, SJ: "Happy to me beyond measure have been the tidings of the coming of the fiftieth anniversary of the founding of St. Ignatius College, so dear to me, and of our church, begun under happy auspices by your worthy fellow citizens. For if, in thought, I dwell on the very abundant and happy fruit which, with God's help, you have reaped in Church and College, and with which the well-known piety and favor of your pupils and fellow citizens have hitherto requited your labors, I cannot but give thanks to Almighty God for the past, and harbor the assured hope that, for the future also, we shall reap equal, yea even more abundant fruit."[22]

Pope Pius X also sent his blessing to SI in August: "In this blessing, therefore, we shall rest, here in the dawn of the coming Jubilee, hoping, as we well may, that its brightness will not be ephemeral; and, that the seeds of sacrifice planted in the last half century of effort will take root and prosper unto the ripened ear of success, for the welfare of Catholicity in San Francisco."

SI, in its jubilee year, was at the pinnacle of its success. It was one of the key centers for San Francisco Catholics who sought to study and worship. It attracted thousands to the various missions and retreats by visiting Jesuits. The famed preacher and future principal of St. Ignatius High School, Fr. Dennis Kavanagh, SJ, wrote the following in an article appearing in the *St. Ignatius Church Calendar* (an expanded church bulletin, published monthly for 70 years): "Perhaps the most striking features of St. Ignatius Church were the solemn services for which it was noted. Who does not recall the male choir of 50 voices under the masterful direction of Fr. Allen and Fr. Coltelli? Who does not remember the solemn occasions like the feast of Corpus Christi when 1,600 sodalists, decorated with medal and badge, moved in solemn procession through the aisles? Who does not know how, on days like Good Friday, the church was filled to overflowing two hours before the services began?

"We cannot explain this enthusiasm better than by attributing it to the well known and universally admitted fact that the Fathers connected with the church were remarkable for their eloquence and zeal and self-sacrificing devotion for the cause of religion. It mattered not whether it was the thundering eloquence of Fr. Bouchard or the whole-hearted appeals of the fervent Fr. Kenna or the gentle exhortations of Fr. Calzia, or the sweet paternal assents of Fr. Varsi or the catechetical instructions of Fr. Prelato — there was a ring of exceptional earnestness in it all which attracted people from all parts of the city."[23]

The school began the weeklong jubilee festivities on October 15, 1905, with a Pontifical Mass of Thanksgiving at St. Ignatius Church celebrated by Coadjutor Archbishop George Montgomery of San Francisco. Many other celebrations and Masses followed and the alumni gathered on the Tuesday of that week. The next day, the Alumni Association took many of the visiting Jesuits, who had come to SI for the celebration, on a San Francisco Bay cruise and, on the following day, to the top of Mt. Tamalpais on the old railroad line that wound its way to the peak.

That Thursday, October 19, the school celebrated with a gala banquet at the St. Francis Hotel, attended by 175 priests, alumni, faculty and friends of the school. The Hon. W. Bourke Cockran, a Congressman from New York and noted orator, was the featured speaker. Judge Jeremiah Sullivan, the first president of the Alumni Association, offered these opening remarks: "Any American citizen who overlooks the portals of the Golden Gate can find much to gratify him both

as an American and a Catholic. As he looks out upon the sea, he reflects that, for over 800 miles, it washes the shore of his beloved California. When he looks back on old Yerba Buena, where the Franciscan friars made their first home, he reflects on the wonderful growth of San Francisco. He looks back to the early days of the city where, closely following the discovery of gold, came the followers of Loyola, — there they laid the foundation of the great institution of learning whose fiftieth anniversary we celebrate tonight."[24] The next day, October 20, the Jesuits held a special commencement ceremony where they awarded nine Master's and Bachelor's degrees and 16 honorary degrees.

On February 10, 1904, the Junior Philhistorian Society staged Sedecias: The Last King of Judah.

IV. 'ALL HELL SEEMED DANCING WITH JOY'

With the jubilee celebration over, the regular routine of school re-established itself in late 1905 and early 1906. The Jesuits even considered moving the high school portion of the school to some available land west of Fillmore Street, or even to Millbrae, and making St. Ignatius College into a university. (In the Consultors' minutes from September 6, 1904, preserved in the Province Archive Room, mention is made that "the advisors think entirely that the high school must be removed, and they propose that now a piece of land be purchased near the city [of] San Francisco, for example, near Millbrae." Two days later, the minutes indicate that "the Superior has read what actions there were in discussion of SI College regarding the proposed high school…. The advisors of this mission praise the actions and the deeds.") In addition, the college considered adding a law school and medical school and offering degrees in those fields.

Mother Earth had other plans for the school. At 5:13 a.m. on the morning of April 18, 1906, three days after Easter Sunday, a fearsome earthquake shook much of the state for 48 seconds and ignited a four-day firestorm that destroyed much of the city. The disaster caused $500 million in damage (more than

$8 billion in today's dollars.) Though accounts at the time put the death toll at just under 700, more than 3,000 people lost their lives in the conflagration, many trapped in tenements that collapsed when the ground beneath them liquefied.

The earthquake caused major, but reparable, damage to the church and college. Plaster fell in the Jesuit residence and college, and cracks widened in the walls. The church roof suffered major damage,

In 1901, SI decorated itself for the visit by President McKinley. It was the finest the school would ever look.

The bell that rung in the second and third campuses came crashing to the ground on April 18, 1906, but survived intact. The Jesuits rescued it and placed it in the current St. Ignatius Church.

The skeleton of City Hall across Van Ness Avenue can be seen in this August 17, 1906, photograph as clean-up efforts continued.

and inside, a small piece of the cornice fell from the northwest corner of the ceiling. Fr. Vincent Testa, SJ, SI's treasurer, was struck on the nose by a falling candlestick while saying Mass at the high altar. McGloin writes that "since he had not reached the Consecration, he took off the vestments and left the church." In the sanctuary, the damage consisted of broken candelabra, candles, flowers, vases and broken glass. The marble statues of Mary and St. Joseph fell to the ground and broke.[1]

Despite this, worshippers and priests had cleared the debris by 6:15 a.m. Four Masses were said in succession for the people of San Francisco, with 300 attending the last Mass. Several priests also heard confessions until 8 a.m.[2]

There is an apocryphal story that Frieden, SI's president, sent a two-word cable to Rome: "*Ignatius fuit!*" ("Ignatius is no more!"), a reworking of Virgil's "*Illium fuit*" regarding Troy's destruction as described in *The Aeneid*. Other facts of that horrific day are certain, as Frieden gave a detailed account of them several years later in a lecture in St. Louis entitled "Some Personal Reminiscences of the Earthquake of San Francisco." What follows is an excerpt of his talk:

"The time was near the hour of sunrise — 5:13 in the morning, Wednesday, the 18th of April. Stillness hovered over the great city…. Everybody at St. Ignatius was astir. Rising at 5 o'clock [the traditional hour for Jesuits in residence to arise], we were engaged in making our toilet. Slight and short earthquakes, of one to five seconds duration, are not a rare occurrence in San Francisco. Half a dozen per annum, or even twice that number, would not startle the average Californian. The practice on such occasions is to cross oneself, and say a short prayer — a couple of seconds, and all would be over. I must admit, however, that I always felt relieved when the earth was once more quiet, in its normal steadiness.

"And so that morning, thirteen minutes after five, when the first indications of the earthquake appeared, I crossed myself, made the wonted aspirations, and continued dressing. But in a few seconds I felt that the quake was sharper than any I had yet experienced. Lo, half clad as I was, I dropped on my knees, at the foot of my bed, and prayed. Then came that crashing, rumbling intonation, so strangely awful and so terrible that it baffles the power of description — none can comprehend it save those who have experienced it. Yet it was but the herald of the terrific convulsion that followed. The great strata of rock and conglomerate that form the peninsula on which San Francisco stands rotated, tilted, twisted, sank and heaved in veriest agony. The massive buildings of St. Ignatius seemed like a piece of shrubbery in an autumn storm.

"Meanwhile I was on my knees, making acts of the love of God and of perfect contrition. 'The end has come,' I said to myself; 'in one short minute I shall stand before the judgment seat of God; every second counts: I must be ready.' Never in my life have I prayed as I did on that occasion. In the past I had visited so many sanctuaries dear to every Catholic and especially to every Jesuit … but nowhere did I pray as I did during the forty-eight seconds of the San Francisco earthquake. To this day I have comfort in the thought that when the crucial moment seemed at hand, I turned to God with all the power of my soul, with my entire being; I turned to Him alone. It was the outcome of the faith that is in you and me; and — be it said in humble thankfulness — God's grace dispelled all terror at having to appear before my Judge.

"But Divine Providence had disposed otherwise. As abruptly as the earthquake came, so it ceased. The troubled ground resumed its normal shape and equilibrium. 'Peace, be still.' The mandate had come from heaven; it was obeyed. No chronicler, nor storyteller, can describe with anything like accuracy the workings of the human mind during that fearful suspense of forty-eight seconds. None but the Almighty can tabulate the agonizing prayers that went up to heaven from so many souls, whose faith bade them turn with all the energy of their beings to Him who alone can guard and ease.

"When the earthquake had subsided, a party of Fathers and Scholastics went through the rooms to see if anyone was injured. Though several doors were jammed in their casings, and had to be forced open to release the occupant, no one had suffered any harm.

All the inmates of the college were accounted for — twenty-one priests, nine scholastics, eleven brothers and seven servants. We were deeply grateful. In the building itself, every room and every corridor showed the confusion, while here and there appeared dangerous looking cracks several inches in width, and running some distance along the walls. The most serious damage was done in the large auditorium, located on the upper story of the college building: the top of the façade had fallen.

"Little or no harm had been done to the church. The towers were intact, the organ in its place. But statues had fallen; and the rich Easter decorations were piled in a heap of broken candelabra, candles, vases and flowers, literally strewing the ample sanctuary with wreckage. My heart was bleeding as I surveyed it all. It was but the beginning of our trials — worse was coming.

"Hundreds of people, men and women, stunned with terror, not knowing what might follow, poured into the church to seek shelter from their very fears — shelter with Him who loved them as His children and who would provide. Every confessional was besieged — all dreaded a repetition of the shock, they wanted to prepare for the worst. Hurriedly we cleared away the debris from the altar, and by 6 o'clock we could begin the Holy Sacrifice. The communion rail was filled again and again at each of the four Masses celebrated at

69

SI President John Frieden, SJ, watched as his beloved school burned to the ground.

the Main Altar that morning. It was a solemn and distressingly pathetic sight. How I could stand the intenseness of the strain I know not. Panic in every face at the railing, tears in every eye as the Blessed Lord came to give Himself to His own, faith through it all — you could feel it, and deep devotion pictured everywhere.

"Meanwhile an emergency hospital had been established in the 'Mechanics Pavilion' — a large armory in the neighborhood of the college. Soon it was filled with wounded and dying men and women. And the cry came for priests. Eight of the Fathers were at once detailed to minister the consolations of religion to the many who were so near their final reckoning. Demands for priestly help came from other quarters as well — in each case I supplied the need. Several of the Fathers were still engaged in their work of zealous charity — in hospitals and in the very street — when their own home at St. Ignatius was nearing its destruction.

"At an early hour, fire had broken out in the eastern part of the city. And into a dense cloud, the truth flashed upon us that the fire department was paralyzed — there was no water. Only a few hundred feet away reposed three fourths of all the water on the surface of the globe; we were powerless to use it. The mains had been broken by the convulsions of the earthquake, and now the horrors of a conflagration would be added to the ruins wrought in the early morning. At the College, however, we had every reason for feeling secure. The fire was a mile and more away, the wind blew from west to east, besides we were separated from the threatened section of the city by an avenue, Van Ness, 120 feet in width. But the danger came quickly, suddenly, from an unexpected quarter.

"Shortly after 10 o'clock fire broke out west of St. Ignatius, half a block from our buildings. The wind had grown into a gale, and in less than half an hour the entire block was one mass of flame. A shower of burning embers rained upon the nearest wooden tower, setting it on fire. A few minutes more and the other tower was wrapped in flames. Our buildings were doomed with all that they contained. Promptly we brought the Blessed Sacrament to a place of safety. With great difficulty some wagons were secured to carry the precious vestments and other costly altar furniture to the Holy Family Convent, west of the College on a steep incline. [The structure, at 890 Hayes and Fillmore Streets, is still standing.] Thousands thronged the streets about St. Ignatius; they were the members of our congregation. All were eager to help, but to lend a helping hand had become impossible."

(Later, San Franciscans called this the "Ham and Eggs Fire" as it started after a woman living at 395 Hayes Street lit her stove that morning to cook breakfast, unaware that the quake had damaged her chimney. This fire destroyed not only SI but also much of the Western Addition.)

"It was now past 11. All at once the cry was raised that our buildings were to be dynamited, so as to arrest the spread of the fire to the adjoining blocks. [While firefighters first planned to dynamite the church and school to prevent the fire from spreading, they later chose a site across the street for demolition.] The church had already been vacated; one by one the members of the Community had left the house. But I was not ready to follow them. How could I be ready to abandon the pile of buildings which obedience had given me in charge with all that they contained? It was like leaving my very self; I was and felt so identified with it all; and now I must make it over to destruction. The forty-four Jesuits of San Francisco were homeless. What it had taken half a century to build up and to equip, lay in ashes. The future was a blank....

"From the church I had rushed to my apartment where important documents were kept for reference. And valuables were there, left in my keeping. These latter I gathered quickly, filling a satchel, which was at hand. The documents, and such other portions of the archives as were in my office, I wrapped in a sheet from my bed in the adjoining room. There was no time to gather more. Writings of a lifetime were there stored away, manuscripts it had taken years to prepare, the varied materials for reference which a Priest and Educator should have at hand as his work goes on, souvenirs also of parents, near relatives and friends already passed away — these and numerous other such articles were there. I knew and realized it, but there was no time nor way of saving them. There was not even time to change my garments. As I was, dressed in the priestly garb, what articles of clothing I could reach flung over my left arm, the satchel in one hand, dragging the archives with the other, I left the house which had become so dear to me, and which I was never to reenter. As I have said already, in the square in front of our buildings a dense mass of humanity had assembled. Hundreds of our friends were there — their sobbing told me as I made my way to a wagon which had been provided."

(Jack O'Dea '28, whose father, Michael, was an SI grad, notes that his father told of watching the school burn down and wondering why the fire department never used any of the water from the swimming pool to extinguish the blaze.)

"All Hell seemed dancing with joy," were the words of SI student Joseph Vaughan, 17, as he watched SI fall to the flames. He later joined the Society of Jesus.

Before & After: The entrance to the college gym.

the fire included 30,686 in the college library and 3,000 in the Ladies Sodality library, along with 7,927 pamphlets.[3]

Another eyewitness was Fr. Joseph Vaughan, SJ, who was a 17-year-old student at SI at the time. Years after the earthquake, he wrote about that terrible day: "I dropped down into Hayes Valley and walked toward St. Ignatius, hidden by smoke welling up on all sides. I met Fr. Kenna [then 62], venerable by years and by accomplishments, whose soft-spoken words and generally unperturbed demeanor revealed the self-control of a saint. We looked up at the fire slowly creeping down the tall tower towards the heroic-size bronze statue of St. Ignatius standing on a small pedestal between the two spires. Flames whipped at the statue, licking it and encircled it with diabolic glee, when suddenly the bluish flame characteristic of copper shot forty feet into the air. All hell seemed dancing with joy, watching this fiery liquidation of the Jesuits in San Francisco, the cataclysmic termination of half a century of labor. But Satan and his hordes should have learned a lesson from four hundred years of Jesuit history! Fr. Kenna, with tears wetting his venerable face, looked up to Heaven and whispered a prayer: God's will be done...."[4]

From their lookout at the Holy Family Convent at 890 Hayes Street, the Jesuits saw the city in flames. Fr. Henry Whittle, SJ, later wrote in his diary that "the city seems a sea of fire." With most of the city residents afraid to re-enter the buildings, and with soldiers

Frieden and several other Jesuits went to the Holy Family Convent on Fillmore Street, which they hoped would be spared the fire. He asked two men to carry the satchels of documents while he carried the Eucharist in its ciborium. As the group walked toward the convent, they passed Catholics who recognized the Blessed Sacrament and either bowed their heads or genuflected as Frieden walked by them.

Fr. Richard Gleeson, SJ, the president of Santa Clara College at the time, offered another account of the earthquake and fire. He had spent the night of April 18 at St. Ignatius College. After witnessing the damage, he wrote that he "saw the college and church catch fire and I assure you that it was a sad sight. We could hardly save anything and the church is gone with its many treasures of art. The grand college went next and then the best physical and chemical department in all the Society, at least in America, and with it three splendid libraries with all their treasures. The loss is, in many regards, simply irreparable." The books destroyed by

shooting looters on sight, the city seemed like a scene from Dante's *Inferno*.

But on the fourth day, the fires finally died out. Fr. Jerome S. Ricard, SJ, a Jesuit at Santa Clara College (where he was known as "Padre of the Rains" for his weather predictions and where he ran the observatory), wrote this to the *San Jose Mercury* on April 22, 1906: "The earthquake period is gone. Once the pent up forces of nature have had a vent, nothing of a serious nature need be apprehended. At the most a succession of minor shocks may be felt and that's all. It is unreasonable, therefore, for people to continue in dread of a new destructive trembler. People should fearlessly go to work and repair mischief done and sleep quietly at night anywhere at all, especially in wooden frame. Never mind foreboders of evil: They do not know what they are talking about. Seismonetry is in its infancy and those therefore who venture out with predictions of future earthquakes when the main shock has taken place ought to be arrested as disturbers of the peace." Ironically, in the 1940s, one Jesuit priest, Fr. Alexis Mei, SJ '16, installed a seismograph in the basement of St. Ignatius Church, and it remained there until the 1960s recording the tremors that regularly jolted San Francisco over the years.

In the end, the Jesuits of San Francisco lost their residence, their church, and their college, including the most comprehensive ornithological collection west of the Mississippi, science laboratories that rivaled any in the country and the beautiful art that adorned the church. Miraculously, no one at SI died in the

earthquake and fire — not one of the 44 Jesuits or teachers or students, though some suffered injury.[5] With an indomitable spirit, the Jesuits went about rebuilding their home, their church and their school for the sake of their students and for the greater glory of God.

The charred rubble of the college and church.

V. The Shirt Factory: The Early Years (1906 ~ 1919)

Five months after the destruction of SI, students celebrate the opening of the Shirt Factory.

The earthquake and fire may have destroyed the beautiful school, but it would not do the same to the spirit of those who taught and studied there. After the earthquake, SI built a "temporary" campus that would last for 23 years and inaugurated a host of new traditions. The school published its first literary work in The Ignatian, re-established its debating society and, for the first time, began distinguishing itself from the college by calling itself "St. Ignatius High School."

Students began formal competition in football, baseball, basketball and track and saw one graduate, Matthew Sullivan, rise to become Chief Justice of the California Supreme Court. The Jesuits began building the grand edifice of St. Ignatius Church, one of the city's most beautiful places of worship, and it would send nearly 400 of its graduates to fight in World War I. Ten of those men would not return.

Rising from the Ashes

We can barely comprehend the feelings of the SI Jesuits as they returned to the ashes of their school once the fire subsided. Imagine them, in their black cassocks, poking through the rubble looking for items they could salvage and grieving over all they had lost. They were able to save vestments, chalices, crucifixes and ciboria that they had pulled out before fire gutted the church. They were also able to save some furniture and the giant bell that had sounded the call to prayer on Hayes Street and, years before, on Market Street. They had it carted it away, knowing full well that they would rebuild. (That bell had fallen to the ground but survived intact and is now in use at St. Ignatius Church.)

Some of the SI student body continued their schooling at Santa Clara College in the days following the earthquake. Fr. Richard Gleeson took in a number of his brother Jesuits from SI and invited the graduating class to finish their term with Fr. Dionysius Mahony, SJ, and Mr. Frederick Ruppert, SJ. Those students were awarded degrees at the end of their

On the first day of school at the Shirt Factory, each class posed for pictures.

term. (Among the members of that class was Bernard Hubbard, later to join the Jesuits and gain fame as "The Glacier Priest" for his explorations of Alaska.)[1]

While those classes were underway, Frieden wrote to Archbishop Patrick William Riordan, Alemany's successor, asking for permission to rebuild the church and college at another site. Earlier, the Jesuits had left their Market Street campus as it had grown too crowded with businesses and, regarding property taxes, too expensive. By the turn of the century, they saw the same thing happen to Van Ness Avenue, and they wished to migrate westward once more.

In a letter to the Archbishop, Frieden wrote that "constant increase of taxes on our property on Van Ness Avenue makes it impossible to rebuild there. We ask permission of Your Grace to change the location of the church and college. That portion of the city bounded by Hayes, Stanyan, McAllister and Masonic

Avenue seems suitable and free from objection. The only block obtainable at present is that bounded by Shrader, Fulton, Cole and Grove, but the steep grade makes it undesirable for building. However, we are compelled to take action at once; we have an option on that block expiring on Monday, May 21st. We ask Your Grace's permission to close the bargain with the further permission to purchase a more suitable block in the same section if, later on, we can do so." (The Jesuits later built the USF Law School on this land, which became known as the "Frieden block.")[2]

In the meantime, 18 SI Jesuits became the guests of Mrs. Bertha Welch, who offered her 57-room home at 1090 Eddy Street in Jefferson Square for their use until new quarters could be built. Others came to the aid of the Jesuits, including the Sisters of Mercy. The sisters offered their property on Hayes Street near Golden Gate Park without rent, but they could only surrender the land for two years as they were already planning for the construction of St. Mary's Hospital for that site. Frieden knew he would need more than two years, as the Grove Street campus would need extensive grading before construction could begin, and he declined the offer.[3]

The land he chose for the fourth campus of St. Ignatius College was at Hayes and Shrader Streets. Frieden leased two lots on June 1, 1906, for five years, and on the same day paid a $1,000 deposit on the Grove Street site. Workers began grading the Hayes and Shrader campus on June 26, with a formal inauguration ceremony on July 1. The *Monitor* covered the event and noted the following: "An immense crowd gathered last Sunday afternoon … to witness the ceremony of breaking ground for the new temporary church, monastery [sic] and college of the Jesuit Fathers of St. Ignatius. The Fathers are at present domiciled in the beautiful home of Mrs. Welch … but they are anxious to get into a home of their own … for this reason, the project initiated last Sunday with enthusiastic fervor will be pushed with all possible dispatch to conclusion. It is hoped to have temporary structures ready for occupancy by September 1."[4]

Among those in attendance was Judge Jeremiah Sullivan who, back in 1863, had acted in the play *Joseph and His Brethren* as part of the end-of-the-term dramatic exhibition that year. Standing before the crowd, he spoke of the Jesuits' history in San Francisco, noting that "these sons of Loyola are now facing the future, ready to begin anew their labors. We here ask all to assist with their fortunes, their honor and their best endeavor the building of the new St. Ignatius."[5]

Frieden followed, adding that "three months ago, no one would have thought we would be ready to build a new St. Ignatius upon this site, but, undaunted by disaster, we are ready for the new work. We have never lost courage, for we know that it is God's work and He has provided. If San Francisco is to live, we live with it; if it passes, we pass with it – but not before."[6]

San Francisco Mayor Eugene Schmitz noted that "from the ashes of the past, there will spring up not only a greater and better city but a greater and a better St. Ignatius College and Church." But the last word, and the most light-hearted, was had by Archbishop Montgomery, who made reference to the school's proximity to Golden Gate Park: "This college dates back through fifty years of wonderful history but, like the course of empire, it now takes its way westward. Horace Greeley has said: "Go west, young man!" and St. Ignatius College had never failed to do so. The

Jesuit Fathers are cousins of St. Francis and always locate in the best place. Nobody should doubt the wisdom of selling the old site for a good price and buying a cheaper place. No one will doubt the wisdom of it when he comes to the new church, says his prayers there and then has a little picnic in the park afterwards."[7]

This fourth campus, a temporary one, would serve the school for 23 years, far longer than anyone anticipated. Shortly after it opened, students began calling the Hayes and Shrader school the "Shirt Factory," as the school building resembled the omnibus factory buildings south of Market Street. (It was also a cold and drafty building according to accounts from that period.) McGloin writes that the school earned this name "because of its pedestrian architecture as well, perhaps, of its rambling dimensions. [I], as a high school graduate of the

Students from the grammar school division on a class picnic to Muir Woods in 1916.

last class to be educated within its drafty confines, can testify to its distinctive appearance as well as to the punishment it successfully survived from 1906–1929. Although legend attributes the name to the characterization given the building by Fr. Victor White, SJ, it is perhaps just as true that, after the fire and earthquake, San Francisco had a number of hastily constructed and strictly utilitarian buildings such as the 'temporary' Jesuit omnibus building at Hayes and Shrader Streets. Actually, some of these were 'shirt factories!'"[8]

To ensure the school would be open by September, construction crews worked seven days a week. Perhaps knowing that they might need the "temporary" school for longer than the five-year lease, the Jesuits purchased the land (measuring 275 by 137.5 feet) for $67,500 from Mr. & Mrs. M.H. deYoung. The

contractors finished, and the building was ready by September 1, opening that Saturday to a large crowd. As Fr. Whittle wrote that day in his diary: "We opened the new college today. We were much rejoiced to see a large attendance. As the building is not sufficiently complete and, more especially, as we could not as yet procure textbooks for the students, the classes were dismissed to open again next Friday."

A famous photograph exists from that opening day ceremony showing the entire student body posing in front of the school; some of these students were sitting on window ledges, on the roof, on gables, and atop construction material. It is hard to imagine any school today, with all the concerns about liability, allowing students to pose for a similar photograph.

During the 1906–07 term, the new school saw 34 Jesuits (18 priests, nine scholastics and seven brothers) ministering to 271 students who attended college, high school and eighth grade classes. These teachers and students found themselves with a revised curriculum, as SI began to follow some academic trends of the time. New electives, as listed in the 1906–07 *Catalogue*, included "higher mathematics, mechanical drawing, advanced physics and chemistry, special laboratory work, physiology, biology, modern languages, Latin, Greek and English literature, constitutional and legal history and other branches suitable to prepare one for the study of Engineering, Medicine or Law."[9]

The first college commencement exercises following the earthquake took place on June 25, 1907, in the Van Ness Theater "on the spot occupied before the fire by the college hall," according to the San Francisco *Bulletin*. The school awarded five Master's and six Bachelor of Arts degrees, and SI alumnus and former Mayor James Phelan spoke about the

Fr. John Ford, SJ (background), and his students in 1907.

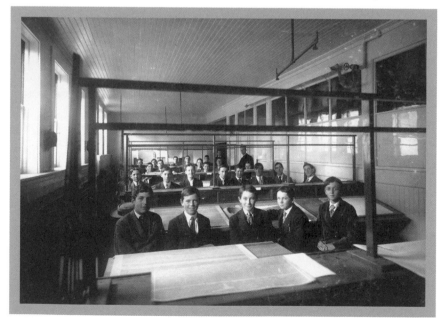

greatness of San Francisco. (The college continued to hold graduation ceremonies in downtown theatres for many years. The high school did not celebrate its own graduation ceremony until 1916.)

A New Site for a New Church

Months earlier, on December 23, 1906, Archbishops Riordan and Montgomery dedicated the 500-seat temporary church, located in the college hall. "We have come today to bless a new church," said Riordan after blessing the interior walls. "It is not like the old one, spacious and beautiful. St. Ignatius has lost a splendid building, a noble college, a great library. But that is all. The spirit that was behind those things is not lost, and, out of that spirit will come grander achievements in the future. And so we can say that we have a nobler temple than the old one."[10] In the months that followed, San Franciscans would flock to this new church. By the end of 1907, the SI Jesuits determined that they had distributed communion 68,000 times that year.

Earlier, as the paint was drying on the Shirt Factory, SI administrators were looking to their next site. On November 16, 1906, they made a final payment of $102,659 on the "Frieden block" (the block bounded by Cole, Grove, Shrader and Fulton Streets). Soon, however, it became apparent that the property's steep slope would add to construction costs. A 46-foot difference existed between Fulton and Grove Streets, and bulkheads and retaining walls would cost $40,000 alone.

Several individuals, including John E. Pope, a San Francisco civil engineer, urged the Jesuits to sell the Frieden block and purchase old cemetery land, owned by the Masonic Cemetery Association, north of Fulton

Street and east of Parker Avenue. The Association was in the process of moving its graves to Colma as part of a citywide effort to relocate all cemeteries outside the city limits. The cemetery site was level and 350 feet higher in elevation than the Grove Street site, allowing the new church to become a city landmark. Pope advised the Jesuits that owners of lots on that block were willing to sell and that the land could be purchased for the same amount as the value of the Frieden block.

(Members of the Cemetery Protective Association, incidentally, were opposed to the sale of the land, even as late as 1928, shortly before the construction of the first college building. According to a May 31, 1928, story in the *San Francisco Chronicle*, the group

The Jesuits broke ground on December 8, 1910, on the current St. Ignatius Church. Upon its completion, it became a new landmark, visible from most parts of the city.

This rare view of the Shirt Factory shows the church on the north end of the property.

Opposite page: A high school class shows its school spirit on the steps of the Shirt Factory.

in 1908 and John Pope's persistent lobbying. Finally, in March 1909, Sasia agreed to sell the Frieden block and spent $138,590 on the new site, measuring 275 by 510 feet. The Jesuits broke ground on the new church in an informal ceremony on December 8, 1910, 61 years to the day after the arrival of Accolti and Nobili to the shores of San Francisco. Sasia, who was infamous for his long sermons, gave a surprisingly brief address during that dedication, after "a sudden gust of wind swept away his manuscript to the four corners of the property."[11]

St. Ignatius Church was formally dedicated on August 2, 1914; at that time, it was the largest church in San Francisco, able to seat 2,000 worshipers, surpassed only in 1971 with the construction of St. Mary's Cathedral. Some critics charged that the construction and decoration costs for St. Ignatius Church delayed the building of a new college. Others countered, according to McGloin, that "such a church is the truest classroom of a Catholic University for, within its walls, have been taught the most significant lessons of all — those involving eternal truths."[12]

What is beyond argument is that the church has become one of San Francisco's most beautiful landmarks, visible from most corners of the city. Elsie Robinson, a columnist for the Hearst chain of newspapers praised the beauty of St. Ignatius Church in a column that ran in many newspapers in the 1940s:

"From where I live, high on the hills of San Francisco, I look across a deep valley and other hills to one which tops them all, and there, tall and gleaming in beauty, rise the spires of St. Ignatius. To you who may not know San Francisco, St.

planned "a determined fight to halt the sale of the old Masonic Cemetery property to St. Ignatius College and also to prevent the removal of bodies from the Old Odd Fellows' Cemetery." The group did not win its fight. Peter Devine '66 recalls that his father and uncle helped to clear out the broken tombstones from this cemetery that remained after the caskets had been removed. The Jesuits had students do this to fulfill the state's physical education requirement and to prepare the land for construction. "These PE classes usually ended up in rock fights," Devine said.)

Despite strong objections by a group of older Italian Jesuits who preferred the Frieden block, two events helped to secure the Parker and Fulton property: the replacement of Frieden with Fr. Joseph Sasia, SJ, as the school's new president

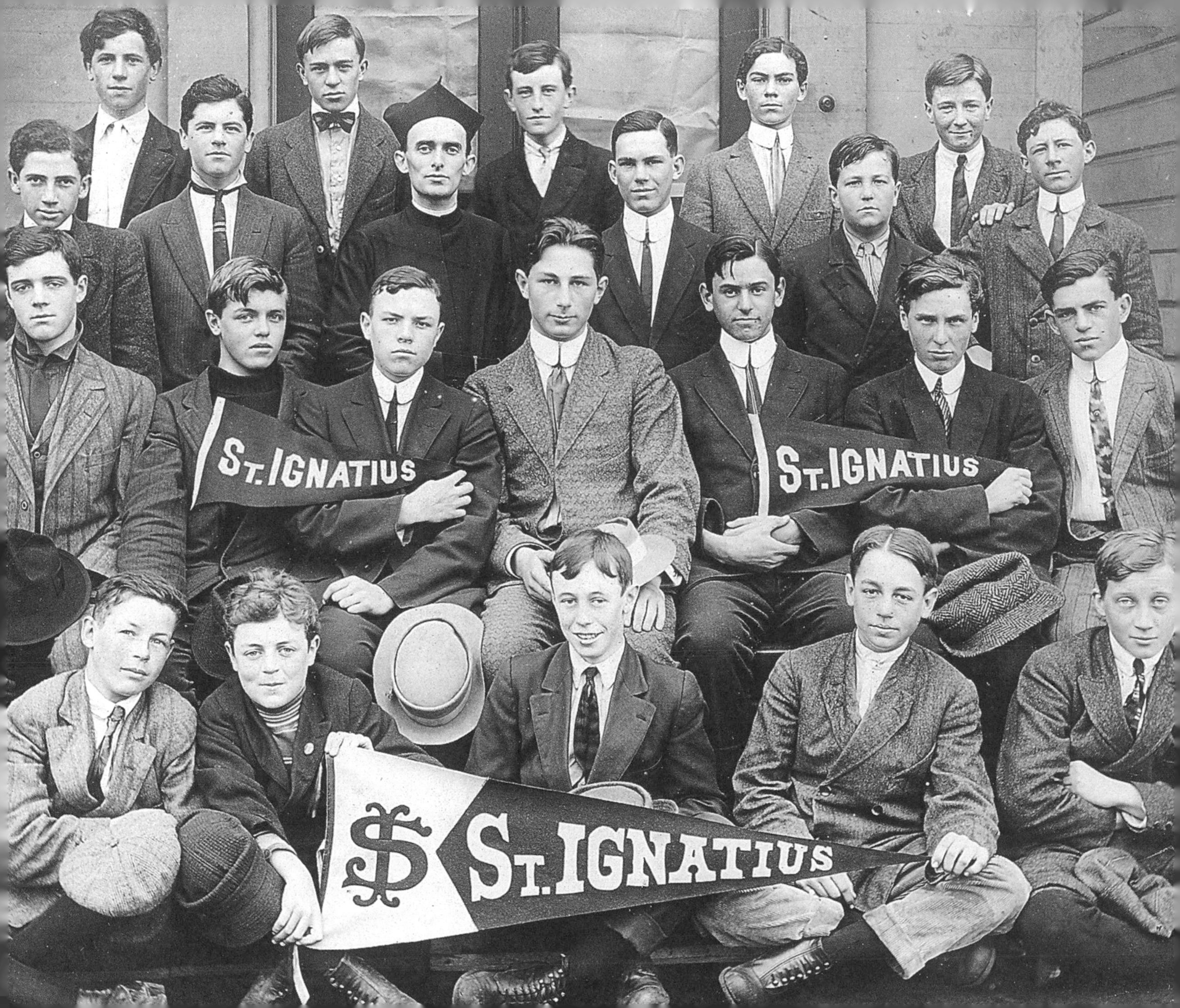
ST. IGNATIUS
ST. IGNATIUS
SI
ST. IGNATIUS

82

Ignatius is one of our oldest and most beautiful churches and colleges. But to us, who live near it daily, those twin spires mean far more. Whatever your creed, they are a symbol of all that is best and bravest in city life. Before they were built, the hill on which they stand was merely sand dunes, littered with rubbish, ugly and forsaken. Then the city began to spread and the vision of men spread with it. And out of that vision came these lovely spires. In the adjacent schoolrooms many a civic leader has been trained. And only God knows how many shamed and bleeding hearts have found comfort before its soaring altar. When the great storms sweep out of the Pacific, darkening the town, or the fog veils the valley in blue mist, I like to look towards those gleaming spires which seem to float in another world."[13]

Students of St. Ignatius High School attended a monthly First Friday Mass at the church and made their confessions there, too. Members of the Sanctuary Society assisted priests as altar boys, and, starting in 1936, seniors celebrated their commencement exercises in that church. All those who marched up its center aisle during these ceremonies sensed the importance of the moment thanks, in large part, to this vast and glorious house of prayer. Today, St. Ignatius Church serves not only SI and USF, but also the people of San Francisco as one of the newest parishes in the archdiocese.

The School Crest and Colors

In 1895, St. Ignatius Chicago used the coat of arms from the House of Loyola to create a college button to commemorate its Silver Jubilee. In the years that followed, other Jesuit schools across the country began using the Loyola crest in their school insignias. SI's crest, designed by George Lyle '09 in 1909, includes the figures of two gray wolves on each side of a large kettle suspended by black pot hooks. The symbol is word play, in that the wolves (*lobo*) combine with the kettle (*olla*) in Spanish to form *lobo y olla* (the wolf and the pot), which, "contracted into Loyola." But the house of Loyola was also known by both the paternal and maternal family names of Oñaz y Loyola, and the crest of the house of Oñaz included seven red bars on a field of gold to honor seven heroes of that family who fought at the Battle of Beotibar in 1321. The kettle also commemorates the House of Loyola's reputation for generosity, as, according to family lore, the family supplied their soldiers with so much food "that the wolves always found something in the kettle to feast on after the soldiers were supplied."[14]

Around 1909, SI adopted red and blue for its school colors. The first issue of *The Ignatian* carried the new crest in red and blue on its cover, and all of the large, ornate, gold plate with cloisonné overlay award medals, given annually to students in the early 20th century, used the red and blue color motif as did the school rings. By the 1920s, the college adopted green and gold for its school colors, while the high school retained red and blue.

School Days

School enrollment increased yearly, climbing from 271 in 1907–08 to 373 the following year and 433 for 1909–1910. The school grew in other ways, too, with the birth of new traditions, the most significant of which, for our concerns, is the first known use of the name "St. Ignatius High School" in the 1909–1910 *Catalogue*. Before that time, St. Ignatius College was divided between the college and preparatory (or high school) divisions. (The name "St. Ignatius Grammar School" also appears in the 1910–1911 *Catalogue*, as the school still taught seventh and eighth graders until 1918.) From this point onward, the high school and college communities began the slow process of separation that continued in 1911 when the college changed its name to the University of St. Ignatius (more on this later). That split widened in 1927 when the college students moved into Campion Hall (on the campus of USF) and when the high school moved, two years later, to Stanyan Street. The high school and university formally split in 1959 into two separate corporations. The final chapter in the separation occurred in 1969 when the high school moved to the Sunset District campus and became known as St. Ignatius College Preparatory. (Even though the name "St. Ignatius High School" did not appear in the official school *Catalogue* until 1909, Fr. Maraschi did refer to the school as "St. Ignatius Grammar and High School" in an 1855

advertisement for the brand-new academy on Market Street.)

Academics

Students in 1910–11 took a familiar course of studies that included religion, Latin, Greek, English, German, Spanish, French, mathematics, civics, elocution, freehand and modern drawing, physical geography, astronomy, physiology, botany, zoology, stenography and bookkeeping, taught by 11 priests and three laymen.

The Shirt Factory was close to Golden Gate Park, and many classes chose to pose in front of McLaren Lodge for school photos.

Admission to the high school seems to have been a rather informal affair. According to the *Catalogue*, "every candidate for admission, who is not personally known to some member of the Faculty, must present testimonials of his good moral character. If he come from another college, he will be required to bring a certificate of good standing from the institution which he has left. Students not of the Catholic faith are expected to conform respectfully to the religious exercises of the College.... For admission into the High School Course a knowledge of English Grammar, Analysis and Composition, of Geography and United States History, and of Arithmetic, is necessary."

The *Catalogue* went on to urge parents to have their sons perform two hours of homework each night and insisted that the following pattern "be exactly followed: Monday — English Composition, Mathematics, Modern Language. Tuesday — Latin Theme, Mathematics, English Exercise. Wednesday — Latin Theme, Mathematics, Modern Language. Friday — Latin Theme, Mathematics, Modern Language. Saturday — Latin Theme, Mathematics, English Exercise."

The *Catalogue* warned that "students who come unprepared to recite, or without having their written exercises ready, are looked upon as morally absent, and like absentees, they must bring satisfactory written excuses from their parents to the Prefect of Studies to avoid censure."

Fr. Charles B. Largan, SJ '14, began his freshman year at SI in 1910 and, as a young man, was an altar server at the dedication of St. Ignatius Church. In an interview published in 1977 in *The 2001* (SI's student newspaper), Fr. Largan recalled that "the only social events were the occasional fistfights, which were a little more grandiose than today's pugilistic contests. The fights would start in the schoolyard and make their way to

Golden Gate Park after school. They were terminated by the police. No one (well, almost no one) knew how to dance in those days so there was no prom. But there was a vote in class to have a dance.... Instead of a dance, the class had a feast at a downtown café. The logic behind this was expressed by ... one boy who said, 'Not all of us can dance, but we all can sure eat.'"

(Fr. Largan taught at SI from 1944 to 1961 and continued living in the Jesuit community, serving as a substitute teacher, unofficial school historian and minister to the sick until his death in 1982. He taught thousands of students, many of whom returned to teach at SI. He also taught Merv Griffin, Sr., the father of the former TV talk show host and producer Merv Griffin. He celebrated his diamond jubilee at SI in 1974, marking the 60-year anniversary of his entry into the Society of Jesus.)

In all, high school life in 1910 and 1911 at 2211 Hayes Street probably didn't seem much different from the school days students experienced at the Market Street or the Van Ness Avenue campuses.

Athletics

The Many Leagues of SI

SI's membership in the various athletic leagues can be a bit confusing. In 1909, SI joined the Catholic Athletic League, and in 1910, the school joined the city's Academic Athletic League (known from 1914 as the San Francisco Athletic League), which was run by student managers. When the Academic Athletic Association formed in 1926, putting the power in the hands of high school principals, SI joined it, though reluctantly because this league prohibited schools from competing against non-AAA teams in playoff games. SI, in 1926, had won the state basketball championship, and students were

Opposite page: Membership in the 1919 boys' 110-pound basketball team, like the 120s and 130s, was based on a complex formula of age, weight, height and ability.

eager for a chance to recapture the crown. But because all other city schools joined the AAA, SI and Lowell had no choice but to go along. SI left the AAA in 1966, in part because only San Francisco residents could compete in that league, leading SI to join the West Catholic Athletic League.

Tennis

Aside from that first football game against Sacred Heart, the earliest records of SI's athletic teams come from the *Ignatian* of 1910, the first student publication. It reported, simply, that "when the High School joined the AAL last year, it was so late in the season that we were able to enter only a tennis team in the tournament at Stanford. The members were the Fotrell brothers, who captured the championship of the California High Schools in both singles and doubles. Thus our prep school's career in the AAL was ushered in most auspiciously."

Basketball

An article in the 1910 *Ignatian* noted that high school basketball "is practically a new game with us and this year marked the advent of a High School team. We entertained very little hope of developing a championship team — not that the players were wanting in quickness of mind and strength of body, two elements of vital necessity to play the game with any degree of success, but because they lacked the experience which tells in tight places. And yet their record is an

enviable one. They finished third in the championship race, yielding only to Cogswell and Wilmerding.... The team consisted of Captain Evans, McGrath, Keating, Noonan, Flood, Foster, Naylor, W. Fotrell

and Harrigan." In 1911, SI's basketball team placed third in the city's league, second in 1916 and first in 1917, coached by W. Thorpe. In 1919, the team had its first star in Jeff Gaffney (who also excelled in baseball), and in 1921, SI beat every other school in the San Francisco Athletic League championship tournament. The basketball program divided students into weight classes, which was the practice of the day, with 100s, 110s, 120s, 130s, and 145s. (In effect, the 145s represented the varsity players, though the weight classifications changed over the years, with the varsity later called the Unlimited. The numbers are a little misleading, as coaches placed students into categories based on a convoluted matrix of height, weight, age and ability.)[15]

The SI rugby team in 1916.

formed the nucleus of the team, their work was gratifying. Their first game was with San Rafael Union High School on September 14. At the end of the game, we were the victors {25–0]. Being the first game of the season, it was devoid of any sensational plays, which generally thrill a spectator at a rugby game. The team on the whole played well, and every man had a hand in scoring."

Football continued through 1916, but was discontinued in 1917 and 1918 in order to provide more athletes for the baseball and basketball teams. It made a brief appearance again in 1919, and again in 1922 before becoming firmly established in 1924 under coach Jimmy Needles (a football star from Santa Clara) and later, his brother Frank Needles.

Football

SI had an on-again, off-again relationship with football (which was played as rugby until the school adopted "American football" in 1919). SI fielded teams in 1908 and 1909, disbanded football in 1910, and reinstated it in 1911 on both the high school and college levels. The December 1911 *Ignatian* reported the following: "Considering the number of novices who

Baseball

We know that baseball began at SI in 1907, one year after the earthquake, thanks to a picture found in the archives of the California Province. The next earliest reference to SI's high school baseball team came in the Easter edition of the 1913 *Ignatian*, which noted that "the doughty little warriors from the high school overcame the onslaught of Poly's host in their first contest and won rather easily [13–6]. A bombardment of John O'Connor's benders in the first inning netted Poly five runs and O'Connor a seat on the bench. Ted Pohlman took up the burden and held Poly safe for the rest of the game." That season, SI finished with 11 wins and four losses. One of those losses, against Oakland High, spurred Warren Brown to write the following in the Easter edition of the 1913 *Ignatian*. "Kids to the right of 'em, trees to the left of 'em, fences in front of 'em, no wonder they blundered. Imagine a baseball game staged on the Scotch bowling green in Golden Gate Park. Picture three primary schools holding picnics on first, second and third bases, and, gentle reader, you have it — Mosswood Park, Oakland, the scene of our second defeat. Words fail to describe the game." Ten years later, in 1923, SI fielded an indoor baseball team briefly.[16]

Track and Field

By Dan Lang '86, Varsity Track and Field Coach

From the earliest days at SI, the track team has enjoyed success thanks to the arduous and anonymous work of dedicated students and coaches. The earliest mention of track competition is in the 1910 *Ignatian,* which refers to the college class of 1913 (then freshmen) that competed on the third annual President's Day. The author notes that "a beautiful and costly trophy offered by Rev. Father Sasia, SJ, [went] to the individual scoring the greatest number of points in the winning class." The freshmen of 1910 so dominated the interclass competition that one of their own, David Barry, was moved to write *The Victors*; a sample reads:

For forty yards the big men ran
And to our joy our Captain, "Stan"
As swift and fleet as the northern wind,
Came first with Milt and Flood behind.

As was the case with most high school programs at the time, SI's track program was organized, judged, scheduled and operated by students. The school also supported the program financially. The December 1911 *Ignatian* noted that "bleachers have been built to accommodate 2,000, thus making the total seating capacity 5,000. It is our intention to put in a cinder track outside the rugby field. We feel proud to assert that our stadium will be the very best in San Francisco."

The earliest reference to an SI high school track team appeared in the 1912 *Ignatian*, which noted

The first baseball team formed in 1907.

that on January 12, 1912, the high school relay team "entered the Olympic Club Indoor Meet and came out victorious, winning the beautiful silver trophy offered for the relay race" against St. Mary's, Lick, Palo Alto and Mission. Stars on that team included Captain McElearney, Chandler, Evans, O'Shea, H. Flood and Keating.

The first student publication appeared in 1910, produced by the college freshman class of 1913.

Just two weeks later the same group of Ignatians took the silver cup at the YMCA indoor meet and tasted victory for the third time at an invitational hosted by *The Examiner*. During the outdoor season (the teams competed in an indoor season in the winter and an outdoor season in the spring), the relay team of 1912 took fourth at the Stanford Interscholastic Meet, a gathering of the "finest athletic talent in the state." (SI teams to this day compete at the Stanford meet, one of the most competitive in the nation.)

The sport continued to develop in popularity, and by 1917 editors of the *Ignatian* proclaimed, "We undoubtedly possess one of the most formidable track teams of the San Francisco high schools…. To encourage track, dual meets have been arranged with Lowell, Humbolt and many other schools for the early spring."

Soon, student coaches would give way to some of the best adult coaches in SI's long history, including world record holders and Olympians such as Emerson "Bud" Spenser and Seattle Seahawks offensive coordinator Gil Haskell.

Terry Ward '63, who coached at SI in the 1970s — and the man whom many consider the Godfather of WCAL track and field — noted that in each of his 37 years coaching track and field, "I try to make the 150 athletes in my charge know that I care for them and want them to succeed. From the fastest runner to the slowest jogger, I live with each step they take."

Julius Yap '74, who coached in the 1980s and 1990s and influenced a new generation of athletes and coaches, echoed that sentiment. "Coach Ward and Coach Haskell also provided the model for me to follow as I returned to teach and coach here at SI. I have had some success here during my 25 years at the prep, and I owe much of that to my two coaches at SI. They taught me the value of hard work. The most important value an SI coach should honor — and this is the top priority of an SI coach — is to care for the student as a person first and an athlete second."

Former head coaches Charles Taylor '88, Tom Fendyan '83 and head coaches Martin Logue '92 and Dan Lang '86 were all athletes under Yap, and each has encouraged his athletes to live out those ideals. In doing so, they practice the Ignatian philosophy of *cura personalis* — care for the whole person.

That philosophy has created a successful program, with the men's team taking 14 varsity league championships and the 1991 Central Coast Section (CCS) title. The women's team won 10 league victories in a row and CCS titles in 1997 and 1998.

Modern track champions include Chris DeMartini '94 for shot put, the only individual state champion in SI history; Olympian Tom McGuirk, who competed in the 400-meter hurdles in Atlanta in 1996 and Sydney in 2000; and Jenna Grimaldi '01, who became the number-one-ranked female high jumper in the nation in her senior year.

If you walk onto the SI track in spring to watch the boys and girls compete, you will find some stark contrasts with the SI track team of 1910. But you will find one thing in common: Much of the work is still done by students. They measure the distance for discus and shot put. They serve as timers for the sprints. They set up and take down hurdles. And they cheer on modern-day Wildcat athletes who, like their counterparts in the Olympics, strive towards their very best.

Extracurriculars

In 1910, the Class of 1913 published a literary journal that, the following year, became the *Ignatian Quarterly*, a combination literary magazine and yearbook. (The publication later dropped *Quarterly* from its title.) The college and high school published this together until 1928 when *The Heights* made its debut, exclusively covering high school life while the *Ignatian* dealt only with college students. (Publication of all high school annuals in the San Francisco Archdiocese ended in 1932 on orders from Archbishop Mitty who hoped to spare Catholic businesses the burden of paying for advertisements.)

Among the articles published in the first issue of the *Ignatian* were essays entitled "The Dangers of Labor Unions" and "Stevenson — An Appreciation," on the writing of Robert Louis Stevenson, along with poems praising Jesus' parents.

The first editorial, written by Adrian Buckley (who received his Bachelor's degree in 1911), noted that "the aim and ambition of the *Ignatian Quarterly* is to be a journalistic success in every sense of the word. In the literary field it certainly has every reason to be sanguine. Many students of St. Ignatius College, who have long desired a wider scope for their literary talents than that afforded by mere class routine, will welcome an opportunity to contribute to a periodical in which their productions will reflect, not only honor on themselves, but also on their Alma Mater. The subjects treated in the *Ignatian Quarterly* will be on interesting topics, and written in a style well calculated to hold the reader's attention throughout."[17]

The journal reported on the various athletic and extracurricular activities, including this report on the Junior Philhistorian Debating Society: "The most important feature of the year was the public interclass debate held in the College Hall on St. Patrick's night. A large and enthusiastic audience was entertained with the question of the fortification of the Panama Canal. Fourth Year High espoused the affirmative, and Third Year High spoke on the negative. The affirmative won."[18]

It also reported on the High School Elocution Contest. The 1920 edition praised the winning student, William O'Brien, "whose clever dialect rendition of the popular piece, 'Rosa,' was capable of stirring the most unresponsive audience." High school students also took part in the Sanctuary So-

The next publication, called The Ignatian, was a combination literary magazine and yearbook.

ciety (serving as altar boys) and the Sodality along with their college counterparts. Finally, students had a rudimentary intramural program, with the high school juniors playing the seniors in the Interclass Basketball, Baseball and Track games, with the winner of the basketball competition receiving the Austin T. Howard trophy, in memory of a deceased professor. In 1922, that interclass track competition became the President's Day games, held at Golden Gate Park Stadium on April 28, pitting high school athletes against their college counterparts. The high school carried the day in nearly all events.[19]

The Sullivans of the State Supreme Court:

Matthew, Jeremiah & Raymond

Even before the 1906 Earthquake, the SI Jesuits saw a need to separate its college from its high school. They came a step closer to that in 1911 by formally changing the name of St. Ignatius College to the University of St. Ignatius (a name used until 1919).

The School of Law began on September 18, 1912, when 29 students gathered in the Grant Building on Market Street for their first class. Serving as the first dean of that school was one of SI's more famous graduates, Matthew I. Sullivan, who received his BA degree in 1876 and who went on to become chief justice of the California Supreme Court.

In 1987, Eric Abrahamson wrote about Matthew Sullivan in *The University of San Francisco School of Law: A History*. In his book, he reveals how SI graduates, such as Sullivan, were growing in political influence in San Francisco. The following is from Abrahamson's book:

"On Sundays, Matt Sullivan went to five o'clock Mass and then walked from the Mission to his office in the Mills Building on Market Street. He worked until noon when his driver would pick him up to carry him home to 920 Guerrero Street where he lived with his brother John and his two sisters, Nora and Julia. From around the corner on Twenty-first Street, Sullivan's nephew-in-law, Eustace Cullinan, Sr., would come with his family to join the party. Sometimes from down the block, 'Sunny Jim' Rolph would drop by, and they would all eat together.

"It was Matt Sullivan, along with attorney Gavin McNab, who convinced Jim Rolph to run for mayor of San Francisco in 1911. A law partner with Theodore Roche and Governor Hiram Johnson, Sullivan was in many ways the workhorse behind a generation of Progressive leaders. He upset the political dynasty of blind boss Chris Buckley in the late 1880s, was appointed to the Board of Supervisors when members of Mayor Schmitz's administration were indicted, and, along with Hiram Johnson, succeeded Francis Heney as special prosecutor in the Abe Ruef trials after Heney was gunned down in court.

"In 1912, after being elected governor, Hiram

Johnson appointed Sullivan president of the Panama-Pacific International Exposition and then, in 1914, appointed him chief justice of the California Supreme Court. When his term expired, however, Sullivan refused to run for the office. According to some, it was against his principles to run for office. According to his grandnephew Vincent Cullinan, 'Uncle Matt knew he could make more money in private practice.'

"In 1912, when the law school at St. Ignatius was begun and Matt Sullivan appointed the first dean, there was hardly a more eminent lawyer in San Francisco, nor was there an attorney more committed to St. Ignatius. Graduated from the college when it was located on Market Street in 1876, Matt Sullivan, along with his brother, Jeremiah (also a justice of the California Supreme Court), played a major role in the formation of the Saint Ignatius College Alumni Association in 1878. Jeremiah served as the first president.

"Like Michael O'Shaughnessey, San Francisco's preeminent engineer who was appointed dean of the College of Engineering in 1912, Sullivan lent his name and respectability to the new school at St. Ignatius but did not engage in the day-to-day administration. Nevertheless, he served as titular dean for 22 years until 1934. His contributions to the college as a whole were so significant — serving as president of the alumni association and engineering the purchase of the Masonic Cemetery land — it seems impossible that he did not play some role in directing the curriculum of the law school."

Finally, Abrahamson notes that Sullivan "may be the unsung workhorse of the Progressive movement in San Francisco, which transformed city government from a patronage system into a modern, professional city management." When Matthew Sullivan died in 1937, he was praised for his service to the city and to SI.[20]

Judge Jeremiah Sullivan (who attended SI for eight years, graduating with his Bachelor's degree in 1870 and his Master's degree two years later), was the first president of the SI Alumni Association. Like his brother, he, too, served on the California Supreme Court and served six years as president of San Francisco Bar Association, which he transformed into an advocacy group. According to Abrahamson, he championed "legal reform and professional improvement," and his reputation led to his election as the first president of the State Bar.

Unrelated to Matthew and Jeremiah was Raymond Sullivan '24, who died October 20, 1999, at the age of 92 after a distinguished career as a justice on the California Supreme Court.

Justice Sullivan was born January 23, 1907, in San Francisco and graduated from SI in 1924 before graduating magna cum laude from USF in 1928. He worked at SI between 1927 and 1935, where he coached the debate team, taught Latin, English, geometry and history, and moderated the senior debating society (the Senate). In the SI student newspaper, the *Red and Blue* of September 21, 1927, he is listed as a

From left, Matthew & Jeremiah Sullivan.

92

"brilliant college student, noted for his forensic ability. Moreover, he will guide the destinies of the Senate during the year."

While on the SI faculty, he received a law degree in 1930 and a Master of Law degree in 1933 from USF. He left teaching in 1935 for private practice and, in 1961, was appointed to the state's First District Court of Appeal, which then covered a swath of Northern California from the Oregon border to the central coast. He became the court's presiding justice in 1966.

He was appointed to the high court in 1966 by Gov. Edmund G. "Pat" Brown and is best remembered for writing the 1971 decision that transformed the way the state's public schools are financed.

An obituary in the *San Francisco Chronicle* noted that Sullivan "'was regarded on the court as a lawyer's lawyer,' said former Supreme Court Justice Joseph Grodin, who served with Justice Sullivan on the faculty of the University of California's Hastings College of the Law. 'He was the court's expert on procedure. He cared a lot about the process of the court. He was also very innovative.'

"In the landmark Serrano-Priest decision, the Supreme Court ruled that California's system of using primarily property tax revenue to finance schools was unconstitutional because school districts in wealthy areas could spend more on a student's education than could a district in a poor area."

He was the recipient of many honors. SI gave him the Christ the King award in 1986 and USF bestowed on him the St. Thomas More Award for legal excellence in 1968 and an honorary doctor of laws degree in 1972. In 1991, Hastings students voted him Outstanding Professor of the Year, and in 1994, the State Bar of California awarded him the Bernard E. Witkin Medal for significant contributions to the quality of justice and legal scholarship of the state. The California Trial Lawyers Association also honored him in 1975 as Appellate Judge of the Year.

World War I

While SI grads such as Matthew Sullivan were thriving in their professional lives, not all was well at the Shirt Factory. Enrollment among university students fell so low that in 1912, the college had only 24 students, including 15 freshmen. During the 1914–1915 school year, there were as many Jesuits teaching high school and college as there were students enrolled in the university — 33 — making it one of the smallest universities in the world. (This was a hard time for many private colleges in the country, and many permanently closed their doors.) During these years, SI high school enrollment fluctuated between 150 and 200 students, a far cry from the heyday of the 1880s when SI was the largest Jesuit college in the U.S. The deficit in students was matched by a financial deficit, and the Jesuits reinstated the Ignatian Society to help raise funds for the school and for the construction of the new church.

World affairs would soon intrude upon SI's crisis. The U.S. entered World War I in 1917, and of the 378 SI grads who fought in Europe, 10 lost their lives. Among those (according to the June 1918 *Ignatian*) was Charles P. McVey who drowned on the *Tuscania*, which was torpedoed on February 5, 1918. The others included William Lasater, George Ross, Frank Cardanali, Harry Heaton, Joseph Hickey, Louis Kengla, William Ketler, Frank Kramer and Frederick Schimetchek. Of these nine, three died of disease, five of wounds and one by accident, crushed by a falling gun carriage. Another alumnus, Lt. Frank A. Flynn, was seriously

Opposite page: Nine grads who fought in WWI were featured in the 1919 Ignatian. *In all, 378 SI grads fought in that war and 10 lost their lives.*

injured in a plane crash and may have died of his injuries.

The highest ranking SI grad to serve in the war was Brigadier General Charles H. McKinstry (SI 1884), who served as 1st Division Commander of the 1st Field Artillery Brigade in 1917. Also serving were the Callaghan brothers, Daniel '07 and William '14, who would distinguish themselves in World War II.

During the war, SI took part in a government program designed to provide military training to college students. The Students Army Training Corps began October 1, 1918, and ended in December, shortly after the November 11 Armistice agreement. In that brief time, military officers trained and drilled students, ending each day at 10 p.m. with taps.

Overseas, Ignatians found hell on earth in that gruesome war. Capt. Joseph Sullivan '11, in the June 1919 *Ignatian*, wrote the following to his brother, Thomas "Sars" Sullivan:

"I do not know whether to be glad or sorry that I was not on the front when the end came. I could not be there on account of my wound. If I had been there, the last shell of the last gun would have riddled me, I am sure. I'm sorry, for there must have been a wild celebration. The fighting where I was, was particularly hard. You know where the First American Army was operating. Well, Sars, they threw the picked Prussian Guard divisions against us, they pounded us with artillery and machine-gun barrages till the very air seemed to be so filled with flying lead that there was not room for more. And they showered us with gas, so that our breathing apparatus became null and void.

Capt. Joseph Sullivan '11 (right), billeted in a German house after a battle, learned that he was staying with the family of a man he had just killed. He later wrote to his mother that he "had a strange feeling, but I had only done my duty."

When my battalion went to the attack, we were war-strength. We had a Major and four Captains. I was Captain of "I" Co., and I was right support company of the battalion. The Boche[21] barrage broke over us for eight hours before the time for attack was set. But my men were dug in, which means that they were in holes in the ground perpendicular to the axis of hostile fire. All through the night the hell continued. The Austrian 88's (whiz-bangs, we call them), just cleared the slope and broke on the reverse side where we were. Frequently I would receive a clod of dirt in the face, which some Boche shell had sent flying. Then the hour of attack came, the battalion rose out the hole and went for the Boche. Such a day and such a night! Captain Sackett, a classmate, led the left support company of the regiment. As we rose, an increase in the Boche barrage was apparent, and Sackett dropped with twenty machine-gun bullets through him. My officers were wonderful. My men — too much cannot be said for them. Of course contact and control were difficult, and as we jumped from crater to crater we could preserve no formation. The ground was a succession of slopes, and over each one the Boche had complete mastery. The Boche had direct fire on us with artillery, and it was deadly. He enfiladed us from the flanks and from the left rear as we progressed, and when we reached our objective the battalion was reduced to 200 men under the command of a 1st Lieutenant. The Major was wounded, I was wounded, Capt. Ed. Leonard, "K" Co., was dead, Capt. Mudge, "L" Co., and Capt. Wilhelm, "M" Co, were wounded, while Lieutenants were strewn over the battlefield.

"Well, it's all over now but the shouting, and I'm sick of war, of its havoc, its ruin and destruction. I want beaucoup peace and quiet, and they are sending me into Germany to get it.

"Sars, it's a funny world. Be good to yourself and take good care of Mother.

"Ever your loving brother, Joe"

Later, he wrote this to his mother with an accompanying photograph:

"In October 1918, at Romagne sous Montfaucon, an isolated "77" was picking off my men. We maneuvered and killed the Boche gunner, and I took his name-tag. Last night I was billeted in this home, and Madam cleaned my clothes. She came across the name-tag and said that it belonged to her son. She knew that he was dead, but she did not know that she was billeting under her roof the man who had killed her son. Mother, I had a strange feeling, but I had only done my duty."

In 1918, the Jesuits in San Francisco suffered under two great strains: an enormous debt and the Great Flu Epidemic that broke out that year. Students and teachers went to St. Mary's Hospital for treatment, and one scholastic died. Others, including Fr. Pius Moore, SJ, who ministered to the Japanese community in San Francisco, "were brought to death's door," as were many family and friends of those connected to the school.[22]

The Jesuits accrued a debt in excess of $1 million due in large measure to church construction. Archbishop Edward J. Hanna, on May 12, 1919, issued a formal proclamation asking the people of San Francisco to help the Jesuits. "Something must be done and done quickly if we are to preserve the old historic institution," he wrote. A fund-raising drive that year netted $200,000, and Fr. Moore, SI's 16th president, sold the Hayes and Van Ness site for $311,014, further cutting the debt to $451,597. By 1925, SI had whittled its debt down to $130,000.

While Fr. Moore was able to address this problem, he was less able to increase the size of the university student body, which in 1919 numbered only 26. He changed the university's name back to St. Ignatius College, and the enrollment grew slowly in the years to follow, with 41 students taking college classes, excluding law students.[23]

St. Ignatius High School, on the other hand, was thriving in the early 1920s. In 1921–22, for instance, student enrollment rose to 357. It began the gradual process of separation from the university in 1916 when the high school held its first graduation exercises. Before that, only students who had earned Bachelor's or Master's degrees received diplomas during the three-day-long-program that marked the end of the school year.

VI. THE FOUNDATION OF TRADITIONS (1920 ~ 1929)

Even though the high school found itself in the ramshackle Shirt Factory, sharing it with the college division, it thrived and began new traditions, such as the creation of the Wildcat mascot. Athletic victories came in the big three sports, with the basketball team taking the state championship in 1926 and a league title in 1927, the first year SI entered the AAA. League crowns also came in baseball (1921 and 1927) and tennis (1926 and 1928). By the end of the decade, SI left the Shirt Factory in 1929 for modern quarters up the hill on Stanyan Street, separating from the college for the first time and cementing its identity as an independent high school. It also found itself, along with the nation, at the start of the Great Depression.

Despite all these calamities, school life proceeded apace. SI started a new tradition in 1919 with its first senior prom after class president George Devine '19 proposed that the school hold a formal graduation prom at the Palace Hotel. The Jesuits wrote to Father-General in Rome for permission, and he agreed that it was part of a young gentleman's education.

The Jesuits Move North to Welch Hall

In 1920 the Jesuits benefited again from the generosity of Mrs. Bertha Welch, who built a residence hall for the priests adjacent to the church. Rather than donate funds to the Jesuits, she oversaw construction herself as while she was "altogether genuinely fond of the Fathers, as she had shown abundantly in the past, she was not overly convinced of their business acumen...."[1]

The former Jesuit residence in the Shirt Factory was turned into classrooms, and the Jesuits expanded the science labs, which while improving the school, also moved it further into debt. Two massive fundraisers, the May Festival, held in 1921 and 1924, took place in the Civic Auditorium, and the SI Jesuits managed to repay a $100,000 loan to the Hibernia Bank.

(Jesuits in both the college and high school communities lived together in Welch Hall from 1921 until 1959 when the USF Jesuits moved to Xavier Hall. The Jesuits teaching at the high school stayed at Welch until 1969 when they moved to McGucken Hall in the Sunset District campus. Welch Hall was demolished in 1970 and the open lawn area is now called Welch

The 130-pound city basketball champions of 1927.

Field. From all reports, Welch Hall offered threadbare accommodations, and some of the high school priests in the 1960s perhaps resented the fact that they had to remain there, with its leaking roof, while their college counterparts moved into modern quarters.)

SI's First Two Principals

The high school department in 1924 was led for the first time not by the college president but by a principal. The first principal, Fr. Cornelius Buckley, SJ, ran the school from 1924 to 1926, presiding over a faculty of 11 Jesuits and 12 laymen.

Fr. Buckley graduated from SI's preparatory de-

partment in 1890 and two years later from SI College. He joined the Society of Jesus in Los Gatos and, after studies in Spokane, returned to SI to teach briefly before leaving to continue his studies in Italy and England. He was ordained in 1908 in Dublin and returned to the Bay Area where he served as dean of students at SCU (1912–1922) and as a teacher of novices (1922–1924) before becoming SI's first principal. He served as a history professor at USF from 1926 until 1935 when heart trouble forced him into early retirement from the classroom. From 1936 until his death, he served as Regent of the USF Law School and as spiritual director of several San Francisco convents.

After his death on January 20, 1947, the following obituary appeared in the *Province News* of the California Province of the Society of Jesus: "Fr. Buckley was a well educated man, both in secular and religious subjects. He was an excellent teacher, and a very popular confessor. In 1946 he heard 18,000 confessions." He used to voice his disapproval of the training that Jesuit seminarians were receiving. "He did this once too often, for the Provincial, Fr. Francis Dillon in 1922, sent him to Los Gatos [for more formation] to remedy the situation."

The author of the obituary noted that Fr. Buckley usually submitted his reports on SI to the Province office late. "The only difficulty was to get the report on time. He was usually one to two years late. Strange to tell, he was up to date when death called him."

Succeeding Fr. Buckley was Fr. Albert Whelan, SJ, the younger brother of Fr.

Edward Whelan, SJ, president of St. Ignatius College. Of Fr. Albert Whelan, McGloin writes the following of this "Prefect of Studies" — another term for principal: "Those who remember the Albert Whelan regime recall that he ran what perhaps may best be described as a 'tight ship' — for he was a disciplinarian par excellence and tolerated little in the way of infractions."

Ken Atwell '29 remembered one incident that illustrates this quality: "One day, after seeing a disturbance in the hallway, Fr. Whelan rushed out and pinned the suspected ringleader to the bulletin board by the neck. The trouble is, he chose the wrong boy. The next day, that boy's father, a wealthy physician showed up and proceeded to tell Fr. Whelan what he thought of him and the institution. He told Fr. Whelan, 'If you take off that collar, I'll give you a whipping.' Fr. Whelan ripped the collar off, but the doctor turned around and left."

Athletics

Basketball: SI Wins its First State Title

SI's basketball teams enjoyed great success in the 1920s. By 1921, SI took first in the city in the 145-pound division with a 67–1 victory over Mission. The unlimited (or varsity) team of 1922, led by "Scotchy" Hamilton and "Goat" Turner, went undefeated to win the league title. In the 1925–26 academic year, Frank Needles led the 145 team to an 8–0 record and then asked state officials if his team could compete in the California Interscholastic Federation playoffs for the state championship. He received permission to play and to include members of the unlimited squad as reserves.

In CIF competition, SI beat Tamalpais Union High School (25–17) and Pacific Grove (31–22) before taking to the road to play Palo Alto High School. Standouts such as Tom Feerick and Ray Maloney helped SI win 32–14. Next came Napa on that school's home court, and SI eked out a 18–16 victory after a tough competition. SI beat Marysville for the Northern California championship at a neutral court in San Francisco. Senior George Olsen helped SI take the day with a 34–22 victory. "A group of us went to Napa on a bus to see SI win," recalls Jack O'Dea '28. "George Olson intercepted a pass and went for a lay-up to win the game. When we got outside, the Napa fans were so angry that they began taking it out on us, riding their motorcycles through our crowd."

Next, on April 3, 1926, came Lemoore, the best team from Southern California. SI won 20–11 in what proved to be the lowest-scoring state championship game in California history. It was also the first state championship for any SI (and San Francisco) team, but not the last; in the 1990s, SI's cross country, crew and lacrosse teams would earn state titles.

SI would continue to shine in basketball, with another league championship in 1927 when the unlimited team beat Galileo 21–18. The Depression would eventually cause SI to reduce the number of teams to

SI won its first state championship in 1926 when the 145-pound team beat Lemoore High 20–11. Pictured above are, top row, M. Leahy, O'Gara, Olson, S. Leahy; bottom row, Burns, Feerick, Maloney, Casey, McMahon.

four — the 110, 120, 130 and varsity), but they would not enjoy league supremacy again until 1943.

Football

In 1923, the school hired Jimmy Needles, ("one of the leading half-backs of the Pacific Coast," according to the September 13, 1923, *Red and Blue*) to serve as football coach for both the college and high school teams. Two years later, when Jimmy decided to work exclusively with the college athletes, the high school hired his younger brother, Frank Needles to replace him. Frank, a star at Gonzaga University, coached both football and basketball for six years. George Malley, the father of Pat Malley '49, succeeded him in 1929. (Pat Malley, a star athlete in his own right, went on to coach football at SI and at SCU where he eventually became athletic director. He was honored posthumously in 1985 with the Christ the King award — SI's highest honor to a graduate.)

Baseball &
The Birth of the Wildcat

The SI baseball team turned in a strong showing in 1924, led by coach "Fat" Varni, taking second to SH in the San Francisco Athletic League led by junior outfielder Frank McGloin, who

In 1925, football coach Frank Needles (pictured) took over from his brother, Jimmy, who coached both the high school and college teams in 1923 and 1924.

would later captain the team in his senior year and manage it from 1930 to 1942. (His son, John Bernard Mc-Gloin '29, would graduate from SI, join the Society of Jesus, teach at USF and author several works including *Jesuits by the Golden Gate*, a primary source for this history.)

In 1927, the baseball team, under coach Lorenzo Malone, SJ, won the AAA championship. The following year marked the birth of the term "Wildcat" as the name for the school's athletic teams. Before that, the teams were called the Gray Fog, a name given to SI by a sports writer. Later teams facetiously called themselves the Foglets and Fogletettes (for lightweight divisions). Sometimes, when they lost, they were known as the Drab Drizzle, according to the January 25, 1928, issue of *The Red and Blue*. That article went on to note that "with the separation of college and high school, it has been found desirable to distinguish the teams more strongly. Since the college was originally dubbed the Gray Fog, the Board of Control thinks it fitting that the college lightweights be called the Foglets, and the name has already been applied to them.

"This leaves the high school in an advantageous position…. and now we have the opportunity to rechristen the teams permanently…. The name Wildcats has been decided upon, as best symbolizing the spirit of the high school teams. They have always been lighter than their opponents, and always been noted for their fighting spirit when in difficulties. Their goal line defense, and last-minute rallies on the basketball court, have been proverbial.

"Moreover, it seems to be the universal custom to name teams after some animal — St. Ignatius can now take her place with the Cogswell Dragons, the Commerce Bulldogs, the Poly Parrots and the Galileo Lions."

Swimming, Track & Tennis

Swimming began in 1924 when football coach Jimmy Needles created SI's first team, though he only coached them that one year. The 1924 *Ignatian* reported that "There is not too much material, but several boys among them being Cole, McGibben and Murphy, are showing quite some form and speed in practice."[2] The team had its first formal coach in 1927 when SI hired Tom Kiernan "a noted developer of many national stars." That year, too, saw the team practice in a new location at the Young Men's Institute.

The track team continued to excel in the '20s, with the 1924 juniors, coached by Charley Hunter, beating Mission 133–24. The following year the lightweight track team beat Lowell in a dual meet.[3]

The tennis team, competing in the courts at Golden Gate Park, won the city championship in 1926 and went on to CIF competition and won the AAA championship in 1928.

Extracurriculars

The Red and Blue

The high school launched a new tradition October 14, 1920, with the publication of its first newspaper, *The Red and Blue*, with Eustace Cullinan, Jr. '21, as the first editor. (Cullinan would later serve as a San Francisco Superior Court judge.) In his inaugural editorial, he sounded a refrain familiar to most editors of student publications when he criticized the student body for lack of school spirit: "This year at St. Ignatius there seems to be something lacking, which ought to be present. There is not the old bustling activity that accompanied scholastic activities. In short, the students of St. Ignatius seem to be lapsing gradually into a lithargy [sic].... We conclude that the cause of the evil must lie with the students. In past years, the very atmosphere of the school was charged with action; a keen, wholesome spirit of interclass rivalry existed, yet, paradoxical as it may seem, the school acted as a harmonious whole; we were all one big family together. We used to hear of 'Buck' and 'Spud' but now we speak of 'O'Brien' and 'Sullivan.'"

Cullinan went on to note that "there is something besides mere knowledge, which is just as great in its own way, and even more apt to benefit us in later life. It is the

In 1927, the SI baseball team, under coach Lorenzo Malone, SJ, won the AAA title.

The student newspaper, The Red and Blue, *debuted October 14, 1920, and published until 1949, when* Inside SI *became the official student publication.*

When the college moved to new quarters in 1928, the high school began its own yearbook and christened it The Heights.

forming of acquaintances and friendships which may endure long after the Greek verbs and rules of Geometry have passed from our minds."

He concluded with the reason for the paper's existence: "to give our school what other high schools have, namely, a monthly publication which will review the student activities, and which will spread the achievements of St. Ignatius far and wide…. The Seniors have taken the initiative and are sponsoring the paper for the first edition, feeling that it was up to them to start the ball a-rolling. However, we expect this to be a school paper wherein every class will take an active part in its publication. Above all, don't be deceived by 'scholastic Bolsheviks,' who may say this is a 'fourth year paper.'"

For all this seriousness, the last page of the four-page broadsheet offered these humorous asides:

"Heard in Trig —

"Joe Meaney — This stuff is killing me by inches.

"Ye Teacher — Cheer up Joe, you have a long way to go!"

"Clarence Gilly requests that his many admirers desist from calling him their 'little lamb' as it makes him feel so 'sheepish like.'"

"This one takes the well-known brown derby. A dainty freshman has declined to play football because the ball is made of pigskin."

In 1920, the same year as *The Red and Blue* saw its first edition, SI was denied accreditation after a visit by "Dr. Thomas" from the University of California on April 13. According to McGloin, Dr. Thomas found that the "subject matter of the courses offered was not sufficiently broad; second, the teachers, with some exceptions, were not regarded as satisfactory." The following year, students, teachers and administrators worked to improve the school and received accreditation in 1921.[4]

The Ignatian & The Heights

The *Ignatian* continued to publish as a yearbook, though it went through a major redesign. From 1910 through 1924, it published as a small pamphlet with a cardboard cover. In 1925 it published in a more traditional yearbook style with larger pages (10.75 x 7.75 inches) and a hardbound cover. From the first, it raised funds through advertisements from local merchants. It reported on both university and high school events, as the two schools shared the same building until 1927 when the college moved to Campion Hall at the USF site. The 1928 *Ignatian* covered only the college events, leaving the high school students to create their own yearbook, in 1928, which they named *The Heights*, in anticipation of the school's move in 1929 to its new, higher location on Stanyan Street.

That first edition included this foreword: "This book purposes to be a record of the school year. A book can be nothing more than a record of the human acts or thoughts, and insomuch as it records them faithfully, therein lies its worth and its reason for being. But a school journal, if it accomplishes this purpose, as we hope this has, is more than a cold, lifeless record. It preserves as

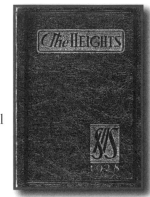

in a bright and deathless looking-glass the brightest and happiest years of our lives, — our school days. That is the reason for the existence of the 1928 *Heights.*"

Edward Sullivan '28 served as the publication's first editor, Charles Casassa '28, later to become a Jesuit and president of Loyola University, was associate sports editor. and H. J. Haley, F. F. Collins and Fr. Harold Ring, SJ, served as moderators.

Music at SI

S I assembled one of its earliest orchestras in 1925 "composed of a small group of willing workers and talented musicians. Many new and difficult pieces were rendered in a manner that showed earnest and hard practice, and the organization merited the highest praise," despite having to cope with "the lack of several instruments, which were so necessary for a balanced orchestra and for properly rendered selections." The orchestra performed at assemblies, oratorical contests and debates under the direction of Mr. A. I. Mei, SJ, a member of the college faculty. Later the orchestra performed at First Friday assemblies while a separate student band played at football and basketball games. In 1926 students formed a boys' choir under the direction of Mr. Paul Descout, SJ, to sing at the many liturgies, and a glee club, which sang at student assemblies.[5]

The Block Club

T he Block Club began in 1925 "to unite all those who have received their awards for athletic prowess into an organization for the furthering of better observance of school spirit and stimulating

The high school faculty in 1928.

athletic interest in the school." Its first officers were Frank Hanlon, Walter Black, Frank Gehres, George Olson and Ulick Kelly; the group consisted of 21 members.

Speech & Debate

S I students took part in a number of oratorical and academic contests that would prepare them for college and for their careers. The big event of the year was the Gold Medal Debate, staged between the Senate (the Senior Debating Society) and the House (the Debating Society of the Junior Class). The victor of this contest received a gold medal, a gift from the Gentlemen's Sodality of St. Ignatius Church. They also took part in a debate with students from Santa Clara (later to become Bellarmine College Preparatory), and vied for other academic awards including the Washington Essay Contest (with the winner receiving a trophy cup given for the best essay on

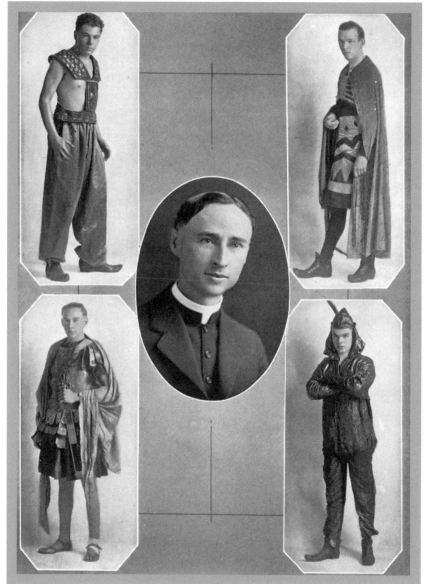

The Pageant of Youth featured a cast of 1,000 students from nearly every parochial school in San Francisco. SI's Rev. T.J. Flaherty, SJ, directed the grand spectacle.

the life of George Washington), the Freshman Elocution Contest (held at the Knights of Columbus Hall) and the Martin Latin Medal (the prize for the best paper in high school Latin).

Other Activities

Other contests included the Dramatic Arts Contest (an award for the best actor), the Outside Debate Team (which competed with other schools), the Loyalty Cup (given to the class "which has shown the most loyalty to the ideals of the school in student activity during the year"), the Museum Essay Contest (sponsored by the M.H. de Young Memorial Museum and won by Daniel Kelleher and George Olson in 1926) and the Senior Memorial Cup (an essay contest to commemorate two deceased members of the class). Other clubs included the Sanctuary Society and Sodality and the rally committees. Students also attended several dances, including the Senior Exclusive ("none but the mighty Senior was admitted"), the Block Club Dance, the Junior Prom, and the Senior Dance.

Along with these official activities were a few unofficial ones. The 1930 *Heights* notes that on October 25, 1929, a dozen "rascally" seniors "imbued with an overdose of school spirit … raided Sacred Heart today with a barrage of tomatoes prior to the football game. Unfortunately, their motives were not approved of by the authorities."

The *Pageant of Youth*

In 1925, the Jesuits looked to another venue to help repay their debt: The *Pageant of Youth* — a lavish play involving 1,000 students from SI and other San Francisco Catholic schools, all under the direction of Fr. T.J. Flaherty, SJ, and written by Fr. Daniel Lord, SJ, a talented young Jesuit of the Missouri Province. Among the stars of *Pageant of Youth* was J. Preston Devine '21, the uncle of former SI drama director and current English teacher Peter Devine '66. Preston played the choicest role in the *Pageant*, that of the devil.

The Red and Blue of February 25, 1925, reported that "when the call for the students was sent out [to audition for the Pageant], the auditorium was filled with the volunteers, forcing the directors to limit the already great number and reserve many for future use."

According to the 1925 *Ignatian*, the *Pageant of Youth*, which had five showings, was "a musical masque, heralded as the greatest religious, educational and dramatic production ever presented in San Francisco…. To accommodate the enormous number of participants, a special stage, 120 feet wide with a depth of 50 feet, the largest ever built in the Civic Auditorium, was constructed. To give a stage opening sufficient to frame the dancing groups and compre-

hend the magnitude of the lavish scenes and lighting effects, the arch was made 70 feet wide and 30 feet high. The rearranged Auditorium had a seating capacity of 6,000 with a perfect view of the stage for all."

In 1927, SI formed the Senior Dramatic Society and presented George Cohan's *Seven Keys to Baldpate* under the direction of Mr. Bart O'Neill, SJ, and Mr. Thomas Foster, with two performances at the Knights of Columbus Hall. A gushing reporter for the *Ignatian* had this to say about the performances of James Ludlow, Garret McEnerney, Frank Silva and Ralph Campiglia: "The players set a precedent which will demand every art from future aspirants to dramatic honors. It is doubtful if the performance will ever be surpassed at St. Ignatius."

Two years later, Mr. Thomas Foster directed *Right on the Button* with a cast, for the first time, that went beyond seniors. Four juniors joined the typically all-senior cast and "a freshman [John McHugh] was chosen to play a juvenile role for which none suitable could be found in the upper division."[6]

Parent Nights

In 1926, SI seniors held a reception to honor their mothers in what was most likely the first mother-son dinner. The *Ignatian* of that year noted that "all semblance of formality was omitted and the meeting was a success as all present entered into the spirit of the occasion. Fr. President spoke in honor of the occasion and praised the efforts of the Seniors and…. implied his sanction for a Mother's Club." The following year, the Class of 1927 held a Fathers' Night devoted "to the honor of that famous family institution, the Dad." The February 9 reception

featured a one-act sketch, a salutatory address and a talk by Father President "outlining the Jesuit ideals of education."

One School Becomes Two

In the 1920s, both students and teachers felt ready to move to new quarters, as the "temporary" Shirt Factory never proved truly satisfactory. Around 1925, Miss Mary Horgan died, leaving the school $25,000 in her will. The Jesuits hoped to ask 300 individuals to donate $1,000 each to help SI begin construction of a new campus, the fifth and final one for the university and the penultimate one for the high school.

In an article in the *St. Ignatius Church Calendar* from July 1926, Fr. Ray Feely, SJ, encouraged parishioners to donate towards this effort by helping to support the training of Jesuits: "To one to whom the name 'St. Ignatius College and High School' carries no significance, it must be a difficult enigma to solve, why over a thousand lads should deliberately pass by the luxurious temples of learning scattered throughout San Francisco and should content themselves to spend the glamorous days of youth in such drab surroundings. The enigma deepens when one learns that these young men are paying for the privilege of attending school in 'a refugee shack' (a reference to the emergency shelters of the 1906 Earthquake), while a short distance away splendid buildings offer them an educa-

tion free and without tuition (i.e., Lowell, Polytechnic and Washington). And all this in an age which values chiefly the superficial, whose standard is the extrinsic and not the intrinsic worth, which is more concerned with the tortoise shell frame than with the accuracy of the lens!

"The answer to this enigma is to be found in two words, 'Jesuit Education….' The point sought to be brought home here is that, in San Francisco as elsewhere, parents and boys alike desire instruction by Jesuit teachers, even if that education demands sacrifices both in the matter of finances and accommodations. The insistence of the people of San Francisco is so strong that dozens are turned away annually from St. Ignatius for lack of classroom space."

Fr. Edward J. Whelan, SJ, the 15th person to serve as president of SI, spearheaded fund-raising for the new college campus (the beginnings of USF) shortly after taking office in 1925, and by 1926, he had raised $10,000, enough to give him hope for the rest. On December 10, 1926, the college celebrated the groundbreaking ceremony for the Liberal Arts building on Ignatian Heights, the name students used to describe the hilltop campus site adjacent to St. Ignatius Church. Among those who spoke that day were Fr. Whelan, Mayor "Sunny Jim" Rolph, Msgr. Michael Connolly of St. Paul's Parish (Archbishop Edward J. Hanna's representative), and Frank Hughes '83, president of the SI Alumni Association.

The new college building (Campion Hall) opened

As construction began on the Stanyan Street campus in 1928, students in the cold and drafty Shirt Factory anticipated their new, modern quarters.

on October 9, 1927, after being blessed by Archbishop Hanna, and student enrollment finally began to increase. That slow growth inspired the college to change its name once again, this time to the University of San Francisco. However, not until the end of World War II and the introduction of the GI Bill did USF's enrollment start to skyrocket, making it one of the premier universities on the West Coast and the next step in formal education for many SI graduates.

Between 1927 and 1929, SI high school students studied at the Shirt Factory awaiting their own new campus. Barrett & Hilp, the construction firm that built Campion Hall, began work on September 11, 1928, on the Stanyan Street campus, located between McAllister and Turk Streets. Designed by Edward F. Eames along "classical lines," the new high school would be in "harmony with the church, the faculty building and the college building."[7] According to the *St. Ignatius Church Calendar* of 1928, planning for the new school involved a careful study "of the plans of schools throughout the country," and visits with "more modern ones in Northern California."

The article described the many state-of-the-art features of the new school: "The building has been designed to accommodate one thousand students and will contain, besides the regular business and administration offices, thirty-five classrooms, physics and chemistry laboratories, mechanical and free-hand drawing departments, library, assembly hall, chapel, cafeteria, co-operative store and book store, band room, winter play room and gymnasium.[8]

"The gymnasium will be the finest in Northern California and one of the finest in the country. In it will be located some seven hundred lockers, besides showers, dressing rooms for visiting teams and coaches' rooms. The main floor will be 60 by 102 feet in the clear, and rising from that will be the grandstands with accommodations for 1,500 spectators." (The school, however, would not muster enough funds to build this gymnasium until the 1950s.)

"The high school will have a frontage of 264 feet on Stanyan Street and 75 feet on Turk Street, and the gymnasium, south of the high school building, will have 130 feet on Turk Street and 104 on Stanyan."

The football field next to the school featured an 8-lane crushed-granite track and wooden bleachers on the east side of the field. It was known as SI Field and later, after the high school moved to the Sunset District, as Loyola Field and then as Negoesco Stadium. (The field now offers stadium lights, seating for 5,000, a concession stand and a pressbox — a far cry from the windswept plain where SI teams battled for 40 years.)

Construction took a year, and the Stanyan Street campus opened August 19, 1929. The *Calendar* extolled its beauty then, noting that the lobby "is done in Sienna marble, the walls being in imitation travertine." It touted the library, which had "accommodations for 10,000 volumes and for 100 students. It is done in the mission style, the woodwork in oak. An Assembly Hall adjoins the Library, a delicately done thing with beamed ceiling, in a grayish color, the drapes for the windows and stage in green."

The article noted the layout of the building, with offices for the principal, vice principal, spiritual director, student body and athletic departments on the first floor along with seven classrooms. The second floor held 15 classrooms, with an addition 12 on the third level. "The Physics and Chemistry Departments, modern and up to the minute in every way, are located on the third floor, and next to them are two drawing rooms, one for mechanical drawing, the other for free-hand drawing.

"The gem of the entire building is the chapel, the entrance to which is on the second floor, but which occupies the space of two floors. It has a gallery, which is entered from the third floor. The harmony of the Chapel, the delicately colored walls, the graceful arches over the windows, the symbolism of the ornaments, all point to it as being something quite distinctive in a Chapel design. But the crowning point of the chapel is the Altar, designed entirely by Mr. Edward Eames....

"In the basement, which is completely above ground, are found the Student's Co-operative Store, the Book Store, the Assembly Room and Library of the Gentlemen's Sodality, a huge winter playground, a Cafeteria completely modern in every detail, the athletic locker and dressing rooms, and the Boiler Room.

"The extensive playgrounds outside of the building contain four basketball courts, three handball courts and a tennis court. And just east is the Athletic Field, which will be used both by the College and High School. The field has been thoroughly graded and planted in grass; in length it is 534 feet, and in width 200 feet. The turf field is encircled by a quarter-mile running track, which has been designed and laid out in accordance with every requirement and is one of the very best tracks in California."

The article concluded with praise for the state-of-the-art public address system "which the principal from his desk can address the students in any particular classroom, or in all the classrooms at once. By means of the loud speaker attachment in all of the rooms connection may be made.... Thus a notice, instead of being sent around by word of mouth to the thirty-five classrooms and consuming a great deal of time, can be delivered simultaneously to all of the classes at the expense of just a few moments of time." The PA also allowed for radio hookups. "Thus if a message should be on the air that would be of great educational advantage to the group studying American History, for instance, or Civics, or Chemistry, that message can be directed to those particular classes. The possibilities of the Public Address System are very great and far-reaching indeed."

Students leaving the Shirt Factory to study on Stanyan Street felt as if they were walking into the Taj Mahal. This landmark school would serve more than 10,000 Ignatians over the next 40 years until 1969 when SI moved to its sixth campus, located in the Sunset District.

James D. Phelan

One generous gift of $100,000 made the Stanyan Street campus possible and paid for nearly a third of the $342,000 construction cost of the school. The donor was former U.S. Senator James D. Phelan, considered by many to be "the foremost citizen of California."[9]

Phelan, who received his A.B. degree in 1881, was one of SI's most famous graduates. Of Phelan's early days, an 1878 story in the *Monitor* reports the following: "We attended the literary entertainment ... on last Monday evening. The College Hall, where it took place, was well crowded, and a highly appreciative audience manifested great interest in the proceedings. The principal feature of the entertainment consisted in a

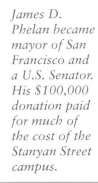

James D. Phelan became mayor of San Francisco and a U.S. Senator. His $100,000 donation paid for much of the cost of the Stanyan Street campus.

debate on the question, 'Has every male adult a right to vote?' and the arguments advanced by the young debaters were very ably and forcibly put. Where all were so excellent, it may be invidious to single out any individual, but the natural, self-possessed and eloquent delivery of Master James D. Phelan elicited general commendation."[10]

Phelan aspired to a literary career, but his father — an Irish immigrant who made his fortune as a trader, banker and merchant shortly after the Gold Rush — convinced him to join the family business in real estate and banking. In his role as businessman, he doubled his family's assets. According to an article in the *San Francisco Chronicle*, Phelan was "San Francisco's greatest host after the death of banker William Ralston [and]… the city's most eligible bachelor who financed California playwrights,

artists and sculptors, filling [his Saratoga home Villa] Montalvo with their creations."[11]

Later, Phelan would serve as San Francisco mayor (1896–1902) where he worked to reform City Hall, improve the economy and pass a new city charter that led to the creation of elected supervisors. He was also California's first popularly elected senator. The Jesuits showed their gratitude to Phelan in 1905 by granting him an honorary degree of Doctor of Law. On the day of the 1906 earthquake, Mayor Eugene Schmitz appointed Phelan head of the relief committee for those made homeless by the fire. The Jesuits paid their final tribute by naming USF's Phelan Hall residential dormitory for him in 1955.

Despite his accomplishments, Phelan remains a controversial figure in city history due to his support of the Chinese Exclusion Act, which drastically reduced the number of immigrants coming from China. After the San Francisco Earthquake, Phelan hoped to relocate the city's Chinese population to Hunter's Point to remove them from the center of the city, and he also warned against the growing influx of Japanese immigrants. Phelan's anti-Asian politics may have been typical for his times, but as USF President Stephen Privett, SJ, noted, Phelan's "explosively rhetorical expressions of exclusionary sentiments have all the appeal to modern ears of fingernails scraping down a blackboard."[12]

After Phelan died on August 7, 1930, at his country home near Saratoga, his remains lay in state at City Hall for three days. A funeral

K.3. Tappa Kega Schwartz, 1928 S.I.

Mass followed, the "largest and most imposing funeral ever seen in San Francisco," on August 11 at St. Ignatius Church attended by California Governor Clement C. Young, Mayor Rolph, and U.S. Senator Samuel D. Shortridge. The Jesuits named nearly 100 honorary pallbearers for this graduate of SI who made possible the construction of the high school's fifth home.[13]

Enrollment Rises as the Old School Falls

In the years before the Depression, enrollment at the high school climbed steadily. In 1909, the high school held 198 students. By the fall of 1922, high school enrollment topped 500 for the first time in the school's history and climbed to 852 in 1931–32. The following year, enrollment fell to 680, but by the mid 1930s, the numbers had recovered somewhat to "considerably above the 700 mark."[14]

The stock market wasn't the only thing to come crashing down in 1929. That same year the Shirt Factory was demolished. An editorial in the September 19 edition of *The Red and Blue* waxed eloquently on this demise: "…we don't forget our athletic ups and downs, our literary, forensic and thespian activities there. A building does not make a school: it is the student body that classifies it. So when you see apartment houses on the south side of Hayes Street opposite St. Mary's Hospital, just remember that all the spirit and loyalty has moved up a block or so, and that the students of the new St. Ignatius High School are even more interested and enthusiastic for bigger and better accomplishments for their new school." In the November 15 edition, as the demolition progressed, *The Red and Blue* struck a lighter tone: "We bid you goodbye, school of cold winters and JUG all the time. The

rambling shack of wood is now a gigantic pile of toothpicks." The paper made no mention of another great demolition — that of the stock market — which occurred two weeks earlier.

Jack O'Dea '28

Fr. Harry Carlin, SJ, and Jack O'Dea at an Alumni Golf Tournament in the 1980s.

Jack O'Dea '28, a longtime supporter of SI who, at the time of this writing, still attends many SI events, recalls performing as a devilish imp in the *Pageant of Youth* in his freshman year at SI. The plot revolved around the devil tempting a youth, and the youth successfully resisting. "In addition to being a lot of fun, it was a great place for high school boys and girls to meet. Many students paired off, thanks to the *Pageant*."

O'Dea also recalls his one algebra teacher at SI who made a big impression on him: David O'Keefe. As a college student at SI, O'Keefe played on the varsity baseball team that took on the Chicago White Sox and nearly won. "As a baseball legend, he inspired fear in us. All he had to do was turn around and look at you and you burned." O'Dea also notes that over the years he has met "so many people who say they played on the team, that it's no wonder they almost won. They must have had outfielders all over the place."

The entire student body, as in years past and years to come, celebrated First Friday Mass together at St. Ignatius Church. (This tradition ended with the move to the Sunset District campus.) O'Dea recalls that afterwards, Fr. Whelan would announce the class

From left, Fr. Thomas Martin, SJ, Fr. William LeVasseur, SJ, & SI Principal Albert Whelan, SJ.

debate that night.

The scores were never high for the games, O'Dea said. "We beat Poly 3–0 in football when Vin Casey dropped-kicked a field goal. We also beat SH that year, though we were never very good. We would always sit together in the rooting section. Fr. Whelan said at one game that he was astounded to see 250 students in the rooting section at Ewing Field (north of the former Presentation High School) even though the school had only sold 25 tickets. It was a pretty high fence to climb, but we made it!" He also recalled the SI baseball team winning the AAA in 1927 with a 3–0 record, coached by Lorenzo Malone, SJ.

The Class of '28 also entertained themselves in other ways. During their lunch break, members of the class would play softball in the enclosed yard behind the school. Toward the back of the field was a shed with a row of toilet stalls with doors that didn't quite reach the ground. "We posted two outfielders on the roof of that shed," said O'Dea, "and one outfielder on the steps leading to the classrooms. Sometimes a ball would be hit and roll under a stall in the outfield. Without a 'by your leave,' an outfielder would kick open the door, regardless of who might be in there, get the ball, and throw it back into play."

O'Dea adds that his four years at SI, from 1924–28, "were the greatest years of my life. We had such camaraderie. At one time there were 700 people in the school, and we knew everyone. I remember one holiday when we all came back to school because we enjoyed being there."

Fourteen of O'Dea's classmates entered the priesthood that year, with most joining the Society of Jesus. Those large numbers were typical of the time, spurred, in part, by active recruiting among the Jesuits and by the example of the young scholastics. O'Dea recalls

awards for the month. As a freshman, O'Dea won the Latin Medal one month for having top marks in his class. Later, back in class, O'Dea listened attentively as his Latin teacher told him, "You fooled me this month O'Dea, but as long as I live, you will never get another medal!"

O'Dea won the Gold Medal Debate in his senior year and led SI in debate against Lowell and Santa Clara. The debates were taken so seriously that Fr. Whelan, the principal, wouldn't let Charlie Casassa (who would join the order after high school and later become president of Loyola University in Los Angeles) or O'Dea play basketball for the 145-pound squad against Polytechnic High School because they had a

the Jesuits taking students out of class to interview them to see if they had an interest in joining. "They never called me out to be interviewed. They called me out for other reasons, though!" His good friend Charles Casassa was one of those interviewed who did join the Society after leaving SI.

O'Dea, 92 at the time of the interview, graduated with a BA and law degree from USF and became an attorney. He sent his sons — John Francis O'Dea Jr. '76 and Thomas Martin O'Dea '79 — and his grandson, Ryan O'Dea '07, to SI. He retired at 82 and is still an active member of the SI alumni association, attending the downtown business lunch and the annual golf and tennis tournament and all-class reunion each June.

Ken Atwell '29

Ken Atwell '29 recalls the nuns in grammar school warning students that they had a choice: either be good students and go to SI or be bad students and end up at reform school.

Atwell also recalls one SI teacher who always wore a black three-piece suit. "He was renowned for his aim. If he had his back to us while writing on the blackboard and heard us talking, he would turn around and throw his chalk, hitting the offender every time."

On another occasion, while sitting in JUG (Justice Under God), the students grew a bit rowdy while memorizing a page of Latin as punishment. The prefect of discipline, Fr. Harold E. Ring, SJ, saw them through the window from his office and raced to the classroom. "He slammed the door open, took one kid's neck in his hands, and slammed him against a blackboard. That quieted us down."

Not all the teachers were tough, though seemingly they had to be to survive. One scholastic made the mistake of treating his young charges as gentlemen. One day, while closing a double-hung window, the ropes broke that held the balancing weights, and the window slammed down on his fingers, trapping him there. "The students debated whether to help him or to leave him there," said Atwell. "We eventually lifted it off his fingers, but he wasn't too happy with us."

Atwell remembers the students sitting on the steps outside the school, chewing tobacco, holding spitting contests and memorizing lessons for homework. "The quality of education wasn't quite up to today's level," he noted.

After graduating from SI and attending St. Ignatius College for a year, Atwell continued his education at UC Berkeley and in Utah. He eventually started a successful commercial construction business before moving to Idaho. He died December 21, 2004, at the age of 92, leaving SI $1 million in his will.

Tom Brady '31

Tom Brady '31, father of Kevin Brady '68, transferred to SI in 1928 after his freshman year when his family moved from Seattle. He was not happy to learn that his sophomore year would begin August 16, three weeks earlier than in Seattle. "I felt cheated to have my summer cut short," he noted in a 2004 interview. He felt even more cheated when he walked into the ramshackle Shirt Factory, but it took him no time at all to fit in. He joined the Sanctuary Society, moderated by Mr. William Huesman, SJ, who made it one of the most sought-after clubs to join by leading students on hikes in Muir Woods and taking them for outings on the bay to Paradise Cove on a tug boat lent by the father of one

Freshman initiation in 1926.

Opposite page: Each year, SI celebrated President's Day, which featured athletic contests between classes. Pictured above is a 1924 tug-of-war.

so we played handball on the old rectory wall. It was only 15 feet wide, so we had to learn to keep our eye on the ball and catch it as it bounced off the back wall.

He took a job working for the Jesuits as a receptionist at Welch Hall and, the following year, at the new school on Stanyan Street, working for the school in a student-run co-op, where he sold candy, cookies, root beer, pineapple juic, watch fobs and pins with the SI insignia. He thought the new school resembled "a palace, with wide halls and lockers up and down the corridor. I knew I wasn't in heaven because we still had class, but it was close."

The new building featured a giant furnace in the basement (which was actually at street level), and as co-op worker (and later manager), he befriended the school janitor, James Aubry McCulley, who lived on campus in one of two rooms in the basement. One of McCulley's jobs was to make a home brew for the Jesuits and to clean up the priests' Villa at Clear Lake. Brady would sometimes accompany McCulley on these trips to help with the clean up.

He was surprised to

of the students.

At lunch and at recess, students played all kinds of games, including football. Brady recalls one large senior, Willie Kennedy, who tossed a football that landed in one of the latrines stationed at the south end of the play area. He also recalls eating Mexican food for the first time in his life — "They didn't have Mexican food in Seattle when I was growing up" — and one food fight that ensued, involving tacos and tamales.

The old school featured handball courts that were built in the interior of the old church (after it had moved to Fulton and Parker). "But even then, there were only three or four courts for the whole school,

see women working in the office at the new school, though he recalls only two — an assistant registrar and a receptionist/secretary.

For his graduation, Brady was disappointed to learn that he would have to go through two ceremonies, one just for SI students and another, by order of the Archbishop, for all Catholic San Francisco high school students at Dreamland (later called Winterland). "It just meant we had to take our Sunday-going-to-meeting suit out one more time."

At SI, Brady found himself impressed with the Jesuits he met — Fr. Charles F. Carroll, SJ, who had been his parish priest in Seattle and who came to SI to teach, Fr. Ed Whelan, SJ, and his brother Fr. Al Whelan, SJ, and Mr. William Huesman, SJ, who inspired many young men to join the order, including Brady. He was one of 17 from his class to join the Society of Jesus, and he stayed in the order for more than 12 years, leaving just six months shy of ordination. He eventually attended law school and became an administrative judge for the Assessment Appeals Board.

A senior class from 1933.

VII. Making a Home on Stanyan Street (1930 ~ 1939)

The decade of the '30s was a time of hardship for San Franciscans, as the Depression cost citizens their jobs and savings. But it was also a time of momentous happenings. The General Strike of 1934 marked a victory for the labor movement with repercussions that were felt for decades. San Francisco, just as it rose from the ashes of the Earthquake and Fire, saw that it could rise to the occasion in the midst of an economic downturn and build two wonders of the world — the world's longest bridge and the longest single-span suspension bridge. It even dredged up Treasure Island from the bottom of the San Francisco Bay and held the Golden Gate International Exposition in 1939 and 1940, celebrating its status as the capital of the Pacific Rim ports of call. All of these events touched the lives of SI students. Still, high school life went on, and SI students enjoyed athletic victories in baseball (1930), tennis (1931 and 1932) and, for the first time, crew, taking the AAA title in 1939 using whaleboats in the San Francisco Bay.

Diamond Jubilee Celebration

SI marked its 75-year anniversary with a series of celebrations starting May 19, 1930, that included a diamond jubilee rally at SI Stadium on October 13; a celebration at the Civic Auditorium on October 17 with Archbishop Hanna, Mayor Rolph and USF President Edward Whelan, SJ; and a parade and Mass

The high school community celebrated the 75-year anniversary of the founding of SI.

SI Principals Fr. Dennis Kavanagh, SJ (top) & Fr. Walter Semeria, SJ

on October 19. St. Ignatius College used this occasion to change its name formally to the University of San Francisco.

Later, on May 22, the Society of California Pioneers dedicated a plaque commemorating the first St. Ignatius Academy of 1855. The plaque was affixed to The Emporium department store, built on the site of that one-room schoolhouse. SI President Fr. Anthony P. Sauer, SJ, rededicated that plaque and installed a new one at The Emporium in 1979, the first year he took office, commemorating the school's 125th anniversary. The plaque bears these words: "The original St. Ignatius College has developed into both the University of San Francisco and St. Ignatius College Preparatory. Placed in honor of their 125th year by both senior classes of 1980. October 15, 1979."

The Case of the Missing Principal

In the 1930–31 school year, SI had three principals. First, Fr. Dennis Sullivan, SJ, who had taught as a regent at SI in the early 1920s, took over in the summer of 1930 but left for Seattle on November 3, possibly for reasons of health, and he died there six years later. Following in his stead was the noted preacher

Fr. Dennis Kavanagh, SJ, but sickness forced him, too, to resign by January. Succeeding him was Fr. Walter Semeria, SJ '15, a legendary figure, known not for his tenure of office, but how he ended his association with the Jesuits.

Not much is known about his two terms as principal. He introduced the practice of mailing report cards home to parents and ended the Friday assemblies at which students received awards and medals for academic achievement. The August 19, 1932, edition of *The Red and Blue*, mentions in passing that he had left for his tertianship studies, and that Fr. James King, SJ, would succeed him as principal.

Four years later, Fr. Semeria disappeared, the apparent victim of a drowning accident on May 15, 1936. The May 27 edition of *The Red and Blue* reported that Fr. Semeria had died, "a victim of the raging Pacific Ocean." It mentions that he had been "burdened with periodic sickness," and had most recently served as "spiritual father of the young men of the University."

What no one knew at the time was that Semeria had faked his death in order to leave town. SI Athletic Director Robert Vergara '76 found out what really happened when, in 1983, he interviewed Fr. William Keenan, SJ, SI's treasurer.

Fr. Keenan told Vergara that Semeria had gone to the beach one day after school and then disappeared, leaving behind a pile of his clothes and a breviary on the sands. The Jesuits, thinking that he had committed suicide, kept the matter quiet. But some, including Fr. Keenan, found it hard to believe Semeria had committed suicide. "It was thought odd, at the time, that Fr. Semeria should go swimming after school that day. He didn't like the water, but his clothes were on the beach, and he disappeared. It was assumed that he had drowned. About 10 years later, however, USF received a request from a Southwestern Bible college for Walter Semeria's transcript — an odd request for a man supposedly 10 years dead. At about the same time, Fr. William Dunne, SJ '15, president of USF and SI (and Semeria's high school classmate at SI), was scheduled to go to Albuquerque, NM, for a conference. While he was there, he took a 'shot in the dark' and looked through the phone book for a Walter Semeria. He found the name, dialed the number, and asked if he could speak with Walter Semeria. When Semeria came to the phone, Fr. Dunne recognized his voice and said, 'Hello ———.' Fr. Dunne called Semeria by a nickname that only the two of them used. Semeria knew the charade was over and agreed to meet with Fr. Dunne. They were together for an hour or two and Fr. Dunne had his say."

Some of the priests in the city had refused to believe that Fr. Semeria had actually pulled this; after Fr. Dunne's meeting, they were convinced. Further confirmation came when some publication ran a photo of a Protestant ministers' conference, and Walter Semeria was clearly visible. He had become an Episcopal minister. Semeria later changed his name, and he never told his family that he was alive, worried, perhaps, that the stigma of being related to a runaway priest would be too much for them to bear.

A Song to Fight Over

In 1932, SI hired Eneas "Red" Kane, a nationally-ranked track athlete who had coached and taught there for several years, as the school's first athletic director. He served in that position until 1936 when he left for a job at City Hall. He was replaced by Richard "Red" Vaccaro, a former star athlete at the college, who held the job until 1953. Following him were J.B. Murphy (1953-1967), Leo LaRocca '53 (1966–2000) and Robert Vergara '76 (2000–). (More on these men in later chapters.)

The school began another sports tradition in 1933 when Fenton Gervase O'Toole '34 wrote the words that generations of Ignatians have sung at rallies and games. The November 8, 1933, edition of *The Red and Blue* reported on this event:

"Here It is:
School Victory Song

To the Red and Blue we'll all be true,
We'll wave her banner to the sky,
We'll fight for you, old Red and Blue,
We'll fight for Saint Ignatius High!
And victory will be our goal —
For we will reach it, if we try,
So let us fight—with all our might—
We're gonna fight, fight, fight, fight, fight!"

Ignatian's Song of Victory Made by F. O'Toole

"The Victory Song's here! A real cheery song of encouragement for the boys who wear the Red and Blue. For a long time loyal Ignatians have been discussing ways and means of instilling more pep and enthusiasm into our student body. Fenton O'Toole '34 has come to the aid of all loyal Ignatians with a new victory song, to be sung at all games and rallies to the tune of a snappy military march.

"You will hear the song at the next rally but in the meantime learn the words so that you can warble the Red and Blue warriors on to victory. Get behind the new school song and make it a real student body accomplishment of the year."

O'Toole, who later changed his first name to Felton, joined the Society of Jesus after graduating from SI and served as a priest for 50 years until his death. He ended his career as an assistant professor of English at SCU from 1975–83.

The Depression

If you ask people who graduated from SI in the 1930s what they recall of the Great Depression, they will not say very much. Most recall times of little hardship for themselves. "That was all we knew. We didn't know we were poor," was the echo of nearly every Ignatian interviewed for this history.

Still SI was not immune from the ravages of the economic downturn. Perhaps the most obvious effect of the Depression on SI was the elimination of the yearbook. The 1932 edition of *The Heights* was to be the last SI yearbook until 1946, when it returned as the renamed *Ignatian*. With Archbishop Edward Hanna's health failing, and with the archdiocese in economic trouble, Bishop John J. Mitty was called in from Utah in 1932 to serve as Hanna's coadjutor and set things in order. On November 6, 1932, in an announcement in *The Monitor*, he ordered all Catholic schools in the archdiocese to stop publishing yearbooks. His reasons: "It has been shown that the preparation of these books has been found to cause a considerable loss of time, on the part of the pupils, a burdensome and useless expense to parents and a great annoyance to merchants who were imposed on to advertise in these books, to defray the cost of printing them."[1]

For similar reasons, he instructed SI in 1936 not

Al Worner '36 helped his parents pay SI's tuition by delivering the Shopping News during the Depression.

to raise funds to build a gym, and the school delayed its fund-raising campaign for several years. (In a terse letter to SI Principal James A. King, SJ, Mitty wrote that "no permission for [the gym fund-raising] drive has been asked or granted.... I hereby forbid this campaign and order it to be discontinued immediately."[2]

SI suffered in other ways. Stan Corriea '34, who attended SI in the early years of the Depression, noted that a small number of his classmates could not afford the jump in tuition, from $5 per month to $7.50, when the school moved from the Shirt Factory to Stanyan Street. Those who could not afford the tuition typically lasted out the school year and did not return the following fall; however, Frank Dowling '36 recalls more than a few mothers coming to SI to withdraw their sons, unable to pay the monthly tuition. "The Jesuits would ask what they could afford. If only $3, the priests would say, fine. Just pay that. We want to keep your boy in school."

Some of those who did have a little extra money spent it, during the last days of Prohibition, on liquor purchased at a speakeasy at the corner of Stockton and Sutter. "We used to go there in high school and buy a quart of whiskey for $1.50," said Corriea.

Peter Devine '66 tells the story of a time when the Jesuits at SI could not afford to pay their electric bill in the mid 1930s: "Several graduates, including my father and uncle, revived the Alumni Association to raise money for the Jesuits. When the mothers in the Loyola Guild learned how hard-pressed the school was, they organized a bake sale. The story goes that the Jesuits spent the night in their chapel praying for money to pay their electric bill. The next morning, the mothers brought them their proceeds from the bake sale, giving them enough to pay it."

Bob Lagomarsino '39 recalled that some of his

classmates put newspaper or cardboard in their shoes when it rained because of the holes in their soles. "But we thought that was normal. We had three square meals a day and didn't know any different. Our parents struggled through the hard times to afford the tuition," which in the late 1930s had risen to $9 per month. "I used to pay for it by working at my dad's store and by selling magazines at Ocean Beach."

Lagomarsino sold *The Saturday Evening Post* and *The Ladies' Home Journal* for 5 cents to people visiting Playland at the Beach. "But not everyone had money to spare, and the magazines were a tough sell."

Al Worner '36, like Lagomarsino, worked to help his parents pay the tuition. Worner delivered the *Shopping News* on Wednesdays and Saturdays. "That was nice money," he noted. "And I used to get 25 cents to cut the front lawns for my neighbors."

In 1935, Worner remembers, SI held its junior prom with a small orchestra in the auditorium at USF due to financial problems. The Depression didn't keep Worner and his classmates from having a good time when school let out. "If one of us could borrow a car from his father, we would drive to Land's End on Saturday afternoons and listen on the radio to the afternoon orchestra from Meadowbrook in New Jersey. Or we'd go out to Playland with our families or to Sutro Baths with our buddies. At Playland, we would ride the giant slides, get lost in the maze of mirrors or try to walk through the spinning barrel and get tossed around.

"On Sundays, we would eat at Lucca's, which offered dinner for 50 cents, including petits fours to take home with you. For 75 cents, you'd get a bottle of wine for dinner.

"If I took a girl on a date, I'd go with a few other couples to a show. Afterwards we would take our dates to the St. Francis or the Mark Hopkins. Six or eight of us would take a table in the dining room, and for $2 we would order a bowl of punch for two and dance to Freddie Martin. The ballrooms loved having us there, because we looked good in our suits and ties, and we kept the places from looking empty. With dinner at $4 or $5, they were having trouble filling those places."

Academics

What did high school students read in their English classes in the 1930s? What electives could they take? According to the *Catalogue* of 1930–31, students read such classics as *The Iliad & The Odyssey, The Aeneid, Everyman, Morte d'Arthur, Pilgrim's Progress, Gulliver's Travels, Robinson Crusoe, The Vicar of Wakefield, The Last Days of Pompeii, Ivanhoe, Treasure Island, Captains Courageous* and *Lorna Doone.* They also read Shakespeare, Austen, Dickens, Hawthorne and a number of poets, such as Tennyson, Arnold, Byron, Coleridge, Pope, Milton and Browning — in short, the Great Books that students had read 30 years previous and would continue to read 30 years hence. This was the same reading list used by every teacher in every school in the province, as they all looked to the *Ratio Studiorum* to guide their curriculum. (Not until the 1960s and 1970s would teachers be allowed to experiment and stray from this norm with authors such as Kate Chopin, e.e. cummings and Allen Ginsberg.)

SI offered a variety of courses over the four years, but students had few options for electives. Subjects

Bob Lagomarsino '39, who also attended SI during the Depression, noticed that his classmates wore cardboard in their shoes when their soles wore thin.

included chemistry, civics, debating, English, French, German, Greek, history, Latin, mathematics, mechanical drawing, music, physics, public speaking, religion, Spanish and social science. In all, 35 teachers and seven administrators helped 850 students march through their four years of high school education.

In 1933, the school changed its curriculum, requiring all students to take Latin, English, history and mathematics in their first two years as core subjects, with honors students taking Greek in their sophomore year. For the junior year, students could choose from three different sets of additional courses, though, as Fr. McGloin notes, "St. Ignatius High School still was determined to retain its character as a college preparatory institution for not one vocational or commercial subject was included in the three groups."[3]

SI also began offering three kinds of diplomas in 1933: a general diploma for students taking fewer than four years of Latin, a classical diploma for four years of Latin study, and the highest award — an honorary classical diploma — for four years of Latin and two of Greek.

In 1938, Fr. Edward B. Rooney, SJ, the national director of the Jesuit Education Association, came to SI to evaluate its programs and facilities. He found that the 704 students and 45 faculty of SI enjoyed a "fine reputation" and that the school "was run exceptionally well." He also noted that SI was "one of the four Jesuit high schools chosen two years ago to participate in the Cooperative Study of Secondary School Standards in some two hundred American high schools. Its rating in this study was quite satisfactory." He hoped that the school would employ more Jesuit priests as teachers, as SI relied heavily on scholastics, whose time at the school lasted only a few years. Those scholastics, however, were crucial to the run-

ning of the school, as they supplied needed manpower and kept tuition costs low. They also served to inspire young men to follow a vocational call to the Society of Jesus as priests and brothers and to become diocesan priests.[4]

Athletics

Football

The football team, which left the AAA after the 1931 season for lack of success against the powerful city teams, went undefeated under Coach George Malley from September 1933 to December 1935, finally losing 12–7 to Loyola High School of Los Angeles in the state Catholic prep grid championship. Coach Malley was so popular in those days that you could hear him being interviewed on Bay Area radio stations. His success prompted SI to return to the AAA in 1936. The *San Francisco Chronicle*, at the end of the 1934 season, likened Malley's team to the "Rockne Ramblers" of Notre Dame. (It seemed in those days as if all Catholic athletes in the U.S. were measured against the exploits of Notre Dame's great teams.) "Today in San Francisco is an unsung, unnoted football team that embodies about everything that Notre Dame teams of years ago stood for — rambling, fight and Irish — and undefeated records. That team belongs to St. Ignatius High School. The Ignatians ramble over California a bit, next year they may even trek to Reno; Irish names dominate the lineup and the record is clean — not even one point is tabbed for opponents."

The lightweight football team also enjoyed success, with the 1933 squad, coached by Eneas "Red" Kane, winning 13 games by shutting out each oppo-

The 1932 Footbal Team.

The Stanyan Street campus and football field.

nent and scoring a total of 219 points. The team was ranked first in Northern California but missed playing Bakersfield for the state championship. SI hoped to raise funds to travel south through the gate receipts of a game against Sacred Heart. When that game was cancelled, SI opted not to make the trip.

Basketball

In 1936, Eneas "Red" Kane, SI's first athletic director, left and was replaced by Richard "Red" Vaccaro '26, who made a name for himself as a football great at SI. In 1924, the year he entered SI as a sophomore, he became the captain of the varsity football team under coach Jimmy Needles. He continued at SI College in 1926 and graduated in 1930 after playing football for SI and the Olympic Club. In 1931 he started teaching at the high school and the following year became assistant to Leo Rooney, SI's head football coach. In 1936, he became both the new athletic director and head football coach (1936–1941) after George Malley left to coach on the college level.

One challenge Vaccaro faced was the lack of a gym for his basketball teams. The school began raising money for a gym, with $70,000 set for the goal, and in the meantime, SI played at the newly-opened Kezar Pavilion and Stadium.

The varsity basketball team of 1935–36 seemed destined for greatness with the hire of Louis Batmale, a member of Lowell's Class of 1930 who was a year out of college. Members of the Class of '36 wondered who this baby-faced choirboy was, as he looked no older than they. Some students began making fun of him behind his

back. One day, they turned all their chairs around to face the back of the room. "We thought it was funny," said Bill Bennett '36. "He did not."

Jack "Doc" Overstreet '36 was one of those who was not immediately impressed by Batmale. "Then one day, I was walking down the hall, and this tall man grabbed me. He said, 'Are you trying to knock me down? That's not going to happen.' No one gave him trouble after that. Later, I realized how much he and all my teachers really cared for us."

Batmale coached the SI basketball team to seven straight wins, leading up to a big game against Lowell. Bob Fair '36, who played for Batmale, remembers Kezar selling out all 5,500 seats, and turning away

The 130-pound basketball team from 1937.

125

10,000 more. Lowell beat SI 29–8 that night. "That was pretty embarrassing for all of us," Fair notes. For Frank Lawson '36, that loss "was the toughest of my life. Over the years I have run into so many people who said they were at that game." SI wouldn't avenge itself until 1943, when Kevin O'Shea '43 would lead the Wildcats to a city championship.

Batmale succeeded as a coach despite having to scrounge around the city for gyms to use. "All we had were two hoops in the schoolyard," he noted. "We would use a gym on Page Street and ones at Kezar, the Governor's Club (now the San Francisco Boy's Club), Roosevelt Jr. High School and, once in a while, Mission High and Everett Junior High."

Batmale also taught English at SI between 1935–39 and recalls the faculty make-up was the ideal mix for Fr. James A. King, SJ, whom Batmale called "a great principal"): one-third priests, one-third scholastics and one-third laymen. Batmale, like all the lay teachers, made just enough to get by: $1,700 per year. "Those were Depression dollars," he added. "An apartment cost $30 a month to rent and a restaurant dinner cost 75 cents." Still, after he married, Fr. King told him this: "Louis, you can't work for the Jesuits all your life. You need to make enough to support a family now." The Jesuits simply couldn't afford to pay lay teachers as much as they deserved, so Batmale left SI, took a job at Commerce High School, and eventually rose through the public school ranks to become president of San Francisco City College, retiring in 1977.

Dr. Louis Batmale, who taught English and coached basketball, was told to look for another job if he hoped to support his family. He eventually became president of San Francisco City College.

Baseball

SI won its first AAA baseball championship under manager Frank McGloin '25, who had been a star on the SI baseball team. The 1930 season began with the Wildcats winning four of their first five games with stars such as Joe Burns, Roy Harrison and team captain Cal Sever, who later played in the Pacific Coast League for the Oakland Oaks. In the league championship, SI beat Galileo two games to one. McGloin said that team was "one of the best I ever coached."[5]

Crew

The SI Rowing Club may have been active informally in the 1920s, but it gained formal status in 1932 when Thomas O'Dwyer, a student at SI, organized the school's first crew, which was coached by William Lenhart. After more than 200 boys tried out, the coach formed two crews, one for the 130-pound weight class and the other an unlimited (varsity) boat. In its first year, rowing in 14–person whaleboats, SI beat Galileo, Lowell, Marin Junior College and several other schools. The team to beat, however, was the crew from Continuation High School, and SI placed second in AAA competition to that school in 1936 through 1938.

James Feehan '32, who died in 2004, was a member of the first crew. His widow, Geraldine, recalls that her husband "practiced with the rowing club every Saturday morning on the Bay with Angel Island their destination. On one trip, the boys stayed too long on the island. Because of changing tides, rowing back was hard and dangerous. They arrived safely, but it was an anxious and worrisome time for everyone awaiting their return at the South End Rowing

Club pier. Monday morning was also an anxious and worrisome time when the team was called to the principal's office for a full accounting of the episode."

In 1939, SI won its first league title by defeating Galileo; SI recaptured the league championship in 1941 and 1942 before disbanding. SI would not compete in crew again until 1979. In the 1990s, SI would prove to be a powerhouse both in California and in the nation, taking first place in the U.S. in 1997, marking SI's only national athletic championship.

Golf

The first mention of a golf team occurs in the 1930 edition of *The Heights*, which noted that the "there aren't too many good golfers in the prep circles around here, and the Wildcats seem to be blessed with an amazing number of them." Standouts included senior Frank Devlin, who already had a hole-in-one to his credit, sophomore George Kuklinsky and junior Neal Lyons. Others on the team were Al Buchner, Joe Kelly, Lee Hoagland, John Duff, Frank Keane, Sid Heller, Gerry Lunch, Fred Cosgrove, Jack Sherry, Ed Gilmore, Bill O'Toole and Jack Freed.

Extracurriculars

CSF

In 1930, SI applied for membership in the California Scholarship Federation and formed its first Honor Society, Chapter 211 of the CSF. According to *The Heights* of that year, the group was "a junior part of the International Phi Beta Kappa Honor Society and any high school member enjoys the help of that body upon his entrance into college." The first five members that year were William Dowling, William Dunbar, James Gallen, George Myers and John O'Connell. In 1942, Edward L. Burke '42, who later

The SI Crew in 1939 after winning the All City Championship. Photo provided by Maureen Revel and Carolyn Coe, whose father, Timothy Sullivan, is pictured (2nd from right, standing). Sullivan's grandchildren are recent SI grads.

served for a time as a Jesuit and a professor at USF, won the CSF's highest prize, the Seymour Memorial Award, honoring him for being the top male student in the state.

Marching for ROTC & Jeans

Fr. King, principal from 1932–1945, added a Military Training Unit to the curriculum in 1935, the genesis of the ROTC program. While students participated in it by the hundreds, they still had a rebellious streak. In March 1937, 50 students came to class wearing blue jeans to protest the strict dress code. When they were told to go home and change, they walked outside and sat in the street. The *Examiner* ran a picture of the students on March 19 with a "Strike for Jeans" sign during their sit-in, and the caption noted that "for a while, they sat in the street wearing out the jeans at strategic points. But all of them were back in class by noon" and that "the principal called it a lark." Those boys spent a day in JUG for every class period they missed.

Speech & Debate

Debate continued to be a primary extracurricular activity. In 1934, SI took on Bellarmine over this proposition: "Resolved, that Hitler is a benefit to Germany." Debaters in the Senate, the senior debating society, gathered first at SI and then at Bellarmine for two nights of arguments. Bellarmine defended the proposition, arguing that Hitler had "checked communism" and had "been a benefit to Germany, financially." SI countered, with Jack Clifford arguing that Hitler's government "was one of oppression," Jack Wade noting that Hitler had "fostered race

Opposite page: St. John Berchmans Sanctuary Society, junior division, in 1932. Several of the members would become Jesuits including, top left, Thomas Reed, future SI principal. Two over is Fenton O'Toole, who wrote the SI fight song and later joined the Society of Jesus. Third row, second from left is Charles Dullea, future USF president; bottom row, third from left is Harry Carlin, future SI president.

hatred," and Jack Barbieri pointing to the trade wall erected by Hitler. SI won that debate round, though it lost the following day to Bellarmine.[6]

The General Strike of 1934

SI students witnessed the historic events of the city in the 1930s, including the General Strike of 1934, when longshoremen began a strike for better wages. That July, street violence broke out and police shot and killed two longshoremen and wounded 109 people. A four-day general strike followed that shut down the city.

Even though his father was a police officer, Bill Bennett '36 had sympathies for the longshoremen and eventually became one. "I thought they were getting screwed," he said. "I was from a working class family just like most of the kids from SI then."

But most of the Jesuits, long opposed to communism, had little sympathy for the longshoremen and their leader, Harry Bridges. "One day they took the students to the chapel and asked us to pray that FDR would not recognize Red Russia," said Bennett. "It didn't work, despite all our prayers."

Few students were touched by the violence, though Bennett did see strikers beat a scab to death, and Bob Lagomarsino '39, while driving with his parents, had a motorcycle cop smash into the back of his car while chasing a striker. Kevin Brady '36 worked for a man who carried a gun while delivering pharmaceuticals to city hospitals. "Whenever strikers stopped him, he told them he had to get the drugs to the hospitals. They let him through, but he had that gun in case there was trouble."

This 1933 shot shows SI, USF, the Golden Gate Bridge & the Masonic Cemetery.
Also seen are the San Francisco College for Women on Lone Mountain, Temple Emanu El & St. Mary's Hospital.

Two Wonders of the World
and a World's Fair

In 1936 and 1937, San Francisco introduced two engineering triumphs to the world with the Bay Bridge (the world's longest bridge at the time) and the Golden Gate Bridge (the longest single-span suspension bridge). *The Red and Blue* of November 6, 1936, ran an editorial drawing a parallel to the Bay Bridge, which would link San Francisco to the East Bay on November 12, to the educational bridge that existed between USF and SI. "Soon a great campus will connect the high school and university, binding them as a great historic sight [sic] in San Francisco… the future!" Little did the writer know that SI and USF would, in 1959, formally separate, becoming two distinct institutions.

To celebrate the construction of both bridges, San Francisco hosted the Golden Gate International Exposition on Treasure Island in both 1939 and 1940, featuring such talents as Johnny Weissmuller and Esther Williams in Billy Rose's Aquacade and Sally Rand's Nude Ranch on the Gayway. Many SI students and families attended this great event, the twin to New York's World Fair, including Leo Carew '40, who went to the Folies Bergere with his cousin. He saw the catcher for the San Francisco Seals, Joe Sprinz (whose son later went to SI), try to catch a ball dropped from a hot air balloon. The ball fell so fast that it shattered Sprinz' jaw and nearly killed him. Carew also saw the first television, invented in San Francisco, and a talking robot called the Voder.

Br. Louis Bueler, SJ, who worked at SI for 30 years, found a job as a gardener at the fair and helped to put out a fire in the California Building. Bob Fair '36 recalls being a contestant in Kay Kyser's Kollege of Musical Knowledge. "I won $50 for answering all the questions right about the Big Band songs. I had a chance to chat with Harry Babbit, who sang with Kyser. Then in 1999, I met him again in San Jose and took part in another contest where I had to name the members of Guy Lombardo's orchestra. I won that contest and, when I got on stage, told Harry that we had met before in 1939. 'Don't you remember me?' I asked him. He thought it was a great coincidence for us to meet 60 years later."

But on this idyllic island, built to celebrate civilizations from around the world, Carew, Bueler and Fair saw signs that all was not well across the ocean. One by one, they saw various countries pull out of the exposition, starting with Czechoslovakia, as Germany began its European conquests.

Richard Egan '39

One of the most famous students to attend SI graduated in 1939. Richard Egan starred in *Love Me Tender* (1956), in which Elvis Presley made his debut, Disney's *Pollyanna* (1960), and *A Summer Place* (1959), playing Sandra Dee's father.

At SI he performed in *The Dragon's Breath* and *The Bat* and won the Freshman Elocution Medal. He got to know all the priests by working the switchboard at Welch Hall. After graduating from USF, where he participated in the College Players Theatre productions, he enlisted in the Army during World War II and served as a judo instructor before being discharged in 1946 with the rank of captain.

He picked up his acting career at Stanford after the war, earning a master's degree in theater history, and at Northwestern University, where he taught and appeared in 30 shows.

A Warner Bros. talent scout eventually spotted

him and signed him to a contract. After a series of supporting roles, he became a star for 20th Century-Fox, which likened him to Clark Gable, and cast him in a number of adventure movies including *A View from Pompey's Head* in 1955, *Esther and the King* in 1960 and *The 300 Spartans* in 1962. He also starred in *Up Front, Hollywood Story, The Devil Makes Three, Seven Cities of Gold, Split Second, The Glory Brigade, Demetrius and the Gladiators,* and *Slaughter on Tenth Avenue.*

Richard Egan '39 starred in Elvis Presley's first film and had his own TV series.

In 1962, Egan began a career in television as Jim Redigo in *Empire,* a contemporary western series; for its second season, the show changed its name to *Redigo.* Toward the end of his career, he played the role of Samuel Clegg II on the soap opera *Capitol* until his death in 1987. Among the pallbearers for his funeral were his close friends Robert Mitchum and boxer Floyd Patterson. (Both Egan and his brother, Fr. Willis Egan, SJ '35, a theology professor at USF, were lifelong fans of boxing. They numbered among their friends many of the champions who fought at the Olympic Auditorium in LA. "I enjoyed watching Richard's boxing movies when we would hold 'Jesuit Night at the Fights' at Loyola University," recalls Fr. Kotlanger. "He was a generous man who frequently attended SI and USF events to boost alumni enthusi-

asm." Fr. Kotlanger also recalls that Herb Caen used to joke that Fr. Willis Egan should have become an actor as he was better looking than his brother.)

During his career he received the Laurel Award and was ranked among the top tier of entertainers by *Good Housekeeping* magazine. He was survived by his five children and by his wife, Patricia, whom he married in 1958 at Star of the Sea Church at a Mass officiated by his brother. His cousin Grace White noted in the spring 1989 issue of *Genesis II* that Egan was happy to land the *Capitol* part as it allowed him to spend more time with his family. "Rich was a wonderful family man," said Mrs. White. "His family meant everything to him. Even though he was in Hollywood, Rich lived a quiet life and was very private. He was a holy man, truly a religious person."

Alfred J. Cleary (SI 1900)

In 1930, Alfred J. Cleary (SI 1900 & grandfather of Board of Regents President Mark Cleary '64) was appointed San Francisco's first chief administrative officer by Mayor Angelo Rossi. Cleary, who had trained at UC Berkeley as a civil engineer, was chief assistant in charge of work on the Hetch Hetchy Dam and the supervisor of the pipeline that carried its water to the Bay Area. He also proposed the Rincon Hill site for the Bay Bridge and created the Mokelumne Water Project, which supplied the East Bay with water.

Under the city's new charter, Cleary wielded considerable power as supervisor of both the SFFD and SFPD, the departments of finance and records, purchasing, public works, health, real estate, electricity, street traffic, welfare, coroner's office and several minor bureaus. *The San Francisco News* praised the appointment in a December 16, 1930, editorial, calling Cleary an "expe-

rienced, successful and highly regarded civil engineer.... In his new post Mr. Cleary will be the real boss of most of the routine work of the city."

Alluding to the corruption inherent in city government at that time, the *News* editorial added this note: "To clean up the Department of Public Works and to apply efficiency and economy to its street and other construction work will be in itself a job to test any man's capacity."

When he died in 1938, 108 honorary pallbearers, including A.P. Giannini (founder of the Bank of Italy which later became the Bank of America), took part in a funeral procession down Van Ness Avenue. Alfred Cleary Street, on the west side of St. Mary's Cathedral, was named for this remarkable civic leader.

Al Wilsey '36

One of SI's greatest supporters over the years was Al Wlsey '36. He died in 2002, but his legacy can still be felt at SI, from the library named in his honor to the many years of service he gave the school as regent and trustee.

At the age of 12, he accepted an eight-year scholarship to SI and USF offered to the brightest incoming freshman. He and his brother, Jack Wilsey '34, traveled daily by ferry from Sausalito to San Francisco to reach SI, and despite the commute, both Wilseys excelled in academics and athletics. In addition to play-

ing football, Al argued on the speech and debate team and was a member of the honor society.[7]

By 1937, Al's first year at USF, both his mother and father had passed away, leaving the Wilsey Bennett Company family butter and egg business to Al and Jack. The company prospered under the direction of the brothers, and after World War II expanded into other products, including margarine, shortening and salad oil. Today, among other things, the Wilsey Bennett Company is involved in real estate development and venture capital investment. In explaining his success, Al characteristically responded, "We were just at the right place at the right time."

In the true Ignatian spirit of service, over the years, Al gave generously of his time, talent, and resources. He served the Fine Arts Museums of San Francisco as a trustee, and a room in the Palace of the Legion of Honor is named for him and his wife, Dede. He was an avid supporter of numerous San Francisco institutions, including the opera and the California Academy of Sciences.

When Fr. Carlin created the Board of Regents in the 1960s, he invited Wilsey to join. Wilsey led both capital campaigns — the one to build the Sunset District campus in the 1960s and the one to remodel it in the 1990s after the school became coeducational. To thank him for his efforts, SI named him a Life Regent and made him one of three lay members of the Board of Trustees — the ownership body of the school — when that group was formed in the late 1990s.

"He is one of the most helpful and considerate alums

Left: Alfred Cleary was the most powerful man in San Francisco besides the mayor in the 1930s.

Al Wilsey '36 became a successful businessman known for his generosity to SI and the city.

I have ever met," said Fr. Sauer on the day Wilsey received the school's Christ the King Award. "He is among the rare individuals who helped us through major hurdles and difficulties of all kinds to allow SI the freedom to concentrate on advancing our mission as an educational institution." His son Alfred S. "Lad" Wilsey, Jr., is a member of the school's Board of Regents.

The Glacier Priest

By Fr. Gerald McKevitt, SJ

Among the famous persons in the United States in the 1930s was Fr. Bernard Hubbard, SJ (SI 1906), popularly known as the "Glacier Priest." Though listed in Santa Clara University's bulletin as a member of the geology department, the peripatetic Hubbard spent most of his time exploring Alaska and lecturing about his travels to audiences across the country.

Hubbard's career as an explorer began when he was a youth climbing the Santa Cruz mountains with camera, gun and dog.[8] Later he was called "Fossil" by his SI classmates and at Santa Clara because of his interest in geology. Hubbard entered the Jesuit order in 1908 when he was 20. Even as a religious, he showed great resourcefulness in finding opportunities for mountain climbing and exploration. Sent to Innsbruck in the 1920s to complete his theological studies, Hubbard devoted more than his spare time to probing and photographing the alpine peaks and glaciers of the Austrian Tyrol. It is here that he earned the nickname *Gletscher Pfarrer* — "Glacier Priest" — which he carried all his life.[9]

In 1926, Hubbard returned to Santa Clara to teach Greek, German and geology, but it was not long before he again pulled on his hiking boots. During summer vacation in 1927, he made his first major expedition to Alaska to explore the Mendenhall and Taku glaciers. That trip, over country never before traversed by man, brought the 39-year-old priest extended publicity. So great was the interest generated by nationwide newspaper coverage of the expedition — beautifully illustrated by Hubbard's own photographs of the glacial wonderland — that another trip was organized the following year.

When Hubbard returned from the Alaskan wilderness in 1928, he announced that he was "the first human being ever to reach the rugged and almost inaccessible interior of Kodiak Island," where he found mountains 6,000 feet high of which "no one had previously known the existence."[10] His knowledge of the Taku River region led the U.S. Coast and Geodetic Survey to seek his services the following summer as a guide for a party erecting triangulation stations there. The summer of 1929 also found Hubbard trekking through the rarely visited and spectacular Valley of Ten Thousand Smokes toward the summit of the towering volcano Mount Katmai.

Frequently accompanied by strapping athletes from the Santa Clara football team ("chosen to stand hardship," a New York paper explained) and occasionally traveling alone (as in 1931, when he mushed a 13-dog-team 1,600 miles from the interior of Alaska to the Bering Sea), Hubbard pursued his interests in both geology and the great outdoors. They had long since overshadowed his devotion to the classroom. In 1930, he was released from teaching at the university for full-time lecturing, writing and further exploration of the Alaskan wilderness.[11]

Financing his trips with proceeds from his public lectures (any surplus was destined for the Jesuit missions in Alaska), Hubbard turned his attention in the early 1930s to the volcano-torn Alaskan Peninsula. He had visited Aniakchak, "the largest active volcano in the world," for the first time in 1930. The next year Aniakchak erupted in a spectacular display of fire and molten rock. Hubbard returned to explore and photograph the volcano's still smoking crater. For two weeks he and his party of university athletes trekked around and through its smoldering dangers. The results of that expedition were described in *National Geographic*.[12] Hubbard returned frequently to the giant craters of Aniakchak, Veniaminof and Katmai in succeeding years, as in 1934, when the National Geographic Society participated in his expedition to explore and map both the Alaskan Peninsula and the adjacent Aleutian Islands, whose topography had been greatly altered by the recent volcanic upheavals.[13]

When the adventures of this unusual Jesuit were serialized in *The Sunday Evening Post* in 1932, the name "Glacier Priest" became a household word. Sponsorship of his lecture tour and radio broadcasts by the National Broadcasting Company that same year enhanced Hubbard's finances as well as his fame. Accompanied by a couple of his Alaskan sled dogs, Hubbard thrilled audiences across the country with stories of how he had traveled with Eskimos on a 2,000-mile trip to the Arctic Circle, celebrated Mass on ice floes, narrowly escaped death while flying an airplane into the crater of a still active volcano and hiked for weeks through the vast center of the mighty Aniakchak. "Half the year the highest paid lecturer in the world, the other half a wanderer among treacherous craters and glaciers": thus *The Literary Digest* described him in 1937. When he stepped down from the lecture platform at New York's Town Hall in May of that year, after eight months on the road, he had delivered more

Fr. Bernard Hubbard, SJ (SI 1906), the Glacier Priest, was the highest paid lecturer in the U.S. in the 1930s. He built his reputation on his explorations of the glaciers and volcanoes of Alaska.

than 275 talks, "probably a world record," the *Digest* surmised.[14] Hubbard also wrote popular accounts of his travels. *Mush You Malemutes*, his first book, appeared in 1932; three years later he wrote *Cradle of the Storms*.

Although scientists occasionally accompanied him (Hubbard himself was largely self-trained), the overall scientific value of his 30-odd expeditions to Alaska was not great. Indeed, his pretensions to expertise on a variety of highly technical subjects, as well as his proclivity for the spectacular and for what appeared to be self-serving publicity, earned him criticism from his fellow Jesuits trained in geology and other scientific fields. Hubbard was effective in other ways, however, for his adventures reaped a harvest of publicity not only for himself but also for Santa Clara and especially Alaska. While SCU's football teams were capturing headlines in newspapers across America, the "Glacier Priest" was making the name of the university known in lecture halls from Los Angeles to New York.

Alaska loved him as its volunteer ambassador because of the worldwide attention he drew to the territory's natural wonders.[15] His lecture tours and radio broadcasts, as well as the coverage he received in magazines and newspapers, led a Juneau daily to con-

Fr. Hubbard, seen here with a Grizzly that he killed, took athletes from SCU's football team on some of his excursions, as they were known "to stand hardship."

Chalk-Dust Memories: The 1930s

Fr. Bernard Hubbard came to SI in 1928 to deliver four illustrated lectures at the Little Theatre at St. Ignatius College dealing with "The Great Gapatsch or Mountain Climbing in the Central Alps," "Conquering the Wild Taku," "Castles and Folk Lore of Central Europe," and "The Wonders of Yellowstone National Park." The last two lectures were illustrated "by 400 colored slides," according to the November 21, 1928, edition of *The Red and Blue.* In the next edition, the paper reported that when Fr. Hubbard taught in Los Angeles, he would "go swimming far out into the Pacific in search of small octopi. Finding one of these, he would let it fasten its tentacles about his arm and would swim back to shore with it. The next day he would exhibit the creature to his students."

Dr. John E. Tobin, Jr. '34

While I was in my second year Latin class in 1932, San Francisco experienced one of its infrequent snowfalls. A student in our class made a large snowball and placed it on the teacher's desk. When the teacher entered the room — Val King, who later edited the archdiocesan newspaper, *The Monitor* — he saw the snowball on his desk and asked who had placed it there. He received no confession, and had the entire class stay after school and write out *The Ancient Mariner.* We all remembered that snowball well; also, we have not forgotten Mr. King.

clude in 1932 that Bernard Hubbard had generated the most extensive effective advertising that Alaska had yet received.[16]

But the most important result of his explorations was the thousands of feet of motion-picture and still film with which he illustrated his lectures. Those materials, which are kept in Santa Clara University's archives, constitute one of the largest collections of images of Alaska in the 1930s. Hubbard's photographs provide a valuable visual record of many aspects of Alaskan geography and the life of its native peoples that have long since disappeared.

Reprinted from Fr. McKevitt's book, The University of Santa Clara: A History 1851–1977, *published by Stanford University Press, 1979.*

Barney Ritter '36

Fr. James Strehl, SJ, the prefect of discipline, kept me on an even keel and got me to quit smoking. I used to get tossed out of class on a regular basis. I wrote from Luzon during the war: "If it hadn't been for you, I don't know where I would be today." He wrote me back: "Barney, if this was the only letter I ever receive, I know my priesthood will have been a tremendous success."

Andy Leoni '36

Three students commuted to SI by ferryboat — Al Wilsey and two others. One day they were late, and Al Wilsey made up a story about how the ferry came in backwards by mistake and had to back out to reenter the port. Mr. Clem Schneider, SJ, a scholastic, swallowed that story hook line and sinker. Everyone knows that ferryboats are designed to allow passengers to embark and disembark from both ends.

Bill Britt '36

We had a great guy named Bill Barry in our class. He was a character, always getting in trouble. Fr. Strehl, who was the prefect of discipline, was always calling his mother to come get him. By the end of his senior year, Bill said, "My mother should have received a diploma. She spent more time at school than I did."

Robert Barbieri '36

Bill Bennett used to get us both in trouble, and we had to go to JUG all the time. He'd hum during class, but because I sat behind him, I would be the one to get in trouble. One year we had Ray Sullivan (who went on to become a California Supreme Court justice) for our teacher. Once, during lunch, we shoved paper in the keyhole of the classroom door to prevent him from opening the room to start class. He worked for 10 minutes on that lock and then got Fr. Strehl, who saw what the problem was and used his knife to extract the paper. We all had to stay until 5 p.m. that day!

Jack "Doc" Overstreet '36

As sophomores, we hung out during lunch at Reds, a small store across the street from the school. We bought cigarettes for a penny apiece. But that got old fast, and one day we went to the reservoir on Folsom to shoot craps. When we came back to school, there was Fr. Strehl telling us to stand out of line. We had no idea how he knew we were playing craps. Then we looked down at our knees and saw the red dust on our pants from the reservoir. "See you at 3 p.m.," he told us.

Owed to JUG

Fie on Thee, Foul Jade!
  Fair Thou never art,
That from Stygian Shade,
  Winged shafts dost dart
To fill with pain my unsophisticated heart.

Thou, the Grim Suppressor
  Of my youthful joys —
Turning each Professor
  'Gainst poor, meek-eyed boys,
When by chance in school, they make the slightest noise.

At the final setting
  Of the Golden Sun,
Must I keep on sweating
  Over lines that stun,
Until it seems my unfair task is never done?

Oft the shades of even
  Melt around my plight,
Till the stars of heaven
  Serve alone for light,
And still I've got about six hundred lines to write.

Waking or asleep,
  Thou dost haunt my soul,
O'er my visions creep,
  Heaping fires of coal
Upon the heartless Prof who sent me to this hole.

Yet Revengeful Powers!
  This one hope I find:
Though I've squandered hours
  'Neath your ruthless grind,
If Winter's in my soul, can Spring be far behind?

The 1932 Heights published this "Owed [sic] to JUG,"
(a parody of Shelley's "To a Skylark," reprinted from
Seattle Prep's 1930 yearbook.

Contemporary Ignatians know it as "detention," but most Ignatians throughout the years called it JUG — the name either derives from Justice Under God or the Latin *ad jugum* or *ad iugum*, which means "under the yoke." Students coming late to class had to write out pages of Latin or copy chapters from books. Bob Lagomarsino '39 (who died in 2004 shortly after being interviewed for this book) recalls being the last one in from PE because he was chasing down a basketball. "My teacher, Eneas Kane, told me, 'You're going to JUG.' I had to write out by hand several chapters of *Treasure Island*. I did that in lieu of homework for about a week. All that for chasing down a basketball after the whistle blew!"

• • •

One semi-official tradition involved the annual hazing of the freshmen. Leo Carew '40 believed, along with many of his classmates, that there really was a swimming pool on the roof. "We were told that you had to be a sophomore or older to go there," Carew said. "We never saw it, but we all believed it for about a week or so!"

Hazing could take a more physical turn, as evidenced by *The Heights* of 1932. It records that on August 24, 1931, freshmen experienced "the prettiest piece of scrub hazing in years — certain scrubs possessing hairy chests were brought to Stow Lake and bound securely. Chicken feed was sprinkled over them — and didn't the ducks have fun!"

Opposite page: The SI Jazz Band in December 1937, directed by Mr. Walter Schmidt, SJ.

Saint Ignatius College Preparatory
Alumni Who Died in World War II

CLASS OF 1907
Adm. Daniel J. Callaghan — Navy

CLASS OF 1910
Lt. Col. James M. Sullivan — Army

CLASS OF 1912
Major Thomas J. Lennon — Army

CLASS OF 1915
Capt. Joseph L. Pritchard — AAF

CLASS OF 1919
Lt. Charles A. Rethers — NAF
Chaplain Fidelis Wieland — Navy

CLASS OF 1925
Sgt. Roy F. Bruneman — Army
S⅟c James A. McLoone — Navy

CLASS OF 1926
Lt. Norbert S. McKenna — Army

CLASS OF 1927
A-B Thomas E. Dorsey — Merchant Marine

CLASS OF 1928
Lt. Hubert L. Murray — Army

CLASS OF 1929
AOM ⅟c Owen P. Stenson — Navy

CLASS OF 1930
Capt. James P. McVeigh — Army
Pvt. Vincent J. Moran — Army

CLASS OF 1931
Pfc. John J. Edmonds — Army

CLASS OF 1932
Sgt. Willis M. O'Brien — AAF
Ens. Thomas H. Topini — NAF
Pvt. Edward J. Toner — Army

CLASS OF 1933
Ph M John F. Kenney — Navy

CLASS OF 1934
Capt. William J. Alton — AAF
SP ⅟c David F. Deasy — Navy
Lt. William G. Drum — AAF
Capt. Elton J. Giusti — AAF
Major Edward L. Larner — AAF
Sgt. J. Paul Paganini — Army

Lt. Deb O'Connor — Navy
A-B Edmund P. Scully — Navy
Capt. John F. Sullivan — AAF

CLASS OF 1935
Ens. William J. Bruce — NAF
Ens. David W. Criswell — NAF
Lt. William E. Griffith — AAF
Lt. Douglas J. Stinson — Army

CLASS OF 1936
Lt. Edwin J. Colson — AAF
Capt. Louis A. Dentoni — AAF
Pvt. Francis E. Eaton — Army
Capt. Joseph T. Golding — Marines
Lt. Joseph R. Hunt — NAF
Pvt. Francis X. Icaza — Marines
Lt. Jack Kerrigan — AAF
F/O Joseph M. Sala — AAF
Lt. James A. Wilson — Army

CLASS OF 1937
Lt. Edmund F. Boyle — AAF
Lt. John T. Connolly — AAF
Ens. Richard J. Fenton — Navy
Lt. Gonzalo Legoretta — AAF
Lt. John A. MacDonald — AAF
Pvt. Chris McKeon — Army
Cpl. Robert S. Salopek — Army
Lt. William R. Telesmanic — AAF

CLASS OF 1938
A-C Donald Carne — AAF
Lt. Mark L. Golden — AAF
F/O George H. Rich — RCAF
A-B Thomas J. Rovere — Merchant Marine
S/Sgt. William J. Sanguinetti — Army
S/Sgt. Robert W. Semple — Army
Lt. Horace W. Smith — Army
Lt. James P. Tierney — Army
Lt. Honore F. Zabala — Army

CLASS OF 1939
Ens. Alfred J. Aniclo — Navy
Lt. Walter D. Brown — Army

Lt. Timothy J. Cavanaugh — AAF
S⅟c Edward J. Dellarocca — Navy
Lt. Robert E. Devlin — AAF
Lt. Bernardo X. Ferrari — AAF
Capt. Warren S. Goepp — AAF
Pfc. Daniel F. Hurst — Army
SM2/c Robert F. MacCarra — Navy
S/Sgt. John H. O'Hara — AAF

CLASS OF 1940
Sgt. John Cleary — AAF
Sgt. Leonard Hovorka — AAF
Lt. Robert D. Kunz — AAF
Lt. James H. Marshel — AAF
Cpl. John C. Santos — Army
Lt. Milton L. Waters — AAF

CLASS OF 1941
S/Sgt. James P. Faulkner — AAF
Sgt. Norman L. Geoffrion — Army
Lt. Albert J. Hogan — AAF
A-C Jeremiah F. Kelly — AAF
Lt. Robert C. Regan — AAF

CLASS OF 1942
Pvt. Andrew Carrigan — Army
Lt. James F. Cross — AAF
Lt. Cornelius E. Donoghue — AAF
Cpl. James J. Floyd — Army
Pfc. Jack F. Holland — Marines
Pfc. James D. Kearney — Army
Lt. Charles M. Mardel — AAF
T/Sgt. Malcolm A. Nicol — AAF
Lt. Ralph H. Schoenstein — AAF
A/c Albert L. Sundstrom — AAF

CLASS OF 1943
Sgt. John J. Beumann — Army
AOM 2/c Thomas J. Ford — Navy
S/Sgt. John S. Gercovich — AAF
Pfc. John F. Keegan — Army
Pvt. James R. Mullane — Army
Pfc. George J. Perasso — Army
AOM 2/c Gerald O. Shea — Navy

This plaque, honoring the 96 Ignatians killed in World War II, is located in the Alfred S. Wilsey library.

VIII. WAR & VALOR (1940 ~ 1949)

The decade of the '40s at SI is a paradox. World War II cast its shadow over the entire nation, and SI was not exempt — approximately 3,000 SI grads served in the Armed Forces and 96 died for their country. Students graduated early to enlist, and they watched as one teacher after another exchanged chalk and eraser for a uniform and rifle. Still, high school boys will be boys, and the Big Game would always mean more than a conflict half a world away. The decade also saw the birth of great traditions, such as the Bruce-Mahoney Trophy, and champion athletes, who would go on to professional sports teams. The basketball team brought home championships in 1943 and 1947, crew in 1941 and 1942, the swimming team in 1943 and 1946–48, and the football team in 1945, capturing its first league title. The decade also saw great teachers who left their mark well past the 1940s. The decade was book-ended by two of these greats: J. B. Murphy, who began his 50-year career in the 1939–40 academic year, and Uncle Frank Corwin, who started his 44-year tenure at SI in 1947.

"Mr. SI": J.B. Murphy

In its 150-year history, the SI faculty has included a number of people who bled red and blue, many of whom were or are alumni or alumnae. But the teacher who has earned the title "Mr. S.I." never attended St. Ignatius. To earn that moniker, he simply put in 50 years on the job, serving as teacher, coach and athletic director (from 1953 to 1967).

Few people know that John Bernard Murphy (universally called J.B.) almost didn't live past his 24th birthday. He entered St. Patrick's seminary after graduating from St. Paul's grammar school, but one year from ordination, J.B. learned that he had bleeding ulcers, and his doctor told him he would die within six months.

He left the seminary and spent the next year and half struggling to recover. When he felt strong enough, he decided to work to help his parents last out the Depression. He sought work as a Latin teacher, given his seminary training. But when he started work on August 16, 1939, at SI, he found himself assigned to history and

J.B. Murphy, who taught at SI for 50 years, served as the school's third athletic director.

PE classes. Two years later, he was assigned to teach math when a scholastic from Spokane called in sick a day before classes began. "The principal looked through his faculty, and I was the only one who had four years of high school math. No one on the faculty had college math," recalled Murphy in an interview published in the summer 1989 issue of *Genesis II*. "He said, 'Murphy, you're teaching five classes of math on Monday at 8:30 a.m.'"

Students soon learned that he was a tough disciplinarian. "I had a volatile temper, but I worked awfully hard when I started teaching to cool it. The very first days I was teaching, one of my students — now a respected lawyer — was making fun of me *sotto voce*, speaking behind his hand. In those days, the teacher's desk was on a platform. I pushed my desk off the platform into the arms of this boy. I went down, picked him out of his desk, took him outside and lifted him by his shirt against the lockers. I said, 'I'm an Irishman and you're a disturbing little runt. If you do that again, I'll separate your head from your shoulders.' Forty-seven years later, he told me that he respected me for what I did."

His close friend and fellow teacher, Frank Corwin ("Uncle Frank" to the students and faculty), tempered this image by noting that "between J.B. and Fr. Tom Reed, our principal at the time, those two knew every family in every parish in San Francisco. J.B. knew everything about each boy at SI, not just the boys in his class. He would know if they had any family problems, such as an alcoholic parent or monetary issues. Because we had no real counselors in those days, J.B. would often go to a student's home to help a boy with family problems. He put in many 16-hour days doing this."

He married Edna Ford in 1940 and they had four children, including Chuck Murphy '61, who has taught math at SI since 1965. Three Murphys made the cover of *Company* magazine (a national magazine for American Jesuits and friends) when it pictured J.B., Chuck, and J.B.'s grandson Matthew Murphy '89 when he enrolled at SI. The first coed class also included Matt's sister, Marielle Murphy '93, who enrolled the year her grandfather retired.

During the war years, J.B. became a favorite of many of the students. "They hung onto us and their parents in those days," he noted. "All of the students had tremendous respect for the Jesuits and were continually afraid that they were going to lose the lay teachers they dearly loved to the draft."

During the war, battleships sailed in and out of San Francisco Bay daily. "You lost your students' attention as soon as a war ship sailed by the Golden Gate. All the boys would look out the window at the

J.B. Murphy in 1961. The Ignatian staff dedicated their yearbook to this venerable math teacher.

ship coming in, and you could see the anguish and pathos in their faces. You lost their attention immediately. It was a poor teacher who tried to bring them back to attention; after the ship sailed past, you could recapture their attention."

J.B. gained coaching experience with the Young Men's Institute swimming team (the precursor to the CYO), and he became SI's third athletic director in 1953. He found himself in contentious meetings with the AAA's other athletic directors, most of whom were from public schools. "When they pushed him, he would push right back again," recalled Frank Corwin. "He wasn't afraid to speak up."

But as an athletic director, he is perhaps most known for never missing a game. And for most of those games, he would wear his trademark yellow tie. He began wearing it in the early 1950s when René Herrerias '44 coached basketball for SI before leaving to coach at UC Berkeley. "We were guests at the tournament of champions at Cal," said J.B. "Against all odds, our team won every game during the morning and afternoon. At dinner, René ribbed me about my flashy yellow tie that I was wearing. That night we won the championship. After ribbing me all day about the yellow tie, he said, 'Any game I coach for the rest of my life and your life, I want you to wear that yellow tie.'"

Pay at SI was low, so J.B. took on several other jobs to support his family. At Hamm's Brewery, he worked on the bottling line during his summers. "I was on the job for three hours when my supervisor asked me why all the other workers were calling me 'Mister.' I told him these boys, students and athletes at SI, knew me as their athletic director." With that, the foreman promoted J.B. to line boss. Even though he made more working for Hamm's for three months

than working for SI for nine, he stayed at SI because, as his son Chuck noted, "there's a real mesh between his philosophy of education and Jesuit philosophy. I've heard Jesuits speak of Ignatian values, and it's obvious to me that they were speaking about the way my father taught."

In his last decade at SI, J.B. taught one class of freshmen for two periods, helping them adjust to life in high school. In 1973, football coach Gil Haskell '61 created the J.B. Murphy Award, which, each year, the team gives to the SI football player who best exemplifies the Ignatian spirit through inspirational leadership on and off the field. Upon his retirement in 1989, the school honored him by naming the football field "J.B. Murphy Field."

The Outbreak of War

At 8 a.m. on December 7, 1941, Jack Grealish '44 was sitting in the pews at Most Holy Redeemer Church for Sunday Mass. When he and his family arrived home, they heard the news that Japan had launched a surprise attack on Pearl Harbor. "We were in shock," said Grealish. "Everyone was in shock. We didn't know how to react." That surprise attack killed thousands of servicemen and launched America into World War II. More than 3,000 SI alumni served in the armed forces and 96 of those men lost their lives.[1]

Despite the conflagration, life at SI did not change drastically during the war. Students still worried about exams and who would win the big game. The war intruded upon their high school lives in several ways, however. Teachers and older brothers left to fight in Africa, Europe and the Pacific Theater. News came back of alumni who had died or had been wounded.

Some alumni officers returned to SI to speak to students or visit their teachers. And every day, war ships sailed in and out of the Golden Gate capturing the attention and imagination of the students, some of whom graduated early to enlist.

The December 19, 1941, edition of *The Red and Blue* barely makes mention of America's entry into the war. The February 14, 1942, edition, however, offered three topical front-page stories. Two of those stories reported on the departure of teachers: David Walker, a history teacher, to the Navy and Fr. Cornelius O'Mara, SJ, to the Chaplain Corps. (Seven other SI alumni also served as chaplains in the war: Lt. Col. William Clasby, Capt. Wilfred Crowley, SJ, Lt. Charles Farrell, Capt. William Hanley, SJ, Capt. Raymond I. McGrorey, SJ, Lt. Col. William J. Reilly, and Lt. Cmdr. Jerome J. Sullivan, SJ.)

The third piece told of a returning alumnus, Richard Treanor '33, who recounted his rescue at sea. Ten days after the attack at Pearl Habor, Treanor, a third mate on the *U.S.S. Manini,* found himself swimming for his life after his ship was destroyed by a Japanese submarine 200 miles southeast of Honolulu. "He told of days of hopeless drifting, of praying, of water shortage; how one of their number died before safety was reached. On Christmas Eve a plane circled overhead while Treanor sent a semaphore with a flashlight. He described the jubilance of the men as they looked forward to being rescued on Christmas, the happiest day of their lives. But hope faltered and disappeared as Christmas came and went. The pilot must have seen them, Treanor explains, but nothing materialized.

"One day, two days more they waited. The water ration was shrinking into nothingness and eating the hardtack was as impossible as gulping bricks. Then on the twenty-seventh of December, they spotted another plane, and this time Uncle Sam's fleet came to the rescue."

The Red and Blue published numerous items on the war, and two Jesuits (Mr. Timothy McDonnell, SJ '36, and Fr. Lloyd Burns, SJ '16) launched a new publication in October 1944 — the *G.I. Wildcat,* a monthly newsletter sent to Ignatian alumni serving in the Armed Forces. (This was the first alumni bulletin to be published and prefigured two later alumni publications.)

In the *G.I. Wildcat's* first issue, the authors reported that of the 400 boys who applied to SI, a record 280 enrolled as freshmen. The Jesuits selected those 280 by having all applicants take an entrance examination for the first time in the school's history. It "seemed to be the only fair way to select the 280 boys that could be accommodated with the limited faculty and limited classroom space. One of the questions on the examination was: 'Why do you wish to attend St. Ignatius High School?' Here is one of the many unusual replies: 'Because I like the Christian Brothers.'"

The one-page, double-sided newsletter reported on visitors, on alumni who had distinguished themselves, and on casualties: "Martin Torti '35 was recently given the Bronze Star for heroism. He was wounded while obtaining ammunition when the supply was exhausted and the squad was under fire." Not all the news was from the front, however. Fr. Burns made sure the alumni kept up with the high school news. In the April 20, 1945, edition, for example, he reported on what may have been the first senior sneak. "Spring Fever has overtaken the City and the boys have their eyes on China Beach and other such spots. A couple of weeks ago, the fever 'got' the senior class so badly that after the First Friday Mass they went AWOL. The TJA (top Jesuit administrator) in the person of the Prefect of Discipline had them sentenced to a full school day on Saturday."

The May 1945 edition had much to celebrate, including "VE Day, Liberated Prisoners, [and] Missing Ignatians Found. We thank God for all of these things. But our war is still only half over, maybe less than that, because it seems a majority of Ignatians are in the Pacific Arena. In the November 1945 edition, Fr. Burns noted that Fr. King, SI's principal, left to serve as dean of faculty at Santa Clara, and that he had been replaced by Fr. Ralph Tichenor '27.

With most alumni back home, Fr. Burns stopped publishing the newsletter in May 1946, but expressed his hope that some sort of alumni publication would continue in the years to come.

SI's Japanese-American Students

For at least two students, the war meant dislocation. Takashi Watanabe '42 and John Morozumi '42 were forced to leave school two months shy of graduation because they were Japanese-Americans. Rather than report to the detention centers which would send them on their way to internment camps, they decided to live freely elsewhere. Both moved further east — Morozumi to Denver and Watanabe to Yerington, Nevada — and both continued their studies at Jesuit Colleges.

"SI was the best time of my life," Watanabe said. He and Morozumi had been friends at Morning Star School in Japantown, where they studied under Irish nuns and converted to Catholicism. Both boys went to SI and found that their classmates accepted them without prejudice. However, Morozumi remembered that he "never entered one of my classmates' homes. That was an unspoken convention."

Both men felt at home at SI. Morozumi joined the debate society and, although not tall, played basketball for two years. "I played against the likes of Kevin O'Shea, a formidable player even in grammar school. I remember getting thoroughly thrashed."

While both boys saw the war coming, they felt removed from it. And they had no doubt whose side they were on. In his junior year, Morozumi joined the ROTC and eventually became a student officer. "My parents, who chose to immigrate to the U.S. and who were ineligible for citizenship because they were Japanese, taught me to have the utmost allegiance to my country of birth and citizenship." He knew the war was inevitable when the government froze all assets of Japanese-Americans and cut all telegraph lines between the U.S. and Japan. "I couldn't withdraw 5 cents if I wanted to, even though I had nothing to do with Japan."

When Japan bombed Pearl Harbor, Watanabe recalled that he "was shocked to hear the report. I didn't realize the significance of it until much later. I was still a little naïve at 17."

Their classmates didn't treat the two differently

Takashi Watanabe and John Morozumi of the Class of 1942 both avoided the internment camps during WWII; they had to leave SI and San Francisco, however, and finished their education elsewhere.

after the attack. "They knew I had nothing to do with it," said Morozumi. "They had no unreasonable biases. I think that speaks to the higher intelligence of the group of boys who went to SI."

In March 1942, all Japanese-Americans living on the West Coast were told of the U.S. government's plan to send them to internment camps. "They felt we constituted a danger," recalled Morozumi. "I was aghast. When I heard this news, I immediately became a rebel. I was not about to be imprisoned. Even though Japanese-Americans were subject to curfews and martial law, I decided not to obey these rules." (Former SI College President Edward Whelan, SJ, protested this policy in the pages of *America* magazine.)

By late March, both boys realized they would not be able to stay in San Francisco in order to finish their last two months at SI, and they knew they would be arrested if they remained in California. Watanbe decided to follow his parents, who had moved to Yerington a month earlier. His father, leaving most of his family's possessions behind, managed to find work at a friend's laundry in Nevada. "We didn't have that much to lose, but it was still devastating," he recalled. "I couldn't finish my schooling. Everything was just gone. Our friends lost their businesses, their homes, their furniture. They were allowed to carry only their personal belongings to camp."

In Yerington, he worked on his friend's ranch — "a good experience for a city boy." Six months later he left for Loyola University in Chicago and, after the war, returned to San Francisco where he received a degree in pharmacy from UCSF.

Morozumi's parents decided to go to the interment camps and reported to the detention center at the Tanforan race track where they were housed in horse stalls. They eventually went to the Topaz internment camp in Utah. Morozumi chose not to follow them. Instead, he went to Regis College in Denver, which accepted him despite his not having a high school diploma. There, he paid his way by working at the college 60 hours a week for $25 room and board. He became classmates once again with Watanabe after transferring to Loyola University in Chicago where he studied medicine.

In 1944, Morozumi, on his second try to enlist, was accepted into the 442nd Regiment, an all-Japanese-American combat team that fought in Africa, Italy, Germany and France. But Morozumi never saw those countries. Instead, the U.S. Army sent him to central China where he worked in intelligence-gathering. A technical sergeant, Morozumi wore both the dog tags of a GI and the uniform of a Chinese officer because he dealt with Chinese officers "who would lose face if they had to deal with a sergeant."

In China he interrogated Japanese prisoners of war to determine their troop strength on the Chinese-Soviet border. "From the information we gathered, we knew that the Japanese were moving their vaunted Manchurian Army from central China to Shanghai, Hong Kong and Japan in preparation for a U.S. invasion. After serving for four years, Morzumi attended both USF and Loyola Chicago, where he earned his degree in medicine.

Both men returned to SI in 1992 for their Golden Diploma. There they also received their high school diplomas 50 years late in a moving ceremony before the surviving members of their class. "It was doubly meaningful to me to receive this," said Morozumi. "It symbolizes the integrity, intellectual honesty, the constant search for truth and veracity and the rejection of expediency that SI instills in its students."

SI students in ROTC uniform in 1944.

While the war did not intrude often into the lives of SI students, more than a few incidents served to remind Ignatians that they were not a world apart. The school conducted air raid drills and continued to train students in ROTC. For Jack Grealish, the war came home when Bill Telasmanic '37, a star end on the football team and catcher on the baseball team at both SI and USF, died in a plane crash in North Africa in the early days of the war. "Everyone felt his loss," said Grealish. "Every day, we would check the newspapers to read the casualty lists. But we were 16, and we tended to focus on our high school problems."

Grealish recalls one alumnus, a Navy officer, visiting his Latin class, taught by Fr. Lloyd Burns, SJ. "Fr. Burns, who was very proud of his Latin class, asked him if Latin had helped him. The officer gave Fr. Burns a funny look and said, 'It hasn't done me any good at all.' That's not what Fr. Burns wanted to hear."

Val Molkenbuhr '43, while jogging around the Beach Chalet, recalls seeing ships coming in and out of the Golden Gate. "Once in awhile we heard of alumni dying in a battle, and we prayed for them."

Bob Lagomarsino '39 lost about a dozen friends to the war, including his good friend, Dan Hurst '39. "We went to grammar school together, and after he enlisted, we corresponded. My mother was the first to hear that he was missing in action, and later we heard that he had been killed in the South Pacific. I was quite upset. I knew his parents and sister and felt so sorry for them."

Grealish, Molkenbuhr and Lagomarsino enlisted, as did thousands of fellow Ignatians, with many graduating early or leaving before graduating to fight what nearly all considered to be a just war against brutal dictatorships. "This wasn't like the Korean War," recalled Grealish. "Everyone was 100 percent behind it."

The specific tragedies of each of the 96 SI alumni deaths were spelled out in *Gold Star Ignatians,* a commemorative pamphlet published in 1947 by the school. (The 96 dead listed in that book also have their names printed on a memorial plaque in the Alfred S. Wilsey Library.) Reading through these names and the circumstances of their deaths, we are reminded of the horror of war in its particulars. These men, some barely out of boyhood, died all over the world, from the Arctic waters off Alaska to the deserts of Africa, from the forests of Germany to the islands of the South Pacific.

Lt. Col. James M. Sullivan '10, a doctor with the Reserve Medical Corps, was one of these men. In May 1941, he was called into service and sent to Sternberg General Hospital in Manila, and then to Base Hospital No. 2 in Bataan. He survived the Bataan Death March and was sent to Cabanatuan and Bilibid Prison Camps. "After surviving three years of imprisonment, he died after reaching Moji, Japan, on January 31, 1945, from fatigue, starvation and wounds received during the sinking of his hospital ship by U.S. forces." Others died in less dramatic ways, from car accidents to illness to being crushed by falling trees in storms, yet their loss, too, was felt by family and friends.

Among the Ignatian servicemen were numerous war heroes, including Capt. Joseph Golding '36 and Sgt. Roy Bruneman '25, who were awarded Silver Stars posthumously in 1944 for gallantry in action in the South Pacific.

The four most famous Wildcats who served in the war were Rear Admiral Daniel Callaghan (SI 1907), his brother, Admiral William Callaghan '14, General Fred Butler '13 and Ensign William Bruce '35.

Admiral Daniel Callaghan (SI 1907

Daniel Callaghan was born in San Francisco on July 26, 1892, and raised in Oakland. He graduated from SI in 1907, having attended both the Van Ness Avenue campus and the Shirt Factory in its first year, commuting to school by ferry and train and using that time to memorize "long skeins of Keats and Tennyson, whole cantos from Longfellow and Scott — or figuring out the all but impossible ways Caesar or Cicero had of constructing sentences for his Latin classes."[2] At SI, Callaghan was "greatly influenced by [his] Jesuit mentors," according to *Fighting Admiral: The Story of Daniel Callaghan.* "Dan had the appearance of being a bit overserious. But actually, in the company of his own crowd, he was jolly enough…. [When] the Ignatian baseball team, which though a secondary [school] affair, took on the junior varsities of the University of California, Santa Clara and Stanford colleges, Dan soon won himself a right fielder's berth. He was also prominent in the 'Gas League' punchball circuit, and especially after making up his mind about going to Annapolis, he was a constant user of the gymnasium, giving himself a thorough physical workout — a habit that became almost a fault throughout his life.

"But for the most part, Dan at high school concentrated on books…. Striding into Fr. John P. Madden's Cicero class on a fine spring morning, Fr. Woods found Dan Callaghan [standing] up, reciting. Fr. Woods took over the book from the slightly startled mentor and popped a question at the strapping youngster in a purposely unintelligible mumble. Dan did not catch it, of course, and stood nervously waiting. To have asked for a repetition of the question would have been an admission of lack of attention. After a moment, the Jesuit repeated the question as indistinctly as before. Dan could only guess at what was wanted, and guessed wrong. Hence his answer was wrong…. The result was a severe going over for not having studied his lessons, much to the amazement of his classmates. But Dan took it well… with the reflection that such 'lacings' were good for the soul, though terribly hard on one's sensibilities."[3]

Dan also experienced the 1906 earthquake while at home in Oakland. He helped his father organize a "sort of vigilante committee to quiet the neighborhood" and to warn people not to light fires in their fireplaces as many of the chimneys had collapsed. (Sadly, just such a fire kindled the conflagration that

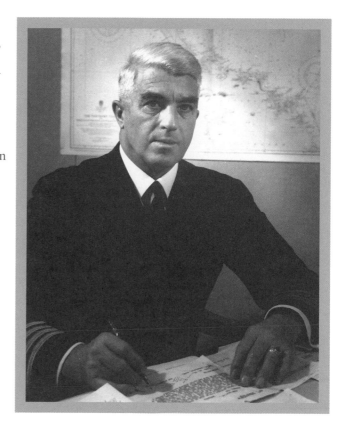

Admiral Daniel Callaghan (SI 1907) received the Medal of Honor posthumously for his bravery during the Battle of Savo Sea.

destroyed SI College across the bay.)[4]

After leaving SI, Dan attended the Naval Academy, graduating in 1911. His distinguished career was marred by one incident that led to a Courts-Martial for allegedly requisitioning the wrong replacement parts, which made his ship, the *Truxton*, unable to continue its trip. He was acquitted of all charges and restored to duty.

Later, he spent three years at UC Berkeley where he served as professor of naval science in the naval ROTC. Then, in 1938, President Roosevelt asked his physician, Ross McIntire, for a recommendation for a Naval Aide, someone who was a "salt-water sailor," rather than an administrative figurehead. McIntire had just the man for the job, and recommended Callaghan. For the next three years, he served the president keeping him "posted on the intimacies of naval matters, domestic as well as foreign," and listening "with intelligence while the President expatiated on the whys and wherefores of Hipper's cruiser tactics at Jutland or the follies of the Russians at Tsushima." Roosevelt wanted "someone who had the feel of the sea in him, and was more than delighted when he found that Dan was a gunnery man and could talk of fleet maneuvers."[5]

Callaghan lived aboard the presidential yacht, the *Potomac* while serving the president, and the two became fast friends. When the U.S. entered World War II in 1941, Roosevelt reluctantly let Callaghan leave the *Potomac* for *U.S.S. San Francisco*, and to serve in the Pacific Theatre. Callaghan's final fitness report included this note from FDR: "It is with great regreat that I am letting Captain Callaghan leave as my Naval Aide. He has given every satisfaction and has performed duties of many varieties with tact and real efficiency. He has shown a real understanding of

the many problems of the service within itself and in relationship to the rest of the Government."[6]

By this time, Callaghan had earned a reputation as a hometown hero. In *Embattled Dreams: California in War and Peace 1940–1950*, historian Kevin Starr (who attended SI in the 1950s and who serves as California State Librarian), noted that "Callaghan was the pre-eminent military figure of Northern California, especially for Catholics, and he was held in awe by San Franciscans just as Patton was held up by Southern Californians as one who "embodied the best possibilities of the region…. Whereas Patton was privileged, flamboyant, profane, and self-regarding, Callaghan was steady, unassuming, pious (avoiding alcohol…), and thoroughly devoted to the welfare of his men, who tended to call him Uncle Dan behind his back. As Patton was devoted to tanks, Callaghan was devoted to the art of gunnery. While other naval colleagues bespoke the future in terms of airplanes and submarines, Dan Callaghan devoted his career to perfecting the art and science of gunnery from surface ships." Callaghan was also a "tall, solid figure, prematurely gray, a Spencer Tracy look-alike, known to the men of the fleet as well as to the brass as a commandingly steady figure, the representative naval officer of his era."

Callaghan served as captain of the heavy cruiser *U.S.S. San Francisco*, which had escaped serious damage in the attack on Pearl Harbor and then spent six months on Vice Admiral William Halsey's staff. In 1942, he returned to the *San Francisco* as commander of Task Force 65, made up of five cruisers and eight destroyers that fought in the first naval battle of Guadalcanal in November 1942. While aboard the *San Francisco*, Callaghan commanded his ships to sweep the waters around Savo Island on November

11 in preparation to block the arrival of a Japanese invasion fleet and to provide cover for the unloading of Marines. The next day, Callaghan's task force was attacked by 25 enemy torpedo bombers, forcing him to get under way.

The Japanese force consisted of two battleships, *Hiei* and *Kirishima*, one light cruiser and 15 destroyers. On November 12, Callaghan ordered his ships back to Savo to meet the enemy. Shortly after 1 a.m. on November 13, one of his ships, the *Helena*, detected the Japanese 27,000 yards away, but Callaghan, whose forces were badly outgunned, didn't know the exact location of the enemy as his ships lacked radar.

The Battle of Savo Sea (also known as the Battle of Sealark Channel) began with the Japanese approaching Sealark Channel in three columns. Callaghan made a daring move and took his fleet, with the *San Francisco* in the lead, between the two outside Japanese columns and head-on toward the third column. (Picture Callaghan's fleet sailing into the middle of an inverted V.) Callaghan hoped to sail through the enemy columns and fire at them before they had time to lower the elevation of their guns. Once past, he hoped "to pit speed, target angle, range and rapidity of fire against bulk and force."[7]

At 1:42 a.m., with one ship 3,400 yards away, Callaghan gave the order to fire torpedoes, later ordering, "We want the big ones." Three minutes later, Japanese searchlights spotted the American fleet and the battle was underway. Callaghan ordered guns on both sides to open fire, hitting the *Yudachi* 3,700 yards away. The Americans were surrounded, firing from both port and starboard. As Starr writes, "Maneuvering was difficult, and the *San Francisco* lacked the latest radar; but whether this was the cause

for what followed or rather whether what followed was due in some measure to Callaghan's gunnery-oriented spirit of the attack, the American force literally sailed into the middle of the Japanese force, as if running a gauntlet. What ensued was perhaps the last ship-to-ship naval engagement in military history as the American ships and the Japanese ships fought through direct searchlight-guided gunfire." It was also the largest night battle in naval history.

At 2 a.m. Callaghan's flagship was struck by a salvo from the *Hiei*, and the bridge took a direct hit from a 14-inch shell immediately killing Callaghan and three of his staff officers and mortally wounding Capt. Cassin Young, the ship's commanding officer. Despite the loss of bridge and commander, the ship continued to fight on, moving closer to the enemy so its 8-inch guns would be more of an even match with

Admiral Daniel Callaghan served as Naval Aide to FDR. He is pictured here with Eleanor Roosevelt, King George VI and Queen Elizabeth on the Presidential yacht, The Potomac (now moored in Oakland).

The USS San Francisco, badly damaged, sails under the Golden Gate Bridge. Part of that ship is now on display in Land's End.

the 14-inch Japanese guns. *The San Francisco* took 47 hits and its crew had to extinguish 25 fires. It stayed afloat, however, and managed to sink one Japanese ship and damage several other ships badly enough to allow an American submarine to sink them. Had *The San Francisco* and the other ships in the task force failed, Guadalcanal would probably have fallen again to the Japanese. The badly damaged ship eventually returned to port under its own power thanks to the quick actions of Herbert E. Schonland, who taught at SI in the 1947–48 academic year and then at Santa Clara University.

Schonland, who retired as a Rear Admiral, also won the Medal of Honor for his actions in that battle. With Callaghan's death, and the death of two other officers, Schonland assumed command of the *San Francisco*. The second deck compartment of the ship had taken on water, nearly sinking it, when in waist-deep water, Schonland secured the deck by pumping off and draining the water, working with only flashlights to help him see. (The bridge of the *San Francisco* is on display at Land's End above the Cliff House in a memorial to Admiral Callaghan and the other Americans who died that day on the *San Francisco*.)

Word came to President Roosevelt of Callaghan's death on November 16, 1942. "There was no one willing to convey the news to the President. When finally word was brought to him officially, he gasped in unaffected consternation. 'I knew it,' he said. 'I knew Dan was too brave a man to live. But I'll bet, as he set his course straight for the enemy, he was thinking of Dewey and Manila, and our constant discussions of such actions.'"

The next day, FDR sent a note to Dan's wife, Mary, that read, "I am very sure I need not tell you of the sense of great personal loss to me. Dan and I had a very wonderful relationship during the years he was at the White House. I took great pride in him, and I must have been nearly as happy as he over his new command. In spite of our grief we will always remember a gallant soul who died leading his ship and his command to a great victory."[8]

Callaghan received the Medal of Honor posthumously for his actions that day. His citation reads as follows: "For extraordinary heroism and conspicuous intrepidity above and beyond the call of duty…. Although out-balanced in strength and numbers by a desperate and determined enemy, Rear Admiral Callaghan, with ingenious tactical skill and superb coordination of the units under his command, led his forces into battle against tremendous odds, thereby contributing decisively to the rout of a powerful invasion fleet, and to the consequent frustration of a formidable Japanese offensive. While faithfully directing close-range operations in the face of furious bombardment by superior enemy firepower, he was killed on the bridge of his flagship. His courageous initiative, inspiring leadership, and judicious foresight in a crisis of grave responsibility were in keeping with the finest traditions of the U.S. Naval Service. He gallantly gave his life in the defense of his country."

In that same battle, the *U.S.S. Juneau*, part of Callaghan's task force, had been sunk by a torpedo, hitting the port side near the forward fire room where ammunition was stored, destroying the ship in a giant fireball and killing the five Sullivan brothers. Only 10 sailors survived that ordeal.

The U.S. Naval Academy later named one of its rooms in honor of Admiral Daniel Callaghan, the hero who helped win the Battle of Guadalcanal, and American Legion Post No. 592 was instituted in his honor on March 23, 1944. On July 24, 2004, the *U.S.S. Potomac* Association celebrated Daniel Callaghan Day with a series of lectures, official proclamations and a Bay cruise aboard the *Potomac,* the boat Adm. Callaghan served on as FDR's aide. More than 20 members of the Callaghan clan attended that celebration, including Caitlin Callaghan '99, Larkin Callaghan '01 and Connor Callaghan '08, great-grandchildren of William Callaghan '14, Daniel's brother.

Admiral William Callaghan '14

Dan Callaghan's brother, William, was also an admiral in the Navy and served as the commander of the *U.S.S. Missouri,* the battleship on which Japanese representatives surrendered to the Allies in Tokyo Bay to mark the end of the war. After attending SI, he graduated from the U.S. Naval Academy in 1918 and served in World War I on a destroyer. In 1936, he received his first command, that of the *U.S.S. Reuben James* (later sunk by a German U-Boat in 1940), and later joined the staff of the Chief of Naval Operations in 1939, where he served as logistics officer for the commander in chief of the Pacific Fleet, receiving the Legion of Merit for his efforts.

He commissioned the *Missouri* in 1944 and led it

in operations against Tokyo, Iwo Jima and Okinawa. During the Battle of Okinawa on April 11, 1945, Callaghan's ship came under kamikaze attack. Fortunately, the 500-pound bomb aboard the plane failed to detonate, but the pilot was killed instantly when his plane crashed into the battleship.

Crewmembers put out the fire around the plane and found the broken body of the Japanese pilot lying on the deck. The crew felt anger and outrage, but Callaghan ordered them to prepare the pilot's body for burial with military honors, "an unprecedented act for an enemy in time of war." Some of the crew grumbled, but others respected Callaghan for doing the right thing. Crewmembers worked at night to create a Japanese flag to drape over the body, and the ships's chaplain offered the prayer, "Commend his body to the deep," while the Missouri's crew saluted and an honor guard fired their rifles to honor this fallen pilot.[9]

"Interestingly, during a September 1998 reunion of former *U.S.S. Missouri* crewmembers at the battleship's new home in Pearl Harbor, many of those who served in World War II told members of the Association that, in retrospect, they felt Captain Callaghan acted correctly," according to Patrick Dugan of the *U.S.S. Missouri* Memorial Association.[10]

Callaghan went on to serve as commander of Naval Forces in the Far East during the Korean War and retired in 1957. He died July 8, 1991, at the age of 93. On April

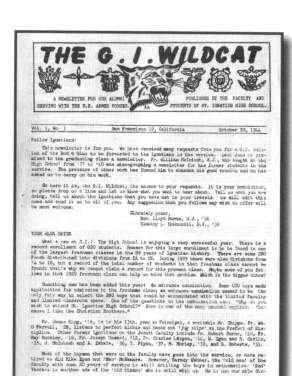

THE G.I. WILDCAT

A NEWSLETTER FOR OUR ALUMNI
SERVING WITH THE U.S. ARMED FORCES.

PUBLISHED BY THE FACULTY AND
STUDENTS OF ST. IGNATIUS HIGH SCHOOL.

Vol. 1, No. 1   San Francisco 17, California   October 20, 1944

Fellow Ignatians:

This newsletter is for you. We have received many requests from you for a G.I. edition of the Red & Blue to be forwarded to the Ignatians in the service. Last June we promised to the graduating class a newsletter. Fr. William McIntosh, S.J., who taught at the High School from '37 to '40 was mimeographing a newsletter for his former students in the service. The pressure of other work has forced him to abandon his good resolve and he has asked us to carry on his work.

So here it is, the G.I. Wildcat, the answer to your requests. It is your newsletter, so please drop us a line and let us know what you want to hear about. Tell us what you are doing, tell us about the Ignatians that you have met in your travels. We will edit this news and send it on to all of you. Any suggestion that you fellows may wish to offer will be most welcome.

Sincerely yours,
Rev. Lloyd Burns, S.J., '16
Timothy L. McDonnell, S.J., '36

YOUR ALMA MATER

What's new at S.I.? The High School is enjoying a very successful year. There is a record enrollment of 820 students. Reason for this large enrollment is to be found in one of the largest freshman classes in the 89 years of Ignatian history. There are some 280 Frosh distributed into divisions from IA to IH. During 1929 there were also divisions from IA to IH, but a record of the total number of students in that freshman class cannot be found; that's why we cannot claim a record for this present class. Maybe some of you fellows in that 1929 freshman class can help us solve that problem. Which is the bigger class?

Something new has been added this year! An entrance examination. Some 400 boys made application for admission to the freshman class; an entrance examination seemed to be the only fair way to select the 280 boys that could be accommodated with the limited faculty and limited classroom space. One of the questions on the examination was: "Why do you wish to attend St. Ignatius High School?" Here is one of the many unusual replies: "Because I like the Christian Brothers."

Fr. James King, '16, is in his 13th year as Principal, a veritable Mr. Chips. Fr. Wm. O'Farrell, '28, listens to perfect alibis and hands out 'jug slips' as the Prefect of Discipline. Other former Ignatians on the Jesuit faculty include Fr. Robert Burns, '10, Fr. Ray Buckley, '16, Fr. Joseph Howard, '12, Fr. Charles Largan, '14, W. Egan and H. Carlin, '35, J. McIntosh and A. Zabala, '36, T. Flynn, '37, M. Morley, '32, and R. Roberts, '31.

Most of the laymen that were on the faculty have gone into the service, or have retired as did Mike Egan and 'Mac' McNamara. However, Barney Wehner, the 'old man' of the faculty with some 20 years of service is still drilling the boys in mathematics. 'Rod' Vaccaro is another one of the 'old timers' who is still with us. He is now our able dir-

The GI Wildcat was SI's first alumni publication, helping to keep Ignatians informed of grads overseas during the war.

12, 2001, he was honored in memoriam at a ceremony aboard the *Missouri*, docked at Pearl Harbor, to commemorate the respect he paid to the Japanese pilot. Since kamikaze pilots wore no identification, the Japanese Navy narrowed the identity of the pilot to three possibilities, and descendents of each of these families attended the ceremony. One family brought water taken from the area where a U.S. submarine had recently surfaced, accidentally sinking a Japanese fishing boat, and that water was poured into Pearl Harbor from the *Missouri*.

General Fred Butler '13

Brigadier General Fred Butler '13 was another SI graduate who played an integral role in the war. After three years in the college division, he graduated from West Point in 1918 and from the U.S. Army Engineer Schools in 1921. He remained in the U.S. Army until his retirement in 1953.

He worked in China and Outer Mongolia with the Army Corps of Engineers and taught at West Point before returning to San Francisco in 1927. He helped to create Treasure Island for the 1939–40 Golden Gate International Exposition and supervised roadwork on Yerba Buena during his stay here. After the fair ended, Treasure Island was sold to the U.S. Navy and became the base of operations for the war in the Pacific Theatre.

In World War II, he was involved in both the African and Italian campaigns and the invasion of Southern France. For his efforts, he received the Distinguished Service Cross, the Legion of Merit, the Oak Leaf Cluster, the Bronze Star and the Purple Heart. France honored him with the Croix de Guerre and the Legion of Honor, and Italy awarded him the Cross of Valor. (The October 20, 1944, edition of the *G.I. Wildcat* reported that "Brig. Gen. Fred Butler has been making the headlines lately. He is the leader of 'Butler's Task Force,' driving up France to Berlin. His son Bill Butler is a member of the senior class at the High School.")

After the war he served as manager of the San Francisco International Airport and as a commissioner for the SFFD. In 1962, Pope John XXIII honored him with the title of Knight of Malta and in 1965, SI gave him the Christ the King Award.

The Class of '42 & The Greatest Generation

In 2004, Dr. Barrett Weber '42 assembled a collection of stories from 26 members of his graduating class from SI who had served in World War II. These stories are available online at www.siprep.org, and they are all noteworthy for their poignancy and patriotism. Among those stories are those of Al Hutter, Marshall Moran and Owen Sullivan.

Hutter, who was part of the 147th Infantry Battalion that landed on Iwo Jima on February 19, 1945, helped the Marines mop up. Later, he was transferred to Tinian where he guarded the runway there. Then, at 2 a.m. on August 6, 1945, "we heard the B29 engines starting and moving about. At 2:45 a.m., a B29 appeared out of the gloom and started down the runway. It seemed that it was too heavily loaded to get airborne, and we all climbed into our shelters in case it ran out of runway. It was agonizingly slow and seemed to strain to become airborne, but it did at the very end of the runway and slowly began to climb into the morning sky." The plane was the *Enola Gay* en route to Hiroshima.

Marshall Moran, as a 19-year-old 1st gunner on a 30-caliber heavy machine gun squad in Germany in September 1944, came under attack from German mortar and artillery fire along with his friend, 19-year-old Bobby Schmidt of Glendale, who "was one step behind and below me. I heard the noise, felt the vacuum and faced the split-second arrival and explosion of an 81-m.m. shell. A piece of shrapnel hit me with the force of a mule kick, passing through my left calf, slamming me to the turf. Other shells followed. Pandemonium set in. Just behind me, Bobby's throat had been cut by the same shrapnel that passed through my leg. I held his unconscious body in my arms as he bled to death. I remember screaming, 'Medic!' to no avail, as we had taken so many casualties."

Later Moran was taken to a hospital that found itself threatened by the German offensive in the Battle of the Bulge. The high command issued all patients .45 caliber pistols to defend themselves from German paratroopers. Moran recalls walking the grounds and passing another patient who "neither looked at me nor acknowledged my existence. Just after passing each other, one shot was fired. I turned to find him on the ground, his foot shattered by a .45-caliber bullet. He was a 'section 8'... who crippled [himself] for life so [he] would not be forced to return for battle."

The captain in charge of this unit insisted that Moran state, under oath, that the soldier had deliberately shot himself. "I refused. The small bones in his left foot were shattered. He'd be a cripple for the rest of his life. My rehabilitation ended abruptly, and I was quickly returned to my unit."

After the war, Moran visited Bobby Schmidt's parents, who had only heard that their son was MIA. "With tears in my eyes, I told them Bob had died in my arms. The three of us cried together."

Owen Sullivan found himself facing a firing squad after his B-24 bomber went down over the Carpathian Mountains in Slovakia on November 20, 1944. On a bombing run to Poland, his plane had caught fire and exploded, burning Sullivan's face and breaking his arm, though he did manage to parachute to safety. "I had no idea what country I was in."

When he landed, villagers aided him, taking him to a creek where he immersed himself to hide his scent. A German patrol and their dogs passed a few feet away but did not spot him. He recuperated in a local farmhouse, learning to speak Slovak from a bilin-

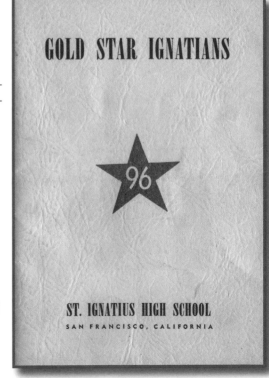

The 96 Wildcats who died in World War II were memorialized in Gold Star Ignatians, published in 1947.

The End of the War & The Birth of the Bruce

After the end of World War II, SI and SH thought of a fitting memorial to the fallen alumni of both schools: a perpetual athletic trophy, given to the school that won at least two of the three games in football, basketball and baseball. This trophy, named for SI's Bill Bruce '35 and SH's Jerry Mahoney, would also commemorate the oldest athletic high school competition west of the Rocky Mountains.

In *The Red and Blue* of January 29, 1947, reporter Watt Clinch '47 predicted that "this trophy, as time goes by, will doubtless come to mean as much to SI and Sacred Heart as the legendary Axe means to Stanford and California and the Old Oaken Bucket means to Indiana and Purdue."

The *Chronicle's* Ken Garcia wrote an article about this trophy in 2001, in which he noted that "Bill Bruce was a gregarious, sharp teenager, who came to SI in 1931 on a scholarship as a virtual unknown. Bruce was an orphan who attended St. Vincent's School near San Rafael, commuting across the Bay by boat. He was a fine student and a good athlete who started as a lineman — defense and offense were not specified in those days since everybody played both ways."

The February 26, 1947, edition of *The Red and Blue* added that while at SI, Bruce "repeated a year of Greek so he could raise his average from a 92 to a 95," and was later elected salutatorian for his class.

"Bruce never made All-City," wrote Garica, "but his charisma and quick mind charmed his classmates who elected him student body president. When he graduated in 1935, Bruce went to Santa Clara University, where he started on the Broncos team that beat LSU 21-14 in the Sugar Bowl. He spent his summers working as a park director at Grattan Playground

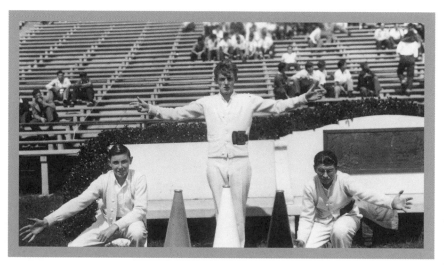

Yell leaders in the 1940s. Photo courtesy of Dick Raffetto '44.

gual Book of Mormon, and he was reunited with three of his 10-man crew. The others had been captured, killed or tortured. "We spent Christmas Eve that year in a pig sty, drinking slivovic, a 105-proof plum brandy, listening to accounts of the Battle of the Bulge on the BBC and roasting a pig," said Sullivan.

Sullivan spent 16 weeks in town, posing as a local, drinking coffee with Germans during the day and, later, taking part in partisan raids against them. On March 24, 1945, the Gestapo caught up with Sullivan and crew member Eugene Hodge. They lined both men up against a wall "pockmarked with bullet holes. A German gunner set a machine gun on a tripod, and as [we] waited execution, the officer in charge decided to lead [us] on a 250-mile march."

During the march, Hodge grew ill and was sent to a German hospital while Sullivan escaped into the woods where he was rescued by Americans in Austria. After the war, the Slovakian Defense Ministry presented Sullivan and four other Americans the Medal of Freedom.

in the Haight, before enlisting in the Navy in 1940, where he became an outstanding fighter pilot.

"'Bill was a natural leader, extremely popular, who just had this air of command,' said Fr. Harry Carlin, SJ, SI's executive vice president, who was one of Bruce's classmates. 'He was a model for students then and he's a model for them now.'

"Bruce flew more than 50 combat missions in Europe during the early '40s before being called back by the Navy to train young pilots at the Naval Air Station in Pasco, Washington, part of the Tri-Cities area in the eastern part of the state that combines desert terrain with steep canyons. And there, on April 14, 1943, Bruce, with a young trainee at the controls, refused to bail out when the pilot could not pull their plane out of a nosedive, and the two men were instantly killed. Bruce was 25."

Garcia added that SH's Jerry Mahoney, who grew up in the Richmond District, was tall enough to start on his school's varsity basketball team as a freshman in 1941, "a feat so uncommon that it stands out almost as much as the fact that he made first team All-City in basketball and football his senior year. 'He was one of the best athletes in the city,' said Jack Grealish, 'and I know, because I played with him and against him.'

"Mahoney enlisted in the Navy and, after boot camp, was assigned to a merchant ship for combat duty. In June 1944, just hours after the *Denny B. Plant* set out from the Atlantic coast, the ship was torpedoed by a German submarine. Every man on board was killed. Mahoney was 18."

Even though the trophy match was not inaugurated until 1947, the schools mark the first year of the match-up as the 1945–46 academic year to commemorate the end of WWII. SH took the trophy that year,

and SI the next. In all, SI has kept the trophy 40 times as of 2005, and SH 18 times.

In 1967 SI joined the West Catholic Athletic League and SH remained in the AAA until 1969. For two years, the schools split ownership of the Trophy, though they didn't play each other on a regular basis during those years. Competition resumed in the 1969–70 academic year when SH joined the WCAL. By the end of that year, the schools had tied in football and split the other two games. SI kept the Trophy that year as it had been the last team to win it back in 1967.

Few traditions capture the joy of high school as this rivalry between SI and SH. If you go to Kezar Stadium, Big Rec Field or Kezar Pavilion for a Bruce-Mahoney match-up, you will find emotions tuned to a fever-pitch, voices hoarse from shouting and athletes primed to play at their peak. You will also find something more — a community of parents, alumni, students and teachers who are part of something special, something that transcends the specific time and place of one game and that connects them to the ideals of service and tradition that both Bill Bruce and Jerry Mahoney stood for in their brief lives and that they upheld in their deaths.

The Age of Athletes

The hardships of World War II brought students together to form some of the closest communities in school history. To this day, alumni from the 1940s gather to talk about old times, just as grads from other eras do, but their spirit and their affection for the school seems stronger, forged from the suffering and prayer that were part of that era.

The 1940s also proved to be a watershed decade for Wildcat sports. The decade that saw the start of the Bruce-Mahoney Trophy games also saw the inauguration of the John E. Brophy Award along with heated basketball match-ups with Kevin O'Shea '43 leading the Wildcats to a celebrated city championship over Lowell and the varsity football team defeating Polytechnic on Thanksgiving Day 1945, 13–7 for the city championship, led by coach John Golden. His team appeared before a crowd of 30,000 at Kezar Stadium with Poly the favorite, having won the Northern California Championship the previous year. But an SI fullback, senior Gordon Machlachlan, helped SI win 13–7 with two touchdowns, including a 48-yard run to the end zone. The basketball team recaptured the AAA crown in 1947, led by coach Phil Woolpert and remarkable play by George Moscone '47, Cap Lavin '48 and All-City Larry Rebholtz '47. (Cap Lavin, recalls classmate John Savant, "was a gifted passer who could get the ball to a teammate under the basket leaving his opponents flatfooted." Lavin went on to become a legendary coach and teacher in Marin and helped to start the Bay Area Writing Project at UC Berkeley.) SI's outstanding "mermen," who included Phil Guererro, Jerry Brucca and Jack McGrowan, helped SI's swimming team finish first in AAA competition in 1946 through 1948.

"This was war time, and outside of the San Francisco Seals, there were no professional teams competing," recalled Grealish, who was named to the San Francisco Prep Hall of Fame in 1995. "The sports pages were pretty tough to fill. More often than not, you'd see banner headlines in the *Chronicle* reading 'SI beats Balboa,' followed by a blow-by-blow description of the game. This attention, and the fact that we beat Lowell in the final seconds in 1943, lent an artificial importance to high school sports. We had a tremendous amount of school spirit. It wasn't uncommon to

see 800 SI students walking down Stanyan Street to Kezar to watch a basketball game. We'd fill an entire side of Kezar with white shirts, and our games would draw capacity crowds of 6,600 fans. I don't know how else to describe that spirit except as a big togetherness that we all felt. Maybe it was because the war was hanging over our heads. Perhaps, because of that spirit, we experienced a lot of success then."

The success was also due to some talented coaches. Alex Schwarz, who served as head varsity football coach from 1942 to 1944, joined the athletic department in September 1940 after a successful career playing for USF. At one point, he coached football and basketball for SI — the sports he excelled in while at Mission High and USF. (Schwarz made the All-Pacific Coast football team in 1936 and 1937 and served as captain of the '37 squad.)

While Schwarz was finishing his degree at USF, coaching frosh football there and working at the Golden Gate International Exposition on Treasure Island (running the lost and found department), his close friend Fr. Ray Feeley, SJ, told him of job openings for football coaches in Los Angeles and Denver. "My wife said she wasn't about to leave San Francisco," said Schwarz. Then in 1940, Fr. Feeley called him again to tell him of another job. "This one you can't turn down," he told me. "It's at SI." The starting monthly pay: $80.

His first year, Schwarz served as the football team's line coach under Red Vaccaro, and in his second year, he took over the JV team. In 1942, when Vaccaro became the athletic director, Schwarz took over the head coach's job. He coached standout players, including Bob Mintun, Don Gordon, Val Molkenbuhr, Charley Helmer, Dan Coleman, Dick Cashman, Bill and Bob Corbett, Jim Canelo and Jack Burke, who was also a champion discus thrower. However, though his expertise was in football, Schwarz gained more fame for coaching basketball when his 1943 team turned in an undefeated season.

Schwarz's basketball career began when one coach left to join the California Highway Patrol mid-season, and Schwarz stepped in, getting advice from Bob Kleckner at USF. "SI had not won a single game that season before I took over, and it didn't win a game when I first started coaching." Despite the regular season losses, Schwarz's team went on to win the Catholic school tournament at St. Mary's College that year.

In 1942, Schwarz's team featured the skillful play of John LoSchiavo '42 (later to become president of USF) and came in second in the league, losing to Poly. "When I came back to school, I saw the principal, Fr. King, who said, "'Tis well we lost. The boys were getting too excited." I responded: "You mean to tell me that you want your debating teams to come in second?"

Schwarz coached without an on-campus gym. He reserved the gym at Everett Junior High on 17th and Church Streets for his basketball team, but with school letting out at 3:15 p.m., students would take an hour by bus to get to the gym, leaving them less than an hour for practice. To speed up their trip, Schwarz bought a 1936 Ford panel truck and put seats in the back to carry two teams and manager Harry "Dutch" Olivier '44 (later to become a Jesuit) to the gym, cutting travel time to 15 minutes.

The opportunity arose in 1943 to buy a bus when Student Body President Val Molkenbuhr '43 convinced his father and uncle to make a donation to the school. "It was a goodly amount, but not quite enough for a new bus," said Schwarz. He later saw an ad for used Army buses and drove down to San Luis Obispo to inspect them. There he ran into a mechanic he knew

from the city who told him to buy a certain bus, as it had a brand-new engine. "I figured with the sale of the truck and the donation, I could swing it," said Schwarz. "I came back and told Fr. King. He had to think it over. A few days later, he told me that my request had been denied. 'You're spoiling the kids,' he told me. 'No Jesuit school has a bus, not even USF.'"

Schwarz's reflection on that decision was simple. "Those were interesting years."

Despite the lack of sophisticated transportation, the 1943 team went undefeated. "You have no idea how exciting that was," said Schwarz, who was carried, along with O'Shea, on the shoulders of rooters to the dressing room. The starting five that year included Kevin O'Shea, Harvey Christensen, Jack Scharfen, Jim Beeson and Tom Flaherty.

O'Shea wasn't the only great athlete to be influenced by Schwarz. Jack Grealish '44, a four-sport

Varsity football players in 1948.

160

The Bruce–Mahoney Trophy is shared between SI and SH (now Sacred Heart Cathedral). The school that wins two of the three games of football, basketball and baseball takes the trophy home for the year.

student, used to play baseball and then have Schwarz drive him in his truck to a track meet, with Grealish changing uniforms in the cab.

Schwarz spotted another great athlete, Joe McNamee '44, playing intramural basketball at SI. "I saw him playing hunch at noontime and asked him to come out for the team. He said he couldn't because he had size 14 feet and couldn't find sneakers big enough to fit him. I called a sporting goods store in the city, and they told me to try a store in Oakland, which did stock shoes that size. I drove there, bought the shoes and gave them to Joe. He joined the team and turned out to be a good player for SI and USF." McNamee eventually played professionally for the Rochester Royals in the 1950–51 season.

Schwarz also had high praise for Rene Herrerias '44, who in February 1944 against the Lincoln Mustangs, was the first lightweight player ever to score 27 points in a single game. "In those days, an entire team might score 25 points in one game." Herrerias later went on to great fame coaching for SI (and later UC Berkeley), leading the Wildcats to four AAA championships (1951 and 1954–56) and two Tournament of Champions victories in 1954 and 1955.

In 2004, Schwarz was inducted into the San Francisco Prep Hall of Fame for his talented coaching at SI, Mission and City College.

The Pride of SI: Charlie Silvera

Frank McGloin '25, who started coaching baseball in 1930 (winning an AAA championship his first year), ended his career as varsity baseball coach in 1942, though he continued to be an avid supporter of SI until his death in 1994. (Each year since 1995, one junior varsity baseball player receives the Frank McGloin Award in honor of this great Ignatian.)

McGloin had many superb players, including pitchers John Collins and Buzz Meagher and first baseman Harvey Christensen, all of whom earned first-team all-league honors. (Christensen '43 also earned all-league honors in basketball. Collins pitched a no-hitter against Balboa in 1938 and earned the league pitching title. Meagher started a triple-play as pitcher in 1939.)

But the most celebrated of them all was Charlie Silvera '42 who went on to become a catcher for the Yankees between 1948 and 1956. As such, he was one of eight Yankees to win five consecutive World Series and six in all. However, Silvera only played in one of those games (in 1949) as he was backup to Yogi Berra, one of the Yankee's greatest players. Still, he served his team with distinction, mainly helping to warm up pitchers in the bullpen. He roomed with Mickey Mantle and Joe DiMaggio, and he traveled on Billy Martin's staff from job to job during that manager's volatile career.

Silvera began playing baseball at Mission Dolores School, and he nearly went to Sacred Heart. "But Bob Dunnigan, who lived down the street, talked to my mother and made sure I went to SI to play for Frank McGloin, who was a great coach. He had a wonderful temperament and was great with kids."

At SI, Silvera played on the varsity team in each of his four years, spending most of the time as catcher. After graduation, he signed with the Yankees, and along with Jerry Coleman and Bob Cherry — Lowell seniors also signed by the Yankees — he took a train on June 20 to Wellsville, NY, to play on the PONY League there in a Yankee farm club for one season.

In 1943, he entered the service and played base-

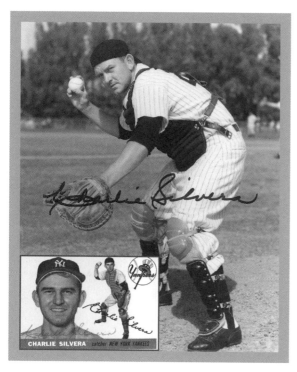

Charlie Silvera played for the Yankees during its glory years, helping his teammates win six World Series.

ball for three years at McClellan Field in Sacramento on the same team as Joe DiMaggio before being transferred to Hawaii, where he continued to play ball with the 7th Air Force.

After the war, he spent several years on farm teams before seeing major league action for the Yankees for the last four games of 1948 to replace an injured catcher. He stayed with the Yankees while they won seven Pennants and six World Series — five of them in his first five years with the team, from 1949–1953, a feat yet to be repeated. (After his fifth World Series ring, he and some of the others asked for silver cigarette cases.)

His teammates called him "Swede," a nickname given him by John Swanson, the owner of the Mission Bowl. Swanson didn't care that Silvera was Portugese-Irish, only that he had blond, wavy hair. "Everyone playing ball in the Mission District had a nickname, and that name stuck with me."

Silvera didn't mind warming the bench watching Yogi Berra play. "After awhile, I tried to hide so they wouldn't discover me. I had sat on the bench so long, I was afraid my tools had grown rusty." During dou-

ble-headers, Berra played the first game, and Silvera would step in for the nightcap. In 1957, the Yankees sold Silvera to the Cubs, and a badly sprained ankle on Memorial Day that year ended his career.

He spent the next several years managing farm teams for the Yankees and the Pirates and then scouted for the Washington Senators until 1968. Billy Martin then asked him to join his team of coaches, and he followed him to Minnesota, Texas and Detroit. "He kept getting fired, and I'd be fired along with him. After 1975, I told him I didn't want to be fired anymore." With that, Silvera returned to scouting and has worked for the Yankees, Brewers, A's, Marlins, Reds and Cubs.

In 2003 he celebrated the 50-year anniversary of the Yankees' five-straight World Series victories and his 62nd year in baseball. If you go to a Giants' game, you can still see him in the seats scouting for talent.

"I always felt that I was born in the greatest city in the world, lived in the greatest district in that city and played for the best team ever in baseball with the greatest catcher who ever lived. And I had an excellent education at SI. I succeeded because of the discipline that started at home and then continued at SI and in the service. That discipline really helped me with the Yankees. We all felt that there are major league ballplayers and then there are Yankees. We felt the same camaraderie on that team as I still feel for my SI classmates — guys like Fr. John LoSchiavo, SJ, and Bill McDonnell."

At his 50-year reunion, Charlie Silvera made this comment about his years at SI: "Great classmates, great school, great teachers and great baseball coach."

(At his class's 63rd reunion in 2005, Silvera presented Fr. Sauer with his SI block for the school archives.)

Silvera wasn't the only major-leaguer to attend SI. Jimmy Mangan '47 played with the Pirates in 1952 and 1954 and with the New York Giants in 1956.

Don Bosch '65 played with the Pirates in 1966, the Mets in 1967 and 1968 and the Expos in 1969. And Allan Gallagher, who played third base for the Giants from 1970–1973, and who finished his career with the Angels, attended SI for part of his high school years before he went on to Mission High School where he became AAA Player of the Year. He returned to the Jesuit fold when he enrolled at SCU.

An Original '49er

Eddie Forrest '39, who died in 2001 a month shy of his 80th birthday, was one of the original members of the San Francisco '49ers. Forrest graduated from Presidio Middle School before coming to SI, where he excelled in basketball and football. At 5-feet, 11-inches and 215 pounds, he wasn't the biggest linebacker SI had ever seen, but he was effective. He made the All-City team during his last three years with the Wildcats, playing for George Malley, and was chosen to play in the high school version of the East-West game, which pitted the best East Bay high school athletes against their San Francisco and Peninsula counterparts. He went on to SCU where he played offensive guard and linebacker for Coach Buck Shaw. He later enlisted during World War II and served as a paratrooper in Europe. In 1944, the Green Bay Packers drafted him, but because he was in the service, the draft wasn't binding. "I was away from home so much, I didn't want to go to Wisconsin to play," he said in a 1992 *Genesis* interview. Then Buck Shaw, who served as the first '49ers' coach, signed him while he was still in Germany. Two years later, when the Niners played their first game, Forrest was in uniform, playing center, guard and linebacker for two seasons in the

All-America Football Conference. He then returned to SCU where he coached with Len Casanova until 1951 following the Broncos' victory over Kentucky in the Orange Bowl.

"I can remember when he used to practice with his team at the Polo Fields," said classmate Bob Lagomarsino. "The '49ers were 33 strong in those days. Eddie was a real rugged guy, but he weighed less than 220 pounds. In those days, you didn't have to be a behemoth to play football."

A member of the San Francisco Prep Hall of Fame and SCU's Athletic Hall of Fame, Forrest always spoke fondly of his days as a '49er. "Most of us were from the Bay Area, and we all knew each other before the '49ers," he said in a 1996 interview in the *San Francisco Chronicle*. "So we were a very, very close team. Since there were no other major-league pro teams here then, we were sort of quasi- or semi-celebrities. People knew us. Anybody in the Bay Area interested in sports knew about the '49ers in those days. From the beginning, we got good crowds. We all lived in Parkmerced. The wives knew each other and socialized together. It was a very happy existence."

Later, Forrest was active as a volunteer with the NFL Alumni Association, and he built a successful career as a savings and loan executive, retiring in the 1990s to spend time with his family.

"He couldn't make too many of our annual reunions because of his bad knees," said Lagomarsino. "But he did come to the 40-year and 50-year reunions. He led the class in singing the fight song. He was one of the most popular guys in the class."

SI had several other athletes play pro football, including Dan Fouts '69, who made the NFL Hall of Fame as quarterback for the San Diego Chargers. Look for more on him in Chapter 10.

Kevin O'Shea '43

Everyone who went to SI in the 1940s knows the name Kevin O'Shea. The great basketball player, who died in 2003, made the All-City Team in his junior and senior years, helped SI earn a number-one ranking in California and led SI to a 1-point victory over Lowell for the AAA title in his senior year.

His classmate Val Molkenbuhr, student body president then, was part of the sold-out crowd that night at Kezar. When O'Shea sank the winning basket in the last second, Molkenbuhr rushed to the locker room and took a shower with the team. "My tears flowed like the shower water," he said.

Looking at the headlines from the *Chronicle* and *Examiner* in those days, you would think O'Shea was the only player on the team. "Wildcats Plus O'Shea Bubble Past Bewildered Bears 36–9," "O'Shea Does It—Ignatians Win!" and "O'Shea Shines in Wildcat Triumph," read a few of the headlines from the 1942–43 season.

For the game against Lowell, sports writer Bob Brachman proclaimed that "Irish Kevin O'Shea is one of the great athletes to enter San Francisco High School portals. The brilliant SI cager proved this last night before 5,000 fans in Kezar Pavilion when, with 10 seconds remaining, he stole the ball from a pileup, dribbled 50 feet through a host of Lowell Indians and tanked a field goal that gave the Ignatians a 23-22 triumph. When the gun sounded signaling the Wildcats' fourth straight victory and the first defeat for Lowell, St. Ignatius rooters lifted coach Alex Schwarz to their shoulders, hoisted O'Shea with him, and triumphantly paraded them to the dressing quarters." That win gave SI its first city crown in 16 years.

After leaving SI, O'Shea went to Notre Dame briefly, and then left to serve in the Coast Guard during the war. He returned to Notre Dame in 1948 where he played until 1950, earning All-American honors in each of his three years there.

In an obituary published by the *San Francisco Chronicle*, former USF player and coach Ross Guidice called O'Shea a "great defensive ballplayer [who was] really quick. And he had an unusual shot — he kind of just spun the ball up there."

After Notre Dame, O'Shea played three years in the NBA for the Minneapolis Lakers, the Milwaukee Hawks and the Baltimore Bullets. Despite being only 6-feet, 1-inch, he was able to score against taller players from inside the key according to John "Joe" McNamee '44, who played with O'Shea on the Bullets. (McNamee also played for the Rochester Royals in the 1950–51 season.)

In his *Chronicle* obituary, O'Shea's son Brian '69 said his father's proudest moment "was the night when he and four other Baltimore Bullets, including Bay Area legend Don Barksdale, played an entire game [which they won] without a substitute, the first and only time that has happened in the NBA."

After leaving basketball in 1953, he entered

the insurance business. He made a brief return to basketball in the early 1960s when he became general manager of the short-lived San Francisco Saints in the American Basketball League and coached *Examiner* basketball camps.

In 1966, he made a foray into politics when Mayor John F. Shelley appointed him to the Board of Supervisors. He lost in his 1968 election bid after initially being declared the winner. "He was too nice a guy to be good in politics," said McNamee in the *Chronicle* story.

His wife, Jeanne O'Shea, said that her husband was "always proud of his association with St. Ignatius High School and St. Ignatius College Prep. One of his favorite stories is that he learned how to study at SI, although his grades did not always indicate that. He liked to say that the basic foundation he received at SI prepared him for Notre Dame and the business world." O'Shea and his wife had five children — Mary Anne, Brian '69, Timothy '71, Kevin '76 and Catherine Franceschi.

In addition to O'Shea and McNamee, two other Wildcats played professional basketball. Fred LaCour '56, who played with the St. Louis Hawks from 1960–62 and the Warriors the following year, tied an AAA record in his junior year at SI against Galileo, scoring 29 points. Also, Bob Portman '65, a first-round draft pick from Creighton, played with the Warriors between 1969 and 1973. (More on these two players later in the book.)

The John Brophy Award

When Kevin O'Shea was leading his team to the city championship, he was doing it, in part, for classmate John Brophy '43, who

The 1942 track team. Photo courtesty of Kerry Hansell, whose father, James G. Kelly '43, is fourth from right in the front row. Kerry, whose three daughters are grads, started coaching high-jump at SI in 2005.

died that February. As a freshman, Brophy developed a serious illness, and doctors had to amputate his leg. He regained his health and took part in the Sodality, Sanctuary Society, debate team and CSF. He also served as a student body officer, a writer for *The Red and Blue* and manager of the swim team, earning membership into the Block Club.

Brophy suffered a relapse in November of his senior year, and the basketball team dedicated its season to him. He died on February 10, 1943. At the end of the year, the Block Club, spurred on by its president, Don Gordon '43, created the John E. Brophy Award to honor this exemplar of Ignatian values. Harvey Christensen '43 was the first recipient, chosen because he modeled Brophy's "loyalty, integrity and unselfish dedication." Christensen made a name for himself as "the greatest natural athlete in the circuit, and without a peer in his position," according to one *Chronicle* reporter. "He looks like an edition of Paul Waner. Bats .536. Can play any position in the field. A heady fielder. A born leader." Christensen also made a name for himself as a star basketball player and swimmer, and earned

The 1941 varsity crew competed in whale boats on the bay.

Right: Bill Morlock '49

All-City honors in all three sports. After high school he played for the St. Louis Brown's minor league team from 1949–51 before serving as a baseball coach at USF and Lincoln, where he eventually became principal. The San Francisco Prep Hall of Fame inducted him in 1993.

Other Sports

Track, swimming, tennis and boxing rounded out the sports program at SI in the 1940s, with golf resurrecting in 1949. Frank Zanazzi, a "curly-haired, Scotch-burred" track coach, came to SI in 1946 after serving as a U.S. Olympics trainer. In his first year, he led SI to a divisional championship but fell just short of taking the AAA title.

"Young Man, Have You Considered the Priesthood?"

William Morlock '49 grew up in the Mission District, the son of an Irish-American mother and German-born father. While he attended dozens of Seals' baseball games (the stadium was walking distance from his home on 22nd Street between Florida and Alabama), he was not the athletic type. He attended SI and found himself in the honors program, taking four years of Latin and three years of Greek. Scholarly and contemplative by nature — he celebrated his 44th year in the classroom at SI in 2005 — he found himself drawn to the Sodality. It did not take the Jesuits long to encourage him to consider a vocation as a priest.

"The school had a clerical atmosphere when I was a student," said Morlock. "All the priests wore cassocks, and most of the lay teachers had left to serve in the war." Those priests were guided by the same counter-reformation philosophy that guided St. Ignatius of Loyola as he founded the Society of Jesus in the 1500s. "We heard time and time again how the Church had been torn asunder by the wicked Protestants," said Morlock. "It was totally pre-Vatican II, with religious instruction consisting of apologetics."

Morlock was impressed by his Jesuit teachers, including the scholastic Albert Zabala, SJ, who would later serve as chairman of the theology department at USF and who founded the USF Summer Theology Program, and Fr. Alexander Cody, SJ, the school's chaplain. "The first

impressed me with his intellectuality, the second with his spirituality. These were ideal Jesuits."

Given Morlock's religious predilections, "it didn't take long for them to apply pressure. The entire Church was dedicated to recruiting boys for the priesthood, and there was a general presumption that if you were religious, you should become a priest." Since its early days, SI had sent its students into the Novitiate, hitting a peak in 1931 with 17 seniors entering the Society of Jesus.

Morlock was one of eight in his class to begin studies toward the priesthood, but he chose the diocesan seminary of St. Joseph's, as he was "put off" by the Jesuit lifestyle. On his first day at St. Joseph's, he heard the news that the Russians had the Bomb. Then he entered the building and barely left for two years, cut-off from most of the outside world, with the exception of trips home for two weeks during Christmas and three months each summer. "I left because I could not adjust to monastic life," he said. "It was almost as bad as the Jesuit novitiate, with a completely regimented life measured by the constant ringing of bells." Morlock, after a stint in the Army, returned to the U.S. and to SI, where he has taught since 1961 in three departments, as a German, church history and world history teacher.

A Tangled Tale of Publications

Despite the war, despite the athletic milestones, high school life continued in the 1940s to be filled with the day-to-day events that never seem to change from decade to decade. These events were recorded in *The Red and Blue* until June 1, 1948, when the newspaper printed its last copy. According to Warren White '39, the moderator of the first *Inside SI*, *The Red and Blue* did not return "partly because it was expensive, and partly because its news was quite old by the time it was published."

The school also had a new publication that was gaining favor: *The Ignatian* (not to be confused with the yearbook of the same name). In 1945, the school published a 36-page literary magazine containing "a student-composed Greek oration, ten types of literary expression, [and] a number of fine-line illustrations."[11] In 1947, the literary magazine became a news magazine, and ran on a quarterly basis until 1950. This publication modeled its design on *Time* magazine; sadly, there was "an uncertain period spent reconnoitering with *Time* about copyrights" in 1947, according to the annual, and it changed its look to avoid legal action.

Another publication, the school yearbook, resurfaced a year later, also calling itself the *Ignatian*. (The school abandoned the name *The Heights*, which it had called its yearbook from 1928 to 1932.)

Students enjoying an edition of The Red and Blue in the 1940s.

The 1943 varsity swim team.

a low priority. In any case, a *Red and Blue* edition might wait several weeks before it cleared to go to print by which time any claim to currency had vaporized."

The in-house nature of the publication gave it its name as did the sly reference to the then very popular John Gunther books (*Inside USA, Inside Europe* and *Inside Latin America*). "By using the 'Inside' title gimmick, the students and I did an end run. If our logic was Jesuitical, well, we had been well taught. Fr. Harrington was, I think, relieved to be rid of the responsibility."

White kept expenses down by mimeographing the publication and producing it in an after-school journalism class. "Students had fun doing it," White added. "They were delighted to have something current to read on Monday mornings." The publication expanded into a four-page magazine in 1950 ("Rag to be Revamped" read the headline of the last one-pager) and continued to grow over the years.

Finally, *The Quill* appeared in 1951 as a literary magazine publishing short stories and poetry. It published until 1954, and then appeared again in 1992 as the school's official literary magazine.

Currently, students receive *Inside SI* in newspaper form, and *The Quill* and *Ignatian* yearbook, which appear annually. SI publishes the *Principal's Newsletter* online three times a year as well as the quarterly *Genesis*, the alumni magazine that started publication in November 1964. (A previous alumni publication, the *Ignatian Bulletin*, was published from 1956 until 1967 when *Genesis* took its place.)

Replacing *The Red and Blue* was a onc-page mimeographed sheet that called itself *Inside SI*, published weekly by the English students of Warren White '39 beginning in 1949 "as a practical task for his Journalism class... reviewing the past week and pre-viewing the week to come," with Bob Amsler '49 as the first editor. White, who taught at SI between 1948 and 1955, volunteered to start the newspaper "so I wouldn't have to supervise JUG," he said in a 2003 interview. The magazine was able to succeed where *The Red and Blue* failed. It published quickly because, as an in-house publication, it did not require review by a professed Jesuit priest. "The concern was that *The Red and Blue* went off campus to other schools in an exchange program and its contents needed to be vetted to insure that they reflected properly the AMDG mission of both SI and of the Order itself," said White. "Fr. Harrington had the misfortune of having the censor duties added to his already considerable responsibilities, and he probably gave them

Uncle Frank

Francis "Uncle Frank" Corwin, one of the best loved teachers in the school's history, began his 44-year teaching career in September 1947. A veteran of World War II, where he served as an MP, Corwin brought to his history classes stories and a demeanor that would frighten, amuse and entrance students (sometimes all at once) until his retirement in 1991. His students knew the truth of a joke told by Bob Sarlatte '68: "Frank Corwin doesn't teach history. He remembers it."

When students recall Corwin, they think about his years serving as detention proctor. Students who received JUG went on a white-knuckle roller-coaster ride of master-sergeant-style badgering and mock abuse.

It went something like this: "Mistah! Sit up straight and let's see the whites of your knuckles! I could shine my shoes between your butt and the back of your chair!"

After leaving the army, Corwin went to Utah to teach. There the chain-smoking teacher found the strict Mormon standards a little too tough to take. Teachers weren't allowed to smoke in public, and twice he was caught and reported to his principal, who warned him that if he smoked in public a third time, he would be fired for moral turpitude.

"That's what they charge pimps and prostitutes with," Frank said in a *Genesis III* interview.[12] "I told myself there were still 47 other states, so I gave notice." He landed a job at SI and started teaching in the fall of 1947. On his first day, he walked into the teachers' room and into a thick cloud of cigarette smoke. "In those days, everyone smoked at SI, including the Jesuits. The smoke was so thick, you could cut it with a knife."

Then he listened to the conversations of the teachers and panicked. He asked himself, "What am I doing here? These teachers are brilliant. I told myself to keep my mouth shut so they wouldn't know how little I knew. From then on, I've always felt privileged to work at SI because we have an excellent faculty."

Corwin began proctoring detention in the early 1950s when Fr. Tichenor asked him to take on the job. Corwin was used to East Coast private school boys "who were little gentlemen. At SI, the boys were live wires, always into mischief and pranks. I could see that they were ready to explode. So when I walked into the detention room, I had every kid freeze in an upright position in his seat with his butt touching the back of his chair, hands folded on the lip of his desk, the whites of his knuckles showing, his shoulders back, feet planted together and staring at a mark I'd made on the blackboard. I'd tell them not to move their eyes from that mark for one hour."

The veteran soldier had his fun with his charges. He'd heap verbal abuse onto his students, but it wouldn't take the students long to realize that behind the bellicose voice lay a heart of gold and a gentle spirit.

Corwin's punishments

Frank Corwin in 1959.

hole, and told the boys to fill the hole up again. When they were done, he asked them what was in the hole. One boy had seen Frank throw the paper into the hole. He got to leave. The other two had to dig the same hole and find the paper.

Principals throughout the years would take visitors to the detention room to show off Corwin's crisp discipline, and parents praised him for the tight control he maintained. "They'd tell me to give their sons the back of my hand if they failed to do their homework," he noted.

Corwin, along with nearly all the faculty in the '40s and '50s, believed in the efficacy of corporal punishment. "If a student missed two homework assignments, he felt the back of my hand," Corwin said. "He always had his homework the next day. And between Fr. Ray Pallas, SJ, and Fr. Leo Marine, SJ, every locker on the third floor of the old school was dented from bodies they sent flying through the air."

The SI faculty honored Frank Corwin on his retirement by wearing dunce caps. Many of these men, when they were students, served detention under Uncle Frank.

grew creative over the years. Leo LaRocca '53, one-time athletic director at SI, remembers Corwin ordering him to go to the ROTC armory, check out an unloaded rifle, and walk back and forth in front of the treasurer's office "guarding it" for one hour.

Another time, Corwin dealt with three boys who were repeat offenders. He used an old Army trick to punish them. He told the boys to dig a hole five feet wide, five feet long and five feet deep. When they were done, he had the boys turn around. He took out a small piece of paper from his pocket, threw it in the

Corwin stopped rapping the boys in the early '60s. "Other teachers still practiced corporal punishment, but I was afraid I might injure someone. I substituted it with screaming and shouting."

In class, Corwin peppered his lectures with stories of Cairo and the war. Those stories brought to life the textbook accounts that students read. He also knew how to capture the imagination of a 15-year-old boy. While teaching a rigorous course of history, which he developed for the archdiocese (the infamous syllabus), he told stories of corpses three-days dead in the desert, of men dying from drinking too much liquor too quickly, and, of course, of Major Lake and his mistress, Sasha.

Corwin soon found that he was the subject of faculty stories. It had as much to do with the love the faculty felt for this grizzly-bear of a man as much as it had to do with the situations in which Frank found himself.

For instance, during one fire alarm drill at the Sunset District campus, Frank directed his students to leave the school and then saw that Fr. Gene Growney, SJ '60, had elected to stay behind because one of his students had a full-length leg cast and could neither walk downstairs nor take the elevator during the drill. Frank and Gene decided to have a smoke in the bathroom while waiting for the drill to end.

"We were talking and didn't hear anyone coming. The next thing we knew, we saw Br. Draper, the fire chief, the battalion chief and his assistant. Boy, were they annoyed. Gene and I were officially cited by the fire department. Two days later, during the faculty dinner, the faculty gave Gene and me fire hats."

The faculty ribbed Frank about that for years. And they didn't let him forget about the time that he woke up, showered and dressed, said goodbye to his wife and left for school. He got to the Stanyan Street campus, found no one there and thought that the entire school was at church for a religious holiday. He raced to St. Ignatius Church and found no one there. He walked back to school and saw a maintenance man. "He asked me what I was doing in school on a Saturday. If I could have physically done so, I would have kicked myself in the butt. When I returned home, my wife was laughing so hard, I thought she'd fall down. I didn't speak to her for two days. And of course it got back to school. Nothing stays a secret."

Frank, who eventually moved to Marin, car-pooled with several other teachers. One day they played a practical joke on Frank. They arranged with Fr. Bill Keenan, SJ '36, the school treasurer, to put a note in Frank's pay envelope indicating that because the school was short on cash, several teachers couldn't be paid for several months.

In the car on the ride back to Marin, each of the teachers pulled out his paycheck and announced that more money had been withheld than they had expected. They watched as Frank took the bait. He reached into his coat pocket and pulled out his pay envelope. He opened it, took one look, and shouted, "Turn this car around!" They were driving on the Golden Gate Bridge at the time. Frank knew he couldn't face his wife without having been paid in full.

In 1987, SI named Frank Corwin as the recipient of the President's Award, the highest honor the school bestows upon a person who has not attended SI. That citation reads, in part, that "as the years passed, students and alumni came to realize Frank's goodness, innate charity and deep humility. It is there that the wizard whose bombast was only an instructional tool was seen to be the teacher *par excellence*, for he showed the scarecrow, the lion and the tin man that the treasure they had been seeking actually had always been deep within them and needed only to be recognized by the one who cared to be self-appropriated. And so the tin man finds his heart, the lion his courage and the scarecrow his brain, thanks to Frank's tutelage."

When he retired in May 1991, the faculty held a surprise going-away party for Frank and for two of his longtime colleagues who were also retiring — Joe Parker and Anny Medina — SI's first full-time female faculty member. Three judges, the Hon.

Timothy Reardon '59, the Hon. William Mallen '54, the Hon. Robert Dossee '52, all former students of Corwin, came to honor this veteran teacher, as did J.B. Murphy, who had retired in 1989 after 50 years at SI. Members of the faculty and the judges all wore dunce caps as they sat in on Uncle Frank's last detention period.

At the party, Judge Mallen recalled his senior year history class with Corwin. "He had one of the greatest scams going. By the time I got to my senior year, I thought I was ready for a break. But Mr. Corwin, on the first day of class, announced that anyone who caught him in a mistake would receive an automatic A for the semester and an exemption on the semester exam.

"From that point on, I sat glued to my chair listening to his every word. Two-thirds through the year in one of his lectures, he referred to Abraham Lincoln who 'served as a colonel' during some battle. I raised my hand. 'Mr. Corwin,' I asked. 'Do you remember the promise you made at the beginning of the year?' He said he did. 'Abraham Lincoln was a captain, not a colonel during that battle.'

"Mr. Corwin looked in his text and announced, 'You're absolutely correct!' He took out his grade book, marked an A in it under my name, and announced that I was exempt from the exam. From that point on, I didn't hear another word of history in that class."

Fr. John Murphy, SJ '59, an extraordinary English teacher at SI at the time of Corwin's retirement, told the story of being in Uncle Frank's class during the 1956-57 paper drive. The winning class, he noted, won the title of the "Loyalty Class." "Mr. Corwin gave threats, appeals and humiliations as motivation to be that class. For instance, he assigned a long term paper that could be waived by meeting our individual quota. We were determined to be the Loyalty Class. To do this, we hired a truck and one of the parents drove. And from early in the morning until late in the afternoon on a fall Saturday, the 30 of us canvassed the Richmond District. We went systematically from Arguello to the beach using Clement as our axis and fanning out and bringing the papers back to the truck by hand and with wagons. The truck got full. In fact, our one class had collected more newspapers than the rest of the school together.

"Well, such a great event could only be capped by an unauthorized, unexpected visit to Mr. Corwin's home. So late Saturday afternoon, sweaty and smudged, we rang the doorbell. When Mrs. Corwin saw us, she called to Frank who came out with some alarm on his face. We presented him with a truckful of paper. Realizing there was no danger to his person or family from us, he assumed his habitual role as omniscient, rotund professor and said, 'Gentlemen, in the history of my years at St. Ignatius, this is an historic event. All records have been shattered. You have done yourselves proud. I am sure the principal and administration will be stunned by such a performance. Thank you gentlemen. I will see you Monday morning.'"

In a *Genesis IV* interview, Frank insisted that his greatest honor was not the recognition he received from San Francisco Mayor Art Agnos a week before his retirement, when he received an honorary proclamation from the City of San Francisco, but the fact that he taught at SI. "I'm very trite," he said. "I've known I've been blessed to have the opportunity to teach at this kind of school. I've taught in public schools where no one seemed to care about anything. Here, there's plenty of care, concern, and most importantly, love."

A senior retreat at El Retiro from February 1, 1948.

Joe McNamee Bob Wiebusch   George Moscone   Cappy Lavin   Harvey Christiansen

Herb Schoenstein   Kevin O'Shea   Ron Maresca   Don Benedetti   Rudy Zanggani

George Moscone & Leo McCarthy

Two of SI's best known politicians graduated in the 1940s — George Moscone '47 and Leo McCarthy '48.

George Moscone's senior yearbook caption included the following: "A devotee to athletics and ROTC, he was mentioned on several All-City basketball selections, having played on various school teams since his freshman year. He won the first year elocution contest and was a three-year baseballer. The 'Bambino' will attend St. Mary's with Herman Wedemeyer."

Born to working-class parents November 24, 1929, Moscone went on to SI where he excelled at basketball, earning all-city honors and an athletic scholarship to college. He played for Phil Woolpert, and, along with Cap Lavin, helped the team earn its second AAA championship. He was also a good speaker, as his victory in the Frosh Elocution Contest indicated.

After graduating from college and Hastings Law School, he married Gina Bodanza, his childhood sweetheart, and they had four children. (Two of those children, Chris Moscone '80 and Jonathan Moscone '82, were in class at SI the day their father died. His granddaughter, Zea Moscone, is a member of SI's class of 2008.)

He became involved in San Francisco politics through John and Phillip Burton and won elections for supervisor, state senator and San Francisco Mayor. A champion for civil rights and the interests of the poor and working class, Moscone was a popular mayor. On November 27, 1978, he and Supervisor Harvey Milk were gunned down by former Supervisor Dan White. That night, 40,000 people marched in a candlelight vigil to honor Moscone and Milk. (More on this in Chapter XI.)

Leo McCarthy was born in Auckland, New Zealand, and immigrated with his parents to California when he was 3 years old. At SI he made the track team and competed in shot put. He later earned a Bachelor's degree in history from

USF in 1955. He married Jacqueline Burke, and they have four children, two of whom attended SI — Adam '83 and Niall '85. (Leo's grandchildren Courtney Allen '97 and Kevin Allen '00 also attended SI.)

In 1964, he was elected to the San Francisco Board of Supervisors (along with Moscone) and later served as California Assembly Speaker for six years in the 1970s followed by a 12-year stint as Lieutenant Governor. In his many years of public service, he is credited for his efforts in education, health and the environment. (He also made a point of driving to his San Francisco home every day from Sacramento to be with his family.) He is a longtime SI supporter who attends many of the school's events and was a featured speaker at a Downtown Business Lunch in the 1990s.

Remembering Saint Ignatius

By J. Hugh Visser '47

In September 1941, Holy Name School opened with 10 boys and 19 girls in the seventh grade, the highest class. Some three months later, December 7, the Japanese bombed Pearl Harbor, and we were suddenly thrust into a new and frightening world. San Francisco, and particularly the outer Sunset, seemed vulnerable to a sudden attack. Volunteers became air-raid wardens; there were blackouts and air-raid drills and, in a short time, rationing of gasoline, red stamps for meat and blue stamps for sugar and butter.

In the spring of our seventh grade year, the school had a newspaper drive, and we collected hundreds of pounds of paper. The money went for a Mass kit for an Army chaplain. One of our parish priests went into the military.

In the following year, when I was an eighth grader,

our teacher, Sr. Canisius told me that there was to be a scholarship examination for Saint Ignatius High School and that she wanted me to take it. Both of my parents were immigrants from Europe and had no knowledge of high schools. Students from the outer Sunset usually went to Polytechnic High School, which we passed on the "N" Judah line as we took the streetcar downtown.

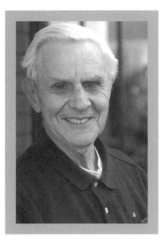

Dr. J. Hugh Visser '47

We had to find out where SI was and how to get there.

On the appointed day I went to SI and took the scholarship exam, which was also an entrance examination. The exam was given in various classrooms, each of which had a platform about 6 feet by 8 feet and raised about a foot above the floor. On this was a desk and chair for the teacher. On the wall of each classroom was an old-fashioned loudspeaker about three feet in diameter over which some of the instructions for the exam and the words to be spelled were announced. At one point after the exam, we were taken into an auditorium and shown movies of school activities, including a basket-ball game starring Kevin O'Shea. He was a senior at SI and an all-city player, but I had never even heard of him. So far as I knew, none of my Holy Name class-mates had ever been to a high school football or bas-ketball game.

A few months later the school received word that I was among the eight winners of a four-year, full-tuition scholarship to SI. I still have the newspaper clipping listing the names of the eight and the value of the full amount — $390 for the whole four years. That August, I went to register for school and met the office staff at that time — two secretaries.

The Class of 1947 at an alumni reunion.

The First Day

On the first day of school, we freshmen found our names and the classrooms to which we were assigned on the main office bulletin board. We found our way to class and took seats. Soon a young Jesuit came into the classroom, took roll and had us sit in alphabetical order. These were to be our seats for the year; we remained in the same classroom and the teachers changed. He told us that he was our registry teacher, that this was a class in Latin, and then told us some of the school rules. Schoolwork was to be done in pencil, homework in ink. Fountain pens and knives would be confiscated on sight. (Ballpoint pens had not been invented yet.) The young Jesuits on their way to the priesthood were "scholastics" and were to be addressed as "Mister." And going out to your locker, except at recess and lunchtime was an offense punishable by JUG, which went from 3:15 to 5 p.m. Greater offenses were punishable by Saturday JUG — from 9 a.m. to noon.

He also wrote a long word in German, *zusammengehörigkeitsgefühl*, across the entire front blackboard. He explained that it meant a feeling of working and belonging together, and this was what he wanted his class to develop. He never did tell us his name. Later we found a schedule of classes and teachers on the class bulletin board and discovered that he was Mr. James Markey, SJ. At that time he stood, while teaching, at the back of the class. A student who misbehaved might find himself hit by a tennis ball or an eraser, which he then had to pick up and carry back to Mr. Markey.

The School Day

The school day consisted of two periods, recess, two more periods and lunch. After lunch came activity period for which the registry teacher reappeared. During this half-hour, you could go to school club meetings or stay in the room and study. Two more regular periods completed the day.

Early in the year we carried home to our parents a notice that if we were not doing at least three hours of homework a night, it was not because it hadn't been assigned.

The Curriculum

The curriculum in those days was standard for everyone. We all took Latin, English and math for four years. Freshmen took PE and a study period, though it was possible to take a semester of typing instead of study period. Mr. Tonge, also the 130s basketball coach, taught us to type on the old-fashioned standard machines.

At the end of our first year, those of us who had

done well academically were put together in 2A or 2B, and Attic Greek was added to our classes. This was not a choice. About 32 of us who had taken two years of Greek *did* choose to take third year Greek from the same teacher. This and typing (instead of study period) were the only electives during the four years.

The science class taken by all freshmen was General Science. As juniors, we took chemistry, and as seniors, physics. No course in biology was ever given. At the same time, no modern language was offered. Some of our classmates could speak Italian, but because of the war and the government posters saying, "don't speak the enemy's language," they didn't advertise this ability. I'm sorry that we didn't get a chance to learn another language at an early age.

Memorization and Translation

Our ability to memorize was valued and stimulated by having to memorize all of the vocabulary words in Latin and Greek together with the various changes in declensions, conjugations and tenses. Our English teachers also frequently had us memorize a daily stanza or two of poetry. You would be called on in class to start or continue the poem. One of the poems assigned by Mr. Willis Egan, SJ (whose less handsome brother was in the movies), was "Mia Carlotta." It was written in Italian-English dialect, but perhaps to avoid hurting the feelings of some of our classmates, it was typically recited very prosaically. But then Mr. Egan called on Aldo Bozzini. Aldo, who later starred in our senior class production of *Henry IV* and went on to direct plays at Holy Names College, stood up and with voice and gesture gave a very dramatic presentation of the poem. He had set a new standard, and from then on everyone followed his example.

One day during our senior year Mr. William Richardson, SJ, our American History teacher, announced that we were going to memorize the names of all the presidents in order. The class emitted a loud groan. He replied, "It's easy. It's like a speech from Shakespeare." Then in a rhythm and using some names as verbs, he had us recite with him:

"It's two –four –two.
Washington Adams
Jefferson Madison Monroe Adams
Jackson VanBuren
Harrison Tyler *Polk* Taylor
Fillmore *Pierce* Buchanan
Oh! Lincoln to Johnson *Grant* Hayes
Garfield Arthur, on to Cleveland,
Harrison, Cleveland
McKinley Roosevelt Taft Wilson
tell him not to be so
Harding on Coolidge
For Hoover, Roosevelt and King Harry." (Harry Truman was then president.)

In 15 minutes everyone in the class knew the presidents in order.

On another day in our senior year, Mr. Thomas Flynn, SJ, our Greek teacher, assigned in class a short passage for translation. He then collected the papers. The following day he had students write certain chosen translations on the board. We then voted for the best translation. When one was chosen, he asked the author to stand. No one did. He asked again that the author should not be bashful — that he should stand. Again, no one did. Then he said, "Maybe the author is standing." He, of course, was the only one standing; it was his translation.

The Faculty

The faculty in 1943 was made up of some Jesuit priests, a large number of young Jesuit scholastics, and a few laymen. The principal was Father James King, SJ, a mild-mannered man, probably a little under 6 feet, who spoke with a slight lisp. He was, however, definitely in charge. On one occasion when I happened to be standing in the main corridor, I heard him speak to a member of the senior class, a student who was a football player and oarsman who stood a good 6 feet, 4 inches. Fr. King looked up at him and said, "child," and then reprimanded him for some transgression. With that one word, I felt he had cut that boy off at the knees. When Fr. King was reassigned during our junior year, a farewell tribute in Greek, written by our teacher, Mr. Thomas Flynn, SJ, was delivered by Jim Fitzpatrick.

Lay faculty members included Mr. Bernie Murphy and Mr. Bernard Wehner, both long-time and excellent math teachers; Mr. Michael McNamara, an elderly teacher who was rumored to have been wounded in the Boer War; and Mr. "Red" Vacarro, Mr. Alex Schwartz and Mr. Walt Tonge, all of whom both taught classes and coached. After the Second World War ended, the school hired a great English teacher, Mr. Warren White, and a physics teacher, Mr. Ward. As seniors in 4A, we thought that Mr. Robert Ward was barely a page or two ahead of us in physics and sent a delegation to the principal, Fr. Ralph Tichenor, SJ, asking that we get Fr. Raymond Buckley, SJ, a long-time physics teacher, instead. He was not at all sympathetic to our plea and essentially told us that he made those decisions, period.

On another occasion the Class of '47 made Fr. Tichenor very angry. As seniors, we made a closed three-day retreat at El Retiro in Los Altos. Nearing the school on the return bus, someone began singing, "Onward Christian Soldiers," and this continued as we started to climb the school steps. Fr. Tichenor came out of the front door, shouted for us to be silent, and threatened to expel anyone who sang or spoke on the way back to our classrooms.

The Jesuit faculty consisted of both priests and scholastics. Fr. William O'Farrell, SJ, the Prefect of Discipline, was known to the students as "Wild Bill." He prowled the corridors reputedly on crepe-soled shoes, and if he caught you out of class, you were sure to end up in JUG. Also among the Jesuits was Fr. Charles McKee, SJ, who taught religion, a short, stocky man who was said to have been a boxer in his youth, who was also the guardian of the front door at noontime. It was the senior privilege to be allowed to leave the building during the lunch break, but you had to pass Fr. McKee, who stood at the front door checking senior IDs. He took no guff from anyone and made all decisions about your leaving. When we did leave at noontime, we often went a few blocks to Rossi Playground to play catch or talk.

Smoking was also strictly forbidden, and if caught doing it, a student would be expelled. Nonetheless, it was reported that at the market across Stanyan you could buy a single cigarette for 5 cents. A pack at that time was about 20 cents. It was, however, a "do as I say, not as I do" rule. Any student who went to the teachers' lounge to speak to a teacher during recess or lunch time would, when the door was opened, be greeted by a huge cloud of smoke.

Another priest who taught religion was Fr. Charles Largan, SJ. He had a hearing problem and wore a hearing aid, a box about two inches square, on his lapel. Sometimes our class would make a low humming sound, and he would start to adjust the controls. A similar reaction followed when a student who had been called on would stand and silently mouth his answer. Several years later, a surgical operation was able to cure the cause of his deafness and he was able to discard the hearing aid.

The Jesuit scholastics were mostly about 8–10 years older than the students. Most of them had themselves gone to SI and were familiar with the school's rules and customs. They taught various subjects, and while some were excellent teachers, others were not. They were, however, devoted to the school and the students, and, in addition to teaching, took on many other jobs. They served as athletic coaches and as moderators of the Sanctuary Society, Sodality, the debating societies and the *Red and Blue* school newspaper. They also coached participants in the Freshman Elocution and Sophomore Oratorical Contests. Some would go with small groups of students to Mill Valley, from where we would hike to Muir Woods or Muir Beach.

At least twice on Holy Thursday, after the Blessed Sacrament had been moved to the Altar of Repose, Mr. Vince McGinty, SJ, led a group of us from St. Ignatius Church across the street to the Carmelite Chapel and then on foot to visit the Altars of Repose at several other churches, a total walk of perhaps 4 or 5 miles.

Mr. McGinty was also the moderator of the *Red and Blue*, the school newspaper. Under editor John Jay O'Connor III, assisted by John Motheral, Watt Clinch, Jim Fitzpatrick and several others, the paper came out once a month. As business manager, I tried to get ads from various stores at $1 per column inch. Roos Bros., Ashley McMullin Undertakers and a barber shop on Grove Street took out an occasional ad. We took the typed stories to Flores Press in the Bayview, got the galley proofs and corrected them, and then returned them to the printer.

Honors

With every report card period the school gave ribbons for first and second honors. If your average was between 85 and 92, you would receive a red ribbon for second honors. An overall average above that earned a blue ribbon for first honors. Names of the winners were announced over the loudspeaker system, and the students who were called went to the principal's office to receive their ribbon.

The week of review work before exams was called "repetitions." If a student kept an "A" average all through the second semester and through repetitions, he could, except for his senior year, be excused from the final exam in June. If you got all "exemptions" in June, you got out of school a week early and got a head start on finding a summer job.

Ed Caldwell, Herb Haskins and Merlin L. (Bud) Henry, all Class of 1950, walking along Market Street in 1947.

In due time, we became aware of the many extra-curricular activities in which we could partici-pate. One of these was the Sanctuary Society (the "Sanc") whose members served Mass at Saint Ignatius Church. The Jesuit scholastics served the 5:30 and 6 a.m. Masses, and for about one week out of every month, each altar boy was assigned to serve a 6:30 or 7 a.m. mass daily at one of the side altars or at the do-mestic chapel in the Jesuit Residence. At about 8 a.m. each day, a breakfast was served behind the residence. Anyone who went to communion had fasted since midnight and was hungry.

Under the main altar was a large room with chairs and a pool table. Here the members of the Sanc could read or play pool or billiards between Masses and be-fore school. Some became real "pool sharks." At the end of the school year there were prizes given to the Sanc members who had served most often. The used basketballs from the intramural games were given to us. You got your pick; those who served most chose first and got the best balls. Bill Healy was often a win-ner.

On each First Friday, the entire student body at-tended the 8 a.m. Mass, which was frequently a *missa cantata* and some of us, directed by Mr. Leo Havorka, sang the Gloria, Credo, Kyrie and responses. After Mass there was time to go for a quick breakfast; Jea-nette's Donut Shop on Geary near 16th was a popular spot for that.

Fr. Alex Cody, SJ, directed the Junior Sodality. At some point, Fr. Cody spoke with each of us about becoming a Jesuit and several of our class did enter the Society. It was custom that on March 19th, St. Joseph's Day, the city officials, mayor, supervisors, fire

and police chiefs and so on would go to St. Anne's Home on Lake Street and serve as waiters for the el-derly residents. Many were long-time San Franciscans who were delighted by this. Fr. Cody brought a group of boys from the Sodality to wash dishes for the day. At Christmas he had a group of Sodalists prepare a short play and some songs which were performed at Notre Dame School on Dolores Street for the girls who were from foreign countries and wouldn't be re-turning home for the holidays.

The school also had three debating societies: Soph-omores belonged to the Congress, juniors to the House, and seniors to the Senate. Each group had a Jesuit scholastic as a moderator, and we participated in inter- and intra-school debates. In the spring, a team from the House debated a team from the Senate in the Gold Medal Debate. One reason to join the debating societies was to be able to attend the House-Senate Dance.

Although various parishes sponsored dances for any high school student, at SI you couldn't attend a school dance until your junior year. The House and Senate held a dance in the fall for members only. There was also the Junior Prom to which juniors or seniors could go, and the Senior Exclusive. These dances were all held at either the school auditorium or the USF au-ditorium and a bid cost about $3 or $4. The commit-tee hired a band, usually made up of college students, for the evening, and the boys came in tuxedos rented from Selix or Uptown Clothiers for about $5. Mr. Murphy stood at the door to enforce the "no corsage" rule. If a boy bought his date a corsage, she was asked to leave it at the door. This prevented competition and saved each student at least $4 or $5. After the dance, we often drove to Mel's Drive-In on Geary for a milk-shake or root beer float before taking our dates home.

Ken Innes was one of the people who pushed to

bring back the yearbook in 1946. His father took the individual pictures of the students.

ROTC

During our second and third years, we were required to take ROTC. We were under the command of Capt. Harold Hamilton, whom we called "Cosmo." The origin of the nickname was his frequent threat that if we misbehaved, he would have us there on Saturday cleaning cosmoline, a thick and tenacious grease, from the M1 rifles. On Wednesdays, the entire ROTC marched in formation. You were supposed to wear your uniforms to and from school, but some students found this onerous, and like Bob Matson, crammed their uniforms into their lockers. The wrinkled uniform then had a "locker press."

At the south end of the field were some telephone poles topped by a transverse piece of lumber from which hung four ropes each about 2-inches thick. As part of our R.OTC training, we had to climb these ropes. We handled real rifles but never fired them. The school's rifle team, which shot .22s, practiced in a range in the school basement.

Athletics

Although only the freshman class at SI took physical education — and this was a mild exercise class because there was no gym and no facilities to shower — there were many opportunities to participate in athletic activities. The intramural program went on all year, but as the courts were outdoors, rain cancelled many games.

On the asphalt-covered yard on the northeast corner of the campus there was a daily noontime soft-

ball game. Homeruns were made when the balls went over the fence, and the players were often indebted to passersby who threw the balls back onto the field. The noon hours were also filled with basketball games, and each year there was a competition for which every registry class fielded a team. The games, played in the center court behind the school building, were well attended and hotly contested. A registry class that happened to have a couple of the stars of the thirties or varsity teams usually did very well and would often emerge as the winner.

Both SI and Sacred Heart were members of the AAA, the Academic Athletic Association. Varsity football games were played at Kezar Stadium and sometimes on the fields of Washington or Balboa High Schools. St. Mary's, USF and Santa Clara also played at Kezar, but there were no professional teams at that

Students playing basketball at the Stanyan Street campus in 1949.

time. I still remember our game against Sacred Heart that opened the season in 1945. The grass at Kezar, especially compared to the field at SI (now Negoesco Field), was so soft and lush that there was little incentive to get up after

The ROTC armory in the 1940s.

Opposite page: Members of the ROTC.

having fallen or having been knocked down. That was the first game of the season in which SI won its first AAA football championship.

Mr. "Red" Vacarro coached the "thirties," the freshman-sophomore team, also known as the "goof squad." The varsity had been coached by Mr. Alex Schwartz until he left for the public school system. Under Mr. John Golden, the varsity won SI's first city football championship in 1945.

The school supplied shoulder and hip pads as well as pants and jerseys. There were perhaps 25 or 30 helmets

for the team. Each player had to find one that fit him, and if you were sent in as a substitute, you either had to find a suitable one or use the one from the player you were replacing. We supplied our own socks, cleats, mouth guards and supporters.

The basketball teams — thirties and varsity — practiced at the Page Street Gym, now the San Francisco Boys and Girls Club. At the time, it was a barn-like building with few amenities. The lightweight teams practiced outside in the schoolyard.

In an effort to equalize competition, basketball players were divided into teams by "exponents." So many exponents were given for age, height and weight. Basketball teams played as the 100s, the 110s, the 120s and the 130s. If a player wanted to make the 130s and was close to the limit, though he couldn't control his age or height, he might, as some did, fast, dehydrate himself or even take laxatives for a short period before the weigh-ins.

Basketball games were played at Kezar Pavilion on Stanyan Street near the stadium. Before big games it was not unusual for a large number of cheering students to march down Stanyan from SI to Kezar. In fact, before basketball and football games, rallies were held at school. Fr. Giambastiani, who was from Italy and taught at USF, was sometimes invited to perform. He would stand in his cassock on the platform that was at the top of the steps above the basketball courts, jut out his chin and have the whole student body standing in the courts below raising their fists in the air, shouting, "Duce! Duce! Duce!" Then he'd quiet the crowd, pretend to give a speech in Italian, pause, and then the students would again shout, "Duce! Duce! Duce!" and this would go on for 10 or 15 minutes. Another frequent speaker was Donald Gordon '43, a member of the U.S. Marines and a former football player at SI. The band, under Mr. Orlando Giosi, played at some rallies and most games, regaling us with renditions of the fight song.

The swim team practiced at a pool in the basement of the YMI Building on Oak Street.

Everything Else

Each year the student body put on a school play under the direction of Mr. James Gill. A large professional-looking glossy program was put out for the play, and students sold ads for the programs. The student raising the most money got a prize. Bob Mitchell, son of the Chief of Police, was a frequent winner. The money from the ads was to help build a gym, but our class had been out of school for a number of years before a gym was finally built.

Our parents came to school events such as the Elocution and Oratorical Contests and the school play; they also came if invited to the principal's office to discuss a son's problems. Mothers of boys at SI and USF also formed the Loyola Guild, and although they held an occasional tea, their main purpose was to raise funds for scholarships. They held an annual rummage sale, first at Polk Hall at Civic Center, and later at the Hall of Flowers. When my mother discovered the source of my scholarship money, she joined the Guild and worked in the furniture section of the sale for the next 40 years.

When we were juniors Mr. McGinty asked several of us to help move furniture and other large items for the sale. Our efforts were rewarded; the Guild had him take us to lunch at the Golden Pheasant and then to see *The Student Prince* at the Curran. This wasn't my first visit to a stage play. During freshman year, Mr. Felton O'Toole SJ, our English teacher, suggested that for extra credit we go to the Geary Theatre to see *The Merchant of Venice*. While sitting in the upper balcony, I recognized several

other SI freshmen nearby also watching John Carradine play the merchant.

Our junior class (3A) also decided to have a picnic at Searsville Lake near Stanford. Each of us put in $3 or $4. The war was over, and someone whose father had connections to a meat market bought T-bone steaks, and someone else bought spaghetti. A couple of us who had driver's licenses went down to a truck rental place on the corner of 9th and Market Streets and arranged to rent a stakebed truck. We invited our registry teacher, Mr. Maurice Belval, SJ, and our chemistry teacher, Mr. Frank Koenig, SJ, to go along.

On the appointed Saturday, we got the truck, drove to SI to pick up the Jesuits and our classmates and drove to the lake, where we swam or played ball and stuffed ourselves, finally coming home in the late afternoon. No one worried about written permission, insurance or liability then. We never knew if the school administration was aware of the picnic or whether the scholastics told anyone.

Graduation

There was no college counseling of any type at that time. Some fellows who wanted to be engineers went to Santa Clara; some from the East Bay enrolled at St. Mary's; a half a dozen went to Cal or Stanford; and the rest of us moved up the hill to USF.

Our graduation ceremony was held

Two students in a trundle seat. Courtesy of Dick Raffetto '44.

Opposite page: Prom night.

twice. In the morning a ceremony was held at St. Ignatius Church, and in the afternoon, as part of a ceremony for all Catholic High Schools, we were given our diplomas by the bishop.

I think we were fortunate to have been at SI when we were. The friendships we formed with our teachers and with each other have lasted for over half a century and are still ongoing.

Chalk-Dust Memories: The 1940s

In 1943, I was in my second year at SI. We had Greek class first period each morning. Mr. Joseph Geary, SJ, then a scholastic, was our instructor.

One Monday morning he came to class a bit early and announced: "No matter what I say, do not turn in any homework for the rest of the week."

He left the room abruptly and returned a short time later.

On Thursday morning of that week, he opened the class with by announcing, "I do not know what is going on here, but no one has turned in any homework so far this week." He then turned to Martin Woods, one of the best Greek students in the class, and asked him if he knew what had happened.

Martin said: "Mr. Geary, on Monday you told us not to turn in any homework this week."

With a huge smile on his face, Mr. Geary said, "Oh no! My twin brother was here this past weekend and got to class before I did." His identical twin brother, John, was a scholastic at Bellarmine down the Peninsula.

— *Joe Stevenot '46*

• • •

In 1946, my freshman religion teacher was Fr. Charles Largan, SJ. Fr. Largan had a hearing problem and wore an old-fashioned hearing aid of that time which consisted of an earpiece with a wire band across the top of the head, much like a hands-free cell phone. At the end of the band opposite the earpiece a cord ran under one's shirt, or cassock in the case of Father, and ended in a microphone-amplifier, clipped on the shirt front. Occasionally a fly would buzz around Fr. Largan's chest near the microphone, and he would wave his hand around his ear attempting to swat the fly. Hilarity ensured.

Each classroom had a two-way communications system to the school office, which consisted of a black box hung up high on the wall. During each period, a voice would ask, "Attendance, please," and the teacher was expected to reply with the names of absent students. Of course, Fr. Largan couldn't hear well enough, so some wise guy would point up at the box, even though no one had asked for attendance, and Father would dutifully report the absences. And, as you might guess, when the office did ask for attendance, no one would call Father's attention to the request, which would drive the office batty.

As one might imagine, a few of us matured to the point that these sophomoric (or is it freshmanic) actions were later regretted. At a reception for the Class of 1950 not too many years ago, who should show up but Fr.

The 1944 varsity baseball team.

English, a few blocks away from USF. The evening before her funeral Mass, the rosary was said for my mother. I was totally taken by surprise when Jesuits started appearing for the rosary. I didn't even know that most of them knew that my mother had died. My guess is that there were well over 60 Jesuits who said the rosary with us for my mother. A number of those Jesuits barely knew me. I shall never forget the spiritual support that they gave my father and me.

—*Donlan F. Jones '48*

• • •

During Oakie Days, we would break the dress code by wearing old clothes and gather in the field at lunchtime to show how we were dressed down. The school grew concerned about our unofficial practice and clamped down on us, threatening to send home anyone who didn't dress properly.

When it was time to order our class rings, we noticed the design had changed. The new design made it look like a girls' school ring instead of the design we were used to. A group got together and found someone to redesign the ring and take orders, which the administration did not appreciate.

— *Tom Bertken '50*

• • •

At the old SI on Stanyan Street, we had to walk up 15 stairs to reach the entrance to the school. From this vantage, you could see into one of the new homes across the street. Inside was a young lady who took her shower every morning at 7:30 a.m. Ordinarily, there would be no one at school that early, and she was in the habit of undressing in front of the curtainless window, showering and then drying off. Mysteriously, students began arriving at school at 7:30 each morning. Mrs. Harrington, the

Largan, and thanks to the wonders of modern science, he had undergone an operation that restored his hearing. With a few of us gathered around him, Father told us, "I remember you guys and all the tricks you used to play on me." But he said it with such good grace and a twinkle in his eye that we knew we were forgiven.

— *I.P. "Bunk" Sicotte, Jr. '50*

• • •

During my freshman and sophomore years at SI, I had a part-time job of running the telephone switchboard at USF. As a result, I got to know not only all the Jesuits who were associated with St. Ignatius High School, but also, to some degree, most all the Jesuits associated with both St. Ignatius Church and USF.

In September 1946, my mother died suddenly. My father had her body prepared for burial at Carew and

principal's secretary, walked up the stairs one morning, looked at us, looked across the street, and said, "Haven't you boys ever seen a naked lady before?" How could we answer that? If we had said, "No," it would show that we were not men of the world. After hearing only total silence, she walked inside. Fr. Gerald Leahy, SJ, the prefect of discipline, wrote a note to our neighbor suggesting she buy shades. All of a sudden, the show stopped.

— *Jack Riordan '44*

• • •

Mr. Carlin was my favorite teacher. In his first year teaching at SI as a scholastic, we used to like to fool around with him. We named him Nilrac — that's Carlin spelled backwards — and everywhere we went, we wrote "Nilrac was here" on the blackboard. He took it in good humor.

Fr. Raymond Buckley, who taught chemistry and physics, stood about 5 feet tall. We respected him because he was really tough. My mother was active in the school in those days, and she had an ulcer as did Fr. Buckley. They would speak to each other about home remedies. After class one day he asked me, "How's your mother's stomach today?" I responded, "That's pretty personal, Father!"

In those days, we had corporal punishment. If any trouble occurred between students or between a teacher and a student, the ROTC sergeant would say, "I'll see you in the armory at 3 p.m., and we'll settle it with gloves on." Whatever disputes we had, we used our fists. Most of the time, the teachers won, but once in awhile, one of the big Irish football players would win.

— *Dick Raffetto '44*

• • •

No one had an automobile in those days. We all

had rationing stamps during the war and people used to trade gas for sugar and meat. We took streetcar 31 to school, which went by Turk and Stanyan. The motorman drove the streetcar and the conductor stood in back and collected fares. If the streetcar trolley came off, the conductor got off, put it back on the wire, got in and rang two bells. One time, in front of SI, someone pulled the trolley off, and the conductor got out. As soon as he hit the wire, someone rang two dings, and the driver went off, leaving the conductor behind.

— *Jack Goodwin '49*

• • •

We used to have ROTC every Wednesday where we marched in a parade in uniform, which included a white shirt and black tie. One day, we were told we weren't going to have a parade but physical exercise instead. They

A 1944 debate.

said, "Everybody, take off your coat." Here is this vast sea of white shirts, with the exception of one guy. He had taken a white shirt, cut out the collar portion that was visible, and wore it with tie under his uniform coat. When he took off his coat, he exposed a t-shirt with large blue and white stripes. He stood out like a sore thumb.

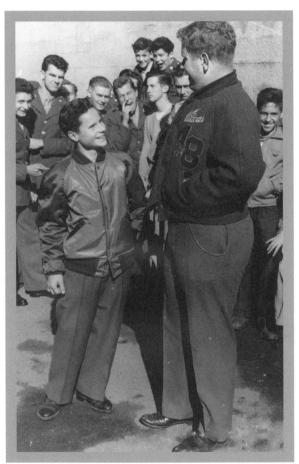

One day, I was thrown out of class for spelling a word right. Fr. Joseph Dondero, SJ, taught sophomore English. He asked the class how to spell "acknowledgment." He went around the class, and when several students spelled it correctly, he said, "That's not right." I quietly borrowed a dictionary from the guy next to me, raised my hand and told him respectfully that the word had been spelled correctly. He threw me out of class and sent me to the principal's office. I told Fr. James King, SJ, that I was thrown out of class for spelling a word right. I didn't want that class to go through life not knowing how to spell that word. [Editor's note: The *Miriam Webster Dictionary* shows two alternative spellings for the word "acknowledgment," either of which is correct.]

— *Claude Boyd '45*

• • •

I really had a strong desire, even as a student at St. Cecilia's, to go to SI. I knew I would know a lot of fellows there, and they helped me when I ran for student body president. One day, after I had made an announcement regarding class pictures, Fr. King said, "Mr. Molkenbuhr, pitchers are what you put water in. Pictures are portraits."

I played football for one year under coach Red Vaccaro. He was a driver. Boy, you had better be pushing all the time. One time he went out on the field, and he saw a guy laying on the ground. He gave him a kick and told him, "You're not hurt. Get up." He got up! Alex Schwarz took over coaching the next year in 1942. He was an all-coast end for USF, first string all conference there. He sure inspired us. He was clean cut and a real gentleman.

My classmates and I talked about what service we were going to enlist in after we finished school. The four years at SI were the best I had. Even though I had to transfer three times on Muni to go there, it was worth it. My mentor was a scholastic, Cornelius "Con" McCarthy. He encouraged me to run for president of the student body, telling me, "Val, you can do it." SI had other really fine Jesuits, holy men, such as Fr. Cody.

I took ROTC from Sgt. Storti, and that helped me when I joined the Marines. He was a short guy who gave us instructions in weapons and drilling. I was a battalion commander, and my good friend Jack Schimelpfenig '43 was in charge of the whole ROTC unit.

— *Val Molkenbuhr '43*

• • •

One of our history tests was administered by our ROTC sergeant. Before he came in, someone wrote out a cheat sheet on the blackboard all in Greek. When the sergeant started to erase the board, we told him he couldn't because our Greek test was next. He didn't have a clue what was going on. We all did well ... too well. The priests knew we had cheated but didn't know how. They asked the sergeant how he could let an entire class cheat. As I recall, we all had to retake the test.

Later that year, the day before Christmas vacation in 1949, I found myself in Fr. "Skipper" Largan's religion class. Someone brought to class one of the very first portable radios, about half the size of a toaster. Shortly after the opening bell, the strains of Christmas carols filled the room. Father was somewhat deaf but heard the music. He just could not identify the origin. He was aided in this by our pointing to the public address system. He closed his book and told us that as long as the office was going to pipe in music, we might as well enjoy it. Unfortunately, a commercial broke in.

At the second commercial, Father got up and left the room, and someone placed the radio on a windowsill. The class then quieted, and we looked very busy. Father returned, said nothing, just opened his book and resumed class with perfect aplomb. The very next class, Fr. Pierre Jacobs, SJ, picked off the culprit immediately as he walked into chemistry. But that is another story.

— Bill Kennedy '50

• • •

The Jesuit Educational Association conducted an evaluation of SI between March 4 and 8 of 1946 and submitted the following in its report:

"One of the most notable things about the high school this year is the lack of tension both among the students and among the faculty. As a result the pupils are apparently working harder with better results and the faculty is much more content than it was last year.... At the same time St. Ignatius' high scholastic standing is being maintained. Graduates entering the University of California last year obtained the highest rank of all those entering from private schools. Two students won awards in the Westinghouse Science Search Tests. In other national and local contests the representatives of the school have given a most satisfactory account of themselves."

The report did offer this mixed evaluation of one teacher: "Mr. ——— has matured considerably during the past three years, but he is apparently unable to adapt himself to the mentality of first year high school students. I doubt that he has any enthusiasm for the subject, and certainly has not communicated any to his pupils; rather, he dampens their enthusiasm by refusing to answer questions."

As to discipline, the report faulted SI for its lack of proper playground facilities: "As a consequence pupils are allowed to come into the school building before classes begin in the morning and to remain in it during the two recess periods. The result is bedlam in the corridors. I hate to think of what it is going to be like if an additional 300 freshman are admitted next year!"

The report also noted the difficulty teachers had "settling the boys down when they have entered the classroom. The boys are supposed to be quiet when they enter the classroom, but that is an almost impossible regulation to enforce ... after shoving one another around in the corridors."

The report also mentioned the contents of one bulletin board, which "for some unknown reason contains the picture of some woman swimming champion!"

Opposite page: Norbert Korte '48, who later became a Jesuit brother, was known as "Red." As head of the IRC (Ignatian Rally Committee), he was SI's best "pepper-pot." He was a four-year Sodalist, a House debator and an ROTC officer.

IX. SUCCESS & DISCONTENT (1950 ~ 1959)

The decade of the 1950s saw a period of stability at both SI and in the nation. Fr. William Finnegan, SJ, took over from Fr. Ralph Tichenor, SJ, as principal, and under his five-year tenure the school finally built its gymnasium. He was succeeded in 1955 by Fr. Robert Leonard, SJ, who had served the school as vice principal for four years.

Another institutional change occurred at SI when the high school and USF formally parted ways by the end of the decade, incorporating as separate institutions. Despite the new gymnasium, administrators felt pressure to move — pressure from USF, which wanted the Stanyan Street structure for its own plans to expand, and pressure from a growing student body eager for a modern campus.

The decade was marked by a string of athletic victories that made SI the athletic powerhouse of the city. The baseball team brought home league crowns in 1954, 1958 and 1959; the basketball team won the league in 1951 and then followed with league and Tournament of Champion wins in 1954 and 1955 (with another league victory in 1956); the swimmers won the AAA in 1953, 1958 and 1959; the golf team dominated the AAA with league victories in 1951, 1952 and 1957–59; and the football team triumphed

SI & USF in 1940.

in 1956, 1958 and 1959. Coaches such as Jim Keating, Rene Herrerias and Pat Malley were the heroes of the day.

SI strove to be an island of tranquility in this decade, as world events, such as the Korean War and the Communist witch-hunts, led by Senator Joseph McCarthy, swirled outside the school's walls. However, many young people in this decade felt a growing unease with the established institutions, and that unease surfaced at SI from time to time.

Academics

The Separation of the Schools

Fr. Edward B. Rooney, SJ, the Jesuit Education Association director who inspected SI in 1938, made a return inspection in 1950. His report praised SI as "unquestionably one of the outstanding Jesuit high schools in the United States … for many years now, it has been building up a fine reputation in the local community and it continues to merit and to enjoy this reputation."[1] Rooney was pleased that the school was willing to dismiss students whose grades did not measure up, but criticized the tendency of stu-

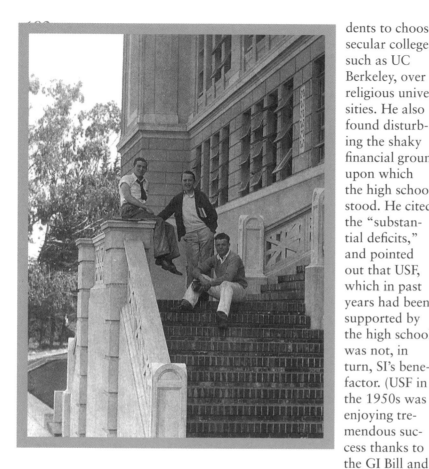

dents to choose secular colleges, such as UC Berkeley, over religious universities. He also found disturbing the shaky financial ground upon which the high school stood. He cited the "substantial deficits," and pointed out that USF, which in past years had been supported by the high school, was not, in turn, SI's benefactor. (USF in the 1950s was enjoying tremendous success thanks to the GI Bill and veterans returning to their studies.)

Rooney recommended that the school adopt and follow annual budgets and raise tuition. He warned that if USF and SI were ever to separate, the high school would be in financial straits. The following summer, SI Treasurer Edward Zeman, SJ, informed parents that the school would raise tuition to $135 per year.

The school also began taking seriously the no-tion of separation from USF, something that had been initially discussed at the turn of the century. As USF's and SI's missions became more specifically focused, this split seemed a natural thing. In fact, the two other province schools that had started as combination college-high schools — Loyola and Santa Clara — both had broken off their preparatory divisions years previous, Bellarmine in 1925 and Loyola High School in 1929. The reasons for those separations were (as Gerald McKevitt, SJ, wrote about the split between Bellarmine and SCU) "as numerous as they were obvious." In his history of SCU, McKevitt noted that "as late as 1915 there were 350 colleges and universities in the United States that still retained 'prep' schools, but such arrangements were becoming increasingly anachronistic." After Santa Clara adopted the title of "university," the school's faculty resented "the intolerable anomaly of a university frequented by boys in knickerbockers." While that tension was lessened in San Francisco by the minor geographic separation between USF and SI, faculty and administrators at both schools saw the handwriting on the wall.[2]

As early as 1950, the SI and USF Jesuits were seriously looking at sites for the relocation of the high school. A memorandum dated November 13, 1950, noted two parcels: a 12-acre Laurel Hill site (now the Laurel Village Shopping Center), costing $450,000, and the 2-acre Masonic Avenue car-barn property, costing $75,000 on which the school considered building a gymnasium and playfield. This second site would allow the SI Jesuits to separate from the USF community "by the erection of a faculty building on the present High School site."[3]

In 1955, the Jesuits of both schools, who were still living as one community in Welch Hall, took the first step toward canonical separation when they received a letter dated August 21, 1955, "to Jesuit superiors from Fr. Vincent McCormick, SJ, American Assistant to Fr. General John B. Janssens, in which he conveyed the latter's decision that the two communities should eventually be so separated."[4]

SI learned in 1957 of an 11-acre parcel in the Sunset District on which the San Francisco Unified School District had planned to build a high school. When the district abandoned its plans, the Jesuits at SI expressed interest in the rolling sand dunes between 37th and 38th Avenues and Pacheco and Riviera Streets. USF President John F.X. Connolly, SJ, approached Mayor George Christopher for help securing the property for SI. On August 11, 1958, Mayor Christopher wrote to Joseph A. Moore, president of the SFUSD Board of Education, encouraging the sale of the "surplus land" to SI and adding that "to this moment, no use has been found for this site." He also warned that San Francisco was in danger of losing SI to another city "unless we are able to cooperate with the University of San Francisco in securing a new location for this time honored school." If that were to happen, he added, "the burden of taking care of its student body may fall on the shoulders of San Francisco taxpayers."[5]

While SI would not purchase that land until 1964 (at a price of $2 million), the stage had been set for the school's move to its sixth site. In the meantime, USF and SI prepared for the eventual move by formally separating on July 1, 1959, as distinct corporations and Jesuit communities after receiving permission from the Father General, thus ending a 104-year relationship between high school and college. Fr. Patrick J. Carroll, SJ '31, became president of St. Ignatius High School and rector of the 40-member SI Jesuit community. (The dual role of rector-president continued until 1985 when the duties were separated

and Fr. Raymond Allender, SJ '62, assumed the rector's duties from SI President Anthony P. Sauer, SJ.) Fr. Carroll, who had taught at SI from 1938 to 1941, served as assistant to the provincial prior to this appointment.[6]

Not every Jesuit was happy to see the two schools part ways. Br. Daniel Peterson, SJ, librarian at SI between 1975 and 2000 and later province archivist, was a student at USF in 1959 during the separation. He recalls his teacher, Fr. Ray Feely, SJ, coming into the classroom, shaking his head and complaining. "They took our preparatory department away from us," he told the class. "He was in a foul mood all day. He thought it was a terrible decision, but I suspect his was a minority opinion."

Fr. George Dennis, SJ, teaches Latin in 1951 to students eager to learn.

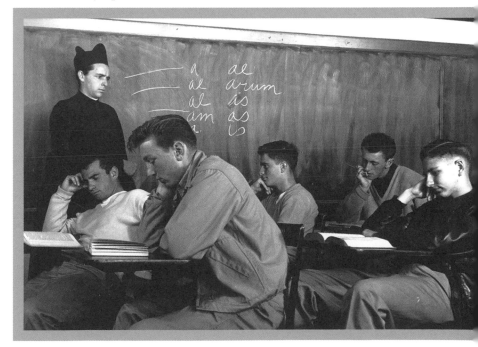

The Preparatory Department
of the University of San Francisco

For many years, SI published a *Catalogue* (also referred to as the *Prospectus*, though it bore no official name), offering a listing of the school's philosophy, organizational structure for the following year and the awards given and student names from the previous year. In July 1951, the document still listed St. Ignatius High School as the "Preparatory Department of the University of San Francisco, Founded October 1855, Conducted by the Jesuit Fathers."

As for its "Educational Aims," the school offered this in the way of a mission statement:

"To mold manhood, to develop the entire man, mind and heart, body and soul; to form as well as to inform;

"To train the mind to analyze rather than memorize, so that it may distinguish truth from error; to strengthen the will that it may have the grit to practice virtue and reject vice; to cultivate the heart that it may love the worthwhile things;

"To instill culture; to stimulate ambition; to disdain mediocrity and develop leadership; to train citizens for times and eternity;

"To maintain high academic standards; to encourage research; to present the technical phases of various fields of knowledge, yet to integrate and make vital education; to present the current and complex problems of modern life, yet assisting youth to solve these problems with principles as eternal as the God that promulgated them — the eternally vital principles of truth and justice;

"To instill into youth the neglected doctrine that morality must govern economics and politics, and that modern ills cannot be cured merely by shifting economic systems and changing political structures: pointing out that every system must be administered by men over men, and that selfishness, greed, dishonesty and lust for power are moral evils which cannot be eliminated by civil legislation but only by moral restraint;

"To rivet to the minds of youth the truth that all hatreds, whether of class or race or creed or foreign nations, rot civilization, and that, irrespective of one's belief, the sole and ultimate solution of economic, political and social ills was epitomized by Him Who said: 'Thou shalt love thy Lord thy God with thy whole heart and thy whole soul and with thy whole mind; — thou shalt love thy neighbor as thyself.'"

That mission statement was at once an ideal and a reality — something evidenced by students and teachers, though certainly not at all times. To help guide the young men toward this goal, the *Prospectus* included sage advice in a section entitled "Methods of Study," listing these six steps:

1. Have a fixed period of study each day....
2. Study in a quiet, well-lighted room.... You cannot concentrate in the face of distractions that come from the blare of a radio or the conversation and laughter of other people.
3. Plan your study according to your needs....
4. Aim at understanding what you study.... Knowledge must be digested and assimilated like food before it becomes a part of you....
5. Use pencil and paper....
6. Review what you have learned. Memory is an elusive thing and sometimes plays tricks on us...."

The *Catalogue* also listed the courses offered for the 1951–52 school year as follows:

First year: religion and public speaking, arithmetic

and grammar review, Latin, English, algebra, ROTC.

Second year: religion and public speaking, Latin, English, geometry, world history, ROTC. (Students aiming for the "Honorary Classical" diploma would substitute Greek for ROTC.)

By junior year, in addition to taking the requisite religion, public speaking, Latin, English and ROTC classes (Greek for honors classes), students had the freedom to choose two of four options: physics, chemistry, algebra or U.S. history-civics.

Seniors likewise had choices to make. Everyone studied religion, public speaking, Latin and English. In addition, they could choose three from the following: U.S. history-civics, chemistry, physics, trigonometry-solid geometry, algebra, economics, ROTC, study hall and Greek for honors classes. Students could also sign up for a typing course.

These courses resembled those at Jesuit schools throughout the U.S. and still reflected the school's roots in the *Ratio Studiorum*. For this education, students paid $140 in tuition and $60 in fees in addition to books. The school advertised its policy "not to exclude any Catholic boy because of his inability to meet tuition requirements." To help meet that promise, the school offered many students financial aid including eight named scholarships established by generous patrons and organizations.

Students continued to compete for 13 academic honors and awards, much like in past decades. These included the General Excellence Award, the Sodality Award, the Sanctuary Award, the Shakespeare Award (for the "best portrayal of a piece from Shakespeare"), the Freshman Elocution Award, the Sophomore Oratorical Award, the Gentlemen's Sodality Debating Award (given to the best debater in the public debate between representatives of the senior and junior class-

es), the Fathers' Club Debating Award (given to the best debater in the public debate between representatives of the sophomore and freshman classes), the Senate Debating Plaque, the Martin Latin Award, the Washington Essay Award, the Science Award and the ROTC Awards.

Fr. Richard Spohn, SJ, in 1955. He built all of his demonstration materials himself and was famous for the meticulous planning of his lectures.

Three Greats: Fr. Spohn, Warren White & Fr. Becker
Fr. Richard Spohn, SJ

Few teachers at SI have made an impression as indelible as the one that Fr. Richard Spohn, SJ '31, made on the 5,000 students he taught between 1947 and 1979. An exacting teacher, he knew what he would be teaching on any given day during the year, and he had a cabinet filled with home-made demonstrations to make concrete the abstract notions of physics. He set off rockets, shot a miniature cannon and recreated famous experiments, inspiring many students to choose careers in science.

Bob Hunter '48, who was a student for Spohn's

second year at SI, noted that "it was tough enough taking both Latin and Greek, so no one wanted to take physics. But he was a great, great teacher who not only knew his physics well, but could teach it well. After we found out how good he was, we filled each of his classes." Hunter also marveled at how Spohn "managed to acquire enough thermodynamic, mechanical and electric equipment to make physics real for us."

Bing Quock '72, head of the Morrison Planetarium, noted that "as far as his demonstrations were concerned, he was the equivalent of Mr. Wizard. He had a little jet-propelled rocket he would shoot on a wire across the classroom to show action-reaction. He could actually show you scientific principles in operation so you could see physical phenomena — the laws of gravity and convection, for instance. You didn't have to learn about them through a book only. You could see them right before your eyes."

Quock remembered Fr. Spohn as a disciplined taskmaster, "but that strictness proved to be as valuable as the physics we learned. He even made sure we put our lab chairs back under the table a certain way. That helped me to be a critical thinker, to approach my work on a meticulous level almost to the point of fussiness. But that's necessary in science."

Laurence Yep '66 wrote about Fr. Spohn in his memoir *The Lost Garden*. "I took physics from a priest who over the years had refined his science demonstrations down to the smallest detail; and they were presented with all the flair and precision of a Broadway show. His example of air pressure was especially memorable because he would place a marshmallow into a bell jar. Slowly he would pump out the air, and the marshmallow, with less and less air pressing at its sides to help it hold its shape, would slowly begin to

swell and expand. By the time most of the air had been taken out from the bell jar, the marshmallow looked as large as a rat. Then he would let in some air; and even that slight amount of air pressure was enough to make the marshmallow collapse into a gooey mess…. However like the good showman he was, he always saved the best for the climax, ending the final class with a bang. During the last day of instruction, he would set off a miniature replica of the atom bomb. There would be a bang and a flash of light and then a pillar of white dust would shoot up toward the ceiling where it spread out into the familiar mushroom shape."

Fr. Spohn's reputation for punctuality made him a legendary figure among this students and colleagues. Fr. Raymond Allender, SJ '62, recalled that "on the last day of school in the 1970s, for instance, the dean of men would call Dick's classroom a few seconds before the final bell rang, just as he was finishing the last sentence of his last lecture. He'd ask, "Dick, have you completed your material?' and Dick would answer, 'Yes, Brother, you may now ring the bell.'" He would then shut his notebook and proclaim, "And gentlemen, that is physics." In 1976, his venerable schedule was thrown off for the first time when Fr. McCurdy made a surprise announcement declaring that the last day of class would be a holiday.

Tom Kennedy '63 recalled that Fr. Spohn "knew that he was going to be absent for a particular class, so he put that day's lecture on a tape recorder so the class would not miss a thing. The class was intently listening and taking notes, and about 20 minutes into this taped lecture, Fr. Spohn's voice boomed out, "Shut up, Brandi!" As you might have guessed, Tom Brandi was talking at this exact moment. Needless to say, both he and the class remained quiet for the rest of the period."

"Dick gave such credibility to the science department and the profession of teaching because he was such a thorough professional," added Fr. Allender. "No doubt about it. He was a dominating figure. He was Jesuit education."

Fr. Spohn made school history by having his class go coed nearly 20 years before the rest of the school. When SI moved to its Sunset District campus, it offered morning physics classes to girls from the city's Catholic high schools. "He loved teaching the girls," said Fr. Allender. "They brought out his gentle side. To him, they were his girls." Fr. Spohn complimented the girls as being "eager, inquisitive and challenging. The worst thing you could do would be to underestimate them."

He retired in 1979 when his diabetes worsened, but he continued to live at SI and helped out in classes while he trained to become a spiritual director. "That was typical of him to start a whole new field once he retired," said Fr. Allender. "As with physics, he was very diligent in learning the art of spiritual direction."

Eventually, he moved to the Jesuit retirement center in Los Gatos, though he kept in touch with former students and sent newspaper clippings to teachers at SI offering ideas for their classes. He died in January 1989, and his memorial Mass was celebrated in Orradre Chapel on the SI campus, presided over by his nephew William Spohn '62.

Warren R. White '39

Fr. Spohn wasn't the only great teacher at SI. Another favorite of many students was Warren White, who taught at the Stanyan Street campus between 1948 and 1955. He was also the originator and first moderator of *Inside SI* and the director of numerous plays. White attended USF and spent three

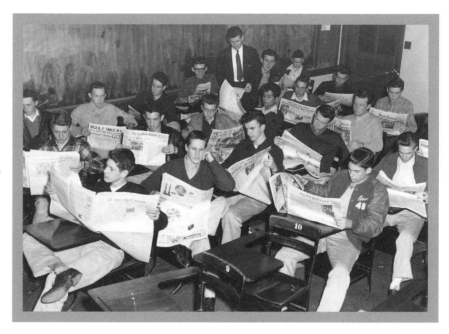

Warren White asked his journalism students to analyze the way different newspapers covered the same story. Photo courtesy of Warren White.

years in the service before returning to SI to teach. "Suddenly, my former teachers were colleagues, including Mr. McNamara, Red Vaccaro, Barney Wehner, Sgt. Storti, Edward Dermot Doyle, Fr. Joe King, SJ, Fr. Alex Cody, SJ, Fr. William O'Neil, SJ, Fr. Ray Buckley, SJ, and President Dunne. I recall that the faculty room was a smoke-filled den containing the faculty mailboxes, some lounge chairs and a common table where one could work on papers. Other than the physics and chemistry rooms, there were no dedicated rooms and the faculty had no offices. The faculty room also served as a lunchroom if you brown-bagged it, but there was a provision of coffee. In the cafeteria, we sat in an area screened off from the students, but it was not very attractive. The Jesuits repaired to their rectory on the Hilltop, and we laymen made do.

"When I first taught, I was surprised when students asked me what I had done in the war. I wondered how they knew I was a veteran. Then I realized I was wearing a lapel pin of an eagle that all veterans received and which we called a 'ruptured duck.'"

"Everyone in the English department used the same anthology — *Literature and Life* — published nationally with separate editions for public and parochial schools. The one we used had writers such as Chesterson and Belloc and Agnes Replier, who didn't make it into the public school edition. One advantage to this was that almost every high school senior in the U.S. would be familiar with at least four plays by Shakespeare, some of the sonnets, Gray's 'Elegy in a Churchyard,' Tennyson's 'Ulysses,' and T.S. Eliot's 'The Hollow Men,' for example. Student choice was honored in the assignment of book reports — at least one a semester. Students could select what they wished, subject to approval. Junior year was devoted to American literature, senior to British."

With the sudden death of James Gill in 1949 (who had directed the school's plays for 20 years), White took over the director's job. He had acted in USF's College Players under Gill's direction. "Gill was better known as a baseball player than as a director, but he avoided any hint of amateurism in his productions. What I knew was what I had learned from him, and it worked for me by and large.

"The annual play was a fund-raiser for the gymnasium and had gone from using the Little Theatre at USF to performing at the Marines Memorial Theatre on Sutter Street. It was my responsibility to select the play and cast, organize a stage crew, build the sets, get the furnishings and props, schedule rehearsals and supervise the move to Marines and back to Stanyan Street. A stipend of $500 was added to my annual pay.

"Shortly after I had replaced Gill, Fr. Joe King came to SI with his enthusiasm for glee clubs and music of all kinds. He started organizing talent shows, and they evolved into musical productions in which I began to take a part. One was called *Win Winsocki*. MGM had produced a "B" list musical set in a small Midwest college whose survival rested with the success of its football team. We ignored the book and the title of the film, but used the fight song, which went, 'You can win Winsocki if you only try,' and other stereotypical sentiments. It was a wonderful song, and it served as the basis for a pastiche of songs, dances, sketches, whatever Fr. King, the students or I could devise. The following year we topped it with a work we called *Souther Pacific*, which combined bits of Rogers and Hart with *The Caine Mutiny, Mr. Roberts*, and other ideas from Fr. King, the students or myself. These performances were at USF's Little Theatre, and it didn't occur to any of us that we should have paid royalties. I trust a statute of limitations applies.

"One year, Bing Crosby wanted to use the Marines Memorial for a broadcast, but we had the lease for the theatre. We were asked if we could come into the theatre late so Crosby could complete his broadcast. We did make up and costume by the swimming pool there and had our sets off to the side in the wings. Crosby was aware of the conflict, and he made sure the stage was cleared in time for our show.

"The Marines Memorial productions included *Yellow Jack*, a Pulitzer-winning play about the conquering of yellow fever in Cuba as a prelude to building the Panama Canal. We did comedies such as *Three Men on a Horse, Here Comes Mr. Jordan*, and *The Gentleman from Athens*. All had been successful on Broadway and had been made into motion pictures. All the female roles had to be changed into male roles.

My last shows at Marines, and I think the last time SI used the hall, was for *Billy Budd*, a man-of-war saga, which had no female parts and needed no altering.

"A Jesuit seminary in the Midwest had established a cottage industry rewriting standard plays to change female roles to male ones. There were many boys' schools and colleges, and thus a demand for scripts with all-male roles existed. The rationale, at least at SI, was that as a school activity, a school play should be open to as many students as possible. Using a girl in a part would exclude one Ignatian, and that didn't seem right. Nor did the thought of female impersonation ever suggest itself. The policy, at least in my years at SI, was never a stratagem for separating the sexes. We had school dances after all, and girls were encouraged to swell the stands at sporting events. In the next few years, Mr. Dick McCurdy, SJ (later principal at SI), having succeeded me, chose to use the more convenient stage of the Presentation Theatre on Turk Street."

Fr. John Becker

In 1958, a young Jesuit came to SI and stayed for 20 years. Fr. John Becker, SJ, was a remarkable English teacher and *Inside SI* moderator known for his propensity for punning, his highly structured curriculum that became the department standard and his manner of inspiring students. Over the years, a number of Ignatians who now write for a living point to Fr. Becker as the man who convinced them they had talent worth pursuing. *Dragonwings* author Laurence Yep '66, *Frasier* creator Peter Casey '68 and *Chronicle* political reporter John Wildermuth '69 are just three who praise Becker for giving them their start.

Fr. Becker was born in Oak Park, Illinois, and

Kevin Tobin

attended St. Philip's in Chicago and St. Monica's High School in Santa Monica before entering the Society on July 1, 1943. He earned a Master's degree in English at Loyola University and has taught high school since 1950, at Bellarmine, SI (from 1958 to 1978) and Brophy. While at SI he moderated *Inside SI* (and taught students to print four-color magazines using a press in the basement of the school), taught English and religious studies and took students to Europe each summer, buying a Volkswagon van in Germany and touring for six weeks with 10 or so students who slept on the floors of Catholic school gymnasiums. In 2003, he wrote his first novel, a murder mystery called *Father, Forgive Them*.

Fr. John Becker, SJ, at a 1965 Christmas Dance.

A Curious Encounter
with the Ladies' Auxiliary of the VFW

By Brian Hassett '59

In 1958, when Fr. John Becker came to teach English at St. Ignatius, I was a senior. The focus of Senior English was writing, a discipline with which I had mixed success. The teaching style of the new teacher would be crucial. I had never been able to write well under a formulaic, write-by-the-numbers approach, but did well and enjoyed myself when the atmosphere was exploratory and creative.

For the first few weeks, the way Fr. Becker operated in the classroom was of high interest to me. Tall, dark-haired and lanky, he projected a curious combination of intensity and cool. His posture was relaxed, but his mind was focused. The issue at hand was always how to communicate effectively in writing. He didn't have all the answers, but he did have questions. How might this scene be rendered so the reader feels he is part of it? How can your position on an issue be presented so the reader looks at it in a new light? There wasn't one right answer or a single approach. Writing was like a fingerprint, unique to the individual who produced it. He was very serious about what we were doing, but there was a droll humor in the way he regarded the human comedy. After those first few weeks I relaxed. This was going to work out fine.

As assignments for his writing workshop, Fr. Becker would have us respond to the prompts of writing contests, and then would actually enter our most promising efforts in the contests. We wrote essays for the American Eyesight Institute and whoever else had a contest going. Well into the school year I was pleased to learn that the five hundred words I'd written on "The Space Age Challenge to America" for the local Ladies' Auxiliary of the Veterans of Foreign Wars had won the second prize of $15. Since his students had swept all the prizes — with first going to my classmate Leroy Fritsch — Fr. Becker accompanied us and our guests to the Friday evening awards ceremony at a meeting room in the San Francisco Opera House.

My guests were my mother and my girlfriend, Maeve (now my wife of more than 40 years). We didn't know what to expect. My mother, straight from a long day in a downtown billing office, was in a Thank-God-It's-Friday mood, wanting nothing more than to unwind and relax. Maeve and I were hoping things would be short but sweet. We joined Fr. Becker on the street and went in to see what awaited us.

We were met in the hallway by a phalanx of six ladies in military outfits of a cut somewhere between the Girl Scouts and a guerilla band of Daughters of the American Revolution. Two ladies took each prizewinner securely by the arms. Then, the ornate doors of the meeting room were thrown open and we were summarily marched into a gallery of 50 or 60 uniformed ladies, who were clapping loudly to a Souza march on the phonograph. After being marched twice around the room, we were led to a platform upon which an elderly woman of commanding figure motioned us to our positions.

Grinning to keep from bursting into laughter, I searched the room for Maeve and my mother, and found them in the visitor's gallery with Father Becker. Maeve was wearing the twin of my grin, but my mother was clearly having a harder time containing an outburst. I looked from them to Fr. Becker, who, cool as always, gave me a nod that said, "We can get through this. Hang in there."

Things unfolded quickly. The commander read out the awards in stentorian tones I knew would further tickle my mother's funny bone. "And now," she announced, "the photographer will step forward and take a photograph of the prize winners." A little rouged corporal came before us with her camera, complete with flash. My mother was doing a little dance to contain herself.

The camera was aimed. The corporal pushed the button, but nothing happened. She tried a second and a third time but nothing happened. At this point in the proceedings, mother had broken into a jig, Maeve's smile was about to burst, and even Fr. Becker's crooked smile was stretched to the limit.

The corporal adjusted the camera and tried yet again to snap the shot. Nothing. Finally the commander descended from the platform, brusquely took the camera, fiddled with it a few seconds, handed it back and returned to her place on the platform. "That should do it," she said confidently.

Smile everyone," said the corporal. I was smiling as broadly as I'd ever smiled in my life. She pushed the button. The camera exploded with a puff of white smoke. Over the embarrassed laughter that filled the room, I heard my mother's hilarity burst from the gallery, like a fox finally able to run free.

As we stood in the street, decompressing before heading home, Fr. Becker smiled his crooked smile and shook his head. As a teacher, whose job was to civilize but not suppress the sensibilities of teenagers, he no doubt had witnessed comic vignettes in the yards and halls of St. Ignatius on a daily basis that rivaled the evening's proceedings with the ladies' auxiliary. You could see him rolling them around in his mind like a piece of candy. His humor had no hard edge, no ridicule. I've tried to maintain that same perspective.

In his 20 years at St. Ignatius, Fr. Becker deeply influenced writers such as Lawrence Yep '66, whose fiction includes the Newbery Honor Book *Dragonwings*, and Peter Casey '68, creator and producer of NBC's *Frasier*. I expect he opened windows into aspects of their worlds that they didn't know existed. That's what he did for me. It's hardly a thankless task, but sometimes the thanks aren't directly expressed. Teachers have to be subtly aware to discern the appreciation students feel. I'm confident, from what I know of Fr. John Becker, that such discernment sweetened his task.

By the way, since I'm crediting Fr. Becker as my first writing teacher, it is germane to note that I went on to earn a doctoral degree in creative writing and to work as a writer and teacher of writing.

Laurence Yep & Peter Casey

on Fr. Becker

From top: Laurence Yep '66 and Peter Casey '68 both credit Fr. Becker with encouraging them to pursue careers in writing.

Laurence Yep '66, the author of *Dragonwings* and dozens of other books, wrote about Fr. Becker in his autobiography, *The Lost Garden*. Here is an excerpt from his book:

"In my senior year, we had Father Becker who taught us English by having us imitate the various writers and various forms. We had to write poems in the complicated rhyme scheme of the sestina; and we had to write scenes

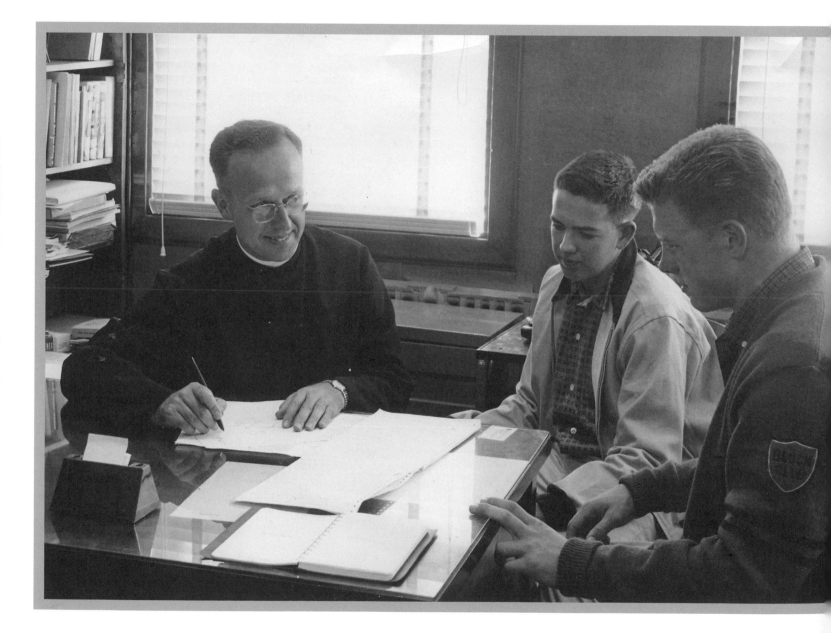

imitating Shakespeare. Our writing would never make anyone forget William or the other greats of English literature; but we learned the nuts and bolts of a style. To this day, I have to be careful what I read because I tend to imitate that writing.

"Early in the semester, Father took some of us aside and said that if we wanted to get an 'A' in his course, we would have to get something accepted by a national magazine. All of us were intimidated by the prospect; but in those days you didn't argue with a Jesuit priest — and you still don't. All of us tried. None of us got anything accepted; and he later retracted the threat and graded us by the same standards he used for the rest of the class. However, I got bitten by the bug and kept on trying."

Peter Casey '68, a writer for *Cheers* and *Wings* and the creator of *Frasier* (the most honored sitcom in TV history), was also a student in Fr. Becker's class. "He was tough," Casey said in an interview that appeared in the Spring '95 *Genesis III*. "He could nail you if you weren't paying attention, but he never did it in a malicious way. I respected his opinion tremendously. When he told me that I could write, it made an impression on me. Heading into college, I wasn't exactly sure what direction I wanted to go. That praise helped steer me to major in journalism at a junior college and in broadcasting when I transferred to San Francisco State University."

On April 20, 1997, SI dedicated a courtyard next to the campus ministry center in honor of Fr. Becker. Casey donated funds for the project, which, with its fountain and benches, is a place that invites students to gather in small groups and discuss a novels and poetry.

& the New Alumni Association

To mark the 100th anniversary of the founding of St. Ignatius College, USF and St. Ignatius High School held a centennial week in October 1955. SI celebrated a solemn Mass on October 13 sung at St. Ignatius Church by Fr. William Tobin, SJ, with a sermon delivered by Fr. Charles Casassa, SJ '28, then president of Loyola University in Los Angeles. SI students also took part in USF's celebrations, which included an October 14 University Memorial Mass for deceased students and an October 16 Mass celebrated by Archbishop John J. Mitty, who was assisted by a former SI religion teacher, the Right Rev. Msgr. Harold Collins.

In the 1955 yearbook, SI Principal Robert Leonard, SJ, asked Ignatians to commemorate the centennial by referring to the key image of the 1950s — the Atom. "This is an Atomic Age: of fusion and fission; of unbounded energies harnessed and exploded; of contracting and scattering; of elements merged and particles ejected. An analogy may be drawn between the atomic process and your lives. Remember, however, it is a resemblance, not a parallel. During your days at St. Ignatius there was a building up of, a search for unity — a fusion — with God, with truth, with one another; in a word, the fusion of faith, hope and charity. Now is the zero hour of fission. You are divided and hurled forth, not to dissipate your substance nor to lose your character in the world, as atomic particles are hurled forth never to return. For you, the bond of these earlier years will never be broken. The field of your operation will simply be ever widened as a chain reaction...."[7]

Fr. Thomas Reed, SJ, speaking with members of the Block Club.

Fr. Robert Leonard, SJ

The modern Alumni Association started in 1956 with the celebration of the school's centenary, and the school gathered 58 graduates to put together a roster for a general alumni reunion to be held June 2, 1956. At that event, alumni gathered by year in classrooms. "These rooms became pretty lively places, and some men who had not seen their classmates for quite a few years were having a field day," reported the *Ignatian Bulletin*, the precursor to the *Genesis* alumni magazine. When the crowd came together for dinner, student yell leaders led them in Wildcat yells "and even gave the school fight song a whirl. Then former yell leaders took over under the leadership of Danny Galvin '42. Dan still [had] the touch, and the alumni responded long and loud." Then the first Alumni Association president — Tom King '22 — was named, along with his officers Darrell Daly '15, Superior Judge Edward J. Molkenbuhr '18, Charles Creighton '30, Richard B. Doyle '21 and Dan O'Hara '35.[8]

Fr. Robert Leonard, SJ
& Fr. Thomas Reed, SJ

In the June 6, 1957, *Inside SI*, editor Dan Flynn '57 paid tribute to outgoing principal, Fr. Robert Leonard, SJ, who had come to SI in 1951 as its vice principal and dean of discipline and who had served as principal starting in 1954. Flynn wrote that students came to respect Fr. Leonard. "For one thing, Father

was a star athlete himself — an All-Stater in Arizona in football, basketball and baseball." When Leonard took over as principal, it was "a popular choice," wrote Flynn. "In the semesters that followed, strange things began to happen. Students were trusted with more and more privileges. SI had a principal who was with and for the students every inch of the way. The main secret of Fr. Leonard's success lay in the fact that he trusted the students. He knew the good, positive method of directing them. Seldom was he heard criticizing the student body on the PA system. Instead of criticism, he boomed out the strong encouraging words which gave the students the confidence they needed."

His replacement would be Fr. Thomas Reed, SJ '34, a native San Franciscan and an SI grad. Born in 1917, Fr. Reed entered the Society after graduating from high school and taught at SI between 1942 and 1944. He studied education at St. Louis University, Stanford and USF where he received a doctoral degree in education counseling and psychology in 1985. He served as principal of SI between 1957 and 1964 before leaving for USF to serve as acting dean of education. In one of his first acts as principal, he created a split lunch period, given the large enrollment of 1957, with seniors and sophomores eating before juniors and freshmen. He also added fluorescent lights to the first floor corridor.

Fr. Reed was known as a forthright man who always spoke his mind, but "his frankness and off-the-cuff manner could be controversial," according to his obituary published in the *National Jesuit News*. He made an unsuccessful bid in 1972 for a seat on the San Francisco Board of Education, but was appointed to the board by Mayor Joseph Alioto to fill a vacancy and served until 1977.

Athletics

Basketball in the New Gym

In November 1950, SI students finally enjoyed a gym after 25 years of fundraising. Construction began in March 1950, with money coming from all sources, including a "till that bulged with greenbacks from the play" and the generous donations of parents and local businesses. The money was not enough to pay the entire cost of construction, and the school still faced a $30,000 debt in 1951. By 1955, however, it cleared the books on that debt.[9]

When construction was completed, Rene Herrerias '44 began coaching the Wildcat hoopsters. After graduating from SI, Herrerias played for USF, where, at 5-feet, 9-inches, "his flashy and sound playing thrilled the crowd at Madison Square Garden when his team won the NIT in 1948." Herrerias returned to coach at SI, succeeding Phil Woolpert, who had left to coach at USF.[10]

In all, Herrerias led the Wildcats to four AAA championships (1951 and 1954–56) and two Tournament of Champions victories in 1954 and 1955). He began his auspicious career in the fall of 1950 by leading the 120s to an undefeated record. (The 110s and 120s played in the fall in those days.) The 120s were captained by Mic Kelly '52 and featured two Prep Hall of Famers, Bernie Simpson '54 and Ray Paxton '54, as well as Steve Moriarty '53 and Jim Stephens '53. The 130s also won their division, captained by Bill Parker '52 and featuring Dan Powers '52, Nils Fernquist '52, Bob Braghetta '53 and Speed DeConti '52.

The varsity made it a trifecta by also winning the AAA. Herrerias captured his first varsity league victory in March 1951 in a 40–37 win against Commerce

(which starred Casey Jones) with the starting five of George Hayes, Bob Wiebusch, Stan Buchanan, Bill Bush and Rudy Zannini, all five of whom matriculated to USF, three on athletic scholarships. (Other stars of that era include Ray Healy and Bill Mallen.)

The shortest among those five was Zannini, who, at 5-feet, 6-inches, averaged 15 points each game, the third highest in the league. He was nicknamed "The Mouse" and "The Watch Guard" by his teammates, but continued to play at USF side-by-side with teammate Bill Russell and later earned entry into the San Francisco Prep Hall of Fame.

The star of the 1954 and 1955 Tournament of Champion teams was Fred LaCour '56, one of the most gifted men to play basketball for SI. (He later

Construction begins on the Stanyan Street gym. Today it is part of the Koret Center.

played with the St. Louis Hawks from 1960–62 and the Warriors the following year.) In 1954, he tied an AAA scoring record in his junior year at SI against Galileo, scoring 29 points. He shot for 22 points against Salinas in the first round of the Tournament of Champions on March 10, 1955, and later shared honors with Team Captain Dan Casey '55, both named as all-tournament players.

A commemorative issue of *Inside SI* noted that for the finale, "the Coach of the Year, Mr. Rene Herrerias, and the Team of the Year, the St. Ignatius Wildcats, [rode] high on the shoulders of the SI students as they triumphantly paraded and cheered through the scene of their glorious victory — champions all!"

In his senior year, LaCour earned All-American honors and led his team to a 7–1 league finish and the championship. His team won the first two games at the Tournament of Champions, but LaCour suffered a broken finger and did not play against El Cerrito, which won 26–20.

No. 3, Rudy Zannini '51, at 5-foot, 6-inches, was one of the stars of his team.

Baseball

After Frank McGloin retired from coaching, SI baseball teams were led by John Golden (who also coached football) and Grove Mohr, who, in 1950, led SI to a 7–2 season. In 1954, Mohr captured the AAA championship with stars such as Ken Dito '54 (who later worked as a broadcaster for KNBR), Ray Paxton '54, Roger Ferrari '55 and Jack Scramaglia '55. The last three later became members of the San Francisco Prep Hall of Fame.

Paxton also played basketball at SI, but his star was brightest on the diamond, and in his junior year he earned a pitching spot on the all-league second team for the AAA after pitching a no-hitter against Lincoln. At one point, he had 21 straight scoreless innings.

In his senior year, he helped SI take both the AAA basketball league crown and the Tournament of Champions. Paxton was named to the All-AAA, All-TOC, All-Metro and All-NorCal teams. Later, pitching for the Wildcats under coach Grove Mohr, Paxton took SI to its first AAA baseball title in 24 years and earned a spot on the all-league first team and on the *Examiner* All-Star team. Also, he was named MVP of the *Chronicle*/Lions Club East–West All-Star game after pitching all nine innings and collecting four hits while leading his team to a 15–4 victory. That victory won him a trip to the World Series in New York where he saw Willie Mays make his famous catch against Cleveland at the Polo Grounds.

Paxton was named both San Francisco and NorCal Athlete of the Year in 1954 before his freshman year at SCU. He later spent a year playing for a Red Sox farm team in Las Vegas but found that baseball had lost its allure.

Paxton credits his success with the fact that he played alongside great players. "Those were special times," Paxton recalls. "The 1950s were so peaceful. Everyone seemed to get along so well, and I had many great friends."

Roger Ferrari, who played his senior year for Jim Keating, was twice selected to play in the San Francisco East–West All-Star game and batted .425 in his senior year, earning All-City honors. He went on to earn MVP status for the East/West game where he hit three for five. As MVP, he represented San Francisco at the Hearst Sandlot Classic at the Polo Grounds in New York.

After graduating from SI, Ferrari attended City College where he made the All-Conference and All-Northern California teams for two seasons. "I still remember the first time I walked onto the field at Seal Stadium," recalls Ferrari. "It was during the CYO championship game in 1951 in my eighth grade year at Sts. Peter and Paul. I thought I had made the big time. That was the year Mickey Rocco was the star first baseman, and I always watched him, trying to imitate his moves. He wore number 4, so that was always the number on my jersey and my lucky number."

Jack Scramaglia played varsity baseball in each of his four years and made the all-city team in both his junior and seniors years. As a senior he hit .464 and led the league in hits. That year, the *Examiner* selected him to play on its all-star team that traveled to New York. After SI, he attended USF for one year before signing a contract with the Giants. He played three seasons in the minor leagues before leaving to become a teacher and coach at Roosevelt Junior High School in San Francisco. In 1997, the San Francisco Prep Hall of Fame inducted him into its ranks.

In 1955, Jim Keating took over as baseball coach. He won his first league championship in 1958 with stars such as Don Leonardini, Ron Cook, Ken Dekker and all-Northern Californian John Giovanola. He recaptured that crown the following year despite predictions in the city papers that SI would never beat SH. Thanks to Chuck Rapp's pitching and Ron Calcagno's hitting, SI won 4–3. (Read more on Jim Keating in the next chapter.)

Golf & Bob Callan '57

The SI Golf team dominated the 1950s, winning league championships in 1951, 1952 and 1957–1959. Bob Callan '57 helped SI in his senior year to take the league crown and also captured the San Francisco City Junior title. While a student at SCU, he led its golf team to three consecutive league titles. He

The 1957 varsity baseball team in the locker room. From left are Assistant Coach and scholastic Mr. Bob Welch, SJ, Br. Lenny Sullivan, SJ, and Coach Jim Keating.

went on to win several city and county titles during his college career and then received a bachelor's degree in business from SCU and a law degree from USF.

Currently a real estate investor, Callan has continued to excel in senior's competition. Consistently ranked as one of the top players in the state, he has been selected to represent the Northern California Golf Association in team competition on 13 occasions. In 2003 he became the first player to win the San Francisco City Senior, Alameda Commuter, San Francisco County Senior and Oakland City Senior championships in the same year. He also won the prestigious Western Seniors title in Guadalajara, Mexico. Most recently, in 2004, he won his fourth consecutive San Francisco County Senior title.

Soccer & Cross Country

Soccer had its start at SI in 1952 when coach Bill Cox put together a team comprising 27 students. The following year, moderator James Straukamp (a Jesuit scholastic, who later became an Anglican priest) came to assist Cox. The 1953 *Ignatian* reported that the all-city captain Bob Braghetta '53 and Class of '52 seniors Barney Vannucci, Steve Sullivan, Jack Murray, Terry Curran, Bob Del Moral and Don Kelleher led the team to a victory against Lowell and a tie with Washington. Aside from Braghetta, standout juniors included Jim Flanagan and Mike Balibrera. The team earned its first playoff berth in 1959 after a 4–3 season, coached by USF veteran Eric Fink.

The first mention of an SI cross country team occurs in the 1955 yearbook with a photograph of the first 21 runners. The following year, *Inside SI* praised the efforts of students Walt Van Zant, Steve Barrett, Jim Leary, Mike Deasy and George De Cat and praised the new cross country course in Golden Gate Park that started at Broom Point and went "through Lindley Meadow, around the police stables, around the middle lake, and then back down the south side of the Polo Fields, through another meadow and finally to the finish line just west of Lloyd Lake," covering "1.9 miles of rough terrain."[11]

Football

One of the stars of the day was Gil Dowd '57 who helped lead SI to the AAA football championship in 1956. Dowd played on the frosh and JV teams and watched as the varsity struggled against strong teams from the AAA. By the time Dowd was a senior, it had been 11 years since SI had captured the league crown.

Something happened in 1956 to change SI's luck. Varsity Coach Sarge MacKenzie left to teach at USF and Pat Malley '49, whose father had coached at SI, took his place. Malley, who had been a star athlete both at SI and SCU, suffered an injury in his senior year at Santa Clara and, after serving in the Army, returned to SI to teach and coach. He brought along Gene Lynch '49, his teammate from SCU.

Early injuries contributed to losses against Poly and Washington, but the Wildcats went undefeated after that and took the city championship by beating Poly and then Balboa for the Turkey Bowl game before a crowd of 30,000. "Coach Malley's squad scored an

Gil Dowd '57

Opposite page: Students formed an SI block in the cheering section for the football games.

early touchdown and had to rely on the defense the rest of the way. With three minutes to go in the game, Balboa had the ball first and goal. With their backs to the wall, SI's defense tightened up and the Bucs were unable to cross the goal line. SI had won its second championship, as the scoreboard read SI 7, Balboa 6."[12]

Dowd, who entered the Prep Hall of Fame in 2003, credited the entire team with the success. "My classmates Ed Rothman and Bob Isola and I each took turns excelling in the backfield. We each did our share of running." Dowd eventually earned All-City honors and was named Player of the Year by two of the city papers. He also earned All Northern California Second Team and All Metro Team honors and was named East Bay–West Bay All Star Game MVP.

George Devine '59 leads cheers at a 1956 football game.

Coach Pat Malley
& his Amazing Bag of Tricks
By Brian Hasset '58

Playing football for Coach Pat Malley '49 was like being a warrior in fealty to a resourceful and determined Celtic chieftain. Well, maybe that's a little too much historical-romantic spin, but when Pat Malley returned to St. Ignatius in 1956, where his father had coached and he had been team captain, he brought a code and style that probably did derive from such roots. It was a good fit.

He was tough but imaginative. Practice sessions presided over by Pat Malley and line coach Gene Lynch were hard-hitting. When you were called to jump into the tackling circle, runners came at you from every direction, helmets lowered and knees pounding. Your job was to tackle one, then spin around and get the next and the next. It was no picnic, but there was also an element of play in those practices that brought out the best in us. Gordie Lau, who would later argue in the Supreme Court about equal educational opportunity, would let out a shout with each tackle, which Coach Malley played up to add a note of levity. Wind sprints sometimes became a game where first the Italians lined up and ran shouting down the field, and then the Irish, and then an ethnic assortment known as "the rest of you guys." Off the practice field, Mr. Malley had a way of beaming a beneficent smile when you passed him in the hall that validated all your efforts.

Our offense was nicely balanced. Mick Doherty and Ron Tocchini were a running tandem that pounded defenses until they broke, and Ron Calcagno at quarterback could air out 30- and 40-yard passes to a talented corps of receivers, including Pete Ackenheil, who doubled as kicker of field goals, PATs (points after touchdown) and booming kickoffs. It was a team deep in athletic talent on which every player had honed his skills to fill a need.

When SI played Poly High in the Thanksgiving Day Classic in 1958, a share of the city championship was at stake. Poly, coached by old-time Santa Clara Bronco Milt Axt, had dominated the city league for years, and we had lost to them in the regular season 9–6. Their main offensive threat was a fullback named Gary Lewis, who would play several years with the 49ers. Like us, they were hard-hitting and seasoned. Their offense wasn't as multi-dimensional as ours, but they were tough on defense and Lewis, a speedster at 6-feet, 3-inches and 220, was a dimension unto himself when he arced off tackle and headed downfield.

Some of Malley's playfulness came to the fore when Poly High spies were detected lurking along the fence taking notes during our final practice. He called a team huddle, concocted four or five off-the-wall plays, and had us run through them, surely flummoxing the spies and very possibly setting up the confusion that Poly experienced in the game two days later. Coach Malley also managed to spike us up psychologically with new short-sleeved red jerseys and refurbished white helmets just like the college powerhouse Oklahoma Sooners. When we ran onto the field before 22,000 fans at Kezar Stadium, we felt sharp and cohesive, especially when we saw the Poly players doing jumping jacks in inexpertly washed uniforms on which red from the numerals had bled pink across the white jerseys. Score a subtle advantage for the Wildcats.

At this late date I can't do a play-by-play description of the game. I don't know if it was Doherty

or Tocchini who tore through the Poly line for the first score. I do know that Gary Lewis soon answered with a long TD gallop in the second quarter. In the third, Coach Malley sent in a newly-installed trick play called Helter Skelter in which the entire line pulled left and Ron Calcagno seemed to be following the flow on a roll out. But then Ron planted his feet and reeled off a long cross field pass to Ed Nevin, who had run left with everyone else, but then cut back into the open flat for a touchdown.

It was a hot Indian summer day. Malley substituted freely, which kept our legs fresh. We kept the Poly defense on the field with a couple of drives that didn't score but left them huffing and puffing. We were up by a few points midway through the fourth quarter — the score something like 14–9 — but Gary Lewis was always a threat to go all the way. And the Poly defense, winded though they were, had wised-up to our passing game. They were yelling, "Watch for Helter Skelter!" when we broke from the huddle in passing situations. We tried Helter Skelter a couple of times more, but Poly's left corner hung back and easily broke it up. That's when Pat Malley came up with an-

From left: Coaches Pat Malley & Gene Lynch

other foxy move in which I played a part that I savor to this day.

I was standing on the sidelines, hoping we could hold the line, when Pat Malley called my name. I ran to his side where Ron Calcagno was standing. Our defense had pushed Poly back around their own 30. Our offense was about to take the field. Coach Malley fixed us with his fierce blue eyes and quickly mapped out a variation on Helter Skelter in which I, at right end, continued across the field, rather than cutting back against the student body left flow.

I hadn't caught a pass all season. The good thing about my sudden insertion into the lineup was that I didn't have time to get too nervous. Calcagno leaned over center Dave Favro, who would go on to play at UC Berkeley, and called the count. The play unfolded in basic high anxiety slow motion. Never fleet of foot, I pounded across the field on a diagonal, head down. At the point when Nevin had earlier cut back, I fired off whatever afterburners I could muster and looked back to where Calcagno had pulled up from his roll out and let fly with a somewhat wobbly pass. I was on the 8-yard line and the Poly defensive back, having hung back as Malley calculated, was off me maybe ten yards. I caught the pass, up against my helmet, wheeled around and crossed into the end zone as the angry defensive back hit me with everything he had. I felt nothing but unadulterated bliss.

Time running out, the Poly Parrots, in their sweaty, vaguely pink jerseys, were starting to wear that dazed look teams get in the final minutes of a losing effort. The sequence of scoring is a little blurred in memory, but at some point Pete Ackenheil kicked a long field goal to put the score somewhere around 23–9. That perfect end-over-end goalpost splitter nicely highlighted the package of skills our team pos-

sessed. We won that game with a beautifully balanced team effort, but also high on the list of positive factors was the craftiness of Pat Malley, who spontaneously responded to the game as it unfolded before him with one brilliant surprise after another. I have had many splendid Thanksgivings in the intervening years, but never have I floated 10 feet off the ground as I, and the rest of our band of warriors, did that day.

Extracurriculars & Campus Ministry

The Senior Retreat

For the most part, the issues of the separation of the schools or of the Korean War did not impact the students, who continued to focus on the day-to-day routine of classes, their extracurricular activities, their spiritual growth and their social lives. The three-day senior retreat continued to be a highlight of their time at SI. In 1950, the yearbook reported on this hallmark of Jesuit education:

"Dear Lord, teach me to be generous. Teach me to serve Thee as Thou deservest, to give and not to count the cost, to labor and not to seek for rest; to toil and not to seek reward, save that of knowing that I do Thy will.

"Long will thoughtful Ignatians remember this short but powerful prayer, the traditional keynote of the annual three-day Senior Retreat at El Retiro.

"They will remember, too, the new but uplifting experience that was theirs during those few days, when far away from the turmoil and nervousness of city life, they turned their minds and hearts to God.

"Some among them, such as Moore, Sheehan, Fazzio and Enright, will remember special duties that helped keep the retreatants in that atmosphere so necessary for a good retreat. All will remember the strict silence, the soul-searching meditations and the impressive Stations of the Cross.

"They will remember especially the spirit of the retreat, which perhaps remained with them after their departure from El Retiro; how it rendered them quiet and thoughtful, anxious to put their retreat resolutions into faithful practice, hopeful some day to return to El Retiro for another 'spiritual checkup.'"[13]

The St. Ignatius Church *Monthly Calendar* ran a few student reflections on this retreat, written by members of the class of 1950. Here are a few excerpts:

"I went to El Retiro to get out of school and to have a good time, but after a few hours I changed my mind. I think the main reason for the change was the total lack of distraction. My thoughts there were more serious than at any other time of my life. I changed my mind, too, as to what made up the important things of life, for the things that seemed so important a few days before now seem to be trifles. I made resolutions; I pray to God that He will give me the strength to keep them."

"I have made many retreats before, but none impressed me so greatly. I think the reason for this is the wonderful atmosphere of the place. I enjoyed the whole retreat, but I especially enjoyed making the out-door Stations of the Cross and saying the rosary while walking through the lovely gardens and visiting the outdoor shrines."

"When I first came to El Retiro, I must admit I was prepared for a rather boring time. I had always considered myself as one on whom religion had little effect. I had never thought much about God, religion or life after death. I just believed them

mechanically, like one believes that two plus two equals four. I never tried to reason any religious matters out, but took the word of the teacher. But as I look back on it now, I didn't really believe my religion, and because I attended a public school for quite some time, I was even at times prone to disbelieve. However, at El Retiro, I had a chance that was never offered me before to *think* these problems out, and today I am convinced that the Catholic Church is the right church, that God exists, and many other matters of Faith on which I was weak…. What at El Retiro helped me clear up my mind? I believe it was the atmosphere. As a mountaineer, I have visited places in the huge canyons of the Sierra where probably no one has ever trod, and

Fr. Newport directed a retreat for freshmen and sophomores in the SI auditorium in the early 1950s.

in these places with a few chosen friends I did most of my thinking…. At El Retiro I believe the atmosphere of the mountains was provided; the guidance of the Church in important matters was added."[14]

Both the Sanctuary Society (which provided the altar servers for the many Masses the priests said) and the Sodalities continued to provide avenues for the boys of SI to serve the Church and grow in faith during the school year. The Junior and Senior Sodalities were much like SI's modern Service Club and CLCs. "Whether it was waiting on tables for the Fathers' Club, washing dishes at the Old Folks Home, or enjoying the convention dances of the Bay Area Catholic High Schools, [members of] the Sodality worked together," strove for "personal sanctification and sanctification of one's neighbor," and held daily noon rosaries during October and May.[15]

This faith life of students in the 1950s was the pre-Vatican II Catholicism of the *Baltimore Catechism*. Spiritual life for the boys would continue much this way until the late 1960s and early 1970s when the effects of Vatican II began to influence the way the Jesuits shared their own rich spiritual traditions with their students.

The program from the 1953 Fight Night.

Fight Night & Rifle Club

SI used the new gym for more than just basketball. It provided Ignatians a place to launch a new event: Senior Fight Night. In March 1953 "the toughest sluggers in the class of '53" took part in a boxing contest. The school borrowed a boxing ring from the Presidio through the help of Capt. Buckley, in charge of ROTC at the school. The evening featured nine bouts. "Some of the glove wars were antics, others full of clever punching and smooth footwork."[16]

Fighting wasn't the only unusual competition held at SI. Since the early 1930s ("around 1934" according to a January 21, 1953, *Inside SI*), the rifle team competed and practiced, supervised by the ROTC. The same edition of *Inside SI* reported on the annual Hearst Rifle match, with "five shots per person in each position," for the 13-man team coached by Sgt. McAllister.

Inside SI & *The Ignatian* Comes of Age

To celebrate the centennial year of the school, *Inside SI* grew from a small 4-page publication into a slick 16-page magazine. Its moderator, Robert Piser, SJ, who later changed his name to Kaiser when he moved to Rome in 1962 — I got tired of everyone calling me Pee-Sair — instigated the change when Fr. Leonard assigned him as moderator of both the literary magazine and the school newspaper. He asked if he could combine budgets and produce one publication, and permission was granted.

Kaiser was a devotee of *Time* and had even written his Master's thesis about the ethics of *Time*-style journalism. "*Inside SI* had a strong resemblance to *Time*," he noted in a 2003 interview. "Writing *Time*-style taught the kids to write colorfully and concretely, and the format helped us organize what we thought was important about SI and its culture."

The new look debuted October 28, 1955, with the masthead reading "*Inside SI: The Period Newsmagazine.*" Editor James O'Brien '56 offered this by way of introduction: "This year we are trying to make our writing so interesting and persuasive that when the fellow who hates football reads *our* article about the sport, and through it feels the exhilarating excitement of the game, he won't be able to see enough football."

The following year, Kaiser and his editors changed the layout to emulate *Sports Illustrated* "because we realized *Time* wasn't the right model. We were so much of a jock school then, and we featured Gil Dowd '57, a star football player, on the cover in a full-page, full-bleed duotone photo. The kids just loved it. We delivered it during class time, and teachers suspended class so that students could read about themselves."

Dan Flynn '57 served as editor in his senior year, and the magazine won national renown in 1957 with an All-American Award from the University of Minnesota. Roy Camozzi also won a $100 scholarship at a Northern California Student Press Conference put on by UC Berkeley for a feature story he wrote. The magazine went on to win first place for its cover photo of Fr. Leonard from the Catholic High School Press Association, which also named the magazine a "Publication of Distinction" among high school and college publications on the Pacific Coast. Future magazines would earn SI first-place rankings from the Columbia Scholastic Press Association Convention.[17]

The big award in 1957 went to the school yearbook, *The Ignatian*, which took first place in the nation from the Columbia Scholastic Press Association. The yearbook featured the first place football and golf teams and a full-color cover, a first for that publication.

The Ignatians over the next few years continued to excel and, at times, offered new ways of showcasing the student body. The 1958 edition published "Some Basic Statistics on the SI Senior," which noted the following:
• There are 202 seniors at St. Ignatius.
• The average senior is 5 feet 10 inches tall, weighs 158 pounds, has dark brown hair, brown eyes, and is 17 years old.
• 51.2 percent of the seniors participated in the SI sports program this past year.
• The percentage of seniors working after school has dwindled during the past 10 years; now it is 10.8 percent.
• The SI senior estimates that he spends on average of 1.5 hours studying each night; time spent in slumber, 7.6 hours.
• Though studies seemed to be more difficult this year, the senior class maintained an average of 84.3 percent in all subjects during the fall semester.
• Seniors seem to be more social now, with 16.3 percent going steady.
• 91.8 percent of SI seniors plan to attend college next year. More than half of these, 58.2 percent, will attend Catholic colleges.

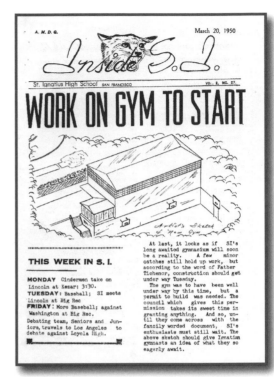

Inside SI debuted this new format in 1950 and then another in 1955, modeling itself after Time Magazine.

Gordon Getty '51 & Sir Paul Getty

Gordon Getty '51

Peter Raven '53 is the director of the Missouri Botanical Garden.

No one knew it at the time, but two brothers in the Class of 1951 belonged to one of the richest families in the country. Both Gordon Getty II and John Paul Getty, Jr., however, didn't grow up wealthy. Their mother, Ann, had divorced J. Paul Getty, and, according to Gordon's good friend and classmate Judge William Newsom '51, "they knew they had a rich, even very rich father, but as he had almost no influence upon their lives, one didn't hear much about him…. Neither Paul nor Gordon seemed particularly concerned about money or the lack of it — nor did they seem to dwell on expectations." Music became a greater part of Gordon's life, and he collected operatic records. The yearbook noted that Gordon came to SI from San Rafael Military Academy where he spent time as a debater. "However, he found time to take an active part in the Fathers' Club Talent Show. As yet he is undecided as to college or profession." His brother went from a wild childhood to a "serious conversion thanks to the Jesuits of St. Ignatius" though he never graduated from the school.[18]

On February 24, 1958, *Time* ran a cover story on J. Paul Getty, ranking him as one of the world's richest men, and Gordon was thrust into the spotlight. He eventually became a noted composer, writing the opera *PlumpJack* based on the character of Falstaff, a 32-song cycle of Emily Dickinson's poems entitled *The White Election* and a play based on Poe's "The Fall of the House of Usher. He has shown great generosity with his many gifts to SI and the art community over the years, and has served the school as a member of the Board of Regents since the 1980s.

Gordon's brother, "Sir Paul," as he was known in England, was knighted by Queen Elizabeth II in 1986 for his charitable work. He was proud of that title because he loved the rich traditions of England, a love he noted that grew from his days as a student in America "where I was captured by the romance of English history and Shakespeare," according to a 1998 interview with the *Sunday Telegraph*. He died at 70 in 2003.

Peter Raven '53

When *Time* named Peter Raven '53 a Hero of the Planet in April 1999, the editors there had good cause. Few other men have done as much as Raven to stop the destruction of rain forests and slow the loss of biodiversity, and hardly anyone is as articulate or as passionate as he is regarding our need to save our planet. Raven's passion and professionalism have won him a litany of awards, honors and posts. Among them:

• Raven was Home Secretary of the National Acad-

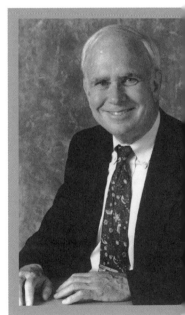

emy of Sciences and a member of President Clinton's Committee of Advisors on Science and Technology.

• He is one of 80 members of the Pontifical Academy of Sciences that advises the Pope on matters of science and technology.

• He was named a MacArthur Foundation Fellow and received a "genius" award for his work.

• The National Geographic Society recently named him chairman of the Committee for Research and Exploration.

• ABC named him a person of the week in 1988, and the *New York Times* ran a story on his achievements on the cover of its "Science Times" section.

• He has authored more than 400 articles and 16 books, including two leading college textbooks and the biology text used at SI.

• Since 1971, he has turned the Missouri Botanical Garden in St. Louis into one of the world's leading centers for plant conservation.

• In 2000, he received the National Medal of Science from President Clinton, recognizing him an authority on plant systematics and evolution and as the originator of the concept of coevolution.

Raven started his remarkable career at age 8 when he enrolled as the youngest member of the student section of the California Academy of Sciences. In his sophomore year at SI, he discovered a species of beetle and a rare shrub in the Presidio — the Presidio Manzanita (*Arctostaphylos hookeri ravenii*). Since then, he has had dozens of newly discovered plants and animals named for him.

After two years at USF, he transferred to UC Berkeley. He has worked at Stanford, in New Zealand and all over South and Central America in his long and successful career.

Bishop Carlos Sevilla, whose parents immigrated to San Francisco from Colima, Mexico, near Guadalajara, is the only SI grad to be named a bishop. (Msgr. Eugene Fahy '29, who died in 1996, was granted many of the powers of a bishop in 1951 for his missionary work in China, though he was never granted the title of bishop given the Church structures there at the time.) He entered the Society of Jesus after graduating from SI and was ordained a priest in 1966. His appointment came Dec. 6, 1988 as auxiliary bishop of San Francisco, and on Dec. 31, 1996, Pope John Paul II named him Bishop of Yakima in Washington State.

Bishop Sevilla is one of 12 bishops who has signed "The Columbia River Watershed: Caring for Creation and the Common Good," published February 2001. The half million residents of the Diocese of Yakima, including 4,000 members of the Yakima Tribe, have much at stake over the fate of the Columbia watershed, as their land fronts more of that river than any other diocese in Oregon or Washington.

Bishop Sevilla and the 11 other co-signatories hoped to offer an opportunity for reflection rather than a call to specific action, and he called for a future where "we hope to see the best of the watershed of the past: living waters of God's creation flowing from meadows and mountains to the ocean while providing for the needs of God's creatures along the way. We ask all people of good will to imagine what they would like the watershed

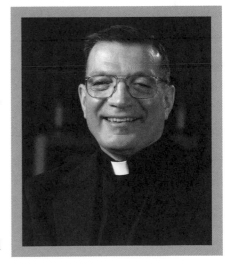

Bishop Carlos Sevilla '53 of Yakima, Washington.

to be like in ten, fifty or one hundred years, and to work conscientiously to make that image a reality."

In his time as bishop in San Francisco and Washington State, Bishop Sevilla has played a prominent role on several committees of the U.S. Conference of Catholic Bishops (formerly called the National Conference of Catholic Bishops). He has served as consultant for the NCCB Committee on Hispanic Affairs, a member of the NCCB Committee on Marriage and Family Life, chairman of the NCCB Committee on Religious Life and Ministry, a member of the NCCB Committee on Social Development and world Peace Domestic Policy, a member of the USCC Catholic Campaign for Human Development, chairman of the Bishop's Subcommittee for Translation of Liturgical Texts Into Spanish, co-chairman of the West Coast Dialogue of Catholics and Muslims and a member of the USCCB Committee for Ecumenical and Interreligious Affairs.

Bob Drucker '58

Bob Drucker '58 is best known as the Wizard of Westlake for leading SI basketball teams from 1966-1986, taking the 'Cats to the NorCal championship and to the state finals in 1984. Drucker got his start in basketball long before coming to SI when, in 1947, his mother took him to the *San Francisco Examiner* basketball camp at the Mission Armory. He won a shooting contest, received a trophy and had his picture in the paper. That first taste of glory got Drucker hooked on the game. Later, as a student at St. Anne's, he found himself in a PE class taught by one of his heroes — Jim Kearney '48 — who won the Brophy Award at

SI (and later the Christ the King award) and played football for USF's undefeated, untied and uninvited football team of 1950–51. (Kearney later became a distinguished principal in several San Francisco high schools.)

"He was a hero back then to all the seventh and eighth graders," recalled Drucker. "We would go to USF football games at Kezar and see him play on the same field the '49ers used, and that was good enough for all of us."

At SI, Drucker played on the 110s, 120s, 130s and varsity teams and trained with Rene Herrerias '44 and Jim Keating. "These men, along with Phil Woolpert, who coached at USF, were the kind of men you admired and respected. They were young and enthusiastic and had a profound influence on me."

Drucker, who served as sports editor for *Inside SI*, did not find scintillating teachers in his classrooms. "They just talked for the entire period. It wasn't even the Socratic method." In his junior year, Drucker found himself in J.B. Murphy's math class. "That was like an island at SI. He would lecture for 5 or 10 minutes and then have us do student-centered work."

Drucker found himself grateful for the help provided by scholastics. "Fr. Ed Malatesta, SJ, knew I was struggling; he took me aside and encouraged me to work harder. He recognized that I could do better, and we became fast friends until his untimely death."

In the 1990s, both Drucker and the late Jim Kearney were inducted together into the Bay Area Prep Hall of Fame. Drucker later coached golf with Kearney's son, Steve Kearney '81. (For Bob Drucker's fabled career as a basketball coach, read the next chapter.)

Opposite page: Bob Drucker '58 served as one of SI's most successful basketball coaches. He is pictured here with Paul La Rocca '84.

Jerry Brown '55

Jerry Brown '55, former governor of California and mayor of Oakland.

The 1955 yearbook lists this for Edmund "Jerry" Brown, Jr.: "Jerry proved his oratorical abilities by winning the Freshman Elocution and Sophomore Oratorical contests, being chosen on the Silver and Gold Medal Debates, and gaining the Degree of Distinction in the National Forensic League. He was also a member of the CSF and the Activities Dance Committee." In his senior year, he was a key member of the SI chapter of the NFL that took the Grand Sweepstakes Award, making it the best team in Northern California.

While Brown was a student at SI, his father served as Attorney General for California and, in 1959, voters elected him Governor. Jerry attended SCU and joined the Society of Jesus for a time. After he left, he earned his B.A. in classics from UC Berkeley in 1961 and then attended Yale Law School in 1964.

Brown received his start in politics in 1969 when voters elected him to the Los Angeles Community College Board of Trustees. In 1970, he was elected California's Secretary of State, and four years later he followed in his father's footsteps to become California governor, earning reelection in 1978.

He came to SI on October 6, 1978, to register students eligible to vote for the upcoming election. He met with Fr. McCurdy and was interviewed by three students for the school newspaper. At recess, he addressed the student body and spoke about the advantages of living in a democratic society.

During Brown's tenure as governor, California produced a quarter of the country's new jobs. Brown established the nation's first agricultural labor relations law and instituted the California Conservation Corp. He helped to preserve the fragile coastline by creating the California Coastal Protection Act and worked to institute the country's first building and appliance energy efficiency standards, making the state the leader in solar and alternative energy. Brown also takes pride in the number of women and minorities he appointed to government positions.

After leaving office, he traveled to Japan and India, where he worked with Mother Teresa. He practiced law in Los Angeles before becoming chairman of the state's Democratic Party in 1989. Two years later, he resigned from that position, citing his "disgust with the growing influence of money in politics."[19]

He ran for president in 1992, making a strong showing thanks, in part, to his refusal to accept contributions larger than $100, and was the only Democratic candidate to pose a serious threat to Bill Clinton. In 1998, Oakland residents elected him as their city's mayor, and he won reelection in 2002 with the goal of revitalizing the city's downtown "in a spirit of elegant diversity."[20]

Korean Conflict

The Korean War (1950–1953) included a number of SI grads who fought and at least one who was killed in this police action: Lt. Roger Kelly '43, who had graduated from West Point in 1949.

The war came home to Ignatians in other ways. Sgt. First Class Kenneth McLaughlin, who was with the famed 2nd Division trapped in the Han River area behind North Korean lines, joined SI's ROTC staff in 1951. During the fighting, he was critically wounded and evacuated to the states, and after his recovery, the Army assigned him to SI.[21]

A number of teachers fought in Korea, including Michael Hemovich, the football coach, who was called up from Army Reserves to serve in the conflict. He was replaced by Robert (Sarge) MacKenzie '31, a veteran coach at SI and Pacific Coast Scout for the Cleveland Browns.[22]

Dr. Barrett Weber '42, who served in World War II along with many of his classmates, also served in Korea, assigned to an infantry clearing station with the 25th Infantry Division as a physician, caring for the sick and wounded and shipping them out to MASH units in the rear. "At first we were quartered in the City Hall at Masan. The floors were covered with litters of wounded men. In the battle for Masan, lasting several weeks, our platoon treated about 5,000 casualties, of whom 1,100 died. Working day and night in the heat of the summer, we were all inexperienced in the ways of war and learned the hard way. The Army was totally ill equipped. For the first few weeks there were no antibiotics, no anti-malaria pills, and we were naïve about food and water handling. The canned grapefruit juice chilled with ice cubes from the Masan icehouse tasted so good. Shortly everyone was violently ill with dysentery. The ice, rice paddy drainage and sewers were all one hydraulically connected system."

Later, Weber drove behind enemy lines to help retrieve 80 American POWs who had been spotted by a reconnaissance patrol. Then, just as the war was about to end, the Chinese broke through in force and ended up in back of Weber's unit, which began "a painful extraction from those frozen mountains.... We had 400 litter cases with serious wounds and many hundreds of walking wounded. There was one road west that was still safe. We told the walking wounded to take off and hike out of there. The remaining infantry were setting up a rear guard holding action. I was faced with a difficult decision. We didn't have the transportation to evacuate the litter cases. Just as the moment came to decide — stay with them and be captured or take off with the platoon — miraculously 20 empty trucks arrived to evacuate the wounded. It was close."

Jesuit Missionaries

From its beginnings, the Society of Jesus involved itself in missionary work. St. Ignatius went to Jerusalem in hopes of converting Muslims to Christianity and later sent St. Francis Xavier to the Far East to share the Gospel of Christ. The Jesuits who

Fr. Jack Clifford, SJ, spent three years in a Chinese prison where he experienced psychological torture.

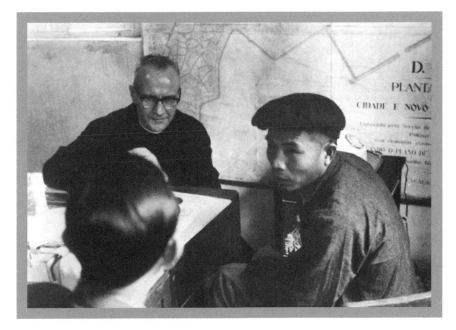

came from Europe to establish schools and parishes throughout California and the Northwest in the 1800s were carrying on that missionary tradition.

Many priests who were SI alumni also served as missionaries starting in 1928 when Joseph Lo Pahong, a Shanghai businessman, persuaded Pope Pius XI and Jesuit General Wlodimir Ledochowski to send California Jesuits overseas to assist the French Jesuits in their efforts in the Shanghai Mission Territory. Their work in China continued through war and revolution, eventually extending from China to Japan, the Philippines and Taiwan.

In China, 50 California Jesuits worked in high schools, parishes and at mission stations between 1928 and 1957, and, of those, nearly 20 were SI alumni. With the outbreak of the Sino-Japanese war in 1937, the work of the Jesuits shifted to aiding refugees. Some Jesuits spent much of World War II in Japanese internment camps in Yangzhou and Shanghai, while others, including Fr. Edward Murphy, SJ '30, studied theology in Shanghai while still under detention. (Fr. Murphy later became the first Jesuit ever to serve in Taiwan since the Jesuits left that island in the 1700s.) When the Communists took over in 1949, the Jesuits struggled to continue their work despite imprisonment, attempted brainwashing and expulsion.

One of the last two Jesuits to be imprisoned by the Red Chinese was Fr. Charles McCarthy, SJ '29. He arrived in China in 1941 and spent more than two years in a Japanese internment camp during WWII. In 1953, while rector of the Bellarmine Theologate in Shanghai, he was jailed by the Chinese Communists, and served four years in five different prisons. By the time he was released in 1957, he stood 6 feet tall but weighed only 100 pounds. After regaining his health and strength in California, he served in the Philippines for more

than 30 years, working for the assimilation and naturalization of Filipino-Chinese, writing three books on the Chinese in South East Asia, and heading various research and educational programs. Walter McCarthy '33 established the Rev. Charles J. McCarthy, SJ, Scholarship in memory of his brother.

Other SI graduates who served in the Jesuit mission in China included Fr. Ralph Brown, SJ '32, Fr. Daniel Clifford, SJ '29, Fr. John W. Clifford, SJ '35, Fr. Albert Corcoran, SJ '21, Fr. Ralph Deward, SJ '25, Fr. George Donohoe, SJ '39, Fr. Joseph Donohoe, SJ '33, Rev. Msgr. Eugene Fahy, SJ '29 (who, with the title vicar apostolic, held the rank of a bishop), Fr. John J. Gordon, SJ '30, Fr. John Lennon, SJ (SI 1905), Fr. John Magner, SJ '20, Fr. John Moholy, SJ '30, Fr. Paul O'Brien, SJ '25 (appointed the first superior of California Jesuits in China in 1945, in charge of all non-Chinese Jesuits), and Fr. Gerald Pope, SJ '27.

The most prominent of the above-mentioned, Rev. Msgr. Fahy, was appointed vicar apostolic to meet the needs of his fellow missionaries by confirming young Catholics and ordaining priests. He began his service in China in 1941, learning Chinese from the French Jesuits at the Maison Chabanel in Beijing. The Japanese interned him in 1942, though he was allowed to continue his theology studies and was ordained in 1945. He received the title Prefecture Apostolic in 1949 and Prefect Apostolic of Yangzhou in 1951, the year he was imprisoned by the Chinese Communist Party. After his expulsion in 1952, he served in Taiwan until 1962 when he left to attend sessions of Vatican II in Rome. He returned to Taiwan in 1963 and remained there until his death in 1996 in Taoyuan; he is buried at Hsinchu.

Of all the Jesuits who served in China, perhaps the most well known to students at SI was Fr. William

Ryan, SJ. Though not an SI grad, he taught and counseled at SI between 1960 and 1989. While serving as prefect of discipline at Aurora Preparatory and as associate pastor at Sacred Heart Church, both in Yangzhou City, Fr. Ryan went on trial, charged with being a spy. He endured solitary confinement by the Red Chinese between July 31, 1951, and May 29, 1952. In a 1988 interview, published in the Winter edition of *Genesis II*, he spoke of his experiences in prison: "I lost track of time, forgot how long I'd been in my cell. They took away our calendars. I had nothing but that cell. Four walls, a floor and a ceiling with a 15-watt bulb way up on top. No books…. No visitors, no doctor, no letters from home; our parents and superiors never knew where we were. Just a big hole, that's all. They wanted to break us down." After a series of brutal interrogations, the authorities released Fr. Ryan in 1952 to Irish Province Jesuits stationed in Hong Kong.

Fr. John Clifford, SJ, also knew the reality of torture. After seven years working in Shanghai, he was arrested on June 15, 1953, in Shanghai and spent three years in prison enduring psychological torture meant to brainwash him. In his book, *In the Presence of My Enemies* (published in 1963 by W.W. Norton & Co.), he told of how he was tossed out of jail in 1956 by his captors who were enraged that he had not "submitted a confession nor given my captors a single fragmentary sentence of propaganda value. They freed me, even though at the last minute I refused to sign the papers they insisted were necessary. In other words, I behaved like a normal, stubborn American — and that is what saved me."[23]

Another noteworthy SI missionary was Fr. John Gordon, SJ. He began his Chinese language studies in 1939 in Beijing and taught in Shanghai before being interned by the Japanese in 1942. He taught English for four years in Nanjing and then left for the Philippines in 1951 after the Communist takeover. While serving as treasurer of Xavier University in Cagayan de Oro City, he helped the impoverished communities living at the town's garbage dump, who combed through the trash each day looking for something to use or sell. Fr. Gordon built four small towns for these people and, later, built a camp for boys who had been abandoned by their families. Assisting him in those efforts was Fr. Gregory Ahern, SJ '44.

Also stationed in Taiwan was Fr. Philip Bourret, SJ '29, now in residence in Los Gatos. He worked in radio and television there between 1950 and 1967, assisted from the states by his classmate Harold De Luca '29 (who is also a generous benefactor to SI). He had 2 million listeners to his show at the peak of his success, and he later traveled for three decades offering help to churches in Third World countries to start their own religious broadcast programs.

Other prominent SI grads who served in the Far East include Fr. Edward Thylstrup, SJ '52, who works as the English language editor for Kuangchi Program Service in Taipei, and the late Fr. Alden Stevenson, SJ '32, an administrator in Hsinchu and editor of the *Jesuit Missions* magazine. After normalization of relations between China and the U.S. in the 1970s, Fr. Stevenson led the first university study

Fr. William Ryan, SJ, taught scores of SI students and told many stories of his imprisonment in China.

Bob Kaiser, a Newsweek editor, taught and coached at SI as a scholastic in the 1950s.

group to China and made several subsequent visits over the next 25 years. He was influential in starting a number of academic exchange programs between Chinese universities and USF before his retirement in 1981. In addition, Br. Richard Devine, SJ '52, has worked in Japan since 1959.

The job of raising funds to support these missionaries fell on the office of the California Jesuit Missionaries, headed by Fr. Ed Murphy, SJ, from 1964 until 1981, and by Fr. Theodore Taheny, SJ '43, from 1981 until 2003. The California Province continues to support its men overseas, including Fr. David Robinson, SJ '70, who works as a parish priest at St. Joseph Catholic Church in Benin City, Nigeria.

The SI-China connection is far from over, however. Br. Daniel Peterson, SJ, who served as a librarian at SI for 25 years and who is now the province archivist, spent several summers in the 1980s and 1990s in the She Shan Regional Seminary in Shanghai helping to catalogue and organize 30,000 books donated by schools and seminaries throughout the U.S. and Europe. Those donations were arranged by the late Fr. Ed Malatesta, SJ, who lived in community with the SI Jesuits while working at USF as the director of the Institute for Chinese-Western Cultural History (now called the Center for the Pacific Rim).[24]

Dissension in the 1950s

SI in the 1950s was a Shangri-La for most students and teachers, but not for all. Not everyone was happy with the conformity and old school ways imposed both by 1950s America and a pre-Vatican II Society of Jesus. Some students rebelled, such as Michael Corrigan '60, who wrote about his displeasure with Jesuit strictness in the semi-fictional *Confessions of a Shanty Irishman*. (He also sang the praises of Fr. Becker in his book for showing him "the magic alchemy in words.") For the young scholastic Robert Kaiser, SI was both an ideal school and a place that tried his patience.

Kaiser arrived at SI with 10 scholastics from his philosophy studies. "Talk about fresh-faced enthusiasm," he said in a 2003 interview while a visiting scholar at USF. "After being cooped up for seven years, we walked with a spring in our step now that we were suddenly in 'the active life' (as opposed to 'the contemplative life'). I threw myself into the job 110 percent, as did the other scholastics. At 24, I looked about the same age as the 17 year olds I was teaching. I remember going to a senior class picnic and grabbing a beer. One of the dads said, 'You can't have a beer.' Then he discovered that I was one of the scholastics."

As a scholastic, Kaiser worked long hours, rising at 5 a.m. and often working until 2 a.m. In his first year, he ran the frosh Sodality and *Inside SI*, was a prefect at the cafeteria at lunch, coached JV football, taught three courses of freshman English, one Virgil course and two more honors classes in senior English.

"Teaching at SI made me feel special," he said. "We had a faculty and student body striving for excellence. We were the best. My main job, as a coach or teacher, was to convince the kids they could do more than they thought they could. And they often did."

Kaiser was closest to his JV football kids. Noontime, they huddled around him in the cafeteria, and they attended '49ers games en masse thanks to free '49er tickets provided to schools by Mayor Christopher's Milk Fund. Coaches from UC Berkeley and Stanford made sure Kaiser got 44 tickets for their games. "The quarterbacks would sit with me, and we'd call the game together. We were like comrades in arms, and I made sure everyone played every game."

The scene was very different at Welch Hall, where Kaiser lived with "some very old and crotchety priests" assigned to USF. "They didn't talk to us very much." He praised some of the priests at SI for their vitality, but they still made the scholastics do most of the grunt work. Their only time off was Friday night when the minister gave the scholastics a case of port or black Muscat from the Novitiate. "There were more than two dozen scholastics then. We could go through a case of port while we played Monopoly or hearts," said Kaiser. "Audie Morris would always try to shoot the moon and, at a penny a point, he'd end up owing us huge amounts of money."

Scholastics then received a $2 weekly allowance to cover "bus fare." Kaiser and Morris didn't use the two bucks for bus fare; they spent their money on movies, borrowing the school's pick-up truck — "the keys were under the mat" — and "tootling down to Market Street Saturday nights in mufti. The movie cost 50 cents and popcorn was a dime. We would have been in trouble if anyone found out we were borrowing the truck, but it was our way of cutting loose at cut rates."

Kaiser soon found life in the order far too rigid.

"We followed the rules woodenly. If I wasn't awake at 5 a.m., I wasn't a good Jesuit. If the minister found I wasn't at Mass at 5:30, I'd be in trouble. Sometimes I was assigned a 6:30 a.m. Mass to serve, and I'd sleep in to 6 a.m, lazy lout that I was. We were then supposed to meditate for one hour before a 7:15 breakfast. But if I slept until 7, after working on *Inside SI* until 2 a.m., I was in trouble. It was all a part of the formalism that prevailed at the time."

The students, for the most part, didn't sense this tension. "The kids were happy kids," said Kaiser. "What was not to be happy about? They were in the best school in the city, getting the best education, envied by all the other kids, and they had an identity. They were from SI and were proud of it."

In his third year, Kaiser decided to leave the order and SI. "The sacrifices of the three vows were ones I was willing to make as long as I felt I was doing something for the Kingdom. When I found out that my superiors were more interested in reveille and taps, than in the work I did running the school magazine, I realized the sacrifices weren't worth it."

Looking back on it now, Kaiser says "there wasn't a lot wrong with SI. It wouldn't have been fair to ask the Jesuits in the 1950s to do what they are doing today. That would be rewriting history. Luckily, the Jesuits have learned new ways of getting spirituality across."

After Kaiser left SI and the Society of Jesus, he went on to a successful career in journalism. He covered Vatican II for *Time* and is now an editor for *Newsweek*. He is the author of 10 books, including *Clerical Error*, which recounts, in part, his years at SI. Kaiser is also the editor of the online magazine www.justgoodcompany.com, published by Westcoast Companeros Inc., a club of more than 200 men who

The SI band performs in the Stanyan Street campus schoolyard.

he was taught. Michael Corrigan '60, the author of *Confessions of a Shanty Irishman* and *The Irish Connection and Other Stories*, also found SI at times to be an oppressive place.

The third critique, by C. T. (Terry) Gillin '62, reflects on the value of Jesuit education in the 1950s; he praises the Jesuits for teaching him to read critically, for encouraging him to evaluate what he was learning and for inspiring him to model his own life after theirs.

SI changed drastically in the 1960s and 1970s to fix the problems discussed by Flynn and Corrigan while keeping alive the core values — the ones Gillin and many others found valuable. Spurring these changes were Vatican II, the needs of a new generation of students, and the desire of Principal Edward McFadden, SJ, and the faculty to turn SI into a modern school.

By Daniel C. Flynn, '57

All in all, I am totally grateful for my years at SI. I just wish the Church at that time hadn't been so uptight about sex. Women were portrayed as "occasions of sin." Good grief. Nevertheless, life has "turned out well" for me and I am completely grateful for the life I have today.

Actually, people of my age were lucky. We were born in the United States of America too late for the Korean War and too early for the Vietnam War. We benefited from America having won World War II and having helped Japan and Germany recover from their defeat. We did suffer from the ailing President Roosevelt's concessions to Stalin, the most malicious dictator of our century, to bring a more rapid end to World War II, but we survived the subsequent Cold War that resulted from those concessions.

First impressions of SI: Fifty years ago, I entered

have left the Jesuits. "It comes out spasmodically," he says. "I still feel I'm a Jesuit at heart," he adds. "And I still have a strong identity with SI. In 2002, I met a guy in a restaurant in Venice who turned out to be a student at SI when I served there as a scholastic. We had a tremendous sense of belonging."

Three Candid Critiques

Dan Flynn '57, who served as editor of *Inside SI* in his senior year, now teaches ESL in Belgium. Looking back on his days at SI, he sees several problems with the way he was taught and with what

St. Ignatius High School at Turk and Stanyan Streets. My first impression was "gray." (I have a picture of our senior retreat at El Retiro taken February 1957. It's a grim gray picture with little evidence of joy.) After I spent eight years in the colorful classrooms of Notre Dame des Victoires and then St. Monica's, the gray, dank rooms of SI stood ominously in stark contrast. (My Belgian friend and former SI classmate George De Cat '57 will tell you that the SI classrooms were fantastic compared to his post-war primary school classrooms in Belgium. It all depends on your life experience and point of view.) Maybe it was the fact that we were no longer in class with beautiful young women — just guys. What were they trying to protect us from? Maybe it was because we had stepped back in time to the Middle Ages or even the Dark Ages when we entered SI. I learned years later that our Jesuit teachers had actually whipped themselves in the seminary for holiness!

Teachers: Mr. Piser, SJ, English, now Robert Blair Kaiser, journalist and author; Mr. Eugene Bianchi, SJ, Sociology and 4-A homeroom teacher, now a layman and professor emeritus at Emory University in Atlanta; Mr. Andrew Dachauer, SJ, chemistry; Mr. Leo Rock, SJ, Latin; Mr. Corwin, history; and Fr. Spohn, physics. Dachauer was a nice guy for me. I wonder where he is today. [Editor's note: Fr. Dachauer is pastor of St. Joseph's Church in Mammoth Lakes, California.]

Moments: Being Editor-in-Chief of *Inside SI* and producing an innovative *Sports Illustrated*-style monthly magazine after Bob (Piser) Kaiser had replaced the typical high school style newsletter with a *Time* magazine-style publication the year before. Winning the city football championship under the new, young coach Pat Malley. Being one of five cheerleaders that season. Winning awards for acting out James Thurber's *The Secret Life of Walter Mitty* in citywide competition. Watching Fred LaCour lead SI to a city championship in basketball. Acquiring a lifelong skill by taking a pre-school morning typing class from Rene Herrerias, the basketball coach. Playing on the SI soccer and tennis teams and winning a block letter.

Classes: Mr. Rock giving up on our 4-A "Honors Program" class in Latin and having us read the rest of Caesar's Gallic Wars in English. The walls of the classroom bending in an earthquake one year.

Antics: The Jesuits trying to teach us that kissing above the neck is a venial sin and below a mortal sin. They couldn't have been serious, but they were, and some of us were so naïve as to have believed them. A Jesuit spiritual director preaching to us that we should pin a scapular to our pajama pants at night to protect us from temptation.

Tragedies: A symbol of the sexual revolution to come — a talented young student who played the guitar was thoroughly punished by the priests and scholastics for a mild imitation of Elvis Presley at a pre-game coed rally one afternoon.

Dan Flynn, center, with classmates Alan Smith and George De Cat in Belgium.

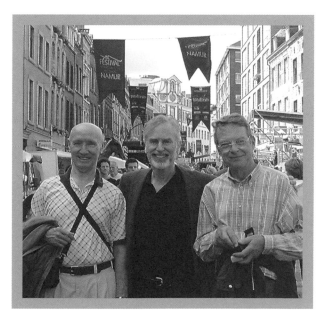

The first SI dance that I invited a date to in my freshman year: the 'dance' was in the stinky gym. There were no decorations, no band, no nothing. My date was not impressed, and I did not see her again until a primary school reunion 50 years later. Having to take Latin and ancient Greek because I was selected for the honors program. How about useful modern languages such as Spanish (third in number of native speakers in the world) or Chinese (first in number of native speakers)? They are just as useful for "training the mind" — the excuse we were given as to why we were being trained in Latin and ancient Greek.

The sex advice I got from Fr. Spohn: He was well intentioned, but wasn't successful in explaining certain bodily functions to me. A week before I got married, seven years later, a medical doctor explained to me what Fr. Spohn had not. (My dad had died when I was 10, and there was no one in the family to counsel me to take the Church's teaching with a grain of salt.) We had a perfectly awful textbook called "Modern Youth and Chastity" to guide us in sexual matters.

Philosophic reflections: It seems our class was near the end of the medieval-style education that the highly educated, but insulated, Jesuits tried to pass on to us. Some Jesuits had worldly experience, but most lived in the luxurious men's club that was known as the Society of Jesus so long as you played by their rules. The world was a shock after I left the Catholic cocoon of the 1950s and entered the Army for two years as an officer. Did I have more talented teachers at SI, especially among the scholastics and lay teachers like Mr. Corwin, than I would have had had I gone to public high school? I sometimes wonder if I wouldn't have gotten a more realistic education at a place like Lowell High School and at San Francisco State rather than Santa Clara University where I went

after SI. It no longer matters. I'm grateful for this free gift of life that I do have. Today, SI appears to be a colorful, lively place. But it also appears to be a school primarily for rich people's children. *(Editor's note: SI may appear this way, but the reality is quite different. SI awards more than $1 million in tuition assistance to about 20 percent of the student body, ensuring that no one is denied an SI education for lack of funding.)*

I wound up winning the General Excellence Award at graduation, but it turned out to be a hollow award for me. I was extremely touched by the award, but I did not feel good about it. Many of my classmates were much more talented than I. I felt alone, apart and alienated from them by the award, while my self-esteem glowed in the false, ephemeral sustenance it gave me. Today, I feel my classmates are loveable guys, and my only regret is that I wasn't capable at the time of getting to know them better. I had won the General Excellence Award by following rules that didn't function well beyond my Catholic cocoon. So, despite the award, I was ill-equipped for the greater world at large. I survived, though, and I have a beautiful life in Europe today with a wonderful wife, and for that I'm grateful.

So, what is the residual value to me of that Jesuit high school education at SI 50 years ago? I still have quite positive memories and souvenirs of my years at SI. I have my big SI block letter that I won in sports and wore on my white cheerleader sweater. I still have copies of all the *Inside SIs* I edited. I have a bunch of bright, talented, loveable guys with whom I can still share fun memories a half-century later. Nonetheless, my two primary school reunions are even more fun. I can share memories with bright, talented, loveable women as well.

By Michael Corrigan '60

I thought the curriculum at SI was broad and scholastically viable, though I didn't want four more years of religion after eight years with the nuns of Notre Dame. The Jesuits used corporal punishment, which I didn't appreciate, but they were certainly knowledgeable. The Modern Youth and Chastity course was ridiculous in retrospect, and the absence of girls and/or sex education was a flaw. I was amused at the quaint term, "self abuse" or "solitary use of the genitive faculty" for masturbation. I wanted to attend a public school but my father wouldn't allow it.

I did like some aspects of SI. The drama teacher was also a singer, and I acted in *Paint Your Wagon*, which only confirmed my lifelong love of professional theatre. Fr. Becker brought literature to life. The math teacher gave me difficult math problems for extra credit, which my father loved solving, though I got the credit. Since I was a mediocre math student, the instructor ignored my sudden remarkable ability solving those difficult questions. Certainly, I did learn the value of discipline that helped me when I decided to take graduate school seriously.

I don't remember much student camaraderie. Two friends left SI in their second year. I did feel somewhat alienated not being a superior athlete, and I was disconnected from SI by my final year, as most of my friends were outside the school.

The school was simply too strict, too much like a military camp for my tastes, though, when I visited SI in March 2004, I found it to be quite remarkable. In an odd way, SI did prompt me to better understand Joyce's *Portrait of the Artist as A Young Man* and Camus' work, which could be used as an argument against the Jesuit style of education in those days.

The Ignatian Spirit . . . Half a Century Later

By C.T. (Terry) Gillin '62

The cast of the 1953 production of Win Winsocki with Mr. Fell, SJ, as musical director.

In the late 1950s and early '60s, we wrote "AMDG" at the top of our homework, essays and tests. *Ad majorem Dei gloriam* ("for the greater glory of God") may be virtually all that remains of my four years of Latin, but it embodies the Ignatian spirit that lingers in my life almost half a century later. "AMDG" was a reminder that the work, however routine, bore the meaning we brought to it with our own intentions. It was a sign that our work was done with respect for ourselves as well as for the assignment.

In 1958, St Ignatius High School took a child and, over four years, turned him into an adult — as Jesuits have been doing for hundreds of years. The lessons of intentionality and responsibility expressed in their motto resonate throughout my life. They can be summarized in three points. First, the Jesuits taught me "to read." Reading is not as simple as it seems; it requires interpreting, making sense out of the story or essay by understanding its assumptions and implications. It implies thinking analytically, applying the meaning of the text to one's own life and contemporary world. Reading is an invitation to think about the kind of person one wants to be and the kind of society one wants to help build.

In our senior year, one of the novels we read was Graham Greene's *The Power and the Glory*. As I recall it, the story concerns a "whiskey priest" caught in the turmoil of Mexico's revolution that has outlawed the Church. The central figure has given up his priestly vows to save his life; he is living with a woman and struggling with his conscience. He hears that an escaped convict is in the mountains and wants to confess before he dies. The priest wonders if he should seek the convict, or if what he's been told is just a trap set by the government to catch him. In the end, the priest chooses to search for the convict and is caught by the government. I remember the way Fr. Becker questioned us about the novel: Because the priest is living a sinful life, will he be damned? Or, because he lays down his life for another, will he be saved? Through the discussion that followed, we were invited to recognize something of the complexity of life, to move beyond the child's world of black-and-white morality, and to think and evaluate for ourselves.

This remembrance leads me to a second point. The Jesuits taught us not only to think but also to evaluate: to recognize that our everyday actions, the ordinary things we think about and do, are important. Each thing we do matters: how I respond to family, friends, colleagues and strangers such as other drivers, people on the street and panhandlers. The Jesuits taught that we are all a little like the whiskey priest. Each day presents opportunities, usually about mundane matters, that

matter. It seems to me, the Ignatian question is, How am I to respond? And the assumption is that we each have deep within ourselves the ability to know how to respond.

Thirdly, I remember being impressed by the Jesuits themselves, their commitment to teaching and their dedication to us, their students. At SI, the Jesuits gave us a place to define ourselves, to be grateful for our accomplishments and to be tolerant of the inevitable mistakes, our own as well as others'. I saw them as role models for a way to live that makes a difference — loving my family, dedicated to my work, contributing to the community, working toward the development of a just world. Inherent in the reading and discernment that they taught are the seeds of the kind of civic community we want to build. It was the experience of my Jesuit teachers that led me to become a teacher and inspired me to understand teaching as more than the transmission of ideas; rather, teaching helps students connect their understanding to their own actions. For me, the "more" (the "*majorem*") in the Jesuit motto is the belief that I can come to a better understanding of my self and the world and that we each can make a difference.

Terry Gillin lives with his wife and son and is a professor of sociology at Ryerson University in Toronto, Canada.

Chalk-Dust Memories: The 1950s

In those days, everyone was unified. Everyone had friends from SH and Riordan, which had just started, and we used to all meet at the dances Friday night at one of the three schools. We were all interested in girls at that time.

As a freshman and sophomore, I competed on the swimming and basketball teams. We used to see Ollie

From left: Class of 1951 grads Bill Reed, Bob Havens, Ed Brown, John Arnerick, Les Rosebold. Bill is the only surviving member of this group.

Matson practice on USF's football field when USF was ranked first in the nation. Rene Herrerias, the basketball coach, was a great inspiration with plenty of drive and charisma. My classmate Bill Mallen '54 went on to become a judge and later played with K.C. Jones for USF's basketball team.

Warren White was an outgoing and inspiring English teacher who took a great interest in the students and ran the playhouse. Mr. Dennis, later Fr. Dennis, ran the paper where I worked drawing cartoons, poking a little editorial fun at the students and staff.

— *Edward Boblits (Jahn) '54*

• • •

We had great young Jesuit scholastics and priests, including Mr. Ed McFadden, Mr. John LoSchiavo and Mr. George Dennis. Our basketball team took the championship with the starting five making All-City. We had a nice contingent of guys who commuted to school from Oakland. Think of the time those guys had to get up in the morning to catch the ferry!

— *Denis Ragan '51*

• • •

Our class started in 1953. The school asked us to us sell tickets to raise funds to build a field house with a swimming pool, with the first prize being a trip to Hawaii. The student who sold the most tickets for his class was given a day off from school. (Jim Gallagher '57, who later served as Sonoma County Assessor for many years, earned that distinction.) We sold tickets for four years and raised thousands and thousands of dollars, but SI never built that field house.

When Pat Malley started coaching, he told us we were going to beat Poly. When we played them the first time, they kicked our behinds. We then played Poly in the semifinals and beat them. That was the happiest day of Pat Malley's life. He had convinced us that we could beat Poly and we believed him. The newspapers used to write about us as the stumbling, bumbling and fumbling team. But under Malley, we had a tremendous defense. Nobody scored much on us. SH had a famous fullback, Walt Arnold, who went on to play at UC Berkeley, and we held him to 6 yards rushing one game. Our fullback, Gil Dowd '57, had a banner day and went on to star at Stanford.

After the earthquake of 1957 our class (4-D) was in the chemistry lab on the fourth floor of the old building on Stanyan Street. After all the beakers and vials stopped shaking, our teacher, a young Jesuit scholastic named Mr. Lentz told us all to sit down and be calm, and he would check out the situation. He proceeded to leave us in the lab, went down the hall, and was not seen again that day.

— *John Strain '57*

• • •

In 1945 when I was 10, I lived close to Kezar, and my uncle, who had graduated from Poly, took me to see what he thought would be a Poly massacre of SI. SI won 13–7 for the city championship. My uncle had a temper, so I had to hold all my joy within, smiling on the way home.

SI was a big ROTC school. After freshman year, you either took Greek or ROTC. Either in my sophomore or junior year, *Life* magazine was going to do a big spread on SI's ROTC program, as it was one of the largest in the country. The photographer stood on top of scaffolding to take a picture out on what is now USF's soccer field. All the ROTC officers assembled us and had us stand at attention looking at the camera. To be funny, one row of 10 or 20 kids faced the opposite direction, away from the camera. The photographer didn't discover this until he developed the prints. The magazine never ran the picture because of that one row. Some students were upset even though no one could have identified himself as the faces would have been so small. But we could have had national exposure.

J.B. Murphy taught me algebra in my freshman year. He was down-to-earth and sincere; he wanted you to succeed. I always respected him. I remember many teachers had to have summer jobs, and I worked side by side with Bernie at Hamms and Burgermeister. It was strange working with him as a colleague.

Frank Corwin was such a great storyteller that students would much rather listen to his stories than pay attention to the course. He told us about the Egyptian red ants that would eat a tire as it moved and about swords that would fly through the air and decapitate someone who spat by mistake in the high holy places in Egypt.

My companions made my time at SI so enjoyable. At my 50-year reunion, I realized just how proud I am to have associated with these people for so long. We now get together four times a year, and we can just be ourselves. If you happen to be well-to-do, great; if not, no big deal.

— *Charlie Leach '53*

• • •

SI's old high school gym was built before USF had its own gym. Fr. Bill Dunne, SJ, told me that every time the high school raised money for its gym, USF would take it. To keep that from happening, the SI Jesuits began putting their money in coffee cans in the principal's office. They did that for 15 years, never showing it to the college president. When they had enough for a down payment on the gym, they brought those coffee cans filled with money to the treasurer's office.

— *Pete Devine '66*

• • •

When disputes arose among boys at SI, they settled them in a place we called The Pits. There had been a large building in Golden Gate Park across from St. Mary's Hospital, but only the foundations remained. It was a big deal in the 1950s and 1960s for kids to go there to fight after school, and sometimes those fights would draw hundreds of students.

— *Chuck Murphy '61*

• • •

My first year at SI was marked by austerity, symbolized by Bellarmine beating us 55–7. We had a small playground but great camaraderie with 1,000 guys from all over the city thrown together. In those days, you stayed together with same 30 people all day and all year, and after four years, the friendships were strong. Pat Malley was one of three lay teachers in the whole school. Even though he taught freshman math and coached football, he also taught religion between the lines, and it was more than I learned in religion class. One day he told about some kids who knocked an old lady down in a bus, and he made an impression about how rotten a thing that was. He explained that war isn't against bad people but against evil.

Because of the lack of facilities, we had to take physics during the upperclass lunch period and had lunch with the lowerclassmen. We never ate anything. About 15 of us would make a mad dash to the basketball courts outside the chapel, to the one good basketball court. The first 10 guys that made a basket got to play, and we'd play the entire lunch period. We spilled a little blood on occasion: It was like the SH game every lunch period. With all I was doing, I felt life was flying by and just wanted to savor every minute. It was also a great way to relieve stress.

— *Fr. Fran Stiegeler, SJ '61*

• • •

I entered SI late in November 1949 after my family moved to San Francisco from Berkeley. I had Frank Corwin for history, and when he found out I had roots in Utah, he told me he had worked there the year before but had been almost fired for "moral turpitude" for smoking. I couldn't believe that anyone would kick out a teacher straight from service in Africa. When I met Fr. Andy Gilligan, SJ, he looked at my name and said, "Oh no, not another Dago!" and he proceeded to tell Leo LaRocca and Frank Ravetti to come up and take care of me. From then on, they were my angels, even though I trembled in

my boots when I saw all 6 feet of Leo.

Mr. Ed McFadden, SJ '41, taught Latin by walking along the railing of the window with a yardstick acting out the role of Caesar. Geometry was taught by Fr. Ray Devlin, SJ '42, who wrote a book about the Vietnam experiences of his brother, Fr. Joe Devlin, SJ. Br. Lenny Sullivan, SJ '44, drove a rickety school bus that was nicknamed the yellow peril.

The classroom was like the movie *The Blackboard Jungle*. It was students against teachers. We had some crazy priests, including Fr. Charlie McKee, SJ, who claimed to be an ex-boxer. This man, who taught a course using *Modern Youth & Chastity*, shoved me down the center stairs and against a locker for something I did that angered him. At one point, he made derogatory remarks about Leo LaRocca's date. Leo reached a point where he had all he could take. He grabbed the priest by the throat and said, "If you weren't wearing this cassock, I'd clobber you," or words to that effect.

The teachers running detention would come up with neat little tricks to punish us. We would kneel on the floor on pencils for 45 minutes, and if you squirmed, you stayed longer. If you got in the way of Fr. Ray Pallas, SJ '32, he'd whack you with his cane.

I had some excellent teachers, such as Fr. Pierre Jacobs, SJ '31, who taught chemistry. I was amazed to earn a "B" in that course, as he was a tough teacher. On the first day of class, he impressed upon us how dangerous the course could be by holding up a pair of pants minus the crotch that had been burned away from an acid spill. Warren White was a fantastic English teacher, and he inspired me to study English at USF. I worked stage crew for him for *Billy Budd* and *Look Homeward Angel* at the Marines Memorial Theatre.

— *Fr. Paul Capitolo, SJ '53*

The backstage crew from Room Service. Photo courtesy of Bob Dawson '52.

X. Stanyan Street Meets Haight & Ashbury (1960 ~ 1969)

In some ways, SI was an island of conservative, traditional values while the changes taking place in San Francisco during the 1960s roiled around it. In other ways, SI was forever changed by those forces of Vatican II, the Civil Rights movement, the protests against the war in Vietnam, and the Summer of Love. Those changes did not evidence themselves so much at SI in the 1960s, but took root, nonetheless, and flowered in the 1970s.

The decade can be summarized by sports, spirituality and school relocation. The sports teams rose to new heights, and school spirit climbed with each success. The football team earned a first-place national ranking in 1962 and won five league championships, the last in the new West Catholic Athletic League after SI left the AAA. The baseball team brought home four league titles, and the basketball team won three championships. Some of the lesser known sports — golf (AAA champs in 1961) and cross country (league

The Stanyan Street campus in the late 1950s.

champs three times) also did well. The most successful sport, however, turned out to be swimming, which took AAA laurels seven times. In all, it was a golden age for SI athletics.

After Vatican II, SI began rethinking the nature of Jesuit education. In past decades, Jesuits shared their unique brand of spirituality mainly during the senior retreats. That started changing slowly in the 1960s as the idea of being "contemplatives in action" grew to encompass the sodalities (which morphed in the CLCs of the 1970s) and the good work they did throughout the city.

The biggest change came at the end of the decade, when SI moved quarters to its sixth campus, located in the sand dunes of the Sunset District. That move changed not only the location but also the name of the school as it christened itself St. Ignatius College Preparatory and set its sights on redefining itself as one of the nation's premier prep schools.

The Move to the Sunset District

In the spring of 1957, 600 boys took the freshmen entrance examination, but because of "limited facilities" the school accepted only 287 students. "The major reason for holding the student body down to this figure is the lack of facilities in the Physics and Chemistry Departments," noted the *Ignatian Bulletin* that year. In the early 1960s, Fr. Patrick Carroll, SJ '31, SI's first president, conducted a study of the school's strengths and weaknesses and long-term needs, spurred by the formal separation of SI and USF. He asked architects to draw plans for remodeling the Stanyan Street campus to include larger classrooms and for a new structure, an eight-story Jesuit residence north of the school. That plan never made it off the drawing boards. After reviewing those plans and the findings of the study, he determined the school had to move to more modern quarters.

SI made a successful move to the Sunset District thanks to Fr. Harry Carlin, SJ.

Fr. Harry V. Carlin, SJ

The task of that move was given to Fr. Carroll's successor, Fr. Harry V. Carlin, SJ '35. Harry Carlin, the youngest of six children born to William and Evelyn Carlin, grew up in Berkeley and moved to St. Agnes Parish in San Francisco at the age of 13. His father worked for the Bannan family at Western Gear Corporation, and years later, Harry would ask Bernard Bannan, the son of the company's founder, to join SI's first Board of Regents.

In 1931, young Harry entered the brand-new SI campus on Stanyan Street, and by his junior year, he knew that he wanted to become a Jesuit. Harry entered the Society after graduating from SI, and his father told him, "Go. I'll see you in a week. You'll miss your movies too much." He worked hard at his studies and at picking grapes with the other novices at Los Gatos. "From early morning to late afternoon, with only a break for lunch, we'd pick grapes," he recalled. "After two weeks, our Levis could stand by themselves from all the dried grape juice on them."

In 1942, Harry returned to SI to teach English and coach basketball, and he led his 110's team to the city championship. From 1945–1949 he studied theology at Alma College, and in 1948 was ordained to the priesthood. Although he felt that teaching was his true calling, Harry was asked in 1950 to serve as Loyola High's vice principal — the school disciplinarian. Strict but always maintaining a sense of humor, Harry spent a combined nine years at Loyola, Brophy and SI, assigning many a rambunctious student JUG. "I used to tell the students that I didn't want to hear their excuses for being late unless their car blew up and they brought in the parts to prove it. The next day one student walked in late rolling a tire. He said his car blew up. I had to let him go. I just laughed at his ingenuity."

In 1957, he returned to SI where he proved a strict taskmaster with both students and faculty, Jesuits included. "If a young scholastic or lay teacher couldn't handle a tough class, Fr. Carlin would give him a quick lesson in classroom management skills," noted veteran SI teacher and coach Bob Drucker '58.

He left in 1959 to work with scholastics as vice president of Alma College, and then was offered the president's job at SI in 1964, which he reluctantly accepted. He had hoped to teach students instead of running a high school.

Fr. Carlin started raising funds for the new school by launching the Genesis campaign in November 1964 and hiring Duane Press, former director of development at St. Mary's College, to help with fund raising as assistant to the president. Together, the two men launched the *Genesis* magazine that year. The first issue included the following by way of explanation of the publication's name: "Because we realize that no four years will be as full, as rich and as vital as those four years when a boy 'begins' his journey to manhood at Saint Ignatius, and because each day we 'renew' our total commitment to the growth and development of the young men entrusted to us, we have chosen to call this report 'Genesis.'"

(The magazine has changed names with each new fund-raising campaign. It changed to *Genesis II* in 1980 just as the Genesis Campaign neared completion of its goal of paying for the new school construction. The Genesis II Campaign sought to raise SI's endowment fund from $1.1 million to $4 million over five years. In December 1990, the school announced the Genesis III campaign to raise $16 million to remodel the campus, and the magazine's name changed, too. Finally, in December 1996, the school launched the Genesis IV campaign — announced in the newly renamed *Genesis IV,* published in January 1997 — that ultimately increased the endowment to $50 million by 2005. Over the years, the magazine has grown from a four-page newsletter to a 56-page quarterly featuring articles on students, faculty and alumni.)

In 1965, the San Francisco Unified School District put up for sale the 11.374-acre Sunset District parcel,

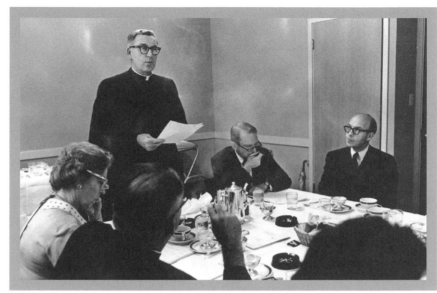

Fr. Carlin formed SI's first Board of Regents in the 1960s.

located on 37th Avenue between Rivera and Pacheco Streets (known as Assessor's Block No. 2094), and asked $2 million for it. Fr. Carlin bid $2,001,100 "just in case someone bid against us," he noted in a 1990 *Genesis IV* interview. "On April 13, 1965, at 7:41 p.m., Commissioner James E. Stratten, Chairman of the Board of Education, rapped his gavel and called the public meeting to order." After announcing that the district had received one sealed bid, he called for any other bids for the property, but none were forthcoming and the property belonged to SI. With that, SI "made its greatest step forward in 110 years."[1]

Now that the school had purchased the land, it had to pay for it. To help dramatize the need for funds, SI staged a photo for the May 1965 cover of *Genesis,* entitled "Exodus!" showing 15 students sitting in chairs in the middle of the sand dunes being taught by a Jesuit (Fr. Bob Mathewson, SJ) wearing his cassock.

To dramatize the need for funds to build the new school, the May 1965 Genesis staged this photo for the cover.

Archbishop Joseph McGucken aided SI in the purchase of the land with a $1 million donation on April 30, 1965, the largest gift the school had ever received, made "in recognition of the contribution of the Jesuit community during their 110 years of service to the city and the archdiocese."

Fr. Carlin also assembled the first SI Board of Regents — men and women whose generosity and talent would prove invaluable to building a new and modern campus. They gathered for the first time in 1966 and reconvened regularly over the years since then to advise the school in its mission. (The first board included Joseph Alioto, Bernard Bannan, Mrs. Fred A. Beronio, Fr. Harry Carlin, SJ, Arthur P. Carroll, Thomas Carroll, John P. Cruden, Henry Doelger, Jr., John J. Ferdon, Charles Gould, John Henning, Fr. Leo Hyde, SJ, W. Dobson Kilduff, Mrs. August Koenig, Mrs. Jules Leonardini, Richard O. Linke, Fr. Edward McFadden, SJ, Felix McGinnis, George McKeon, George Millay, Francis J. Murphy (who helped oversee construction of the new campus), Thomas J. Murtagh, Hugh O'Donnell, Daniel O'Hara, Charles Paganini, Frank Paganini, Charles Quarré, James Rudden, Vincent Sullivan, Al Wilsey, and chairman William Zellerbach.)

For money and advice to build the $8.1 million campus, Fr. Carlin relied heavily on his board, and he hired Henry Doelger of Doelger Enterprises as Special Advisor, responsible for the planning and construction phases of the new campus. (Doelger had attended 6th, 7th and 8th grades at SI's shirt factory campus but left school to support his family when his father died. His firm developed much of the Sunset District and Daly City.)

In July 1965, Fr. Carlin and his consultant, Dr. John Butler (who was given the title of "school planner"), hired Corwin Booth and Associates Architects to design the campus. John Walsh, Jr., served as project architect with Richard Blanchard, and the two designed a campus that combined the old and the new, with "arches, pitched roofs, colonnades… suggested by the mission style, but [with a] contemporary impression." Blanchard wanted "those elements in the mission style [to be] translated into modern form, using contemporary construction methods and materials."[2]

He also hoped to keep maintenance costs down on the 192,000-square-foot structure by using bricks and stucco on the exterior and to maximize classroom space through "minimum waste on corridors." He also gave SI a unique roof design with connecting "self-supporting square pyramids with skylights at the apex… supported by post-tensioned cross beams, permitting longer bridging…."[3]

Fr. Carlin worried that he didn't have enough money to build the entire project, and initially planned to construct the library and Commons at a later date. "I thought we could use one or two classrooms as a library. But the board advised me to borrow the money to build it all. 'It will never be cheaper,' they told me. I'm glad we did. We saved a lot of money in the long run. Had we built SI today, it would cost $80 million."[4]

Carlin soon became famous among SI alumni

for being an effective fund raiser. "At first I didn't like doing it, but I got used to it, as I knew we had a good cause." One of his strategies was to ask certain donors to pay the interest on the debt while the school worked to pay the principal. "People responded well to that idea."

Generous donors included Mr. & Mrs. Joseph Alioto ($110,000), the estate of Joseph E. Krout ($171,000) and Mr. & Mrs. Michel Orradre, who gave $95,600 towards the construction of the chapel in memory of their son, Stephen, who had died in a car accident in 1964. Even the students raised $28,000 on their own to pay for their new campus. Later, SI sold its Stanyan Street site to USF for $1.8 million to help pay for the Sunset District school.

Bulldozers began work in July 1967 grading the football field and track, under the supervision of Hudson, Brennan and Yee, Inc., the low-bidders for the job at $167,100. The architects decided to build the field first to allow two years for grass to establish. (That grass field was replaced in 2002 in favor of FieldTurf.) Williams & Burrows (low bidders at $5,198,000 with final costs coming in at $6,100,000) began construction on the school building February 13, 1968, after delays caused by financial problems, and on March 21, 1968, the school held a formal ground-breaking ceremony with California Provincial Patrick Donohoe, SJ, blessing the site from a PG&E aerial lift.[5]

While classes opened September 13, 1969, much of the campus still had not been finished, and the 1,185 students left at 1 p.m. to allow workers time to finish the newly-named St. Ignatius College Preparatory. (The Board of Regents approved the name change in May 1969.) The first thing to impress students were the carpets that covered the floors of the

halls and classrooms — a far cry from the hard floors of the Stanyan Street campus. John Butler, who helped determine the specifications for the new school, chose carpeting "not only because it is the best acoustical material, but because this keeps down maintenance costs." Students also discovered the value of rubber-soled shoes after a few static-electric shocks.[6]

Fr. Carlin, who ushered in the modern age of St. Ignatius, stayed on as president until 1970, the

241

Work on the Sunset District campus did not finish until 1970.

Fr. Carlin and members of the Board of Regents tour the construction site.

Tom Carroll '43 served on the Alumni Board and on the Board of Regents. A San Francisco firefighter, Tom recalls spending many enjoyable off-duty hours driving Fr. Carlin as he visited parents and other potential benefactors while fund-raising for the new SI campus. "For 10 years, from 1965 to 1975, Fr. Carlin and I would leave SI around 9 a.m. and head for downtown to begin a full day of visits. He would generally see three people in the morning and another couple after lunch. Sometimes he would even visit a family in their home in the evening.

"Fr. Carlin had great success in these fund-raising efforts because he was so personable and friendly. It was my great pleasure to spend those days with him. We enjoyed lots of good conversation, and he was like a father and brother to me. I am very fortunate to be able to call him my good friend."

Thanks to Fr. Carlin's efforts, SI paid its debt in full in 1981. Fr. Carlin kept the last cancelled check as a memento of all those years of planning, building and paying off the 2001 37th Avenue campus.

"It's amazing what he did with no experience," said former SI principal Fr. Edward McFadden, SJ, in a 1990 interview. "Without him, there would be no new SI campus."

end of his six-year term of office. When he returned from summer vacation, he discovered that the school had named the Commons in his honor. "It was a nice gesture," he said, "But we probably could have raised money by naming it after someone else."

Even though SI had a new president in Fr. Cornelius M. Buckley, SJ, Fr. Carlin's days at SI were far from over. "The provincial told me, 'You built this; now you pay for it,'" as SI still owed $1.7 million for the school and the $550 annual tuition didn't even cover the real costs of educating each student. Since then, Fr. Carlin has served as executive vice president, working in the development office and raising money through Cadillac Raffles, Stagecoach West fund raisers, auctions and by the time-honored method of shaking hands, looking people in the eyes and asking for donations. Many of those who met this determined man ended up digging deep to help the school.

The Christel the King Award

"By means of a striking gold medal, a citation of Merit, and a reverent, dignified ceremony, the Alumni Association each year pays homage to one of its own who has distinguished himself in his Community, has brought honor and credit to his Alma Mater and has rendered outstanding service to the School."[7] With this announcement, SI established the Christ the King Award as the highest honor it bestows upon a graduate, and its first recipient was Dr. Edmund Morrissey '16, a world-renowned brain surgeon and chief of staff at St. Mary's Hospital. The school presented the award to him on the Feast of Christ the King in 1960 during the First Annual Family Communion Breakfast and Alumni Mass.

SI's Parent Clubs

The Loyola Guild

The Loyola Guild began in October 1925 for mothers of sons who attended either the high school or the college (though wives of graduates and lay professors could join as well). According to the 1925 *Ignatian*, the group existed to "foster a deeper acquaintance with all in touch with St. Ignatius College, and to cooperate with its officers to the effect that faculty and parents may work in harmony for the best interests of the school and students." They held a monthly meeting followed by a concert or a lecture and raised money in all sorts of ways to help the Jesuits. During the Depression they held a bake sale to help the school pay its electrical bill. One year, the mothers raised enough money to buy uniforms for the college band. "Back in the 1920s, these mothers had a great love for the Jesuits and their mission, just as we still have today," said Guild President Connie Mack.

At its peak, the Guild boasted 1,200 members and was one of the elite women's clubs in San Francisco. "It was a white-glove organization," added Mrs. Mack. "The Guild's annual tea at the Palace Hotel drew a thousand women and sold out every year at $5 a ticket. For many women, it was *the* club to join."

Currently the group has 750 members across the country and raises money to endow scholarships at SI and USF. The group held a gala celebration at SI in 2000 to mark their 75th anniversary, drawing 15 past presidents including Katherine Walsh, who would soon celebrate her 100th birthday.

The Guild still organizes rummage sales, Christmas house tours and fashion shows to raise funds, each year collecting approximately $15,000 to split between SI and USF. Since its inception, the group has raised nearly $500,000 for SI alone, providing 375 full scholarships to SI students in addition to 750 partial scholarships to students at USF.

The Ignatian Guild

In 1959, when SI formally split from USF, Fr. Patrick Carroll created a subcommittee of the Loyola Guild made up of SI mothers who would raise funds only for SI, and he asked Mrs. Dorothy Leonar-

Stagecoach West served as one of SI's most important fund-raisers.

dini to serve as the group's first president. In 1961, this subcommittee became a separate group, the Mothers' Advisory Council, and the following year its name changed to the St. Ignatius Mothers' Club. Three years later, in 1965, Theresa Caldarola — who had a passion for helping educational causes — pioneered the Ignatian Guild and oversaw the creation of the group's constitution and by-laws. That year the group held a celebrity auction and, at the Fairmont Hotel, its first fashion show, sponsored by Lili of Shanghai. The raffle for the event earned $20,000 to support the school.

The Ignatian Guild continues to hold two successful fashion shows each year — a Saturday dinner and a Sunday luncheon — during the first weekend of November. It also sponsors many other events, including the International Food Faire, which celebrates the diverse cultures that make up the SI community.

The Ignatian Guild also ran Stagecoach West, which started in 1972. The fund-raising dinner featured the Wells Fargo stagecoach, a Western barbeque, gaming tables and dancing. It also sold a cookbook for $5 entitled *Food for Thought*, assembled by its members and featuring recipes such as Mulligatawny Soup by Mrs. Jerry Cole and Potage Vichyssoise Josephine, by Mrs. Josephine Araldo (a Cordon Bleu graduate and French cooking instructor). The book received favorable reviews in the press, including one from James Beard of the *Examiner*. In 1977, the Ignatian Guild put out a second edition of the book with additional recipes.

Other Ignatian Guild fund raisers over the years have included the Dorothy Leonardini Scholarship Fund, the Salesmen's Samples Sale, the annual Christmas Celebration in the Carlin Commons and the Rummage Sale at the Hall of Flowers — run jointly by the Ignatian and Loyola Guilds. The Ignatian Guild

Opposite page: Fr. Victor White, SJ, was the guest speaker at a father-son gathering on Oct. 16, 1949. After the meal, the Jesuits dedicated the baseball backstop in honor of Edward McQuade '24.

also sponsors a Day of Recollection each year for its members and celebrates new officers at an installation Mass and luncheon in May. Other Guild events include the mother-student communion breakfast, the mother-daughter night and the mother-son night.

The Fathers' Club

The school began a new tradition in 1937 with the institution of Father's Night, featuring science project displays, elocution contests, Sodality activities, and performances by actors, singers, musicians and members of the ROTC. This was a return, of sorts, to the three-day commencement ceremonies that ended the terms for SI students who graduated from the Market Street and Van Ness Avenue campuses. Two years later, the event evolved into the annual Fathers' Club Talent Show, where students competed for prizes. Fr. Harold E. Ring, SJ, president of SI and USF at the time, hoped that it would become the foundation of an SI Fathers' Club. The night also featured a sports review and a talk by Fr. William Dunne, SJ, who would succeed Ring as president. The April 1939 *Monthly Calendar* for St. Ignatius Church reported that "no alumni meeting brings together more of the 'Old Boys' than Fathers' Night at the High School. The fathers are always surprised to find out what their sons are doing and what they can do in a modern high school. Fathers' Night is only three years old, but each time it has been an overwhelming success."

The Fathers' Club formally began in 1948 in part to help SI complete the fund-raising drive to build the gym. (By then, the school only had one-fifth of the money needed.) Edward Turkington, father of Ned Turkington '49, was one of the founders of the Fathers' Club, according to Edward's grandson, Ted

Turkington (who joined SI in 2003 as the head varsity baseball coach). The group received help from its first moderator, Fr. Fred Cosgrove, SJ, and organized a Father-Son Communion Breakfast in October 1948, with more than 700 attending the Mass and outdoor feast that followed. Before the November Poly football game, the group organized a rally, held in the St. Dominic's auditorium. According to the 1949 *Ignatian,* the group also offered sports clinics, a picnic and an Ignatian Heights Talent Show featuring "vaudeville, music, mimicry and general entertainment." By the 1950s, with the help of moderator Donald O'Gara, SJ, the Fathers' Club also sponsored dinner dances, a festival and the Cana Conferences.

The group earned money for the school in the 1950s by using the SI schoolyard to park cars for the '49er games at Kezar. Dr. Elmer Bricca, president in 1954–55 (the uncle of Steve Leveroni '69, who served as president in 2003–2004) had the dads park the cars together as close as they could. "They would then leave until the game ended," said Leveroni. "Someone invariably would want to leave early, and mass confusion would ensue."

The group launched the Cadillac Raffle in 1957 when Fathers' Club President Bernard

McCann '31 and Remo Tocchini (president in 1958) persuaded a local dealer to donate a car to the school. The first winners, who split a ticket, were Ernest Granucci and Dr. Leo Chelini, both relatives of Steve Leveroni. This event continued as the group's primary fund raiser until the 1980s.

The Fathers' Club arranged to have Jim Nabors

(TV's Gomer Pyle) come to the 1966 Cadillac Raffle, where Nabors drew the winning ticket; the event raised $20,000 for the school.

In 1970, after the school moved to its new quarters, SI inaugurated an auction, raising $40,000 that year. The first chairman was Joseph R. Bisho with Mrs. Eugene J. Marty, Jr., and Mrs. L. Cal Lalanne serving as co-chairs. The Ignatian Guild continued this event for a number of years. Then in 1997, the Fathers' Club began sponsoring the auction, and it has become one of the most important fund raisers for the school thanks to auction chairmen Fred Tocchini '66, Al Clifford '73, Scott Erickson '73, Joe McMonigle, Joe Toboni '70, Bert Keane '68, Sal Rizzo and David Pacini. In 2004, the auction helped raise more than a half million dollars to help the Genesis IV endowment campaign. These sold-out auctions have also been successful at bringing diverse members of the SI community together to create a fun-filled evening of food, entertainment and fast-paced bidding.

The Fathers' Club, moderated by Br. Douglas Draper, SJ, since 1971, holds several major gatherings each year for its members, including two barbecues, a Crab 'n' Cards night and a father-son dinner featuring a guest speaker. (In 2004, '49ers' quarterback Joe Montana spoke of his relationship with his father and regaled the audience with stories of his days playing at Candlestick Park.)

In 1993 the Fathers' Club began running the concession stand during the football and basketball games, with proceeds benefiting the school, and it joins with the SHC parents' club to run concessions during the Bruce-Mahoney football game at Kezar.

Fred Tocchini '66, who followed in his dad's footsteps as Fathers' Club president, thinks that the group has become successful over the years because of the "vast resources that lie within the parent community. Also, the group has camaraderie because members are willing to be a part of this long tradition of service to the school. Not everyone can write a big check, but many are willing and able to work hard to help SI in whatever way they can."

For Tocchini, who served as chairman of the Sesquicentennial Committee and Regent, being a member and president of the Fathers' Club "was an important part of my life. My older brothers attended SI in the 1950s, and I felt a part of the SI community even before I attended the school."

Athletics

SI Football Ranked First in Nation

Despite the plans to move the school in the 1960s, life continued its normal routine, especially in the realm of football. After Pat Malley left SI, the school hired Larry McInerney as head coach and Vince Tringali (a member of USF's famous "Undefeated, Untied and Uninvited" football team) as his assistant. McInerney's teams won the round-robin championships in the AAA for two years, in 1959 and 1960, but never won a Turkey Bowl championship game. Then, in 1962, Tringali took over as head coach and hired a remarkable assistant — Robert H. "Doc" Erskine, who left semi-retirement after many years of coaching college ball. Together, they helped SI in 1962

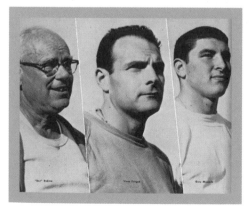

From left, varsity football coaches Doc Erskine, Vince Tringali and Gary Musante.

and 1963 win 19 straight games in two undefeated seasons and win consecutive AAA championships. (For each of those 19 games, Coach Tringali wore his trademark red Alpine hat.) On January 4, 1963, *The San Francisco Chronicle* announced that SI had tied with Miami High School of Florida for first place in the Imperial Sports Syndicate's 1962 U.S. interscholastic football ratings based on votes from 56 coaches and sportswriters across the country.

The following is an excerpt from "Remembering the glory years of SI football," first published in the Fall '88 *Genesis II*:

By Robert Vergara '76

The 'Cats opened the 1962 season against Balboa, and with three touchdowns in the second quarter, went on to a 29–6 win. Galileo and Polytechnic were SI's next victims, with the Lions going down to a 39–0 defeat and the Parrots suffering a 26–0 shutout.

By the time the 'Cats defeated Lincoln in their fourth game of the season, it was clear that they were a major force in the league. In the team's first four games, SI had scored 107 points to their opponents' 12. Quarterbacks Lee French and Ray Calcagno and fullback Tom Kennedy sparked the Wildcat offense, aided in no small measure by one of the finest lines in SI football history — Bud Baccitich, Rudy Labrado and Gene Maher, to name a few of the stalwarts.

The 'Cats next took on Mission. Although the Bears had been picked by many to win the league, they too were bested by SI 49–0.

The following week, the Wildcats faced archrival Sacred Heart in a game televised as KGO-TV's "Prep Game of the Week." In those days, Channel 7 taped a high school football game played on a Thursday or Friday and broadcast the game the following Saturday morning with Bud Foster and Bob Fouts (the father of Dan Fouts '69) doing the play-by-play. The TV audience saw the Wildcats defeat the Irish 22–6.

By this time, sportswriters, who early in the season had called SI a "good team," were now agreeing with the *Examiner's* Bob Sprenger when he wrote that SI's 1962 football squad "has to be one of SI's best teams in history."

Next came the Washington game, which led to another victory for SI, and the 'Cats found themselves in the last game of the regular season. That contest, against Lowell, would decide the round-robin champion.

The score was close throughout. Finally, with less than 5 minutes remaining in the game, Ray Calcagno connected with Charlie Parks on a 48-yard pass to set up the winning touchdown. Final score: SI 19, Lowell 13.

The Indians fell into a three-way tie for second place with Mission and Lincoln. At that time the AAA had no structure for a four-team playoff. Only the top two teams met on Thanksgiving Day to decide the championship. Lowell won the draw and met SI at Kezar Stadium before more than 16,000 fans to battle for the title.

SI scored in the first quarter when Calcagno threw

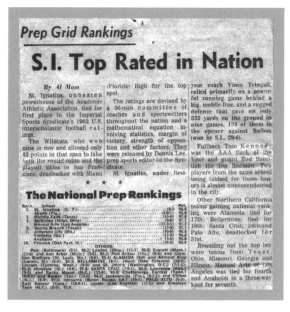

In 1962 and 1963, the SI football team did not lose a single game and earned a number-one ranking from the nation's sportswriters.

In 1962, SI was ranked first in the nation among high school football teams.

a 30-yard pass to Charlie Parks, putting the Wildcats on the Indians' 2-yard line. Mike Sullivan scored on the next play, and Calcagno kicked the extra point, which turned out to be the margin of victory.

Lowell scored in the last minute of the first half, but the snap for the PAT was too high, and the Indians had to settle for six points. It was a defensive battle from then on as SI held on to a 7–6 victory.

The win gave the Wildcats the AAA championship, a 9–0 record and the first perfect season in SI football history. It was an auspicious start for Vince Tringali's tenure as head coach of the SI football program.

Those who doubted that SI could continue its success into 1963 were jolted back to reality with the Wildcats' first game of the new season against Mission, which had been a playoff contender in 1962. In the AAA opener for 1963, Mission fell to SI 58–0, and SI established two yet-to-be-broken records for most points scored and the largest margin of victory in a game.

Next, SI prevailed over Lincoln and Galileo. Once more the Wildcats and the Irish were television stars as they continued their ancient rivalry, featured in the "Prep Game of the Week." SI maintained its dominance in a 35–0 whitewash. And once more the Wildcat defense — among them Greg Kolar, Dennis Brooks and Bob Unruh — excelled, prompting Bob Sprenger to call the SI line "possibly the finest collection of athletes in the City league in years."

SI continued its winning ways against Balboa and previously undefeated Washington for its 15th and 16th consecutive victories. Playing in the rain at muddy Galileo field, the 'Cats finished the regular season by downing Lowell 27–6. Calcagno went over the 1,000-yard passing mark for the season as SI sewed up the round-robin championship.

The AAA returned to a four-team playoff format

in 1963, and SI was paired with Lincoln while Sacred Heart and Washington were matched in the other playoff contest. The Irish and the Eagles met on Thursday, November 21, with Washington emerging victorious. The next day, SI and Lincoln were scheduled to meet to decide who would take on the Eagles for the title on Turkey Day.

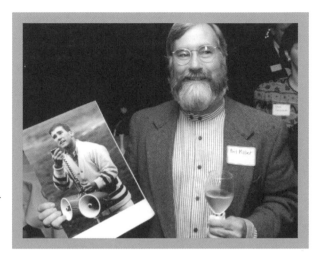

Former SI cheerleader Bill Miller '66 holding a picture of himself leading cheers during a 1966 football game. Photo by Kevin Tobin, taken at the 35-year class reunion in 2001.

But the stunning news from Dallas that morning altered the plans. Along with a host of other events across the nation, the playoff game was postponed as San Francisco joined in mourning the assassination of President John F. Kennedy.

Thus, for the first time in many years, Thanksgiving Day in the city did not see the AAA football championship game. Instead, the postponed playoff game was held. The Wildcats easily handled the Mustangs 33–6, thereby earning their fourth straight appearance in the title game.

Nine days later, SI and Washington met for the crown, and 8,000 Kezar Stadium fans saw the Wildcats methodically put the Eagles away. SI scored once in the second quarter and twice in the fourth in rolling up a 21–0 shutout. It was SI's 19th consecutive victory over a two-year period — another Wildcat football record, and SI finished as the top Northern California team.

The Doc Erskine Trophy

Robert H. "Doc" Erskine joined the SI coaching staff in 1962 after having retired from coaching college football, and he worked closely with Ray Calcagno, the quarterback for the Wildcats in his junior and senior years in the days

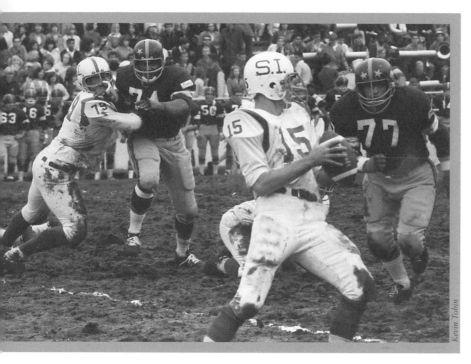

QB Jim Nevin '66 in the 1965 playoff game against Lincoln.

Kevin Tobin

when quarterbacks called their own plays. To learn what plays to call, Calcagno spent hours with Doc, who was a master strategist. "He gave me a good feel for the game," said Calcagno, "and he influenced my decision to become a coach."

Doc also had a good sense of humor. During a game against Galileo, Calcagno called a play-action pass. "All three of my receivers were open, and I threw it between two of them for an incomplete. When I came off the field a few plays later, I got on the phone with Doc, and he kindly reminded me that any one of those three could have caught the ball for a touchdown."

After Erskine left SI, he became a successful head coach at Riordan before retiring in 1969 with a high school record of 29–6–1. The following year, SI and Riordan established the Doc Erskine Trophy to the school that won that year's football game to honor an individual known for his generous spirit, gentlemanly qualities and knowledge of the game.

Even though Doc Erskine only coached at SI for a brief period, his legacy continues. "I've learned a lot about Doc through those whom he coached and influenced," said Joe Vollert '84, former head football coach. "There wasn't any showmanship or flash to Doc. He coached players to execute their fundamentals well and to know their plays — elements that have been the cornerstone of SI's program since he helped coach some of our all-time great SI teams. He influenced such people as Riordan's head coach Frank Oross, former SI head coach and Seattle Seahawk offensive coordinator Gil Haskell '61, and my head coach when I played for SI, Ray Calcagno. Ray had a large influence on me and what I did as a coach just as Doc had that influence on him. I've always hoped to carry on his legacy."

From the AAA to the WCAL

Tringali had two lean years after his twin undefeated seasons but returned with another pair of league championships. This time, however, those championships came in different leagues. The 1966–67 season was the final time SI competed in the AAA. The following year, SI joined the West Catholic Athletic League as 121 of its students lived outside the city, and AAA rules (instituted in 1959) barred them from athletic competition.

For years, SI tried to change the rule, but to no avail. Even State Senator J.F. McCarthy, an SI grad, tried to repeal the rule, but failed. The issue came to a head after a March 21, 1966, baseball game that SI won 4–3. The losing team later filed a complaint that two boys on the team did not live inside the city. The league found merit in the complaint and fined SI a three-game forfeit.

Fr. Carlin asked that the forfeits and rules be overturned, and after some hard-fought negotiations, he hammered out a compromise with George Canrinus, the AAA coordinator of athletics, at a June 3, 1966, meeting. He offered Carlin a deal: extend the residency borders to include Daly City and Pacifica. Fr. Carlin checked his records and found that 125 students lived in those two towns and agreed to the compromise.

At a subsequent meeting of the AAA principals, however, that compromise was never put on the table. Instead, the principals voted only on the question of the repeal of the residency requirement, and that measure lost 7–3.

SI found itself in a tough spot. It had been a charter member of the AAA since 1923, and leaving would mean competing in a much stronger Catholic Athletic League. After the vote, SI chose to leave, despite arguments by alumni that the school would lose money by competing outside the city. In an *Inside SI* article in 1966, (Vol. 19, No. 2, p 6) Fr. Carlin argued that "it has become increasingly clear that while the residency rule has not affected the athletic program at St.

Ignatius High School, it is having a serious effect on a school's central purpose. Under these restrictions, the school cannot offer every boy a full educational experience. He is forced to become a spectator in activities that have an important bearing on his social and physical development." He also noted that colleges look favorably on boys with athletic experience and that graduates who lived outside the city limits would be less inclined to send their sons to SI.

The Championship Seasons of 1966 and 1967

SI's Board of Regents voted unanimously on October 6, 1966, to leave the league. But SI football left with a bang, winning the round robin with a 7–2 season and earning a spot against Lowell at Kezar in the Turkey Day game — the last time SI would ever compete in that city championship match. For this game, Tringali once again wore his lucky red hat that he had donned during his 19-game streak.

The Wildcats had lost key players to injuries, including first-string QB John Cercos, fullback Paul Schneider and right guard Jeff Braccia. Nonetheless, SI fought Lowell to a 14–14 standoff late in the fourth quarter. Then, with seconds remaining, QB Paul Contreras threw to Tom Schwab. A defender tipped the ball, and it went into the arms of SI's Gary Hughes, who ran 23 yards to score a touchdown with 40 seconds left on the clock.

"It was an incredible moment," said Boris Koodrin '67, who played linebacker and left guard for the team. "The crowd tore down the goal posts, and we carried coach Vince Tringali around before a crowd of 10,000. I'm not sure if he liked being carried

252

around, as he wasn't the touchy-feely type."

"It was the most exciting sports moment of my entire life," added Fr. Sauer, then a scholastic at SI.

Kevin Tolm

KGO-TV televised a high school "Game of the Week" each Saturday.

Opposite page: Vince Tringali in 1966.

"We all went wild, and although we scholastics were assigned to guard the goal posts, one was demolished by the crowd."

The following year, SI was not expected to do well in the much stronger WCAL. In fact, some at SI argued that the school should remain in the AAA for fear of being dominated by the Peninsula and South Bay teams. However, in that first year in the WCAL, SI took first in football and basketball and had strong showings in all other sports.

The victories began in the fall with a football team that included all-league stars Mike Ryan '69, Ray Washmera '69, Bob Giorgetti '68, Jim Figoni '68, Mike Matza '68, Randy Fry '68, Mike Mitchell '69, Dan Driscoll '69, Bob Sarlatte '68, Rick Arrieta '68

and a junior quarterback named Dan Fouts '69 (more on him later). After going 3–1 in preseason, the 'Cats went 6–0 in regular season play, beating both St. Francis and Riordan 26–20, St. Mary's 35–6, Serra 27–7, Bellarmine 28–21 and Mitty 41–0.

Tringali stayed with SI one final year before leaving in 1969, with a record of 54–14–1, to help USF resurrect its football program. Jim McDonald '55 took over for two years and Tom Kennedy '63 for two more before Gil Haskell '61 stepped in as head coach between 1973 and 1977. As testimony to Tringali's legacy, both Haskell and Alan Saunders '64 sent Tringali a photo of a game between the Kansas City Chiefs and the Seattle Seahawks played on November 24, 2002. Haskell was the offensive coordinator for the Seahawks and Saunders had the same position with the Chiefs. (He had also served as head coach for the San Diego Chargers). During that game, the two teams earned a combined 64 first downs, an NFL record. In the photo are both Haskell and Saunders and this inscription: "To Vince Tringali, in sincere appreciation for your leadership, guidance and support throughout the years. You've made a difference in our lives."

Tringali, long after leaving SI, continues to make a difference in the lives of football players. Thanks to his intervention, Igor Olshansky '00 made history as the first Soviet-born person ever chosen by the NFL when the San Diego Chargers tapped him in 2004 in the second round of the draft.

Born in Dnepropetrovsk, Ukraine, Olshansky came to the U.S. when he was 7 in 1989, and enrolled at SI for his freshman year. On his 15th birthday, he stood 6-foot, 6-inches tall and weighed 240 pounds. At an SI football game, Tringali ran into him and asked him if he had a son playing football.

"When I found out he was a student, I asked

him why he wasn't out there playing football," said Tringali. "He told me he was a basketball player, and I said whoever told you that lied to you." The next year Olshansky joined the SI football team, and he struggled a bit learning the techniques and rules, but it didn't take long for the colleges to come knocking. He signed with the University of Oregon, the same school Fouts had attended, and became a favorite of fans there who chanted "I-gor" at each game. After Olshansky left college, Tringali was at his family home, sitting right beside him during the draft, when Igor got the call from the Chargers who eventually made him a starter on the defensive line. "And God help any quarterback he hits," added Tringali.

Vince Tringali: The Other Side of Fear

By Boris Koodrin '67

Everyone has certain experiences along the way that they can look back on as milestones on their personal landscape. Playing football for Vince Tringali was one such landmark, and it has had a lasting effect on my life, the meaning of which continues to unfold. At the time it offered me the opportunity to face certain fears head on and come out on the other side. Tringali was an especially tough coach and was not known for his softness. But as any wise person can tell you, the ability to tell a convincing story is every bit as important to a teacher as are any of the other skills needed to pull someone through the eye of a needle.

Vince Tringali was a rite of passage. If nothing else, when we hit the field on any given Friday, we believed in our hearts that no team was better prepared to win. Practice was almost as tough as he

was. I remember at one point Coach Tringali spent an incredible amount of energy inserting vertical slats into the cyclone fence surrounding the practice

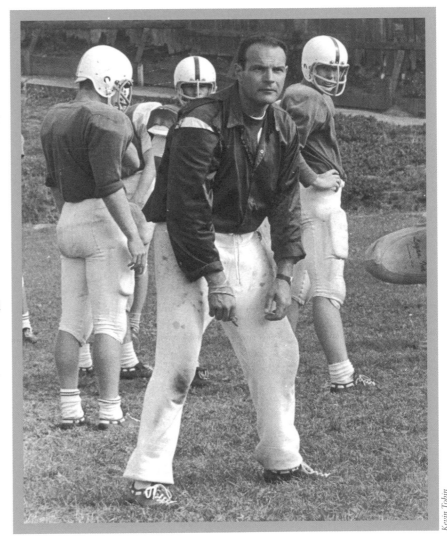

Kevin Tobin

field across from USF. I was never quite sure if that was intended to keep out the prying eyes of opposing scouts or of the parents who would line up to watch their kids practice during the week. Whatever it was that he was planning, it called for a lack of witnesses and that, in itself, was a pretty unsettling thought.

One thing he provided to many of his young players was consistency. His way was black or white, and it left little room for any gray. His greatest contribution, however, was the high level of expectation that he held over our heads, and the intensity with which he would get us to rise to that level. Perhaps the most vivid memory I have of those days is of Vince Tringali delivering an inspirational pre-game speech about going beyond the pain and reaching down deep and delivering more than we had to give — you know, the usual stuff. He was asking the impossible from us because, in his book, that was what was required. I can't really recall his words. What has stuck in my mind all these years is the sight of him holding his hand in the fire that he had built on the locker room floor. His hand remained fixed in the center of that fire the entire time he was addressing us. To this day I remember the intensity of the moment as I watched the glow slowly spread across the cold concrete like some primal ooze that was being unleashed in front of us. Transfixed, I succumbed to the moment and fell victim to the surge of raw invincibility that had taken over the room. I was recently reminiscing about that day with my good friend, Rocky Wair '67, who played at left guard. As he recalls it: "I don't know about you, but I remember that we literally flew out of that locker room on fire. Nobody in the world could have beaten us that day."

I graduated SI having been touched by Tringali's fire. Over the years that symbol has resurfaced many times to pull me through difficult situations. When push comes to shove, the strength of your personal fire can get you through anything, especially when facing life-threatening situations. Interestingly enough, I spend time these days teaching incarcerated gang members how to make fire using a primitive bow drill. Through dedication, discipline and a healthy dose of faith, they discover the ability to create their own physical fire. Fire has the ability to transform because it takes a certain amount of passion and commitment to achieve it. It can turn a hopeless survival situation into a picnic. When you learn about fire, it has the tendency to jump inside of you and become your teacher. And it can likewise transform a timid heart into a raging furnace.

I don't remember what teams we played or what the score was the day Tringali built up our team's fire, but it has remained an important personal symbol. Each one of us walked into Vince Tringali's fire in our own way back then. The fears and doubts that once caused me to walk away from my life's desire have now become the fuel that drives my own creativity. For me, it started an endless chain of fires that has taken me to the other side of my fears. Perhaps, just as importantly, it has convinced me of the power that an equally good story can have on one's own students.

Dan Fouts, NFL Hall of Famer

The greatest quarterback ever to play for SI is undoubtedly Dan Fouts '69, who went on to the University of Oregon and to the San Diego Chargers (where he played his final year under head coach and fellow Ignatian Alan Saunders '64), setting numerous records and earning entry into the NFL Hall of Fame in 1993.

It's no cliché to say that Fouts was born to play the game. His father, Bob Fouts, was an announcer for the '49ers and for other sporting events, and he grew up around pro football players. "I'd like to take credit for teaching him how to throw," said Tringali. "But I can't. He picked up the sport through osmosis." Fouts also met sports greats Wilt Chamberlain and Willie Mays through his father.

Dan transferred to SI in his sophomore year and started playing for Tringali. But because the coach didn't favor a passing game, college scouts didn't take much notice of him. "I begged USC to take Danny. I told them he can throw like the wind. He was tall but lanky — he wasn't that big, but he was tough."

Fouts loved his days at SI. "They were great years," he recalled in a 1993 *Genesis III* interview. "The thing I appreciate most was the attitude that we had. It was one of confidence bordering on cockiness and arrogance. 'We are SI.' We are something special. And in those days, athletically, we were untouchable. We worked hard and had a great coach in Vince Tringali. That foundation really carried me a long way."

He never threw an interception in his senior year at SI, and he helped SI earn the league title in his junior yera by beating a Serra team that featured Jesse Freitas and Lynn Swann. He ended up at Oregon, earning one of two athletic scholarships the school offered and setting 19 school records. The Chargers took him as a third-round draft pick in 1973, and he found himself playing alongside Johnny Unitas, then in his last season. By the time Fouts retired at the end of the 1987 season, he had become one of the league's best quarterbacks, setting 42 team records and eight NFL records, including most 300-yard

passing games. He helped the Chargers rise from the basement of the AFC West to become three-time AFC West champions. In all, as commander of Air Coryell, he passed for 43,040 yards and became the second-highest passer in NFL history. He is the third player ever to pass for more than 40,000 yards. He was selected to the Pro Bowl six times and made AFC Player of the Year in 1979 and again in 1982, this time for both the NFL and AFC. Three times he earned All-Pro honors. The year after he retired, the Chargers retired Fouts' number 14, which he had worn from 1973 to 1987. He was inducted into the NFL Hall of Fame in 1993 in his first year of eligibility.

Fouts credits his success with "being at the right place at the right time and then taking advantage of the opportunities. I played for one team for 15 years, and that's kind of unusual. When Don Coryell came to San Diego in 1978, he really made a difference in my career. We had good players and played an exciting brand of football. It was bombs away."

After leaving football, he served as KPIX sports

Dan Fouts '69, a star quarterback with the San Diego Chargers, is in the NFL Hall of Fame.

anchor, earning two Emmys, and anchored the Bay to Breakers coverage and the San Francisco Marathon. He hosted *Game Day with Dan Fouts* and found himself doing his father's job, covering play-by-play for Niners' preseason games. He left for ABC in 1997, first to announce college ball and then as expert analyst for Monday Night Football with Al Michaels and Dennis Miller for the 2000 and 2001 seasons. He had a small role in the Adam Sandler movie *The Waterboy* along with Brent Musberger and appeared in a Miller Lite Beer commercial with Ken Stabler of the Raiders. He continues to announce college and pro football for the NFL Network. He has received numerous honors over the years, including induction into the San Francisco Bay Area Sports Hall of Fame in 1997.

Dennis Carter died shortly before half-time during a basketball game against Bishop O'Dowd.

Dennis Carter

One month after the assassination of John F. Kennedy, SI lost one of its own. While playing basketball for SI against Bishop O'Dowd on December 20, 1963, Denny Carter collapsed and died 5 seconds before the start of half-time with his parents watching in the stands. Charlie Dullea '65, his teammate, noted that "everyone just waited for him to get up. The Bishop O'Dowd players covered him with their warm-up jackets as our team just sat on the bench stunned. When the firemen came to work on him, our team went into the locker room and said a rosary. While driving home, I heard the news on the radio that he was dead-on-arrival at Park Emergency near Kezar. His death had a dramatic impact on me and my friends."

The priests and scholastics at SI spent the next few months doing grief counseling, though no one called it that. "Two scholastics, Jack Keating, SJ, and John Coleman, SJ, who, under the guise of playing Pedro with us on the football field, would engage us in conversation and get us to talk about Dennis' death," added Dullea. "They helped me get through the first traumatic experience of my life."

In 1964, the basketball team inaugurated the Dennis Carter Award, with Edward Engler '64 as the first recipient. Since then, the team has given the award to the player who has demonstrated sustained excellence in leadership, spirit and commitment to his fellow players and the school.

Basketball

SI won three basketball league championships in the 1960s, the first in 1960 with Stan Buchanan as coach and the second in 1965 with Bernie Simpson '54 as coach. Playing for him were Charlie Dullea '65, who would go on to become SI's first lay principal, and Bob Portman '65, a first-round draft pick from Creighton, who played with the Warriors between 1969 and 1973. Also on the team were Bruce Scollin, Mike Doherty, Frank O'Malley and junior Rich Ames. Ironically, the toughest game of the season was the first league game against Balboa, whose star player, Willie Wise, would go on to play professional basketball. At a packed Kezar Pavilion, Portman fouled out with 2 minutes left on the clock, but SI prevailed to win by 2. SI lost only one game that season against Lincoln and the Wildcats found

Bernie Simpson (head coach) and Dante Belluomini (assistant coach) led the SI basketball squad of 1964-65 to the Tournament of Champions runner-up position. This squad included current principal Mr. Charles Dullea (back row, third player from the left). Most of the starters from this squad went on to play in Division 1 NCAA Programs. From left standing: John Westerhouse, Jim Ducker, Dullea, Jim Nevin, Don Carlson, Tim Lavelle, Bill Marra, Tom Kilker, & Bernie Simpson. Front row, from left: Dennis Dolan, Rich Ames, Tom Lynch, Frank O'Malley, Mike Doherty, Bruce Scollin, Bob Portman & Tom Gibson.

themselves playing an undefeated SH at the end of the regular season. A last-second 15-footer by Portman put SI ahead at the final buzzer. SI proceeded to win the city championship, beating Wilson and Lowell, and went on to the Tournament of Champions to beat Gilroy and Richmond before losing the NorCal crown to Fremont of Oakland.

SI won a league championship again in 1967 under Bob Drucker '58 in his first year leading the Wildcats. The basketball court in the McCullough Gymnasium bears Drucker's name for good reason. In his 20 years coaching at SI between 1966 and 1986, Drucker turned in a 394–150 record, taking SI to eight league titles, two CCS championships and one NorCal win. Drucker earned the title "Wizard of Westlake" when Bob Enright '76 gave him the nickname based on John Wooden's moniker, the Wizard of Westwood.

After a stint in the Army, Drucker applied for a job at St. Cecilia's where he coached basketball while earning his degree at USF. In 1965, he came to SI along with Leo La Rocca, and the following year, Fr. McFadden selected him to coach the varsity basketball team. (Fr. McFadden had a rule preventing first year teachers from coaching.) The victories came as did the satisfaction of seeing young boys grow into fine men. One example, Drucker recalled, was Levy Middlebrooks '84. "He came as a big, shy freshman with some skill, but he struggled a bit when he played on the freshman team. As a sophomore, he still was a little timid. Then something happened in the middle of the season that year. He improved right in front of our eyes. His confidence grew, as did his presence on the court. At the end of the regular season, I moved him up to varsity to help the team practice. Even the varsity kids were noting his improvement. Paul Fortier '82 became his mentor, and Paul's determination

to help him improve was inspirational. Most kids I coached went through that kind of transformation, but not in such a dramatic way."

After 20 years of dragging his own children to his games, Drucker was ready to retire from the sport, and he returned to the classroom in 1986. In 1992, he went from teaching history and counseling to working as a full-time counselor, but he returned to the classroom in 2003 as a full-time history teacher. He served as assistant coach to Jim Dekker in 2002 when the SI varsity girls basketball team took first in CCS, and he now serves as the boys' varsity golf coach.

"It was difficult to 'retire' at age 46," said Drucker. "But I was an intense coach, and my father died at 58. In the back of my mind, I thought that would happen to me if I had continued coaching basketball."

His intensity, he said, comes from the passion he has for the game. "I love how creative basketball is. Some people paint, and others write. For me, X's and O's are an art form. But drawing plays on cocktail napkins while taking my wife out to dinner was not the way to win her heart. The game consumed me."

Coaching golf is different, he noted. "We're not allowed to coach on the course during competition. Sometimes I think the most important service I offer our golfers is driving the van."

Nearly all the Drucker family is involved in SI. Bob's son, Joe, graduated in 1990, his daughter Chrissy graduated with the first coed class in 1993, and his daughter Katie Kohmann works in the school's development office as alumni coordinator. His wife, Kathy, and his daughter Molly might as well be honorary SI alumni for all the time they've spent at SI watching Bob coach in his distinguished 40-year career.

James Keating & Baseball

Between 1955 and 1974, James Keating helped his varsity baseball team reach the playoffs 15 times and took them to league championships six times between 1959 and 1967. Keating made a name for himself as an outstanding track star and football, basketball and baseball player at Commerce High School and at San Francisco State College. He then played for the Detroit Tigers organization and coached in the San Francisco Unified School District before coming to SI.

In the 1960s, his teams drew crowds by the thousands to watch the Wildcats beat AAA and WCAL opponents. In 1962, for instance, more than 4,000 fans watched SI beat Balboa 2–0, led by junior pitcher John Gualco and slugger Bob Ignaffo. In 1965, Vince Bigone '65 helped SI win another league championship by turning in a 13–1 pitching record and batting .426. The AAA named him the league's most valuable player.

In 1966, the team was forced to forfeit three games after a complaint was filed that two members lived outside San Francisco city limits. That decision led to SI's leaving the league, as has already been discussed. In 1967, SI played its final year of baseball in the AAA, with Jim Dekker '68 and Joe Dutto '67 helping the Wildcats to a 19–1 record. In championship match, Poly scored four runs in the fourth inning. SI answered with four runs of its own in the bottom of that inning and five more runs in the seventh to win the league title.

In a 1988 *Genesis II* article, Dekker, who later coached with his mentor, recalled Keating's "standard coaching outfit of black Converse sneakers, khaki or grey pants and white tee-shirt." He would end prayers with "St. Jude, pray for us," and encourage his team by telling them, "Keep going; it'll blow over," whenever it started to rain. "He never wanted to stop practice for

any reason," added Dekker. "The teams he coached thought he was invincible. We defeated opponents not necessarily because we were more talented, but because we were prepared and took the field with confidence."

Dekker's fondest memory of Keating is of a time in 1968. "He asked me to be the godfather to his new daughter, Shannon, and I felt honored that he and his wife, Betty, would even consider me. We held the baptism at the Keating's parish church, and I thought that after the ceremony we would have a small party or gathering. Like most high school players, I was unsure about being with a coach in a setting other than the playing field. I shouldn't have been so nervous; instead of returning to the Keating home after the ceremony, we proceeded directly to Marin Catholic's baseball field to take Sunday batting practice, with most of Coach Keating's children shagging balls. He must have thrown to me for at least two hours. Only after batting practice did we celebrate in the customary fashion.

To honor him, Jim Dekker '68, who took over as head coach, instituted the Keating Award in 1975, with Stephen Baccari '75 as the first recipient. Jim Keating died in 1988 after a four-year battle with cancer, and was buried in his coaching uniform along with his glove and bat. The 1989 varsity

Veteran baseball coach Jim Keating.

baseball team wore a black armband all season in Keating's memory. "Knowing Jim, he would probably be embarrassed by the attention," said Dekker.

Swimming

SI's swimming team enjoyed a remarkable run in the 1960s, taking first in 1960–61 and 1963-67. In 1965, Coach Bill Love '59 helped the team break or tie nine city records and score the highest point total ever recorded in the city. SI's nearest competitor trailed by 90 points at the finals. In 1968 in the WCAL, SI came in second to Bellarmine despite outstanding efforts by swimmers such as Mick Lavelle, who later returned to coach along with Robert Gogin. SI wouldn't find gold until 1984, but the team still enjoyed success in the 1970s thanks to swimmers such as Mark Harris, Mark Yuschenkoff and Glenn Ackerman who continued to compete despite the lack of facilities and dwindling interest in the sport, as membership declined from 60 to a dozen members.

Leo La Rocca '53

Leo La Rocca, who served as SI's Athletic Director for 34 years, first came to SI as a teacher in 1965 and quickly became known as "The Godfather." It's not just because this towering man's grandparents came from Sicily. Leo is the least threatening man you could meet. He was, however, the man to go to if you wanted a favor done. He gained a reputation as someone who could provide help with just one phone call, whether it was finding a donor for a scholarship for a senior whose father had just died or finding a job around campus for a freshman who had a hard time fitting in.

As a 6-foot, 3-inch sophomore, Leo helped his basketball team take second in the Tournament of Champions. He also made the all-league baseball team in his junior and senior years and boxed for the Olympic Club on the side. In 1965 he left his family's seafood business and found a job at SI teaching English along with fellow first-year teachers Tony Sauer, Bob Drucker, Chuck Murphy and Riley Sutthoff.

In his second year on the job, both he and Drucker were vying for the varsity basketball coach's job when Fr. McFadden called him into his office for a chat. "He said to me, 'You really don't want to coach basketball, do you Leo?' I said, 'Yes I do.' 'Wouldn't you rather be athletic director?' Little did anyone know that J.B. Murphy was stepping down."

For the next 34 years, Leo scheduled games, reserved fields, hired coaches and supplied teams with equipment. He also attended thousands of games, including all but one of Drucker's basketball games. "I was sick one day," Leo explains.

In his long tenure as AD, he saw many changes, including the move from the AAA to the WCAL, the shift to coeducation and the increase in the number of teams and sports. When Leo first began at SI, only a small fraction of the SI student body competed in track, baseball, football and basketball. Now there are 13 boys' sports and 13 girls' sports, and nearly 900 of the 1,400 students participate in the athletics program. To assist him in this transition, SI hired Teresa Garrett in 1989 as associate athletic director, and when she left that position, Bob Vergara stepped into the job.

LaRocca never judged his success by whether his teams won or lost. "Driving home after a basketball game, I couldn't tell you the final score. I get the most satisfaction not from watching a team win, but from watching kids play as hard as they could, win or lose. Championships are nice, but it's far more gratifying watching kids grow into men and women, have families, be happy and do well professionally. I only hope that I've been a little part of their success."

To honor him, SI renamed its winter basketball tournament the Leo A. La Rocca Sand Dune Classic, and the SI crew named a boat for him. He also received the Christ the King Award in 2004, the highest honor the school can bestow on an alumnus.

Fr. Mario Prietto, SJ, who served as SI principal for 13 of La Rocca's 35 years at SI, announced on the day he got the job that "as long as I'm principal, Leo La Rocca is the AD. I've never regretted that decision. Leo is one of the kindest, most loyal persons I know. His devotion to SI has always been a great source of strength and inspiration for me. His heart is like his hands — big, warm and outstretched in service."

Cross Country & Riley Sutthoff '60

Each year since 1971, the cross country and track and field teams honor a "most inspirational" athlete with the Riley Sutthoff Award, named in honor of a man who started teaching French and coaching cross country at SI in 1965 before his tragic death in a car accident in 1970.

Terry Ward '63, Bellarmine's athletic director and track coach and a former SI coach and teacher, was a freshman runner when Riley was a senior. "When you are a freshman, it is easy to be in awe of seniors," he noted. " I ran very well as a freshman and was the city champion in the 660-yard run. One of the major reasons why I competed so well was the tutoring Riley gave me. Riley would always say hello to me and would compliment me when I did

Opposite page: Leo La Rocca at a faculty-student basketball game in the 1960s.

well. In the early '60s the classes did not mix and to have someone who was about to graduate validate what I was doing left a lasting impression on me. In my junior and senior year, I made it a point to always help younger athletes. What Riley did for me, I wanted to do for others. This is my 35th year coaching track and field, and every day I try to make the 150 athletes in my charge know that I care for them and want them to succeed. From the fastest runner to the slowest jogger, I live with each step they take, just like Riley lived with me in the 1960s. I was very proud to succeed Riley as cross country coach. Riley was a great man whom many of us still miss."

Academics

Fr. Tom Reed, SJ

Fr. Reed (whose life is detailed in the previous chapter) served as principal between 1957 and 1964. Paul Vangelisti '63, who has gained fame as a poet, recalls being sent to him for discipline one day.

"Fr. Reed was more liberal than he let on. One day in religion class, our teacher was absent, and we thought we would have the period to study for physics. Suddenly we see an old priest sent in to proctor who, years previous, had been tortured by the Chinese. We were a little rowdy, but we studied hard. He decided he was going to have a class on religion and talk about Mary. That was the last thing we felt we needed. He started by asking each of us for an exclusive definition of 'man.' By the time he got to me — with my last name starting with a 'V,' I was at the end of the line — every definition had been exhausted, so I said, 'Man is the only animal that habitually copulates

in more than one position.' The whole class went ballistic. He threw me out and told me to go to Fr. Reed.

"When Fr. Reed saw me, he said, 'Paul, you're a good boy. Why are you bothering me?' I explained, and he walked back to the classroom with me. To the priest he said, 'Father, we may punish boys for some things, but we don't punish them for showing intelligence. Sit down Vangelisti. Father, I want to speak with you outside.' I've always had a soft spot for Fr. Reed since then."

Bill Kennedy '50, who taught at SI between 1960 and 1997, recalls his first year working for Fr. Reed, who was a little behind on his accreditation report that year. He enlisted Kennedy to help him. "I had to go to several older Jesuits for information," said Kennedy. "It was the first time they had ever been approached by a lay person asking for accreditation data. I amassed all the material and wrote some of it, but it was a very slap-dash affair as I was teaching a full load at the time. It was an absolute disaster, as the school was ill prepared for that accreditation. We got it, but it was a dicey proposition."

The Death of JFK

After President John F. Kennedy was assassinated on November 22, 1963, students attended a memorial Mass on November 26 with Fr. Reed delivering the eulogy. An *Inside SI* article noted that "everyone in the church was moved to tears as [Fr. Reed] recounted a little anecdote about 'John-John.'" Mark Murphy '64 eulogized him in *Inside SI* by noting that "not one of us knew the man. There were 1,100 of us clustered around radios that day, listening to the broadcast of the assassination. Each one felt a curious sense of personal loss. None of us had voted for him: we were too young. Had we been old enough, perhaps many of us would not have voted for him. And yet, the very fact that we, as Americans, can have the freedom to choose, made the loss more acute…. Perhaps it was because he was a young man that we could feel a close identity with him. He played football, he sailed a boat, and he was a man we could understand. We could have sat down and talked to him; we could have argued with him, exchanged opinions; he would have understood. He was so young to die that somehow our youth binds us closely to his memory…. No more work was done that day. Bunches of tight-lipped students went over the tragedy in low tones. Teachers gave up their classes to study periods or to discussion groups. Because it wasn't necessary, no attempt was made to keep order or silence. The classrooms, which on a typical day might have been filled with spitballs, wisecracks and paper airplanes, were strangely silent and devoid of any light-heartedness."[8]

Fr. Ed McFadden, SJ

In the 1960s and 1970s, SI turned from a good city school into a great regional school; much of that was due to the efforts of Fr. Ed McFadden, SJ '41, who served as principal between 1964 and 1976. He helped usher in the modern era of high school administration at SI. "When we grew up in post WWII America, many men, including priests, were products of the military," said his close friend Bob Drucker '58. "Their watchwords were power and obedience and authority. Relationships between scholastics and priests and students and teachers were adversarial. That waned with the '60s when people questioned authority and with the advent of Vatican II when rela-

tionships became more collegial and collaborative."

Drucker found this true in his relationship with Fr. McFadden, whom he grew to respect. "He was a vi-

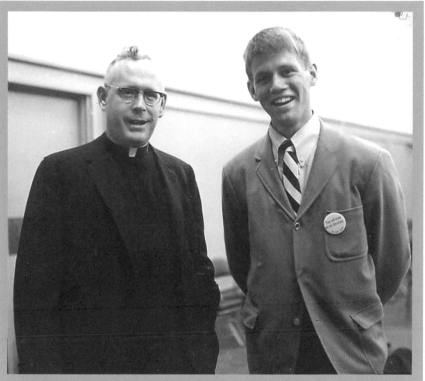

sionary who recognized the need for more laymen and the need for a professional counseling office. He knew we needed to expand the language department to include more modern languages and hired Riley Sutthoff to teach French. He saw the need for more honors and AP courses, and he was a pioneer in the Jesuit Secondary Education Association."

Fr. Ed McFadden, SJ, and a young Michael Shaughnessy '67 (who works at SI as a campus minister.

Drucker most appreciated Fr. McFadden's hands-on advice he would give to new teachers. "He'd give you a few suggestions after visiting your class, and he would choose what classes you would teach each year. He cultivated his faculty in that manner, hiring young laymen such as Chuck Murphy and myself."

Fr. McFadden gained a reputation as a blunt but loving teacher and administrator who traumatized freshmen but who gained the love and respect of his students as they became upperclassmen. A Jesuit for 60 years, Fr. McFadden entered the Society of Jesus after graduating from SI in 1941. As a student at SI, he wrote a column for *The Red and Blue* called "Doings from Other Campi," filled with topical jokes, puns and witty comments. Later, as principal of SI, that sense of humor would surface whenever he signed notes to coaches as "The Owner." Later, as a teacher at Bellarmine College Preparatory in San Jose, he signed his notes with "Edward the Professor."

After his ordination to the priesthood in 1954, he began his life-long work as a high school teacher and administrator, working as prefect of discipline and principal at Loyola High School in Los Angeles before coming to SI to serve as principal. (He eventually earned SI's highest honor, the Christ the King award, in 2000.)

Throughout his career as an educator, he was known for his one-line advice to novice teachers: "Don't smile until Christmas." His take on students' rights sometimes came as a shock to student councils when he emphasized, "One man, one vote. Mine!" And whenever a teacher complained about the dog-days of April, he would simply advise, "Get in there and pitch."

His friend, Fr. John "Jack" Mitchell, SJ '58, recalls that after Fr. McFadden left administration in

Fr. Leo Hyde, SJ, awaiting the arrival of an SI student.

1977, he had a special way of starting the year with his freshmen at Bellarmine. Even the seniors each year would gather outside on the first day of class to watch. "Ed would enter the classroom hardly even glancing at the students sitting nervously at their desks. (Actually, Ed was more nervous than they were, but they did not know that.) He would walk directly to the board and write on it while saying aloud, 'Summer is over.' Then he would write down an assignment due the first day of class and walk out of the room. The freshmen would wear wide-eyed expressions of wonder at what had transpired and what it portended for the future, and the seniors outside would roar with laughter."

"He used to scare the freshmen to death. He kept the kids on their toes and just expected the best of them," Fr. Sauer said. "There was a method in his madness.

"I came to teach in 1965 with Bob Drucker, Chuck Murphy, Leo La Rocca, Riley Sutthoff and great young Jesuits," added Fr. Sauer. "Fr. McFadden was our mentor and my friend for many years. For a long time, he was the only principal I knew. He was at my side at my first Mass in 1971, and I was honored to give the homily at his funeral Mass."

SI in the early 1960s had "a lot of male testosterone in the halls with a militaristic atmosphere," noted Peter Devine '66. "Some of that changed when Fr. McFadden became principal. He emphasized academics and promoted the arts and *Inside SI*. He softened the hard edge and hired good laymen. The school needed that infusion because it had been slipping academically."

Devine added that Fr. McFadden was clever in advancing his agenda. "He threatened to have us wear uniforms with blazers and ties. That was a smoke-screen for what he really wanted to do. While students were busy protesting the uniforms, he made a host of changes, including having students, and not teachers, move between classrooms from period to period. He asked students to take a third year of a foreign language and biology in their sophomore year. He encouraged the lay faculty to be experts in their fields, so we started having better quality teaching. In the old days, the principal would hand a textbook to some poor scholastic and tell him to keep a day ahead of the students. At the end of the year, he told students that he was a principal who listens, and that he wouldn't ask students to wear uniforms. They loved him for that."

Leo Hyde '47

For SI grads from the 1970s to the present, Dean of Students Douglas Draper, SJ, is synonymous with discipline. But for those who attended SI in the 1960s, Fr. Hyde holds that distinction. He was in charge of keeping discipline, of punishing offenders and, at times, of showing mercy when it was most needed.

In one sense, Leo Hyde's SI history mirrors that of the Stanyan Street campus. He and his twin brother Robert Hyde '47, were born at St. Mary's Hospital in October 1929, across the street from the Shirt Factory, which had just been vacated as students left for the new Stanyan Street campus, and he was instrumental in supervising construction of and transfer to the 2001 37th Avenue campus.

As a student at SI, Leo Hyde was a member of the Sanctuary Society, which Fr. Carlin (then a scholastic) moderated, and through that organization, he grew friendly with many priests such as Fr. Ray Buckley, SJ, and Fr. Charles Largan, SJ. Hyde joined the order

Kevin Tobin

upon his graduation from SI and was ordained in 1960. He returned to SI in 1962 and served as prefect of discipline and as assistant principal until 1970 when he left SI. (He left the Society of Jesus in 1971 to wed, and he and his wife, Gail, now have two children, Jennifer and Kym, and one grandson.)

"Students were a bit afraid of me when I came to SI," Hyde noted. He was tough but fair, and as one student wrote to him years later, "You were never an SOB. You always let us talk and explain why we were in trouble. You might send us to JUG, but we always had a chance to explain ourselves."

For a young Peter Devine, on his first day at SI, there was nothing more frightening than Fr. Hyde. "He lined us all up in back of north schoolyard, military style. He walked down the line looking at each boy, shouting out his infraction: 'Shirt!' 'Tie!' 'Haircut!' Every so often, he would tell one boy to go to the office. He looked as if he were throwing someone out of school. We didn't know it, but that boy was simply missing a medical form. To us, it looked like a random expulsion."

Hyde did impose what he called Martial Law during fire drills. "If a teacher reported a student to me for fooling around or talking, then that boy was automatically and instantly suspended from school."

Outside his office was an infamous bench where students would sit while waiting to meet with him. (That bench was moved to the Sunset District campus in the 1990s and now sits outside the deans' office, a gift from Bill McDonnell, who bought it at a USF auction. Students lounge on that bench to chat with friends, something they would never do at the Stanyan Street campus.)

Sometimes discipline problems involved more than mere tardiness. One day a teacher punched a student in the hall, and the student responded by hitting him back. "He was sent to the office, but the priest involved saw me right away," said Hyde. "He told me it wasn't the kid's fault. I treated that case as if it were self-defense."

Later, at the famous Turkey Bowl game of 1967, when students began tearing down the goal post, Hyde ran down to the field along with two police officers and grabbed the first kid he saw. "I handed him to the police officer and said, 'As acting principal, I'm making a citizen's arrest.' That broke up the mayhem. I was afraid someone would get hurt and that we would have to pay to rebuild the goal post. Later that day, I drove by the police station to make sure the police had released the young man. It turned out he was an SCU student who had had a few beers by halftime."

Hyde made a point of not keeping the discipline records on file for long, as he did not want to see students damaged by youthful exuberance years later. "By state law, it was automatic suspension for smoking within three blocks of a school," said Hyde. "I didn't feel a suspension for that reason or for serving JUG should go into a permanent file."

During the construction of the Sunset District campus, Hyde would visit every Saturday with plans in hand to inspect the work. "I knew all the contractors and all the architects. I had always been interested in the maintenance and was in charge of all the maintenance at the Stanyan Street campus."

The 37th Avenue site had been a dumping ground of sorts, and for every truck load of debris removed, new sand had to be hauled in so the site would settle evenly, according to Hyde.

Hyde stayed on as assistant principal for one year when the school community moved to the Sunset District campus, and Br. Draper, who came to SI in 1966, succeeded him in the newly created post of dean of students.

After leaving SI, Hyde worked at the Provincial's office for one year before deciding to leave the order. He then found work with his classmate George Millay '47, the founder of San Diego's SeaWorld, as a construction supervisor and, later, as manager of planning, construction and facilities for Magic Mountain, which Millay helped create.

Fr. Anthony P. Sauer, SJ

Fr. Anthony P. Sauer, who has served SI for the past 26 years as president — by far the longest of any of its administrators — first came to SI in 1965 after philosophy studies in St. Louis. A graduate of Loyola High School and Santa Clara University, Fr. Sauer had served as a lieutenant in Korea in the 13th Field Artillery supporting the 19th Infantry Regiment at Observation Post Lola at the Demilitarized Zone, 2,000 meters from North Korea. "I had more power at 21 than I've ever had since then," he said. "That's why I don't take myself too seriously today."

After leaving the Army he taught for a time at Loyola High School and was briefly engaged before deciding to join the Society of Jesus. He studied English at USC and at St. Louis University. The day he arrived at SI as a young scholastic, race riots were breaking out in Los Angeles and tanks were driving up and down Stanyan Street to prevent the riots from spreading to San Francisco.

He found himself teaching sophomore and junior English (and, later, senior English) and helping to moderate *Inside SI* and the Sanctuary Society. He liked his first two years so much that he asked to stay a third. Two weeks before school started in his third year, Fr. McFadden told him that he would be the school's only counselor, the admissions director and the person in charge of scheduling classes. On top of that, he had one English class to teach. "I had to learn college counseling really fast," he noted.

Mr. Sauer was a far cry from the traditional Jesuits of the 1950s. Robert Thomas '68, now a prize-winning poet, had Fr. Sauer for senior English and recalled that he and his classmates didn't use the stodgy textbooks other English classes used. "He had us use a new textbook that included poetry of Wallace Stevens, William Carlos Williams, T.S. Eliot and e.e. cummings," said Thomas. "That was my first exposure to those poets." Mr. Sauer even taught Ginsberg's controversial poem *Howl*, much to the chagrin of a few parents and faculty.

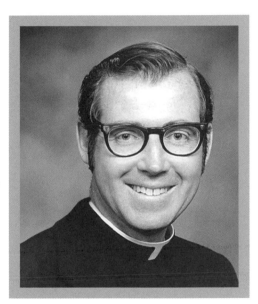

Fr. Anthony Sauer, SJ, in 1979.

Boris Koodrin '67 also enjoyed Mr. Sauer's English class. "I had never been inspired by a teacher the way Tony inspired me. I had never experienced academics the way I did in his class. It was no struggle at all. He had a way of seeing you for who you were. It was an uplifting experience. I'll always be indebted to him for giving me something I really needed."

Koodrin's classmate, Michael Shaughnessy '67 (a teacher and campus minister at SI since 1981) calls Tony Sauer "my personal hero. When he came to SI, everyone was scared of him. I swear he used a riding crop as a pointer and slammed it on desks to get our attention. He worked our fingers to the bone, but you could tell he cared about us, not just as students but as people. Now I am very lucky to be professionally related to him. He's been a remarkable president, and I feel cared about and cared for."

When students asked their teacher to consider the poetry of modern rock songs, Mr. Sauer agreed. He listened to the Beatles and Bob Dylan and even staged a debate between juniors Tom Schaefer '67 and Shaughnessy as to whose poetry was better: Dylan Thomas or Bob Dylan.

He attended the Human Be-In in Golden Gate Park in January 1967 when Timothy Leary arrived in a hot air balloon, he saw what was happening during the Summer of Love in the Haight, and he counseled students who considered applying for conscientious objector status for the Vietnam War. He left in 1968 to study at the Jesuit School of Theology in Berkeley and to be ordained, but he would return in 1971 for his second stint as a teacher.

SI's First Female Teacher

In 1965, SI hired its first female member of the faculty. Mrs. Marjorie Buley (the wife of chemistry teacher Horace Buley) taught biology, though only for one year. Still, the school had a number of women working there. The 1966 yearbook lists nine women: Mrs. Emma Basso (registrar), Mrs. Dolores Bloom (bookkeeper), Miss Judy Galassi (alumni secretary), Mrs. N. Hauck (switchboard), Mrs. J. Jeffs (development secretary), Mrs. Frances McCausland (bookkeeper), Mrs. A. Murphy (president's secretary), Mrs. A. Schmidt, (assistant principal's secretary) and Miss C. Swanson (school nurse).

Extracurriculars

Speech and Debate

From its beginnings, SI has had a proud tradition of argumentation and public speaking. The student forums and debate teams did well in past decades, and in the 1960s, students in the SI Forum continued to excel under the guidance of former Jesuit Charles Henry '38. In the 1962–63 school year, for instance, students who excelled included seniors Gerry London, Rick Del Bonta, Paul Vangelisti and Robert Carson — the latter two well-known poets — juniors David Mezzera and John Scalia and sophomores Frank Gollop and Eugene Payne. The debate team of Mezzera and Scalia "merited not only state acclaim but also national recognition," according to the *Ignatian*, and SI received an invitation for the first time in its history to attend the Georgetown University Debate Tournament along with two dozen other schools in the country. In their senior year, both Mezzera and Scalia debated in the National Tournament in Akron, Ohio. Mezzera returned to SI in 1970 to teach public speaking and moderate the SI Forum. In the 1970s, SI sent speakers and debate teams to compete in the nationals every year except 1973 and 1979. In 1972, seniors Stephen Schori and Gerald Posner (the author of *Case Closed* and many other books) took third in the National Forensic League finals at Wake Forest University.

The Ignatian & Inside SI

Inside SI started a new tradition in 1963 when Fr. John Becker took over as moderator. He would continue in that role (with the exception of a few years) until 1975. In 1963, the school received a donated press and, with the addition of more equipment in 1967, students began producing the newspaper in-house. They typeset the magazine, made negatives from the pages using a process camera, burnt plates using a carbon arc, printed full-color pages and bound and trimmed the issues. The magazine covered the controversies of the day that ranged from the Block Club being an elitist organization to the Student Council being a do-nothing organization.

The Ignatian continued to excel in the 1960s, with the 1964 yearbook including color pages for the first time. One yearbook generated discussion that continued for years. In 1967, the yearbook staff produced a large, linen-covered tome that contained beautiful black and white photographs and almost no text. Students and teachers either loved it or hated it. The young scholastic in charge, Dennis Alvernaz, and editor Richard Robinson '67, had one thought in mind while working on it. "We wanted to create a family album," said Alvernaz, now a retired Catholic priest. "You don't find captions in a family photo album. In those days, we felt like a family. It was a wonderful time, just before the decline of everything. It was the last hurrah of the WWII generation and their children, and a spirit of camaraderie filled the halls."

To produce a larger book, both in terms of format and page count, Robinson, Alvernaz and their staff (including ace photographer Vince Piantaneda '69) stretched their budget by learning to develop their own film and make their own prints. They used a small darkroom on campus and drove a few miles to a public darkroom to rent facilities. They also did their own layouts and turned in camera-ready art to the yearbook company.

They began their book with a 16-page photo essay that included some of the only text (aside from names) found in the document. In it, Alvernaz offered this wisdom: "It was better, he [Christ] thought, to

Kevin Tobin

fail in attempting exquisite things than to succeed in the department of the utterly contemptible." Alvernaz hoped that the introduction would spiritually challenge students and ask them to be self-critical.

Visiting coeds in the Inside SI office.

Because of the mixed reaction to the nearly wordless yearbook, Alvernaz returned to a more traditional tome for the 1968 edition with editor Bob Cooney '68. He and Cooney later collaborated on two more unusual yearbooks, this time at SCU where Cooney was yearbook editor and Alvernaz, once again, moderator, while studying theology at Alma College. The two published yearboxes — boxes in which students would find several spiral-bound books.

Rocket Club

In the fall of 1961, SI students formed the Rocket Club, moderated by chemistry teacher Horace MacPherson "Mac" Buley. Club members spent the first six months experimenting with various fuel mixes and named their first rocket the TR1 in honor of Principal Tom Reed, SJ. They launched that rocket in May 1962 in Nevada. (California law prohibited vertical rocket launches, so the boys experimented with horizontal flights in San Francisco and traveled to Nevada to see if their machines had the right stuff.) While the first stage of that May launch was successful, the second stage blew up after traveling 1,000 feet high. They planned an October launch with a mouse and a parachute ejection system "so that we can recover him," reported the October 5, 1962, *Inside SI*. Then, on January 18, 1963, the club launched a six-foot rocket a mile high into space, making it the "second largest amateur solid fuel rocket ever fired in the U.S." They worked on another rocket, dubbed "Big Mac" after their moderator. It stood 18 feet high and included two stages and a nose cone with a guidance system that students could control from the ground.[9]

Theatre

Peter Devine, who performed in many of the plays in the 1960s, recalled that all the plays at SI were done with an all-male cast until 1964. "I was in the last all-male show, *Little Mary Sunshine*, performing the role of Madame Ernestine in the spring of 1964." In the fall of 1964, Fr. Bill Breault, SJ, the new drama director, wrote to Rome to ask permission for women to be allowed to act in plays at SI. He received permission, and the first show to feature actresses was *Charlie's Aunt*, which, added Devine, "is

SI staged Damn Yankees in 1967. Photo by Kevin Tobin.

about a guy who dresses as his aunt to fool the girls into thinking they have a chaperone." It also starred SI fine arts teacher Katie Wolf, who was then a junior at St. Rose Academy and whose mother, Jean Wolf, was costume designer at SI.

"Once the shows became coed, the musicals started growing in size," Devine added. In 1965, SI staged an original musical, *Margo and Me*, written by Tom Calderola '65, Dave Miller '66 and Phil Kelsey '66. The show was performed at Marina Junior High School and proved so successful that the next year SI staged *Oklahoma!* at the Marines Memorial Theatre. SI was the last amateur group to play that theatre because ACT acquired it the following year and unionized. "When we went to put our sets and lights in for *Oklahoma!* in 1966, the union tried to stop us. Fr. Carlin then placed one phone call and took care of it. The union never bothered us after that."

The theatre department produced a number of wonderful shows during the 1960s including the student-authored *Margo and Me* and *Arsenic and Old Lace*. The 1966 production of *Oklahoma!* Directed by Nicholas Weber, SJ, was one of the best shows produced by SI. According to the 1966 *Ignatian*, *Oklahoma!* featured students Norice Moore, Peggy Walsh, Willie Morrissey, Glen Howell, Mike Yalon and Dave Miller, who "exhibited the talent that has been waiting to be expressed at SI musically and dramatically." The show also featured Peter Devine and Katie Wolf, who would both continue their careers at SI.

In 1967, students attended a school rooted in 400 years of Jesuit tradition. Then at lunch and after school they would walk to Golden Gate Park or to Haight Street and find a different world, one that involved protest, drugs and rock and roll.

"I could walk to the park as a senior during lunch and watch hippies dancing around," said Robert Thomas, who identified with the youth movement both at SI and, later, at UC Santa Cruz where he studied English, attended Grateful Dead concerts and protested the Vietnam War.

Boris Koodrin '67, a lineman for the football team at SI, noted that much of San Francisco "was a whole different world. We were close to Haight-Ashbury and to Golden Gate Park where it was a clash of worlds, not that there was any antagonism, between students and hippies."

Ron Elliott '62 was the songwriter & guitarist for the Beau Brummels.

As a student, Koodrin and many others attended a legendary concert — a fund raiser for SI — at USF's Memorial Gymnasium on April 7, 1967, that brought Buffalo Springfield and the Jefferson Airplane to SI, with a lightshow by Headlights. "They were up-and-coming artists, not that big yet," said Koodrin. Still, the two groups drew 4,000 fans to the benefit concert for SI's building fund. "Several faculty members eyed Haight-Ashbury's shaggy contingent with glazed optics and twitchy clipper fingers," wrote Charlie Gavin in the *Inside SI* concert review.

John Wildermuth '69, now a political reporter for the *San Francisco Chronicle*, recalls that cross country coach Riley Sutthoff would have his team avoid running near Haight Street. "Everywhere we saw guys selling the *Oracle* and the *Berkeley Barb* or guys asking for contributions to build a new temple. We saw the Grateful Dead perform on top of a flatbed truck on Stanyan Street and saw the Diggers perform."

Students and teachers at SI also saw the ugly side of the movement, especially regarding the drug scene. On a Saturday morning in 1967, one of Bob Drucker's players, Steve McCarthy, cut his eye. "I took him to Park Emergency. When I walked in, I saw a beautiful 18-year-old girl reciting nursery rhymes; she was so out of it from drugs. I had never seen anyone like this. At 27, I was frightened; this was my neighborhood, but I had no idea what was going on as I was a bit naïve."

Fr. Bill Muller, SJ, who taught at SI as a scholastic in the late 1960s, saw both sides of the changing times. "I used to go walking from Welch Hall out into the Haight, and it dawned on me one night that I shouldn't be doing this. The kids changed in just those two years. They developed a social consciousness and an awareness of the world around them. They paid attention to the Vietnam War, Robert Kennedy and Martin Luther King."

SI did contribute to the music scene of San Francisco in the 1960s with Ron Elliott '62. Elliott and Sal Spampinato (who later changed his name to Sal Valentino) formed the group the Beau Brummels and had several hit songs, including "Laugh, Laugh" and "Just a Little" in 1965, which Eliott co-wrote with classmate Bob Durand '62. After the Beau Brummels broke up, Elliott pursued other musical avenues, including country rock, and recorded and released *The Candlestick Maker*.

Vietnam

Many SI alumni served in the armed forces during the Vietnam War but only three are known to have died: Denis O'Connor '58, Richard Bloom '60 and Richard Arthur Timboe '62. In addition, one other grad, Frederick John Riley '51, a retired Navy pilot, served in the CIA's Air America and was killed in Laos.

Frederick John Riley '51

Frederick Riley grew up close to SI near Haight and Ashbury. As a senior, he served as a cheerleader, and he was a member of the 130s basketball team and the rally committee. He joined the Navy while still in college, according to his close friend Richard Howard '52.

In the 1960s, he left the Navy to join in the CIA's secret war in Laos, supporting Laotians in their struggle against the North Vietnamese. Riley flew C-123s into Laos carrying supplies. On November 27, 1962, his plane was damaged by Neutralist anti-aircraft fire while on approach to land at Xieng Khoung. He was mortally injured in the ensuing crash. "He was a hell of a good guy," said Howard. "He had no business being killed like that."

Riley is memorialized on the Wall of Honor at an Air America memorial in Texas. He had no siblings and his parents, who have since passed away, "suffered immensely after Fred's death, as he was their only son," added Howard.

"Fred's case has always troubled me. I saw many people die on ships. I lost my wingman during the war and saw a lot of blood spilled. Those people were all remembered and honored, but those who died in Air America were, for the most part, performing an admirable and honorable task for our government. Whether or not you agree with their mission, they were heroes of the first rank and never recognized. It's heartbreaking."

Denis O'Connor '58

Denis O'Connor was born May 3, 1940, and grew up in San Francisco with his parents and six sisters. In a '57 Chevy that was the envy of his class, he would drive many of his sisters to a bus stop near SI every morning on his way to school. "It says a lot about him that he risked his 'coolness' by

Denis O'Conor and his wife, Patricia.

performing this task in his even cooler '57 Chevy filled with other SI boys," said his sister Brenda MacLean. "He had a wonderfully sarcastic humor and his little sisters were treated to the daily observations of the world by him and his friends." His sister Mary Pratto recalls his pride in wearing his junior jacket and his desire to study engineering at SCU. "Having three sisters older and three younger, Denis established himself at a young age as a strong individual," she added. At SI he also participated in the Sanctuary Society and the Sodality and held a number of class offices.

Denis' father, Jim, was a concrete contractor and the owner of D. O'Connor and Son, and Denis worked for him every summer from the time he was 5 to learn the business. After college, he planned to enter the family business and then go into San Francisco politics. "He believed it was possible for an honest patriot to make a difference in San Francisco and even in the country," said his widow, Patricia (Patty) Ekenberg, who was in her first year at the University of Detroit when she met Denis, a senior.

A finance major, he was active in ROTC, and after college he was commissioned a Second Lieutenant and stationed in Wiesbaden, Germany. Patty and he were married there in 1964, and they had two daughters — Elizabeth, born in 1965, and Christine, born in 1966.

Denis had a great sense of humor, according to Patty. "Not only was he funny, but he also loved music. He prided himself on knowing the words to every song in every Broadway show and every movie musical."

As a member of the 101st Airborne Division, Denis was transferred to Fort Sill, Oklahoma, in 1966 before shipping out to Vietnam for his first tour of duty in 1967. He was killed three months later, on October 10, 1967, from an explosion in Quang Nam, possibly from a grenade or an artillery shell.

"Denis was one of the lucky people in this world who defined his priorities at a young age," said Patty. "He told me that his first duty was to God, his second duty was to his country and his third duty was to his family. I understood taking a back seat to God, but was a bit miffed to be behind country, especially when he volunteered for Vietnam. His values would not have allowed any other decision. It wasn't easy, but it was simple. He volunteered for service because he thought that for the defense of our country, we had to help rid the world of communism. He was a man of great honor and principle. He had to do the right thing."

Patty, who had moved to Sonoma with Denis shortly before his leaving for Vietnam, vividly recalls the day she learned of his death. "It was horrible. The minute I saw the uniformed men coming to the door, I knew what it was. I was numb."

Years later, one of Denis' sisters introduced Patty to a family friend and Lowell grad, Don Nelson. Patty married him, and the two had a son.

She maintained close ties to Denis' sisters. "Our son, Curt, called the O'Connor sisters 'auntie' and Don adopted our girls." Sadly Don died in 1996 and Patty endured another visit to her door to inform her of a husband's death. She later married a close friend of Don's mother in 2000 and continues to make her home in Sonoma.

She and the sisters continue to honor the memory of Denis. "He was the best brother and is missed every day of these past 37 years," said Brenda MacLean. His daughter, Beth, added that "a family gathering doesn't go by without stories told of him (always accompanied by plenty of laughter and tears)." His sister

Mary added that "Denis was very loved by all of us. I still miss and remember him to this day." His name appears on the Vietnam Veterans Memorial on Panel 27E, Row 85.

Richard Bloom '60

The October 7, 1966, *Inside SI* included the following notice: "Rich Bloom was in many ways a typical SI student. He was active in his school life, rifle team, track and football, and received fairly good grades in his studies…. When the war in Vietnam began to get hotter, he was sent to fight. It was there that he was killed in action in service to his country and ideals. *Inside SI* salutes Rich Bloom, a true Ignatian, who gave his life that others might be free." — *Joe Cordes '67*

Born in 1942, Richard Bloom grew up on 35th Avenue and attended Holy Name Church. His mother, Dolores, a third-generation San Franciscan, worked at SI in the treasurer's office, and his father, a San Francisco policeman, came from West Marin. His friends included Dick Lynch '60 and Bill Foehr '60. Lynch recalls that Bloom and his father were "more devoted to one another than any father and son that I've ever met."

At 6-feet, 2-inches and 190 pounds, Richard was "solid as a cement block and an exceptional athlete. As a defensive back at SI, he could run as fast backwards as I could forwards," said his Marine buddy Richard Torykian. Lynch recalls that he was "very friendly, not too studious, a great athlete and hunter and very into automobiles. He had a '49 Ford hotrod that we rebuilt."

After SI, he attended USF for two years where he continued to play football before enlisting in the Marine Corps Officer Training Program. According to his sister, Katherine Bloom, he hoped to become a pilot. He had a girlfriend, but didn't want to marry until he came back from the war.

He first trained in Pensacola, Florida, to fly the A4E Skyhawk and F8 Crusader and then went to El Toro with the First Marine Division. There he hooked up with Torykian, who recalls the day he met Richard Bloom. "My roommates, two fighter pilots, and I went to a bar one night where I ran into Dick Bloom. We got into a little bit of an argument when I told him his date was ugly. You had to know him to understand how he took it. He had so much life in him and an enormous sense of humor."

At El Toro the two used to play handball on Friday nights after work and share a few drinks at the Officers' Club. "When he smiled, his whole face smiled," noted Torykian. "We talked about going deer hunting with his dad in Olema after the war."

Torykian thought that Bloom was "an outstand-

Richard Bloom died when his plane crashed in the jungles of Vietnam.

ing aviator. We struck up a great friendship." The two were roommates in Laguna Beach until March 1965 when President Johnson sent elements of the Third Marine Division to Vietnam. Richard went to Vietnam in early 1966 and flew 70 combat missions in two months with Marine Attack Squadron 224 before being killed on September 20, 1966, flying support for ground troops near Chu Lai. Bloom's aircraft was hit during his third run against a truck park near the village of Ha Tinh, about 20 miles southwest of Danang. According to Bloom's wingman, small arms fire downed the plane. Bloom's body was never recovered. Torykian believes the plane burrowed into the soft jungle ground and buried Bloom in his cockpit.

Katherine, his sister, remembers the day two men in full dress uniforms came to the door to inform the family of Richard's death. "They rang my doorbell, and I heard my mother scream. I ran to the door. It was horrible. I'll never forget that day. I adored my brother."

Dick Lynch found out about his friend's death two weeks after he married. Then, two months later, he received his wedding present from Bloom. "That was really hard. His death was such a useless tragedy."

Torykian, on his way home from the war, stopped in San Francisco to spend time with the Bloom family, answering their questions about how their son had died. He made a point of visiting them every five years. Both he and Lynch became surrogate sons to Bloom's father, and both spent time hunting with him.

Years later, someone called Bloom's family claiming to have his dog tags and offering to recover the body for $50,000. The family called Torykian, who knew it was a scam, and authorities arrested the caller. "Dick's remains are gone," said Torykian. "They are a part of the earth. But I still remember him as a vibrant man and great athlete. Everybody loved him. He was a courageous person who feared nothing. I lost a great friend and the country lost a great American."

His name can be found on the Vietnam Veterans Memorial on Panel 10E, Line 123.

Richard Arthur Timboe '62

Born March 23, 1944, he was known as "Rich" at SI, "Art" at USF and "Tim" at home and in the military. Richard Arthur Timboe is also remembered as a hero for giving up his life while trying to save a soldier in the South Vietnamese Army.

Timboe grew up an Army brat in the Presidio along with Margo McRice, whom he later married. "It was like growing up in a little village inside a big city," said Margo. "No one locked the doors." Tim played Little League baseball and ran track at SI, and his best friend was Terry Gillin '62, now a professor of sociology at Ryerson University in Canada, who knew him as a quiet guy. "It blew everyone's mind when Margo and he eloped a year after he graduated from SI."

In 1963, after returning from Mexico, Tim and Margo moved in with Tim's parents while Tim continued his studies in political science at USF. Their son Michael Arthur Timboe was born in late 1963 and Brian William Timboe was born the following year. Tim graduated in 1966 and entered the Army after receiving his ROTC commission.

He went to Ft. Benning, Georgia, for infantry training and then to Ft. Campbell, Kentucky, to the 101st Airborne Division for jump school training. As a first lieutenant and pathfinder, he went to Vietnam in November 1967, assigned as an advisor to a village north of Saigon to work with the South Vietnamese Army as part of Advisory Team 70. He slept and ate with the villagers and wrote home about drinking homemade liquor. His wife sent him care packages of San Francisco items: copies of the *Chronicle*, Ghirardelli chocolate bars and sourdough bread.

On January 30, 1968, the North Vietnamese launched the Tet Offensive. On February 1, the Vietnamese commander of Tim's unit sent out a light machine gun unit to try to capture Viet Cong. One gunner was hit and Tim ran out to carry him to safety. He hoisted the man onto his shoulders and was running back when he was shot and killed. For his bravery, he was awarded the Silver Star.

"He was really friendly and didn't have an enemy in the world," said his son, Brian. "He died doing exactly what he wanted to do. All he ever wanted to do in his whole life was serve in the Army."

Timboe's family was first told that he was missing in action. Five days later, word came that he had died. "This poor soul in uniform came to the door," said Margo. "He was a basket case. I was his first case ever, and I had to call my father to take him to a bar to calm him down. He didn't know what to say. It was probably for the best, as it took my mind away from my own loss worrying about this poor guy.

"Fr. Eugene Schallert, SJ, at USF was such a good help during this time," added Margo. "He told me not to wallow in self pity and to focus on taking care of my children." Fr. Schallert presided over the funeral Mass at St. Ignatius Church February 14.

For Gillin, the loss of his best friend was a hard one to take. "I was in grad school when Margo called me. Like so many at that time, I had a kind of confusion about opposing the war while still struggling to honor those who were fighting. I had a tremendous sense of loss and a sense of ambivalence over whether or not he had died for a good and just cause. Part of

my sadness was that I thought his death was unnecessary because the war was inappropriate. We need to honor people like Tim who have served their county so selflessly while, at the same time, remain free to intellectually and morally challenge the rightness of any war." Margo chose to involve herself with Swords into Plowshares. "They know how to heal everyone, even widows."

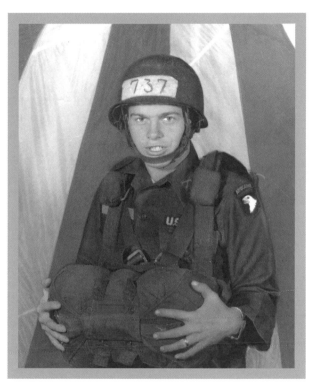

Richard Arthur Timboe died while trying to save the life of a comrade.

Richard Arthur Timboe is buried in the San Francisco National Cemetery in the Presidio, Plot WS 636-B, and his name can be found on the Vietnam Veterans Memorial, Panel 36E, Line 62. He is also survived by his two grandsons — Christopher and Dylan.

In addition to having their names appear on the Vietnam Veterans Memorial in Washington, D.C. and in Sacramento, Denis O'Connor, Richard Bloom and Richard Arthur Timboe have their names inscribed on a memorial in Justin Herman Plaza along with 160 other San Franciscans who died in Vietnam. Brian Timboe spoke at the 2001 dedication of that memorial, telling a cheering crowd of 500 that "there's nothing to be ashamed of, to be a Vietnam vet. I just want to say this to you: 'Hold your heads high!'" His father is also remembered in a memorial at USF.

Chalk-Dust Memories: The 1960s

Michael Shaughnessy '67

(Michael Shaughnessy is part of the Campus Ministry team at SI. He has taught religious studies at SI since 1980.)

Some students considered resisting the draft, but most would have gone willingly had they been drafted, including Michael Shaughnessy '67. "Had I been drafted straight out of high school, I would have gone without thinking about it a second time," he noted. Now a religious studies teacher and part of SI's campus ministry team, Shaughnessy has actively opposed the U.S. war in Iraq and encourages his students to judge conflicts in light of the Just War Theory. "As a student at SI, I had never heard of 'Just War Theory' or the Catholic peace tradition," he noted. "The bishops came out with a letter in 1970 saying no kid should graduate from a Catholic high school without knowing about these traditions. That's when I knew what I was going to do with my life: Teach at a Catholic high school, particularly teaching moral decision-making and encouraging people to take ownership of moral decisions and citizenship. That's what I've been trying to do at SI."

The son of Bert Shaughnessy '31, Shag, as he is known to colleagues and students, felt an adversarial relationship between teachers and students in his days at SI. "We were brutal to our teachers. We kept track of teachers who either quit or cried, and we would try to make them do one or the other. There was no sense of *cura personalis,* and much of our education resembled the Baltimore Catechism. It made no difference whether or not you understood what you were memorizing. The only teachers who challenged me to think and not just do rote memory were Jesuit scholastics. Tony Sauer was one of them. Looking back, I did learn more than I thought at the time. I learned how to write a 5-paragraph essay and enough information to win at Trivial Pursuits or Jeopardy. But a big part of my attitude was formed then."

Shaughnessy describes himself as having been a smartass in class. "One teacher kept throwing me out of class and wanted me suspended. Fr. Hyde didn't suspend me, because he thought the teacher was at least half at fault for not controlling the class. I had scores of detentions, including one on game day that meant I couldn't go to the game. I was a cheerleader and went anyway. Fr. Hyde saw me there and gave me five days detention. He said, 'I'll see you tomorrow.' Some days I started and ended my day with Uncle Frank."

Shaughnessy recalls playing freshman soccer and attending *Margo and Me*, a play written by students and performed at the Marina Middle School. At school he found himself in a class filled with other Irish kids while another class had all Italians. "It was the first and last year they tried doing that. There was 1D for Dagos and 1G for Gaels. They put a Japanese boy named Shigiyo in the Italian class because his name looked Italian. One African American with the last name of Grogan found himself in the Irish class. Ironically, Fr. John Enright, SJ, was trying to promote Civil

Kevin Tobin

Rights and integration, and he brought kids in the Sodalities to marches to carry banners. It was through the Sodality that I first heard of Cesar Chavez and the UFW, and we collected money to give to farm workers' families."

Shaughnessy is glad that the relationships between students and teachers at SI are more collegial and less adversarial than in his day. "Education at SI is far beyond mere rote memory. We know about Bloom's taxonomy and higher levels of learning. And there's a real respect and care for one another. People are conscious of *cura personalis* now."

Bill Kennedy '50

(Bill Kennedy taught Earth Science at SI, along with math, history, chemistry and drivers' education, from 1960 until 1997.)

It seems to me that in the 1960s, the students were really almost like a band of brothers. The Jesuit community was great in number and included a number of historical, famous and, of course, talented members. They accepted and respected the lay faculty although we were in the minority. I always thought there was tremendous collaboration between the Jesuit and lay teachers. I don't think we ever saw them as the opposition. The 1970s was a time of stress for the Jesuits, with some of the priests leaving the order. Some retreats were tough in those years for the lay faculty who were, along with the Jesuits, dealing with the tough transitions brought on by Vatican II.

We managed to have a lot of fun, though. Bill Love, for instance, had a great sense of humor. One day, after Fr. Hyde said he was sick and tired of guys smoking one block from school, Bill and I got in his car along with a big camera. We drove down the street about 20 minutes before school began. We zipped down Arguello, hopped a right and saw 20 students smoking on a stoop in front of a house. As we raced by, I took seven pictures. We had those students nailed to the wall. The next several days, everyone approached Bill Love and me, begging us not to share those pictures with Fr. Hyde. They never went back there to smoke. They knew we had them. They were fortunate that they were never punished.

Chuck Murphy '61

(Chuck Murphy has served as teacher, coach and administrator at SI since 1965.)

When I started at SI, only four or five lay teachers were on the faculty. Most had another job. Some worked for the *Chronicle* delivering papers in a truck; my dad worked for Hamm's and Burgermeister Breweries. I was in a unique position being the first (and at the time, the only) child of a faculty member to attend SI. The school, in those days, represented much of what it does today: strong academics with extracurricular involvement. As an eighth grader, I had to decide which high school to attend when I took the entrance exam. It wasn't a hard decision. I always wanted to go to SI because my dad worked here, and SI sports were always in the news.

Kids today don't realize the impact the media had on high school sports. Every week in the *News* or *Call*, you would have two full pages on high school sports coverage, where you would see caricatures of star athletes. They were bigger than life. I knew who all the top high school athletes were in the city. The coverage rivaled that of the pro teams.

Schools competed to see which game would draw the highest percentage of students to attend. SI and SH would always win the award and always tie each other with 100 percent attendance. The numbers were huge.

The climate in the school was very much top to bottom. You knew your place. Seniors were gods, the Block Club was the most powerful organization in the student body — much more powerful than the Student Council. Everyone knew who the Block Club officers were, but not the Student Council officers. Rallies were optional and not always attended by everyone. SI could be a hard place for some kids. It took a strong kid to break away from the mainstream, as there was tremendous pressure to be a part of the team as a spectator. It gave you a feeling of togetherness. When SI won, you felt you had a part in the victory.

Art Cecchin '63

(Art Cecchin came to SI in 1973 as director of scheduling and has since served as a coach, Social Science Department Chairman, teacher and sports editor for Genesis IV.*)*

In our senior year, we were in charge of breaking in a new dean, Leo Hyde. Before him we had John Hanley, who was tough — he never smiled — although he stood about 5-feet, 5-inches. Leo came in and smiled, and we thought we had it easy. We broke him in and taught him all the ropes.

In our junior year, someone made an emergency call that sent ambulances and fire engines to Frank Corwin's house. We almost lost our prom until the guy who did it admitted it. Dick Spohn was the best teacher I ever had. He scared the hell out of me but made physics informative. We had to build an electric motor from scratch. If it spun, you received an A. If it didn't, you got an F. Mine spun, and that's why I became a science major.

Students at work in the library at the Stanyan Street campus.

Paul Vangelisti '63

(Paul Vangelisti is a noted poet, editor and teacher living in Southern California.)

Fr. Jake Enright was Caryl Chessman's confessor. He was a liberal priest who came to SI by way of Los Angeles. Whenever he taught a lesson on birth control, we would all snicker as he drew diagrams of a penis and vagina that weren't very good. Another guy, Mr. Thomas Franxman, knew dozens of languages even though he was only 27. He could write Greek with either hand from either direction. He was gearing up to become a New Testament scholar and was the most brilliant man I ever met at SI, and that's saying a lot.

Gathering in the gym for a rally in 1966.

Kevin Tobin

Mark Cleary '64

(Mark Cleary is the chairman of SI's Board of Regents.)

One of Vince Tringali's axioms was for his football players to be "fast getting off the line." If we were to go on the "first count," he wanted us to go on the first noise we heard. One day during practice while I was on the line, he came out with a starter's pistol hidden in his pocket and got down behind us. We didn't see the gun, but when we heard the shot, we certainly were fast getting off the line.

We also had isometric bars in the field against the gym made of 1-inch thick tempered steel bars. Part of our training was to squat under them and try to stand up. John Deschler, our All City tight end, stood up and bent the bar. He didn't know he couldn't do it, so he did it.

Our time at SI was also marked by the assassination of President Kennedy and the tragic death of Denny Carter on the basketball floor. Denny was a good friend, and I served as one of the pall bearers. The entire school participated in mourning him.

David Mezzera '64

(Dave Mezzera taught at SI between 1970 and 2002, moderated the the speech and debate team and served as Community Service Director.)

On football games days, we followed an activity schedule and finished school 20 minutes earlier than on regular class days. The entire student body would proceed to the gym for a spirit rally, and from there would march en masse down Stanyan Street and directly into Kezar Stadium for the football game. About 85–90 percent of the student body would join in the police-escorted march down to Golden Gate Park to enter the cheering section. The cheerleaders would lead the pack, carrying the SI banner to the game. Block SI's really worked in the cheering section at football games: Seniors and juniors wore their red and blue jackets to form the block SI and underclassmen would all wear white shirts to provide the background. To me, that was what school spirit was all about.

Due to the ingenuity and contacts of Fr. Richard Spohn, SJ, SI had its own ruby laser rod in 1964 and was able to display holographic images.

Rainy day schedule still existed in the early 1960s. The last 20 minutes of the school day, titled Activities Period, would be canceled on a rainy day or before a big game to give us an early start.

SI's librarian in the 1960s, Br. Len Sullivan, SJ '44, would not allow students to take textbooks into the Stanyan Street campus first floor library. He would announce that "the library is for library books, not to do homework!" Also, students were not allowed above the basement in the Stanyan Street building until the first bell rang to begin the school day unless going to the library, main office or vice-principal's office.

Each school year began with a fund raiser, and we sold World's Finest Chocolates. Once, when I rang a doorbell in the Sunset District trying to sell a candy bar "to raise funds for a new field house," the occupant of the home said that that was the same excuse he used when he was an SI student a number of years prior, and SI still hadn't built the new field house.

On May 30 and June 1 and 2, 1963, the Stanyan Street gymnasium was transformed into an ice arena, with a portable ice rink brought in and assembled on the floor of the gym and a portable compressor up on the field to run the brine through the pipes and freeze the ice. A hole was punched through the wall of the gym to accommodate the pipes and hoses, which caused all sorts of consternation from SI. A local ice skating school used the venue to put on its yearly ice review mainly for parents of the young skaters. The company cut a deal with SI that year — all profits would benefit the SI building fund, and students were given quotas to sell two ads in the program and to purchase two tickets for the show, with chairs set up around the rink and the bleachers of the gym pulled out for more seating. For each ad sold, students received a raffle ticket for a scooter. Charlie Dullea, who only sold one ad, won the contest. Prior to the event, in order to pique SI student curiosity, a dozen or so teenaged girls performing in the show came to an SI rally in costume and were introduced to the catcalls of the SI students. The idea was to encourage students to buy tickets to see the show. Three SI students ended up skating. I had a solo and did a pair routine with a partner. Also, for each night of the show, the names of two SI students were drawn from a hat and ice skates were placed on their feet as young ladies gave them a quick skating lesson. The whole thing was a setup; Paul Hanley and Phil Woodard were chosen each night and took part in a well-rehearsed skit featuring pratfalls, real and spontaneous. Some of the young women in the show, many years later, sent their children to SI, and one of the skaters later married Ray Calcagno. The June 1964 fund raiser was a concert production held at USF's Memorial Gymnasium featuring Vince Guaraldi, Ronnie Shell, the Gateway Singers and Bola Sete.

Peter Devine '66

(Peter Devine has taught English and drama at SI since 1976 and directed 100 plays over a 25-year period.)

Peter Devine kicks up his heels at a school dance.

Kevin Tobin

This was the time of Coach Tringali when football was king of the school. Some teachers demanded to see our tickets to that afternoon's football game. If we didn't have them, they would give us extra homework. On the other hand, those football games were exciting because our team was nationally ranked. We used to march from Stanyan Street after weekly rallies with freshmen and sophomores wearing white dress shirts and juniors and seniors in their red or blue jackets. We would form a block SI in the rooting section every week and have on average a thousand kids at every game. We had to sit in the rooting section. If you didn't, if you sat with your girlfriend instead, catcalls would bring you back to the rooting section. The Jesuits would line the section to keep order.

When I was a student, women could come up the front staircase and into the main office. They would then receive permission to enter one classroom only on the first floor where they worked on costumes. They weren't allowed anywhere else. The locker room was reserved for only some teams, so guys changed clothes in the hallways for sports or stage crew.

We loved to play pranks on our teachers. Students stayed in the classroom, and teachers moved between periods. We had all the time in the world to plan pranks between classes. We would deliberately move the teacher's desk so that as soon as he put books on it, it would fall off the platform, or we put tacks on his seat. Sometimes we would turn our desks to the back of the room, especially when we had a young scholastic. He would enter the room, see us facing the back wall, and then walk down the middle aisle. Just as he got to the middle, we turned our desks to surround him. We drove two poor scholastics to tears, and one had a nervous breakdown. SI could be a rough school. Fr. McFadden told teachers never to smile before Christmas for a reason. I recall one scholastic, a brilliant physicist, who couldn't keep one study hall under control. Fr. McFadden walked by and, rather than disciplining us, told the teacher, "Can't you keep the animals in their cages?"

As a student, we had the rigid Fr. Becker English system: a nightly paragraph, five vocabulary words, five lines of poetry memorization, a short story or chapter to read, plus outside reading on the novel of the month — primarily Catholic authors. For example, even though junior year was supposed to be American Literature, we read several of the IMAGE series books on Jesuit Saints in England resisting the Protestant Reformation. We only read one Hemingway — *Old Man and the Sea* — for the Christ symbols. We also read the "Catholic" interpretation of *The Great Gatsby* (a man who lost his soul for materialism and modernism), and we read every Graham Greene, every Evelyn Waugh and lots of Shakespeare. (He was a secret Catholic, as our senior English teacher informed us.)

The nightly paragraph writing that we did freshman and sophomore year proved a great practice. We had to memorize rules in the Brown Bible (the grammar text), use one rule and underline it in the nightly paragraph. Each paragraph was an assigned subject with an assigned format, each vocabulary word had to be used and underlined and each topic sentence had to be underlined. By junior and senior years, we had to write longer essays: the 5-paragraph essay with an assigned topic due every Friday. Some of the assigned topics included "Spirit at SI," "Interview with the SI Dolly" (a student body president at another Catholic high school) and "Hamlet and Jesus." Our teacher handed back each weekly essay on the next Monday or Tuesday, and our rewrites were due on Thursday. No exceptions to this: every week one essay and every week one rewrite. For every grammatical error, we had to write the rule out from the Brown Bible 10 times with the corrected sentence.

Parts of that system are now worthy of satire, but that solid curriculum helped us to learn how to write and prepared us for college writing. Unfortunately, we were limited in our experience of authors, except Shakespeare and the Greeks, and read no contemporary novels except *The Power and the Glory* by Greene. However, we were very well prepared for the survey of British Literature in college having read *Beowulf, The Inferno, Le Morte d'Arthur* and at least eight Shakespeare plays over the course of four years.

Boris Koodrin '67

(Boris Koodrin is an artist who painted the sesquicentennial mural, which is the cover of this book.)

The senior retreat towards the end of the year was very important to me. I started by fooling around with the group, but when we were split up into our separate rooms, I found that the introspection really touched me. It woke something in me that was very powerful. That's one of my fondest memories of being at SI. It set me on a deeper search for meaning.

Fr. Tom Carroll, SJ '68

(Fr. Tom Carroll, SJ, is a retreat director at El Retiro in Los Altos.)

When SI moved to the new school, my parents, Tom '43 and Peg, wanted to celebrate the occasion with a gift to the school. I suggested the gift of a chalice and paten, the chalice to feature on opposite sides simple crosses centered on two styles of SI rings. One of the rings had belonged to a cousin, Roger Carroll '14.

I designed the chalice and paten in 1969, and my parents had them fashioned in a metalsmith's shop in San Francisco, right near the Bluxome Street firehouse where my father worked. The chalice

Below is an SI ring from the 1930s. The style changed several times over the century.

features the face of my father's ring, with its SI block relief on one side, and the face of my own class of '68 ring, with its red stone, on the other side.

When the chalice and paten had been completed, my parents gave them to Fr. Harry Carlin, SJ, then the president, for the use by the school. It was presented not on any major occasion, but just in an informal visit to Fr. Carlin's office. Our family has borrowed the chalice and paten on a number of occasions, using them for family weddings and for my first Mass at St. Gabriel Church in 1984.

John Wildermuth '69

(John Wildermuth is a political writer for the San Francisco Chronicle.*)*

Everyone has seen priests on the altar at a parish, but Fr. Pallas gave me a different view of a priest. He was a wisecracking guy. I remember coming to school on a Saturday and seeing a guy wearing a watch cap and a beat up old sweatshirt sweeping the corridors. He looked up, and I saw it was Fr. Pallas. He growled, "Get out of the way." He told corny jokes and related with kids on a personal level. Sometimes you forgot to wear a tie on First Friday, and you tried to get through the entire day without a teacher noticing you and sending you to Leo Hyde for detention. Anyone who had Fr. Pallas would try to make a trade for a tie, because he would notice.

Fr. Becker ran the English Department, which had a heavy emphasis on writing in each of the four years. Each week, freshmen wrote 100-word essays, sophomores wrote three 100-word essays, juniors 500-word essays with a first draft, and seniors had various styles of writing to emulate. That helped me in college be-

The March 1966 SI band concert directed by Robert Houston.

cause I was used to putting words on paper. He was a kind man, not a "jump-on-top-of-you" guy, who gave you the idea that writing was important and that anyone could do it. And with his syllabus, even some rookie, not too experienced (or even trained) teachers could learn how to teach English by following Fr. Becker's very detailed day-by-day routine of memory work, vocabulary, grammar, literature and writing.

I stayed in 1F with the same guys all day, every class, for my first year. Then SI began offering modern languages to freshmen in my sophomore year; from then on, you didn't stay with the same group for all your classes because of the language alternatives. It could have been worse. When my father went to SI, he stayed in the same classroom and the teachers switched. Anyone who did well in Latin had to take Greek. That wasn't my concern. In the 1960s, kids who didn't do well in Latin as freshmen had to take double English with Leo LaRocca in their sophomore year. The "powers that be" dumped our second year Latin class and replaced it with a second English course. It was the same English class everyone else took, only taken twice as slowly. There were few future valedictorians in the class. I did poorly in English and Latin my freshman year, and when I found myself in double English, I looked at the people around me, and said, "Jeez! They think I'm like one of these guys?" That jump-started my stalled academic career at SI. When I was at Loyola University and editing the college newspaper, I was told by some younger, Latin-phobic friends that La Rocca was showing his students my name in the newspaper staff box to prove there was academic life after double English.

We had an active life outside SI. Even though we attended an all-boys school, we weren't in the seminary. We saw plenty of girls at the games, and teen

club dances were big in the parishes. They were a great meeting place for kids from all the high schools. They even provided a popular teen basketball league for the kids who weren't good enough to play for the school.

We were supposed to be the first class to graduate from the new school, but construction problems prevented that. I think it's better that we graduated from the old school. We're part of the history of Stanyan Street.

Michael Thomas '71

(Michael Thomas has been a counselor and coach at SI since 1979. He is also the director of the Peer Assistance Center.)

It never entered my mind that we needed a new school. The old place had a mystique to it. My brother had gone there, and it was full of tradition. I had great teachers, such as Michael Burke for history, Bill Muller, SJ, for English, Bob Grady and Gene Growney, SJ. Then we'd get ready for the rallies, conducted by Vince Tringali in the old gym. You had to experience it — 1,000 guys in the gym and you could hear a pin drop. He would talk for 40 minutes every Friday before the game. During one game I recall being at the top of the SI block that we formed in the stands — we were told what to wear: either a white shirt or school jacket to form the block. I was picked up and passed all the way down to the first row within seconds.

I can't remember ever being called in by a counselor, but Fr. Becker took me under his wing. I worked in the print shop over the summer, and he taught me how to run the old printing presses and burn plates. I would have been in his first group to go to Europe in the summer of 1970, but I had to cancel.

I loved the all-male environment. Teaching at a coed school is wonderful, but I wouldn't trade those four years for anything. I had a cross section of friends then (they are still my friends today) who made my time wonderful.

"There are places I remember . . . "

By Curtis J. Mallegni '67

The sharp ring of the alarm clock cut through the quiet stillness of the early morning air. It was a typical start of a fog-infused summer day in San Francisco: 6:30 a.m. in June of 1963. Today was my maiden voyage to the fortress at 222 Stanyan Street known as St. Ignatius High. I hurried out of our flat at 3216 Fillmore Street and across the street, to board the 22 Fillmore bus with thoughts of high school running through my head. Equipped with fresh school supplies, clean clothes and the promise and wonder of a new educational adventure, I was ready for any challenge. At Ellis Street I transferred from the electrical 22 Fillmore bus, to the careening, diesel-powered juggernaut known as the 31 Balboa. The note I received from SI said to get off at Stanyan. When I arrived, I beheld the fort: 222 Stanyan Street — St Ignatius High. It would become the hub of my life for the next four years. Without a clue as to what lay ahead, my momentum took me to the front door and through the portals of Jesuit education.

My admission letter indicated that I would have to attend, and successfully complete, summer school to be admitted to the freshman class at SI. I was committed to whatever it took. Wandering through the halls with other bewildered classmates, I had to make

Mr. John Spinetta, SJ, teaching Latin in the 1960s.

it to the right classroom and be on time. The letter I received read Room 310 — Mr. Corwin.

Using my modest instincts of direction, I found the classroom at the end of the third floor facing out over a parking lot with a beautiful view of Turk Street. The smell was of musty chalk dust, cleaning solvent and furniture polish. The classroom was four rows of eight undersized desks of what seemed like early American colonial and probably doubled as a stockade for recalcitrant settlers. I was a rather robust youngster in my tender years (although that has all changed now), so needless to say the fit of the desk was rather snug.

Kevin Tobin

Mr. Richard Blinn, SJ, on upright bass in Oklahoma.

At the front of the room, there was a lonely, larger, but still undersized, desk. It had the effect of making the teacher look much more imposing, perfect for intimidating youngsters. The desk was occupied by a pensive, bespectacled, owlish looking man with a stern look. He wore a herringbone sport coat that had high mileage, standard issue teacher tie, and the balance of appropriate pedagogical attire. He surveyed the room with an expressionless but all-consuming look. Little did I know or realize I was about

to get my first introduction to "Uncle Frank." The settling-in rustle continued for a few more moments. There was an air of nervous angst among the summer schoolers. The Frank Corwin Experience was about to begin.

Then a scarcely audible mutter came from the front desk, which initially failed to quell the student din. Finally in booming Bostonian diction, Corwin announced "Room 310, Mr. Frank Corwin, St. Ignatius summer school," closely followed by a shrill alarm bell. Class was now formally in session, the honorable M. Francis Corwin presiding. A heavy, nervous silence ensued. Corwin held the attendance folder in his hand and examined it closely.

"I will call your name, and you will answer 'present.' If you are absent, don't answer." he bellowed. Whatever could he mean by, "Don't answer if absent"? As confusion reigned, he continued. "As I call your name and you answer, I want you to move to the next available desk so that the class will be seated in exact alphabetical order. Understood?" Once again, Uncle Frank surveyed the perplexed adolescent faces. He was thoroughly amused.

Corwin then proceeded to read off the names with perfect inflection and accent. I knew, as good as he was, he would certainly stumble on my name as did every teacher I had since kindergarten. Then he loudly proclaimed, "Mr. Mallegni, (Ma-len-yee)." Perfect. "Here," I peeped, and meekly took my place right behind the L's.

With roll call completed, he placed the absentee slip in the doorjamb outside, and then pulled the door shut. Class was formally in session. To begin, he outlined some basic ground rules: "Buttocks all the way back in the chair, eyes front, back straight." We sat in silence and watched his every move. He slowly walked around the room, intently looking into our faces as if he were looking for something he had lost.

He carefully perused the grade book in the stilled silence of the classroom. Finally, he stopped and looked up. Then it happened. My worst nightmare. Like a cannon shot, Uncle Frank boomed, "MR. MAL-LEN-YEEEEE! ON YOUR FEET, SUH." I rose in silence although I felt like Ralph Cramden in the "homina-homina-homina" mode, dumbstruck, gasping for air.

He continued with perfect diction at high volume, "In the great tradition of Jesuit education, do you know where the division between the Pacific and Indian Oceans is located?" I stood in pallid consternation. My paralyzed mind labored for a relevant thought. The stunned silence continued. Beads of perspiration sprung from my brow. Uncle Frank continued to scour the faces of the class as he paced up and down the rows, waiting, waiting. Finally, my jaws separated. and, with what seemed like the creak of an old barn door, I said, "I don't know."

"You don't know?!!!" he thundered. "You don't know?!!!" he repeated with a questioning upwards inflection for emphasis. "You *must* know this, Mr. Mal-len-yee! This is part of a well-rounded education. Your homework assignment, and that for all your classmates, is to determine the boundary line of the Pacific and Indian Oceans, Mr. MAL-LEN-YEE!! Take your seat, sir (suh)." Gladly, I thought.

With the passage of time, I could put this in perspective and appreciate my first SI encounter with the legendary Frank Corwin. As I got to know him better, I came to a fuller appreciation of his larger-than-life impact on so many of us. There was a tinge of self-deprecation in his style and delivery as if he were taking a shot at the potential for pomposity in academia.

Yet he understood the benefits of order and discipline in academic achievement. Uncle Frank had made his point. The bar had been raised considerably. This was very different from grammar school, and it was adapt or perish. Whatever it was, he left an enduring impression that carried me into freshman year.

With summer school under my belt, I felt like a seasoned SI veteran. I knew the floor plan of the school, including the location of the vice principal's and principal's offices and, most importantly, the basement vending machines. With brimming confidence, I was ready for a full load of classes, which included some new and mysterious fields of study such as Latin.

In my freshman year, my first period class was Latin taught by Mr. Morlock. Yes, THE Mr. Morlock. I always admired his persistence in trying to teach us a language that for most of us was really conceived on another planet. The classroom was set up included long white Formica-type desks that faced the front of the room and seated about 8 to 10 across. Each student was assigned a number, and Mr. Morlock would have a corresponding number on the blackboard. (It was actually a green board as I recall.) We would put on the headphones and listen to spoken Latin phrases. If Mr. Morlock pointed to your

At a 1966 rally mixer.

Kevin Tobin

number, you would have to repeat in Latin the phrase you had just heard over the headphones. If you did it reasonably well, you got a check. If you missed it

Kevin Tobin

From left, Class of 1965 members Mike Mullins, Phil Rossi, Tom Bone, Rick Chiles, Steve Campi & Dennis Conway by the south yard on Stanyan Street.

badly or botched it, you got a 0. He was very efficient, so each of us would get three or so at-bats with each session.

The great thing about this approach is it provides immediate feedback, requiring deft intellectual agility and total concentration. I got off to a rocky start. When Mr. Morlock pointed to my number the first few times, I just smiled and waved. I promptly got 0's: instant feedback. I picked up three or four goose eggs before I realized I was supposed to repeat the phrase. It was time to get on the stick. Carpe Diem! Then my Italian genes kicked in and I was able to hold my own.

To this day, I remember many useful Latin phrases

that I use as ice-breakers at cocktail parties and other social gatherings. Some of my favorites are *"vestis virum facit"* (clothes make the man), or *"mens sana in corpore sano"* (sound mind, sound body, or something like that). Here's one that appealed to our sense of adventure: *"A cane non magno saepe tenetur aper"* (a small dog often scares a wild pig). If you want to get the hors d'oerves all to yourself, try that one sometime. And finally, one of my personal favorites: *"Caelo fulmen scriptumque tyrannis"* (lightening is the writing of the gods.) This one is instant social currency.

Anyone who has studied, or speaks another language appreciates the mental agility required to express oneself in a foreign language. It's another way of looking at things, a different worldview. I don't think there are many chat rooms in Latin these days, but like summer school, it was another growing experience, stretching our pliable intellects into new and exotic domains.

Webster's dictionary defines sophomoric as "conceited and overconfident of knowledge but poorly informed and immature." Pondering the nuances of isosceles triangles and other geometric mysteries in my sophomore year illuminated this condition all too well. The illuminator was Fr. Pierre Jacobs, SJ, and he was the perfect antidote for our sophomoric tendencies.

Fr. Jacobs was an Old-World gentleman in the fullest sense, carrying himself with utmost poise and dignity. I can still see the image of Fr. Jacobs coming across the football field to class with beret and flowing cassock as if he were floating on air. His appearance projected precision and efficiency in all things. His beret, rimless glasses and perfectly groomed flattop haircut, chiseled a formidable image of intellectual acumen against a backdrop of the rampant and diffuse trappings of sophomoritis. He was the intellectual razor's edge.

Amid the unsettled din of the initial moments of class, he would quietly wait for antsy students to settle, and they gradually did. He then proceeded with taking attendance, pausing to look at the faces so as to remember them in his steel-trap memory. He pronounced the names perfectly. Fr Jacobs was pleasant, balanced, mature and always in control. There was no time for foolishness, and he acted as if he were telling us, "When you're in my class, you have to grow up for 45 minutes."

Fr. Jacobs was instinctively fascinated with the mysteries of geometry. He was always pleased when he completed the solution to a difficult problem as if to say, "Isn't it wonderful the way that falls into place?" He reveled in the precise language of mathematics. In his sonorous Belgian accent, he would wonderfully pronounce the language of the trade: isosceles, hypotenuse, circumference and Pythagoras (PI-THAG-O-RUSS). It was all music to my ears, although these concepts elude me to this day.

He had all the geometric trade implements: a compass, a ruler and a protractor. Despite Fr. Jacobs' insistence on focused attention and calm in pondering mathematical mysteries, one of us would inevitably drop one of these tools on the floor where it would land with a rattle. In quintessential Fr. Jacobs style, he would respond, "Put the toys away, child." Enough said. The geometric "tools of the trade" could also be used to inflict short jolts of discomfort to classmates. There was nothing like letting the guy in front of you "accidentally" back into your compass at about 9 a.m. — a rude wake-up call.

Affixed to the midriff of Fr. Jacob's cassock was a small metal tube that held a piece of chalk, attached to a retractable metal chain and used to facilitate the drawing of geometric shapes as needed. As he discussed various shapes, Fr. Jacobs would quickly pull out the cylinder holding the chalk, and by placing his thumb as an anchor on a portion of the chain, draw near perfect triangles, circles and other objects to demonstrate his point. A picture was worth a thousand words, and he knew it.

The highlight of the class was working the geometry problems en masse. Fr. Jacobs would posit the mathematical conundrum, and we would quietly try to solve it using our books, our instruments and our sophomoric guile. You could hear our brains working hard, as Fr. Jacobs strolled the classroom looking over our work with a discerning eye.

After about 5 minutes, he would verbalize what he was seeing and sensing. As he'd peer over someone's work, he would announce to the rest of the class, "We have one correct an-

A dress code advisory from the 1960s.

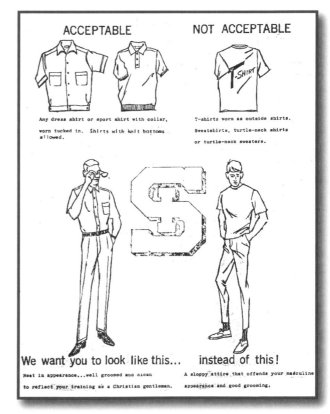

swer." This person would have a gleaming, gloating smile on his face. The rest of us would look on with perplexed resentment. Fr. Jacobs would continue his stroll through the aisles, stop and take a look, then announce, "We have one INcorrect answer." The student would look befuddled at the master, and, if inclined, Fr. Jacobs would offer a suggestion or two to facilitate the solution.

Finally he would stop at my desk. He'd peer down, look at me directly, shake his head and say, "We have one UNBELIEVABLE answer." The place would go nuts (for a very short period), and then Fr. Jacobs would say with great sarcasm, "Settle down, children." And thus was the extent of my enigmatic foray into geometry. In all, Fr. Jacobs greatly helped us in overcoming our sophomoric proclivities, and some of us had lucid but brief moments of geometric understanding. More importantly, he did much to get us farther down the road to maturity and junior year.

As we gingerly made the transition from overconfident sophomores to under-confident juniors, my sojourn in the mysterious world of mathematics continued. The next stop was "advanced" algebra, or Algebra II with Bill Lamon.

Mr. Lamon had been a pilot in the Belgian Airforce. He was the epitome of Old-World dignified honor and expected his students to be of similar mien. He carried himself with the dash and aplomb of the fighter pilot he had been. Some might have characterized him as a mite stuffy, but his standards were high and

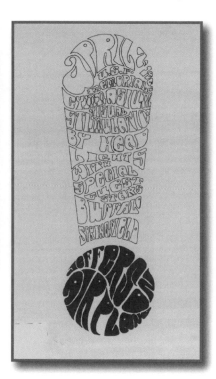

A poster for the Jefferson Airplane and Buffalo Springfield concert to benefit SI.

out of reach for most of us. No doubt our profound mystification with the enigmatic world of mathematics continued with Mr. Lamon.

In keeping with his Old-World tendencies, Mr. Lamon was inclined to read, for all the class to hear, the results of major exams. Our mathematical foibles were exposed to the not-so-tender mercies of our fellow classmates.

He would read the names and proclaim the grades with great drama and formality. Some of the names have been changed to protect the not-so-innocent. With a heavy Belgian accent, he proceeded: "Let's see … Mr. McArthur. Where is Mr. McArthur?" McArthur would sheepishly raise his hand. "Oh yes." Lamon would take a measured look at McArthur, and then, using his pencil, he would scroll down the attendance book and then stop. "Mr. McArthur … a DEEEEE! Ah, you need to do much better, much better." McArthur ignominiously slunk deeply into his chair.

And so he continued, "Mr. Johnson … a DEEEEE! Same problem. You need to work much harder." Johnson accepted his sentence with a bewildered look on his face. Mr. Scarpone … a DEEEEE-MINUS! Terrible!" a D-minus mathematically is about 0.5 grade points (see I did learn some math). As such, it does not make a great difference in advancing the cause of civilization, yet many got the D-minus. On the other hand, it gave new meaning and significance to the upside of getting a straight D.

After about 20 or so grades were read, all in the lower reaches of the grade spectrum, he would pause for a little editorializing. "It's unbelievable to me that these grades are so poor. You need to do a better job of applying yourselves. It is your honor, your pride." We looked on profoundly bewildered, like a herd of deer starkly frozen in the headlights of Mr. Lamon's grade book.

Exhaling in disgust and shaking his head, Mr. Lamon continued and finally got around to yours truly. "Mr. Malignant ... how in da hell do you pronounce dat name?" This was something I had become quite used to, so I tried one of the most successful techniques to facilitate the pronunciation of a nice Ma-len-yee. "Mr. Lamon, think of lasagna. The gn is fused together to produce a n-y sound — like la-sahn-ya."

"Oh yes. This is very helpful. Let me see." He scrolls down the grade book. "Yes, Mr. Malignee — EFFF, a complete fah-lure." With a dumbfounded look, I accepted my fate. Despite the ignominy of COMPLETE failure, my classmates were actually very understanding, themselves all lurking in the D and D-minus neighborhood. With heavy hearts and dizzy heads, we pressed on, determined to improve.

Among other junior year adventures was chemistry class. Who could forget the wily Mr. Buley asking in his smoke-burnished voice, "God ******! Why don't you guys get this? What the hell is going on?" With his drawn, compassionate face, he asked the critical existential questions. Through the sulphur bombs and titrations, I honestly had no idea what the hell was going on. It was hard enough just memorizing the elements. Just when you had it under your belt, some guy at Berkeley would discover a new one ... Seaborgonium or Berkulonium! Yikes! Mr. Buley looked on dolefully as we sustained our profound confusion.

And there was the youngish and very patient Mr. Capitolo: Cappy, The Bear. We were not well suited to English, but he tried to make it fit. Some rubbed off, but most rolled off. Cappy was the embodiment of patience as a virtue.

In senior year we were graced with the young, erudite scholastic Mr. Tony Sauer. He called me either "Chief," or "Big Curt," or "Curt babes." He humored himself with our names as well as our own adolescent attempts to be cool. Little did we realize we were in the midst of such a formidable wit and intellect who

By the end of the decade, construction of the Sunset District campus neared completion. The football field is visible through the arch of what would become a classroom window.

Construction neared completion in 1969. Pictured here is the western side of McGucken Hall.

would become the intellectual beacon of SI. He was way ahead of us, and we rarely got "his drift" as hard as we tried. Yet he endured as one of the truly great friends of our class, then and now. If only we could go back and take it all in anew with a slightly better chance of understanding what he was talking about. We pondered the Canterbury Tales, the Rime of the Ancient Mariner and Macbeth. We memorized "Tomorrow and tomorrow and tomorrow creeps in this petty pace," and we imagined Lady Macbeth out outing the damn spot. Great stuff indeed, if only we had known.

There were the personalities for the ages, like the diminutive and fiery Padre Luis Peinado, SJ, and the chanting of Machu Pichu; the young Bob Drucker; and Chuck Murphy cum venerable SI legend Pere Bernie; the super-organized scholastic Randy Roche; Tringali's English class; the way-over-our-heads American History with Mr. Buckley; followed closely by Fr. George Lee's "why anything" religion class; or the not-so-silent retreats with Fr. Hanley; the so-quiet-you-could-hear-a-pin-drop library under the watchful eye of Br. Sullivan; and the stern but abundantly fair Clark Kent look-alike, Fr. Leo Hyde, and his then understudy and legend-in-the-making Br. Douglas Draper.

Some places I'll never forget: the Pits, the field house, the gym, the sandwich place (sign knocked out every few days from a pine cone volley), Kezar Pavilion and the side doors that breathed when the crowd roared, the vending machines in the basement, the chapel and the Fr. Hyde sit-down-and-cool-off bench (now outside Br. Draper's office on 37th Avenue).

One day the Red and Blue flag came down at the fort at 222 Stanyan and it was all different and yet fatefully necessary. The place had taken us as far as it could. The Red and Blue was hoisted again at the dunes on 37th Avenue, and the lore, legends and memories of old SI followed the flag to the Sunset.

In those great days in the mid-1960s, our lives were imbued with the music of the Beatles. They captured our hopes, our fears and the spirit of the era. The music often expressed what we could not. Their song "In My Life" from the *Rubber Soul* album expresses best what SI was for me then and now:

There are places I remember
All my life though some have changed
Some forever not for better
Some have gone and some remain
All these places have their moments
With lovers and friends I still can recall
Some are dead and some are living
In my life I've loved them all.

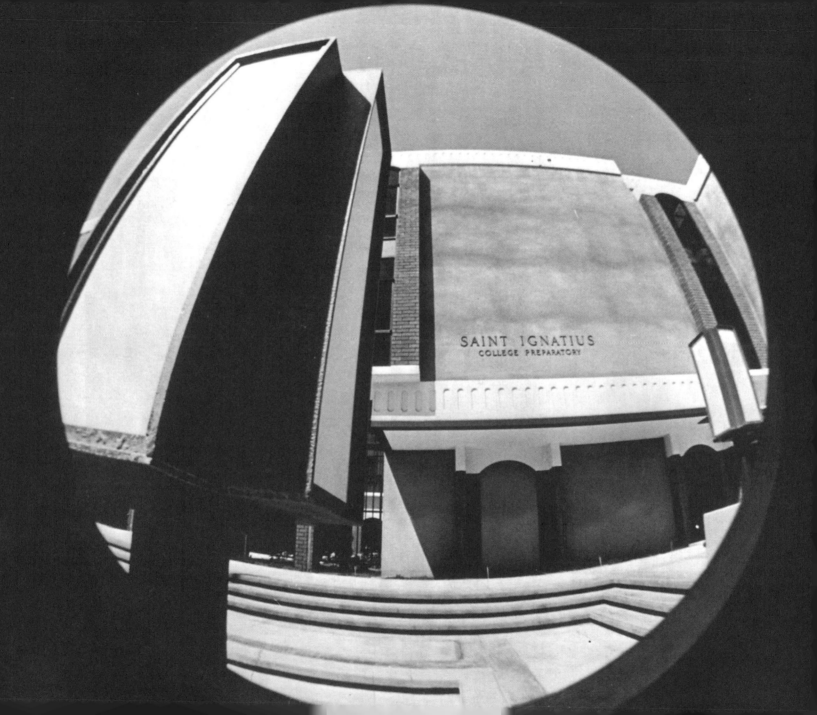

XI. REDEFINING JESUIT EDUCATION (1970 ~ 1979)

The 1970s saw SI complete its first decade at its brand new campus at 2001 37th Avenue, built atop some of the last inland sand dunes San Franciscans would ever see. Rising from the grains was a modern facility and a new name — St. Ignatius College Preparatory. Inside the new buildings, tensions flared amongst the faculty as the dynamics of the times played themselves out between the older and younger teachers. The decade saw several changes in leadership with no fewer than four presidents and two principals trying to steer the Good Ship SI into calmer waters.

Students continued excelling at classes and extracurriculars. Peter Devine '66 joined the faculty in 1976 and began a remarkable 25-year run directing 100 plays. Inside SI faded from sight, replaced by a series of newspapers, and students found new homes in the various ethnic clubs that were outgrowths of the Civil Rights movement.

SI was changing in a more profound way, too,

as Jesuit schools all over the U.S. reexamined their mission. In a remarkable document called "The Preamble," Jesuits and lay teachers redefined Jesuit education for a modern world. At SI, that meant the creation of the Community Service Program, Sunday Night Liturgies, SI Outbound and Christian Life Communities (CLCs).

In athletics, SI dominated in track and field, with coach Terry Ward '63 and his boys taking the league championship seven times. Under Coach Luis Sagastume, the soccer team prevailed, winning league crowns three times, and the golf team locked up league honors from 1977 to 1979. The basketball team generated the most excitement by also taking laurels three times and coming close to being NorCal Champs. While the football team did not win a championship, it captured the hearts and minds of many Wildcats with several outstanding seasons under coaches Tom Kennedy '63, Jim McDonald '55 and Gil Haskell '61.

St. Ignatius College Preparatory from the 1971 Ignatian yearbook.

Changes in Leadership

SI students, well into their first year in their new quarters, held a dance in the Carlin Commons on April 15, 1970. The school then opened its doors to the public on April 18 and 19 for an Open House, drawing 7,000 to inspect the still unfinished structures. Then, on June 6, 248 members of the class of '70 took part in the school's 111th commencement exercises at St. Ignatius Church, and many returned to SI June 9 when Archbishop McGucken blessed the school. The ceremony apparently took many hours as he blessed and dedicated each classroom, laboratory and office as well as the Stephen Orradre Memorial Chapel where he concelebrated Mass with the SI Jesuits. At the end, the announcement was made that the Jesuit residence would be named McGucken Hall in honor of the Archbishop's financial and moral support.

(That chapel, incidentally, features 12 brilliant faceted glass windows created and installed in 1970 by Carl Huneke. Each window holds "inch-thick glass set in a thin epoxy matrix that allowed the chipped edges of the glass to refract light in radiant colors. The saints depicted in the windows are Jesuit saints except for St. Stephen, who was selected in honor of Stephen Orradre."[1] The saints include St. Ignatius, St. Francis Xavier, St. Alphonsus Rodriguez, St. Peter Claver, St. John Brébeuf, St. Isaac Jogues, St. Stephen, St. John Berchmans, St. Stanislaus Kostka, St. Peter Canisius, St. Robert Bellarmine and St. Aloysius Gonzaga. The artist, who died shortly after the new campus opened, was born in Achim bei Bremen, Germany, where he started his apprenticeship at age 13. After immigrating to San Francisco, he opened the Century Stained Glass Studio on Fillmore Street where he created windows for more than 70 California churches and two additional windows in the Jesuit chapel in McGucken Hall.)

Fr. Edward McFadden, SJ, continued to serve as principal until 1976, when Fr. Richard McCurdy, SJ, succeeded him. The Office of the President saw five occupants in the 1970s. Fr. Cornelius Michael Buckley, SJ, who led the school as president between 1970 and 1973, had taught at SI from 1956 to 1959 before being ordained in France in 1962. Fr. James R. Hanley, SJ, who succeeded him, was a native San Franciscan who had taught theology at SI between 1960 and 1968. He served until 1975 and was succeeded by Fr. Russell Roide, SJ, who served until 1979. Fr. Anthony P. Sauer, SJ, who had taught at SI in the 1960s and early '70s, returned in 1979 to serve as president, and his record 26-year tenure in that office has provided the school with leadership in key moments in the school's history.

Changes were taking place, too, on the academic side of the school, with the creation of two new positions — assistant principal for academics and assistant principal for student activities. Fr. Charles R. Gagan, SJ '55 (who, at the time of this writing, is pastor of St. Ignatius Church), held the former position, supervising faculty, and Fr. Roide held the latter position, supervising all extracurricular activities, including athletics.

The administration and faculty were still primarily Jesuit with 39 religious and 34 laymen serving the school, a far cry from the school's early days, when SI employed a handful of laymen; but by the end of the

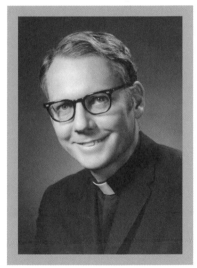

Fr. Cornelius Michael Buckley, SJ, succeeded Fr. Carlin as president of SI.

The Sodalities became the Christian Life Communities, and students continued to serve people in need.

decade, those numbers would shift dramatically, with 51 lay faculty, administrators and staff and only 29 Jesuits. The 1979 faculty also included three women — Anny Medina (French), Carolyn Rocca (Italian) and Katie Wolf (Art & Architecture). In addition, two women worked in the library (Renate Morlock and Geraldine Ferring), nine served as secretaries and one served as the registrar.

Jesuit Education Redefines Itself

The social activism of the 1960s carried over into the new decade and led to the birth of SI Outbound, which had taken the place of the student Sodality of the Blessed Virgin. Students in this organization worked as tutors in grammar schools throughout the city, visited the elderly and did other acts of community service. The success of this program led to the creation of the Community Service Program in 1980, with every student asked to complete 100 hours of ministry. (This office was renamed the Christian Service Program in 2003.)

One of its creators, Michael Mandala, a scholastic at the time, hoped that SI students would contribute "to the betterment of the San Francisco community" by tutoring students from economically disadvantaged neighborhoods. In its first year, the program attracted 80 students and offered academic credit to 25 seniors. It also helped the school attract students of diverse ethnicities and races, something SI had pursued actively since the 1960s.

The start of SI Outbound was a reflection of a profound change that was taking place at SI and at other Jesuit schools. The tenor of Jesuit education had been slowly changing across the country, spurred both by Vatican II and by financial troubles at some of the high schools. In 1969, the Jesuit Educational Association, made up of colleges and high schools, disbanded when the universities left to form their own organization. In 1970, representatives of the Jesuit high schools gathered in Scottsdale, Arizona, to discuss the creation of a new organization to be called the Jesuit Secondary Education Association. (The first president of the JSEA was an SI grad — Fr. Edwin McDermott, SJ '36.)

One of those in attendance, Robert "Jerry" Starratt, principal of Fairfield Prep in Connecticut, recalled one shocking announcement at that meeting, made by a friend of his, a Jesuit principal in New York. He told Starratt and the others assembled that "morale in his school was at an all-time low … and that if he didn't come away from the meeting with any sense of direction, he was going to go back and close his school."

Starratt had just read an essay by Fr. Jim Connor, SJ, the Maryland provincial at the time, "who wrote that no matter what ministry Jesuits are engaged in, they're basically giving the Spiritual Exercises," noted Starratt. "I began talking about what that might mean in a high school setting, citing themes from the Exercises such as the Call to the Kingdom, Finding God in All Things, Contemplatives in Action and Carrying the Cross with Christ. I spoke off the top of my head about how to translate the Exercises into the curriculum and pedagogy of a Jesuit school and thereby to recapture the Jesuit identity of our work."

His friends told him to go to his room and put those ideas into writing. "I went to my room and said, 'My God, what have I gotten myself into!' The trouble was that I couldn't remember what I had just said." When he returned to the meeting, Starratt had in his hand what became the Preamble to the JSEA's Constitution — one of the key documents that gave those assembled a reason to continue assembling.

The response to that document was electric. "The Preamble became a rallying cry for the schools," said Joe O'Connell, SJ, the JSEA President who honored Starratt in 2001 with its Ignatian Educator Award. "It proved to be a transformational point for Jesuit secondary education in the United States. Had it not been for Jerry's inspiration, we would have been in a very different place than we are now."

That Preamble and the Constitution for the new JSEA became a catalyst for change throughout the decade of the '70s for SI and for Jesuit schools across the country. The Preamble asks schools to "go beyond the criteria of academic excellence, important as this is, to the far more challenging task of bringing about a true *metanoia* [a fundamental change of character] in their students...." It also asks Jesuit schools to "move more vigorously towards participation in community affairs" and to "honestly evaluate their efforts according to the criteria of both the Christian reform of social structures and renewal of the church."

In 1973, during the first mandatory faculty retreat, teachers discussed the Preamble and made it "the ultimate criterion for all of our future decisions," wrote Fr. McCurdy in the December 1973 *Genesis* magazine. When the faculty returned to SI, they formed committees to "evaluate every aspect of the school in the light of our stated values and goals."

Charlie Dullea, then in his first year teaching at SI, attended those meetings and recalls how revolutionary the document was. "It was filled with ideas that today we take for granted. But that was the first time we heard of the concept of 'magis.' In our meetings we discussed the need for a community service requirement as a prerequisite to graduation." Dullea was most struck by this statement from the Preamble: "If the faculty at a Jesuit school are men and women whose lives are inspired by the Ignatian vision, then the question about the percentage of Jesuits on the faculty is not an overriding issue. It is more a question of the quality of the lives of the faculty, both Jesuit and lay. The school will be Jesuit if the lives of its teachers exemplify and communicate to the students the vision of Ignatius."

"For me, this meant I should learn the craft of teaching *and* develop spirituality in concert with my colleagues," said Dullea. "Thirty three years later we have an Adult Spirituality Office that serves the spiritual needs of the entire faculty, outside of the classroom."

The establishment of SI Outbound, and later, of the Community Service Program, was only a part of SI's response to this call to action. In the 1960s and earlier, students and priests may have had informal conversations about religion, and certainly friendships developed and grew among them. Rarely, however, did Jesuits share their unique brand of spirituality with students beyond the senior retreat. That changed with the birth of the Christian Life Communities in the early 1970s and a new kind of senior retreat.

Christian Life Communities

The Christian Life Community movement traces its roots to 1563 when Fr. John Leunis, SJ, founded the first Sodality of Our Lady by "gathering a group of young lay students at the Roman College to help them unite their lives."[2] The first Sodalities at SI were among the 80,000 Sodalities that prospered around the world into the early 20th century.

By the 1950s, more than 2 million American teens were members of Sodalities. Some Church leaders, responding to Vatican II, felt these groups would work better as smaller communities, and the CLC movement began. For the first few years of the 1970s, SI students used the words "Sodality" and "CLCs" interchangeably, but by the mid-70s, the name change took hold for good.

CLCs prospered at SI because they involved smaller communities than the Sodality. A dozen or so students met weekly with one or more moderators — priest or lay teachers — to discuss matters spiritual, go on retreats or simply enjoy each others' company. These CLCs grew in popularity with students at SI (there were 10 active CLCs by 1979) in part because they stressed six points that are at the heart of Ignatian spirituality: Finding God in all things, following the Spirit

(to hear and respond to any call), collaboration with Jesus to further God's kingdom, ordering relationships by living and choosing in loving collaboration with Jesus, living in the freedom for which we are created, and making retreats along the lines of the Spiritual Exercises.

CLCs remain popular at SI to this day. "My fondest memory of SI was my involvement with CLCs," said Elwyn Cabebe, MD '92. "As a freshman, I joined Lucie Rosa-Stagi's CLC, which at the time had only four members. After the first meeting, by default, I became the CLC leader and continued on until senior year. By senior year, however, it had grown to more than 100 members. It served a social function and fostered empowerment. It also taught us that our community extends well beyond the walls of SI."

Cabebe's group raised money towards tuition for a girl in South America, volunteered at community events, had discussions about spirituality and learned to pray together. "My CLC gave me the tools and encouragement to become involved in my community and build on the relationship that God has with all of us," he added. "For that, I am truly grateful."

The CLCs (and the Sodalities of past years) held an annual Christmas food drive to help San Francisco families of limited means. The food baskets, with the help of Fathers' Club drivers, now help families who come to the Christmas Store at St. Dominic's Church in a program devised by Sr. Cathryn deBack who, in 1981, became the first sister hired at SI. (She received the President's Award in 1998 for her service to the city and the school.)

A New Kind of Retreat

The senior retreat in the 1960s wasn't much different from retreats of decades past. In the early 1970s, the retreats changed to reflect the Preamble and Vatican II. Teachers such as Frank Kavanagh and Charlie Dullea told stories from their lives of how they lived out Gospel values, and students had opportunities not only to reflect but also to share their reflections with teachers and friends. "We really got close to students during these retreats," says Dullea. "We tried to do more than merely preach to students." Those changes ultimately led to the Kairos retreat — encouraged by SI Principal Steven Nejasmich — which began at SI in 1999, modeled after a program pioneered at St. Ignatius College Preparatory in Chicago. The senior Kairos retreat now runs four days and is one of the watershed events for seniors at SI. The name comes from a Greek word meaning "decisive time," and the campus ministry team has created a retreat that they believe is "filled with opportunity, that requires both discernment and bold action" and that offers high school students "the opportunity to examine, develop and deepen their commitment to the Lord."[3]

Fr. Pedro Arrupe & the Call to Action

Fr. Pedro Arrupe, SJ, the Jesuit Superior General from 1965 to 1981, gave SI another reason to move in this new direction. He visited SI in 1971 where he told students that if we have "suicidal blind irresponsibility and lack of courage, we will have no right at some later date to mourn the passing of our schools." Two years later, in a speech to the Tenth International Congress of Jesuit Alumni of Europe in Valencia, Spain, he spoke to alumni from Jesuit high schools and universities, many of whom felt that their primary duty as Jesuit supporters was to donate money. He challenged them to do far more, to dedicate themselves to become "men for others" and to rise out of their complacency. He asked his listeners — and challenged those who taught and studied at Jesuit schools — to live simply "and in this way to stop short, or at least to slow down, the expanding spiral of luxurious living and social competition" and to "draw no profit whatever from clearly unjust sources. Not only that, but going further, to diminish progressively our share in the benefits of an economic and

Students in SI Outbound also participated in service work.

social system in which the rewards of production accrue to those already rich, while the cost of production lies heavily on the poor." He asked all to be "agents of change in society; not merely resisting unjust structures and arrangements, but actively undertaking to reform them."

Priests at SI, like Jesuits throughout the world, were unclear on how to respond immediately to Arrupe's words. Some priests at SI embraced the speech and invited students to become these "men for others." Priests invited students to join picket lines in support of the United Farm Workers' grape boycott, and others created more opportunities for SI students to minister to those in need.

"Whose side are you on?"

For the first year at the new campus, SI held half-day sessions to let workers finish the building. The Jesuits also had to adjust their schedules, eating their meals at the Holy Name Parish Center, as workers still had not finished the kitchen in the Jesuit residence. "Each morning we would board a bus at Welch Hall and drive to Holy Name," said Fr. Charles Gagan, SJ '55. "It was an old bus and pretty grim."

In 1970, the school began a new tradition and one that would last until the 1990s. The Sunday Evening Liturgy began not in Orradre Chapel, which was still unfinished, but in a double classroom on the second floor. Every Sunday, Fr. Gagan had students move the altar from the small Jensen Chapel to the classroom and then move it back. A priest in charge of the chapel complained to the rector each Monday that the altar hadn't been replaced correctly. "He was very careful about Jensen Chapel," said Fr. Gagan, "and if we put the altar back one inch from where it had been, I

would hear about it."

Within a few weeks, students began crowding into the classroom every Sunday night for Mass. "We were addressing a need not being addressed by parishes at the time," he added. "This became a sore point, as pastors in the area resented their parishioners coming to us. Now that I'm a pastor, I see their point."

It didn't take long before the double classroom proved too small to fit all those who came to Sunday Evening Liturgy. To accommodate the crowds, Fr. Gagan had the chairs moved outside and invited people to sit on the floor. "Even then it was crowded. We didn't really have enough room until we moved into the chapel." Mercy student Mame Campbell Salin preferred "sitting on the floor to pews" and she liked the fact that Masses were celebrated at night. "That seemed to make it special for some reason."

The same priest who was in charge of Jensen Chapel was also placed in charge of Orradre Chapel, and he again proved an adversary to Fr. Gagan. "We argued over the number of confessionals for the chapel, and he insisted that the altar be set in cement on top of the stairs, so we had to use a second altar, as we didn't want to celebrate Mass that way. We asked for a portable altar, and this created controversy in the community. This was a time of tension in the Church between the old and the new when changes in the liturgy brought on by Vatican II were still being promulgated."

Fr. Gagan wasn't the only one to sense the tension. Many in the administration were used to a pre-Vatican II way of doing business, while many of the young priests, scholastics and teachers were ready for a change. Colleagues soon found themselves in adversarial roles, fighting over all sorts of issues — from the plays performed to the dress code among priests, some of whom did not feel the need to wear a Roman collar all day.

Tensions came to a head in 1972 when Nick Weber, then a Jesuit, put on *The Fantasticks*. Controversy arose when the Jesuit administration told Weber to cut a few risqué lines and the show was nearly cancelled. (Nick left SI after another fight over the play *Celebration* when the administration objected to a sexual reference in the play's opening line.)

Charlie Dullea '65, recalls being pulled aside by a colleague during the first mandatory faculty retreat shortly after he was hired in 1972 and asked, "Whose side are you on?" "He wanted to know if I supported the old guard or the younger priests who were pushing for change."

Fr. Gagan praised Fr. Sauer and Fr. McCurdy for helping to restore peace between the factions in the years that followed. "In addition, a tremendous group of lay faculty helped spread the Jesuit message," said Fr. Gagan. "Some of them understood the Jesuit message better than the Jesuits did. When I look at other schools, I'd say that one of Fr. McFadden's strong points was that he hired good teachers. He also refused to take sides. He hated conflict. At the time, some found that diffidence infuriating, but his care and concern for individual teachers was outstanding."

The struggle between old and new was inevitable, Fr. Gagan adds. "Looking back, I don't see how we could have avoided it. We had to enter it and come out. Those who did were better off than those who pretended that Vatican II had never taken place."

Fr. Gagan's fondness for SI stems from his happy experiences there both as a student and scholastic. "I received my vocation at SI. And I loved teaching under Fr. Reed in the 1960s." But the best was yet to come, he noted. "Some say Jesuit schools live on

a great reputation. In the 1970s, SI began to deserve its reputation. It improved academically under Fr. McCurdy, and the ideas of 'Men for Others,' of social ministry and faith that does justice distinguished us from other schools and made us successful. In years past, the Sodalities did outreach work. In the 1970s, that spirit of outreach permeated the entire school."

Br. Douglas Draper, SJ

Br. Draper is perhaps the best-known dean of discipline in the U.S. For the past few years he's also served as minister of the Jesuit community, assisting the rector in the day-to-day business matters affecting the residents of McGucken Hall.

Beginning in 1969 when he took over as dean, students have known the power of his voice over the public address system as he runs down the list of students to be called to his office. And while most students may fear hearing their names on that list, they respect the man who reads it.

"They feel this way because he's a fair, honest and loving human being," said his close friend, Fr. Paul Capitolo, SJ. "That's what allows him to be dean as long as he has — the longest reigning dean in any Jesuit school in America."

"I'm always puzzled when someone asks me why I became a brother," said Br. Draper (who is also known as the Duke of Discipline, or, simply the Duke.) "It's a

Br. Douglas Draper, SJ, succeeded Fr. Hyde as Dean of Students.

vocation, just like a vocation to the priesthood. I knew that God called me to a religious state as a brother, and I knew I could be happy doing this work."

When Br. Draper started as SI's dean in 1969, he was "absolutely petrified. But over the years, I've seen the seeds we've planted come to fruition. We do instill values in them. And when you make a friend with a student, you have a friend for life."

Br. Draper is also known for his sense of humor when it comes to catching rule-breakers. For the 1973 prom, dozens of students rented a penthouse room at a hotel on Sutter Street. As they continued celebrating there with their dates, Br. Draper received a call alerting him to the situation. He and Fr. Gene Growney, SJ, drove to the hotel and finally convinced the manager to give them permission to raid the party. "Just as he gave us permission, we heard that the students called for room service. A waiter in a green jacket wheeled his cart out, and I borrowed his jacket," recalled Br. Draper. Then he and Fr. Growney took the elevator to the penthouse, knocked on the door and announced that room service had arrived. "When the door opened, I burst through and saw everyone dive for cover. I opened the door to the bathroom and found a young man, fully clothed, sitting on the toilet with his date on his lap. I told him if he sat there too long, he would get hemorrhoids."

The next year, after the last final exams for the Class of 1974, the seniors brought a keg to the top of Strawberry Hill in Golden Gate Park. "Fr. McFadden heard about it and told me to do my job." He and Fr. Capitolo walked up the hill, found the boys and poured out the keg. Br. Draper then realized that, in his cassock, he was unable to walk down the hill. One of the students, John Stiegeler '74 (who teaches history and coaches soccer at SI) hoisted Br. Draper on his back and carried him down the hill.

In 2000, Pope John Paul II honored Br. Draper in a ceremony at St. Mary's Cathedral along with 50 other Bay Area priests, religious and lay people as part of the Great Jubilee of the Year 2000 celebration. Br. Draper received the Pro Eclesia et Pontifice papal honor (for individuals who have served the Church and the Pope with distinction) along with four alumni — Frank Heffernan '48, Robert McCullough '48, Michael D. Nevin '61 and Dr. Collin Poy Quock '57 — and former regent H. Welton Flynn '71 at St. Mary's Cathedral on September 17, 2000. The Pope also honored several SI parents and one alumnus by naming them to the Order of St. Gregory the Great, including Suzanne and Louis Giraudo '64, Richard J. Dunn and the late Marygrace Dunn, and Mary Anne Schwab (an SI mother and grandmother).

"I was certainly humbled by this honor," said Br. Draper, "but I wasn't really struck by the significance of it until SI's Mass of the Holy Spirit when the student body gave me a standing ovation."

When he heard that he was to receive the honor, Br. Draper asked himself, "Why me, Lord? My life is very ordinary. I sow seeds of discipline for the young men and women at our school. But I imagine that that's the point of the award — to honor people who do ordinary things that really do matter." Br. Draper accepted the award "in the name of the many students, parents and faculty members, both lay and Jesuit, who have touched my life so deeply during my time at SI."

At the ceremony, presided over by Archbishop William Levada, the recipients sat together. "There I was," said Br. Draper, "near Welton Flynn, the former SI Fathers' Club President. I realized all the good he and all the other honorees had done for the Church, especially those who work with high school students. The seeds we sow will come to fruition in later years." In addition to a cape and medallion, Br. Draper received a scroll, which he hangs proudly in his office.

Fr. Richard McCurdy, SJ

Fr. Richard McCurdy, SJ, who succeeded Fr. McFadden in 1976 as principal, attended high school in San Diego and had taught English and directed plays as a layman at SI between 1954 and 1956. He then entered the Society of Jesus and came back to teach at SI as a scholastic between 1962 and 1964. He returned in 1972 to serve as assistant principal for academics for a year and executive vice principal for a year. "I was lucky to be Fr. McFadden's assistant. He, like me, had his eccentricities, but he taught me much more than anyone else about being a principal. I loved him and owe him a great deal." Fr. McCurdy then left for Brophy in 1974 and returned to SI in 1976 to serve as principal, a job he held until 1981.

With each return, Fr. McCurdy felt delighted to work with colleagues, some of whom had been students of his. "In 1954, the only laymen aside from myself were J.B. Murphy, Frank Corwin and Rene Herrerias. But when I returned in the 1970s, I was teaching alongside Bob Drucker, Chuck Murphy and other familiar faces. By the time I was principal, I felt as if I knew everyone and had even hired a few of them. Being principal was like a homecoming for me."

Thanks to Fr. McCurdy, academics continued to improve and SI began living up to its new name as a college preparatory. As a member of the Commission on Research and Development (a part of the Jesuit Secondary Education Association), Fr. McCurdy

helped to pioneer what became known as the CIP — the Curriculum Improvement Process. In 1977, he started a yearlong reevaluation of what was taught at SI and how it was taught, and he asked Assistant Principal for Academics Steve Lovette '63 to administer the self-study.

"As a result of the CIP, SI changed in many ways," said Fr. McCurdy. "This was the first real step towards collegiality between Jesuits and lay people. Every member of the faculty was involved in the CIP. We met in departments and in larger groups to critique our curriculum and to relate it to the seminal documents coming out of the JSEA on faith and justice. We had to see if we were doing what Fr. Arrupe suggested we should be doing. It was tedious at times, looking at every single aspect of the school, but it was necessary."

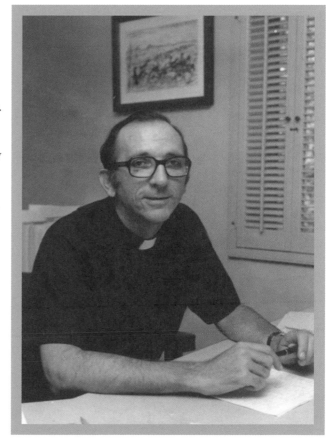

Fr. Dick McCurdy, SJ, became principal in 1976.

Students in 1978 probably didn't notice too much of a change in their classes. "The classes didn't change, but their focus did," says Fr. McCurdy. "For instance, we wondered how to change math classes so that they could teach social justice. We wondered if word problems should deal with hunger or the percentage of disadvantaged in the world."

Fr. McCurdy also briefly considered having SI become a coeducational school. "The biggest problem we faced was what the consequences would be for the girls' schools." He also stepped up his efforts to recruit students from diverse backgrounds. "When I came as a layman, the population was working class Italian and Irish. However, the composition of the city had changed, and I went to every grammar school each year to talk to principals to encourage their students to come to SI."

Sr. Cathryn deBack, OP, principal at Sacred Heart School in the Fillmore, didn't believe SI would be a welcoming place for students from disadvantaged

Sr. Cathryn deBack received SI's President's Award for her service to the community.

backgrounds. "I told her I would accept any student she recommended," said Fr. McCurdy. "She didn't believe me. Still, she recommended some students, and I took them in. That was a breakthrough for her. Later, she came to SI to tutor students after school and that began her much stronger involvement with SI. She proved influential in talking with other principals, telling them that we meant what we said."

McCurdy worked hard to keep the college preparatory from becoming preppy. "I was anxious that it should not turn elitist. I feared it might if we could not continue to diversify. I thought that taking in economically disadvantaged students was crucial" and toward that end he asked Steve Phelps to accelerate his recruitment efforts.

Fr. McCurdy continued the improvements to the counseling department inaugurated by Fr. McFadden. In the mid-1970s, Brian Robinson and Fr. Curtis Bryant, SJ, came to SI trained in counseling, and, as the school hired other trained counselors, the department grew more professional under Fr. Bryant's direction. He also set up a mentoring program in which he trained students to run group discussions among freshmen to help them fit in, and he instituted an alcohol education program that debuted in early 1975.

The faculty never had a tenure process until Fr. McCurdy established a five-year renewable tenure system in 1977. "Teachers walked in to the tenure meetings feeling challenged but left feeling supported," said Charlie Dullea, head of the English Department in the '70s. "You had a chance to review your past few years and plan for the next five."

Fr. McCurdy also lobbied the Board of Regents for permission to raise faculty salaries. "The trouble was that each time we raised salaries, tuition went up. This was at a time when I was doing everything I could to beg, borrow and steal scholarship money so poor students could come to SI. But we had to help our teachers as the salaries we were paying weren't just."

Fr. McCurdy praised Lovette for pushing through many of these needed changes. "He was absolutely wonderful. He has a love for the school that goes beyond what most people understand. I leaned on him tremendously. Everything that I'm proud of accomplishing, he was a big part of." (Steve Lovette now serves the school as Vice President of Development.) Fr. McCurdy also praised several other faculty leaders, including Bob Drucker, Charlie Dullea, Chuck Murphy and Bill Morlock. He saved his highest praise for Fr. Carlin. "He made it possible for us to do all that we did. He is a great hero for me who worked unceasingly with great success. He stands in gigantic proportion, and SI is what it is thanks to him."

McCurdy also hired his share of wonderful teachers, and he points to Peter Devine '66 and Katie Wolf as two who helped SI advance in theatre arts and fine arts over the years. "In the 1950s, the arts were present but they were a bit extraneous. Thanks to Peter and Katie, they became an integral part of an SI education. They added to the great program that Nick Sablinsky began after Fr. McFadden hired him."

McCurdy grew close to many students and faculty, and he treasures those relationships to this day. "I think of Stan Raggio '73 and Burl Toler '74, who were on the SI Board of Regents and have become great supporters of the school. And I appreciate those teachers who worked for so little in the beginnings of their careers. My greatest memory is the community that was formed by the Jesuits, faculty and students. That is what I most treasure."

McCurdy developed a severe case of mononucleosis in 1980 and recommended that Fr. Mario Prietto, SJ, the assistant principal for student affairs, take over as principal the following year. "I'm very fond of Mario and thought he had great potential to lead the school. Fortunately, Fr. Sauer agreed."

After SI, McCurdy served as assistant to the provincial for four years before going to Jesuit High School in Sacramento where he continues to work as an English teacher.

Athletics

Football

Varsity football head coaches in the 1970s included Tom Kennedy '63, Jim McDonald '55 and Gil Haskell '61. While their teams never won a league championship, they made their mark as exemplary and memorable coaches, especially Haskell, who coached from 1973 to 1977. "Anybody who played for him would tell you that his enthusiasm was infectious," says SI Athletic Director Robert Vergara '76. "He had the kind of personality that made you want to play hard for him."

As a player at SI, Haskell grew frustrated with one of his coaches and, according to Vince Tringali, was ready to walk off the field and quit. "I told him that I thought he was a great football player. I told him not to worry about what the coach said, to keep his mouth shut and do what he said." Haskell followed that advice and enjoyed much success at SI, making all-city in his senior year. At San Francisco State College, his team won three championships, and he played briefly in 1966 with the '49ers and joined SI's coaching staff in 1969. At SI he used coaching techniques he learned from '49ers' coaches Frankie Albert and Dick Nolan

and his SI coach, Pat Malley.

After leaving SI, Haskell coached for USC, the LA Rams, the Green Bay Packers, the Carolina Panthers and the Seattle Seahawks, where he is the offensive coordinator working with Seahawks' head coach and Lincoln grad Mike Holmgren and former SI coach Bill Laveroni '66. In his first year with the Seahawks, Haskell coordinated the AFC's top-ranked red zone offense, which gained 292.5 yards per game.

Backfield in Motion – Again

By Bob Lalanne '73

(Bob Lalanne delivered this address to a meeting of the Board of Regents in 2002 after noting that among the regents were several members of the SI backfield from his days at SI.)

The most successful SI football season since the last WCAL Championship Team in 1967 took place in 1972 when the 'Cats went 8–2. The 1984 Wildcats were also 8 and 2 but also had one tie. Coach Tringali always said a tie is worse than a loss and that any team that would play for a tie is not worthy and are just a bunch of measly…. Unfortunately that tie greatly tarnishes that 1984 record.

At this meeting are regents who were also members of that record-breaking 1972 Wishbone backfield-in-motion, who dazzled the opponents with speed and smarts: quarterback Stan Raggio '73, fullback Al Clifford '73 and halfbacks Sam Coffey '74 and Burl Toler '74. I was a defensive lineman from that 1972 team, so I have some inside information I can share with you.

In 1971 we were 1–7–1. Most of us were juniors, so we had the seniors to blame. Head coach was Tom

Kennedy who coached the offense and the backs, and Gil Haskell served as line coach. Gil, a great guy who now coaches for the Seahawks, was always full of energy and enthusiasm.

In spite of the poor 1971 season, Tom Kennedy saw something in these guys. Given their intelligence and ability to perform, Tom decided to throw out the entire offensive system from 1971 and over the summer install a version of the highly complex Wishbone offense. He also brought in a past SI and collegiate lineman to coach the line — Bill Laveroni.

Coach Kennedy, an SI and Santa Clara football great, was a super coach and had a great influence on us as players. He was incredibly organized, neat, in fantastic physical shape, a hard worker and very disciplined. He reminded me of Bill Walsh: He was a professor of the game who ran a tight ship.

Coach Bill Laveroni had a heart of gold. He was a classic, burly offensive lineman, a standout at SI who had a great career with UC Berkeley's Golden Bears. His experience enabled him to share with the linemen the real tricks of the trade in the trenches. We felt that with Coach Laveroni we had a competitive advantage and a loyal teacher.

Fr. Sauer taught most of us English, but we also learned poetry from our coaches who told us we had to be "mobile, agile and hostile." Our coaches also expanded our vocabulary. Coach Bill's favorite word was "doofus." He called me a doofus so many times that I began to believe him.

Stan, Al, Sam and Burl were a real combo, all fast and smart. Stan "the Man" was brilliant. He was always walking the halls with either Coach Kennedy's playbook or his college level Greek and Latin books. As a defensive player, how many times have you looked across the offensive line and seen a wily quarterback who also majored in the classics and then went off to Dartmouth? Stan was smooth.

Al was like Linus in Peanuts, always muddy, curled in a ball, low to the ground and constantly pounding his helmet into lineman and linebackers so that Sam and Burl could run for glory. Al was relentless, and when he did carry the ball, you hardly knew

Football coaches Gil Haskell and Bill Laveroni.

it because he never changed his pounding style.

Sam Coffey had style and a constant grin on his face, even when he took a hit. Do you remember the old black-and-white glossy action football photos in yearbooks from the '50s? Even when Sam cut up the field, he had the unique ability to cut, freeze (to let the photographer shoot) and then score. He was another

of Coach Kennedy's backfield who would study at Dartmouth.

And finally there was Burl Toler, Jr. He was all business, and nobody could catch him. Coach Laveroni always said the first priority as a defensive end was to turn the halfback up-field and to never, never let him get outside and around you. I liked that approach, because if I turned Burl to the inside, even if I missed tackling him, I was successful in containing the perimeter, and the inside linebacker would then have to catch him.

Burl had a great career as a running back at SI, and he had even a greater career at UC Berkeley as linebacker. When he showed up at UC Berkeley the year after me, he was just as quick as ever but 40 pounds heavier. He was moved to linebacker and became the quarterback of the defense not only because of his athletic ability but also because of his smarts. Yet another Jesuit trained athlete.

We went 8–2 and were very close to going 10–0. We barely lost to Serra in a mud bowl, missing a long field goal with little time remaining. We were convinced Serra watered down their field on top of the recent rainstorms to slow down the Regent backfield.

We beat Mitty and SH and shut out Bellarmine at Kezar 21–0. Against Bellarmine, I tipped a pass and intercepted it — a defensive end's dream. After spinning, faking, juking and pulling a "Sam Coffey," I returned the ball up the sidelines for a 3-yard return. I could have gone all the way, but fellow defensive lineman and future 4-year starter at Stanford, Alex Karakozoff, and Tom Corsiglia '73, a future Santa Clara lineman, tackled me out of shear excitement.

The week before our championship game against Riordan, we played St. Francis under the lights. They had a very good team, but we just rolled over them.

We were hitting on all cylinders. Our final game was the WCAL championship game against Riordan the following week. It took place at Lowell because Kezar was just too wet and the '49ers were playing the next day. The SI stadium couldn't hold enough people. It was a very full house.

Riordan had a great quarterback in Mike Carey who later played at USC. They were coached by Bob Toledo who, until recently, coached at UCLA for years and won a few Rose Bowls. It was one of those games that whoever had the ball last on offense would probably win. I forget the final score. Maybe it was 28 to 24. Some might remember that late in the fourth quarter Stan and Xonie Lloyd, our wide receiver who later tutored Jerry Rice, barely missed hooking up on a deep sideline route with us down by a few points.

In any event, one summer 30 years ago, Tom Kennedy saw in these four athletes something special. I can't think of a better place for the wishbone backfield of '72 to reunite than here on the SI Board of Regents. May the four of you continue to help bring SI across the goal line for years to come.

By Loring R. Tocchini '80

(Loring Tocchini was the fifth member of the Tocchini family to graduate from SI.)

I was a freshman in the fall of 1976, and the varsity football team was preparing for a home game against Bellarmine. The varsity squad was in a position to capture the first championship football title for the school since moving from the Stanyan Street campus. I remember the excitement around the school that week was intense. There were articles in the paper about the upcoming game as well. SI had come out of the 1950s and 1960s with many football championships, but none so far in the '70s.

The roster of names for that team read like an "Old San Francisco" ethnic montage: Cipolla, Barberini, Rocca, Shannon, Murphy, Clancy, Garvey … the list goes on. It's trite but true: Each member of that squad brought something special to that team, but they shared in common a strong work ethic. They came from families with proud ethnic heritages that are very much a part of the make-up of our country, city and school. They were also young men whom a freshman could look up to and try to emulate.

Coach Gil Haskell worked the varsity squad hard that week. I was a member of the frosh football club that year, and I can remember heading home each night that week after practice and seeing the varsity still at it. I would stop and watch for a while from the top of the stadium stands. You could smell the scent of cut grass coming off the field in the cool fall air. The stadium had no lights, and nightfall, as it always does that time of year, would come on fast. The only thing you could see were the silhouettes of these athletes running through their drills with the backdrop of the Pacific Ocean behind them. If the play didn't run smoothly, you could hear coach Haskell yell, "Run it again!" This went on each afternoon that week until there wasn't any more light to work with at the end of each day. After rigorous wind sprints, these guys would come off the field looking as if they had just been through battle.

Coach Haskell was preparing them for what he knew was going to be a tough game. He was always upbeat as he would say, "Men, enthusiasm is the force that drives momentum." He preached it to his squad and insisted the other coaches approach their daily routine on the field the same way. That attitude became infectious. Every player did his best to encourage his partner to take his game to the next level, especially that week.

Game day came on Friday. There were banners all over school proclaiming, "Beat the Bells!" and "Ring the Bells!" I can remember the stands at the beginning of the game being packed on both sides of the field with students, family, alumni and friends from both schools. The stadium went from crowded to standing room only as the game wore on. In fact, during the last half of the game there were people standing on the track, sitting on the cyclone fences at the south end of the field and standing all over the grassy sections at each end of the field. There were even people in their front room windows on Rivera Street watching the game.

The cheering went back and forth from each side of the field. I can remember the head cheerleader for SI, John Forsyth, yelling to the student body that he wanted "echo quality" cheers. "Go Cats!" "Smash the Bells!" The cheers rang out. When the student body cheered loud enough, the cheer would echo off the houses on 39th Avenue. It was unreal.

SI led for most of the game, but the Bells fought back to a 15–15 tie as the final gun sounded. Nightfall was descending quickly upon the stadium, and emotions from both sides of the stadium were running high. Since a championship was on the line, a "California tie-breaker" was instituted. Each squad had four plays to advance the football. The football was placed on the 50-yard line, and the team that advanced the ball the furthest would win the game. All I could see on the field were the silhouettes battling back and forth, just as I had seen during practice.

When it was all over, SI had lost by what someone said was about a foot. My voice was gone from yelling cheers. I remember seeing our players coming off the field with tears in their eyes, exhausted. They had given everything they had on that field that afternoon and there was nothing left to give. Coach Haskell led his team into the field house at the north end of the field after they had congratulated the other team, and then they closed the doors. After a brief moment of silence, you could hear the school fight song rising over the stadium, sung by the players inside the field house. You couldn't have written a better script to this game except to include a win. These men were proud of themselves and the school they represented.

I felt proud of those guys and proud to be associated with SI. Revenge can be somewhat sweet though. The following year, although there wasn't a championship on the line for SI, we traveled to Buck Shaw Stadium at Santa Clara University to face Bellarmine, then ranked the number-one high school football team in the country. No one gave us a chance of winning. We shut the Bells out 8–0 in a defensive struggle. It was one of hardest hitting games I have ever seen.

The 1974-75 & 1975-76 Basketball Teams

By Mark Hazelwood '80

St. Ignatius has had a rich sports history, and in particular a great basketball tradition. City high school legends — from Kevin O'Shea, Fred LaCour, Bob Portman, Paul Fortier and Levy Middlebrooks to Jesse Lopez Low, Nico Mizono and the rest of the 2004 CCS champion Wildcats — have "laced 'em up" for the Wildcats over the past 60 years.

Never, however, has SI ever had a greater run of hoop success than during the years 1974–75 and

1975–76. These two teams, coached by the "Wizard of Westlake" Bob Drucker, set a standard of success that has never been duplicated.

In the fall of 1974, Coach Drucker was beginning his ninth season as coach. He had enjoyed great success in those first eight years, winning a WCAL title in 1968, and never suffering a losing record. In 1974, he welcomed back four returning seniors: forwards Juan Mitchell and Tony Passanisi, center Michael Bowie and point-guard Dan Buick. This group had helped lead SI to an impressive 20-win season and a second-place finish the year before. It was not, however, a championship, and Drucker continually reminded his players of this as the '74–'75 season progressed.

Joining the returning seniors were a powerful group of players moving up from the JVs: forward/ center Billy O'Neill; forwards Kurt Bruneman, Tom Stack and Bob Enright; and guards Mike McEvoy, Craig Bianchi, Louie Carella and Dan Abela.

During pre-season play, Drucker tried to find the right mix. The team struggled early on against Marin Catholic and Redwood before earning comeback wins. As the pre-season progressed, the team improved offensively. Buick and Bowie started to develop some chemistry with Buick looking to give what was called the "Bowie Lob" as often as he could to the 6-foot, 7-inch senior. SI finished the 12–0 pre-season, with 30-point wins over Mills and Carlmont.

As always, the WCAL would be a tough fight every night. Right away, SI was matched up against archrival Sacred Heart at Kezar. On January 3, 1975, a capacity crowd of 5,000 watched one of the great basketball games in the storied history of the two schools. During regulation, no team led by more than 6 points. With Bill Duffy and Bill Duggan, the Irish

hung in there with the 'Cats and, with 26 seconds left, pulled ahead 52–50. Senior Tony Passanisi responded and nailed a jumper from the corner to put the game into overtime.

Duggan returned the favor for SH by hitting a 30-footer at the buzzer to send the game into a second overtime. As the second overtime wound down, SI trailed 61–60. With less than 10 seconds left, Kurt Bruneman fired up a shot that bounced off the rim.

Juan Mitchell celebrates the league championship in 1975.

Out of nowhere came Bill O'Neill, who pulled down the rebound, and put it back in to clinch the victory. Looking back at all the games he coached, Drucker called this a classic.

The 'Cats then rattled off seven more wins, including a 90–32 trouncing of Bellarmine. SI clinched the regular season WCAL title, whipping St. Francis. In the final regular game of the season, SI traveled to Serra hoping to be the first city team to go undefeated since Wilson in 1968. A hostile "Jungle" crowd helped the Padres move out to an early lead. Juan Mitchell led the 'Cats back to send the game to overtime. Unfortunately, Serra guard John O'Leary hit five free throws, and Serra pulled the upset, ruining the perfect season.

After the game, Drucker told the press: "It's like getting the monkey off our back. When the guys left the locker room, I could see relief on their faces. We're going to be all right." SI's colorful coach was prophetic.

In the WCAL semi-final playoff game the following week, Michael Bowie poured in 33 points, grabbed 14 rebounds and had three blocks as SI clobbered Mitty 70–40. Drucker's crew was then paired up once again with Serra in the finals at USF. With 5,000 mostly SI partisan fans looking on, SI jumped out to a 47–36 lead before hanging on to nip the Padres 54–52, earning both revenge and the WCAL title.

SI then moved to the Central Coast Section Tournament. First up in Region I was San Mateo High, featuring star forward Sylvester "Sly" Pritchett. Holding Pritchett to eight points, the 'Cats pulled away late and won 84–75. Unfortunately, SI lost Dan Buick for the rest of the playoffs to a broken hand.

Facing Westmoor in the next round, Drucker

worried about the loss of Buick and about his team growing overconfident, as SI had beaten the Rams earlier in the season. As they had all season, the team responded. Stepping in for Buick, junior guard Mike McEvoy recorded 19 points and five steals to lead the 'Cats to the Region I title.

Not satisfied, SI then advanced to the CCS final tournament at Maples Pavilion. In the semifinal contest, the Wildcats took on Region III champ Gilroy. Showing great leadership, Billy O'Neill led SI with 13 points in a defensive struggle as the 'Cats prevailed 57–40.

In the season finale at Maples Pavilion, SI faced Cupertino, led by All Northern California performer and future Los Angeles Laker Kurt Rambis. Rambis, a junior, had played superbly all season in leading Cupertino to a 27–1 record, nearly identical to SI's 28–1 record. In front of a sold-out crowd of 6,500, SI's front-line held the Pioneers' big man in check and the 'Cats matched Cupertino point for point.

As the game wound down to the 1-minute mark, Juan Mitchell committed his fifth foul, putting guard Mike Saladino to the line. Saladino missed the free throw, but Rambis tipped in the basket, giving Cupertino a 61–60 victory. Despite the CCS final loss, SI ended with an incredible record of 28–2. No St. Ignatius team had ever won so many games.

With the beginning of the 1975–76 school year, Drucker said good-bye to starters Mitchell, Bowie, Passanisi and Buick. The 1975–76 team returned McEvoy, O'Neill, Carella, Abela, Bianchi, Enright and Bruneman, who gained so much experience from the year before. Drucker now added Craig Wallsten, Alan Smoot, Chris LaRocca, Brad Levesque, Dan Hurley, John Skapik and sophomore Tony Zanze.

The fantastic season the year before led to high

Opposite page: Dan Abela '76 helped his team to a league title.

expectations. SI was picked as the fourth-ranked high school team in Northern California by the *San Francisco Examiner*. Without Bowie and Mitchell, Drucker knew this team needed to win with defense and good outside shooting.

SI started the pre-season right where it left off the year before with impressive wins over St. Joseph's, Marin Catholic and Washington. Despite a loss in the El Camino Tournament to Westmoor, SI finished the pre-season 12–1.

The 'Cats opened the defense of their WCAL crown against St. Francis. In what would be a typical, unselfish performance for this team, SI had five scorers in double figures, led by Mike McEvoy with 18 points. SI won 68–59.

SI continued its winning ways and eventually took on archrival Sacred Heart. Extracting revenge for a JV championship loss two years earlier, Bill O'Neill scored 20 points and SI whipped SH 68–56 at Kezar. After cruising past St. Francis and Riordan and edging Serra twice, an undefeated WCAL season came down to the final game against Mitty. A year earlier, the 'Cats had fallen just short of this goal. This time McEvoy and O'Neill saw to it that there would be no letdown. Combining for 34 points, the senior leaders led SI to win 68–50 and the perfect league record, a feat never before accomplished in the history of the WCAL.

The Wildcats went on to face Bellarmine in the WCAL Tournament's final game at USF. SI kept the Bells close in the first half, shooting just 11 for 31 from the field. In the second half, playoff hero Craig Bianchi came through, scoring 17 points to lead the 'Cats to their second straight title with a 47–40 victory.

Drucker's boys, now an amazing 26–1 returned

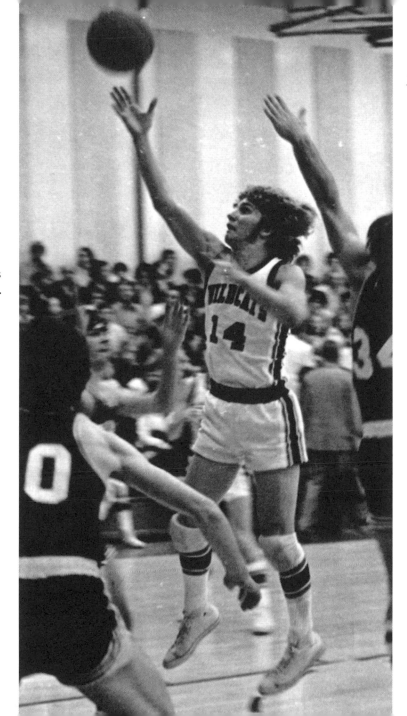

to the CCS tournament to face a familiar opponent, Westmoor, which had an impressive 25–1 record. The Rams took it to SI early on, leading 30–27 at the half. The Wildcats then tightened their defense, holding Westmoor to eight points in the third quarter. McEvoy, Bruneman, and O'Neill once again came through with big shots down the stretch and the 'Cats, avenging their early season loss to the Rams, claimed the Division I title for the second straight season.

Next up for SI was Region III winner Carmel. Again playing great defense, the Wildcats allowed their lowest point total of the year, winning 49–31 and setting up another showdown with Kurt Rambis and Cupertino in the CCS final at Maples Pavilion. SI kept Cupertino's high powered offense under control in the first half, but simply could not generate enough offense. Eventually, Rambis, who would score 27 points and grab 12 rebounds, wore SI out and led the Pioneers to a second straight CCS title over a disappointed Wildcat squad.

The loss was especially tough for senior O'Neill. "We didn't really care about Carmel," O'Neill told Ray Ratto of the *San Francisco Examiner*. "I mean Carmel is where you go on your honeymoon. Nobody plays basketball there. But Cupertino was the big one for us."

SI's season did not end with the loss to Cupertino as it had the previous year. The 'Cats were invited as an "at-large" team to the Tournament of Champions. It was SI's first invite to the tournament since 1965 when the 'Cats were led by Bob Portman. As Drucker would lament later, his team was simply not able to get over the Cupertino loss. With an ill O'Neill playing only limited minutes, the 'Cats lost to Del Mar in the first round, playing their worst game of the season.

Showing typical pride, SI rebounded in the double elimination tournament by whipping St. Mary's of Stockton in the next game 81–46, giving the Wildcats their 29th win of the season and earning another shot at Rambis and Cupertino. Unfortunately, SI would have little left in the tank, losing to the Pioneers 64–55. The loss did not erase the accomplishments of the long season, which included the WCAL title, the perfect conference record, the all-league performances of O'Neill, McEvoy and Bianchi and the tremendous showing in the CCS.

Over the 2-year span, SI had won 57 games and lost 6. From the inside play of Bowie, Mitchell and O'Neill to the outside shooting of Passanisi, McEvoy and Bianchi, they had played at a level of basketball that had not been seen before at the Prep. It may never be seen again.

Track

The SI track and field team took league championships seven times in the 1970s with Terry Ward '63 coaching most of those teams. Ward got his start at SI by running the 4x800 relay with three seniors and setting the school record in his sophomore year under coach Roger Hoy. In his senior year, Ward competed for Fr. Ray Devlin, SJ '42, who took over the program. (His brother, Fr. Joe Devlin, SJ, was the track coach at Bellarmine.) In 1963, SI sent five athletes to the state meet, and Ward became city champion in the 800-meter event.

After studying and coaching at SFSU, Ward joined the SI faculty in 1969 and coached track for Gil Haskell until 1973 when they shared the head coaching job. Ward ran the program between 1974 and 1978, but credits his coaching staff for much of the program's success. "We had guys like Gil Haskell,

Tom Kennedy, Jim Walsh, Mike Lewis, Br. Charlie Jackson, SJ, and Dick Howard," says Ward. "They paid attention not just to the stars but to all the athletes."

While some of SI's success can be attributed to the depth of the program, Ward also credits the boys' attitudes. "We loved having stars, but we also loved working with kids who weren't stars. These guys sometimes worked all summer and came back as ready to go as some of the previous year's standouts."

Ward let his athletes know his priorities by making sure, at the end of a race, to congratulate the runner who finished last and then move up the line to congratulate the first-place runner.

Ward enjoyed coaching at SI. "It always seemed like a family affair, especially since I had so many relatives on my teams. If a problem arose, we could talk about it because we all knew each other. It was always fun being with those guys."

Ward left SI for Bellarmine in 1980 for a change of climate, thinking that he would stay there for 10 years before moving on. He has never left and now serves as Bellarmine's athletic director.

Track Stars of the 1970s

Coach Terry Ward sang the praises of many of his athletes, including the following:
All-Americans: Chris Cole '72, Mike Porter '72, Dan Graham '72, John McVeigh '73 and Jim Hannawalt '78.
School Record Holders: David Gherardi '72, Chris Cole '72, Paul McCarthy '75, Bruce Parker '78, Brendan Ward '71, Julius Yap '74 and Paul Roache '78.
State Meet Qualifiers and Finalists: David Gherardi '72, Chris Cole '72, Xonie Lloyd '73 and Bruce Parker '78

Sprinters: Dan Magee '76, Gil Pacaldo '79, Charles Taylor '88, Mike Kelly '72 and Brian Sampson '78.
Middle Distance: Dennis Burns '76, Pat Linehan '76, Aleo Brugnara '79 and Tony Fotinos '73.
Pole Vaulter: Frank Lawler '71.
Shot and Discus: Peter DeMartini '76, Aldo Congi '72 and Tom Lagomarsino '72.[4]
Distance Runners: Yannick Loyer '80, Ernie Stanton '81, Mark Gillis '81, Phil Bennett '77 and Bill Magee '74.
Hurdlers: Juan Mitchell '75, Bill Ryan '77 and John Goldberg '75.
Jumpers: Peter Imperial '77, Jim Paver '74, Sean Laughlin '82 and Don Vidal '77.
All Time Team Leader: Rob Hickox '72.

By Julius Yap '74

The 1970s cross country and track and field program at SI had perhaps the biggest impact on the person I have become today. All SI athletic experiences have a positive effect on its students but Cross Country and Track and Field are unique in that freshmen, sophomores, juniors and seniors all work out together.

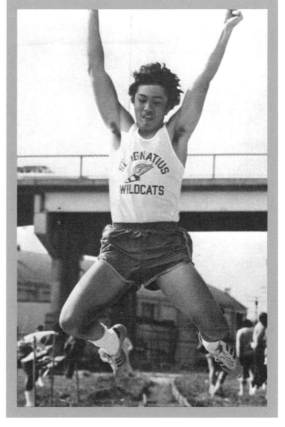

Julius Yap '74 in a long-jump competition during his senior year.

I learned the values an Ignatian is supposed to have by watching the upper classmen live those values every day, so I grew up not only learning those values but

With the move to the Sunset District, SI's baseball team began competing and practicing at West Sunset Field.

also understanding that it was my responsibility to make sure that those who followed would find those values in me. Coach Ward and Coach Haskell also provided the model for me to follow as I returned to teach and coach here at SI. I have had some success here during my 25 years at the prep, and I owe much of that to my two coaches at SI. They taught me the value of hard work. The most important value an SI coach should honor — and this is the top priority of an SI coach — is to care for the student as a person first and an athlete second.

Baseball

In 1974, Coach Jim Keating retired and Jim Dekker '68 stepped in to lead the Varsity Boys Baseball Team for the next 20 years (with the exception of a 3-year leave of absence when Len Christensen was

head coach). Dekker played three years of varsity for Keating starting in his freshman year. As a junior centerfielder and .375 lead-off hitter, he made the all-city team and helped his team take the league championship with a 20–1 record. (That record stood until Dekker's last year as a coach in 1993 when his team won 25 games.)

In his junior year, Dekker won the race for student body president and was being eyed by scouts for professional baseball. Any hopes of turning pro, however, were crushed the summer between his junior and senior years when a car accident left Dekker severely injured. That Dekker can now walk is a tribute to Dr. C. Allen Wall '46, a vascular surgeon. While recuperating, Joe DiMaggio came to visit Dekker and present him with the batting trophy from the first-ever Joe DiMaggio League that Dekker had won that summer.

While a student at Santa Clara University, Dekker commuted to SI to coach with Keating, and after graduating with his degree in English, he returned to SI to teach and coach. When Keating retired in 1974, Dekker took over and led his team in numerous successful seasons, including the 1977 season when SI tied for first place with Serra at the end of the round-robin in the WCAL. Team leaders included George Torassa '77, who eventually signed and played three years in the San Francisco Giants' farm system.

Soccer

In 1967, Luis Sagastume began teaching Spanish and coaching soccer at SI. He came to the U.S. at age 11 from Guatemala and played soccer at USF. As captain there, he led that school to an NCAA national championship. His assistant, Fr. Francis

Stiegeler, SJ, wrote in a 1974 *Genesis* article that "his professional attitude and low-key personal approach immediately injected a transfusion into the moribund soccer program and the subsequent revival of the program has been truly phenomenal. From one team of 18 players in 1969, the soccer program has grown in 1974 to six teams with more than 140 participating players. Along with its growth in size, SI soccer has dominated the WCAL since its inception, winning the varsity title three times in six years and compiling a remarkable record of only six losses in 67 league matches."

Sagastume's 1973 team went undefeated, earning 43 goals and allowing only four against them on their way to a second-place finish in the CCS. The following year, the 'Cats went 12–1–1 to win the league with offensive stars such as Bill Magee '74 (a high school All-American and league MVP), Jim Paver '74 (who scored 13 goals in the '74 season), Connie Konstin '75, Bob Bustamante '76, John Kolenda '75, Dan Salvemini '75 and Rob Fetter '74.

Sagastume left SI for Chico State in 1975 where he received a Master's degree in physical education and returned in 1977. That fall, word got around school that Sagastume had invited a few students out to West Sunset to kick around a few soccer balls. "That word spread around campus and more than 40 students showed up," said Joe Totah '78. "Everyone wanted to be on his team as he had become a legend."

Totah was among those who played for him in 1978 when SI came in second in the league. He praised Sagastume for emphasizing technique and strategy. "He brought each individual player and the team as a whole to a new level. He made sure each player understood his position and was as skillful as possible." Sagastume also taught by example the

virtue of good sportsmanship. "He was very patient on the sidelines," recalls Totah. "He wasn't animated, running up and down screaming. He was very quiet and let the team play. He carried himself professionally and demanded the same of his players both on and off the field."

Sagastume also coached at Chico State and SFSU before leaving for the Air Force Academy in 1979, where he continues to coach soccer. Since then, he has led the Falcons to more than 270 victories in 26 seasons. Taking over for him was Rob Hickox '72, who continues to head the Boys' Soccer Program. He led the 'Cats to championships in 1981 and 2005 and many CCS semifinals.

In addition to Sagastume, Fr. Paul Capitolo, SJ '53, has played a large role in SI soccer starting in November 1973, when Steve Nejasmich and Fran Stiegeler, SJ, asked him to coach in the newly-formed soph-frosh program. He and Dennis Sweeney coached the SI Tigers until 1982 when the WCAL expanded to include a freshman soccer component. Fr. Capitolo moved on to become moderator for the entire boys' soccer program, and is known affectionately by players and coaches as "Cappy Bear" and "The Grand Pooh Bah."

After coaching soccer at SI, Luis Sagastume left to coach at the Air Force Academy.

S I, which had won six league victories in golf between 1951 and 1961, finally got back on track, capturing three league crowns between 1977 and 1979, as well as the CCS championship in 1979, led by Fr. Roland P. Dodd, SJ. Standouts on the team included Tom Sheppard, Manuel Neves, Mike Cinelli, Joe Slane, Joe Vetrano, Sean Sarsfield, Kevin McWalters, Mike Modesti, Pat Doherty, Russ Tominaga, Matt Healy, Glenn Schuldt, Joe Vetrano and Joe Luceti.

Over the years others would step in to coach boys' golf, including Bob Drucker and Julius Yap, who, in 2001, oversaw the creation of the girls' golf program, which won the league, CCS and NorCal championship in 2003.

Lacrosse

By Stephen Finnegan '88

(This article was first published in the Summer 2003 Genesis IV to commemorate the 25th anniversary of the Lacrosse team.)

A s Will McMinn '79 gazed out the window toward the Pacific Ocean from Fr. Dominic Harrington's math class in the spring of 1979, he heard an announcement over the PA that perked up his senior year at SI and his college years at UC Santa Barbara.

"All those students interested in forming a lacrosse club, please report to the student activities office after school." McMinn daydreamed as he continued to look out over the sand dunes that would later become the field where SI would play many of its lacrosse games. McMinn hoped that his father, who had not let him play football, would let him play lacrosse.

On April 19, 2003, McMinn returned to SI and played in the 15th annual alumni lacrosse game on the new FieldTurf of J.B. Murphy Field. Before the game began, he reflected on his early memories of lacrosse at SI. He started by holding up the first jersey from 1979, which resembled a wool football uniform shirt, and then he and others thanked the many people who were instrumental in the program's creation.

Ken Ross '79 was one such pioneer who started the lacrosse team "to help the younger guys play an alternative to football or baseball that would make them proud and build their confidence." He went to Chuck Murphy '61, the student activities director at the time, and asked about buying gym mats for a wrestling team. Murphy told Ross that he was concerned about the "liability of a bunch of guys throwing each other around." Then Ross remembered reading that football legend Jim Brown had played lacrosse along with football while at Syracuse University. Ross returned to Murphy, who always listened to students, and asked about forming a lacrosse club.

Murphy gave the go-ahead, but because lacrosse did not begin as an official school sport, he could offer no funding. Ross's father made a large contribution, and Ross solicited donations from Financial District law and accounting firms. He found that SI's reputation helped him in his fund-raising efforts.

Ross sought advice from University High School Lacrosse Coach Mike Gotlieb (who would be a perennial rival), and he referred him to Bruce Nelson, who coordinated lacrosse leagues around the Bay Area. He assisted Ross in purchasing discounted lacrosse equipment. All Ross needed now was a coach.

By this time Sam Coffey '74, who had played football for Dartmouth College, was teaching history and coaching freshman football at SI. He had heard about Ross's search for a coach and introduced him to John Carney, who had played football with Coffey in college and also played lacrosse at Dartmouth as an All-American.

Carney agreed to coach the "lads" as Ross remembered Carney's term for the ragtag group of SI players (delivered in his East Coast accent). Ross went to every class to recruit players and found nearly 30 athletes who, along with McMinn, showed up to the first meeting.

"We had guys playing in their corduroy pants and button down shirts," said Ross. "A couple of times, midway through the season, we would trade for players with the opposing team to level the talent pool."

Bruce Burns, a freshman at the time, was one of the team's best ball handlers. "We had Jim Hill, John Kapulica, Frank Hseih, John Clark, Rich Alden, Jim Kearney, Tim McInerney, Bill Mazzetti, Mike Patt and many others. The one player on the team who exemplified what we were all about was Kevin Barberini, who, sadly, passed away from cancer several years out of SI. Kevin had a great sense of humor that represented the positive attitude of our program."

In the spring of 2004, SI lacrosse celebrated its 25th anniversary. There have been so many players, coaches, parents and friends who contributed over the years, not only to SI lacrosse, but also to the overall growth of the game on the West Coast.

Many players have handed down their old lacrosse gear to their younger brothers. Bruce Burns '82, who later went on to expand lacrosse at UOP, gave his old gear to his brother Todd '87. Jim Kircher '82, who started lacrosse at Humboldt State, handed down his gear to his brother Glenn '87.

Steve Wynne '90 (younger brother of lacrosse alumnus Ed Wynne '84) came back to SI as a coach to

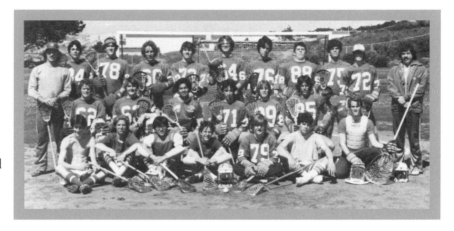

In 1980, the lacrosse team posed for its first yearbook photo.

help Dave Giarrusso lead the Wildcats to three of their four state championships.

Other Lacrosse alumni include Willie Wade '85 and his brother, Yancey '88, who was named High School All-American. Trevor Buck '93 went on to play at Hobart; his father, Stockton Buck, helped build the SI program as a coach for many years.

One family best represents the SI lacrosse tradition. The Merrion clan, who all showed up for the 2003 game, includes Mark '82, whose son and daughter played catch with lacrosse sticks after the game, John '86, who was named High School All-American, and Paul '92 who looked up to his older brothers playing lacrosse. These brothers all took the field and scored goals in this most recent game.

Each year when the varsity and the alumni come together to play, we remember and honor those who came before us. When we pray the prayer of St. Ignatius, we honor the founder of the Jesuits whose missionaries and martyrs were some of the first Europeans to see the game of lacrosse.

We know that we are part of a large extended family of SI alumni, and we wish future teams good luck. We are grateful to the parents and SI for providing us with a beautiful field. We look forward to future seasons and say thank you to McMinn, Ross, Coffey, Carney (now lieutenant governor of Delaware) and all those who made the first 25 years of lacrosse at SI possible.

All-Sports Trophy

In 1977, SI won the WCAL All-Sports Trophy for the first time. The WCAL gave the award to the school that won the most league championships in one year. The WCAL in the 1980s discontinued that award as the two most powerful schools in the league — Bellarmine and St. Francis — typically traded the trophy each year.

Extracurriculars

Birth of the BSU

Fr. Buckley, SI's president, noted in the September 1972 *Genesis* that "today there is a strong emphasis in secondary education on areas of study outside the merely academic. This emphasis finds an echo in the traditional Jesuit philosophy of training graduates who have internalized attitudes of deep and universal compassion for the poor, the victims of injustice, and those in our society who suffer oppression. We plan bold new programs this year to realize better our own Jesuit tradition...."

Those programs included SI Outbound and some-

thing new to the SI landscape: the Black Students Union. The BSU reflected the times and the needs of the students and was the first of many ethnic-based clubs to start at SI in the 1970s. (The Black Students Union in 1992 changed its name to the Association of African American Students.) Other organizations included the Spanish Club (later called the Association of Latin American Students), the Asian Students Coalition, the Irish Club and the Italian Club. Some of these groups had their origin in the Civil Rights movement and in the growing sense that Jesuit schools needed to support the rights of and provide equal opportunity for underrepresented groups. The first of these clubs, the BSU, began as a response to a parody of *Huckleberry Finn* that appeared in 1970 in *Soph Press*, a short-lived sophomore publication. The parody included the N-word and drew strong reaction from African American students, including Eric Goosby '70.

The following year, two students — Timothy Alan Simon '73 and Welton Flynn '71— began talking about the need for a support group for black students at SI. Simon's sister, a Presentation High School grad and a student at San Francisco State University, was involved with activists there, and Simon met many of them around his parents' dining room table discussing Ralph Ellison and W.E.B. DuBois. "It was a vibrant time for intellectual discourse," said Simon. "I was surrounded by black nationalistic thought, and I saw the need for black students at SI to have resources that we could utilize to increase our academic success."

Before the club formed, Simon, Flynn and others participated in forums, moderated by Scott Wood, Chuck Murphy and Bill Kennedy, regarding the need for such a support group. "Many white students asked why we needed to have a separate organization," said Simon. "Now that I'm 49, I see that their arguments

were sincere. SI was there for all of us. But we still faced racism. For example, we had no courses that put any focus on contributions from African Americans who gave 300 years of slave labor to build this country. On a more personal level, we were rarely invited to parties, and interracial dating was still a big issue."

Simon, now an attorney, law professor and elected member of the San Francisco Republican County Committee, found supporters in SI Principal Edward McFadden, SJ, counselor (and future Regent) Lou Giraudo '64, English teacher Scott Wood and Fr. Cornelius Buckley, SJ. "Scott Wood did so much for us. What a saint," said Simon. "Also, Fr. Buckley and I met on a regular basis. This relationship continued through my collegiate and law school years. My family was from Louisiana and drenched in Francophone

The officers of the first Black Students Union in 1973. Timothy Simon is front and center.

culture. This was a scholarly interest of Fr. Buckley's." Later, when Steve Phelps joined the faculty in 1972, his long history of working with African American students led Fr. McFadden to make him BSU moderator. Phelps also coached the BSU basketball team that competed in the CYO Teenage Leagues.

Simon felt tremendous support from the Society of Jesus and the Church. "The BSU became in many ways an outreach of Jesuit ministry," he noted. "Fr. Buckley recognized that our pursuits were not only honorable but also reflective of Christ's teachings. We were even featured on a television program on what is now KBHK, hosted by famed Bay Area and national journalist Sam Skinner."

English teacher Frank Kavanagh '46 also provided support for the group in its first year of existence (1971–72) by donating his collection of black literature to the students. "He came into the English Center, where we started holding meetings, holding a box of books," said Simon. "Then he asked us to come to his car for more boxes." The group then appointed Alan Robinson '73 as librarian, and he wasted no time in creating a Library of Congress Card Catalogue system. "He would track you down if you were overdue in returning a book," recalled Simon.

The club used those books to help educate its members on black history and culture, offering book report presentations on *The Invisible Man* and poetry presentations by Jerome Williams '75 and Gregory Sullivan '73. The group invited political activists visiting the U.S. from Angola and Mozambique to speak to students, and in the 1972–73 school year, they began working with other schools to help them form their own BSUs. They even held a Saturday gathering at SI bringing 100 students from Northern California to the school for an all-day conference featuring Raye

Richardson, the owner of Marcus Bookstore in San Francisco. African American students came from El Cerrito, Stockton and Seaside to listen to him and to a host of student speakers.

In 1972, the club became officially sanctioned and joined the Student Council. Still, some students continued to resent Simon for creating a club that they believed divided the SI community along color lines. "When Bill Kennedy read off grades in class one day, I heard a hiss from some students when he got to my name. He stopped right there and said, 'I want to take my hat off to these students for creating the BSU and for discussing racism at SI.' In his own quirky way, he was an extraordinary supporter of our cause."

Simon worked hard to keep academics the focus of the club, and he praised Xonie Lloyd '73 and future BSU leaders Burl Toler '74, Rod Carter '74, Jerome Williams '75, Kevin Goosby '77, Juan Mitchell '75, Michael Bowie '75 and others for picking up the baton. "Those guys were in the top of the class from the day they stepped on campus."

That the BSU is active in the new millennium is a testament to its success. Simon praised the support given it by parents, who now have their own organization at SI — the Parents of the Association of African American Students (PAAAS). "Black parents in the early days of the BSU did not always support us," he added. "They felt we were putting a top-rated education at risk by challenging students on issues of race. Now the parents, along with alumni and students, support the organization wholeheartedly, and the BSU has helped many students excel. That is the group's lasting legacy and what makes it a proud part of the Ignatian tradition."

A few key events define the era for Simon. "When Eric Goosby '70 (who served as AIDS Czar in the

Clinton administration) started wearing an afro, that was a major event. He identified with his African American roots. Timothy's cousin Gerald Simon '72 (who would become the Fire Chief for Santa Clara and Oakland) was a mentor and exemplar for all of us, especially for freshmen who found coming to SI a tough transition from their grammar schools. The BSU helped students matriculate, which sounds like a contradiction. How can you matriculate if you separate yourself? But through the process of separating, we found common issues and common solutions. We couldn't have found those otherwise. I think that's why other ethnic groups formed."

SI made a commitment in 1972 to support African American students at SI by hiring Susan Johnson, a Boalt Hall Law Student and the first African American woman to join SI's faculty, as a part-time teacher of Afro-American literature. The school also hired a young blond-haired coach named Steve Phelps, whom colleagues later nicknamed the White Shadow after a popular TV show.

A USF grad, Phelps had earlier worked at Hunter's Point and in the Fillmore District as a recreation director. He encouraged some of his best kids to apply to SI and other academically strong high schools. When he approached Fr. McFadden in 1969, the principal told Phelps that SI would accept as many kids as he could send. Phelps insisted that SI offer services to students from these neighborhoods to help them survive in a culture very different from their own and help students preserve their racial identities. "SI wisely agreed," said Phelps, and as a result, SI had, and still has, a higher retention rate of students of color than other schools.

Phelps also started SI Uplift, a summer school program designed to improve diversity at SI. That program, now called Magis, is still in existence at SI,

under the direction of Emily Behr '93, the first member of the pioneer coed class to work full time at SI, and her assistant, Chris Delaney, a faculty member since 2003.

The Rise of Other Ethnic Clubs

Phelps served as BSU moderator for nine years starting in 1972. In 1973 two freshmen approached him looking to form their own organization — the Asian Students Coalition (ASC). Phelps agreed to serve as moderator and soon found himself advising 50 students who modeled their club along the same lines as the BSU. Soon after that, the

Spanish Club started at SI, which later changed its name to the Association of Latin-American Students (ALAS), and the Italian Club also formed.

From the onset, students at SI debated the usefulness of these ethnic clubs. Some wondered if they exacerbated, rather than healed, divisions among students. "The merits of the BSU are debatable," wrote one student in a 1972 *Inside SI* article. "A

The Spanish Club in 1973.

more serious conflict might arise from the formation of the Irish Students Union, who, although they claim that no mockery is intended [of] the BSU, exist as a living statement to say that they do not want a Black Students Union at SI."

Timothy Simon, who founded the BSU, nevertheless supported the Irish Student Union. "I was educated by the Daughters of Mary and Joseph at St. Michael the Archangel. They were predominately Irish among many Irish students and parish members, and that helped me become sensitive to the plight of the Irish. Black students felt an oppression similar to theirs. Some people opposed the formation of the ISU, but I supported it. Why shouldn't they get together and celebrate their culture just as we were doing?"

Bill Love '59 & the Environmental Movement

The modern environmental movement began in the early 1960s with the publication of *Silent Spring* by Rachel Carson. In the 1970s, SI's own Peter Raven '53 (now the director of the Missouri Botanical Garden) warned against the twin dangers of rainforest deforestation and species eradication. At SI, Bill Love '59 was leading the charge to help students grow as stewards of the planet. In 1972 he participated in a unique program in environmental education with the public elementary schools' Science Resource Center. Each week, he took grammar school students to Lake Merced to study the flora and fauna, guided by SI students who had taken Love's Field Ecology course. Those same Ignatians then visited grammar schools to continue the lessons regarding pollution and habitat preservation and tried to provide students, according to Love, "with a new set of standards — a measure stick — which they can apply

Opposite page: Block Club member Robert Vergara '76 hard at work. He would later become Block Club moderator and athletic director at SI.

to their home environments."

Ambient, an environmental club that stressed recycling, formed on January 29, 1972, "with member Tom Yasumura standing in front of the school building, anxiously awaiting the arrival of the first [member]. His patience was well-rewarded as senior Nick Carouba drove up and left a trunk-load of cans and bottles at his feet."[5] Ambient continued over the years, and the group, now called the SI Environmental Club, focuses on recycling, native plant restoration, reduction of consumption and composting.

Newspapers, Magazines, Radio & TV

Inside SI continued to publish for the first half of the 1970s, but it took a six-year hiatus between 1975 and 1981. The SI administration ended its long run in favor of a new publication — a tabloid newspaper first called *SI News* (for the first five issues), and then *The 2001* before a final name change to *The OceanSIder* in 1979 when rookie faculty member Michael Shaughnessy won the Name That Paper Contest with that offering. (The winning prize in that contest was a six-pack of "his favorite beer.") In 1981, the name changed back to *Inside SI* and the publication has come out in both magazine and tabloid formats since then.

For the final edition of *Inside SI* in 1975, students went all-out and printed a 104-page magazine with a full-color cover and featuring a Stonehenge game (based on lectures on that topic by Fr. Spohn) and a bumper sticker. All the work was done in-house, from typesetting to printing and binding, with students using the printing presses, carbon arcs, process cameras and light tables. After 1975, all production for student publications occurred off campus.

In October 1973, a new media outlet broadcast at SI when KZIC (later called KRSI) went into operation. The radio station was actually a public address system with two speakers in the Carlin Commons that "broadcast" during the two lunch periods. After Mark Roos '75 set up the equipment, the station took requests from its collection of 38 records. Also, SITV debuted in 1971 when Mr. Art Encinas, SJ, set up a TV studio in a classroom. It expanded in February 1974, when students in an advanced television production course, taught by Br. Sullivan, broadcast 10-minute news shows in the Carlin Commons at lunch twice each week.

Other Clubs

By 1979, in addition to the clubs mentioned above, students had a wide selection of groups they could join. In 1975, Fr. Russell Roide, SJ, SI's new president, created the Service Club as a way for students who weren't members of the Block Club to serve the school. Students had to have good grades and recommendations from teachers. They wore blue blazers with the Service Club emblem and came to school events to serve as ushers and hosts. Since then, the Service Club has become one of the most active organizations at SI.

Gone were the Sanctuary Society (1975) and the Sodality (which became the CLCs), but according to the *Ignatians* from those years, the following organizations were going strong: CLCs, Block Club, Service Club, CSF, Forum, Cheerleaders, Art and Publicity, Dance Committee, Spirit Club, Rally Committee, Math Club, Frosh Press, Science Fiction Club, Military Service Club, Liturgy Group, Chess Club, Rod and Gun Club, Computer Club, Language Club, Stage Crew, Ski Club, Bike Club, and intramurals.

From its earliest years, SI has been a school that has stressed the fine arts, and the student musicals and plays throughout the years showed a commitment to excellence by the students and directors. In the 1970s and 1980s, that strong tradition provided a foundation for a remarkable

Opposite page: Fr. Fran Stiegeler, SJ.

cultural renaissance at SI, one involving four outstanding teachers who inspired students to excel in music, drama and the visual arts.

The Service Club in 1977.

Janet & Nicholas Sablinsky '64

The first band was formed at SI on Feb. 12, 1874, "to cultivate music for innocent social enjoyment and to add solemnity to civil and religious festivals" and was directed by Mr. L. Von der Mehden.[6] That the school did not assemble the band each year is evidenced by a 1962 *Inside SI* story on the school's reconstituted band program, then in its second year: "Perhaps you don't realize this, but SI *does* have a band. It is young and small, but dedicated. Our band practices forty minutes a day to be able to play

Nick Sablinsky has directed the SI orchestra since coming to SI in 1973.

for our enjoyment at school functions…. This year the band plans a formal concert, perhaps a joint concert with Riordan, and a Pops Concert. The Pops Concert will probably be held in December with guest artists, professional singers and all types of music."

Before 1972, SI student musicians played in a concert band primarily at the rallies and games, performing Sousa marches and the fight song. All

that changed when SI hired Nick Sablinsky '64. As a student, he had played piano and percussion for the 20-piece SI band, led by Dennis Monk. Now, he felt, SI needed a full-fledged orchestra, and he combined students from the girls' schools with SI boys to perform for *Fiddler on the Roof* in 1973. (That show, performed at SI, was directed by Peter Devine '66 who was then teaching at Convent of the Sacred Heart.) In prior years, adult musicians were brought in for the shows, and this was the first SI musical to feature an all-student orchestra, according to Sablinsky.

For the next five years, SI musicians had a busy spring. After they played in the spring musical, they put on a spring concert. That changed in 1978 with the introduction of the Winter Pops Concert, which also featured the SI Jazz Band.

Nick's wife, Janet, served as a vocal coach starting in 1972, and in 1992 SI hired her to start a formal choral program. In the first year she directed one large choral group that over the years has branched into the advanced Chamber Singers, the Men's Choir, the Men's Quartet, the Mixed Chorus and the Women's Chorus. In 1994 she introduced the Handbell Choir to the Winter Pop's repertoire and added a spring choral concert to the litany of shows at SI.

For many students, the highlight of their four years here has been playing for Nick or singing for Janet Sablinsky in such shows as *The King and I* (1977), *Cabaret* (1985), *1776* (1987), *My Fair Lady* (1988), *Evita* (1996) and *The Secret Garden* (1998). The Winter Pops Concert features nearly 200 singers and musicians and is a perennial highlight of the school year. In their 30-plus years at SI, the Sablinskys have fashioned one of the best high school music programs in the country, and future students will profit from their talent, energy and commitment.

Peter Devine '66

Peter Devine '66 directed his 100th play, *Man of La Mancha*, in 1998 after a remarkable 25-year run as director of SI's theatre department. His love of the theatre began when his mother took him to see Mary Martin in the stage play *Peter Pan* when he was 5 years old. "When I saw her fly through the doors into Wendy's room, I was hooked on theatre," said Devine. "That was pure magic."

Devine was steeped in theatre, too, through his relatives. His granduncle Martin Merle served as drama director at SCU and directed the school's annual Mission and Passion plays and the 1925 *Pageant of Youth* in San Francisco. Another granduncle, Martin Flavin, won the Pulitzer Prize for writing the Broadway play *The Criminal Code*.

As a young actor at SI, Devine performed in many plays including *Arsenic and Old Lace, Oklahoma* and *Margo and Me*. "He was an inspiration for me," said Ron Lagomarsino '69, who directed the Tony-Award winning play *Last Night of Ballyhoo*. "He was the lead in several plays when I was a freshman, and he was wonderful and very funny. He was in the first play I ever saw, and he made me want to work in the theatre."

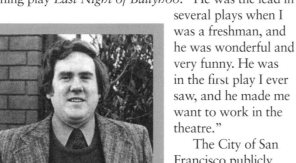

The City of San Francisco publicly recognized Devine for his contribution to the school and to the city in 1987 when it awarded him a citation and issued a proclamation. One year later, he received another, and perhaps greater, distinction when Herb Caen waxed eloquently in his column about Devine's production of *My Fair Lady*. "The best entertainment in our town last week was not in the usual haunts but at 37th and Rivera in the Sunset … where a wildly talented bunch of teenagers from

that school did nightly performances of *My Fair Lady* at a level not far below professional. A lot of people in the audience were moved to observe that 'There's nothing wrong with the kids of today!' which is certainly as true as most clichés. They may even be better than the kids of yesterday, despite the bad press they get so often. All I know is that the senior class at Sacramento High in 1932 never came close to putting on anything resembling the ambitious show at St. Ignatius last week."

After graduating from SI, Devine continued to perform at USF while also majoring in English and theatre. He went on to study at the American Conservatory Theatre and later received his teaching credential. He has continued his drama studies at various workshops, including ones at ACT, Stanford, SCU and the Good Speed Opera

Peter Devine directed 100 plays in 25 years at SI including this 1973 production of Fiddler on the Roof.

House in Connecticut.

Devine joined the SI faculty in 1974 after working at Convent of the Sacred Heart and Mercy where he staged

Katie Wolf, since 1977, has helped students develop themselves as artists.

musicals featuring students from those schools acting alongside SI boys. Students in his program flourished, Devine noted, "because we did a number of shows every year and because we took what we did seriously. We respected students and the dignity of their work. I think that rubs off on them, and they learn to respect themselves as artists and as human beings."

Those who worked with Devine feel the same way toward him. Faculty member Kevin Quattrin '78, who oversees the backstage crew, got his start building sets for Devine back in the 1970s. "Peter's approach to teaching has always been that the student comes first," said Quattrin. "He teaches the person, not just the subject. Working with him in the theatre has taught me more about humanity and ministry than anything else in my life."

Devine believes students create both spiritual and artistic communities in the two downstairs theatres at SI. For example, on the closing night of his spring musicals, the students gathered for an end-of-the-year Mass in the theatre. "The junior who had been in the program the longest led the seniors from the stage to the seats to mark the fact that they would never again walk those boards as actors. They were, from that point on, part of the audience at SI and had to find another theatre. The juniors, sophomores and freshmen then gave them their blessing."

Thanks to foundations built by Devine and those who came before him, the theatre department continues to thrive under the leadership of Marc Bauman, who joined SI in 2000.

Katie Wolf

In 1977, Katie Wolf offered to develop a course of study in visual arts for SI students. Kate was a St. Rose graduate who had studied fine arts at Santa Clara University and had earned an MFA at the San Francisco Art Institute. She had acted in plays at SI and, later, assisted Peter Devine by designing sets. For nearly 30 years, she has developed curriculum and taught the creative process to thousands of young artists whose work has earned national honors.

"I had great visions of presenting a variety of art styles that would generate the students' interest in the process of creativity," she wrote in a *Genesis II* story. "Who wouldn't get excited about works by Picasso,

Matisse, Magritte, Miro and Munch? I remember presenting posters of abstract and non-objective paintings for class critique, hoping to stir up some insightful discussions on color, form, line quality and feeling. I was rather surprised when a student called upon had the following comment: 'Miss Wolf, why is that art? My 8-year-old sister could paint something like that!' I then realized I had some attitudes to change…."[7]

Since 1978, Wolf has taught several classes, including Art and Architecture, 3D Studies, Studio Art, Sacred Symbols, and Art and Nature, taking students on an inner journey to discover their own creativity and on hundreds of journeys beyond the school walls to see art firsthand in museums and buildings around the Bay Area.

In the 1990s she led a summer workshop for students who designed large-scale outdoor pieces that are on permanent display around the school. In the summer of 2003, she and a group of students were artists in residence at the NorCal Transfer Station near Candlestick Park where they transformed trash into works of art. In 1993 the San Francisco Unified School District honored her as the Outstanding Art Teacher of the Year and featured the work of SI students at the de Young Museum. St. Mary's Cathedral also chose her to be its official fabric artist for San Francisco's cathedral, and all the banners and in that building are her creations. Her work ranges from environmental fabric designs at St. Mary's to stained-glass pieces, steel sculpture and Byzantine icons in intimate sacred spaces. She redesigned Jensen Chapel on the SI campus in 2003 when the school moved that facility from the second floor to the Student Activities Center, and her work incorporated her sense of the natural and the sacred.

Wolf is a working artist who continues her personal expression through printmaking, large format acrylic canvases, theatrical set design and the design and construction of wearable art. She also spent her 2003–2004 sabbatical year investigating ways sustainability and nature could enter into the artistic process. From her studies, she designed a new course that asks students to involve those concepts in their sculpture to experience "nature as master designer" and to help students "experience growth in awareness of the creative process."

Nostalgia at the Prep

In the 1970s, a nostalgia fad swept America. The play *Grease* (and later the movie) was making the rounds, as was Sha Na Na, a '50s revival band. Locally, Butch Whacks and the Glass Packs, formed in 1971 at St. Mary's College, featured Class of 1968 members Bob Sarlatte and Craig Martin as well as John Buick III '70 who died in 1989. SI students began forming their own music groups. In 1971, Gary and the Greasers made their debut with Jim McManus, Charlie Caldarola, Tom McManus, Kevin Bravo, Joe Caldarola and Steve Aveson. "To round out the group," reported an *Inside SI* article, was "vocalist Carol Devincenzi. If there was ever a cross between Janis Joplin and Grace Slick, here she is."[8] (Devencenzi now teaches religious studies at SI.) In 1975 Johnny B. and the Speedshifters formed

The 1950s had a revival in the 1970s.

with members of the Class of '75 that included Peter Radsliffe, Jim Lawrie, Tom Stone, John Bacchini, Julio Bandoni, John Agostini, Jean-Louis Casabonne, Jim Farrell and John Flynn. As a fun diversion, SI would occasionally hold "1950s Days" with students coming to school wearing slicked-back hair, rolled up cuffs and leather jackets.

The Blood Drive

Also in 1974, the school began a new tradition, one that continues to this day: the blood drive. From that year on, blood banks have visited SI to ask for volunteers from the student body, some of whom felt it served three purposes: getting out of class, munching on cookies and helping people in need.

The Nightmare of November 1978

Tragedy struck the Bay Area twice in nine days in November 1978, first with the Jonestown holocaust and then the slayings of Mayor George Moscone and Supervisor Harvey Milk. On November 18, Jim Jones, the leader of the Peoples Temple, ordered more than 900 of his followers to drink punch laced with cyanide shortly after some of them assassinated U.S. Congressman Leo Ryan and four people traveling with him to investigate abuses at Jonestown in Guyana. Among those wounded in that attack was Tim Reiterman '65, a reporter for the *Examiner*. As Reiterman accompanied Ryan and several Jonestown defectors to an airfield, a truckload of People's Temple members drove up and approached the planes. "We suspected that they were there to prevent those defectors from leaving and telling their stories about what was really going on in Jonestown," said Reiterman.

"As we were loading passengers on the larger of the two planes, some shots rang out and we had no time to do anything but react. I ran and dove trying to get my head behind one of the plane's wheels." A bullet hit Reiterman in his left arm and wrist and shrapnel entered his right shoulder. "People around me were being hit; there were screaming and rolling amidst a lot of confusion. I bounced up as fast as I could and sprinted for the tall grass around the airstrip. I dove in as soon as I was close enough and crawled into the jungle." There he found a clump of trees where he could gather himself. He wrapped a belt around his arm to stop the bleeding and listened as the shooting subsided. Suddenly he heard several more shots. "I later learned that those were gunmen finishing off a number of the wounded."

When the gunmen left, he returned to the planes and found among the dead Leo Ryan, *Examiner* photographer and close friend Greg Robinson, NBC cameraman Bob Brown, reporter Don Harris and one of the defectors. Of those who survived, 10 were wounded, including Ryan's aide, Jackie Speier, who later became a state senator. Reiterman and most of the other survivors hid in a small rum shop that night along with some of the defectors. "We didn't know if the gunmen would return, but the defectors told us that this would trigger mass suicides in Jonestown, which, in fact, happened." Reiterman returned to the Bay Area, and in 1982, he and fellow reporter John Jacobs (now deceased) wrote *Raven: The Untold Story of Reverend Jim Jones and His People*. Reiterman has kept in contact with survivors and relatives of those who died and has written about the incident from time to time. He serves as a writer for the *Los Angeles*

Times and teaches investigative reporting at the UC Berkeley Graduate School of Journalism. (His daughter, Amanda is a member of the Class of 1998.)

Nine days later, tragedy struck again. On November 27 former Supervisor Dan White killed Supervisor Harvey Milk and Mayor George Moscone '47. The Mayor's sons — Chris '80 and Jonathon '82 — were students at SI at the time. Matthew Bernstein '81 was one of Chris's friends. "I arrived to my fourth period French, and a minute later, Chris followed. He had not been seated more than a minute or two when Leo La Rocca entered the room and whispered in Anny Medina's ear. He then asked Chris to leave with him. I believe they then went directly to the Dean's office. About 10 minutes later, Fr. McCurdy announced through the loudspeakers that the Mayor had been fatally shot. I remember going to see Chris that evening at his house. Several of his classmates were also there. That weekend, we had a basketball game at Bishop O'Dowd. I vividly recall several of O'Dowd's cheerleaders openly rooting for Chris when he entered the game. I also believe they gave him cards and balloons."

A week later, Fr. McCurdy announced on the loudspeaker that the father of Marty Healy '80, had been shot by a disgruntled coworker. "It was certainly a sad time for us," added Bernstein. "I drove home with Chris that evening, and he was amazed that this tragedy could repeat itself so quickly. Whenever Fr. McCurdy made an announcement during the remainder of that year, many of us were quite tense not knowing what tragedy was to be announced. Happily, though, I believe none followed these two tragic events. Yet, it was a very sad week in our school's and city's history and one that I will never forget."

Tim Crudo '80 eulogized the Mayor in *The 2001*

that December. "Always in attendance at such social gatherings as the Communion Breakfasts, George Moscone especially loved to watch his son, Chris, play basketball. As a freshman, I was fortunate enough to meet Mr. Moscone. I had had many previous notions about what to expect, but I had all images except the right one: the father of a friend. Out of City Hall, he was no different from any other father…. At the last basketball game he was to see, he came up to me and began a conversation that lasted but a brief time. But during that time he managed to seem more concerned with my wellbeing than I thought possible. This encounter, though brief, was the highlight of my week. The mayor of a vast and wonderful city taking time out to talk to me, just a friend of his son's."

A Step Toward Coeducation

A few of the Catholic girls' schools in 1969 started sending students to SI to take physics from Fr. Spohn during the first period of the school day. The first class consisted of 32 girls and eight boys who gathered at the school's new campus. Mame Campbell Salin (Mercy '72) was among 19 girls to take a class at the new SI in her senior year. (Mame's SI connections include brothers Ron '71 and Steve '76 and sons Zach '05 and Jared '06.) Mame recalls walking down the halls as freshmen shot rubber bands at her legs. "Before coming to SI, I had this notion that the 20 of us would be treated like princesses by the thousand boys. I thought doors would open for us everywhere we went." The freshmen, she added, "just wanted some attention. They weren't angry that we were there; they were just a little uncomfortable around us. I never felt any

resentment from the juniors or seniors about our being there."

She was impressed both with the stadium seating that resembled a college classroom and with Fr. Spohn's precise lessons. Her brother, Ron, had had Fr. Spohn the year before and had kept all his notes and tests. Mame was amazed that Fr. Spohn's schedule her year was never more than a day away from the lessons her brother had. "I knew about the rocket experiment and told my friends what would happen," she noted. "As a result, we didn't ooh and ahh as much as Fr. Spohn expected us to."

Like most Catholic high school students then, Mame never questioned the logic of single-sex high schools. But taking physics at SI surprised her because it was "a normal class, like any other. For the first time, I wondered why all my classes weren't coed."

Homecoming Queens

In the 1960s and the first half of the 1970s, girls schools sent candidates to SI to compete to be Homecoming Queen. In the fall of 1973, Convent of the Sacred Heart decided not to send candidates to the three boys' schools. "We felt as if it were a meat market," said Lola Giusti, who was a senior at Convent then and who was originally selected to represent her school in the competition. Giusti was familiar with SI both because her father, Bob

Giusti '48, was a graduate and her brother, Bob '76, was a sophomore. She also studied physics with Fr. Spohn in the mornings. She met with several teachers and seniors to tell them that Convent would no longer participate. "Some students reacted with incredulity, others with derision and still others with quiet respect."

Giusti had a fondness for SI, but also wanted the school "to be better for those who followed. SI could be a harsh place, with whistles and derogatory comments as I walked from my car to class." She even found herself parodied on the cover of the December 1973 *Inside SI* for her involvement in Convent's withdrawal from the contest.

In September 1975, the administration ended that contest because of the reaction from Convent and partly because "the contest is a humiliating experience for the girls involved," said Chuck Murphy, then the assistant principal for student activities."[9]

Giusti, whose children are Mia Kosmas '04 and Matthew Kosmas '07, is pleased the school has come so far. "My daughter, who was a part of the dance and drill team as a freshman, asked one priest why SI didn't have cheerleaders. The priest told her that the school doesn't have cheerleaders for the same reason we no longer have homecoming queens — it's not keeping within the school's mission."

Now a professor at UOP's dental school in San Francisco, Giusti has carried on the legacy of Fr. Spohn by teaching several SI grads, including Catherine and Michael Vista, Kevin Growney and Claire Roberts. "Because I had such an inspirational mentor in Fr. Spohn, I am able to give back to the SI community as well as to my profession."

341

Opposite page: In 1970, SI hosted an Open House to show off the new school. Fr. Spohn also greeted parents of young women who, for the first time, were taking physics at SI.

Left: Lola Giusti, DDS

Women at SI & the Coed Issue

The move represented a shift in attitude toward women at SI. Not surprisingly, that attitude changed along with the demographics of the faculty. In 1973, Anny Medina joined the faculty as a Spanish and French teacher, and in 1976, Carolyn Rocca came as a part-time Italian teacher. In 1978, three more women joined the faculty and staff: Julia Maionchi (Italian), Katie Robinson (counseling) and Katie Wolf (studio art).

In 1979, Mary Husung McCarty joined the faculty as a Latin teacher. She did not find it strange teaching at an all-male school, as she was the only woman in her graduate program and had taught three years at an all-boys school. She recalls that "a few kids developed crushes, as they definitely weren't used to having a young, female, single teacher, but I was used to dealing with boys, so it didn't rattle me much." She did receive a few love letters and one boy hung around the classroom and left notes on her car. "I much prefer teaching at a coed school," said McCarty. "It's more normal to have girls and boys in the same room, and they are more fun to teach together."

While SI would not admit girls until 1989, students and faculty discussed the possibility of coeducation throughout the 1970s. The April 27, 1971, *Inside SI* ran a column entitled "Girls at SI?" and the December 16, 1976, issue of *The 2001* ran a story by Phil Bennett '77 (now the managing editor of *The Washington Post)* with this headline: "The Question Remains: Coeducation?" Several faculty offered their reflections, including Charlie Dullea, who noted that "coeducation would be a logical step in the progress of the school in light of the recent changes under the stimulus of the *Preamble*. Women are certainly a part of the community we are tasked to serve."

Others disagreed, including math teacher Col. Vern Gilbert, who feared that going coed would dilute the sports program. SI Chaplain Gordon Bennett, SJ (now the bishop of the Diocese of Mandeville in Jamaica), noted that he had spent two years researching the subject and found no conclusive evidence regarding whether coed or single sex schools worked better. "I personally favor coeducation at SI for reasons that are particular to the city of San Francisco. I am also convinced that, because of the lack of direct evidence, that SI will not become coeducational until financial circumstances indicate that the school must change or face oblivion...."

President's Award

In 1972, SI instituted the President's Award, given each year at graduation "to a non-alumnus who has distinguished himself in some special manner in civic life and has aided St. Ignatius College Preparatory in realizing its goals and objectives." The first recipient was Benjamin H. Swig who was honored as an "outstanding humanitarian, civic leader, hotelier, philanthropist and ecumenist." The inscription read *"Pace tanti viri"* — "With due respect to so great a man." Over the years, SI has given the award to a host of individuals, some who have served the school and others the greater community. The full list of winners appears in the appendix.[10]

Career Day

SI launched a new program on March 2, 1978, with the first Career Day, sponsored by the counseling department. More than 40 people — many of them alumni — representing 25 professions came to SI to speak to juniors. "Some students were discouraged by the prospect of eight or 10 more years of schooling required for certain professions, but most felt the requirements were realistic," wrote English teacher Bob Grady and counselor Andy Dworak in the March 1978 edition of *Genesis*. The program continues under the direction of counselor Michael Thomas '71 and is held every other year. In March 2003, 74 people came to speak at SI, 22 of whom were SI grads.

Night Classes for Parents

SI President Russell Roide, SJ, took seriously the job of communicating the Jesuit mission and vision to the broader community. He instituted a series of adult faith formation classes in the evenings for SI parents, taught by priests on the faculty. He also supported the Sunday Evening Liturgy and encouraged students to attend the Friday Morning Liturgies. Under his administration, the job of bringing Vatican II to life became more fully realized.

125-Year Celebration & Community Service

In 1979, SI celebrated its 125-year anniversary with the coming of a new president, Fr. Anthony P. Sauer, SJ, who had taught at SI in the 1960s and early in the 1970s. In a report to the Board of Regents in his first year in office, Fr. Sauer noted that "our sense of community is strong at SI, but good feelings alone will not ensure excellence. If SI is to be more than a pleasant cocoon, if it is to have a lasting impact, and if it is to live up to its ideals of excellence and ser-

Mayor Dianne Feinstein and Fr. Sauer at the 125th anniversary dedication in front of The Emporium.

vice, then it requires a rigorous commitment to high academic standards and to high moral and religious principles.... One of my highest priorities, therefore is a renewal of SI's commitment to the Jesuit tradition of educating the leaders of society who will go forth to serve."

He referred to the jubilee year by noting that "125 years ago, the wisdom and wealth of generous

benefactors and the dedication of the Society of Jesus working with an equally devoted lay faculty built this Eucharistic haven by the Bay. Let us commit ourselves this afternoon to carry on the work so nobly begun in 1855 as we move into a new era for St. Ignatius College Preparatory in the City of San Francisco."

To give flesh to those words, SI used the 125th anniversary to launch the Community Service Program (later renamed the Christian Service Program). In order to graduate, students, starting with the Class of 1981, would need to perform 100 hours of service "for those members of our human community who are disadvantaged by poverty, old age, poor health, discrimination or physical and mental handicaps," wrote Art Cecchin '63, SI's first CSP director. This new requirement became an extension of the work done in past decades by the Sodalities, SI Outbound and the CLCs at the Little Sisters of the Poor, Laguna Honda Hospital and Helpers' Home. Cecchin believed that "through the performance of service, the student gains a first-hand experiential knowledge of the inequities and injustices in society. Through [reflecting on these injustices] the student can contemplate and discuss the reasons for the existence of these injustices and is challenged to understand that Christ calls each of us to be a man for others."[11]

SI commemorated the 125th anniversary in other ways. Fr. Sauer, Fr. Largan, Board of Regents Chairman Gene Lynch, Finance Chairman Hugh O'Donnell and senior class president Timothy P. Crudo '80, along with San Francisco Mayor Dianne Feinstein, unveiled a plaque at The Emporium on Market Street, the site of the first school. (The 1955 plaque, placed on the Emporium façade for the centennial, was affixed to the new plaque.) The plaque, which will appear on the side of the new Bloomingdales when it opens, bears these words: "The original St. Ignatius College has developed into both the University of San Francisco and St. Ignatius College Preparatory. Placed in honor of their 125th year by both senior classes of 1980. October 15, 1979." Bartley S. Durant, chairman of the Emporium, accepted the award on the behalf of the store, and Dr. Albert Shumate, a director of the California Society of Pioneers, spoke on the history of SI. Fr. Sauer also spoke on the importance of religion in the founding of educational institutions.

A month later, on November 13, SI held a grand celebration at Bimbo's 365 Club with Harry James and his Big Band, featuring singer Phil Harris, organized by Ursula Marsten and Wolfgang Fliess. At the event, Fr. Carlin received the Key to the City, a plaque from the California Legislature, a proclamation from the Mayor's Office and the Citizen of the Day Award from radio station KABL.

Chalk-Dust Memories

Michael Thomas '71

I spent two years at the old school and two years at the new school. We loved the half-day sessions in our first year at the new school. We started at 8:10 a.m. and ended at 12:10 p.m. with no lunch or recess. After we left, work could continue on the school. When we had basketball practice, we would hop in Leo La Rocca's car and drive to Glen Park to practice there because SI's gym wasn't finished.

Fr. McFadden didn't talk to me until I was a senior, and Br. Draper commanded respect from the first. We had an elevator at the new school, and in the very early days, students were never allowed to use it. To be on that elevator was a privileged experience. My buddy Mark Stahl and I were there after hours, and somehow we managed to get on the elevator. In typical 16-year-old fashion, we kept telling ourselves, "This is so great!" Then the elevator opened at the third floor, and we saw Fr. Spohn standing there. We hit the "close door" button and hightailed it out of there as soon as we got off on the first floor.

Fr. Francis Stiegeler, SJ '61

(Fr. Stiegeler taught English and coached soccer at SI between 1973 and 1975 before returning to teach in the 1990s. He has taught at all five schools in the California Province.)

When I came back to SI, I found that it still had the same spirit as when I was a student. You still asked what parish the students came from. I was here with nine young Jesuits, and I recall Fr. Curtis Bryant, SJ, coming to SI wearing a mustache. He wasn't going to shave it off, and that opened the door for the rest of us to wear one.

I don't see much difference now that we are coed. Possibly the boys are more subdued. When SI was all boys, the school was like a living organism that rolls through the doors each morning. The student body had great camaraderie, with boys patting each other on the back and punching each other on the shoulders like a bunch of pups.

Opposite page: The physics lab circa 1970.

Arthur Cecchin '63

(Art Cecchin came to SI in 1973 and has served as tennis coach, director of scheduling, director of community service and chairman of the social science department.)

Fr. Richard McCurdy, SJ, asked me to facilitate the Colloquium on the Ministry of Teaching for eight years. In that program, new teachers from SI met new teachers from other province schools and learned about Ignatian education. He took SI to a new philosophical level with the Preamble and the Jesuit Secondary Education Association.

Peter Schwab '71

There was a certain amount of traditional lawlessness at the old school, with food fights and senior sneaks. When we came to the new school, we found it well lit with carpets and an administration that tried to create a professional atmosphere by coming down a little harder on us when we tried to stretch the rules. The day before our first senior sneak, we heard from the administration if we didn't come to class, we would be suspended and lose our prom. We had a meeting in Room 214 with most of the seniors (it was a double room), and one person said that his girlfriend would kill him if he didn't take her to the prom. Another student quoted the Third Rule of Mao. We called them on their bluff and had our sneak anyway. About 150 of us met at The Circle at 7:30 a.m. and drove in a car parade up 37th Avenue to Santiago. There, we got out of the cars and marched to school singing "We Shall Overcome" and the fight song. We all violated the dress code as much as we could, with most of us wearing shorts. We got to school just as the first bell sounded. Then the announcement came that we had 20 minutes to be appropriately attired. Some guys changed and ran to class and others returned to the Circle and then went to the beach. Eventually, 40 seniors were suspended and had to write out *Macbeth* in order to return to school.

Gary Brickley '71

During the rocket demonstration in Fr. Spohn's class, he was so focused on one aspect of the experiment that he didn't notice that, at the last second, someone had snipped the string and the rocket flew out the window. He never found out who did it.

By Alfred Pace '74

My First Day

In order to attend SI, it was necessary for me to take a series of buses and the L Taraval from Forest Hill Station. Upon arriving at Forest Hill Station, I was confused about which direction and which car I should take. Within moments, I observed several students wearing red and blue SI jackets ... clearly juniors or seniors. Thus it was that I got onto that car, presuming we would arrive at SI in short order. Wrong. The students had just completed photo day and were going downtown. I found myself on Market Street "dazed and confused." A Muni driver provided the correct info and I took the L back to the Forest Hill Station Tunnel. At that point, I was told we had to disembark as the car was no longer "in service." As the time was now approaching 9 a.m., I decided to run from the station to SI, a distance of about 28 city blocks.

Of course, this resulted in my first encounter with J.B. Murphy and Br. Draper, whose quote rings in my head to this day: "Mr. Pace, this is *not* the way to begin your 4-year career at St. Ignatius Prep. JUG for five days." But because of that lengthy run (my first, ever), I decided to go out for the cross country team.

Hair & Grooming Regulations

From time to time during the 4th and 5th period lunch breaks, the doors of Carlin Commons would abruptly and simultaneously close, virtually trapping the students inside with the teachers and faculty standing guard. Swiftly, Br. Draper would enter, black book in hand and with an air of élan, plug in a microphone and announce, "Gentlemen, this is a grooming inspection!" Brother would then make the rounds, entering into his black book those students whose hair was too long and those who were showing the first signs of facial hair. Of course, this became a bit of an event and a number of students would begin to chant the names of those they thought warranted the attention of Br. Draper.

Such it was one day the doors of Carlin Commons closed and the faculty stood guard. It was not long before some students began to chant "Pace, Pace, Pace!" Brother wandered over and suggested, "Get a haircut by Monday."

I failed to get the haircut. Monday arrived and at the end of second period, Br. Draper made his usual intercom announcements of the day and then asked those who had been asked to get a haircut or shave to come down to his office. Yikes!

Upon arrival, Brother correctly observed that I had not complied with his request. Accordingly, he asked me to enter his office and sit down, at which

The SI Forum in 1977.

time he proceeded to cut off a portion of my dangling locks. Frankly, this is an area where Brother has little talent. The result was a clearly lopsided, partial haircut. Brother then said, "Mr. Pace, I suggest you get the rest done by a professional."

I did.

I also remember the following miscellaneous events: Aldo Congi '72 and the SI Juke Box dancing to "Rock around the Clock" during lunch in Carlin Commons; Mark (now Father) Taheny '74 climbing the exterior corner of the gymnasium, using only his hands and feet; Stan Raggio '73, several other students and I in Stan's yellow Plymouth hemi-head Duster listening to Led Zeppelin's "Whole Lotta Love" blaring out of the 8-track; the Circle; races at

Brotherhood Way; my first fistfight on the second floor of the school building; and Mr. Kennedy's biology class where we launched a boat and deployed a seine net in Middle Lake at Golden Gate Park. The police arrived shortly thereafter urging us to bring the boat and net ashore.

Dan Tracey '77

Fr. Gordon Bennett, SJ, our chaplain, was young and approachable and got along with kids. Mike Silvestri helped me out after school with math problems I didn't understand in class. We played Riordan on Halloween night in 1975, and I recall Coach Haskell saying the SH and Riordan games were special because players from those teams would be our buddies after graduation. We beat Riordan 27–0 that night. The day before, Bob Drucker had predicted the score and had written it on the chalkboard in the coach's room.

Kevin Quattrin '78

I recall trying out for frosh football with 130 kids playing for Fran Stiegeler and Steve Nejasmich, our line coach. He figured out who the best five offensive linemen were and prepared them for the first game. Then Brad Carter, who played left guard, pulled a hamstring in the warm-ups before our first game at Bellarmine. They put in the next guy in line, who had almost no practice time and knew none of the plays. I always made sure as a coach not to do that.

Peter Devine's English class was very engaging and humorous. There was a playfulness between students and teachers that didn't exist in grammar school with nuns.

One year, my classmate Brian Duddy died in a car accident. I had been to funerals for old people, but that was my first experience of mortality for people my age. Our whole class went to the funeral. I remember not being able to sleep that night, thinking what a waste and asking why did these things happen.

Ugo Pignati '69

One of my most memorable experiences at SI occurred after I graduated in 1969, the last class to graduate from the Stanyan Street campus (we had been promised to be the first class to graduate out of the new SI, but the new school wasn't yet completed). I had come to SI in 1967 for junior year, having arrived from Italy in 1963. Being Italian, I loved playing soccer, and in senior year was on the varsity and made All-WCAL. That year, our team won the first WCAL Soccer Championship in SI history After I graduated, soccer coach Luis Sagastume asked me to return to SI and coach the junior varsity. I jumped at the chance and agreed to take on the JV team. The first thing I did was to try to put together some uniforms for the team. The shirts my team had worn the previous year had been bought by Coach Sagastume in Mexico, and we were lucky to inherit these. (The soccer jackets we wore as seniors were hand-me-downs from the basketball team). The problem was finding the shorts, since there was really no budget for the JVs. I had been given a few hundred dollars as "salary" so I went to a store on Taraval Street, used my money to buy blue shorts for the team, and had the SI soccer logo put on them. Despite our "mix and match" uniforms from two countries, the JVs played quite well, and I was very proud to lead the Class of 1970 team to the first-ever WCAL JV soccer championship in SI history.

Anne Phipps,

Ignatian Guild President 1980–81

I served as chairman of the February 24, 1979, fashion show, which offered a New Orleans theme, and for that show we offered cookbooks as favors and featured, for the first time, Jesuits as models. We

had a Dixieland band from the Fairmont Hotel featuring Jimmy Diamond playing individual songs for each Jesuit. For Fr. Carlin, we played "I'm Just Wild About Harry," and Mr. Kevin Dilworth, SJ, a youngish scholastic, strolled down the runway to "You Make Me Feel So Young." Everyone seemed to love the show, and more than 700 attended. The show was a labor of love, and it was so gratifying to be involved in such a successful event.

I also helped to re-establish links between the Loyola and Ignatian Guilds and worked on the rummage sale with them in the Hall of Flowers in Golden Gate Park, selling items donated by SI families, local businesses and organizations and members of the Loyola Guild. A highlight for our generous Loyola Guild team was a "fashion show" at USF for fun, using rummage clothes.

For all Ignatian Guild events, I encouraged the participation of women who reflected the diversity of the SI community and of San Francisco. I was also privileged to have introduced to the Guild the establishment of the Dorothy Leonardini Scholarship to honor our first president and to assist needy students.

Peter Devine '66

When I first started teaching at SI in 1974, the English Department had gone through a major revamping. Fr. Becker and others were still doing the old curriculum, but the young faculty were doing the Moffet system. Students only wrote when moved to write. They read no literature not written in their lifetime (meaning 1950 on). *The Catcher in the Rye* was part of that curriculum, but we were not allowed to read or teach it.

The faculty did not teach grammar. Students learned it by writing, by discovering their mistakes and by wanting to correct them out of their "natural curiosity." We had senior electives such as Cowboy Literature, Science Fiction and Fantasy and Film Literature. Fr. Becker, in revolt, took his old courses and renamed them. "Mindbending" was his senior elective, because Shakespeare and the other British writers bent

Left: Anne Phipps receives a bouquet for her work as fashion show chairman.

Below: Tom O'Neill '74 in a biology class. He later joined the Jesuits and is president of SI's Board of Trustees.

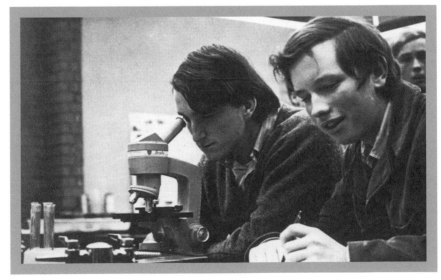

349

your mind to great thoughts; "Pretzels" was his junior course in American Literature (American thought was like a pretzel, heavily salted, going in circles).

Admiring scooters at an SI auction.

By 1977, when SAT scores had declined, Principal McCurdy asked the department to bring back a more traditional approach in the lower division with more emphasis on grammar and writing. Upper division electives were maintained but tightened. We adopted Sir Francis Drake High School's Writing Project (pioneered by Cap Lavin '48), adopted minimum proficiency standards for grammar and writing, and standardized the reading list to include both modern and classic works. We instituted standard department exams, emphasized literary terms from the Oregon Curriculum series and taught grammar and writing terms from the Warriner's Grammar series.

Fr. McCurdy introduced teacher evaluations, and not every teacher was happy about this. However, the exam results, the evaluations and the school-wide writing exam led to many refinements of the curriculum. These changes continued in the late 1970s with the introduction of the Bay Area Writers' Project that started at UC Berkeley. The department began offering the Advanced Placement English test in the spring of 1978 and taught its first AP English course in 1979. Some members of the department resisted "pulling out the bright lights" from the regular classes, since mainstreaming was big at that time; however, parents and the principal wanted an AP program for seniors. We had two sections, each with 45 students. At that time, we only had one lower division honors class sophomore year and no frosh or junior honors classes. We finally did institute a junior honors class and found that the SAT scores went back up.

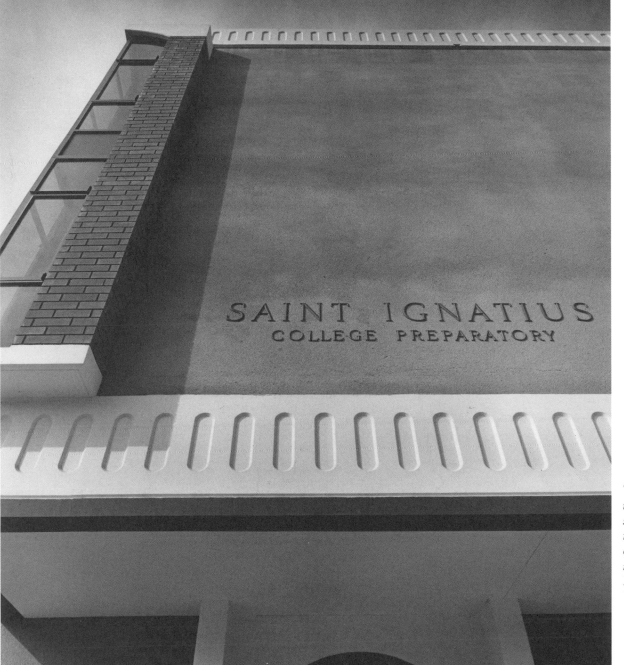

This photo was taken shortly before the dedication of the school in 1970. Photo by John Wright.

XII. THE MOVE TO COEDUCATION (1980 ~ 1989)

In 1989, SI became the first (and still the only) coeducational Jesuit high school in the California Province, and much of the history of SI in the 1980s concerns that historic event. However, life continued routinely for the boys of SI. In fact, with the transition to the new school complete, the school was enjoying some of its best years. Ironically, with families moving to the suburbs and having fewer children, the number of students applying to SI was slowly diminishing. Those low figures weren't the only factors prompting administrators here to re-examine the school's mission. Alumni with daughters were also interested in a Jesuit education for their girls, and the school responded to their needs.

Academically, SI continued to excel with a steady growth in the Advanced Placement Program, and it was recognized as one of the 60 best prep schools in the nation by the U.S. Department of Education in 1984.

SI athletes also excelled, with the boys basketball team winning the league four straight years and taking two CCS crowns and the Northern California Championship (1984). Swimmers took six league championships, soccer won the WCAL in 1981, and the track team won two league crowns. Ray Calcagno '64 and Jim Dekker '68 continued to coach successful football and baseball teams, and new sports began making their marks.

Leading SI throughout the 1980s were Principal Mario Prietto, SJ, and President Tony Sauer, SJ. Together, this duo from Southern California prepared SI for coeducation and launched a $16 million building campaign that, by 1994, would lead SI to new heights.

Fr. Mario Prietto, SJ

Fr. Prietto first came to SI in 1968 as a scholastic. He taught Spanish and Latin, coached golf and helped SI move from the old school to the new Sunset District campus. Those years were hard ones for the Jesuit community, he said, and he watched five brother Jesuits leave the order. "There were people who were resisting the changes called for by Vatican II and others who wanted change now." He recalled the older Jesuits keeping him and the other scholastics "on a tight leash. We had to be back by 10 p.m. and had to get permission to go out in the evening with lay friends. At one point, we didn't have house keys. If you came back after doors were locked, you had to go through a window in Welch Hall, which we called Squelch Hall."

Opposite page: Cheerleaders Bart Murphy, Eamon Corry, John Dedo and Chris Kanelopoulos in 1980.

Though he liked blowing off steam in the recreation room with the other scholastics, he was glad to leave Welch Hall for new quarters on 37th Avenue. But even in these new quarters, Prietto's superiors made it clear that they still ran the show. "There was a real us-versus-them mentality, with the governance of the community being very authoritarian, with no dialog, no question of young people having a voice. The Jesuit community continued to be old school."

He left SI, was ordained in 1973 and worked for five years at Loyola High School before entering Fordham's Jesuit Secondary Administrator's Program. When he returned in 1980 as the assistant principal for student affairs, he found an SI changed for the better. By the end of that year, Fr. McCurdy was forced to step down for health reasons, and the job was offered to Fr. Prietto. At 37, he became the youngest principal in the history of the school when he took office in August 1981. ("Although I was 37, I looked as if I were 24," he wrote in *Headmaster/Heartmaster*, his memoir of his years as principal. "Here I was, the principal of the oldest high school in the San Francisco Bay Area, with teachers on the faculty who were old enough to be my parents.")

At the graduation that June, Dick McCurdy took off his ring and handed it to Mario in a symbolic passing of the torch as they sat at the altar. Prietto, in turn, passed on his job as assistant principal for student activities to Charlie Dullea.

From the start, Fr. Prietto made it clear to the teachers and students that he was, first and foremost, a priest and a minister. Whether hiring a new chemistry teacher, preparing for a WASC accreditation or chatting with a student, Mario knew that his most important badge of office was the collar around his neck.

He credited Fr. McCurdy with laying the foundations in the 1970s for the work that took place in the 1980s. "Dick McCurdy was the one who really connected us to the JSEA," said Fr. Prietto. "Some people made fun of SI by calling it 'Preamble Prep,' but McCurdy never wavered in his commitment to the initiatives that came out of the JSEA, which included the Colloquium and the Curriculum Improvement Process. SI benefited profoundly because the lay faculty were well instructed in the Jesuit foundations. This, for me, was the beginning of colleagueship. I inherited a school and a faculty committed to advancing SI's Jesuit mission."

Fr. Prietto also wielded a sharp axe, and he did not renew the contracts for several teachers he felt were not doing their jobs. He credits Steve Lovette '63, the assistant principal for academics, and the department chairs, with helping him make the faculty more professional through the hiring of a number of excellent teachers. With the new renewable tenure system, SI's teachers had a chance every five years to come up for scrutiny and be challenged to continue growing in their professions.

He also reinstated the admissions test, which the admissions department had earlier dropped in favor of an interview process. That had mixed success, and, in an effort to return to a more traditional and rigorous application process, Fr. Prietto ended the interviews altogether.

In his second year as principal, Fr. Prietto and the SI community faced several tragedies in the deaths of two faculty wives, senior Chuck Simon, former faculty member Carolyn Rocca (who had retired the previous June) and a student's father. Then, on April 4, 1983, 33-year-old Katie Robinson, a member of the counseling department, died after a brief illness. Fr. Prietto describes that year as one of "unbelievable pain. We somehow not only got through it but also emerged with a deeper, closer bond. The young principal did a lot of growing up as well." Longtime SI counselor Phyllis Molinelli described that year as feeling like "the end of Camelot."

A Top 60 School

Fr. Prietto's efforts paid off in 1984 when SI was named one of the top-60 private schools from among the 6,000 in the country. Of the 60 schools receiving the award, given through the Exemplary Private School Recognition Project, half were Catholic and five were Jesuit. The award recognized SI's commitment to excellence in education, supporting a diverse student body, and the help it gave needy students through financial aid. On August 27, 1984, Frs. Sauer and Prietto traveled to Washington, D.C., to receive a banner (which Fr. Prietto hung above the door to his office), and a plaque from President Reagan and Secretary of Education Terrell H. Bell. (Fr. Sauer recalls that their luggage was lost on the flight over and they had to borrow black suits from brother Jesuits in Washington, D.C.)

The award on the plaque reads:

To Saint Ignatius College Preparatory,
San Francisco, California
For Recognition by its Peers in Education
As an Exemplary Secondary School
For the Exemplary Private School Recognition Project
1983–1984
Council for American Private Education
Washington, D.C.

Starting in the 1970s when San Franciscans began moving to the suburbs, SI's demographics began changing, with more and more students coming from Marin and San Mateo Counties. SI struggled to find a way to afford a bus service, but each time it ran the numbers, the program proved too costly. Then, in 1984, the Youth Activities Department of the Catholic Youth Organization called SI with the offer of an affordable chartered bus service. The school subsidized the service, charging students $3 per day for round-trip service and $2 for one-way travel. On August 23, 1984, one bus left the parking lot at the Hillsdale Shopping Center in San Mateo and another left Terra Linda to pick up a total of 60 students on their way to SI, and those buses have continued making their runs for the past 20 years.

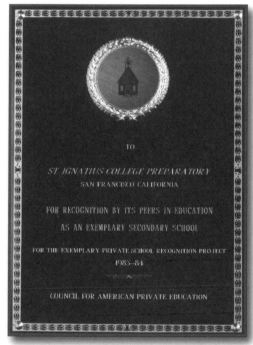

The bus service helped SI respond to its growing popularity among students from outside San Francisco. As home prices in San Francisco rose in the 1980s, many alumni moved to the suburbs but still wanted their children to attend SI. In 1988, for instance, 225 freshmen came to SI from San Francisco schools, while only 150 city students entered in 2004.

In 1984, SI received recognition as one of the 60 best prep schools in the United States.

The number of freshmen between 1988 and 2004 coming to SI from Marin County rose from 16 to 59, with similar increases for San Mateo County (66 to 126) and the East Bay (4 to 14) over that same time period.

The Move Towards Coeducation

Just as SI in the 1960s and 1970s reflected the turbulence of the society that surrounded it, SI in the 1980s enjoyed a period of stability along with the rest of the nation. SI's boat didn't start rocking until June 5, 1985, when, after an end-of-the-year debriefing, the subject of coeducation arose. Someone

The 1981 Liturgy Class.

asked, "What will SI be like in five years?" recalled Fr. Prietto. Another staffer said that, inevitably, SI would be coed by then. Thus, just as the meeting was about to end, a new discussion arose concerning SI's future.

Because the school was doing well, the administrative staff concluded that they should "take the bull by the horns and be pro-active rather than reactive," said Prietto. If SI were to go coed, "we should do it the right way and for the right reasons."[1]

Fr. Prietto felt "in a state of shock after that discussion…. To have this radical consideration at that particular time was for me both disconcerting and exhilarating." The staff agreed that for discussion to continue, Frs. Prietto, Carlin and Sauer would have to be on board. "It was decided that I would approach Fr. Carlin, who was not at the meeting," said Prietto. (At the time, before the formation of the Board of Trustees, these three men, and later Fr. Raymond Allender, SJ, who became rector of the Jesuit community in June 1985, constituted the ownership body of the school and made all the major decisions.)

A week later, walking into Fr. Carlin's office, Mario expected Fr. Carlin to dismiss the idea out of hand. "After I carefully reviewed our staff discussion and recommendation, [Fr. Carlin] looked at me from behind those thick glasses and very calmly responded, 'That seems like a good thing to consider. Let's see where it goes.' You could have knocked me over with a feather!"

Also, the all-boys' school Sacred Heart had just announced it was considering a merger with the all-girls' Cathedral School, and Br. Philip Clarke, principal of SH, had noted in his alumni magazine that, after the merger, "Sacred Heart would be the College Prep of San Francisco." (The two schools eventually merged in 1987.) This made Fr. Prietto more determined than ever to pursue the idea of SI going coed, though he ruled out the idea of merging with one of the city's Catholic girls' schools for fear that SI might lose its Jesuit identity.

In September 1985, Mario asked Steve Lovette to be a part of the deliberations. Lovette, who had been student body president in 1963 and a tight end on the '61–'63 football teams, came to SI in 1969 as a teacher and counselor. He rose through the ranks to become assistant principal for academics after earning a doctoral degree in administration from his alma mater, UC Berkeley. "Steve is a person of great intelligence and deep loyalty to SI," said Mario. "Through all the ups and down of SI going coed, Steve was a consistent voice of reason and innovation." (Since 1988, Lovette has served SI as Vice President for Development and has guided the school through two successful fund-raising campaigns — Genesis III: Building for the Future and Genesis IV: Endow SI.)

Spurring the move toward coeducation was a sudden shift in demographics over the next few years. The number of non-Catholic students had risen from 16 percent for the class of 1986 to 24 percent for the class of 1989. Coupled with that were declining numbers of students applying for admission to SI. On March 22, 1986, a week and a half after the admissions letters went out, SI invited all those accepted to come to school for registration. Both Mario and Art Cecchin, then admissions director, were shocked at how many no-shows they had. After the third tally, "we looked at one another with a feeling of dread and shock," says Mario. "It was as if someone had taken the wind out of our sails on a hot day in the middle of the ocean."[2] Cecchin, who had earlier stated in the faculty room, "Better dead than coed," started rethinking his position and eventually came around to support the move. (His daughter, Meredith Cecchin '97, enrolled in the fifth coed class and now teaches dance at SI.) But for Mario and Steve Lovette, those low numbers made them "more and more convinced that coeducation was inevitable and [we] felt the urgency to move things forward expeditiously."[3]

Fr. Sauer, however, was less enthused by the idea and asked Mario and Steve to write a *Five-Year Plan* for SI to examine the various ramifications of such a drastic change. "It is a credit to Tony's shrewdness and sagacity that we did this," said Mario. Steve Lovette began that study in September 1986, and Mario, in the ensuing months, told several people in confidence about the study and the possibility of SI going coed, including the head of the California Province of the Society of Jesus, the principal at Mercy High School, the superintendent of schools for the San Francisco Archdiocese and Archbishop John Quinn.

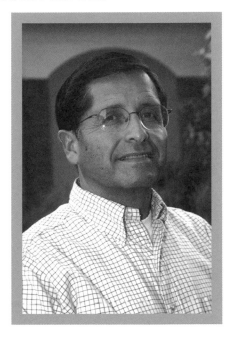

Fr. Mario Prietto, SJ, made sure that SI's transition to coeducation was a smooth one.

In April 1987, that *Five-Year Plan* was complete. It recommended that "the best way to ensure a solid market for our services for the next 15 years would be to begin coeducation as soon as possible" and that coeducation should be undertaken while the school was "in a strong and stable posture" and not "as a last resort."

Frs. Prietto and Sauer discussed the *Five-Year Plan* with the Board of Regents in May 1987 and soon after publicly announced in *Genesis II* that SI was considering the coed question and planned to make a decision by November 1, 1987. In his letter to the alumni, Fr. Sauer asked for comments. He received a flurry of letters from parents, alumni and others with

74 opposed to and 49 in favor of admitting girls to SI. The most heated responses came from the administrators of the girls' schools. On May 29,

From left: Fr. Prietto with Mike Gong, Sherman Chan, Mike Andraychak and Niall McCarthy in 1985.

a meeting was held at SI with the archdiocesan officials and principals from St. Rose and Mercy, two of the schools that would be most affected by a coed SI. Fr. Sauer, in a letter to Archbishop Quinn, described the meeting as "a quite frank interchange [that took] place [over] a good two hours, which was continued over lunch for those who could stay." Clearly the girls' schools were not happy with the prospect of competing for students with SI. As Fr. Sauer noted, "Dr. McLeod (principal of St. Rose)

expressed the view that any SI coeducation would have a deleterious effect on St. Rose applications. Her view that admitting girls in all four years at SI would harm St. Rose admissions [was] listened to closely and sympathetically." He then suggested to the Archbishop a compromise: "Perhaps a gradual transitional phase-in, *if* SI were to go coed." The group agreed to reconvene in September, but in June, several of the principals wrote to the Archbishop complaining that "appropriate consultation [had] not taken place."[4]

In September, Mario met privately with the Jesuit community, which offered an 11–8 vote (with 5 undecided) in favor of coeducation. The faculty, too, met in the fall to discuss the issue and they generally favored the transition. "Over the years, I learned never to underestimate the insight and perspicacity of a Jesuit high school faculty," wrote Prietto. "They would drive me crazy from time to time, but when it came to SI going coed, they were on the forefront of the battle lines, right at my side."

The English Department's report particularly impressed Prietto with its insightfulness. In it, the department noted that "segregation of the sexes no longer fits the social matrix of our world. When SI was founded, and in the subsequent decades, the world was segregated socially. That situation simply has passed; we must assume our place in that new situation, and we must prepare men and women to work in that world with skills and attitudes that can foster Christian and reflective social values."[5]

At the first faculty meeting, Mario was touched by Tony Sauer's candor in explaining how he had at first been opposed to coeducation, but was doing his best — in true Jesuit fashion — to discern the right course. He encouraged the faculty to be open to the process and told them "to this minute I have not made up my mind, but we're all trying to stretch and do the right thing for SI *vis-à-vis* the Archdiocese.... I trust the process as I trust you." Mario was moved by Tony's words and noted that SI "was blessed with a courageous and holy leader during those crucial times of fundamental change."

Students also met to discuss the issue. The Student Council took a straw poll. The results: 2 in favor, 18 opposed and 7 undecided. Members of the senior liturgy group also discussed the issue. At the end, they were split 15–15 with six undecided. At a parents' meeting, most of those who came expressed their opposition to the move, though one parent noted that she "came into this meeting opposed to going coed. After listening to the weak arguments against it, I've changed my mind."[6]

In mid-October 1987, SI received word that the California Province approved the *Five-Year Plan* and "expressed support for whatever decision the SI trustees made." Then Sr. Glenn Anne McPhee, OP, the new superintendent of schools for the Archdiocese, called for an October 26 meeting of all the principals of the Catholic high schools, major superiors and directors of education. Those individuals met with Archbishop Quinn to begin a "collaborative planning process to insure quality Catholic education for the archdiocese." As Fr. Prietto recalled, "the atmosphere was tense. SI was definitely on the hot seat.... That very day the Archbishop had received a letter signed by 150 students at St. Rose imploring him not to let SI go coed." At the meeting the group discussed the "grim picture" regarding declining enrollment and demographics facing all archdiocesan schools. Later, Fr. Prietto wrote to the SI faculty that the discussion at the meeting was "candid, frank and charitable. Certainly there are strong feelings about our coed

decision, but people were reasonable and open...."

The next day, at an October 27 Board of Regents meeting, with 33 of the 36 regents in attendance, the group discussed coeducation and then voted on the issue. The result: 27–5 in favor of the change. (The group, at that time, included only four women regents, and, of those, three voted for the change.)

Then, on November 1, the four SI Trustees — Frs. Sauer, Carlin, Prietto and Allender — met at their Villa (the Jesuit term for a vacation home) in Novato for a day of "prayer, discernment and decision."[7] The group went over all the reasons for and against going coeducational and soon found themselves split 2–2, with Frs. Prietto and Allender for the change and Frs. Carlin and Sauer opposed. "I wasn't really for it at first," Fr. Sauer noted. "But after much prayer and reflection, I came to think it was the best thing to do." Fr. Carlin followed suit and the vote became unanimous. SI, they hoped, would go coed by September 1989. The four decided to wait that extra year "because of the possible adverse effects on the admissions pools of the local Catholic girls' high schools." On November 2, Fr. Prietto alerted the SI faculty of the vote and of the school's desire to seek approval from the Archbishop.[8]

The following night, November 3, Fr. John Murphy, SJ (chairman of the SI English Department), and Fr. Ed Malatesta, SJ (a professor at USF), had dinner with the Archbishop where they informed him of the trustees' vote. The Archbishop was not pleased and asked SI to delay its decision and to continue collaborating with the girls' schools. In the spirit of Jesuit obedience, the trustees agreed, and on November 4, published this document: "In the past year, the Saint Ignatius College Preparatory school community ... has decided to delay any decision on

360   coeducation until further dialogue with the other Catholic high schools can take place." The following day Archbishop Quinn met with all archdiocesan

Class of 1988 Inside SI members Jason Muscat, Dave Pendergast, Dan Saffer and Paul Aquino.

clergy to announce that he was taking a six-month sabbatical for health reasons.[9]

Nearly everyone at SI who had been in favor of coeducation felt battered and beaten and that the years and months of discernment had come to a disappointing end. Fr. Sauer, however, was not among this group. In a memo, he noted that "SI must go coed for itself, but I felt myself we must delay to help the sisters…. The change the Archbishop made in the

proposal we trustees presented to him was essentially making it more open-ended, less definitive as to time."[10]

The girls' schools responded with relief and gratitude, and Fr. Prietto received letter after letter thanking him for the delayed decision. He also received a November 6 letter from Sr. Glenn Anne McPhee inviting SI and 16 other schools to attend a December 10 meeting at USF. That meeting would be the first of many held over a five-month period. Sr. Glenn Anne, a member of the San Rafael Dominicans (the same order that administered St. Rose Academy), proved to be a stellar moderator of these meetings. "We could not have gotten through the trying times … were it not for the patience, wisdom and foresight of this wonderful educator," wrote Fr. Prietto. (SI showed its appreciation to Sr. Glenn Anne during the commencement exercises for the first coed class in 1993 when it bestowed upon her the President's Award.)[11]

The December 10 meeting ended with the decision that each school would submit a statement of its plans for the next two years. At the January 20, 1988, meeting, Fr. Prietto addressed those assembled explaining the reasons for SI's decision to go coed, noting that he "cherished many fond memories of the camaraderie, bonding, spirit and deep friendships that are made [at an all-male high school]…. I've also become aware of certain attitudes towards women that seem to be endemic to an all-male environment. Too often women are looked upon as inferior, that they are threats or simply objects as distinct from a viewpoint that sees them as equals, friends and colleagues." He told the group of principals that he had come to the conclusion that "maleness is not the essence of Jesuit education" and told them of Mike Shaughnessy's daughter, Martha, asking why she couldn't attend SI and his inability to give her a convincing answer. "Finally, I cited the example of an alumnus of the school, who was a lawyer downtown and a graduate of a prestigious eastern law school. He had called to tell me why he would advise against going coed. He told me about the 'pushy, aggressive female lawyers and how difficult they were to deal with. And I shared my response: 'Maybe your inability to deal with your female colleagues might have something to do with the all-male high school you attended…. I'm not saying that women need SI or Jesuit education, for that matter. If anything, SI needs women." The group offered a mixed (sometimes combative) response to Fr. Prietto's talk, and the meeting ended with a call for two studies — one short-term, looking at the effects of SI admitting girls, and one long-term examining the future of secondary education in the archdiocese. But for Fr. Prietto, this meeting proved a decisive turning point thanks to support from Sr. Glenn Anne and Assistant Superintendent Paul Bergez '64.[12]

At subsequent meetings, SI heard requests from the girls' schools not to accept transfer students from their high schools, but only freshmen. SI had planned to accept as many as 100 older girls, who would be role models for the younger coeds, but the girls' schools argued that even this small number, taken from their ranks, would hurt them. SI agreed to this request at a March 29 meeting, and Sr. Glenn Anne asked that SI make public its decision to go coed no later than June 2. After that meeting, Fr. Prietto went "back to my car in the parking lot of the Chancery…. I remember sitting in my car, unbuttoning my collar and saying to myself: 'My God! We are actually going to go coed. I can't believe it!' A feeling of quiet relief came upon me. The next week would be Holy Week.

The joy and freedom of the Resurrection was on the horizon!"[13]

That April, SI formed a Transition Team to prepare for the move to coeducation. Then, on May 10, Sr. Glenn Anne met with Archbishop Quinn, who had just returned from his sabbatical, informing him of the meetings. Sr. Glenn Anne told the Archbishop that she supported SI's decision, and the Archbishop gave his blessing. (The previous week, the Archbishop had attended SI's spring musical, *My Fair Lady*.) In a May 13 letter to the Archbishop, Fr. Prietto thanked the Archbishop for his support and offered this reflection: "Needless to say, the past seven months have not been without their difficulties. However, as I look back upon it all, it is clear to me that the decision to delay our announcement was providential. A new working relationship has been established among all the Catholic high schools, and, I believe, the religious communities that staff them. This augurs well for the future of secondary education in our archdiocese." The Archbishop wrote back on May 17 thanking Fr. Prietto "for the collaborative effort in which this final decision was made."[14] SI made the announcement to go coed May 26 to the faculty, May 27 to the regents and Archdiocesan principals, and in July to the general public through the summer 1988 *Genesis II*. In that magazine, Fr. Sauer wrote the following: "We commit the school's significant resources to the development of programs, facilities and staff that will ensure the same quality of education for young women as that presently available for young men." Over the next academic year, SI made good its promise, preparing teachers with in-services and drawing up plans to remodel the school with the help of the $16 million Genesis III capital campaign.

Preparing for the Girls

In a very real sense, the door closed on the last all-male class with the retirement of J.B. Murphy, who left after 50 years of service. The last all-male student body honored him at the Awards Assembly in May 1989 by leaping to their feet for a standing ovation after Fr. Prietto introduced him. At the end

A 1989 rally in the gymnasium.

of his speech he lifted his arm and shouted: "Go SI! Go coed!" His legacy continued both through his son, Chuck Murphy '61, who represented SI at the archdiocesan coed discussion meetings, and through his grandchildren who attended SI — Matt '87 and Marielle '93, a member of the first coed class.

The girls arrived (175 in a class of 375 in a student body of 1225) for their frosh orientation August 22, 1989. Accompanying them were TV

reporters and cameras to cover the historic event. "As long as I live, I shall never forget watching the Class of 1993 file into Orradre Chapel the next morning," said Prietto. "Steve Lovette was standing next to me, and I told him: 'Doctor, I can't believe my eyes. They're actually here.' Then I thought about all the work that lay ahead of us and added, 'I sure wish it were four years from now.'"

To prepare for that first class, Prietto had formed a Task Force among the faculty and administrators that included Phyllis Molinelli, the chair of the counseling department. The group met for the first time on April 21, 1988, and debated issues big and small, from dress code to off-campus lunch privileges. The school decided not to require uniforms for either boys or girls but did revoke off-campus lunch privileges. "The boys blamed the girls for the rule changes," said Molinelli. "They were furious about losing their off-campus privileges and about having to wear, and tuck in, shirts with collars. And the girls tested every rule there was. Years later, we had to go to polo shirts for both boys and girls."

Molinelli added that "there was a little fear before the girls came, but when they finally arrived, the tension was gone. Teachers who had never taught girls realized that it wasn't that much different from teaching boys."

The school also looked to hire women as administrators, teachers and coaches. In the years leading up to and immediately following the move to coeducation, the school gave leadership roles to the following women: Donna Ravetti Murphy (assistant admissions director and later assistant dean and activities coordinator), Teresa Mullin Garrett (associate athletic director), Kathleen Purcell (head of the campus ministry team), Karen Cota (associate dean) and Kate Kelly Kodros (assistant principal for academics). "If women were truly to be part of the formerly all-male bastion, they had to have positions of real power and authority," wrote Prietto.

Many others at SI proved instrumental to the success of coeducation among the faculty, counselors and staff. In addition, the school brought in outside experts to help prepare the faculty for the girls. In the spring of 1989 three women spoke to the faculty including Phyllis Molinelli's daughter Cathy Molinelli (then dean of students at Notre Dame High School in Southern California); Mary Lamia, a clinical psychologist; and Rita Dollard O'Malley, the former director of campus ministry at St. Ignatius College Prep in Chicago. O'Malley had helped St. Ignatius in Chicago go coed in the early 1980s, and she answered questions from a wary faculty. "I thought it was an engaging dialogue," said O'Malley. "They asked serious questions and were honest about their concerns. They wondered if girls' needs were different from boys' needs. They showed a great deal of respect and a little healthy fear. They wanted the school to become coed the right way. They did ask some unrealistic questions, such as 'Am I going to be as effective a teacher of girls as I am with boys?'"

O'Malley was among seven women hired in 1989 to teach at SI, extending the total number of female faculty from 11 to 18. They now constituted nearly a quarter of the faculty, and that figure, over the next few years, would almost double. (Currently, SI employs 66 men and 55 women who work directly with students, including faculty, counselors, administrators and librarians, not counting off-campus coaches.) O'Malley recalls the "energy and investment put into making the freshman class feel welcome. It was a healthy transition despite the fact that these freshman girls had no older girls to serve as mentors." She recalls the excitement of the early days. "We all had a sense that we were entering into a new era. The students had a great deal of confidence about being pioneers. They knew they were special, and we showed them a great deal of care and concern with focus groups for the girls and boys to talk about how they felt being in this new environment."

Not everyone was happy with the change, including some of the older boys who felt that the focus had shifted from the upperclassmen to the freshmen. A handful of students reacted badly, vandalizing one female teacher's classroom while she was away at the faculty retreat and writing "we don't want women" on papers in her file cabinet.

To aid in their transition to SI, the girls were divided into 10 support groups, each led by a female faculty member. Erika Drous '93, a member of that first coed class, praised her group's leader, Donna Murphy "who did a great job making sure the girls felt welcomed." (Drous, by the way, made SI history by being the first girl to be handed a detention slip for the offense of not having her book in English class. She never served detention, however, as that infraction wasn't one punishable by detention.) Drous enjoyed the fact that her class was the only coed one in the school. "Everyone wanted to accommodate us and attend to our needs."

Molinelli and others felt, however, that SI's eagerness to accommodate the girls was a mistake. "From the moment they walked through the doors, we treated those girls as if they were seniors. We tried to be inclusive, but I think we gave them too much too soon. Still, I think the transition was a success. All the fears proved false — that girls would prove a distraction or that athletic participation would

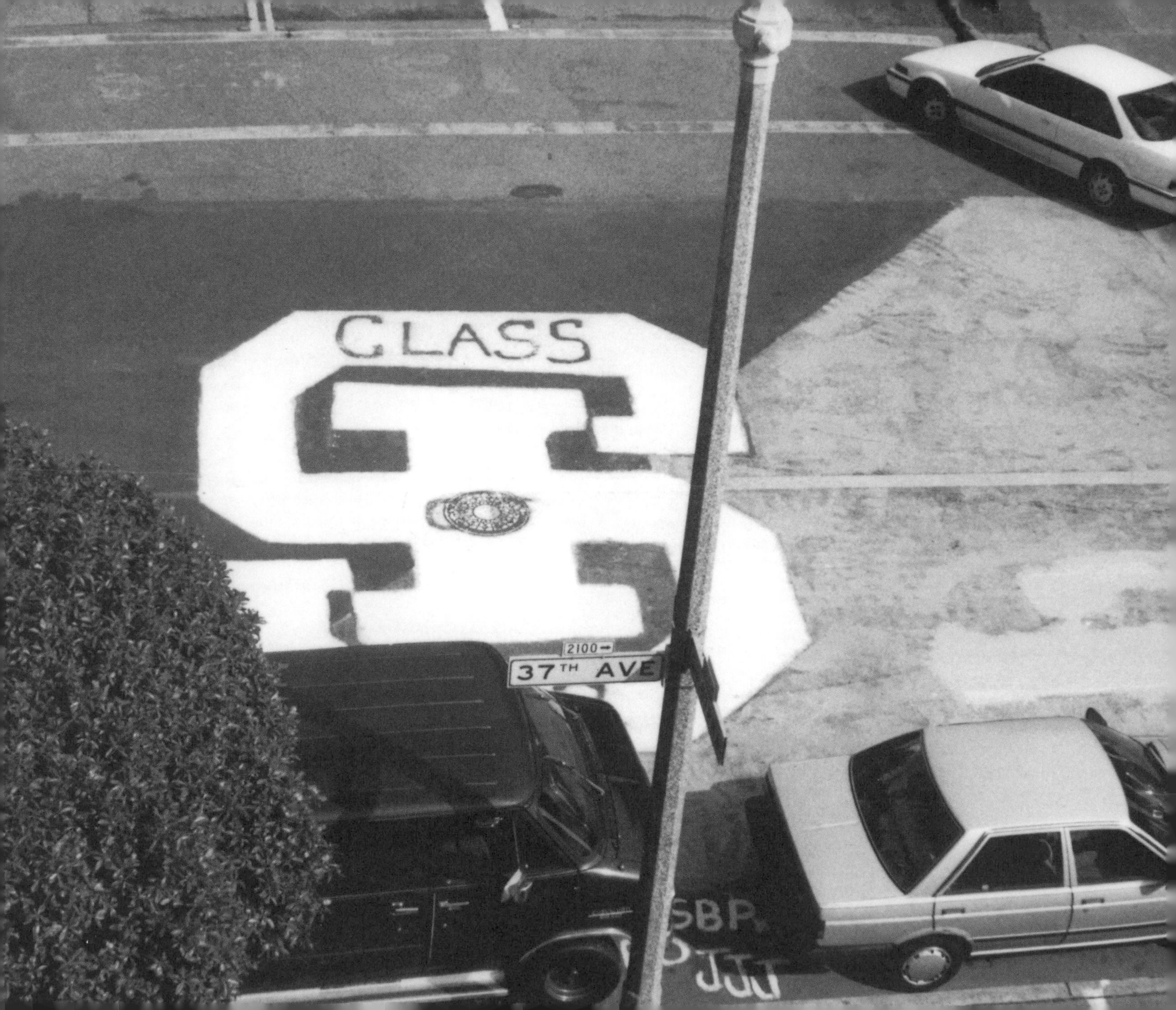
CLASS
2100
37TH AVE
SBP

decrease. The opposite proved true. The SAT scores, AP results and GPAs all rose thanks to coeducation and our teams continued to excel."

Teresa Mullin Garrett, who served as assistant (and then associate) athletic director, helped the first girls' teams get started. The freshmen girls competed on the JV level in their first year and on the varsity as sophomores in volleyball, cross country, tennis, basketball, soccer, softball and track. In later years would they compete in swimming, field hockey, lacrosse, crew, golf, water polo and diving.

O'Malley left the faculty after two years and returned eight years later to direct the Adult Ministry Program. "When I returned, no one was talking about coeducation. That was a sign of progress. Instead of talking about it, we were doing it." Mario Prietto knew that the school had made the right decision. "I myself am a '62 graduate of [the all-male] Loyola High School in Los Angeles. I cherish the time I had there and wouldn't change it for the world. But I am convinced more than ever of the rightness of our decision." SI went coed, in part, because of demographic reasons. "But ... it is far better to go coed for the best reason. That is, because it is the right thing to do. We claim that we are in the business of educating leaders for the future, which has to include the other half of the human race."

Molinelli has also seen the fruits of coeducation: "Some people worried that a coed SI would never have the camaraderie it enjoyed as an all-male institution. I see a different kind of camaraderie. They keep in touch all the time, and close friends remain close. Some of the best friendships are between men and women. The men have learned to look at women differently, and they are called to task when they don't."

One symbol of SI's successful transition to coeducation can be found in the ranks of the student body officers for the 1996–1997 school year. They included Laura Jones as student body president, Katie Watson as vice president, Sally Prowitt as treasurer, Emily Dunn as sergeant-at-arms and Rowena Ocampo as secretary, forming the first all-female collection of student body officers in the school's history.

By Emily Behr '93

I'll never forget August 22, 1989. I was a member of the first co-ed class at SI, one of 175 girls in a school of 1,225 students. On our first day of orientation, we were greeted by nervous yet expectant teachers, excited juniors and seniors and the news media. They literally greeted us — they stood on the front steps of school and watched us arrive that first morning. After 134 years of single-sex education, everyone was ready to get a good look at us. As I reflect back, I also recognize God's welcoming presence. He was in the face of Fr. Mario Prietto, SJ, SI's principal, who welcomed us that first day in Orradre Chapel and did everything in his power to make us feel comfortable. He was in the face of our teachers who banded together to form female 'support groups' to make sure that we were able to adjust and integrate into the historically male-dominated school environment and support us through a difficult school transition. He was even there in the very pink walls of our brand new locker room — such a well-intentioned (yet slightly misguided) gesture by the school administration to 'rebrand' facilities for girls — to let us know they had planned for our arrival and were welcoming us with open arms. All girls must love pink, right?

Last March, I had the opportunity to lead a Kai-

For many years, seniors painted a large SI block on the street in front of the school shortly before graduation.

ros retreat for some of our seniors, and I shared the above reflection with them about my first day at SI. As a naïve and oblivious eighth grader living in Marin County, I had no idea what I was getting into when I accepted a place in SI's "pioneer" class of 1993. Today I feel incredibly grateful, blessed and proud that I was able to be a part of this incredible class.

At our 10-year reunion in October 2003, *Genesis IV* editor Paul Totah interviewed several of my classmates about their experiences at SI. As one would expect, our class experienced our share of challenges and struggles as we lived through SI's growing pains. Amber Clisura, now a textile and fashion designer, recalled, "It was a trial by fire. The faculty wasn't sure how to handle 175 girls, and we weren't sure how to handle the faculty."

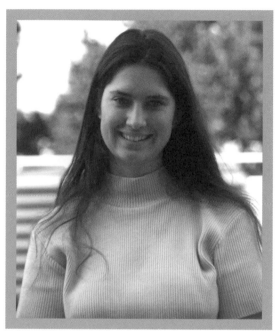

Emily Behr, one of SI's first coeds, heads the school's Magis Program.

During our first few years, the school paid so much attention to the female members of our class that, at times, the boys in our class lived in the shadows. David Ciappara, who today works as a paramedic, remembered, "As a guy, you melted into the background. With so many guys there, the girls paid attention to the older guys. You were like a number almost unless you played sports." For MelissAnne Gallo, "it was eye opening to see that not all of us were welcomed at first. On my freshman retreat, a senior admitted that he [at first] didn't want us to be there and that he agreed with all the alumni [who also protested SI's decision to go coed], but he now saw that it was a good thing."

For the most part, our experiences were overwhelmingly positive. Adversity that we faced made us stronger as individuals and as a class. Attorney Tiffany Cheung reflected that being at SI "taught me to be a stronger woman. As a freshman, I was surrounded by men, so I learned to speak out for myself and to be independent." Despite her trial by fire, Amber Clisura believes that her teachers "prepared me for the world in unexpected ways. I received an education in finding my principles and sticking to them. My teachers taught me not to be afraid to do that, and I'm thankful for them." Jean-Paul Bergez, who owns his own landscape design business, was grateful for the extra attention we received. "People warned us that being a freshman is rough, but it was easy [for us] because people treated us so well. No one gave us an initiation process. Everyone patted us on the back telling us we were special, instead of knocking us down because we were freshmen."

For me, the most incredible thing about being part of this historic class was the myriad opportunities that we were offered. Erica Drous noted that "we had a better high school experience because we never had to be the youngest girls." For four years, our class, particularly the girls, served as the school's guiding force. We served on varsity sports teams as underclassmen, gaining valuable experience that earned our teams championships during our final two years. As freshmen, Blair Wilde and I were the only two girls admitted to Service Club for our sophomore year. Because there was no female representation on student council (made up primarily of seniors), we were invited to attend the student council retreat as sophomores.

Cross country standout Alicia Stanfill and track star Lorelei Suarez were the first girls selected for the Block Club. At times Stanfill felt the pressure of being the first to break tradition. "I knew I was setting precedent and that I couldn't screw up and ruin it for everyone else," but she also knew that she was consistently "supported and given all of the coaching and equal opportunities" afforded older students.

I fondly recall having Fr. John Murphy, SJ '59, as my English teacher freshman year. For years, the brilliant and dedicated Fr. Murphy only taught juniors and seniors. As department chair in 1989, he added one freshman English class to his own schedule because he wanted to see what it was like to teach a coed class. The 30 of us in his class had been blessed with unparalleled intellectual challenges coupled with Fr. Murphy's caring, generous and loving spirit.

Our class was a class of firsts, but our experiences were much like every other graduating class at the Prep. We studied as much as necessary, immersed ourselves in theater, athletics and other activities, celebrated liturgies, prayed together, laughed together, cried together and made lasting friendships. Bryan Giraudo, now an investment banker, marvels at how typical our experience was. "There was beauty in what Fr. Prietto and Fr. Sauer did. They did not make [co-education] an exception, other than the speech on the first day. As I recall, the first day there were TV cameras and then class. It didn't matter the next day."

Emily Behr is a member of SI's first coed class and the first one from that class to work full time for SI. A Stanford graduate, Behr first worked in the school's admission's office and now directs the SI Magis Program.

By Lorelei Suarez '93

As a member of SI's first coed class, I had the good fortune of having Fr. John Murphy, SJ, as an English teacher for three of my four years of English at SI. I enjoyed his rigorous lessons, and he taught us how to write far better than any of my professors at UC Berkeley. I treasure this memory, among others, from my four years at SI — years that changed my life and formed me in ways that I will never forget. My time at SI, I am certain, made me the woman I am today.

My closest friends remain the girls I met those first weeks as a freshman Wildcat. Moira O'Neil is working on her Ph.D. in Santa Barbara, Alicia Thomas just celebrated her one-year wedding anniversary, Monette Benitez is a mom, and Dina Calvin is engaged. When we get together to celebrate one of our life's great moments, as we do to this day, in many ways we are still those 14- and 15-year-old girls who played basketball, danced in 3 Shades, monopolized talent shows, pulled all-nighters writing term papers, and, most importantly, created the first generation of female Wildcats.

I am one of very few women in my occupation. I am by far the youngest employee and the only minority in my office. I am also successful. Ask me where I learned how to succeed, how to lead, how to rise above, and my answer will always be: the halls of SI. Corporate America isn't the first time I demanded to be accepted by a male-dominated organization. Until Alicia Stanfill and I joined SI's Block Club, it was the only all-male club left at SI. She and I made the cut, and the rest is history. We were given an extraordinary opportunity (just as we were in Fr. Murphy's English class) by being in the right place at the right time to own a special place in the SI memoirs.

We started as eighth graders by answering the call to be part of a pioneer class. As freshmen, we found ourselves outnumbered seven to one by the boys. As sophomores, we paved a path for those who would follow, redefining the school's identity while honoring its past. How many chances does someone really get to change history and to do it as part of one's high school experience?

I know how blessed I was for being a part of the Class of '93. Like all teenagers, my high school years were filled with angst, peer pressure, doubt, fear and pain. Some of my experiences were perhaps even more painful than they might have been elsewhere. But as the years continue to pass, and as I face the world and everything it throws my way, I am convinced that my time at SI was close to perfect. Without those heartaches and tears, along with the joys and triumphs, I might not be the confident and strong person I am today.

My time at SI provided me with rare opportunities to be a leader, to set new standards, to create new paradigms and to discover new frontiers. At SI I learned that I could transform the world in limitless ways because I was the magic wand. SI generously gave me the gifts of self-reliance, self-sufficiency and self-esteem. As a result of molding us into such strong individuals, our educators succeeded in shaping us into young adults with the experience, faith and conviction to change the world, just as Ignatius hoped we would and just as we prayed each day when we asked: "Lord, teach me to be generous. Teach me to serve You as You deserve; to give and not to count the cost; to fight and not to heed the wounds; to toil and not to seek for rest; to labor and not to seek reward; save that of knowing that I do Your will, O God."

SI, you taught me well.

Bill McDonnell '42 led the Board of Regents through the 1980s.

Lorelei Suarez is a business consultant in human resources, employment practices and employer liabilities. She also is the founder of Emerging Professionals In Collaboration, a networking organization for young professionals supported by the San Francisco Chamber of Commerce.

Genesis II Campaign

As Hugh O'Donnell '37, finance chairman for the Board of Regents, wrote in the October 1979 issue of *Genesis*, "though the debt on our beautiful campus is nearly retired, this is no time to retreat from the task of providing excellent educational opportunities in the SI tradition.... Shortly, SI will announce a new program, Genesis II, that will enable our school to enhance its reputation, solidify its financial position and keep the devastations of inflation from sending tuition costs out of sight."

SI liquidated its debt for the new school on December 31, 1980, and then launched the Genesis II campaign to raise SI's endowment from $1.1 million to $4.5 million by 1985. The school would use the interest from the fund for "scholarships, facilities maintenance and to offset rising salaries." In addition, the school hoped to raise an additional $250,000 each year to help keep pace with inflation.[15]

The Alumni Association pitched in by launching the first annual Golf and Tennis Tournament on June 6, 1983. The event is still held and is now billed as the All Class Reunion and Sports Day, bringing alumni from all eras back to SI.

Key to the success of the Genesis II campaign was William McDonnell '42, Chairman of the Board of Regents from 1980 through 1991. After graduating from SI and USF, he and Gene McAteer became partners in Tarantino's and The Spinnaker restaurants. (William's son, Tim McDonnell '71, now manages those businesses.) McDonnell joined the Board of Regents in 1973, chaired then by the Hon. Eugene Lynch '49. When Fr. Sauer asked McDonnell to serve as chairman, he and regent Hugh O'Donnell tried to assess the school's financial situation — not an easy task given the accounting practices at the time. He then worked with Fr. Sauer to bring people to the board who had a variety of talents that could serve the school over the years including Bill McInerney, a talented lawyer; Paul Hazen, president of Wells Fargo Bank; and Martin D. "Pete" Murphy, senior partner of Tobin & Tobin, who would succeed McDonnell as chairman.

McDonnell praises Steve Lovette and Frs. Prietto, Carlin and Sauer for the success of the Genesis II, III and IV campaigns. "They made an amazing team. They understood the problems and suffered through many meetings to arrive at creative answers." He also encouraged the business office to adopt modern accounting procedures, and Michael Silvestri '67 was made business manager in 1985.

SI Goes High Tech

SI received its first computers in the 1970s for a summer session computer science class. According to an *Inside SI* article, "The students struggled with four Heathkits (made by Zenith and a gift of Don Ruder) and one Apple II computer in the back room of the library."[16]

An anonymous gift of $50,000 to the Genesis II campaign helped SI purchase its first computer lab in 1982, made up of 30 Apple II Plus computers linked by a Corvus server. Biology teacher William Love '59 set up the $100,000 lab and began teaching a computer course. "We are at the onset of a major revolution in education," he wrote in *Genesis II*. "The computer will be the instrument of this revolution." In 1987, thanks to a grant from the E.L. Wiegand Foundation, SI created a second lab comprising 28 Macintosh SE computers. By the end of the decade, all the offices had personal computers to supplement the VAX server the school used for its primary database.

SI's first computer lab.

Those early computers at SI allowed *Inside SI* to switch to desktop publishing in 1986 using a Macintosh Plus and Apple's first laser printer. Over the years, computers would become ubiquitous around campus. In 2001, the school issued laptops to nearly every faculty member, and the campus network went wireless in 2003. Currently, SI has two computer labs, with more computers available in the Wilsey Library and in various classrooms to help prepare students for the realities of the new millennium.

In the 1980s and 1990s, many SI grads found

themselves working for Silicon Valley's biggest computer firms. Charlie Jadallah '77 and Mike Homer '76 were key players in the early days of Netscape, and and Gary Roberts '75 worked his way up the ranks at Oracle. In 2002, Paul Otellini '68 was named president and chief operating officer of Intel after 27 years working for that company, and in 2004 he became the company's CEO.

The Graduate at Graduation

Between 1980 and 1983, the SI faculty met from time to time to hammer out a document that, over the years, has become known as the "Grad-at-Grad." The JSEA asked each of the Jesuit high schools in the nation to create a "Profile of the Graduate at Graduation," and Fr. McCurdy made this a part of SI's Curriculum Improvement Process.

Teachers met to discuss what qualities a student would have upon graduation from SI. Each student, according to the document would be open to growth, intellectually competent, religious, loving and committed to doing justice and to the pursuit of leadership. For each of these topics, the faculty wrote 10 or so descriptors. That document became the cornerstone of education at SI for many years, shaping curricular and extracurricular decisions.

"This process asked the faculty to examine the bigger picture of Jesuit education," said Fr. Prietto. "It resembled the accreditation process, but we looked at SI through the lens of Jesuit secondary education to see how we fared as a Jesuit school. It is an important document, and I'm quite proud of it."

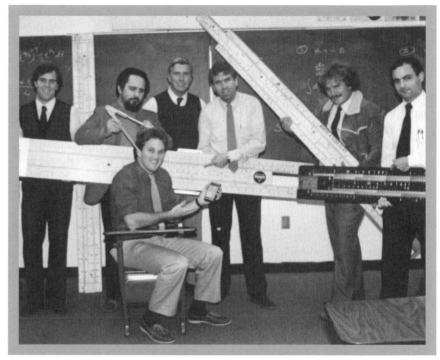

Athletics

Baseball

After a 3-year hiatus, Jim Dekker '68 returned as head coach of the varsity baseball team in 1983. The team that year finished 13-10 and included such standouts as Chris Gaggero '83, who led the league in strikeouts, and Duffy Aceret '83, who was the team's leading hitter. Tim Reardon '86 and Arnie Sambel '86 were outstanding players three years later. Sambel, according to Dekker, was the best player of that decade, a strong pitcher and outfielder. He earned a four-year scholarship to USF

Math teachers in 1986 show off technology, old and new.

Opposite page: The 1985 baseball team posed in front of the Stanyan Street campus two years before it was demolished.

where he still holds many university records. Also, Jun Dasalla '87 had a great senior year and still holds the record for batting average and the most doubles in the triple-round format. (In 1987 the WCAL went from a double round-robin format to a triple round-robin, meaning that SI played each rival three times.)

Basketball

The basketball team would win the WCAL title four straight times between 1981 and 1984, culminating in the greatest victory in modern times for any SI hoops team since the school won the state title in 1926.

In 1981, the team earned the nickname the "Cardiac 'Cats" after clawing their way to co-champion status in the WCAL. Seniors Jeff Thilgen, Frank Byrne, Tom Feeney, Rob Mascheroni, Hugh Campbell and Dean Klisura were seasoned veterans, having played varsity the previous year. Joining them were senior Ray Arata and juniors Mike Radonovich, Gino Cerchiai, David Hamilton, Damien Haitsuka, Rob Ennis and Paul Fortier. They led SI to an 11–1 pre-season finish and an 11–1 round-robin finish before beating Bellarmine (57–50). A 39–38 loss to Riordan forced one more game against the Crusaders. SI won that match 64–44 for the league crown before heading to Stanford's Maples Pavilion for the final two CCS games. There, SI beat Fremont 58–49 and followed with a 54–52 win over Gunn High School for the school's first CCS crown. Fortier, Thilgen and Mascheroni made the All-Tournament Team for their efforts.

The next year, Bob Drucker and assistant coach Shel Zatkin again led the 'Cats to a WCAL title, with Drucker winning his 300th game along the way by defeating Riordan 54–47. Drucker and Zatkin won again in 1983 after a 9–3 round-robin finish and a 50–44 victory over SH in the playoffs. The team won the first two CCS games but lost 46–45 to Fremont of Sunnyvale for the sectional championship.

In 1984, SI's starting-five included standouts Levy Middlebrooks, David Wilson, Dan Oyharcabal, Paul La Rocca and Joe Vollert who helped SI to a 10–2 pre-league record. The league games included a triple-overtime cliffhanger against St. Francis that SI won thanks to the inside domination of Middlebrooks. SI lost its final league game to SH to spoil an otherwise undefeated season, but the team had its revenge in the first playoff game against the Irish. It was déjà vu all over again when SI lost to Riordan and then came back to beat the Crusaders for the league crown. In CCS competition, SI beat Milpitas and Cupertino before besting Riordan once again for the sectional title.

At the Oakland Coliseum, SI won the Northern California Championship (formerly named the Tournament of Champions) by beating Rancho Cordova, St. Elizabeth's and Amador Valley. It was the first TOC win since Rene Herrerias led the Wildcats to that victory 29 years previous. Even though SI fell 65–45 to Long Beach Poly at the Oakland Coliseum on March 17 for the state title, it enjoyed a remarkable run and a phenomenal season to which future teams would aspire but never quite achieve.

The Man Who Helps SI Play by the Numbers

By King Thompson, San Francisco Examiner

(Dr. Robert Jeffrey served as statistician and Sports Information Director for SI between 1969 and 1994. He received the President's Award in 1986 and continued to serve the school until his death. The following article appeared in 1981 in The San Francisco Examiner.*)*

The world's most organized high school sports information director sits hunched in the stands, his black felt pen poised for action over the book of lined binder paper that rests in his lap.

As the referee tosses the basketball in the air for the opening tip-off, the pen begins to squeak across the page, noting such things as who received the tip and whether the team on defense opens with a man-to-man or zone configuration.

For the next 90 minutes or so, Dr. Robert A. Jeffrey, Jr., head of the pathology department at St. Mary's Hospital, is a man avidly pursuing his chosen avocation. Some men play golf or go fishing; Dr. Jeffrey spends his free time chronicling the exploits of the St. Ignatius High football and basketball teams.

All professional sports franchises have statisticians and publicity men, and almost all universities employ sports information directors. But none of them has anything over Dr. Jeffrey when it comes to detailed information.

You want statistics? Dr. Jeffrey has statistics. Lots of them.

He can tell you the usual stuff — average points per game, field goal percentages, rebounds, and so forth. But he doesn't stop there.

Besides a roster and list of probable starters for each team, there is a breakdown — non-league, league and totals for the season — of how every SI player rates in 12 separate categories. Not only can Dr. Jeffrey tell you each player's scoring average or shooting percentage, but also available is such esoterica as how many times a team member has forced a jump ball, how many times he has controlled a tip, how many times he has deflected a pass and how many times he has taken an offensive foul. As if that weren't enough, there is also a rundown on the opposition players, which Dr. Jeffrey labels "Coach Drucker's Pocket Guide" to whatever team he happens to be playing. At the bottom of this sheet there is a list entitled, "Pecking Order for Fouls." It is divided into two categories: "Worst Men to Foul" and "Best Men to Foul." In an instant, you can tell which opposing players are good free-throw shooters and which are not.

Are these mounds of numbers really valuable in terms of winning and losing games? Drucker doesn't think there is any question about it.

"I'll say this much: Our success in athletics can be traced directly to this man's tireless work," he said in 1976.

Things haven't changed in the interim. The Wildcats won the WCAL and CCS Championships and finished 29–5 overall (in 1981).

Reprinted with permission from the San Francisco Examiner.

Football

Though SI failed to win a league championship in the 1980s or 1990s, most athletes from those years would say they played for a winning

He went to SCU, graduating in 1972 with a degree in business, though his college career was interrupted by a stint in Vietnam, where he served with the Army's 101st Airborne Division. Upon returning to the U.S., he coached at USF, finished his degree at SCU and then coached at St. Francis High School for seven years alongside his brother, Ron Calcagno '60.

He led the varsity Wildcats at SI between 1979 and 1986 and then again from 1989 until 1992. He took SI to its first CCS appearance in 1983 after a 7–2–1 record. Selected as a Division I at-large team, SI upset Los Gatos 18–14 led by sophomore quarterback Dan Vaughn who ran for one touchdown and threw a 74-yard touchdown pass to junior tailback Tyrone Taylor. In CCS quarterfinal action against Saratoga, SI lost with 2 seconds remaining after Saratoga scored a field goal to win 10–7.

Another favorite memory for Calcagno was the reopening of Kezar Stadium, which had closed in 1989 for remodeling and opened one year later. SI played the first day game and first night game in that newly remodeled stadium, with the Wildcats walking through the same tunnel trod on by generations of '49ers.

His best memories, he says, are of the boys he coached and the men he coached with. A resident of Mountain View, he decided to leave SI to avoid the grueling commute. He coached football at Mountain View High School between 1992 and 1996 and still works there teaching PE.

team. They would point to Ray Calcagno '64 as the reason why.

Calcagno was a star on SI's number-one ranked football team as a junior and senior. In 1963, he completed 75 of 117 passes for 1,290 yards and 18 touchdowns, making him the top Northern California high school quarterback for passing percentage.

Crew

SI competed in crew beginning in 1932 and continuing through the 1940s before the school dropped the sport. In 1979, SI took up crew

Ray Calcagno, a star player in the 1960s for SI, returned to coach the varsity football team in 1979.

once again with coach Mark Bruneman '73 at the helm. More than 200 students came to try out for 17 slots. The team began practicing at Lake Merced, the Oakland Estuary and Lexington Reservoir alongside the SCU crew. In its first years, crew competed as a club sport, sponsored by the Dolphin Club, which provided boats and equipment. Early members included Boat House Captain Pat Bennett, Morgan Petiti, Kevin O'Kelly, Ed Navarrete and Ben Harrison. SI competed against such teams as the Oakland Strokes and the Pacific Rowing Club through the California Junior Rowing Association. Matt Carrado and Greg Bonfiglio, SJ (now president of Jesuit High School in Sacramento), teammates on SCU's 1982 nationally-ranked lightweight eight shell, began coaching in 1985, leading their boys in 5:30 a.m. practices on the lake. The 1980s proved growth years for the sport, with SI crew rising to state and national prominence in the 1990s.

Swimming

The varsity swim team stopped competing in 1980 due, in part, to the lack of a nearby pool in which to practice and compete. (The 1979 *OceanSIder* reported in its October 31, 1979, issue that the league nearly decided not to hold finals as only four teams — Serra, Bellarmine, SI and St. Francis — had teams; of those, SI was the only school that did not have its own pool.) In 1982, the sport picked up again thanks, in large measure, to the late Bill Schuppel '83. SI's natatorium was years away, so the squad practiced at Hamilton Pool each Thursday and at facilities closer to team members' homes. The team proceeded to win the league championship each year between 1984 and 1991, propelled, perhaps, by

a name change. The team first called itself the Catfish but "the title was changed because, according to team captain Conor O'Kelly '85, catfish are 'low-life fish who suck sludge off the bottom.'" The team changed its name to the Aqualads based on the comic book hero Aquaman. (Aqualad was his trusty young assistant.) "He fit the image we wanted," said Kelly in a Spring 1985 *Genesis II* interview.

Extracurriculars
National Championship in Debate

In 1986, SI's Speech and Debate Program won the National Championship Sweepstakes Trophy from the National Forensic League in Tulsa, Oklahoma, recognizing SI as the top school in the country in legislative debate in a field of 1,500 competitors. The award paid tribute to a dozen years of excellence by past members of SI debate teams.

To win the award, SI sent debaters to 10 of the 13 national tournaments between 1974 and 1986 and eight Wildcats captured individual awards at those events, placing in the top 10 of the best debaters from the U.S. Those winners included Timothy Murphy (1974), Brian McCaffery (1975), Fred Schluep (1976), James Fazackerley (1977), Michael Schwartz (1977), Anthony Cistaro (1981), Michael Boro (1982), Clayton Chan (1983), Jonathan Nicolas (1984), James Farrell (1985 and 1986) and Jeffrey Bryan (1986).

In 1987, SI continued the winning tradition in speech and debate when high school students from 21 states met in Philadelphia to compete in the National Bicentennial Constitutional Student Congress to commemorate the original signing of the Constitution in 1787. California sent two representatives, both from SI — Janar Wasito '87 and Robert Forni '88. After two days of competitive speaking on 10 legislative topics, Wasito took second place honors and Forni earned third place.

The national trophy and other awards are on permanent display in the Speech and Debate display case at SI. They are a testament to the students who earned these honors and to David Mezzera '64, who coached debate at SI between 1970 and 1986 and who retired in 2002.

David Mezzera '64

David Mezzera is the author of *Student Congress and Lincoln–Douglas Debate*, published by the National Textbook Company. That book and Mezzera's passion for student congress competition helped re-establish the credibility of that competitive speech event in California. Because of his many years helping students hone their public speaking and debate skills, the California High School Speech Association inducted Mezzera April 30, 2000, into its Coaches' Hall of Fame.

Mezzera began his auspicious career by attending, as a sophomore, the state speech and debate finals, and he made repeat appearances there as a junior and senior while he was president of the SI Forum. In his senior year, he competed in a national invitational debate tournament in Washington, DC, taking 10th place.

While studying at USF, he helped SI speech coach Charles Henry '38 (then Fr. Henry), and joined the SI faculty in 1970. In 1973, when Henry left SI, Mezzera inherited the program and helped students prepare for debates and congresses while also teaching public speaking and American government. He left those du-

The 1986 Forum: From left are Robert Forni, Peter Gliksthern, Janar Wasito, moderator David Mezzera and Jim Farrell.

ties in 1986 when he became director of the Community Service Program.

During Mezzera's 17-year tenure as speech coach, SI students qualified for the national debate tournament in 14 of those years, and these students enjoyed their greatest success in student congress — the category for which Mezzera wrote the rules.

California Hall of Fame President John Cardoza wrote the following to Mezzera: "Your concern for your students, the success they have realized because of your tutelage, the mentoring you have provided, the growth of quality speech education programs in your league and throughout the state — these are just a few of the reasons for the high esteem with which you are regarded by your friends and fellow teachers."

Cardoza isn't alone in his praise of Mezzera. Simon Chiu '88, a former SI English teacher who coached speech and debate for seven years and who debated for Mezzera, also sang the virtues of his former mentor.

"Besides being my high school speech coach, Dave has quietly and unassumingly mentored me over many years," said Chiu. "I know that he left coaching because he was tired of the weekly grind of going to tournaments and being away from his own family so often, but he has never lost his enthusiasm and passion for competitive public speaking. Dave never forgot why a coach does what he does — for the kids. He has never let the ethos of competition distract him from ministering to his students and teaching the skills they need to succeed not only in a contest but also in life. His success as a coach is commendable; his success as a teacher and educator is admirable."

Mezzera sees the Hall of Fame honor as an affirmation of the importance not only of speech programs in high schools but also of public speaking classes. "When I see high school students (SI and others) struggling with having to speak in public, I'm reminded of the value of taking a public speaking class or participating in a debate program. When I encounter former students (which is rather frequently), most will provide me with anecdotes about how the ability to feel comfortable with speaking in public has helped them as a person and as a professional."

Mezzera continues to stay active in the field, serving as clerk for the San Francisco Bay's District Student Congress, teaching parliamentary procedure pro-fessionally and administering congressional workshop debates during June and July for the Junior Statesmen of America's summer schools.

Publications

The school newspaper went through several incarnations in the 1970s and 1980s. In 1979, the *2001* changed its name to the *OceanSIder* and in 1982 back to *Inside SI* and appeared in both magazine and tabloid formats. SI also launched a video yearbook in 1989 called *'Cat's Eye '89*, produced by the SI Video Yearbook Club and moderated by Br. Thomas Koller, SJ. The videotape sold for $34.95 and featured video clips of games, rallies, fine arts activities, graduation and other gatherings, all set to music. The *Ignatian* continued producing quality yearbooks throughout the 1980s, and a few attempts were made to establish a new literary magazine. When English teachers began publishing one in the 1990s, they called it *The Quill* after the literary magazine of the 1950s.

Theatre

Much has already been written about the Drama Department at SI. For many students, however, the thrill of working in theatre did not lie in the glare of the spotlights, but behind them working on the lighting crew or hammering away as part of the stage crew. Kevin Quattrin '78 made his theatrical debut as a page-turner for a pianist in his junior year. As a junior, he worked with Tony Remedios '77 building roof sets for *The King and I*, the last musical SI would stage with Mercy.

He liked the backstage atmosphere "because these

were down-to-earth guys who treated each other well. I was a newcomer, and they welcomed me right away." Quattrin, who played football as a student (and who served as a football coach at SI from 1978–2004), likened the backstage crew to the offensive line. "We didn't get any recognition and were perfectly happy that way." He credits theatre veterans Bill Raffetto '69, Mark Roos '75 and Phil Bailey '76 with helping to establish that esprit de corps and to train the next generation of technicians and carpenters. Colleges knew they could rely on SI for reliable people for their theatre programs, and many of these people ended up in the profession, such as Dan Michalske '72, Ken Ryan '78 and Brendan Quigley '78.

"Peter Devine encouraged us to learn the traditions of the backstage," added Quattrin. "You treat new people well, and you train them to take your place. He taught us that the theatre was there before us and that it would be there after we left. It was our job to leave it in better shape for the next crew. His philosophy fit right in to the Ignatian mission and vision. He encouraged us to give everything we had to something bigger than us. It's not about glory or about needing people to tell you how important you are."

The crew did enjoy playing pranks during the shows. During *The King and I*, actors portray a scene from *Uncle Tom's Cabin* where Eliza runs away from Simon Legree. "The music sounded just like the music from *Jaws*," recalled Quattrin. "We built a shark fin and ran it across the stage just as Eliza runs across the ice. Only 10 of us knew of the prank, including the lighting people, who put a spotlight on the fin as it raced along the stage. The orchestra burst into laughter, and even Pete Devine loved it."

Quattrin returned to SI's back stage in 1981 as the technical director for *Oliver* and worked the following year on *Bells Are Ringing*. In 1983 he helped Bart Sher '77 with *Working* and later, in 1984, he assisted with *110 in the Shade*. He also worked as a lighting designer, set designer and sound designer over the years, and he teaches students how to hang and focus lights and how to build sets. "There have been so many kids who have moved me with how much they have grown," he added. "Peter had a way of guiding kids to us who needed a place to belong." Quattrin did his part, too, asking his football players to help with the spring musical to move sets. "They would discover how much fun it is and stay."

The Costumers

Jean Wolf, mother of SI Grad Steve Wolf '63 and Katie Wolf (SI faculty since 1978), headed the SI costume department for 19 years, starting in 1961 with *High Button Shoes*, directed by Fr. Fred Tollini, SJ '52. She began designing for Fr. Richard McCurdy's productions of

Jean Wolf puts the finishing touches on Peter Devine's costume in 1966.

HMS *Pinafore, Journey's End,* and *Little Mary Sunshine* when SI boys still played the women's roles. When SI received permission for girls to be in the productions, Jean continued designing the costumes, and her daughter, Katie, was in the first coed cast of *Charley's Aunt* in the fall of 1964. Her final production was for the fall 1979 production of *Death of a Salesman.* Some of her most notable shows include *Fiddler on the Roof, Oklahoma, Teahouse of the August Moon, Carnival, Hello, Dolly! The King and I, Rainmaker* and *Luther.*

Rod Arriaga led CSF at SI and as state president.

Nelia Schubert, the mother of Sergio Schubert '81, began costume design with SI's first production of *My Fair Lady* to celebrate the school's 125th anniversary. She continued designing costumes from 1980 thru 1999. Nelia was born and raised in Italy, but moved to Brazil after WWII where she met and married her husband, a refugee from Communist Czechoslovakia. She worked in semi-professional theatre costumes there for several years before she and her husband came to San Francisco where their son was born. When he became involved in theatre through the stage crew, she decided to assist Jean and then became the designer for the next 19 years. She especially enjoyed designing period costumes and designed and constructed more than 100 medieval costumes for SI's production of *Camelot* — each designed and sewn by her hands alone. Among her most notable productions were *Camelot, My Fair Lady,* *Adventures of Nicholas Nickelby, Cyrano de Bergerac, Cabaret, Man for All Seasons, Secret Garden, 1776, Mack and Mabel, Man of La Mancha* and *Evita.*

California Scholarship Federation

In the 1980s CSF turned into one of the more dynamic organizations on the SI campus thanks, in large measure, to its adviser, Rod Arriaga, who took charge of the organization at the start of the decade. In 1980, a group of students approached Arriaga wanting to become more involved in the school. Arriaga and a delegation of students soon began attending meetings with other San Francisco CSF chapters, which led, in turn, to field trips, college visits and student exchanges.

At SI, the group kept active by tutoring students both at school and at the adjacent A.P. Giannini Middle School, and members raised funds through Candygrams, car washes and dances for scholarships given to graduating Life Members. CSF members also organized blanket and clothing drives for St. Anthony's and started an end-of-the-year awards-night that featured a guest speaker to honor Life Members. By the end of the decade, between 40 and 50 percent of the student body qualified as members and more than 90 percent of those enrolled in the club.

"CSF's motto is 'Scholarship for Service,'" said Arriaga. "It's a secular organization, but its aim is wonderfully consistent with what we do as Jesuit educators and with Ignatian philosophy. We take those who are academically distinguished, acknowledge accomplishments and encourage them to give back to their communities. Promoting all of this in a place such as SI was a natural."

State CSF officials were so impressed by Arriaga's

achievements that, in 1985, they asked him to serve as a member (and later chairman) of the Seymour Memorial Awards Committee, and in 1989 he began a 6-year stint as CSF state president (two years as president elect, two years as president and two years as past president). From 1995 to 1997, he served as the group's historian and archivist and then retired as CSF adviser at SI in 2001 and from teaching in 2005. Carol Quattrin now serves as moderator, carrying on the traditions established by her predecessor.

And All the Rest

Aside from all the activities already mentioned, students could join a host of other clubs. The roster from the 1980s included all the traditional ones previously mentioned as well as ethnic clubs (AAAS, ALAS, ASC & the Irish Club), Amnesty International, Art and Publicity, the Dance Committee, the CB Club, the Sci-Fi/Fantasy Club, Dungeons and Dragons, the Pro Life Club, Sailing, Bowling, the Surf Club, Musical Theatre Workshop, Cheerleaders, Pep Band, the Movie Club, the TV Club, the Computer Club, Peace and Social Justice, the Rally Committee, the Liturgy Group, the Military Service Club, the Pep Band, Big Brothers, Junior Statesmen of America, the Model UN, the Young Republicans, the Democratic Youth Rally, the Hockey Club, 8-Ball Society, Club Med, the Dart Club, the Chess Club, the Spirit Club, the Card Club, the Ski Club, the Young Entrepreneur Club, Wrestling, the Bike Team, the French Club, the Italian Club, the Wilderness Club, the Hiking Club, the Science Club and a few others of limited duration, such as the Film Makers' Club, the Pun and Hibachi Club, the Backgammon Club, the Dred Society, the Python Club (made up of wrestling fans), the Elvis is King Club and the Deep Club whose origins and purpose are a mystery.

Awareness Days

SI set aside one day each year from 1985 to 1987 and again in 1995 as an Awareness Day, with each event dedicated to one issue. They focused on, in order, the arms race, drug abuse, racism, and tolerance. The days proved popular with students who, aside from appreciating the break from classes, spent the day listening to speakers and talking about issues that went to the heart of their Jesuit education.

The Pope Comes to Town

On September 17 and 18, 1987, Pope John Paul II made a historic visit to San Francisco and celebrated Mass at Candlestick Park. More than 120 SI students and a host of faculty served as volunteers for the event as ushers, traffic directors, security assistants, schedule coordinators, resident experts and entertainers during the two-day visit.

Two weeks before the event, Msgr. Jim McKay called Block Club moderator Robert Vergara asking for 40 student volunteers to help direct traffic. A week later, Vergara received a request for an additional 12 students to assist police at six security stations. Vergara, with only 28 members in his club, solicited help from the freshmen class and "in no time, I had twice as many volunteers as I needed."[17]

An additional 75 students served as ushers as part of a 324-member team made up of local Catholic high school students, organized by SI's Art Cecchin. Br. Draper also helped by leading a 70-member team of priests, nuns and brothers (including a dozen SI priests) who also worked as ushers, helping to seat 3,000 priests and religious for a prayer service in the Cathedral. In addition, SI faculty David Mezzera and Michael Shaughnessy acted as experts for media covering the event, and one SI student and two alumni (Dan Guiney '88, Dan Linehan '83 and Brendan Kenneally '82) performed Irish dance for the Pope at the Candlestick Park Mass.

The night before this performance, the Pope celebrated a liturgy at the cathedral for diocesan priests and members of religious orders. Br. Draper spent six hours before the event as head usher, and before the Mass, he and a friend went downstairs for a quick smoke. (He has since quit smoking.)

As they chatted and smoked, they saw a lone figure round the corner of the room they were in. It was Pope John Paul II. "He looked at us and said, 'Fuma! Fuma!'" recalled Br. Draper. "My friend quickly put out his cigarette. However, I knew he smoked, so I went up to him and asked him if he wanted a cigarette. He nodded, and I offered him one of mine. Then he said, 'I only smoke Camels,' and left us there. Later, after Mass, the Archbishop introduced me to him as the prefect of discipline at SI. He told me, 'Stay with it. The children are our future.'"

Earthquake

On Tuesday, October 17, 1989, at 5:04 p.m., a 7.1 earthquake hit the Santa Cruz area, sending shockwaves through the Bay Area and killing 63 people. Fr. Prietto was jogging at the time and recalls that "the jolt of the earthquake was so strong it literally knocked me off my feet." Power went out all over the city, including SI, which was spared significant damage. (A few books fell from bookshelves in the library and several glass beakers broke in the labs.) Three high-rise towers in Parkmerced did not prove as fortunate, and residents had to be evacuated. Capt. Michael Yalon '66, then in charge of the Taraval Police Station, told Sgt. Matthew Perez to find shelter for these residents. He told him, "Try SI."

Sgt. Perez drove to SI, and Br. Draper spoke to him from the balcony of McGucken Hall. "I asked him if we could house 150 people at SI," said Perez. "Br. Draper said, 'Of course.' With that, my dispatcher radioed in and asked if we had any power out there. I looked up at Brother and he looked back at me. Just then the lights went on all over the school and the neighborhood. It was absolutely amazing. It was like a miracle."[18]

"I can't believe how SI bent over backwards to help these people," said Sgt. Perez. "We thought they would open their hearts to the homeless, and they did." For Br. Dan Peterson, SJ, the minister of the Jesuit community, the decision to close the school to help these people was an easy one. "People needed the shelter, and we had the facility. Of course we were going to open up to them. I didn't have to think twice about it."

When Sgt. Perez went to the Parkmerced towers, he faced a new problem: They elderly residents there did not want to leave. Because many of them played Bingo at SI, the police asked Br. Draper to drive to Parkmerced. "When I arrived there, the police introduced me as the Bingo Brother from SI. They told the Parkmerced residents that they would sleep in the same place where they played Bingo. Only then did they agree to leave."[19]

School was suspended for one week while students and faculty aided the Red Cross and St. Vincent de

Paul over the next four days to shelter and feed 200 Parkmerced residents in the Carlin Commons. (The Commons was one of three shelters used by city residents in the aftermath of the Loma Prieta Earthquake.)

Br. Peterson drove through darkened streets to bring cots from the Red Cross and St. Vincent de Paul offices back to SI, and he directed student volunteers to make all parts of the SI campus available to SI's newest residents. Community Service Director David Mezzera '64 and Fr. Robert Walsh, SJ '68, in residence at SI, spent the night with the homeless, offering support and comfort. Also, members of SI's Bread Connection made runs that night to local food markets that opened their shelves and sent donated items to the McGucken Hall kitchen to feed the temporary residents for the next week.

SI students Mike Cogliandro '93, John Vito '90, Rob Newsom '91, Andrew Nielsen '92, John McConneloug '91, Benny Wong '92 and Mark Beering '92 were among dozens of students who mopped floors, folded blankets, sorted food and clothing donations and ran errands for the Parkmerced residents. Alumni also pitched in, including Ken Ross '79, George Torassa '77 and Jeff McDonnell '84.

Among the many faculty who came to SI to help was Jim McGarry, who rushed back to SI Tuesday night from a senior retreat. He and Assistant Campus Minister Peter Devine returned to call the parents of the retreatants to tell them their boys were fine.

By Thursday, the number of people needing shelter fell to 80, and by Friday at noon, the Parkmerced

residents began moving back into their apartments after city engineers ruled them structurally safe. By 3 p.m., the last SI guest, an elderly woman, boarded the MUNI bus used to shuttle residents back to their apartments. "I helped her get on the bus," Br. Draper recalled. "She said to me, 'If we're still here on Monday, I'll see you at Bingo, Bingo priest.' Then she kissed me. I was weary but happy that it was finally over."[20]

The Murder of the Priests

On November 16, 1989, Salvadoran soldiers murdered six Jesuits and their two co-workers at the University of Central America during that country's civil war. Dick Howard '67, then a Jesuit priest, was one of the first on the scene the

Class of 1992 members Benny Wong, Andrew Nielsen and Mark Beering were among the SI volunteers who helped at the Carlin Commons shelter after the Loma Prieta Earthquake.

morning after the shooting. "I couldn't believe it," he said in a *Genesis II* interview.[21] "I knew all of them.... I went to see the bodies and identified them. Then the

From left, Fr Carlin, Archbishop Quinn, Fr. Prietto, Fr. Kolvenbach, Fr. Sauer and Bishop Sevilla.

provincial asked me to tell the archbishop." One of the first reporters on scene was Phil Bennett '77, who, at the time, was the Latin-American correspondent for *The Boston Globe*. (He is now the managing editor of *The Washington Post*.) Bennett recalls running into another journalist who had heard "a report that eight people had been killed overnight. I drove up to UCA and walked through the back gate to the Jesuit residence, probably the same gate the killers had come through. There I saw five bodies lying on the lawn by the back of the study center where the rectory was, and I saw the other three bodies inside. After four years of working in war zones, this was the most gruesome scene I had ever witnessed. There was a

sense of real desecration."

Two of the six priests, Ignacio Ellacuría, SJ (rector of the Jesuit community at UCA), and Ignacio Martín-Baró, SJ, were among "the smartest people in the country, and their killers silenced two of the strongest voices in El Salvador," said Bennett. "These were powerful intellects, and their murder left us all feeling vulnerable."[22]

The SI community reacted with shock and sadness to these killings. The Friday after the murder, Fr. Andrew Sotelo, SJ, dedicated the Friday Morning Liturgy at SI to the slain men and women. The next Monday, a busload of SI students and teachers went to San Francisco's Federal Building to participate in a prayer vigil. At the end of the school year, SI presented the President's Award to Fr. Jon Sobrino, SJ, a colleague of the slain priests, who was also targeted for assassination. He survived only because he was out of the country that night.

Fr. Sobrino returned to SI on November 30, 1992, to speak to the student body. Fr. Sauer, who had studied philosophy under him in St. Louis in the 1960s, introduced him as the "living embodiment of the hopes and aspirations of the 80,000 El Salvadoran people killed in a decade of civil war, and of a nation's poor, striving for a just society." Sobrino's talk, according to Fr. Prietto, was one of the most powerful statements on justice ever offered at SI.

In 1999, SI students and faculty began taking part in protests first at the Pentagon in Washington, D.C., and later at the U.S. Army School of the Americas, based in Fort Benning, Georgia, which trained some of the officers responsible for the deaths of the Jesuits and thousands of other innocent people. Each year, the Jesuit Assistancy in the U.S. asks that every Jesuit high school and college send a delegation to participate in the protest, held in November on the anniversary of the martyrdom of the Jesuits. A highlight of this protest is the Ignatian Family Teach-In, which draws a crowd of 2,000 to listen to speakers address human rights concerns. SI, to this day, continues to attend these gatherings to urge Congress to close the school, and, since 2003, the SI student-faculty contingent has met with a dozen SI alumni who attend the event as representatives from their colleges. "Our students see the legacy of Ignatian education here," said SI religious studies teacher Mary Ahlbach, who helps to organize the SI delegation. "This event tells me that there is reason to hope and that our efforts are worth it."

Fr. Kolvenbach Visits SI

For the second time in SI's history, the Superior General of the Society of Jesus came to visit. (The first was a 1971 visit by Fr. Pedro Arrupe, SJ.) Fr. Peter-Hans Kolvenbach, SJ, Fr. General of the Jesuits, toured high schools and colleges in the California Province between November 28 and December 2, 1989, stopping by SI on December 1 where he spoke about the school's move to coeducation, the martyrdom of the priests in El Salvador and the rich diversity of the SI student body. Among the dignitaries who came to SI for the event were San Francisco Archbishop John Quinn, Auxiliary Bishop Carlos Sevilla, SJ '53, and California Provincial Paul Belcher, SJ.

As Fr. Kolvenbach entered the Commons, he was greeted by an 8-foot-by-6-foot mural-collage painted by students in Katie Wolf's art class, made up of 48 1-square-foot sections, with each section painted by a different student. That piece is now on permanent display at SI in the walkway between the Commons and the Jesuit residence.

In his address, Fr. Kolvenbach told the students that he was impressed by the cheer, "We are SI." "In loss it asks you to look beyond the defeat to your greater unity, and in victory — which I hope is often — it reminds you more than a win of any individual team, your genuine spirit is found again in your spiritual unity and in the rich diversity of your many clubs, sports and activities. Indeed, with the recent, welcome move to coeducation, diversity is ever more the hallmark of your school."

The Fight Against AIDS

In the 1980s, the AIDS epidemic struck the U.S. with a vengeance, with ground zero in San Francisco. Two SI grads, over the years, have

Dr. Eric Goosby '70 led the fight against AIDS in the 1990s.

led the fight against this terrible disease — Dr. Eric Goosby '70 and Dr. Joseph O'Neill '71 — as AIDS Czars in the Clinton and Bush administrations.

In the 1980s, Dr. Goosby worked as an assistant professor at UCSF and in the AIDS Oncology Division at San Francisco General Hospital as Director of the Human Immunodeficiency Virus/Intravenous Drug Using Clinic. He discovered new methods for treating HIV-infected intravenous drug users before becoming, in 1991, director of HIV Services at the U.S. Public Health Service/Health Resources and Service Administration. Three years later, he became director of the Office of HIV/AIDS Policy in the Department of Health and Human Services where he fought for HIV/AIDS prevention, treatment and research. In 1997, while still with the HHS, he acted as interim director of the National AIDS Policy Office at the White House, reporting directly to President Clinton as his senior advisor on HIV-related issues. He later served as deputy director of the National AIDS Policy Office in the White House before moving back to the Bay Area where he now works as CEO of the Pangaea Global AIDS Foundation.

Dr. O'Neill took on the job of Director of the Office of National AIDS Policy in July 2002, and he has worked to influence President Bush's agenda in the fight against this disease. He helped to secure $15 billion to combat AIDS in African and Caribbean countries. This desire to stem the pandemic abroad came after O'Neill visited Africa in 1996, seeing firsthand the effects of this disease. In addition, he spends his Fridays treating HIV infected patients at the Johns Hopkins University School of Medicine's free clinic. He does this, in part, to draw attention to the fact that the disease targets the poorest Americans who make up the majority of the 40,000 people who

contract this disease each year in the U.S.

O'Neill's two brothers are both Jesuit priests and SI grads: Fr. Tom O'Neill, SJ '74, who teaches fine arts at USF and is chairman of SI's Board of Trustees, and Fr. William O'Neill '70, who teaches theology at the Jesuit School of Theology in Berkeley. Also, Dr. O'Neill's parents, Margaret and Bill, are members of SI's Heritage Society.

The Old School Comes Down

Some SI alumni cringed in disbelief and others were first in line on March 13, 1987, when USF announced the Wrecker's Ball to demolish Loyola Hall, the site of the fifth SI campus on Stanyan Street. The college wanted to tear down the old school to make way for the Koret Health and Recreation Center. USF sent out invitations offering a "sledgehammer concession outside the old building for those of you who would like to take one last swipe at the former SI." The evening also offered a silent auction of building memorabilia, though the most valuable item, the bench that graced the outside of the dean's office (on which many penitent Ignatians sat waiting for an ominous interview) went to SI, thanks to a winning bid by Board Chairman Bill McDonnell '42, who donated it to the school.

Fr. Paul Capitolo, SJ, and Bob Vergara also managed to salvage a door with a frosted glass window featuring an etched cross, stained glass windows and an altar triptych oil painting from the old school. The first item became the entrance to the Jesuit community chapel in McGucken Hall and the latter two were used to decorate the faculty dining room in the Jesuit residence.

Opposite page: USF knocked down the Stanyan Street school to make way for the Koret Recreational and Health Center.

Phyllis Molinelli

Phyllis Molinelli started working at SI in 1978 as a secretary for counseling, campus ministry and student activities. In 1983 she became a sophomore counselor and has, over the years, served as department chair and head of various counseling task forces. She retired in 2005.

When I first started working at SI, I felt like a mother to all the students. I was in heaven because I am a mother, and boys have a tendency to invite you to mother them. I used to bake cakes for kids when they had birthdays. It was a smaller school then, and the teachers knew every student.

The atmosphere was also more relaxed than today. We used to string popcorn and cranberries for the school Christmas tree. The faculty used to play practical jokes on each other. Frank Corwin and Bill Love used to put frogs in the detention box to scare whoever was doing detention. One day Katie Robinson and I rearranged furniture in the faculty lounge to resemble an airplane, with Frank Corwin and J.B. Murphy as pilots, with their chairs in the front.

Adding women to the faculty has tempered the male energy and has calmed the storm. Students are more comfortable expressing affection for one another. People hug each other and hold hands, and the guys don't hesitate to offer a hug at Mass during the sign of peace. When we were an all-male school, that just wasn't done.

I was in Steve Phelps social sciences/history class as a freshman (1978-1979). Steve was talking about guerilla warfare, and I asked if that had anything to do with monkeys. That question got me a detention.

I took Fr. Dodd for Homeric Greek, and one of my classmates, who was not doing well in the class, tried to bribe him with a bottle of Greek wine. I reminded Fr. Dodd, "Never trust a Greek bearing gifts."

I attended college at Loyola Marymount University with a pre-med and chemistry major. One of the required courses was a physics laboratory. Predictably, the midterm test was very difficult. A couple of days later, classmates in another section came up to me and congratulated me. I asked them to explain. The instructor said that I earned the high score on the exam. He explained that people criticize American education, but that I was an exception because I had attended SI and studied Latin and Greek.

Latin is actually very useful in the medical profession, despite being a "dead language." During a pre-med course in alcohol/drug studies, the instructor asked what NPO meant. I reflexively responded, "*Nihil per orum.*" After observing a puzzled look on her face, I translated, "the patient can't eat or drink anything."

Fr. Harrington taught me the classical pronunciation of Latin (1978–1979). We learned it so well that I cringed when I heard Ecclesiastical Latin pronounced. During medical school, we studied myasthenia gravis, a neurological disorder. Classmates didn't understand me when I pronounced the letter "v" in gravis as a "w." We proceeded to have a discussion about the merits of classical Latin as opposed to Ecclesiatical Latin. I still pronounce the disorder as "myasthenia grawis."

Opposite page: The pioneer Class of 1993 in their senior year by the old pressbox.

XIII. Focus on the Faculty (1990 ~ 1999)

The decade of the 1990s could be split into two halves. For the first half, the school worked to smooth the transition from a single-sex to a coeducational institution, with the last all-male class graduating in June 1992. Students and faculty saw change everywhere — from the new buildings rising up on the south end of the campus to changes in program and personnel. In the latter half, the faculty found new opportunities for growth in the Professional Development Program that has become a model for schools in California and for the 47 Jesuit high schools across the nation.

The '90s also saw a change in leadership with the departure of Fr. Prietto, the arrival of Steve Nejasmich '65 and the promotion of SI's first lay principal, Charlie Dullea '65.

Academically, the school enjoyed remarkable success, especially with Advanced Placement tests. SI ranked among the top 20 schools in the nation in terms of the number of tests students took and passed, and students continued to find entry into the nation's top colleges.

They found success in other venues, too. Campus Ministry flourished in the 1990s with the creation of the Immersion Program, which sent juniors all over the world to experience life in Third World communities. The senior retreat program changed formats to a Kairos experience, and the retreat program grew at every class level.

Thanks to coeducation, new athletic traditions began at SI with the creation of the field hockey and softball teams and with girls forming volleyball, soccer, basketball, tennis, swimming, water polo, lacrosse, track and field, cross country, crew and golf teams. The decade also saw SI's first athletic national championship when the boys' crew took gold medals in Cincinnati in 1997 and three state championships. The girls' crew also excelled, winning two state titles.

The boys' cross country team brought home a state championship in 1996 — only the second time any SI team had ever done so. The boys also won the league title four times and the CCS title three times. The girls' cross country team turned in 10 straight league victories between 1991 and 2000 and six sectional titles, a remarkable achievement.

The boys' lacrosse team won the state championship three years running, from 1999 to 2001 as well as league titles in 1990 through 1992, and the girls' team won its league five straight years, from 1997 through 2001. Basketball continued to generate excitement with the boys earning league crowns and a CCS championship in 1998. A young girls' program proved its strength from the start, taking two CCS titles. A host of other sports also enjoyed tremendous success, from basketball, softball, tennis, swimming, soccer, field hockey and volleyball, each winning league or sectional championships.

Opposite page: Members of the Class of 1999 along with Br. Draper at the Baccalaureate Mass.

Genesis III Capital Campaign

Before SI went coed, it had a student body of around 1,100 boys. After coeducation began, enrollment soared to 1,450 boys and girls. When the trustees voted to allow girls, they knew they would have to build to accommodate the larger and more diverse population.

In planning for the construction, the development office hired a consulting firm to help determine the scope of the project. That firm advised the school against aiming for the $16 million mark, believing it was too high. Fortunately, the development staff ignored the advice and went ahead, launching, on December 1, 1990, the Genesis III: Building for the Future capital campaign — a $16 million fund-raising drive to pay for a new theatre, pool, garage, tennis courts and gym and to remodel the Student Activities Center, the first and third floors of the school and the campus ministry center.

The school hired the architecture firm of Corlett, Skaer and DeVoto Architects and put much of the planning in the hands of Randy DeVoto '68. DeVoto's firm had designed the Glen Park and Balboa Park BART stations, the 1960 Winter Olympics facility at Squaw Valley and educational and government buildings throughout California.

DeVoto had to figure out a way to allow for construction with minimal disruption to classes and extracurricular events. He split the project into three phases, the first involving the construction of a parking garage at the southern end of the campus with four rooftop tennis courts, with work beginning in 1989. The second phase included the remodeling of the first and third floors of the school building, the student activities center and the campus ministry center. For the final and largest phase, the school hoped to build a second gym, a pool and a black box theatre. The project also involved updating the library, science labs, energy conservation system and the interior corridor.

DeVoto hoped his redesign would reorient the campus around an interior pedestrian circulation spine that would allow students to reach every part of the campus without having to go outside the school. "We accomplished this by demolishing a classroom at the south end of the first floor of the academic building and extending the existing corridor through it," said DeVoto. "This new extended corridor, which connected to the new student center, served as a hub for students to gather."

To raise funds for this project, the school asked Steve Lovette '63 to make a move from the south end of the campus, where he served as assistant principal for academics, to a new office at the north end of campus as the school's vice president for development. In his 15 years in the Development Office, Lovette has led the school through two successful campaigns including Genesis IV: Endow SI, which brought the school's endowment to the $50 million mark. Both

Frs. Sauer and Carlin, along with Bill McDonnell, Pete Murphy and architect Randy De-Voto launch Genesis III.

Fr. Prietto and Fr. Sauer praise him for his unfailing loyalty to the school, the professionalism with which he performs his job and the intelligence and foresight he has shown in preparing SI for the challenges of the new millennium.

Assisting Lovette and Fr. Sauer was a new Development team that formed in the late 1980s. In 1987, Paul Totah '75 (the author of this book) began editing the *Genesis* magazine, and two years later Jim Dekker '68 took over as Alumni Director. Bob Graby, a foreign language teacher and counselor, joined the staff to write grants, and Stella Muscat was hired to oversee all special events, such as the auction and President's Cabinet Dinner. Shirley Minger, Katie Kohmann and Concie Tarantino continue to do a remarkable job helping as part of the Development staff.

Leading the drive for funds was Martin D. "Pete" Murphy '52, senior partner of Tobin & Tobin and president of the law firm. As chairman of the Board of Regents between 1991 and 1996, he made sure that SI would earn enough money to pay for the facilities it needed. Murphy, who served as chairman of the Genesis III: Building for the Future capital campaign, was aided by assistant chairman Jay Fritz, honorary chairman Al Wilscy and the entire Board of Regents. Before the school announced the $16 million campaign, these men raised $2.5 million from the members of the Board of Regents in 1989. "The regents came through because they believed in the school," said Murphy. "They made fund-raising easier when people saw the level of support coming from those regents."

Key to financing the project was a $7 million line of credit from Wells Fargo, secured thanks to Wells' Chairman Carl Reichardt, President Paul Hazen and Senior Vice President Paul Watson '57. Fortunately, too, for SI, the construction industry was in a lull. For the largest and final phase, seven companies bid, with

Webcor turning in the lowest figure at $7 million, a full $2 million under the architect's estimate. Webcor finished on time and with no cost overruns. "We couldn't have built at a better time," said Murphy.

"When we started, the $16 million figure seemed like $600 million," Murphy added. "The school had never raised that much money that quickly. But we finished with only a small amount of disruption to the school, and we ended up raising close to $20 million, giving us a jump start on the next campaign to increase the endowment. I've run four capital

The third phase of construction included a second gymnasium, pool and black box theatre.

campaigns in my life, and this was the best. We had a real spirit of optimism. Much of that credit goes to the SI community. People really care about the school."

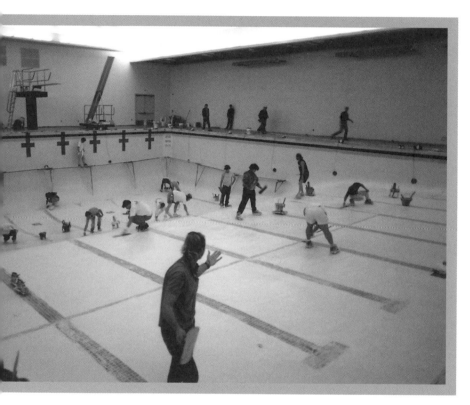

Workers put the finishing touches on the Herbst Natatorium. Opposite page: Photo by Douglas A. Salin.

Murphy could have stayed on longer as board chairman, but he believed the regents needed new blood and stepped down in 1996. The school, grateful for his counsel and leadership, asked him in 1998 to become one of the first lay members of a reorganized Board of Trustees, and he has served the school in that capacity and as a lifetime member of the Board of Regents since then.

Assisting Murphy through his years at SI was his wife, Joanne, who served as chairwoman of an Ignatian Guild fashion show, created the first International Food Faire and chaired the groundbreaking ceremony in 1989. Murphy is also proud of his long association with the Jesuits. He spent 11 years in Jesuit schools — four at SI, four at SCU and three at USF law school — and his three sons (Martin '84, John '86 and Pat '91) are all SI grads.

From Groundbreaking to Christening

April 22, 1990, was a landmark day at SI for several reasons. First, the Ignatian world celebrated the 500th anniversary of the birth of St. Ignatius Loyola and the 450th anniversary of the founding of the Society of Jesus. And at SI, a steam shovel broke ground in the parking lot to begin the first phase of the Genesis III building project. The day began with a procession of students, faculty and administrators down 37th Avenue. Comedian Bob Sarlatte '68 served as emcee and offered humorous commentary as each dignitary took a golden shovel and broke ground. After the backhoe dug up the first shovelful of dirt, Archbishop John Quinn, flanked by Frs. Sauer and Carlin, blessed the site, and Frank Corwin, who would retire that June, spoke at the ceremony. The success of the event foreshadowed the success of the entire building project.

By October 1990, the $1.4 million four-court tennis facility, built by the Amoroso Corporation, sat atop the new student parking complex, completing the first phase of the project. (The four courts were named for the Brusati, Christen, Kelleher and Kitt families.) Work then progressed to the second phase, which

Douglas A. Salin

Douglas A

included a newly remodeled campus ministry center (named for the Nejasmich family) on the north end of the campus. Most of the first floor of the school enjoyed a makeover, with a new Fine Arts Wing (named for the Barbara and Jay Fritz Family) emerging on the southwest corner of the campus complete with a sculpture studio and display cases. Workers built a roof over the student activities center, where the bookstore, yearbook and athletic offices were, and created one of the most attractive centers in the school, complete with skylights and arches. To remake this center, the Herrera Bros. Construction Company had to tear down a load-bearing wall between the school and the center, opening up the campus and allowing for one long breezeway between the southern and northern ends (now called the Ann Eve and Paul Hazen Student Concourse). Workers completed this $2.2 million project in 1992. That year also marked the graduation of the last all-male class, the beginning of a completely coeducational school, and the start of the third and final phase of the building project.

For years, SI students joked about a rooftop swimming pool. (A typical senior prank was to sell fourth floor pool passes to freshmen to this fabled oasis.) In September 1992, work began in earnest on a pool, one named for the Herbst Foundation. It would serve the SI and San Francisco communities as both a school facility and a public natatorium. Webcor Builders also began construction on a new gym (later named for Barbara and Robert McCullough '48) that would seat 2,650 and allow for two full-court practice sessions. That third phase, costing $12.3 million, also included a theatre (named for the E.L. Wiegand Foundation), a fine arts pavilion (named for Mr. & Mrs. Martin D. "Pete" Murphy) and a remodeled library (named for Alfred S. Wilsey).

The SI administration also decided to spend an additional $1.2 million to remodel the third floor science labs (later named the Spohn Science Center in honor of famed physics teacher Fr. Richard Spohn, SJ) to double the space available for labs. The school then repaved the track and named it in honor of Jack Wilsey '34, who had captained his high school track team.

The school formally dedicated the new buildings and the newly remodeled science labs at the President's Cabinet Dinner on December 11, 1993, though the pool and gym would not formally open until March 30, 1994. At the spring ceremony, Matt McCabe '67, a former SI swimmer, brought a 5-gallon glass jug containing water from Fleishhacker Pool that he collected shortly before that pool was demolished. Over the years, he filled that container with $100 in silver coins and gave it to Fr. Sauer to pour into SI's new pool. At a rally before the entire student body, Fr. Sauer showed off that bottle and announced that he would unite two Sunset district pools, one long past and one quite present. He asked a swim team captain James Fussell '94 to carry that bottle to the pool. A tad out of breath, Fussell put the bottle down a little too quickly, shattering the glass and sending the water and coins slipping, rather unceremoniously, into the pool. Buildings and grounds workers quickly gathered the broken glass, and thus the new pool was christened, marking the end of the Genesis III building project, but not the end of the capital campaign, which still had to raise $4.4 million to pay for the new structures. In what the Development Office termed its "full-court press," the school raised enough funds to pay for Genesis III in full by December 1995. In all, the school raised $15,980,240 in five years to ready the Sunset District campus to meet the challenges of the new millennium.

Above: A tee-shirt honoring the last all-male class.

Opposite page: The Student Activites Center.

The Legacy of Fr. Prietto

After 13 years at the helm, Fr. Prietto stepped down as principal of SI in June 1994 and received the President's Award at the commencement ceremony. The citation praised him for being "first and foremost, a priest and minister."

Fr. Prietto could look back with pride on how far SI rose in the ranks regarding Advanced Placement testing. In the 1970s and early 1980s, SI did not emphasize those exams. In 1980, for example, only 139 students took an AP exam and, of those, 54 percent passed. When he came into office, Fr. Prietto asked counselor Andy Dworak to serve as AP Coordinator and to place a new emphasis on the program. By 1994, SI's numbers had risen dramatically, with students taking 567 tests and achieving an 88 percent pass rate. Those numbers put SI in the top 50 high schools in the country regarding the number of AP exams offered. In 1999, boys and girls at SI passed 813 tests, ranking SI 19th in the nation in terms of number of tests given and 16th for the number of tests passed. "What made this ranking even more extraordinary is the fact that SI competes with 25,000 schools in the country, some of which have student bodies as large as 4,000," said AP Coordinator Andy Dworak. To this day, the school can point to the AP program as an objective measure of its academic success, and parents can breathe a sigh of relief as students earn college credit while in high school and save thousands of dollars on college tuition.

Opposite page: Students excelled at AP tests during the 1990s, placing SI among the top schools in the nation.

Genesis IV: Endow SI

The SI Development staff rested one year after finishing the Genesis III campaign and launched its most ambitious fund-raising effort in December 1996 — the Genesis IV: Endow SI campaign, which sought to raise the endowment fund to $50 million over 10 years.

By 1996, the endowment stood at $11 million. The school, which depended on interest of that investment to fund the scholarship program, needed to raise the endowment substantially. Fr. Sauer and Steve Lovette did not need a crystal ball to tell them that costs were going up. SI would have to raise salaries to help teachers afford to buy homes in one of the most expensive markets in the nation, and SI would have to offer far more in the way of scholarships to keep SI a school for all students.

Initially, the program sought to increase the endowment for four funds. SI declared a goal to bring the Tuition Assistance Fund to $31.8 million, the Curriculum and Program Fund to $3.7 million, the Excellence in Teaching Fund to $5 million and the Campus Maintenance Fund to $4.5 million. In 2001, the Board of Regents approved the creation of an additional Faculty Housing Fund, with a $5 million goal, making for a grand total of $50 million.

Leading the charge for this new campaign were two men dedicated to SI: John Christen III '61, who succeeded Pete Murphy in 1996, and Mark Cleary '64, who succeeded Christen as chairman of the Board of Regents in 2002. (Read more about Mark Cleary in the next chapter.)

Christen, a one-time math teacher and longtime realtor in San Francisco, joined the Board of Regents in 1989 and served on the finance and executive com-

mittees. He also served as president of the Alumni Association. "The motivation for the campaign was simple," Christen said. "We needed to make sure

The Board of Trustees in 2004. (Missing is Fr. Michael Turnacliff, SJ).

Opposite page: The Jesuit community in 1988.

everyone could afford an SI education, we needed to ensure that the older teachers could retire with dignity, and we needed to help young faculty in a difficult housing market. Based on the success of the Genesis III campaign, we knew we could reach our goal."

That earlier campaign, he added, "planted many seeds that later bore fruit. People seemed happy to donate to the school. Genesis IV was never a hard sell. People understand the value of an endowment fund. In many ways, the sale had already been made." He also praised the Development Office for working "like a well-oiled machine" and the school for offering a top-notch Jesuit education. "SI was in great demand

because people know that it is a wonderful institution that is always seeking to better itself. I'm happy to be associated with the school just for that reason." (Christen's sons — John '89, Anthony '91, Paul '92 and Matthew '94 — all went to SI. He and his late wife, Marilyn, who served as Ignatian Guild president and helped SI in innumerable ways, also have a daughter, Jennifer, who graduated from Convent of the Sacred Heart in 1987.)

Christen praised the efforts of his predecessor, Pete Murphy, as well as Al Wilsey and Bill Barulich. "Bill isn't an SI alumnus, and he sits on the board of another school. But he has done so much for the Jesuits, including helping to sponsor SI's Comedy Night. He, like so many other donors, appreciates what SI has done for his children." After Al Wilsey died, Christen joined the Board of Trustees, the ownership body of the school. "As I grow older, I appreciate even more what SI does. I am proud that the institution is growing and is vibrant."

The Board of Trustees

As part of a worldwide effort by the Society of Jesus to put an indelible Jesuit stamp on its secondary schools and, at the same time, to invite lay people to help run these schools, SI changed in 1998 the make-up and role of its two governing bodies — the Board of Trustees (the ownership body, which oversees the president) and the Board of Regents (which oversees matters pertaining to the principal and his staff).

This change came as a result of the 34th General Congregation — a worldwide gathering of Jesuits — that took place in 1995. At that meeting, the Jesuit delegates, together with Father General Peter-

Hans Kolvenbach, SJ, emphasized the importance of maintaining the Jesuit character of the order's high schools and increasing cooperation with laity. Fr. John Privett, SJ, the head of the California Province at the time, asked the administrators at SI and the other four schools in California and Arizona to consider these priorities in the make-up of their boards of trustees. Toward that end, SI's four-man Board of Trustees voted May 12, 1998, to expand to include lay people.

The board, as of 2005, includes Fr. Thomas O'Neill, SJ '74, as chairman, and Fr. Harry Carlin, SJ, Fr. Michael Gilson, SJ, Fr. Anthony P. Sauer, SJ, and Fr. Michael Turnacliff, SJ, as well as two past regent chairmen — Martin D. "Pete" Murphy and John Christen — and Board of Regents Chairman, Mark Cleary. Fr. Greg Goethals, SJ, who had served on the board since its inception, left the board when he went on sabbatical in 2005.

Before the change, Fr. Kolvenbach voiced his support of the new trustees. "I commend you," he wrote, "for this move towards a greater involvement of lay people in this dimension of our schools." The formation of a Board of Trustees did not in any way diminish the necessary work of the Board of Regents with its myriad committees on which the school's operations depend.

New Opportunities to be Part of SI

In 1995, Principal Steve Nejasmich, SJ, asked English teacher Simon Chiu '88 to resurrect the **Uplift Program** that Steve Phelps had created in the 1970s to encourage students from underrepresented areas of the city to apply to SI by offering them a summer school program in their 7th and 8th grade years. That program's goals shifted in the 1980s when it became Summer Prep. Chiu brought back the name and the original purpose. Dozens of students from this program matriculated to SI as this program continued to grow and succeed.

In 2000, Principal Charlie Dullea hired Emily Behr '93 to head the program, now called **Magis.** It continues to work with low-income and first-generation college bound middle-school students to provide year-round support and preparation for a college prep high school. It supports Magis graduates who attend SI, providing them with tutoring, social and cultural events, positive mentors and role models and individual advocacy. The program helps SI achieve its goal of offering "a preferential option for the poor," which is an intrinsic goal of the Society of Jesus. It also helps provide SI with a richness that comes from ethnic and socio-economic diversity.

As a way of reaching out to SI grads who work downtown, the school's Development Office began sponsoring the **Annual Downtown Business Lunch** on September 26, 1990. State Court of Appeals Judge William Newsom '51 spoke before 130 alumni and friends in the Bank of America building. Later speakers included Wells Fargo President Paul Hazen, author Jerry Posner '72, San Francisco Mayor Gavin Newsom (then a supervisor) and NFL Hall of Famer Dan Fouts '69.

On June 21, 1996, the Alumni Association, under the leadership of John Christen, turned its annual golf tournament into an **All-Class Reunion and Sports Day.** About 170 alumni took part in golf, tennis, basketball or swimming and came to a dinner at the SI Commons. The event has grown each year, with the 2004 event drawing more than 400 for golf, basketball and dinner and the annual

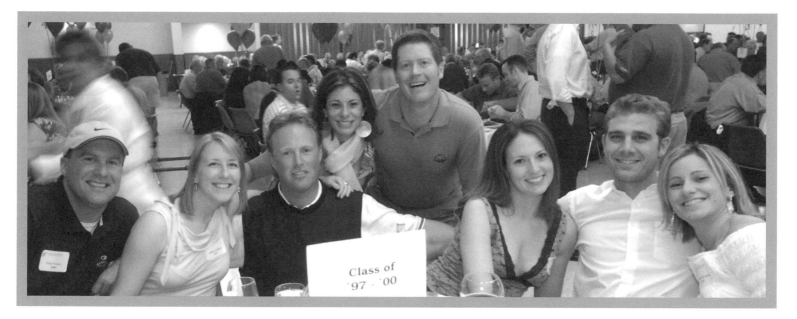

Class of
'97 - '00

bestowing of the "honorary alumnus" status to a worthy recipient.

Alumni and parents also could take part in the school in a new way by visiting **SI's Prep Shop,** inaugurated in 1996 by the Ignatian Guild. The shop offers clothing, buttons, water bottles and decals with SI insignia, and the operation, run entirely by Guild volunteers, has grown over the years. It now sells through the SI bookstore and website and at the various Ignatian Guild and school functions.

That same year, SI launched the **Heritage Society,** made up of individuals who have named the school as a beneficiary in their wills or estates. SI honored the first 30 members of this group with a reception at the Pacific Heights home of Dorothy and Ted Kitt '50 on June 9, 1996. At the gathering, Steve Lovette thanked the members for "discovering dynamic ways

to memorialize family members or to perpetuate their own memories. These people, rather than building monuments to themselves, offer the gift of education to others — one that endures like no other gift and is passed on through the families. Education is the best preventative medicine for society's ills, and these generous people understand that." The group has grown since then and now includes more than 80 families and individuals.

The International Food Faire, sponsored by the Ignatian Guild, has, since 1993, become one of the most popular events of the year. More than 1,000 students, parents and siblings attend this celebration of the diverse cultures of SI with food and entertainment. Each year young Irish dancers perform jigs and reels, Chinese lion dancers amaze audiences with intricate costumes and choreography,

The All-Alumni Reunion brings together grads from all classes each June.

The International Food Faire celebrates SI's diverse cultures.

group exists to assist SI in recruiting students of color and to help them stay and succeed at SI once they enroll. In 2002, under the leadership of executive board members Carmen Jordan-Cox, Anthony Rawls, Lynetta Johnson and Manny Fortes, the group began holding monthly meetings for parents and students to hear speakers, discuss issues or just have fun.

The Immersion Program

In 1990, SI Principal Mario Prietto, SJ, asked the campus ministry staff to intensify its focus on issues of social justice. The campus ministry team responded with an innovative program in the summer of 1992 that sent students and teachers to El Salvador, Mexico and inner-city San Francisco for what would prove to be the first steps of the fledgling Immersion Program. The brainchild of Spanish teacher Susan Ackerman and campus minister Kathleen Purcell, the trips took students to live in community with the poor to expose them to the injustices that cause poverty. Ackerman, a native of Peru, argued that "our students need to accompany people who live in oppression so that we can allow them to teach us, to transform us, to open us to rethinking what are our priorities and responsibilities towards each other."

Since that first summer, hundreds of SI students have spent the summer between their junior and senior years in places such as Peru, Mexico, Guatemala, El Salvador, Appalachia, New Mexico, South-Central Los Angeles, Quebec and Northern Ireland. Fr. Prietto, who went to Guaymas, Mexico, that first year, saw the program as broadening SI's response to issues of civil rights and social justice outside the city of San Francisco. "We needed to become aware of the world outside the U.S.," said Fr. Prietto. "In past years,

and many other performers celebrate their cultures through dance and song.

The **PAAAS** (the Parents of the Association of African American Students) began in early 1990s as a way of helping SI better support African American students. The

we had taught our students about the injustice that exists in our borders concerning women, immigrants, minorities, handicapped, homosexuals and the homeless. Thanks to the Immersion Program, we were able to show our students the substandard conditions that exist in the Third World and have given them the opportunity to learn and serve."

Student-Centered Retreats

Up until the 1960s, only priests served as retreat directors, giving talks and leading discussions. "We never had lay people talk during my senior retreat," said Charlie Dullea. "It was a silent retreat, with a talk by an older priest that we would reflect on. We never had time to discuss our reflections with classmates or other priests. This regimented program was probably the same retreat my father went on in 1937."

In the 1970s, lay faculty, including Dullea, began planning and directing retreats. He recalled trying "to reach kids by talking about their feelings and trying to understand them rather than just preaching to them. We told 'Christ-in-my-life' stories, and many of the students connected more with the young faculty."

The retreat program continued to evolve in the 1990s with the advent of student-led retreats for freshmen, sophomores and juniors. Adults directed senior retreats until 1997 when the school adopted the Kairos retreat structure. By February 2002, the senior retreat grew to comprise four days. (No matter the length or form, the senior retreat continues to be a peak experience for most SI students.) Shaping the retreat program throughout the latter part of the 1990s and the early part of the next decade were Michael Shaughnessy, Michael Gilson, SJ, Rita O'Malley and Sarah Curran.

On March 21, 1996, Bishop Carlos Sevilla, SJ (himself an SI grad), called Fr. Sauer to pass along a request from Archbishop Levada that SI discontinue its Sunday Night Liturgy program. The Archbishop hoped that teenagers would celebrate Mass with their families in their home parishes. Fr. Sauer, who celebrated the March 24 SNL, announced the Archbishop's request to those in attendance and added that SI would comply with the request, thus ending a 25-year tradition. Students continue to attend Friday Morning Liturgies at SI and also have the option of attending 8 a.m. Mass at Jensen Chapel during weekdays.

Students now participate as leaders for all the SI retreats.

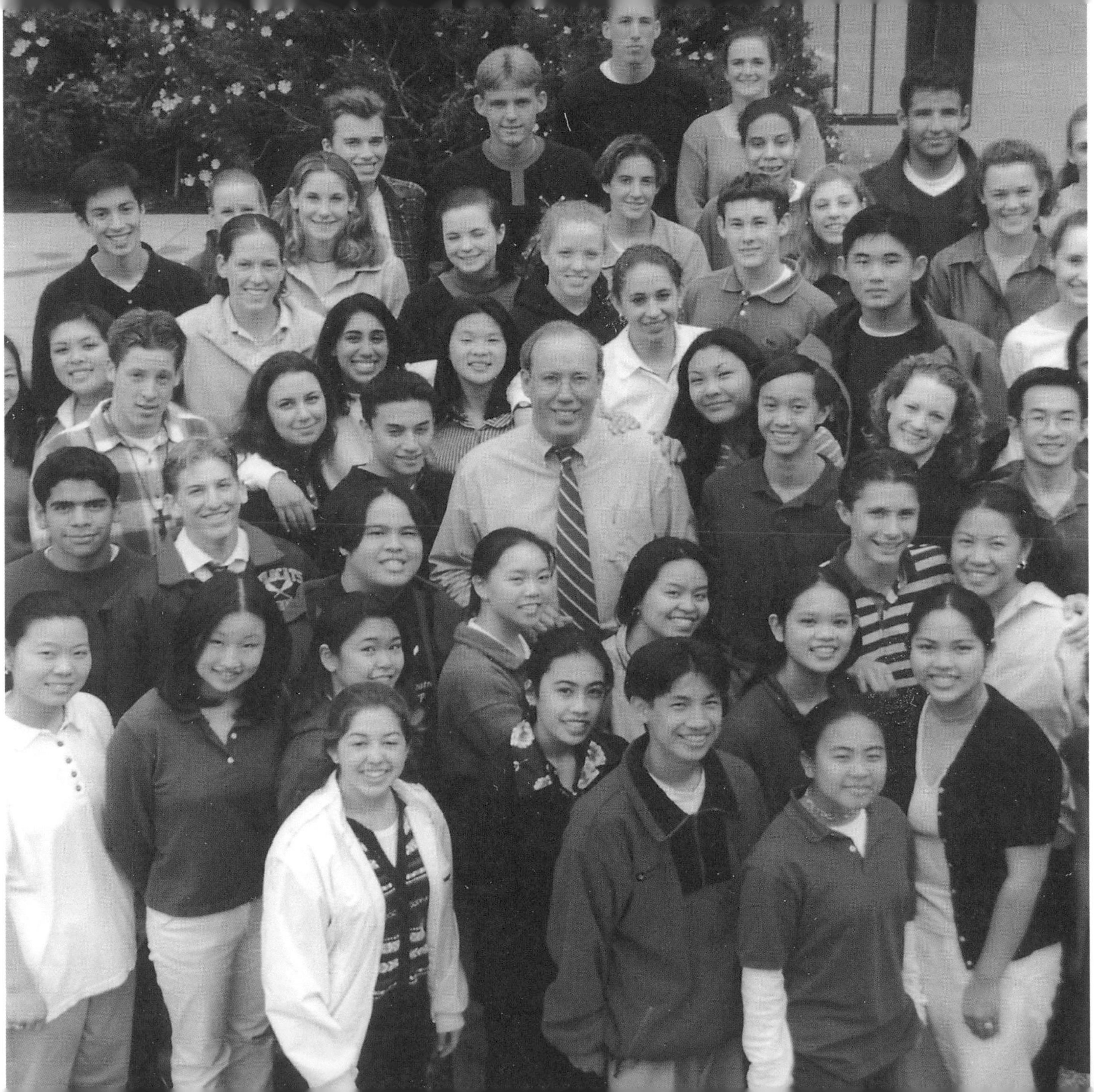

Owen, Julio & Adam

The first coed Class of 1993 attended three funerals for members of the class, the first following the November 28, 1990, death of sophomore Owen Fitzgerald, who suffered a cardiac arrhythmia after collapsing in front of the school. A gifted athlete on the track and basketball teams, Owen was a personable young man, and his death stunned the school.

Then, on November 8, 1992, seniors Adam Powers and Julio Calvo-Perez were killed in a traffic accident on Monterey Boulevard. Alcohol contributed to the accident, and the tragedy served as a heart-breaking wake-up call to the SI community. The counseling department soon began a series of programs designed to educate students and parents about the dangers of drinking. As the school mourned the early deaths of these good men, it also turned a critical eye on itself to see how it could prevent future accidents from occurring. In the years that followed, SI would create a Drug and Alcohol Taskforce, a Community of Concern comprising 43 Northern California schools, an in-house program for drug education and testing, and a breathalyzer policy for school dances. "These programs have been a godsend," said SI counselor Phyllis Molinelli. "For a long time, we did not focus our efforts in these areas, hoping alcohol abuse wouldn't be a problem. But these deaths brought the issue to the surface. We are trying to address these issues as matters concerning health, instead of using fear, and students are helping us by telling us what works."

The First Lay Principal: Charlie Dullea

Steven Nejasmich '65 (then a Jesuit priest) arrived in the fall of 1994 to replace Fr. Prietto as principal. In his three years on the job, he instituted several innovative programs and traditions, including the Fine Arts Assembly, which gave the entire school the opportunity to see student singers, dancers and musicians perform in the McCullough Gymnasium. He also created the position of Director of Professional Development and gave his support to Steve Phelps in that office. He instituted the Transition Liturgy to honor the senior class and mark the junior class's new status as leaders of the school, and he fine-tuned the way department chairs were trained. In November 1997, however, he announced a leave of absence from the Jesuits to revisit his vocation and asked assistant principal for student affairs Charlie Dullea to serve as acting principal.

Dullea had an open-door policy with the students as assistant principal, and that continued after he moved offices. "I think my secretary had a hard time dealing with all the seniors sitting in my office." Dullea formally applied for the job that February and was chosen from among three finalists to lead SI as the first lay principal in the school's 143-year history.

On May 1, before the assembled faculty, Fr. Anthony P. Sauer, SJ, announced Dullea's appointment and praised him for his 26 years at SI where he had worked as chairman of the English department, director of the summer school and assistant principal for student activities.

Dullea, a fifth-generation San Franciscan and a resident of San Carlos, graduated from SI in 1965. Dullea's grandfather, Charles Dullea, served as San

In 1998 Charlie Dullea became the first lay principal of SI.

Francisco's chief of police in the 1940s, and two of his uncles were Jesuit priests: the late Fr. Charles W. Dullea, SJ '34, served as president and chancellor of USF in the 1960s, and Fr. John Dullea '46, is a college counselor at Verbum Dei in Los Angeles. Dullea's father, Edward, graduated from SI in 1937

Members of the swim team shaved their heads in 1999 to support a teammate who had lost her hair after chemotherapy to combat Hodgkin's lymphoma.

and worked in San Francisco as an attorney in private practice.

While the appointment of a lay person marked an historic first for the Sunset District campus, the move was not unusual among the nation's 47 Jesuit high schools. Of those schools, 38 had, at the time, lay principals and three had lay presidents.

After graduating from SI, Dullea received his bachelor's degree from USF in 1969 and then received a commission in the U.S. Army where he served for two years, earning the rank of captain. After his discharge, he received his teaching credential in 1972 and started working at SI that year.

Since the founding of SI, the Jesuit provincial for California had determined who would be principal at the school. In December 1997, Fr. Sauer, in conjunction with the school's Board of Regents, appointed an 11-member search committee, chaired by Mark Cleary '64, that interviewed several candidates for the job. Eventually, the search committee selected three candidates, all of whom met with faculty and students. The search committee then gave the three candidates' names to Fr. Sauer, and he made the final selection.

"I believe Charlie Dullea has the vision, the wisdom and the goodness to continue the good programs of our school and introduce new programs to forward our mission," said Fr. Sauer in his remarks to the faculty.

After his appointment, Dullea said he was "delighted by the new challenge. I know the community well, having come up through the ranks. I've grown up with the institution not only educationally but also spiritually. It will be a wonderful challenge to serve as principal of my alma mater and of a community in which I've invested the majority of my adult life."

His job as principal, he said, "is to keep alive the rich traditions of a school such as St. Ignatius but also to incorporate the innovations that will take us into the 21st century. To do this, my primary focus will be to serve the teachers at SI and to challenge them to be the best in their ministerial profession that they can be."

Dullea's wife, Pattie, is the assistant principal at La Entrada Middle School in Menlo Park, and their daughter, Jennifer, works in human resources for the Gap Corporation. Dullea also has a brother who graduated from SI — Edward Dullea '62 who is retired from the San Francisco Police Department.

Dullea, early on, challenged his teachers not to rest on their laurels but to continue to improve. He started the Excellence in Teaching Program and asked teachers to set and meet a new goal each year while continuing to learn better ways of teaching. "There are more than 100 teachers at SI, and they are in the front line dealing with kids. We expect them to have mastery of their subject, be involved in extracurriculars and develop their spiritual lives." To help them towards the first two of these goals, he asked Steve Phelps to continue in his role as Director of Professional Development. For the third goal, he asked Fr. Greg Goethals, SJ, and Rita O'Malley to form the Adult Ministry Office in 2000.

Kate Kodros

In the spring of 1995, SI promoted Kate Kodros from senior counselor to assistant principal for academics, making her the first woman assistant principal in the California Province high schools. A native of Los Angeles, Kodros attended Immaculate Heart High School and Santa Clara University where she earned her Bachelor's degree in history. She taught at St. Rose Academy from 1976 to 1988 before coming to SI and took over the assistant principal's job when Tom Murphy '76 moved to Rockhurst High School in Kansas City, Missouri, to serve as principal there.

"She has been the right person in the right job for SI," said Steve Phelps, the director of SI's professional development office. "She has modeled professionalism, emotional maturity, confidentiality and collaborative leadership skills. She, as much as anyone, has been responsible for the strong and effective voice of women in every area of the school. Her goal has been that every single teacher and curriculum be excellent for every student. It is no accident that under her watch curriculum, instruction and professional development at SI have earned local, national and international respect."

Kodros had a direct hand in helping teachers develop curriculum and translate that coursework into better teaching. She has helped teachers understand that lecturing for 50 minutes no longer works, and that students learn best when teachers incorporate data from research regarding the functioning of the human brain into their classrooms. "Students remember best what they hear at the beginning and end of a class," said Kodros. "Teachers know the value of making connections between current and past lessons and of personalizing the material for their students."

Kodros is proud of the SI faculty for their collaboration. "Teaching used to be a very isolated job," she noted. "Thanks to increased collaboration, the curriculum and lesson plans are better. Teachers are looking ahead to the skills students need to survive in college and beyond, and they are offering those skills. They are teaching critical thinking, communication and technology skills. And much of this is due to the advent of professional development at SI and to Steve Phelps."

Professional Development

Steve Phelps, who came to SI in 1972, accepted the first sabbatical the school ever offered in 1994. He taught halftime and spent the remaining time visiting high schools around the country looking for examples of programs and practices that would support the SI faculty in meeting the needs of a new generation of students.

He discovered a rich depository of literature and coursework in the area of professional development,

Latin teachers Grace Curcio & Mary McCarty, along with their students, keep Latin alive.

and he brought back to SI the idea of starting a professional development office. In 1995 Steve Nejasmich asked him to do just that and continue to teach two psychology classes to seniors.

"We weren't a school in crisis," said Phelps. "We were an excellent school that could be better." He first determined what sorts of credentials and degrees the faculty had, and he then encouraged young teachers to earn credentials and advanced degrees that would deepen their expertise in curriculum and instruction.

He worked with USF and San Francisco State University to offer a number of credential and Master's classes at SI, and many teachers — from SI and other Catholic high schools — enrolled and went on to earn advanced degrees thanks to those evening and Saturday classes.

He also set up workshops to train SI faculty in the best ways to use technology in their classrooms, and, along with Charlie Dullea, Kate Kodros and Fr. Ed Fassett, SJ, he helped develop the Excellence in Teaching program. He organized Skillful Teacher classes and, with the Board of Regents, established a summer grant program for teachers working collaboratively to develop new and relevant curriculum.

In 1999 he and Kodros helped Charlie Dullea put into place the Five to Four program, lessening the teaching load by asking faculty to teach four, rather than five, classes, and to use their time for continually improving curriculum and instruction and for collaborative and interdepartmental projects. Because of the cost to the school, that program was phased in over four years, beginning with the English and Language departments. He also worked with representatives from the Jesuit Secondary Education Association to bring leadership training seminars and academies to SI, and he has arranged for dozens of professional workshops for teachers to attend both on and off campus. In short, he has supported the SI teachers in their quest to learn more about their craft and to excel. And it has worked.

"All of this has contributed to a culture at SI where people are eager to learn, from the president to the youngest teacher," said Phelps. "In years past, some teachers may have thought they knew it all. Now we're learning so much that we don't even question the process. It's part of the culture. The process has both improved our relationship with other schools and given SI a national reputation for excellence. Administrators from all over the country come here because we have become a school that seeks both to learn from others and to share freely."

It did not take long for those efforts to bear fruit. In 1998–99, SAT scores climbed to record highs, with students scoring, on average, 602 on the verbal section and 592 on math, for a total of 1194, up 14 points from the previous year. In contrast, the average among all Jesuit schools that year was 1174, and the national and state averages were 1016 and 1005 respectively. In 2004, those numbers climbed to 1207 for SI students, nearly 200 points higher than the national (1026) and state (1020) averages.

Steve Phelps likes these numbers, but he tests their accuracy by conducting a simple poll. Each year he walks down the halls of SI and asks students how many of their teachers are excellent. To qualify, he explains, teachers must know their subject well and be gifted at teaching that information. "On average, students tell me that four of their six teachers are excellent. Some say all six. I ask that question to students in other schools, and I'll hear from zero to four. Simply put, we have superb teachers at SI because we work hard to support and reward excellence."

Those rewards come in all shapes and sizes, from a reduced workload and fair pay to help with housing. At SI, a first-year teacher with 30 units beyond

a Bachelor's degree earned more than $50,000 in the 2004–2005 school year. A teacher with 60 units beyond a Bachelor's degree and 13 years' experience earned nearly $84,000 that year. In comparison, the average salary for high school teachers in California during the 2002–2003 school year was $55,000.

Phelps also has been rewarded for his efforts. *Today's Catholic Teacher* magazine named SI as one of 12 schools nationwide honored for excellence and innovation in education. The magazine praised SI for "embarking on a unique approach to forming a school that learns," for "rooting professional growth in every aspect of school culture," and for "learning from the best models available, both locally and nationally." Phelps was also individually honored by the National Catholic Educational Association, which gave him its Secondary School Department Award, citing his "significant contribution to American Catholic secondary education."

Celebrating a Legacy of Scholarship & Creativity

In the 1980s and 1990s, Br. Dan Peterson, SJ, the former archivist and librarian at SI, compiled a collection of 92 SI authors who, as of 2000, had published 435 books. (The complete list is available on the SI web site.) Below are some of the more prominent scholars, novelists, non-fiction authors and poets on that list, followed by just one of their best-known works. The list is a testament to the legacy of scholarship and creativity that has always been a part of SI.

Scholars

Fr. Austin Fagothy, SJ '17, author of *Right and Reason*, a landmark textbook on ethics used in many universities that has gone through 9 editions since 1953.

Robert T. Orr '25, senior scientist with the California Academy of Sciences; former professor of biology at USF and the author of *The Animal Kingdom*.

Robert A. Graham '29, a writer and researcher in Church history and the co-editor of the *Actes et Documents du Saint Siège Relatifs à la Seconde Guerre Mondiale*, the primary sources concerning the Church and the Axis powers.

Harold Harper '29, editor of *Harper's Review of Biochemistry*, a popular medical school textbook that has sold more than a million copies since its introduction in 1939. (Harper started editing it in 1951, marking the date the text changed its name.)

Fr. John McGloin, SJ '29, history professor at USF until his death and the author of *Jesuits by the Golden Gate* (a primary source for this book).

Fr. Robert Ignatius Burns, SJ '39, a preeminent scholar on medieval Spain at UCLA and the author of *The Crusader Kingdom of Valencia*.

Robert J. Brophy '46, Professor of English, California State University, Long Beach and the author of numerous texts on the poet Robinson Jeffers.

Eugene C. Bianchi '48, Professor of Religion, Emory University, Atlanta, the author of *Aging as a Spiritual Journey*.

David Herlihy '48, a prominent Renaissance historian, who taught during his career at the University of Wisconsin, Harvard University, and Brown University. He is the author of *The Black Death and the Transformation of the West*.

Peter Raven '53, director of the Missouri Botanical Garden and the author of *Biology*, a popular textbook used at SI and at numerous schools around the country.

Fr. John A. Coleman, SJ '54, professor at Loyola-Marymount University and editor of *One Hundred Years of Catholic Social Thought*.

James J. Sheehan '54, professor of history at Stanford University and the co-editor of *The Boundaries of Humanity*.

Dudley L. Poston '58, professor at the University of Texas and the author of *The Population of Modern China*.

Non-Fiction Writers

Ted Wurm '37, *The Crookedest Railroad in the World*
Gerald Posner '72 *Case Closed*
John Van der Zee '53, *The Gate*

Novelists

Laurence Yep '66 *Dragonwings*
Phillip O'Connor '50, *Stealing Home*

Poets

John Savant '48, *Brendan's Voyage and Other Poems*
Fr. James Torrens, SJ '48, *The Run of the City*
Fr. Robert Fabing, SJ '60, *Be Like the Sun*
Robert M. Carson '63 *The Waterfront Writers*
Paul Vangelisti '63, *The Extravagant Room*
Robert Thomas '68, *Door to Door*
Vince Gotera '71, *Dragonfly*
Eugene Gloria '77, *Drivers at the Short-Time Motel*

Opposite page: Br. Daniel Peterson, SJ, helped collect books written by and about SI grads. He received the President's Award for his 25 years of devoted service to the students of SI.

Women on the Front Lines

Everyone knows that the people who make any company work smoothly are the secretaries. While that is also true at SI, the secretaries, especially in the days before coeducation, provided

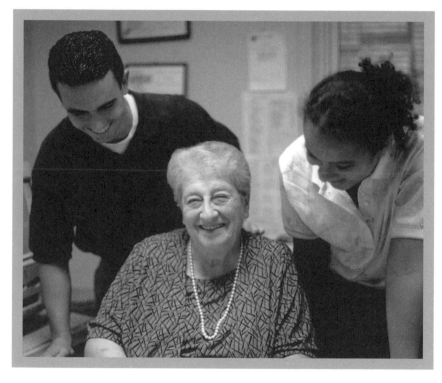

Mrs. Eda Bottini has worked as a secretary at SI since the 1960s.

other essential services. For many of the boys, they were surrogate mothers, bandaging skinned knees, offering support and making the school a friendlier place.

Eda Bottini is the dean of these women. She began her career at SI on June 28, 1966, to help her sister, Emma Basso (then secretary to Principal Ed McFadden) work on the accreditation report. She and a young Mr. Sauer worked together on that document. In 1969, she went to work in the Dean's office for Br. Draper. She left SI for one year, in 1977, and returned the following year to work for Fr. Carlin in the Development Office. She stayed there until 1984 when she returned to assist Br. Draper.

In 2004, Mrs. Bottini turned 81 and continued to commute to SI five days a week from her Redwood City home. "I always enjoy coming to work," she noted. "If I ever retire, I think I'd be lost without SI." She loves her job, she added, because "the students need mothering. I love working with them. They treat me with such respect, and I appreciate them."

She also praised her colleagues on the clerical staff for working hard and as "fun to be with. I enjoy them all." Br. Draper, with whom she has worked for 37 years, "is like a member of my family. I can always talk to Brother and confide in him. He has always been very kind to me." Br. Draper and Fr. Carlin were among the Jesuits who consoled Eda when her husband died in 1990.

Mrs. Bottini loves working with the two deans — Br. Draper and Karen Cota — and with Fr. Warren Wright, SJ, who also assists in that office. While that office is among the busiest at SI, dealing with attendance and discipline, Mrs. Bottini never seems frazzled. She is the calm eye in the center of the hurricane, sitting quietly at her desk, getting her job done, helping, along with all the other secretaries, in the behind-the-scenes running of the school.

"Eda is surely the mother of SI," said her good friend and secretary to the principal Karen Fisher. "She is a warm and welcoming face to students and parents, an antidote to the fear of being called down by Br. Draper to the Deans' Office. Her mind and wit are sharp, and her stamina is amazing to continue to commute from Redwood City and work a full day."

www.siprep.org

In 1996, religious studies teacher Paul Hanley '63 created and published SI's first web site. In its first year, 4,000 people visited it. While that figure may not seem great, back in the mid-'90s, those numbers were respectable. Hanley, who taught himself HTML editing, used animation and music to enhance the site, and he gathered students in the first web club and gave them a chance to have a hand in the web design. Europe Online ASBL honored Hanley for another of his web sites that offered information on Gaelic folklore and culture, giving it a "Best of Europe" designation. Thanks to Hanley, SI became one of the first Jesuit schools with a web presence and laid the groundwork for the www.siprep.org, now used by nearly every teacher and student to extend learning beyond the classroom.

Computer Coordinator Janet Reid and Fr. Ed Fassett, SJ, assistant to the principal, also worked in 1997 to modernize the school's computer and phone network, adding fiber optic cables to bring the Internet to all the computers at SI, to create email accounts for all faculty, and to install a modern voice mail system. Reid spent much of her time training students and faculty to understand how best to integrate computers and the Internet into their curriculum.

During the summer of 1998, physics and computer science teacher Mike Ugawa developed the curriculum for a Science Research program, expanding on the work begun by Tom Murphy '76, the former science department chairman. Ugawa received the Spohn Excellence in Teaching Award and used the award funds to purchase state-of-the art apparatus used to perform experiments in quantum theory and relativity. These experiments formed the core of the curriculum, representing a unique opportunity for high school students to perform experiments in areas of science normally not accessible until college.

"The traditional physics curriculum is based upon the work of Galileo, Newton, Maxwell and others representing ideas developed in the 16th through 19th Centuries," said Ugawa. "The scientific revolution of the 20th Century — work that was done by Plank, Bohr, Schrödinger, Einstein and others — is largely neglected in traditional high school physics programs though it forms the basis for modern technology such as solid state electronics and computers. The Science Research program represents a step toward integrating these exciting topics into our science curriculum."

Ugawa designed the course to help students develop skills necessary for research in any discipline. The students review research literature, develop a protocol, collect and analyze data and present their findings by writing a journal-style article and by giving an oral presentation in the semi-annual Science Research Seminar. "All of these skills are useful in any field of academic or industrial research that the student may pursue in the future," Ugawa added.

SI has offered the Science Research program every semester since its inception; the program has expanded the curriculum beyond the sciences to include projects from various fields of engineering. The Science Research program has distinguished SI as one of the few schools in the nation where students have the opportunity to demonstrate research experience at the high school level.

For his Science Research work, as well as his general leadership in the local physics education community, Ugawa was able to make SI a center for the advancement of physics education in the Bay Area beginning in the summer of 2000 when he was named Physics Teaching Resource Agent for the American Association of Physics Teachers. As one of only 18 teachers selected for the honor from across the nation that year, Ugawa is now among the top 200 physics teachers in the U.S. and works to improve the quality of physics education by offering training and support to teachers in urban centers throughout the country. The U.S. Congress praised this program as one of the few educational reform projects producing substantial results.

"Students in inner-city schools are typically among the most disadvantaged in the nation," noted Ugawa. "This is an opportunity to make a significant contribution toward the improvement of the quality of education received by these students and to increase their chances of success." From 2000 through 2004, Ugawa continued to offer workshops on weekends at SI for teachers from urban schools in the Bay Area. During this time, he was one of the region's leading science educators, serving as the President of the Northern California/Nevada Section of the American Association of Physics Teachers.

Athletics (1999–2005)

The Rise of Girls' Sports

Girls at SI began competing in sports as early as fall 1989 in volleyball, cross country and tennis. The winter season saw the rise of girls' basketball and soccer, and in the spring of 1990, competition began in softball and track. In later years, girls participated in swimming, lacrosse, crew, golf, water polo, diving and field hockey. Three of those sports were new to SI: field hockey, water polo and softball.

Field Hockey

Mrs. Trish Intemann, mother of Fergus '93 and Conor '96, helped form the first SI field hockey team as a club sport in 1993. Intemann, a veteran of the sport, played in high school in Dublin and in nursing school in London. She gained

Kobie Flowers & Tim O'Brien (Class of 1990) bring the Bruce back from SH.

her coaching experience at two Marin County grammar schools and in 1982 started a women's league for the Marin Field Hockey Club. In 1992, while watching her son Conor play lacrosse, she was approached by students who had heard of her enthusiasm for the sport and who asked her to coach an SI team. In 1993, 22 girls formed an unofficial "hackers team," as Intemann called them for their tendency to hit their opponents' sticks rather than the ball. That team won two of its three games and inspired more students to try out for the sport and to petition the school to make it an official team. That happened in 1995, and two first-year Spanish teachers, Shelley Tucker and Linda Neilan, took over coaching duties. In 1997, SI finished first in an informal four-school league. In 1998, the girls joined the Blossom Valley Athletic League in San Jose — the nearest league that offered the sport — winning the league championship that year.

Softball

Girls' softball began in the spring of 1990 coached by English teacher Elizabeth (Sheehan) Swarthout. The team, made up entirely of freshmen, formed a varsity squad, playing against seniors and juniors in the Catholic Girls Athletic League, which only offered competition on the varsity level. Despite being younger than all their competitors, SI's girls finished 9–5, taking second place.

Diving

The SI diving team made its debut in the spring of 1994 when coach David Bispiel took four boys to league competition. The following fall saw the start of the Girls' Diving Team; those girls made

a splash by winning their league and taking fourth in CCS competition. The team included Lisa Wilson, who placed first in the GPSL meet and fifth in CCS competition, Sabrina Soulis '95 (who placed third in the league meet), Nicole Larramendi '95 (who placed fourth), Megan Terheyden '98 and Dawn Matsui '97.

Water Polo

Water polo began first with a boys' program in the fall of 1994 with 11 boys on the varsity and 11 on JVs, with both teams coached by Stephen Psomas. The spring of 1995 saw the start of the girls' water polo team, also coached by Psomas. At the start of the season, 30 girls tried out for this

The Varsity Girls' Field Hockey team.

new sport, with half joining the varsity and half the JV team. The varsity finished a surprising second in the Blossom Valley Athletic League after losing 13–12 in sudden death triple overtime to league champion Leland High School. Standouts on the girls' squad included Kirsten Filak '96, Jamie Chavez '96, Christine Caurant '96 and Kimiko Nakai '96.

Cross Country & Track and Field

The 1990s proved a powerhouse decade for SI's cross country and track and field teams. The boys' cross country team won CCS championships four times in that decade and one state championship in 1996. Long before that state victory, Coach Brian Richter knew he had a talented squad early in the season when, at the Stanford Invitational, all five runners crossed the finish line within 12 seconds of each other to help SI take first at that event. The team went on to win the league and CCS and was ranked number one the entire season. Runners who led SI to that state title included seniors Brad Hansen, Brendan Fitzgibbon, Derek Drummond and Brian Mulry, juniors Brendan Wells and Matt Chen and frosh phenom Neil McDonagh, who finished fourth in the CCS. The victory marked the second time that SI won a state title in a California Interscholastic Federation sport. (The first victory occurred in basketball in 1926. SI did win the state title in crew in 1995, but crew was not administered by CIF at that time.)

The girls' cross country team also made history by winning six straight CCS titles between 1993 and 1998, the first for any school in the section. Many of these runners crossed over into track and field in the spring where the girls took first place in their league between 1991 and 2002 and brought home two sectional championships.

Boys' track took first in the WCAL five times in the 1990s and made history in 1991 by taking the CCS title. This victory, coupled with the cross country CCS title in the fall of 1990, marked the first time SI had captured two CCS crowns in the same year, a feat no other school had ever accomplished. Between 1994 and 1997, the boy's track team finished four undefeated seasons, a first for the school. Much of the credit goes to a talented line-up of coaches that included Julius Yap '74, Brian Richter, Aldo Congi '72, Steve Bluford '84, James Quanico '86, Charles Taylor '88, Martin Logue '92 and Tom Fendyan '83. Yap, who served as head coach for many of those teams over the decade, amassed 29 league and CCS titles in five sports (boys' and girls' track, boys' and girls' cross country and girls' golf), more than any other coach in SI history. In 2005 the city of Pacifica inducted him into its Sports Hall of Fame.

SI senior Chris DeMartini '94 achieved a status no other Wildcat had ever earned: individual honors as a state champion. Earlier in the season, he had been ranked first in the nation in discus, but he finished first in shot put at the California Track and Field State Championships at Cerritos College in Norwalk on June 4, 1994, with a throw of 58-feet, 11.5 inches on the last of his six throws. He also finished second in discus after having an "off day," according to his coach, Brian Richter.

Football

In 1992, Ray Calcagno '64 left SI and Joe Vollert '84 became one of the youngest men, at 26, ever to serve as varsity football coach. Vollert had played under Calcagno and at SCU under Pat Malley '49 and

The Girls' Cross Country Team competing at the Polo Field.

his son Terry Malley. As a senior at SI, Vollert earned both the Brophy Award and the General Excellence Award. He made a name for himself early on as a new kind of coach, one who taught Ignatian values both indirectly, through example, and directly, by stressing them to his athletes. When he retired in 2004, he had earned the respect of hundreds of athletes and of all of his coaching staff who admired the calm attitude and healthy values he brought to each game.

One of Vollert's early tests came in his first year as coach. SI and SH marked the 100th anniversary (albeit one year early due to a typographical error in one newspaper story) of the first time the two schools met back in 1893 for a St. Patrick's Day rugby game. The Irish of Sacred Heart came decked out just for the event with special jerseys reading "Beat SI" on the fronts and "Mahoney" on the backs in memory of their deceased alumnus Jerry Mahoney of Bruce-Mahoney fame. SI may have lost that first match-up in 1893, but the special jerseys didn't provide the Irish with luck this time around. SI beat SH 7–3 before a crowd of 7,000 at Kezar Stadium and kept the Bruce-Mahoney Trophy at SI that year.

Vollert's favorite memories of that decade include Joe Dekker '98 carrying 33 times against St. Francis when SI won 19–0, Joe Lourdeaux '98 kicking four field goals in that game, Alex Buich '98 playing a great game to beat Bellarmine at Kezar in 1996, Drew Virk '99 and Tripp Jones '99 stopping Bellarmine on the goal line to seal a 21–14 win, Anthony Devora '99 returning a punt to ignite SI against San Lorenzo Valley, and Sean Pailhe '97 catching a fake punt for a key play against Del Mar in the CCS playoffs.

"I'm also very proud of some of the teams that struggled," Vollert said in a *Genesis IV* interview. "One of the best teams had guys who stuck together

despite a 1–8–1 season. No one wants to lose games, but I was proud of how those players took care of one another and of how hard they practiced and played. I was just as proud of them as teams that went 8–4."

Vollert also took pride in how well his players combined scholarship with athletics. With the exception of one year, he had one or more players named as scholar athletes by the National Football Hall of Fame in each year he coached. "We preach all the time about integrity: If you're going to work hard on the field, it's a matter of integrity to work hard in the classroom. Our scholar-athletes represented that success."

In 2004 Joe Vollert retired from the varsity coaching job after a dozen years as head coach, the longest anyone has ever held that job in the school's history. Steve Bluford '84, who served with Vollert as co-captain in his senior year at SI, took over the job. When Vollert received the head-coaching job, the first call he made was to Bluford to convince him to leave a career in physical therapy to teach and coach at his alma mater.

Bluford, the school's first African-American varsity coach, also ran track at SI and played football at UC Santa Barbara where he received his Bachelor's degree in psychology. A longtime psychology teacher, PE teacher and department chairman — as well as moderator of the Association of African American Students — Bluford also served as head JV coach from 1994 to 2001, leading his team to the WCAL championship in 1995. He proved his ability to lead the varsity Wildcats in 2004 by beating Sacred Heart 34–0 at the September Bruce-Mahoney game and finishing the league 4–2, including a 61–26 drubbing of St. Francis, setting a school record for the most points scored in a varsity football game.

Opposite page: An October 2001 rally for the football team before the Bruce-Mahoney game.

The baseball team celebrates after winning the Bruce in 2001.

"Steve cares deeply for his players because he blends teaching, motivation and discipline better than any coach I've ever worked with," said Vollert. "He demands the most out of the kids, and they really respond. I've seen over the years that he has a way of getting their hearts. They really love him."

Baseball

Baseball between 1990 and 2005 had its share of magic moments. In 1991, senior Tony Rhein pitched the Bruce-Mahoney game with rain threatening throughout the day. Earlier that day, Tony had attended his grandfather's funeral, and he was determined to pitch the game in his honor. SI went on to beat SH 5–2 on a 3-run homer by Joe Donnelly '91 before a crowd of thousands at West Sunset Field.

Jim Dekker retired as head varsity baseball coach in 1993 after 16 years leading the Wildcats to more than 200 victories, including a second-place finish in CCS that year and a 25–7 season. No team from San Francisco ever went as far in the CCS as the Wildcats of 1993. John Grealish '79, who played for Dekker in his senior year, would follow in his stead until 1998, when he was appointed assistant principal for student activities. Veteran English teacher Jim Bjorkquist '65, who coached alongside Dekker and Grealish, then took over the team for two years.

In 2000, Bjorkquist's team won the league, the first championship since 1967 and SI's first WCAL baseball championship ever. That team also went on to the final game of the CCS championships, losing 6–5 to Leigh of San Jose to take second in the section. The victory came despite several setbacks, including the loss of several key players due to injuries. "We had to regroup time and time again to rebuild the team,"

said Bjorkquist. Standouts included Joe Jacobitz '00, who went on to play at USF and be drafted by the Seattle Mariners; Dave McMonigle '00, who hit .395; Brent Sullivan '00, who had 4 homeruns and 17 RBIs; Paolo Lucchesi '00; Jim Goethals '00; Chris Watters '01; and Michael Tursi '00. As well as the team did in the league, Bjorkquist was just as proud of the team earning CCS Scholastic Championship honors with the highest collective GPA (3.35) of any team in the region.

Lacrosse

In the 1990s, SI boys' and girls' lacrosse became the dominant program in the Bay Area and in the state. Between 1990 and 2004, the boys' varsity won nine league titles and three state championships, with the girls' program, under Coach Colleen Niklaus, winning eight league championships and becoming the top team in Northern California between 1997 and 2004. Much of the credit belongs to boys' head coach David Giarrusso, who came to SI in 1996 to teach history and who became a local legend for his passion for the sport and prowess as a coach. Thanks to his regional leadership, the number of lacrosse teams in the Bay Area rose from eight to 40 in his six years as varsity lacrosse coach between 1996 and 2002, with many of those players learning the game at one of his summer SI lacrosse camps.

Over a six-year period, Giarrusso's teams won 90 games and lost 9. His program became so strong that in his last year coaching, SI's four teams — the varsity and JV girls' and boys' teams — each won the Northern California championship. U.S. Lacrosse named Giarrusso Coach of the Year in Northern California in 1997, 1999 and 2000 and as Man of the

Year in 2002. Giarrusso also served as president of the California Junior Lacrosse Association from 1999 to 2001. When he and his wife, Suzanne Abell (who also coached field hockey and lacrosse at SI) moved to the East Coast to be closer to their families, the SI lacrosse community mourned, but honored Giarrusso's legacy by continuing to excel. In 2004, for example, the boys' team finished 8–0 in the league under the able leadership of head coach Greg Angilly. Niklaus led the varsity girls to a 25–4–1 season in 2003 and helped junior Katie McGovern earn All American First Team honors.

SI lacrosse players excelled in college athletics in both the boys' and girls' programs. In 2002 and 2003, Bridget Mulhern '00, a Cal Poly San Luis Obispo student, was named the U.S. Lacrosse Intercollegiate Associates' Player of the Year and was featured in *Sports Illustrated*. In 2004 she led her team to its fourth national championship, earning first team All-American honors and MVP status of the national championship tournament. Elsa Beyer '01, who played for UCLA, earned second team All American honors in 2004.

SI grads on UC Santa Barbara's lacrosse team helped that school win the U.S. Lacrosse Men's Division Intercollegiate Associates National Championships in 2004. Players included team co-captain Tycho Suter '00 (first team All-American defenseman) Luke Wilson '01 (first team All-American attack honors), Hank Caulkins '00, Ryan Brittain '01, Damon Conklin-Moragne '02 (each an All American), Matt Wagner '00, and Alex Wilson '99.

Other college standouts include Chris Bauman '01, Matt Selig '99, Eric Dahm '00, Peter Langkammerer '01, Brian Bianchi '00, Kevin Clifford '02 and Ben Horn '01, a star on the Naval Academy's lacrosse team.

Soccer

Both Jan Mullen and Rob Hickox '72, the coaches for the girls' and boys' varsity soccer teams, earned more than mere victories for their teams. Each earned the distinction of being named Honor Coach by the Central Coast Section, Hickox in 1994 and Mullen in 1996. The award recognizes coaches "who have made contributions to the growth and development of their sport and their athletes within the school, community and section." Both Hickox and Mullen have dedicated themselves not only to SI soccer but also to a host of community soccer programs, and that dedication has earned them the respect of their peers throughout the state.

Opposite page: The Varsity Boys' Lacrosse Team and coach Dave Giarrusso win the state championship.

Below: The soccer teams play, rain or shine.

Mullen's teams did remarkably well, taking league championships in 1992–1996 and 1998–1999. In the past five years, the boys' varsity soccer team made it to CCS competition four times, to the semifinals twice and to the finals once in 2000 after a 16–5–4 season. Then, on February 10, 2005, the Varsity Boys' Soccer Team became WCAL co-champions for the first since 1981 by beating Bellarmine 2–1 in San Jose.

John Stiegeler '74, a talented history teacher at SI, is a 20-year veteran of the soccer program and Hickox's assistant varsity coach. Hickox praised Stiegeler both for his talented defensive coaching and for helping to support alumni who played soccer at SI and who gather once a year for an alumni soccer game on the Saturday after Thanksgiving. Stiegeler also sends an e-mail report of each game to all alumni soccer players. (Other alumni sporting events include the alumni basketball game the Wednesday before Thanksgiving, the alumni baseball game in April and the alumni lacrosse game in May.)

Volleyball

The volleyball program was the first sport to include SI's girls. Coached by Teresa (Mullin) Garrett, the team grew in ability over its first four years. By the fall of 1992, the team faced its greatest moment when it took on the girls of Mitty, beating them in four games. Playing for the Monarchs was sophomore Kerry Walsh, who, in 2004 in Athens, went on to win an Olympic gold medal in beach volleyball with her partner, Misty May. "We were an unknown team, and Mitty was a powerhouse," said Garrett. "Our victory shocked everyone and put us on the map. Stars of that team included Chrissy Drucker '93 and Robin Harvey '93, who helped their team finish

second in the league and make it to the quarterfinals of CCS play. In 1998, under head coaches Karen Cota and Louie Valiao, the team won its first league championship. The girls came in second place in 1999 and recaptured the crown in 2000.

Cota praised Valiao as being one of the most respected coaches in the league and Aimee Castro and Chris Goethals for developing players, leading the JV program since the 1990s, and taking their team to the championship in 2001. Many players have gone on to compete at the collegiate level, including Julie Guevara '94, Karen Chen '96, Allison Cota '99, Lindsey Cope '01, Monica Charlton '01 and Kelly Kramer '02.

Chris Goethals, who joined the program in 1999 as JV coach and who led her team to a league championship in 2001 along with Aimee Castro, noted that the team has come "a long way over the years under Karen Cota's helm, and the girls now play a high-powered, specialized game." Goethals also praised coach Valiao, who joined the team in 1998 and whose "extensive background in volleyball helped SI compete at a higher level, taking its first league championship in 1999 against the Gators of Sacred Heart Prep." Goethals praised outside hitters Natalie Charlton and Gina Sigillo and setter Allison Cota for leading that team to victory.

In 2000, SI joined the WCAL and found itself against Mitty, St. Francis, Presentation of San Jose and Valley Christian. "We were now competing against nationally-ranked teams," said Goethals. "At first it was a shock to be up against the likes of these schools, but our program hung tough and continued to improve. Through it all, Karen Cota's leadership encouraged a Christian spirit among players and coaches. Trying to go to new heights as a competitive volleyball program was not going to be done at the expense of losing our

Opposite page: The Varsity Girls' Volleyball Team in 1999.

SI Varsity Crew won a national championship in 1997.

Ignatian values." In 2004 Cota stepped down as varsity girls' coach but continued to head the program, and Teresa Garrett, the first girls' volleyball coach, returned to lead the team.

The boys' volleyball team had its genesis in 1976 when English teacher Bob Grady, while refereeing a girls' volleyball game at University High School, spoke with the coach there about forming a boys' league for the city. Grady called the coach at Lick Wilmerding and at Athenian High School in Danville to form the first unofficial league, borrowing uniforms from the JV basketball team. Grady paid for all the volleyballs himself, started practicing in February 1977,

and held competitions March through May. The next year Washington High School joined the league. Star players over the years have included Steve McFeely '87 and John DeBenedetti '83. In 1990, SI joined the SERVE league (Secondary Education Radical Volleyball Experiment), comprising five teams. Standouts Tom Kovats '90, Jeff Spaulding '91 and Sam Yen '91 helped SI to finish first that year.

Crew

In the 1990s, SI's crew reached unparalleled heights due, in large measure, to SI teacher and coach John Pescatore, who won the Olympic bronze medal in

1988 as a member of the U.S. 8-man boat. SI's varsity 8 boys also won the state championship in 1994, 1995 and 1997.

In 1997, the boys' varsity 8 went on to compete in the U.S. Rowing Junior Invitational Regatta in Cincinnati, Ohio, beating out the best crews from around the country and giving SI its only national championship. The boat featured Kevin Schmidt '97, Alex Bea '97, John Paul Sekulich '97, Eric Tiret '97, David Reynolds '97, Patrick Reid '98 and Greg Chiarella '98, John Cranston '99 and coxswain Franco Arieta '97. Alternates were A.J. Hubner '97, Chris Murphy '98 and Joshua Stamer '98. In 2004, the boy's varsity 8 returned to Cincinnati where they finished third in the nation after a second-place state finish. That boat, coached by Tom O'Connell, featured senior coxswain Jesse Burdick and rowers Joe Dudley '04, Mike Snyder '05, Mike Gilson '06, Derek Johnson '06, Jim Terheyden '04, Noel Castro '04, Ryan McQuaid '04 and Mike Tate '05.

The girls' varsity 8 brought home gold in 1995, 1999 and 2000, led by Coach Jen Hayden. In those last two years, they also traveled to Cincinnati to compete in the National Invitational Championships where they placed third in the nation both times. Star rowers on those boats included Betsy Dimalanta '99, Patsy McGuire '99, Katie Waller '99, Giselle Talkoff '99, Becky O'Neill '00, Lauren Labagh '00, Jenny Draxl '00, Ellen Mulvanny '01, Katie Yrazabal '01, Mary Kate Sullivan '01, Dinah Dimalanta '01, Laura Terheyden '01 and Mithu Tharayil '00 with coxswains Marie Mahoney '00 and Sheila Clifford '99. Many of the women in the program went on to excel in college crews and have staged mini SI reunions at the various regattas.

Basketball

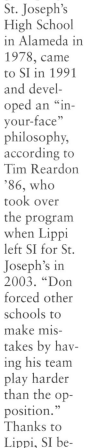

Basketball fever seemed to grip the school in the 1990s with nationally-ranked players and teams taking SI to five league and two CCS championships between 1992 and 2004 for the boys' program and one league and three CCS championships for the girls' program. Don Lippi, who started coaching at St. Joseph's High School in Alameda in 1978, came to SI in 1991 and developed an "in-your-face" philosophy, according to Tim Reardon '86, who took over the program when Lippi left SI for St. Joseph's in 2003. "Don forced other schools to make mistakes by having his team play harder than the opposition." Thanks to Lippi, SI be-

The Boys' Varsity Basketball Team took 2nd in NorCal in 2004.

came one of the premiere high schools for basketball in the Bay Area. "Before Don took over the program, the team had a few tough seasons," said Reardon. "After his first year, we were back to being one of the most respected programs in the Bay Area. For four years, I coached the varsity girls while he coached the varsity boys. In each of those years, the *Chronicle* ranked both SI teams in the top 10 in the Bay Area. SI was the place to go to play basketball."

The Girls' Basketball Team won the league and CCS titles in 2002.

Lippi earned local and national news in 1999 when SI, with a 28–1 record and undefeated in league play, was ranked in the top 10 of all the high schools in the U.S. and number one in Northern California. Players such as Luke Whitehead (a star at University of Louisville and slated for the NBA draft at the time of this writing), Joe Skiffer, Robert Sayle, Anthony Devora and Nick Errico led the team to a second place CCS finish and to NorCal competition. In 2000, Lippi received the Boys' Basketball Coach of the Year Award from the California Coaches Association for his "coaching excellence and professional con-

tributions of time, service and dedication to the profession and athletics."

Reardon stepped in as varsity boys' coach after Lippi left, and led his team in 2004 to both the league and CCS championship — the first time that had happened since 1984. He finished second in NorCal play in a remarkable first year as the boys' coach. He credits the team's success to the combined efforts of the players. "Someone pointed out to me that *The San Francisco Chronicle* ran six stories on our team, highlighting a different player each time. This is a testament to how the athletes needed each other to be successful." The Wildcats finished 11–6 in league play and 23–11 overall that year before going on to beat Mitty for the league championship; Evergreen Valley, North Monterey County, Pioneer and Burlingame for the CCS championship; and Northgate and Foothill in NorCal play before being stopped by Bishop O'Dowd for the NorCal crown. Jesse Lopez-Low '04, a 6-7 senior, Max Mizono '04, Brian Wilhelm '04, Matt Jones '06, Danny Zatkin '04 and Tim Szarnicki '04 were among the standouts on that team.

SI's girls did not win a league championship until 2002, but because the top two teams go on to sectional competition, they did win the CCS championship both in 1996 and 1998. Their first CCS championship came with coach Steve Phelps and players Juliann Busch '96, Kimiko Nakai '96, Liz Lee '97, Kristy Cahill '98 and Maya Fok '98. Tim Reardon, who coached in 1998, won another CCS crown despite having five players sidelined with injuries. Frosh Jacquelyn Hontalas '01, who scored 17 points in her first game, Fok, Cahill, Julie Yap '99, Kirsten Maciejewski '00 and Jessica Libien '99 helped establish the Wildcats as a dominant force in the GPSL with a 25–6 record.

In 2002, under head coach Jim Dekker, the 'Cats had their best season ever, taking both the league, with an 8–0 record, and the CCS championship. That year was the first that all three teams in the program (frosh, JV and varsity) won league championships, the first time league coaches voted unanimously on who should be the MVP (senior Katie Meinhardt), the first time an SI student (Meinhardt) received a full scholarship to a Division I college and the first time the *San Jose Mercury News* chose someone from SI as its girls' basketball coach of the year. Dekker stepped down in favor of Julie Guevara '94, a veteran SI player, who finished her third year as head coach in 2005.

Fifteen years since its inception, the girls' program now has a strong base of alumnae players, many of whom return for the homecoming game the day before Thanksgiving each year to take on the varsity girls' team. The alumnae women played their first game against the Wildcats in 2001, losing 56–23 against the varsity.

Tennis

Both boys' and girls' tennis excelled in the 1990s and beyond, with the boys winning the WCAL in 1992, 1994, 1996, and 1998, and the girls' taking first in 1993 and 2003. The boys won their first league meet in 1992 coached by Art Cecchin '63 after an 18–3 season thanks to Elwyn Cababe '92, Aaron White '92, Derek Bertelsen '92, Chris Zonnas '93, Trevor Hewitt '94, Martin Burke '92, Aric Zurek '92, Jon Weinstein '94 and Chris Jew '94.

The next year, Cecchin, now the girls' head coach, led SI to its first GPSL tennis championship with Lisa Monfredini '96, Sarah Warren '96, Anne Warren '94, Francesca Crisera '95, Mimi Dang '95, Jocelyn Sideco '95 and Kacey Callinan '94.

In 1994 Mike Thomas '71 led the boys to another league title after a 12–0 league finish and a 21–2 overall finish with Jon Weinstein '94, Trevor Hewitt '94, Jason Horn '94, Chris Jew '94, Opara Green '96, Adrian Gonzales '96, Tomo Tom '97, Wesley Chu '96, Mark Kasprowicz '96, Elliot Chun '96, Riley Hurd '95 and several of the players from the '92 championship team. Thomas repeated that trick two years later, going 12–0 in league play and 18–2 overall with number one and two players Adrian Gonzales and Brad White '97 along with doubles' teams of Rob Estrella '96 and Mark Kasprowicz and Elliot Chun and Mike Duffy '97. He also praised Tomo Tom, Wesley Chu and Brandon Chu '98 for helping SI finish among the top eight in CCS play.

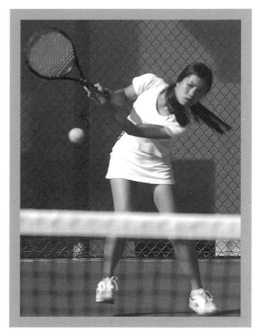

In 1998 Thomas' team once again took first in the league with Brandon Chu, Daniel Ho '00, Jeff Curtiss '98, Omid Talai '98, Jeff Duerson '99, Jason Buick '98, Victor Santore '99, James Shinbori '98 and Scott Li '00.

The girls won the WCAL championship in 2003 with Coach Hillary McKinney helping the 'Cats to a 13–1 season thanks to the power play of Stefanie Ordoveza '04, Donna Verdiano '05, Katy Kilgore '05 and Maggie McAteer '04. Bill Haardt, currently the boys'

The Girls' tennis program won the WCAL championship in 2003.

432

In 2003, the
Girls' Golf
Team took
first in NorCal
and fourth in
the state.

head coach, led his team to a third-place WCAL finish in 2004 after an 11–3 season. Craig Law '84 (who coaches JV girls and boys) and Br. Artie Lee, SJ, have also been instrumental to the success of the program.

Golf

The boys' golf program enjoyed its last league championship in 1979, but continued to excel with star golfers such as Peter Andersen '87, Tim O'Riordan '88, Josh Levin '94 and Mike Sica '99 under coaches Fr. Roland Dodd, SJ, Bob Drucker '58 and Julius Yap '74.

A few girls, such as Judette Tobes '98 and Annie Donnelly '95, played on a coed golf team until 2001 when SI formed a separate girls' team. Elaine Harris '04 and her father, an All-American golfer at Stanford, along with Carolyn Thamkul '03 encouraged Yap to start a girls' team. On the first day of tryouts, 35 girls came out for the team and 24 stuck with it. That year, SI took second in the GPSL. Harris, then a sophomore, took first at the league championship and fourth in CCS play.

In 2002, SI left the GPSL for the WCAL and finished as co-champions with Notre Dame High School, Belmont, before taking third in CCS play and ninth in NorCal competition. The following year, the girls outdid themselves, taking first in league, first in CCS and first in Northern California competition before winding down a remarkable season with a fourth-place finish in the state thanks to the talented play of Harris, Ai Chen '04, Katie Cavallero '04, Dana Fisco '04, Colleen McHugh '05, Katie Moran '05, Patti Pang '05, Keiko Fukuda '06 and frosh phenom Rosalie Tolentino '07.

The Wall of Champions

After the homecoming football game of October 21, 1995, SI dedicated the Wall of Champions in the Martin D. Murphy Pavilion. The series of plaques honor each varsity team that won a league, sectional, state or national championship. Block Club Moderator Robert Vergara '76 did the research for the wall and gave a stirring speech in which he noted that "in recognizing these champions, we honor *all* those who have worn the Red and Blue, whether their team finished in first place or last. For if winning championships were our only goal, our athletic program would be a richly decorated but empty shell. What we celebrate today, along with our championships, is the hard work, the self-sacrifice and the commitment to Ignatian values that are the mark of all truly great St. Ignatius teams."

A Change of Leadership

Robert Vergara '76, Leo La Rocca's assistant AD, took over the job in June 1999 as SI's fifth athletic director. As a student, Vergara served as manager for the baseball and football teams and as a basketball statistician. That began his long love with the SI sports tradition. "I used to go into Leo's office before he knew who I was and look at all the great stuff in his room. I'd look up Dan Fouts in the 1969 yearbook and read about the 1926 basketball team that won the state championship. I loved learning about the great teams from the 1950s and '60s." Vergara returned to SI in 1982 after graduating with his bachelor's degree in history from USF, and, since then, he has taught English, history and public speaking and served as scheduling director for 14 years and as associate athletic director since 1997. As AD, he now works with 96 coaches, 62 teams, 25 sports and 870 students — nearly 60 percent of the student body who play at least one sport. Perhaps Vergara's greatest strength lies in his belief that coaches need to do more than win games. They need to instill Ignatian values in their students, extending the lessons of the classrooms onto the playing field. Helping him in this mission is John Mulkerrins '89, who stepped into Vergara's old job as assistant AD.

SI's Olympians: Tom McGuirk, Sebastian Bea & John Pescatore

Two SI students and one faculty member have competed in the Olympics over the years. John Pescatore, who taught math and coached crew at SI in the 1990s, won a bronze medal in 1988 in Seoul as part of the U.S. team's 8-man boat. Four years later, in Barcelona, he finished sixth in the pairs event. Before the start of the 1996 games in Atlanta, Pescatore carried the Olympic torch 1 kilometer, down Haight Street from Masonic to Divisadero.

In Atlanta, Tom McGuirk '89 raced in the 400-meter hurdles for Ireland — he holds dual citizenship — and he also competed four years later in the 2000 games in Sydney. He was not the only Wildcat there. Sebastian Bea '95 won a silver medal in the pairs rowing event. His victory was all the more remarkable given how much pain he had suffered just three weeks prior. As his plane landed in Sydney, he was stretched out on the floor of the jet, all 6-foot, 6-inches of him, his face contorted in agony and his back on fire with muscle spasms. "The pain almost broke me in half. Passengers had to step over me to exit." Thanks to

SI's Olympians include, from left, John Pescatore (crew coach), Tom McGuirk (hurdles – opposite page top), and Sebastian Bea (crew – opposite page right).

muscle relaxants and a back brace, Bea healed enough to compete and bring home the only medal won by the U.S. men's rowing team at those games. Bea's coach, incidentally, was John Pescatore, who was part of the Olympic Training Center in Princeton, New Jersey. Both McGuirk and Bea have returned to SI often — Bea spoke at a Father-Son Dinner and McGuirk has

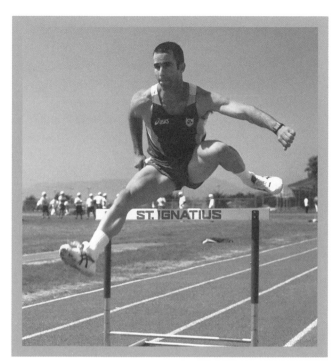

returned to SI to serve as the girls' weight coach, offering his expertise in discus and shot to both boys and girls.

435

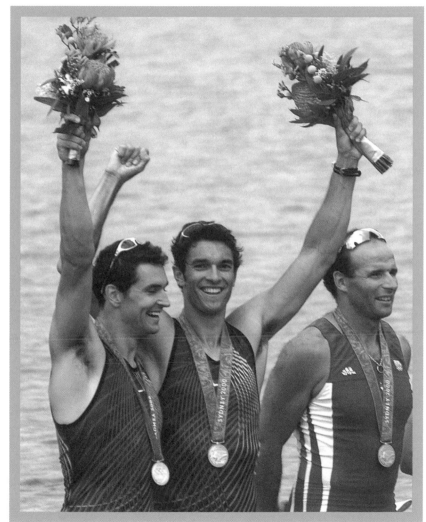

helped out coaching track and field.

Other SI athletes made various Olympic teams. The Salvemini brothers — Len '71 and Dan '75 — both made the U.S. Olympic Soccer Team, though, for different reasons, neither competed in the Olympics. Only the best 25 soccer teams in the world make it to the Olympics. Len's team was eliminated from the 1976 Montreal games when Mexico beat the U.S. in 1975, and Dan's 1980 team boycotted the Moscow games along with all the other U.S. teams that year.

Also, Mike Gravelle '83 became the U.S. national discus champion in 1994 at the USA-Mobil Outdoor Track and Field Championships in Knoxville, Tennessee, with a throw of 201 feet, 4 inches. Gravelle

Extracurriculars

Drama

In 2000, Marc Bauman joined the Fine Arts faculty, teaching acting full time and directing the fall play, the spring musical and advising student directors during the Winter One-Act Festival. Bauman performed with Marcel Marceau on his 1999 North American tour and is one of four Americans to have ever received a diploma from his international theatre school in Paris — L'Ecole Internationale de Mimodrame de Paris Marcel Marceau, an MFA equivalent. A gifted actor and mime, Bauman has been featured on *Entertainment Tonight* (NBC) and *Sunday Times* on CBS. He has performed in many plays, including ACT's production of *The Tempest* and the San Francisco Opera's productions of *The Fiery Angel and Ruslan and Ludmila.*

Opposite page: The 2001 production of Guys & Dolls. This page: The 2002 production of The Pajama Game. Both shows were directed and produced by Marc Bauman.

A dancer goes airborne in the 2002 dance concert, directed by Meredith Cecchin.

Since 1983, Bauman has taught acting and movement throughout the U.S. and Europe, including UCLA, USC and ACT in San Francisco where he has also served as project director. Since his arrival at SI, he has produced and directed many plays and musicals, including *The Miracle Worker, Guys and Dolls, Servant of Two Masters, The Pajama Game, Ascension Day, Chess, Rumors, The Music Man* and *The Diary of Anne Frank* as well as five winter one-act festivals.

Dance

By Meredith Cecchin '97

Those who did not spend the majority of their high school years in the underground cata-combs of SI Fine Arts might assume that SI did not dance until it went co-ed. Those who preferred the spotlight over daylight, however, might remember that SI students, like the fog, have danced on cat feet for decades.

SI hired its first choreographer, John Ellis, to join the farmers and the cowhands in friendship in 1966's production of *Oklahoma!* From 1966 through the '70s, student and faculty choreographers took on the task of choreographing the musicals and musical revues. Marianne Schwarz made a significant imprint on SI dance by choreographing musicals and Musical Theatre Workshops during the late '70s and early '80s including *My Fair Lady, Carnival* and *Hello, Dolly!* Around this time Schwarz was also the first choreographer hired to teach a formal dance class after school for the young men of St. Ignatius.

Ted Curry '82 returned to SI in 1983 to choreograph *110 in the Shade, Cabaret, Mack and Mabel* and several musical theatre revues. Curry was also

the first to choreograph SI students as dancers in the Ignatian Guild Fashion Show in 1984, a tradition that continues to this day. Musical Theatre Workshop performances began to include dance numbers that stood apart from the musical scenes. The first year, dancers performed sections from *A Chorus Line* and *Cats.* (This would not be the last time that Wildcats would perform in ears and tails!) Michelle Stubbs began choreographing musicals and fashion shows in 1987 and took SI dancers into the coeducational transition. Stubbs began the tradition of Saturday morning dance classes, and for 15 years SI's advanced dancers have shown their dedication by rising early to practice on weekends as well as after school.

In 1990, Julie Ferrari was hired after students lobbied for a dance class. When Ferrari (who also taught religious studies) joined the faculty, students finally had the opportunity to take dance classes during the school day. Beginning-level students were able to take classes to complete the Fine Arts portion of their graduation requirement, and Ferrari continued to teach more advanced classes on Saturdays. At this time, classes were held in Bannan Theatre or on the then-carpeted floor of the Band Room. Neither was an ideal space for dancers, so when construction began in the early 1990s, plans included the spacious Wiegand Theatre with its sprung floor and mirrors for the dancers. Wiegand Theatre opened in late 1993, but a swimming pool mishap soon flooded it, warping its floor. The room reopened in 1994, and finally, SI's dancers had their own home.

1994 brought another milestone in SI dance. Julie Ferrari and her dance classes presented SI's first dance concert titled *Baseball, Broadway, and the Blues Brothers.* This was the first dance performance that did not include dramatic performances as well (though it did include a reading of "Casey at the Bat" by faculty member Steve Kearney). Erik DeLong '97 was a freshman dancer in the show and recalls being one of four or five boys in the class and performing numbers from *Damn Yankees* and *42ⁿᵈ Street*.

Angela Brizuela Delphino joined the faculty as SI's first full time dance teacher in the fall of 1994 and continued to develop the tradition of the annual dance concert with elaborate musical numbers and costumes. In both 1995 and 1999, SI dancers would again prowl and pounce to the music of *Cats*. Veronica Esmero '03 recalls performing that *Cats* piece in front of the entire student body in the Fine Arts Assembly her freshman year wearing her "most embarrassing costume," including fur, ears and tail. Delphino expanded the dance program to include two levels of dance classes during the school day and added an additional class after school. More and more SI students were getting the opportunity to dance.

Meredith Cecchin '97 joined the faculty in 2001 and continued the expansion of SI dance. By 2003 the program offered two levels of dance to students during the school day and four levels after school and on weekends. SI Dance Alumni Ted Curry and Lizette Ortega '94 both returned to their dance roots upon joining the faculty at SI. Over 100 students of varying levels participate annually in one or both of two annual dance concerts. SI dancers continue to perform in the Spring Musical and Fine Arts Assembly and continue to develop as choreographers as well as dancers. The dance program continued its feline tradition in 2005 with the January concert *wildCATS*, which featured pieces from Broadway musicals including, predictably, *Cats*.

Though some musical choices might remain the same, SI's dance program has advanced and grown

since that first choreographer was hired 40 years ago. Jesuit schools have always held the performing arts in high regard as important for student development. It is such thinking by administrators, faculty, parents and students that allows the dance program to continue to expand and excel. SI's dancers live out the truth in Albert Einstein's words when he proclaimed that "dancers are the athletes of God."

And All the Rest

Ignatians showed creativity in organizing new clubs from 1990 through 2005. The following clubs made their debut (and some, their exit) in this period: Web Design, InSIgnis, Insignis Core, Wildcat Welcoming Club, Dance and Drill, United Cultures of St. Ignatius, the French Honor Society and Christmas Choir, Spanish Honor Society, Japanese Honor Society, Junior Statesmen of America, the Junior Classical League, Amnesty International, Social Justice, School of the Americas Protest, the Left, C is for Cookie, Martial Arts, Cycling, Animé, Donuts and Coffee, Teen Angel, Paint Ball, Rock and Roll, Diner's Club, Bread Connection, Boys State, Girls State, San Francisco Exchange Program, Academic Decathlon, Ambassador Club, the Quill, Conservative Students' Coalition, Guitar Club & Ensemble, Biology Club, Science Club, Big Sisters, Protosite, Ecology Club, Jewish Life Club, L'Chaim, Yoga, Film, SI Card Club, Mentoring, Pub Club, Interact, Armenian Students Association, Photo Club, Hackey Cats, SI Aquarium Society, Psychology Club, PCMUG, Polo Club, Pep Band and Student Trainers (an innovative program using students as athletic trainers, under the supervision of Marla Bottner and Robert Assadurian, to accompany teams to their games and help with first aid and conditioning).

Opposite page: The Wildcat Welcoming Committee offers tours to 8th graders who come to learn about the school.

XIV. The New Millennium

In the first five years of the new millennium, SI experienced successes that promise a bright future for the school. Those years saw a continued progression of the changes initiated in the 1990s, with the school excelling on all fronts. In 2004, students earned their highest SAT scores and passed more AP tests than ever before. The boys' basketball team in 2004 took the league and CCS championships for the first time in 20 years. Workers put the finishing touches on the campus by tearing up the grass and installing FieldTurf and a new track. And the school announced that it would celebrate the completion, one year ahead of schedule, of the Genesis IV Endow SI campaign in December 2005.

Still, the first few years offered one major challenge. For the first time in its modern history, the SI faculty included no Jesuit scholastics, and the number of priests at SI continued to decline. The Society of Jesus, like all religious orders, does not have the manpower it once had. SI found an answer to this challenge in the Adult Ministry Program. Begun in 2001, this innovative project seeks to train lay faculty and staff in Ignatian spirituality so that SI will always remain a Jesuit school, even with fewer priests and brothers.

In 2005 the school marked the 26th year of Fr. Sauer's tenure as president. He has steered SI since 1979, for one-sixth of the school's history, longer than any of his predecessors. He is not the only person responsible for SI's success, but no one could lay greater claim to it than he. In 2004, the school kicked off its yearlong sesquicentennial celebration at the December 3 President's Cabinet Dinner. Midway through the year, the school held a giant birthday party for itself with the June 4, 2005, Day on the Boulevard event for the entire SI community (thanks to the leadership of SI Regent Fred Tocchini '66 and his Sesquicentennial Committee), and it ended the celebratory year with the December 2005 President's Cabinet Dinner.

Opposite page: In 2003, SI refurbished the track and field, installing FieldTurf to allow for all-weather competition.

Genesis IV Campaign
& The Sesquicentennial Celebration

Thanks to the leadership of Board of Regents' Chairman Mark Cleary '64 and the generosity of SI's donor community, SI is well on its way to reaching the $50 million goal for the Genesis IV: Endow SI campaign. The success of the endowment campaign comes as a result of generous individuals and foundations, and their donations, large and small. Since SI's move to the Sunset District, gifts or pledges of $1 million or more — in single gifts or over several years — have come to SI from Mr. & Mrs. Henry J. Budde, Mr. Charles H. Luchessa '23, the Josephine McCormick Trust, the William G. Irwin Charity Foundation, the Arline & Thomas J. Bannan Foundation, the Henry Doelger Trust, Mr. & Mrs. Michel Orradre, Archbishop Joseph McGucken, Mr. & Mrs. Robert F. McCullough, Sr. '48, Mr. & Mrs. John Gibbons '37 and the Jesuit Community of St. Ignatius (who donate their salaries back to the school).

Because scholarships for needy students come from a school's endowment fund, "endowment is the key to the success of any school," said Mark Cleary. However, two challenges faced the Development office in raising funds for the Genesis IV campaign. "First, it is sometimes hard to do fund-raising for financial aid, as donors do not see a building rise up from

Mark Cleary, was named chairman of the Board of Regents in 2002.

their donations," said Cleary. Secondly, a new challenge arose in the late 1990s with the dot-com bust. "The economy worked against us. People were not flush with disposable income. We finished well because of Tony Sauer and Steve Lovette. Tony retains personal contact with an awful lot of people, yet he's not a high-pressure person when it comes to asking for money. Tony helps people feel good about the school, and he is appreciative for any gift, large or small."

Cleary has also helped bring new people to the Board of Regents who offered diverse talents. "They represented a broad matrix. People such as Clark Callander '76 have stepped up both with money and expertise. We have an investment committee that major universities would envy. Tom Bertlesen's competence in taking care of our funds is incredible. Of all the boards I have served on, SI's is the easiest because everything is so well run."

Despite the tough economy, the campaign had a few early successes, allowing the school to add on the $5 million Faculty Housing Fund to the Genesis IV campaign to help young teachers who faced one of the hottest housing markets in the world. "We did that to help keep SI in the forefront of education," said Cleary. "We need to attract and keep the best teachers we can find."

Cleary praised the work of his predecessors on the Board of Regents who "reconnected with friends of SI during the capital campaign. When we returned to them, we discovered that SI was on their minds, and we encouraged them to join the Heritage Society or to create an endowed scholarship."

Fr. Sauer praised Cleary for his dedication to the school, and noted that his SI roots go back nearly as far as the school's beginnings. His great uncle, Frank Cleary, graduated from St. Ignatius College

in 1882, and his grandfather, Alfred J. Cleary, followed in 1900. Since then six Clearys and one cousin have graced the halls of SI including Mark's father, Alfred J. Cleary, Jr. '37, Mark's two uncles, Louis Cleary '39 and William Reilly '51, Mark's brother, Alfred J. Cleary III '61, and Mark's son, Sean Cleary '99. "These men all had one thing in common," said Cleary. "We were all taught to give something back to the community."

The Sesquicentennial Committee, from left: Jim Dekker, Gary Brickley, Al Clifford, Catherine Vollert, Cynthia Fitzgibbon, Tom McGuigan, Fr. Paul Capitolo, SJ, Fred Tocchini (chairman), Stella Agius Muscat, Peter Devine, Randy DeVoto, Stephen Leveroni (vice chairman), James Monfredini (assistant to the chairman) and Paul Totah.

Each Christmas season, SI students collect food for needy families in San Francisco

Adult Ministry

Given the declining numbers of priests and religious at SI, the question arose: How can SI remain a Jesuit school with few Jesuits? SI answered that question with the Adult Ministry Program, which had its start in 1998, when Fr. Greg Goethals, SJ, the rector of the SI Jesuit community, attended a meeting where he heard one administrator proclaim that the five Province high schools 20 years down the road "will soon be Catholic at best but not Jesuit."

"That got me to thinking about what makes a Jesuit school Ignatian," said Goethals. "His pronouncement disturbed me. Why should I give my life to a cause that will be over in 20 years?" Goethals realized that Jesuits share much in common with other religious traditions, but that they also have one thing unique to their Order: the Spiritual Exercises. "The question then became: How can we figure out a way to give as many people as possible the Exercises? Ignatius founded his institutions primarily as a means of offering the Exercises, to give people the radical experience of God's love in their lives."

Goethals then created an Adult Ministry Office, funded through $50,000 of donated Jesuit salaries, so that he and a co-director could begin leading retreats and prayer services for SI's faculty. "I wanted to put my money where my mouth was," he added. He then hired Rita O'Malley, a former SI faculty member, to work with him to begin the task of helping the faculty become more fully Ignatian.

It did not take long before faculty recognized the need for this office. For the first time in its modern history, not a single scholastic worked at SI starting with the 2002-2003 school year. In 2005, only one Jesuit

served as a full-time faculty member, and three priests taught part time. (Other Jesuits, both brothers and priests, also work at SI in a variety of capacities.) If

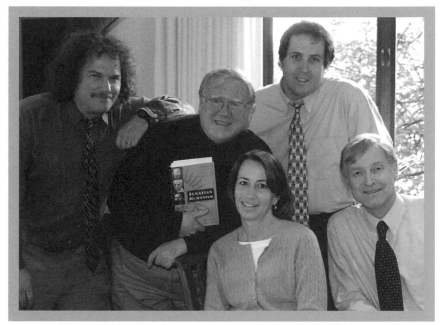

SI were to stay Jesuit, the faculty would have to learn even better how to grow as Ignatian ministers.

In the first few years of its existence, about 80 of the 120 faculty participated voluntarily in at least one of the several programs offered by Greg Goethals, Rita O'Malley and, later, by Mary Abinante, who became a part-time member of that office. Faculty lined up for retreats ranging from the full 30-day Spiritual Exercises to shorter, individually-directed experiences. They participated in prayer groups during Advent and Lent, and they met with priests or with members of the Adult Ministry Team for spiritual direction.

Rita O'Malley (center) guides teachers in Ignatian spirituality. From left are Kevin Quattrin, Peter Devine, Byron Philhour and Steve Phelps.

To allow the faculty to go on extended retreats, Fr. Goethals established a fund so that "teachers would have as few obstacles as possible to perform the Spiri-

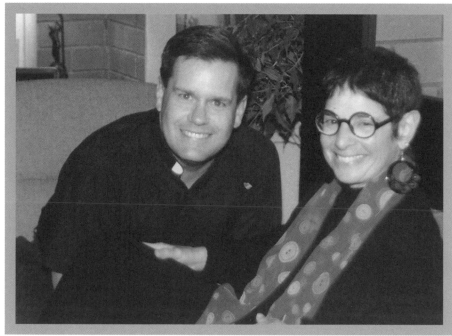

Fr. Greg Goethals, SJ, and French teacher Shelley Friedman.

tual Exercises. This is a legacy that will keep SI Ignatian and keep the charism alive and vibrant."

The Adult Spirituality Office now offers 19th Annotation Retreats (year-long versions of the 30-day retreat), the Arrupe Project, summer eight-day silent retreats, individual spiritual direction, a morning prayer group for young faculty called Lightworks, Advent and Lunch prayer groups and group retreats for administrators, women faculty and male teachers. In addition, all teachers take part in Ignatian Evenings, the faculty retreat and ministry mornings.

"We're not turning lay teachers into Jesuits," Fr. Goethals added. "We're providing people the opportunity to participate in Ignatian spirituality. St. Ignatius was a layman when he created the Exercises and when he directed his followers in their practice. The Exercises are easily translated into the lives of everyday people. Teachers now know how to speak the Ignatian language. They know what *cura personalis* and *magis* really mean, and they see their jobs as ministry, not merely as careers. Kate Kodros, the assistant principal, says that teachers with good spiritual lives are better teachers. They don't see themselves as having a product to give students but as human beings offering a connection to students. They also are better at ministering to students on retreats because they, themselves, are in formation."

Fr. Goethals praised O'Malley and Abinante for their contributions to the Adult Ministry Office. "Rita was hired because, as a mother, wife, woman and lay person, she can relate to the faculty in ways that I can't. Mary has helped us institutionalize the office, to make it more based on programs rather than personalities."

O'Malley believes that this office is unique among all the U.S. Jesuit high schools in that it involves a layperson and a priest and is funded entirely by the Jesuit community. "Greg Goethals envisioned this as a pioneer project. Other schools do similar things, but on a less formal basis. The credit goes to the Jesuit community for supporting us the way it does." For his sabbatical in 2005, Fr. Goethals hopes to translate SI's program to other schools as they, too, face the same challenges as SI.

The Greater Good

The spirit of *magis* permeates each department at SI. Each year, teachers ask themselves how they can choose the greater good, how they can make choices that improve their classrooms and their departments and how they can better serve students. Each department over the past 20 years has made major strides that that are worth noting.

Campus Ministry

Campus ministry used to be the responsibility of one priest. Now, nearly half the senior class and the great majority of faculty assist a diverse campus ministry team in caring for the entire community. "It's no longer a one-man show," said Fr. Greg Goethals, who served as campus minister from 1997 to 2000. He credits George Horsfall '74, a former Jesuit and campus minister, with beginning the transition, forming the first campus ministry team in the early 1990s and overseeing the remodeling of the campus ministry center.

You can see this change reflected in the senior retreat. Up until the 1970s, one priest typically led a silent retreat for a group of seniors. In the early 1970s, a few faculty started sharing their stories with students. In the late 1970s, Fr. Gordon Bennett, SJ, (now a bishop in Jamaica) created a senior retreat program that lasted for 25 years based loosely on the Spiritual Exercises. Then, in 1996, Michael Shaughnessy '67, a member of the campus ministry team and campus minister between 2000 and 2004, went to Bellarmine to learn

about the Kairos Retreat program there and found it worked because it was student-centered. In the fall of 1997, SI offered its first 3-day Kairos Retreat to seniors, and in February 2002, expanded the retreat to four days. The retreats are led by members of InSIgnis, made up of half the senior class, who also run freshman orientation and serve as leaders on the freshman, sophomore and junior retreats. Both the junior and senior retreats are optional, but 95 percent of the members of those classes choose to attend them.

"With the start of the Immersion Program," said Shaughnessy, "we began to think of our role as walking alongside the students rather than leading them." Most students, he added, "come to SI for the academics or co-curriculars. Many students leave saying that their most significant memories are from Campus Ministry activities. We exceed expectations for most students and families."

Students say The Our Father at the 2004 Thanksgiving Liturgy in the McCullough Gymnasium.

Christian Service Program

As of fall 2004, seniors, juniors and sophomores at SI had accumulated nearly 100,000 hours annually of service to our local communities, helping more than 150 charities and agencies through volunteer work during the summer and after school. Of the current seniors, nearly one-third have achieved 200-Hour Service Honors, having served twice as many hours as required for graduation. Over the years, many students have gone well beyond even this generous number and have logged upwards of 1,000 hours of service to their communities.

Students also have the opportunity to participate in SI's faith immersion trips, a program run out of the Campus Ministry office. For the summer of 2004,

64 students and 16 adults visited eight communities as part of this program — Birmingham, Costa Rica, East Los Angeles, Northern Ireland, Sacramento, San Francisco, Tacoma and Tijuana. Living in simplicity and solidarity with their hosts, these groups spend two weeks in service and prayer. Immersion has become a hallmark experience for SI students and faculty, challenging them to more deeply and intentionally learn and address social justice in our society.

Over the years, under the direction of Art Cecchin '63, David Mezzera '64 and now Jenny Girard, student involvement has deepened. SI graduates spend a minimum of 40 hours volunteering with one nonprofit agency working directly with marginalized communities and addressing justice issues such as homelessness, healthcare and education. Students keep a reflection journal while they service these core hours, and are asked to complete all 100 hours by the start of their senior year.

The CSP center received a name change in 2004 to the Thomas J. Reed, SJ, Christian Service Center thanks to an endowment by the Leonardini family. Each year, beginning in 2005, two seniors — male and female — will be chosen as exemplars of the ideals of the program and the values of Fr. Reed, who served as principal between 1957 and 1964. SI will give each student $1,000 that they will, in turn, donate to the organization where they served the majority of their community service hours.

Students in the "Music for Others" group performed for the elderly in 2002.

Counseling

SI offers a professionally trained counseling staff in a modern center that opened in the fall of 2001 after a $400,000 gift from The Carl and Celia Berta Gellert Foundation (named for them and in honor of Alberta and Peter Brusati '43).

"When I need to gather the lower division counselors together for a quick meeting, I can do this immediately because everyone is so close," said Counseling Department Chair Donna Murphy. "It also allows us to deal with students in crisis situations. If I need someone to stay with a student while I get a parent, that can readily happen."

SI boasts one of the best student-to-counselor ratios in the state, with 130–1 for upper division students and 188–1 for lower division students. Each counselor has certification or a Master's degree, and some have specialized training, such as Phyllis Molinelli and Mike Thomas, who are licensed marriage-family-child counselors, and Cally Salzman, the learning specialist and Academic Support Service Coordinator, who works with 100 students with documented learning differences.

Students, rather than changing counselors each year, stay with one counselor for the freshman and sophomore years and then switch to another person, specially trained in college counseling, for their junior and senior years. Counselors offer help with scholarships and college applications and train students to use a subscription web site called myroads.com that helps them decide which college to attend and prepares them for the application process.

Mike Thomas serves as the department's health education coordinator and runs the Drug and Alcohol Taskforce. He works with students in the Peer Assistance Center and with C Is For Cookie as they help their classmates with issues ranging from stress and eating disorders to peer pressure. He also works with

Members of the SI Counseling Department in 2003.

the Northern California Community of Concern — a consortium of 43 high schools that share resources in dealing with issues common to all students.

English

If you look at the reading list from the English Department in the 1980s, you will find books tailored to adolescent boys, from *Lord of the Flies* to *A Separate Peace*. With the advent of coeducation, much about the department changed, from the reading list (which now includes books by and about women and people of color) to the ratio of men and women faculty, with greater gender parity than ever before.

In the 1980s, under the leadership of Fr. John Murphy, SJ '59, the department made huge strides. The curric-

ulum continued to develop during his tenure with a heavy emphasis on the classics, solid writing and reading skills and active learning. Under his watch the school adopted the Junior Writing Exam, which identifies juniors who have yet to master composition skills and to teach them those skills by the time they graduate.

Jim Bjorkquist '65 further developed the curriculum with the establishment of one-semester senior electives such as Fiction into Film, Short Fiction, Shakespeare and Poetry. He tied American Literature to American History in the junior year, and he also encouraged teachers to teach upper and lower division so that teachers would experience students on both levels. Department Chairs Matt Barmore '76, Elizabeth Purcell and Bobby Gavin continued the work of their predecessors, making the department a hallmark of collaboration among its members and between departments. English teachers worked with colleagues in the Religious Studies and Social Science Departments to prepare interdisciplinary curriculum when the junior class attended the play *Miss Saigon* in 2000 and *Ragtime* in 2001 and 2002. The department also launched a speakers' series to bring authors and college professors to SI. In the 1990s, the department resurrected *The Quill*, the student literary magazine, and faculty moderators help student editors select poems, short stories and illustrations for publication in the annual magazine.

While the English Department has had success helping students pass the AP English Language exam in their junior year and the AP English Literature exam in their senior years, teachers measure their success by the passion engendered in students for great literature and its ability to shape lives.

Since the 1970s, the SI Fine Arts Department has expanded from its long tradition of excellent theatre, dance and music offerings to include a full complement of visual arts ranging from art and architecture to photography and sculpture. Ignatians can also learn about making buildings and art objects in a wilderness environment through an Art in Nature seminar. In 2002, students took part in an artist-in-residency program at the San Francisco Transfer Station where they gave new life to cast-offs by turning trash into innovative sculptures.

The fine arts faculty, by teaching creative expression, is furthering the Jesuit mission and vision by educating the whole person. "We are grateful to SI for giving us this opportunity and for supporting us," said Katie Wolf, who heads the department. "SI allows us to give our students the experience of discovering and sharing their own creativity. They become aware that they are the shining reflection of the Creator."

The annual Winter Pops Concert, featuring the choir (left) and orchestra (below), is a highlight of the Christmas season at SI.

With the new millennium came a new name for the Foreign Language Department, which now calls itself the Language Department. "There's nothing foreign about us," notes Department Chairwoman Theresa Tai.

For Tai, the department's success can be measured both in its remarkable AP scores (with several 100 percent pass rates over the years) and by the extent that teachers collaborate on grade level exams, semester exams and projects. The department was in the forefront of collaboration, Tai added, before it became the norm.

Over the past several years, the department has worked to incorporate technology into the classroom, with students learning grammar and conversation using a host of software products and making movies of themselves speaking their language in a variety of contexts. For a few years the department staged its own Oscar awards for the best of those movies.

The languages offered in the 2004–05 academic year included Spanish, French, Latin, Japanese and German. A survey of recent SI grads revealed that 80 percent would make the same choice of language that they made as incoming freshmen and that they felt cared for and challenged by their teachers.

Tai credits the department's success to the colleagueship of her professional staff, which now includes four men in what had been an all-female department. "We all really like each other, and everyone acts with superb professionalism. Each member offers his or her unique sets of skills and resources, from planning curriculum to teaching to working with cutting edge technology that enhances student learning."

The growth of the Internet hasn't made SI's library (or any library for that matter) obsolete. If you visit the Alfred S. Wilsey library before, during and after school, you will find it packed with students searching for and reading books as well as doing Internet searches or writing papers.

The three librarians — Richard Raiter, Virtudes Gomez and Renate Morlock — have become expert at helping students narrow Internet searches, judge the information they find and use it for their homework assignments. Raiter, the department chairman, teaches every freshman that the best onramp onto the information superhighway is not always Google but the SI library web page, which offers free to students a number of subscription-based resources as well as a handy collection of search engines and links to local libraries, newspapers and books by SI alumni authors.

Students also learn how to use the online catalog to search for books by title, author or subject and how to access that catalog from home. Students may also take advantage of the library's expanded hours, from 7:30 a.m. to 5 p.m. The library offers wireless Internet access to students and faculty and soon hopes to offer laptop computer loaners to students.

The library boasts a wonderful collection of books, adding several hundred new titles each year that include recreational novels and college-level texts. Helping the staff are 30 volunteer parents who assist students at lunch and after school, work on special projects and decorate the display cases each month. In addition, 10 student helpers restock and check out books before and after school each day.

Opposite page: Students in French class, such as the ones pictured here, learn French culture as well as language.

Mathematics

In 1988, only two teachers out of 11 in the math department had tenure. The department was young and relatively inexperienced. As of 2004, all but two of the 14 math teachers have tenure in what has become an excellent department.

"When I first came to SI, our Math Analysis (main senior) course was not really prepping anyone for college calculus," said department chairman Kevin Quattrin '78. When the first coed class became seniors, Assistant Principal for Academics Tom Murphy '76 asked him to beef up the department offerings.

The department sent out the first Math Alumni Survey to SI students in their freshman year of college, a practice the department has continued to this day. "We found that the honors kids who had gotten to AP Calculus were well prepared and happy, but few others felt as satisfied." The department responded by offering its own PreCalculus textbook in 1997 and a 2004 textbook on trigonometry, authored by Quattrin. In 2005, the department hopes to offer a third textbook, this one for honors geometry students.

With the Class of 2000, the department reinstituted AP Calculus BC, which it had dropped after 1990. The AP pass rate has gone up over the years, with 47 of 48 passing it in 2004, 21 with a top score of 5.

The department's college survey now includes questions about technology use and cooperative learning experiences in college. "We are being proactive to stay ahead of the curve," Quattrin added.

The department stresses consistency among classes by offering common final exams at all levels. "We were also the first department to establish formal level coordinators who are responsible for monthly meetings among teachers of the same course to fix pac-ing and curriculum issues, as well as formalizing the textbook selection process," said Quattrin. "We also reinstituted the use of the UC Diagnostic test at the beginning of each year to check retention and establish baseline competencies across the student body."

In the late 1990s, the department started offering a summer Advanced Algebra class for sophomores entering their junior year to help them move into and stay in honors-level courses. "This class is, in part, responsible for a jump in the retention rate (of students staying in the honors track) from 30 percent to 92 percent over the past six years, and we hope next year to turn this into an online course."

The department has also responded to the Archdiocesan mandate that all grammar schools teach Algebra 1 to eighth graders. At the request of Steve Phelps, the SI math department designed and presented two summer workshops for eighth grade teachers. Schools that sent their teachers to SI have had a significant increase in placement of their students into SI's honors class over those schools that did not.

As a result, the number of freshmen testing into honors algebra has jumped from 100 in 1998 to 200 in 2004. "This increase has ballooned our calculus classes from 90 students to 170 in six sections," said Quattrin. "Several of our teachers had to retrain to move up into higher-level classes than they were used to teaching. They have done so admirably. Nearly a third of the Class of 2004 passed an AP Calculus test, thanks to four years of solid math education."

Physical Education

Those who attended SI in the early 1970s recall rudimentary PE classes that involved basic physical fitness activities. That changed in the late 1970s when Michael Thomas '71 became department chairman. Later department chairmen, from Rob Hickox '72 to Jan Mullen, improved the department further.

Thomas adopted the textbook *Fitness for Life* and stressed that philosophy to the students. He felt that PE classes should do two things: help students understand the need for physical fitness and give them exposure to activities that they could do on their own throughout their lives. Towards that end, he stressed running, tennis and golf. Later, when SI built its pool, the PE department began teaching swimming and diving and trained students to become lifeguards. With the addition of a modern weight room, the program added weight training to its regimen, with classes taught both by Steve Bluford '84 and Tony Calvello '84.

The addition of the pool and weight room weren't the only physical changes to the school that aided the department. The second gym and new tennis courts, coupled with the two fields covered in all-weather FieldTurf, gave the department the ability to teach classes come rain or shine. Those facilities also allowed for a variety of electives that include weight training, beginning and advanced aquatics, recreational and competitive sports (where students learn to run all sorts of games and team sports), and a women's fitness class.

PE 1, which all freshmen take, and each of the electives offer information on nutrition, drugs and alcohol and other health issues. Students take midterm and final exams that include academic components and do oral presentations on health issues related to physical activity. Students also receive certification in CPR or first aid or the equivalency (such as becoming a lifeguard) in each of the electives.

The instructors don't measure success by how many pounds students can benchpress. "We want students to improve from whatever point they enter the class," said Hickox. The department uses a point

system that allows any student to earn an A no matter his or her ability. The department also teaches students to evaluate their level of fitness and to determine their individual threshold and target zones. "These courses are more important than ever given how many kids

The PE Department offers weight training as an elective.

have sedentary lifestyles," said Thomas. "Once they get in shape, they realize how much better they can feel."

Religious Studies

The consistency in curriculum in the math department is echoed in the religious studies department, where curriculum for classes is the same across the board for each of the first three years, regardless of the teacher, thanks to improved collaboration among department members.

Mary Ahlbach, a recent department chairwoman, praised religious studies teachers for their professionalism and for keeping themselves up-to-date by taking classes that have helped them improve as both teachers and scholars. "Teaching religion is more challenging than other subjects," Ahlbach said. "What we teach isn't as black and white as other disciplines. Our curriculum involves the heart and soul and the personal journey of faith, which is impossible to grade."

Ahlbach is also proud of the addition of social justice and service components to most classes. Each class performs some direct service, from assisting the Comfort Run, which provides juice and sandwiches each Thursday morning to people waiting in line at St. Anthony's, to working at St. Anthony's kitchen during the day. Students each year also take part in a Holocaust speaker series instituted by Jim McGarry in the 1990s.

The department uses textbooks "that go beyond the basic information offered by so many other books," said Ahlbach. "We have created our own readers, use college-level textbooks and include literature such as *The Chosen, Inherit the Wind* and *City of Joy*."

Students also learn how to pray using meditation and contemplation — hallmarks of the Spiritual Exercises. "We aren't afraid to take time to do this because we realize how much our students hunger for this experience. We used to be embarrassed to take academic time to pray, and that has changed." The department also teaches students about the life of Christ, as evidenced in the Gospels, and the lives of saints, such as St. Ignatius of Loyola, "so that when they leave SI, they know Ignatius' spirituality, mentality and charism."

Ahlbach points to the school's graduates as evidence of the department's success. "We sow seeds that may not sprout and bear fruit until years after graduation. Many students attend Jesuit universities and then join the Jesuit Volunteer Corps. Some return to host Immersion trips for SI students. At the School of the Americas protest, we often meet many SI alumni, and some graduates major in peace studies in college inspired by their junior year social justice course."

Science

For Science Department Chairman Deirdre McGovern, the strength of her department lies in its young, vibrant faculty, made up of six women and eight men, with six of the teachers also serving as coaches. All but one of the faculty have a Master's degree, two hold doctoral degrees and one is a dissertation away from her Ph.D. "When I started working at SI 16 years ago, I was the first woman in the department," McGovern noted. "Now there's far better gender parity."

In 2003, the department radically altered the way it structured its courses. In past years, most freshmen would take an Introduction to Science course, with a

Opposite: Associate Dean Karen Cota, wearing a protective suit, gets a charge out of a physics demonstration.

handful of their classmates taking biology. Now, all freshmen take biology, sophomores take chemistry and juniors study physics. As seniors, students may choose to take an Advanced Placement science course or one of several electives, such as Marine Biology, Anatomy/Physiology, Astronomy and Science Research. As a result of these changes, students now take four full years of science.

Students also have the option of studying biology or chemistry in summer school, giving them more options to enroll in Advanced Placement courses during the school year. For instance, a student who signs up for chemistry during the summer could

choose to take AP Chemistry during the year. Students in calculus-based AP Physics also have the advantage of taking two separate AP tests: Mechanics and Electricity & Magnetism.

"The department does so well because our teachers thrive on collaboration," added McGovern, pointing to the restructured biology program pioneered by Ryan O'Malley and Patricia Kennedy and the physics text authored by Byron Philhour, James Dann and Dann's father (a physics teacher for 30 years). "These teachers have devised creative and innovative projects that teach lessons in engaging ways." For example, students in physics build catapults to hurl tennis balls across the football field and devise weather-balloon experiments to make more concrete the abstract concepts in their texts. Chemistry students build hot-air balloons and explore alternative energy sources.

McGovern also pointed to the quality of the lab facilities, which went from three to six after the 1994 school remodel. The labs offer a greater opportunity for cooperative learning, as the lab stations are located on the periphery of the classroom, so teachers can go from lecture to lab by moving a few feet.

The Tech Team, aided by student volunteers, help train faculty to use their new laptop computers.

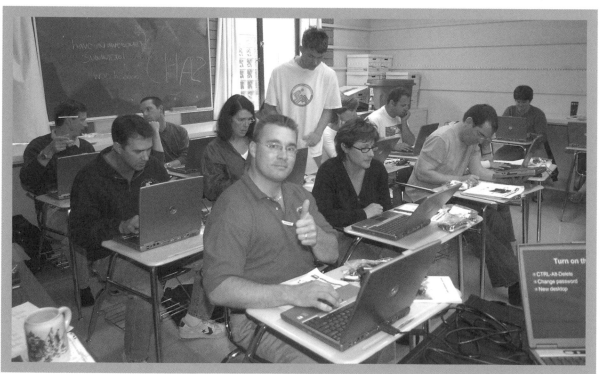

Years ago, history was taught by lecture, using a chronological approach, and focusing primarily on America and Europe. Today, the department teaches according to major themes, from ecology to economics. Students also explore the world outside Europe and now learn the history of the Middle East, Far East, South America and Africa, studying how their history relates to the history of the world and to current events.

Freshmen take a full year and sophomores have one semester of world history. Juniors study American history, and seniors have the option of taking government or psychology for one or two semesters or a one-semester European History Seminar for college credit taught by John Stiegeler '74. Students who earn a B or higher earn three college units from USF.

No other AP exam draws as many students as the AP U.S. History test. Last year, for instance, 280 juniors took the exam. Seniors may take the AP Government or AP Psychology test and generally achieve high pass rates.

The department has sponsored a speakers' program for several years and has hosted U.S. Rep. Tom Lantos, KGO talk-show host Bernie Ward '69 and Assemblyman Leland Yee. It has also worked with the English and religious studies departments on interdisciplinary projects

When SI purchased its first computer back in the 1970s, it became the center of attention, as did the first computer lab set up by William Love '59. Technology at SI has advanced far from those days, evidenced by the fact that computers are everywhere yet no one gives them a second look. They have become as ubiquitous and as useful as pencils, and students and teachers use them as naturally as they would their No. 2 graphite. In short, students see and use the computer for what it is — a tool that can enhance the learning experience without taking the focus away from the subject.

The change came incrementally. After the first two computer labs were set up, the tech team worked to network them and then network the entire school. SI teachers were the first to receive e-mail accounts, with students receiving their "@siprep.org" accounts in 2002. By 2004, most teachers had web pages, and students could check grades and homework assignments online. With the wireless network, established in 2003, teachers and students could use the equipment more easily than ever before. The tech team now comprises four highly-skilled computer experts, aided by a talented group of students who install software, train faculty and solve problems. The technology department, which offers courses from web design to multimedia, also oversees a student computer club. To see for yourself the advances SI has made, go to www. siprep.org and explore the virtual SI community.

Fr. Anthony P. Sauer, SJ, has served as SI's president for 26 years, nearly one-sixth of the school's history.

Opposite page: Fr. Sauer in 1966.

Two Tributes to Fr. Sauer

Former SI principal Mario Prietto, SJ, has this to say about Fr. Sauer, who has served as SI's president since 1979: "No one has taught me more about what it means to be a Jesuit, a priest and a good human being than Tony. He is the best. He is an extraordinary person — not without flaws and a character of the first order — but he is a deeply spiritual man, a great Jesuit, an Irish poet to the core and a man who does not toot his horn even though he has a lot to toot about. You never hear Tony talk about what he has been doing, unlike people in his position who brag about their latest accomplishments. Tony never talks about himself, but when you find out about all the lives he has influenced, all the weddings, baptisms, hospitals and games he goes to, his love is so incredible that it takes my breath away. I get emotional thinking about Tony! He is extraordinary. He is something else."

Fr. Prietto is not alone in his praise. When Fr. Sauer turned 70 in 2004, the SI faculty surprised him with a tribute book, with letters from teachers whose lives he has touched in profound ways. These letters

reflect just why Fr. Sauer succeeds as president and priest. He, like the school itself, has the gift of staying true to core values as well as the flexibility to change with the times. He also has the great gift of looking you in the eyes and making you feel as if you're the only one who matters. Teachers and students at SI know they

have a real friend in Fr. Sauer, not someone merely interested in making them happy. That is why he is the first person they call for baptisms, weddings and funerals, for times of celebration and commiseration. And, unlike some imperial presidents, Fr. Sauer believes in sharing the wealth, empowering all to serve with him as Christ's ministers.

Among those who celebrated Tony Sauer at the faculty party were Bob Drucker, Phyllis Molinelli, Bobby Gavin and Carole Nickolai. Each offered a moving tribute, two of which are reprinted below.

By Bobby Gavin

My first memory of Tony is my interview with him. I meet Fr. Sauer in his office. It is early in the morning. I am on time. I get into his office and he is just finishing up the act of putting on his collar. His back is to me. "Do you want some coffee, my man?" The memory strikes me as typical of Tony because it was altogether casual and disarming. More importantly, he had a rhythm about his life that others entered into, and that rhythm, that dance, felt comfortable. He was late, but he felt early. I liked him right away. I don't think he had any questions prepared for me, but we talked without missing a beat, and I walked out of there thinking: If this guy is in charge, I want to work here.

My next memory: Tony greets the new teachers in the campus ministry meeting room. He introduces himself, offers one piece of advice and exits. He says: "Love your students." I think, "Cool. I can do that." I attempt to implement the technique during the next week, and my freshman English class turns me into a rag doll for nine months. But at the first Mass I attend where Fr. Sauer is the celebrant, his homily weaves to-

gether James Joyce with Bob Dylan. I think to myself: How cool can this guy be?

Let me share a story with you. This last summer, Fr. Sauer, Kevin Feeney '04 and I were scheduled to attend a Bloomsday event at the Mechanics' Library. The festivities are hosted by a good friend of mine, and the party is held to honor Joyce's *Ulysses*. After it was over, Fr. Sauer insisted that I get him my friend's name and address so he could send a thank you note. I eventually got around to it, but after I did, my friend Mark had a thank you note in his hand the next day. He called to tell me that the school's president was "the most courteous man in the world," but, he added, "I honestly can't make heads or tails out of any of it." We all know the experience of this. There is something magical about a Sauer note. You take it to a friend: "What do you think this says? And this here,

is this my name?" but you feel that love he recommended from the first day.

It seems effortless, doesn't it? He might be the hardest working man I know, and yet it truly seems effortless. He seems to be at every SI event, wearing a pair of shorts no matter what the weather and with a lilt in his step. There is a lighthearted joyfulness in the way he carries himself. That lightheartedness transcends his entire life. I marvel at his leadership skills. I have never seen him lose his temper, and he only exercises his power when it is absolutely needed. He has the ability to participate in an English department meeting, and everyone treats him as an equal. Somehow he disarms you of the stigma that he is your boss and a priest. But isn't that Tony's great gift?

And he is not a boastful man. Maybe that is why it is so easy to tell him the truth. Fr. Sauer seemed to

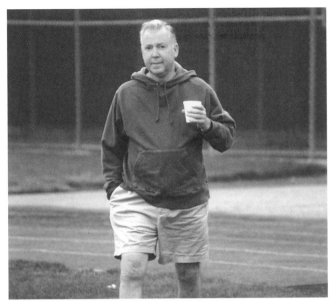

learn early on that it doesn't help to let people at a table know that you are the smartest person there. But I'll bet you he is, and that's one of his secrets.

Fr. Sauer is truly an educator. If there is one thing he is competitive about, it is the notion of improving himself in the classroom. He refuses to grow old in the classroom. He constantly changes his texts. He takes his student evaluations eminently seriously, and he will tell me: "I know they want more discussion. I'm going to create more discussion." There is a fire in his belly. Do you know that he has had a 100 percent pass rate with his AP students for at least three years running? Do you know how hard that is to do? It is not luck. Stand outside of Room 109 right at the end of 4th period and you'll see him in there going over a paper with a student. And he doesn't pull any punches. "What do you mean with this word? Be concise. Too

flabby here." He takes the necessary time, and they learn how to write.

I love to walk in that room and see a line of poetry scrawled across the blackboard with its scansion marked. Invariably I ask one of my students what it says, and he won't be quite sure: "It's Latin I think." Nobody knows poetry like Tony Sauer. If you want to know where he lives and breathes, it is within poetry. I walked in his office yesterday, and he dashed off a couplet from *King Lear* to me. "I have somebody coming in a minute," he said. "The lines you want are 'as flies to wanton boys are we to the gods; they kill us for their sport.' Okay? Thanks babes." And it's time to leave. To him it's as easy as drinking a glass of milk.

But not milk tonight Fr. Sauer. I invite you all to raise your glasses to this great man. Happy birthday Fr. Sauer. We love you.

By Carole Nickolai

I first met Tony during my interview process quite a long time ago. He put a naïve, nervous young woman at ease, and my meeting with the "President" evolved into a discussion about the role of Ebonics vs. Standard English and the decline of the written word. Referring to a recently graded red-marked paper with a huge "D" on it, Fr. Sauer noted that there was "just no hope. He'll never learn to write." He then asked me, "What do you think?" Although my immediate thought was, "Does this mean I'm hired?" I was able to muster some probably obtuse reply. During that brief meeting, Tony treated me not as a mere potential hire, but as a colleague.

I was soon to learn that his ability to shift roles, wear different hats ranging from president to priest, fundraiser to friend, is truly amazing. Over the past years, we've seen him strut his stuff as a model on the runway, be the star attraction at the pre-auction photo-shoots, sit attentively in Mrs. Purcell's cushy leather seat with a clever quip on the tip of his tongue at department meetings and inspire us with his words from the pulpit during "hour with Sauer" Masses. His sermons with multiple literary allusions bring me closer to God. He has sent me birthday cards and letters of support. The bottom line is that he makes me, as well as everyone else here, feel valued. He keeps our community alive and loving.

No one knows this more than his students. Today, no fewer than three of my former students came up to me and said, "I'm so excited to have Fr. Sauer. It's going to be a great year," to which I immediately replied, "Yes, it will." Imagine if we could all inspire such simple optimism in our students merely by handing out a syllabus. Little do those students know what they are in for: the red pen, Homer, Dante, Shakespeare, and other assorted classical and modern lovelies, especially one of Fr. Sauer's favorites, Yeats, and his poem, "Crazy Jane Talks with the Bishop." Fr. Sauer once explained the poem to me. However, his students read the poem and wonder what's going on: Who is Jane? Is Jane sleeping with the bishop? Is Jane the bishop? Did they have women bishops back then?

But I know what the poem means. The poem relates specifically to Fr. Sauer, and his connection is not to the bishop, as some of you may think, but to Crazy Jane. Rebutting the bishop, Jane argues that one finds God not from worshipping in a beautiful cathedral, divorced from people, but from living life and experiencing suffering and joy. She says, "For nothing can be sole or whole / That has not been rent." Tony, you represent that view of spirituality to me, *not* to say that you are "rent"! You, though, *are* someone who embodies the essence of our shared humanity, the grittiness of life and the grace of God.

The faculty celebrated Fr. Sauer's 70th birthday in 2004. From left are Bob Drucker, Bobby Gavin, Phyllis Molinelli, Fr. Sauer, Carole Nickolai and Chuck Murphy.

Thus, on this grace note for Fr. Sauer, we celebrate 150 years of SI's service to the good people of the San Francisco Bay Area. We are grateful for this privilege and thankful that so many people have supported the school in its mission of turning boys and girls into men and women dedicated to lives of service, leadership and faith.

This book records only the first years of what we hope will be a very long and bountiful history for the school, yet we know, too, that this is not the complete history. It can't be. Too much has happened. It is impossible to include the stories of so many people who have taught, studied, performed, coached and competed at SI over the years. Our apologies to those whose stories have yet to be told. To these individuals, we offer this option: Soon the SI web site will offer a Living History section for SI grads to share stories and photos of their time here. We hope this will grow and become something much larger than any book, something that, 150 years from now, people will read and enjoy. Those future readers will, we trust, find an SI that has grown and adapted while staying true to its Ignatian heart — just as we find the same spirit of *magis* and AMDG as present today as it was in 1855.

Why write so much about St. Ignatius College Preparatory? Certainly other high schools succeed just as well as SI. In doing my research, I've seen, time and time again, the quality that distinguishes and defines SI: sharpness. SI sharpens its students. It readies them for the tasks and trials and tribulations of life. Moreover, SI has a certain energy different from other schools. Just walk the halls on any given day and you can feel the static in the air buzzing from classroom to playing field to laboratory to stage. The source of that energy, the dynamo that drives the school, the whetstone that sharpens and shapes, is simply this: AMDG — For the Greater Glory of God. SI, in turning girls and boys into women and men, does this and more. It turns them into people with purpose, with a drive to be a part of the divine plan, to resolve the paradox of doing great things while not thinking about greatness for themselves. AMDG, the gift of SI and the Jesuits, helps us be ourselves in the most profound way we can be. It's why so many grads come back to teach. It's why so many want their sons and daughters to come to SI. It's why, years after graduation, alumni come to reunions and sports days and auctions and fashion shows and international food faires. They come because the goodness of the school stays with them. And they seek the greater good, the *magis*, that is the title of this book and the theme of their lives. I've always known there's something special about this place. Now I've had the luxury to stare at it long enough to put a name to it. Sharpness. *Magis*. AMDG. Go Cats!

— *Paul Totah '75*

Acknowledgements

I could not have written a book of this scope without assistance from a host of talented individuals. First thanks go to the Class of 1955, which raised the funds among its members to pay for the printing of this book. The upgraded paper stock, the duotone process and the hardcover binding are all a result of the generosity of these alumni.

Throughout my research and writing, three archivists provided invaluable aid: Fr. Michael Kotlanger, SJ (archivist at SI and USF), Fr. Gerald McKevitt, SJ (former archivist at SCU, where he now teaches history), and Br. Daniel Peterson, SJ (former librarian at SI and current archivist for the California Province). Each of these three men provided me with background materials and insights into the early days of the Jesuit mission in California and the culture of Jesuit education in the 1800s.

Several individuals provided key proofreading of the text, as well as advice and insights, including Bob Drucker '58, Bob Vergara '76, Peter Devine '66, David Mezzera '64, Kathryn Totah and Mame Campbell Salin. Mame's husband, Douglas, served as the book's designer. If the book reads well and looks good, it is to their credit.

Key people put up with all my hair-pulling over the two years of research and writing, especially my wonderful wife, Kathryn, and my two patient children, Lauren '07 and Michael. The development staff at SI, including Steve Lovette '63, Jim Dekker '68, Stella Muscat, Shirley Minger, Concie Tarantino and Katie Kohmann, also proved most patient with me and provided me with information that ranged from advice on whom to interview to years of graduation for the many people included herein.

My thanks go out to all the individuals interviewed for this book (too numerous to name) and all those who contributed essays, including (in order of appearance in the book) Dan Lang '86, Hugh Visser '47, Brian Hassett '59, Daniel C. Flynn '57, Michael Corrigan '60, C.T. (Terry) Gillin '62, David Mezzera '64, Boris Koodrin '67 (who also painted the mural that graces the cover of this book and the first floor of the school), Curtis J. Mallegni '67, Bob Lalanne '73, Loring R. Tocchini '80, Mark Hazelwood '80, Stephen Finnigan '88, Alfred Pace '74, Emily Behr '93, Lorelei Suarez '93, Meredith Cecchin '97, Bobby Gavin and Carole Nickolai. Also, Kevin Tobin '66 provided me with hundreds of photographs that he had taken as a student working for the *Ignatian*.

I am also indebted to two giants on whose shoulders I stand: Fr. Joseph Riordan, SJ, the author of *The First Half Century*, and Fr. John McGloin, SJ '29, the author of *Jesuits by the Golden Gate*. For much of the early history, I am not so much an author as an editor, repackaging the foundational histories written by these two men.

I was fortunate enough to have a companion on this journey — Alan Zaijka, special assistant to the president at USF. Alan is the author of *150 Vignettes*, which tells the story USF, and (up until 1927) of SI as well. His perspectives proved quite helpful, especially regarding the tensions between the Jesuits and Archbishop Alemany.

Former SI Principal Mario Prietto, SJ, and current principal Charles Dullea '65 both provided me with much help, especially regarding the transition to coeducation and the school's growth and direction in the 1980s and 1990s.

Finally, the one man to whom I am most grateful, and to whom this book is dedicated, is Fr. Anthony P. Sauer, SJ. He granted me a sabbatical from my normal duties to start this project, and he proofread every word on every page, as he does with *Genesis*. At times, after receiving a handful of pages with his inscrutable red corrections, I felt as if I were one of the students in his class, as his advice and comments were more than informative; they helped me become a better writer by urging me to tighten my prose.

To all those named above and to all those unnamed who played a part in this book, thank you.

About the Author

Paul Totah graduated from SI in 1975 and returned to teach at his alma mater 10 years later after a stint as a reporter and as a Catholic Worker. In his 20 years at SI, he has moderated *Inside SI*, taught English, helped to launch the Nature/Nexus course, and edited *Genesis IV*, the school's alumni magazine. He is the co-editor of *The San Francisco Fair: Treasure Island 1939–1940*. He and his wife, Kathryn, have two children — Lauren '07 and Michael.

About the Cover "Spiritus Magis"

The mural depicts the Jesuit concept of Magis (the greater good) and translates to "more breath." It is shown as a strong wind blowing across time, from 1855 to the present and into the future. Important historical figures shown are Fr. Michael Accolti, SJ, and Fr. John Nobili, SJ, upon their arrival in "Babylon"; Fr. James Bouchard, SJ, being inspired by his mother, Mary Bucheur, to become the great evangelist of the West Coast; and Fr. Anthony Maraschi, SJ, keeping SI College from sinking into the sands. God's grace is depicted as leaves blown across the mural from left to right, from past to present, where present-day students are busy carving various aspects of the SI education into stone blocks. The staircase is representative of the path of knowledge and ultimately leads one to the place of devotion. The final destination in the mural is the large star above the left steeple of Saint Ignatius Church, in this case the star Sirius, which is seen along with the constellation of Orion in the night sky. Some Catholic astronomers believe that Sirius was the Star of Bethlehem. An ultimate leap of faith is needed to get there from the uppermost stone block, but the stars of Orion's belt point us in the right direction. Mary Bucheur points specifically to the word 'seek' on the mural. Her advice offers us a second way to reach the same destination.

About the Artist

Boris Koodrin graduated from SI in 1967 and spent 30 years in the commercial world of screen printing, glass sand-carving and graphic design. He has studied various religious philosophies along the way and has spent several years learning the skills of native tracking, survival and spirituality. Today he is fully dedicated to expressing the subtleties of the mystical path through his work as a fine artist. His penchant for detail and storytelling is well documented in his mural "Spiritus Magis."

The above mural, completed in 2005 to commemorate the school's sesquicentennial, can be found on the first floor of the academic building. It invites students to search for hidden symbols and signs, both in the work and in their own lives.

APPENDICES

SI Presidents

Presidents of St. Ignatius Academy, College, High School & College Preparatory.

Rev. Anthony Maraschi, SJ (1855–1862)
Rev. Nicholas Congiato, SJ (1862–1865 & 1866–1869)
Rev. Burchard Villiger, SJ (1865–66)
Rev. Joseph Bayma, SJ (1869–1873)
Rev. Aloysius Masnata, SJ (1873–1876)
Rev. John Pinasco, SJ (1876–1880)
Rev. Robert E. Kenna, SJ (1880–1883)
Rev. Joseph C. Sasia, SJ (1883–1887 & 1908–1911)
Rev. Henry Imoda, SJ (1887–1893)
Rev. Edward P. Allen, SJ (1893–1896)
Rev. John P. Frieden, SJ (1896–1908)
Rev. Albert F. Trivelli, SJ (1911–1915)
Rev. Patrick J. Foote, SJ (1915–1919)
Rev. Pius L. Moore, SJ (1919–1925)
Rev. Edward J. Whelan, SJ (1925–1932)
Rev. William I. Lonergan, SJ (1932–1934)
Rev. Harold E. Ring, SJ (1934–1938)
Rev. William J. Dunne, SJ (1938–1954)
Rev. John F. X. Connolly, SJ (1954–1963)

(In 1959, USF and SI formally separated and the high school appointed its first president; before this point, the high school was under the college president's jurisdiction.)

Rev. Patrick J. Carroll, SJ (1959–1964)
Rev. Harry V. Carlin, SJ (1964–70)
Rev. Cornelius M. Buckley, SJ (1970–73)

Rev. James R. Hanley, SJ (1973–1975)
Rev. Russell J. Roide, SJ (1975-1979)
Rev. Anthony P. Sauer, SJ (1979–)

SI Principals

Before 1924, a Prefect of Studies acted as principal and administered the preparatory division of the college.

Fr. Cornelius Buckley, SJ (1924–26)
Fr. Albert I. Whelan, SJ (1926–30)
Fr. Dennis J. Kavanagh, SJ (1930–31)
Fr. Walter E. Semeria, SJ (1931–32)
Fr. James A. King, SJ (1932–1945)
Fr. Ralph T. Tichenor, SJ (1945–50)
Fr. William J. Finnegan, SJ (1950–55)
Fr. Robert R. Leonard, SJ (1955–57)
Fr. Thomas A. Reed, SJ (1957–64)
Fr. Edward J. McFadden, SJ (1964–76)
Fr. Richard L. McCurdy, SJ (1976–1981)
Fr. Mario J. Prietto, SJ (1981–1994)
Fr. Steven J. Nejasmich, SJ (1994–1997)
Mr. Charles W. Dullea (1997–)

SI Rectors

In 1985, the duties of the Rector-President were separated.

Fr. Raymond P. Allender, SJ (1985–1991)
Fr. William V. Thom, SJ (1991–1995)
Fr. Mark F. Toohey, SJ (1995–1997)
Fr. Gregory M. Goethals, SJ (1998–2004)
Fr. Gerald P. McCourt, SJ (2005–)

*"The award is presented annually by the Alumni Association and the School
to honor a graduate who has distinguished himself or herself professionally
and who best exemplifies the ideal of service to God and Fellow Man."*

1960 Dr. Edmund Morrissey

1961 Hon. C. Harold Caulfied

1962 Mr.Eugene Corbett

1963 Dr. Harold A. Harper

1964 Rt. Rev. Msgr. William J. Clasby

1965 Brig. Gen. Frederic B. Butler

1966 Mr. Thomas I. King

1967 Hon. Raymond J. O'Connor

1968 Hon. Raymond. D. Williamson

1969 Rev. Lloyd R. Burns, SJ; Rev. William J. Dunne, SJ;
     Rev. Charles B. Largan, SJ

1970 Mr. Edmund A. Rossi

1971 Hon. Edward M. Molkenbuhr

1972 Mr. Renolds Barbieri

1973 Mr. Darrell W. Daly

1974 Mr. Thomas J. Carroll

1975 Rev. Msgr. Peter C. Armstrong

1976 Mr. Joseph R. Bisho

1977 Dr. Maurice R. Growney, Sr.

1978 Mr. Stanley A. Roualdes

1979 Mr. Eugene J. Marty, Jr. & Dr. James J. Raggio

1980 Mr. Francis J. Murphy

1981 Mr. Peter J. Brusati

1982 Hon. Eugene F. Lynch

1983 Hon. Preston Devine

1984 Mr. Jerome K. Doolan

1985 Mr. George "Pat" Malley

1986 Hon. Raymond L. Sullivan

1987 Mr. George M. O'Brien, Sr.

1988 Mr. John F. O'Dea

1989 Mr. Raymond T. Allender

1990 Mr. William E. McDonnell

1991 Mr. Robert A. Smith

1992 Mr. Robert A. Halsing

1993 Dr. Robert R. Wall

1994 Mr. James W. Kearney

1995 Martin D. Murphy, Esq.

1996 Mr. Arthur J. Fritz III

1997 Msgr. John J. O'Hare

1998 Mr. Alfred S. Wilsey

1999 Rev. Harry V. Carlin, SJ

2000 Rev. Edward J. McFadden, SJ

2001 Mr. Donald J. Gordon

2002 Mr. Edward J. Dunne

2003 Mr. John Christen III

2004 Mr. Leo A. La Rocca

President's Award Recipients

"The President's Award shall be conferred upon non-alumni
who have distinguished themselves in the service of the greater community."

1972 Mr. Benjamin Swig

1973 Mr. William J. Zellerbach

1974 Mr. John Bernard Murphy

1975 Jules and Dorothy Leonardini

1976 Rev. Alfred Boeddeker, O.F.M.

1977 Louis F. Batmale, Ph.D.

1978 Sr. M. Geraldine McDonnell, S.M.

1979 Br. Douglas E. Draper, S.J.

1980 Michel and Mary Orradre

1981 Rev. Monsignor Richard W. Power

1982 Most Rev. Joseph T. McGucken, S.T.D.

1983 Rev. Robert J. Shinney, S.J.

1984 Mrs. Janet Pomeroy

1985 Col. Vernon Gilbert, USA

1986 Robert A. Jeffrey, M.D.

1987 Mr. M. Francis Corwin

1988 Mayor Dianne Feinstein

1989 Rev. William D. Ryan, S.J.

1990 Mrs. Ralph K. Davies

1991 Rev. Jon Sobrino, S.J.

1992 Most Rev. John R. Quinn, D.D.

1993 Sr. Glenn Anne McPhee, O.P.

1994 Rev. Mario J. Prietto, S.J.

1995 Sr. Mary Peter Traviss, O.P.

1996 Mr. Burl A. Toler, Sr.

1997 Mrs. Ernest (Jenny) Go

1998 Sr. Cathryn deBack, O.P.

1999 Helen and Joseph Bernstein

2000 Br. Daniel Peterson, SJ

2001 Mr. Paul Hazen

2002 Mr. Thomas Bertelsen, Jr.

2003 Bishop Ignatius Wang, DD

2004 Fr. John S. Hardin, OFM

(The year indicated is the year each team placed first in its league or section. For example, the SI football team, which won a championship in the fall of 1966, is listed in 1966, even though seniors on that team graduated in 1967.)

Baseball

SF Athletic League: 1921; AAA 1927, 1930, 1954, 1958, 1959, 1962, 1963, 1965, 1967
WCAL: 2000

Softball

GPSL: 1994

Basketball

Boys:
State Title: 1926
AAA: 1927, 1943, 1947, 1951, 1954 (ToC), 1955 (ToC), 1956, 1960, 1965,
WCAL: 1968, 1975, 1976, 1978, 1981 (CCS), 1982, 1983, 1984 (CCS & NorCal), 1992, 1993, 1999, 2000, 2004 (CCS)
CCS only: 1998

Girls
GPSL: 2002 (CCS)
CCS only: 1996, 1998

Tennis

Boys
AAA: 1928, 1931, 1932
WCAL: 1992, 1994, 1996, 1998

Girls
GPSL: 1993, 2003

Crew

Boys
AAA: 1939, 1941, 1942
CJRA: 1994, 1995, 1997 (U.S. Rowing Youth Invitational)

Girls
CJRA: 1995, 1999, 2000

Swimming

Boys
AAA: 1943, 1946, 1947, 1948, 1953, 1958, 1959, 1960, 1961, 1963, 1964, 1965, 1966, 1967
NPL: 1984, 1985, 1986, 1987, 1988, 1989, 1990, 1991

Girls
GPSL: 1994, 1995

Football

AAA: 1945, 1956, 1958, 1959, 1960, 1962, 1963, 1966
WCAL: 1967

Golf

Boys
AAA: 1951, 1952, 1957, 1958, 1959, 1961
WCAL: 1977, 1978, 1979 (CCS)

Girls
WCAL: 2002, 2003 (CCS & NorCal)

Cross Country

Boys
AAA: 1964, 1965, 1966
WCAL: 1971, 1990 (CCS), 1991, 1995 (CCS), 1996 (CCS & State), 2002 (CCS); CCS only: 1999

Girls
GPSL: 1991, 1992, 1993 (CCS), 1994 (CCS), 1995 (CCS), 1996 (CCS), 1997 (CCS), 1998 (CCS), 1999, 2000, 2002; CCS only: 2003

Soccer

Boys
WCAL: 1969, 1973, 1974, 1979, 1981, 2005

Girls
GPSL: 1992, 1993, 1994, 1995, 1996, 1998, 1999

Track

Boys
WCAL: 1971, 1972, 1973, 1975, 1976, 1977, 1978, 1984, 1985, 1991 (CCS), 1992, 1996, 1997, 1999

Girls
GPSL: 1991, 1992, 1993, 1994, 1995, 1996, 1997 (CCS), 1998 (CCS), 1999, 2000, 2001, 2002

Lacrosse

Boys
NCJLA: 90, 91, 92, 99 (State), 00 (State), 01 (State)

Girls
NCGLA: 97, 8, 99, 00, 01

Field Hockey

BVAL: 1998

Volleyball

Girls
GPSL 1998, 2000

Richard Bassi '59

Donald Benedetti '50

Ronald Calcagno '60

Harvey Christensen '43

Gil Dowd '57

Robert Drucker '58

Roger Ferrari '55

Ed Forrest '39

Jack Grealish '44

Joseph Gualco '63

James Kearney '48

James Keating (SI baseball coach)

Fred LaCour '56

Albert "Cap" Lavin '48

Ray Maloney '27

Kevin O'Shea '43

Ray Paxton '54

Robert Portman '65

Jack Scramaglia '55

Charles Silvera '42

Bernard Simpson '54

Rudy Zannini '51

Al Schwartz (SI basketball & football coach)

Introduction

1 Fr. Fran Daly, SJ, from his column "Ignatian Insight" published in *St. Xavier High School Magazine,* Cincinnati, Summer 2002.

2 Daly.

Chapter I

1 Joseph W. Riordan, SJ, *The First Half Century of St. Ignatius Church and College.* San Francisco: H.S. Crocker Co., 1905. 11-12.

2 Riordan, 19.

3 Riordan, 20.

4 Gerald McKevitt, SJ. *The University of Santa Clara: A History 1851-1977.* Stanford: Stanford University Press, 1979. 17.

5 McKevitt, *Santa Clara,* 18.

6 John McGloin, SJ. *The Eloquent Indian: the Life of James Bouchard. California Jesuit.* Stanford: Stanford University, 1949. 22.

7 Riordan, 26.

8 Riordan, 30.

9 Riordan, 31-31.

10 John McGloin, SJ. *Jesuits by the Golden Gate: The Society of Jesus in San Francisco 1849-1969.* San Francisco: University of San Francisco, 1972. 39.

11 Ironically, after Accolti received commitment from the Society of Jesus to commit men to California, he spent the remainder of his life doing parish work. Never again was he a superior in a Jesuit house.

12 Riordan, 61.

13 *Woodstock Letters,* Volume 26, 1897.

14 Cornelius Michael Buckley, SJ. "Joseph Bixio, Furtive Founder of the University of San Francisco," *California History,* Spring 1999.

15 Riordan, 71.

16 McGloin, *Jesuits,* 10.

17 Riordan, 74.

18 Riordan, 74.

19 McGloin, *Jesuits,* 11 & Riordan, 75-76.

20 Buckley.

21 McKevitt, *Santa Clara,* 74.

22 McGloin, *Jesuits,* 12.

23 McGloin, *Jesuits,* 13.

24 McKevitt, *Santa Clara,* 3.

25 John Atteberry & John Russell, editors. *Ratio Studiorum, Jesuit Education, 1540-1773,* Boston: Boston College, 1999. 10.

26 Alexander J. Cody, SJ. *A Memoir: Richard A. Gleeson, SJ: 1861–1945.* San Francisco: University of San Francisco Press, 1950. 29.

27 Gerald McKevitt, SJ. "Across the Rockies: Italian Jesuits in the American West," *Company Magazine,* October 2001.

28 McGloin, *Jesuits.* 30.

29 McGloin, *Jesuits.* 18.

30 McKevitt, "Across the Rockies."

31 McKevitt, "Across the Rockies."

32 McKevitt, *Santa Clara.* 52.

33 McKevitt, "Across the Rockies."

34 McKevitt, *Santa Clara.* 53, 71-73.

35 McKevitt, "Across the Rockies."

36 Riordan, 83.

37 Riordan, 90.

38 McGloin, *Jesuits.* 14.

39 McGloin, *Jesuits.* 14-15.

40 Riordan, 99.

41 Riordan, 94-95.

42 McGloin, *Jesuits.* 16.

43 McGloin, *Jesuits.* 20.

44 McGloin, *Jesuits.* 23-24.

45 Riordan, 117.

46 McKevitt, "Across the Rockies."

47 Riordan, 106-107.

48 Riordan, 115-116.

49 Riordan, 102.

50 Riordan, 286.

51 McGloin, *Eloquent Indian.* 112-113.

52 John McGloin, SJ. *California's First Archbishop: The Life of Joseph Sadoc Alemany, O.P., 1814-1888.* New York: Herder and Herder, 1966. 198-199.

53 McGloin, *Alemany.* 199.

54 McGloin, *Alemany.* 206.

55 McGloin, *Alemany.* 210.

56 McGloin, *Eloquent Indian.* 114.

57 McGloin, *Eloquent Indian.* 121-122. Fr. Bouchard may have cut his beard after all. Fr. McKevitt recalls seeing a photograph of Fr. Bouchard on ebay in which the aged priest was clean-shaven. Sadly, Fr. McKevitt's bid was not high enough to secure the photograph.

Chapter II

1 Riordan, 105-106.

2 McGloin, *Jesuits.* 19.

3 Riordan, 116. & Fr. Fabian Stan Parmisano, OP. *Mission West: The Western Dominican Province 1850-1966.* Oakland: Western Dominican Province, 1995. 120.

4 Riordan, 118.

5 Riordan, 121-122.

6 Riordan, 122.

7 Riordan, 132.

8 McGloin, *Jesuits.* 22.

9 Riordan, 93.

10 Riordan, 133.

11 McGloin, *Jesuits.* 28.

12 Riordan, 139.

13 Riordan 403-404.

14 McGloin, *Jesuits.* 129-130.

15 Initially, SI College was not unique in granting a Master's degree with no studies done on campus. The school worked in the European model in which a scholar would go and do reading for a year or two anywhere (but usually some prominent institution with a library). They would present themselves to the school from which they had earned their Bachelor's of Arts degree and then would be awarded a Master's degree. The same was done at the other Jesuit schools. Since SIC did not really have sufficient facilities for a student to earn a medical degree, SI graduates matriculated elsewhere, did their studies, and took a Master's degree in medicine from SIC almost as an honorary degree. Had it not been for the earthquake, the college probably would have opened some kind of medical or dental school in the early 20th century like the Jesuit institu-

tion in St. Louis. SIC always followed the SLU model of Jesuit University programs. — *Fr. Michael Kotlanger, SJ*

16 Riordan, 155.
17 Riordan, 161.
18 Riordan, 162.
19 Riordan, 170.
20 Riordan, 197.
21 McGloin, *Jesuits.* 31.
22 *The Catholic Encyclopedia, Vol. II,* online edition.
23 *Woodstock Letters,* Volume 49, Number 2, June 1920. 242-246.
24 *Woodstock Letters.*
25 Arthur Spearman, SJ. *John Joseph Montgomery: Father of Basic Flying, 1858–1911.* Santa Clara: University of Santa Clara, 1967. 18.
26 Riordan, 194 & Spearman, 18.
27 Riordan, 188.
28 *Woodstock Letters.*
29 McGloin, *Jesuits,* 30.
30 Riordan, 198-199.
31 McGloin, *Jesuits,* 33.
32 Parmisano.
33 The original letter is in the collect in the Archive Room of the California Province of the Society of Jesus in Los Gatos.
34 Cody, 11.
35 Richard A. Gleeson, SJ. *My Golden Jubilee Thoughts.* Private Printing, 1927. 17.
36 Cody, 13-15.
37 Riordan, 216.
38 Riordan, 219-220.
39 Riordan, 222.
40 Riordan, 221.
41 Riordan, 222.
42 McGloin, *Jesuits,* 39.

43 Riordan, 317.
44 McGloin, *Jesuits,* 41.

Chapter III
1 Theodore W. Fuller. *San Diego Originals.* California Profiles Publication, 1987. www.sandiegohistory.org/bio/montgomery/montgomery.htm.
2 Spearman, 7.
3 McKevitt, *Santa Clara,* 138.
4 Spearman, 124.
5 McKevitt, *Santa Clara,* 140.
6 Riordan, 240.
7 Riordan, 246.
8 McGloin, *Jesuits,* 56, 60.
9 Riordan, 247.
10 McGloin, Jesuits, 55.
11 Riordan, 248.
12 Riordan, 253.
13 *Woodstock Letters,* Volume 13, 1884. 425.
14 Riordan, 288.
15 McGloin, Jesuits, 63.
16 McGloin, Jesuits, 50.
17 Riordan, 320.
18 Riordan, 322.
19 Riordan, 323.
20 Riordan, 339.
21 Riordan, 346.
22 Riordan, 363.
23 McGloin, Jesuits, 52.
24 McGloin, Jesuits, 69-70.

Chapter IV
1 McGloin, *Jesuits,* 74.
2 McGloin, *Jesuits,* 74.
3 McGloin, *Jesuits,* 65.
4 McGloin, *Jesuits,* 79.
5 Alan Zaijka. *150 Vignettes.* San Francisco: University of San Francisco, 2005.

Chapter V
1 Cody, 81.
2 McGloin, *Jesuits,* 83.
3 McGloin, *Jesuits,* 84.
4 McGloin, *Jesuits,* 85.
5 McGloin, *Jesuits,* 86.
6 McGloin, *Jesuits,* 86.
7 McGloin, *Jesuits,* 87.
8 McGloin, *Jesuits,* 96.
9 McGloin, *Jesuits,* 97.
10 McGloin, Jesuits, 89.
11 McGloin, *Jesuits,* 95.
12 McGloin, *Jesuits,* 114.
13 McGloin, *Jesuits,* 114.
14 *Woodstock Letters,* Volume XXIX, Number 1. 2-3.
15 *Ignatian,* 1910–11, 66; 1917, 78. *Genesis II,* May 1980.
16 *Ignatian,* 1913, 75; 1923, 97.
17 *Ignatian,* 1911, Volume 1, Number 1. 43-44.
18 *Ignatian,* 1911, Volume 1, Number 1. 58.
19 *Ignatian,* June 1920. 86 & 97.
20 Eric Abrahamson, *The University of San Francisco School of Law: A History 1912-1987.* San Francisco: The University of San Francisco School of Law, 1987. 19-20.
21 "Boche" was a disparaging term for Germans during World War I.
22 Cody, 128.
23 Cody, 130.

Chapter VI
1 McGloin, *Jesuits,* 107-108.
2 *Ignatian,* 1924. 135.
3 *Ignatian,* 1924. 136; 1925. 124.
4 McGloin, *Jesuits,* 139.
5 *Ignatian,* 1925. 101; 1926. 107-109.

6 *The Heights,* 1929. 66.
7 McGloin, *Jesuits,* 142.
8 While the gymnasium was part of the original design, the school did not build one until the 1950s.
9 *San Francisco Chronicle,* "Early Baron's Homes on the Range." September 25, 2004. F1.
10 Riordan, 212.
11 "Early Baron's," F1.
12 Fr. Privett made this remark in an email he sent to members of the USF community regarding a student-led protest to rename Phelan Hall.
13 McGloin, *Jesuits,* 122; "Early Baron's," F6.
14 McGloin, *Jesuits,* 140.

Chapter VII
1 *Red and Blue,* November 16, 1932. 1.
2 The letter is in the SI Archives.
3 McGloin, *Jesuits,* 144.
4 McGloin, *Jesuits,* 144-145.
5 *The OceanSIder,* March 7, 1980. 12.
6 *The Red and Blue,* November 26, 1934.
7 Among those who received the 8-year scholarship to SI, in addition to Wilsey, were Loyola University President Charles Casassa, SJ '28, USF President Charles Dullea, SJ '34, and SCU President Patrick Donohoe, SJ '31.
8 *Literary Digest,* Volume 123, May 8, 1937. 25-28.
9 Arthur Spearman, SJ, "Father Bernard R. Hubbard: 1888-1962," *Woodstock Letters,* Volume 93, Fall 1965. 466-73.

[10] Biographical notes in SCU clipping scrapbook and *The Redwood*, 1929 and 1930.

[11] *New York Times*, October 1, 1930 & Bernard R. Hubbard, SJ, "A World Inside a Mountain: Aniakchak, the New Volcanic Wonderland of the Alaska Peninsula, is Explored," *National Geographic*, Volume 60, September 1931. 319

[12] *National Geographic*, Volume 60, September 1931. 319.

[13] *National Geographic*, Volume 65, May, 1934. 625-26.

[14] *The Literary Digest*, Volume 123, May, 8, 1937. 26.

[15] *Daily Alaska Empire* (Juneau), 1930.

[16] *Daily Alaska Empire* (Juneau), *ca.* September 1932.

Chapter VIII

[1] McGloin, *Jesuits,* 123.

[2] Francis X. Murphy, *The Fighting Admiral: the Story of Dan Callaghan.* New York: Vantage Press, Inc. 1952. 11.

[3] Murphy, 12-13.

[4] Murphy, 15.

[5] Murphy, 110.

[6] Murphy, 152.

[7] Murphy, 190.

[8] Murphy, 203-204.

[9] From *Courage, Honor and Compassion: a Tribute to Vice Admiral William M. Callaghan,* 2001, a brochure used at the ceremony honoring Callaghan.

[10] http://www.ussmissouri.com/press/2001/27Mar.htm

[11] *1946 Ignatian* yearbook

[12] Genesis III, Summer 1991.

Chapter IX

[1] Rooney Report, May 29, 1950, located in the USF Archives, also cited in McGloin, *Jesuits,* 145.

[2] McKevitt, *Santa Clara,* 204.

[3] SI Archives.

[4] McGloin, *Jesuits,* 146.

[5] McGloin, *Jesuits,* 147.

[6] McGloin, *Jesuits,* 147.

[7] *Ignatian,* 1955. 8.

[8] *Ignatian Bulletin,* December 1956.

[9] *Inside SI,* March 20, 1950; April 13, 1951; & February 15, 1955.

[10] *Inside SI,* May 5, 1950

[11] *Inside SI,* Sept. 20, 1956. 8.

[12] *Inside SI,* "SI Football: A 55 Year Tradition," by Mark Hazelwood '79, September 14, 1979. 8.

[13] *Ignatian,* 1950

[14] *St. Ignatius Church Monthly Calendar,* 1950. 172-173.

[15] *Ignatian,* 1950.

[16] *Inside SI,* March 27, 1953.

[17] *Inside SI,* January & April 1958.

[18] John Pearson, *Painfully Rich: The Outrageous Fortune and Misfortunes of the Heirs of J. Paul Getty.* New York: St. Martin's Press, 1995. 74, 76.

[19] Biographical information from the City of Oakland's web site.

[20] City of Oakland web site.

[21] *Inside SI,* March 16, 1951.

[22] *Inside SI,* January 12, 1951.

[23] Fr. John W. Clifford, SJ. *In the Presence of My Enemies.* New York: W.W. Norton & Co., 1963. 8.

[24] Peter Fleming, SJ. *Chosen for China: The California Province Jesuits in China, 1928-1957 — A Case Study in Mission and Culture.* Berkeley: Graduate Theological Union, 1987. The work is Fr. Fleming's doctoral dissertation and can be found in the USF Archives.

Chapter X

[1] *Ignatian Bulletin,* April 1965.

[2] *Genesis,* February 1970.

[3] *Genesis,* February 1970.

[4] *Genesis II,* Summer 1990.

[5] McGloin, *Jesuits,* 180.

[6] *Genesis,* February & July 1970.

[7] *Ignatian Bulletin,* April 1962.

[8] *Inside SI,* December 18, 1963. 3.

[9] *Inside SI,* Volume 15, Number 5. 8.

Chapter XI

[1] SI Archives.

[2] http://www.clc-usa.org/

[3] Campus Ministry Team brochure.

[4] Coach Ward also praised Tom Lagomarsino for serving as assistant SI track coach while in college and, later, as a teacher at SI.

[5] *Inside SI,* February 30, 1972. 7.

[6] Riordan, 197.

[7] *Genesis II,* Spring 1989. 16.

[8] *Inside SI,* May 19, 1971.

[9] *(2001, September 24, 1975, p. 1)*

[10] *Genesis,* July 1972.

[11] *Genesis,* October 1979.

Chapter XII

[1] Mario Prietto, SJ. *A Jesuit Prep Goes Coed: Labor of Love and Justice.* July 31, 2000. 5-6. Unpublished manuscript in the SI Archives.

[2] Prietto, *Jesuit Prep,* 18.

[3] Prietto, *Jesuit Prep,* 19.

[4] Correspondence from SI Archives.

[5] English Department Minutes, September 30, 1987, 2. SI Archives.

[6] Prietto, *Jesuit Prep,* 47.

[7] Prietto, *Jesuit Prep,* 65.

[8] Prietto, *Jesuit Prep,* 67.

[9] Prietto, *Jesuit Prep,* 69.

[10] SI Archives.

[11] Prietto, *Jesuit Prep,* 79.

[12] Prietto, *Jesuit Prep,* 102-110.

[13] Prietto, *Jesuit Prep,* 121.

[14] SI Archives.

[15] *Genesis* October 1979 & July 1981.

[16] *Inside SI,* October 1982. 8.

[17] *Genesis II,* Winter 1987. 8.

[18] *Genesis II,* Winter 1989. 3.

[19] *Genesis II,* Winter 1989. 4.

[20] *Genesis II,* Winter 1989. 5.

[21] *Genesis II,* Spring 1990. 12.

[22] *Genesis II,* Winter 1990. 14.